Communications
in Computer and Information Science   1419

More information about this series at http://www.springer.com/series/7899

Constantine Stephanidis ·
Margherita Antona · Stavroula Ntoa (Eds.)

HCI International 2021 - Posters

23rd HCI International Conference, HCII 2021
Virtual Event, July 24–29, 2021
Proceedings, Part I

 Springer

Editors
Constantine Stephanidis
University of Crete and Foundation
for Research and Technology – Hellas
(FORTH)
Heraklion, Crete, Greece

Margherita Antona
Foundation for Research
and Technology – Hellas (FORTH)
Heraklion, Crete, Greece

Stavroula Ntoa
Foundation for Research
and Technology – Hellas (FORTH)
Heraklion, Crete, Greece

ISSN 1865-0929   ISSN 1865-0937 (electronic)
Communications in Computer and Information Science
ISBN 978-3-030-78634-2   ISBN 978-3-030-78635-9 (eBook)
https://doi.org/10.1007/978-3-030-78635-9

Foreword

Human-Computer Interaction (HCI) is acquiring an ever-increasing scientific and industrial importance, and having more impact on people's everyday life, as an ever-growing number of human activities are progressively moving from the physical to the digital world. This process, which has been ongoing for some time now, has been dramatically accelerated by the COVID-19 pandemic. The HCI International (HCII) conference series, held yearly, aims to respond to the compelling need to advance the exchange of knowledge and research and development efforts on the human aspects of design and use of computing systems.

The 23rd International Conference on Human-Computer Interaction, HCI International 2021 (HCII 2021), was planned to be held at the Washington Hilton Hotel, Washington DC, USA, during July 24–29, 2021. Due to the COVID-19 pandemic and with everyone's health and safety in mind, HCII 2021 was organized and run as a virtual conference. It incorporated the 21 thematic areas and affiliated conferences listed on the following page.

A total of 5222 individuals from academia, research institutes, industry, and governmental agencies from 81 countries submitted contributions, and 1276 papers and 241 posters were included in the proceedings to appear just before the start of the conference. The contributions thoroughly cover the entire field of HCI, addressing major advances in knowledge and effective use of computers in a variety of application areas. These papers provide academics, researchers, engineers, scientists, practitioners, and students with state-of-the-art information on the most recent advances in HCI. The volumes constituting the set of proceedings to appear before the start of the conference are listed in the following pages.

The HCI International (HCII) conference also offers the option of 'Late Breaking Work' which applies both for papers and posters, and the corresponding volume(s) of the proceedings will appear after the conference. Full papers will be included in the 'HCII 2021 - Late Breaking Papers' volumes of the proceedings to be published in the Springer LNCS series, while 'Poster Extended Abstracts' will be included as short research papers in the 'HCII 2021 - Late Breaking Posters' volumes to be published in the Springer CCIS series.

I would also like to thank the Program Board Chairs and the members of the Program Boards of all thematic areas and affiliated conferences for their contribution towards the highest scientific quality and overall success of the HCI International 2021 conference.

This conference would not have been possible without the continuous and unwavering support and advice of Gavriel Salvendy, founder, General Chair Emeritus, and Scientific Advisor. For his outstanding efforts, I would like to express my appreciation to Abbas Moallem, Communications Chair and Editor of HCI International News.

July 2021   Constantine Stephanidis

HCI International 2021 Thematic Areas and Affiliated Conferences

Thematic Areas

- HCI: Human-Computer Interaction
- HIMI: Human Interface and the Management of Information

Affiliated Conferences

- EPCE: 18th International Conference on Engineering Psychology and Cognitive Ergonomics
- UAHCI: 15th International Conference on Universal Access in Human-Computer Interaction
- VAMR: 13th International Conference on Virtual, Augmented and Mixed Reality
- CCD: 13th International Conference on Cross-Cultural Design
- SCSM: 13th International Conference on Social Computing and Social Media
- AC: 15th International Conference on Augmented Cognition
- DHM: 12th International Conference on Digital Human Modeling and Applications in Health, Safety, Ergonomics and Risk Management
- DUXU: 10th International Conference on Design, User Experience, and Usability
- DAPI: 9th International Conference on Distributed, Ambient and Pervasive Interactions
- HCIBGO: 8th International Conference on HCI in Business, Government and Organizations
- LCT: 8th International Conference on Learning and Collaboration Technologies
- ITAP: 7th International Conference on Human Aspects of IT for the Aged Population
- HCI-CPT: 3rd International Conference on HCI for Cybersecurity, Privacy and Trust
- HCI-Games: 3rd International Conference on HCI in Games
- MobiTAS: 3rd International Conference on HCI in Mobility, Transport and Automotive Systems
- AIS: 3rd International Conference on Adaptive Instructional Systems
- C&C: 9th International Conference on Culture and Computing
- MOBILE: 2nd International Conference on Design, Operation and Evaluation of Mobile Communications
- AI-HCI: 2nd International Conference on Artificial Intelligence in HCI

List of Conference Proceedings Volumes Appearing Before the Conference

1. LNCS 12762, Human-Computer Interaction: Theory, Methods and Tools (Part I), edited by Masaaki Kurosu
2. LNCS 12763, Human-Computer Interaction: Interaction Techniques and Novel Applications (Part II), edited by Masaaki Kurosu
3. LNCS 12764, Human-Computer Interaction: Design and User Experience Case Studies (Part III), edited by Masaaki Kurosu
4. LNCS 12765, Human Interface and the Management of Information: Information Presentation and Visualization (Part I), edited by Sakae Yamamoto and Hirohiko Mori
5. LNCS 12766, Human Interface and the Management of Information: Information-rich and Intelligent Environments (Part II), edited by Sakae Yamamoto and Hirohiko Mori
6. LNAI 12767, Engineering Psychology and Cognitive Ergonomics, edited by Don Harris and Wen-Chin Li
7. LNCS 12768, Universal Access in Human-Computer Interaction: Design Methods and User Experience (Part I), edited by Margherita Antona and Constantine Stephanidis
8. LNCS 12769, Universal Access in Human-Computer Interaction: Access to Media, Learning and Assistive Environments (Part II), edited by Margherita Antona and Constantine Stephanidis
9. LNCS 12770, Virtual, Augmented and Mixed Reality, edited by Jessie Y. C. Chen and Gino Fragomeni
10. LNCS 12771, Cross-Cultural Design: Experience and Product Design Across Cultures (Part I), edited by P. L. Patrick Rau
11. LNCS 12772, Cross-Cultural Design: Applications in Arts, Learning, Well-being, and Social Development (Part II), edited by P. L. Patrick Rau
12. LNCS 12773, Cross-Cultural Design: Applications in Cultural Heritage, Tourism, Autonomous Vehicles, and Intelligent Agents (Part III), edited by P. L. Patrick Rau
13. LNCS 12774, Social Computing and Social Media: Experience Design and Social Network Analysis (Part I), edited by Gabriele Meiselwitz
14. LNCS 12775, Social Computing and Social Media: Applications in Marketing, Learning, and Health (Part II), edited by Gabriele Meiselwitz
15. LNAI 12776, Augmented Cognition, edited by Dylan D. Schmorrow and Cali M. Fidopiastis
16. LNCS 12777, Digital Human Modeling and Applications in Health, Safety, Ergonomics and Risk Management: Human Body, Motion and Behavior (Part I), edited by Vincent G. Duffy
17. LNCS 12778, Digital Human Modeling and Applications in Health, Safety, Ergonomics and Risk Management: AI, Product and Service (Part II), edited by Vincent G. Duffy

http://2021.hci.international/proceedings

23rd International Conference on Human-Computer Interaction (HCII 2021)

The full list with the Program Board Chairs and the members of the Program Boards of all thematic areas and affiliated conferences is available online at:

http://www.hci.international/board-members-2021.php

HCI International 2022

The 24th International Conference on Human-Computer Interaction, HCI International 2022, will be held jointly with the affiliated conferences at the Gothia Towers Hotel and Swedish Exhibition & Congress Centre, Gothenburg, Sweden, June 26 – July 1, 2022. It will cover a broad spectrum of themes related to Human-Computer Interaction, including theoretical issues, methods, tools, processes, and case studies in HCI design, as well as novel interaction techniques, interfaces, and applications. The proceedings will be published by Springer. More information will be available on the conference website: http://2022.hci.international/:

General Chair
Prof. Constantine Stephanidis
University of Crete and ICS-FORTH
Heraklion, Crete, Greece
Email: general_chair@hcii2022.org

http://2022.hci.international/

Contents – Part I

Perceptual, Cognitive and Psychophisiological Aspects of Interaction

Designing for Older People

Design Case Studies

Dimensions of User Experience

Information, Language, Culture and Media

Contents – Part II

Virtual, Augmented and Mixed Reality

Security and Privacy Issues in HCI

AI and Machine Learning in HCI

Contents – Part III

Interacting and Learning

Interacting and Driving

Digital Wellbeing, eHealth and mHealth

Interacting and Shopping

HCI, Safety and Sustainability

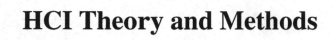

HCI Theory and Methods

Transform Motion Design into Ready-to-Go Assets

Andrii Bogachenko[1]([⊠]) [iD], Inna Bondarenko[1] [iD], Daria Voskoboinikova[1] [iD],
Yevhenii Buhera[1] [iD], Dongjoo Ko[2] [iD], and Svitlana Alkhimova[1] [iD]

[1] Samsung R&D Institute Ukraine (SRK), 57, Lva Tolstogo Street, Kyiv 01032, Ukraine
{an.bogachenk,i.bondarenko,d.voskoboyni,y.buhera,
s.alkhimova}@samsung.com
[2] Samsung Electronics, Seoul R&D Campus, 33 Seongchon-gil, Seocho-gu, Seoul 06765, Korea
dongjoo.ko@samsung.com

Abstract. Motion design development is a time-consuming and challenging process. We analyze problems that usually happen in scope of motion design development and discuss commonly used approaches to solve these problems. We propose an approach to facilitate design-developer collaboration. The main idea of the approach is to create ready-to-go assets of motion design, which are targeted to the Android platform. Our approach extracts and decomposes Adobe After Effects data, rebuilds it into the hierarchical structure of the graphics objects, and assembles obtained data into ready-to-go Android Vector Drawable assets. A user study shows that most participants prefer this approach and think that it saves time (91%) and simplifies the process (100%) of animation development. The implementation shows almost two times better performance on animation playing compared to Lottie's solution. Creation of ready-to-go assets with the proposed approach improved human-computer interaction for designers and developers, allowing them to simplify development of motion design.

Keywords: Motion design · Interaction design · Designer-developer collaboration · Software development processes · Human-computer interaction

1 Introduction

Design plays one of the key factors that have the most notable influence on consumer choice [1]. That's why design development becomes more and more important. Although user experience and graphic user interface designs are well thought out, investing in motion design is not widespread nowadays. However, this branch of design is crucial for making user interactions more convenient and intuitive [2].

Motion design development is a complex process that involves tight design-developer collaboration and needs interaction with a lot of different tools for creating and sharing design artifacts. Usually, motion design is only a part of designer's responsibility. At the same time, preparing documentation and artifacts on motion design (i.e., creating animation) to developers is a time-consuming and challenging process. Animation implementation is in the scope of developer's responsibility, but it is not so obvious and

© Springer Nature Switzerland AG 2021
C. Stephanidis et al. (Eds.): HCII 2021, CCIS 1419, pp. 3–11, 2021.
https://doi.org/10.1007/978-3-030-78635-9_1

may require additional collaboration between developer and designer. All of that entails to research the solutions that simplify processes of sharing and implementing motion design [3, 4].

In the current study, an efficient and self-consistent approach is presented to obtain assets for Android platform directly from software for motion design creation. We conducted a study that evaluates the effectiveness of the proposed approach, comparing it with existing solutions and with regular motion design sharing practices.

2 Related Work

The research by Leiva et al. [5, 6] describes most common problems regarding designer-developer collaboration and groups them in two categories. The first category describes items related to spent time and redundant information upon preparing design documentation. The second category describes breakdowns such as missing details, ignoring edge cases, and implementation constraints. There are several common approaches to solve these problems.

The first approach is preparing documentation with all details about design values, measurements, and other important information (i.e., animation elements, durations, interpolations) manually. The result of this process is a design specification. It can be docx, pptx, png, pdf, or other file formats to share with a developer. Often a specification is not enough. This approach also needs a video for better understanding and proper implementation of the planned animation. It requires additional time for its rendering.

The second approach is to use hand-off tools for sharing motions design. Most popular tools like Zeplin[1] and InVision[2] allow browsing information about animation details. Tools like ProtoPie[3] or Web VI guide [7] additionally allow playing the animation. Nevertheless, all described tools have limitations in terms of getting ready-to-go assets for motion design.

Another approach is creating ready-to-go assets, which are self-contained code targeting a specific platform. The code can be imported directly into an integrated development environment that is used for software development. This highly simplifies motion design development for both developers and designers. Lottie[4] is widely used to create ready-to-go assets [8]. The main disadvantage is that Lottie operates with JSON data exported by Bodymovin[5] from Adobe After Effects[6] (AAE). It gives an additional dependency to the software that utilizes such assets and requires extra time to set up and run assets on the target platform [9]. Furthermore, the JSON format is less dev-friendly than the native animation format of the specific platform.

Among the considered approaches, the last one is the most promising. It can reduce developer's work, allowing not to implement animation from scratch, but only to integrate it into the code. However, the main difficulty of this approach is that assets should be

---

[1] https://zeplin.io/.

[2] https://www.invisionapp.com/.

[3] https://www.protopie.io/.

[4] https://airbnb.io/lottie/.

[5] https://aescripts.com/bodymovin/.

[6] https://www.adobe.com/products/aftereffects.html.

adapted to the target platform. This process may have technical restrictions such as performance constraints, technology differences, limited feature set for motion design implementation on the platform. These restrictions hinder the creation of complex ready-to-go assets. Therefore, research of new solutions to the mentioned issues is important to further simplify the motion design creation.

3 Proposed Approach

One of the most powerful tools for motion design development is AAE. It offers the ability to extend its functionality through modern web development technologies like HTML5, JavaScript, and ExtendScript, without the need for C++ [10]. We utilized this possibility for our approach. We developed a web extension for exporting AAE animation objects into Android Vector Drawable (AVD), which is a native animation format for Android. This is the conceptual difference of the proposed approach compared to the existing Lottie's solution (Fig. 1).

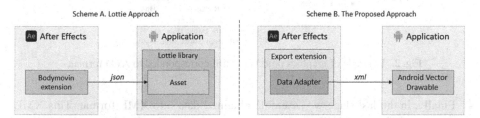

Fig. 1. Comparison of the proposed approach with Lottie.

In the proposed approach the process of getting a ready-to-go asset from created motion design can be separated into four stages.

The target of the first stage is to select the AAE layers that should be transformed into vector graphics. Depending on the AAE layer type, we extract data required to rebuild graphics and animations in AVD format. For example, only size, color and position are required to be extracted in case of solid layer export. Processing of the shape layer should be considered separately because it is the main layer type to be exported. The Shape layer consists of groups, shapes, paths and different properties: fills, strokes, trim paths, merge paths, etc. The combination of those layers and their properties allows the creation of complex graphics compositions. All of them should be extracted properly, taking into account complex dependencies between them.

The second stage relates to the AAE's power as a tool for motion design development. It has plenty of features, styles, and visual effects that allow creating graphics of different levels of complexity. AVD is based on the Scalable Vector Graphics, which is limited compared to AAE in terms of the feature set. Therefore, in the second stage, Data Adapter divides the data extracted from the previous step into simple separated entities. This decomposition allows determining and rebuilding the hierarchical structure of the graphics object according to the AVD format in the next stage.

In the third stage, we rebuild the hierarchical structure. This process is one of the biggest challenges for motion design transfer from AAE to AVD. AAE and AVD provide different ways to organize the hierarchical structure of graphics objects. To replicate the animation, we rebuild the structure of graphics objects to correspond to the AVD format (Fig. 2). For example, in AAE layer structure Fill property located under the shape path on the same level is applied to each of the upper shapes by cascade nesting. On the other hand, to apply such properties in AVD format, we need to propagate them to all the paths explicitly. As a result, structures in AVD may have many more graphics objects with independent properties. This makes the structure more complex, but allows saving the possibility to animate all the features properly.

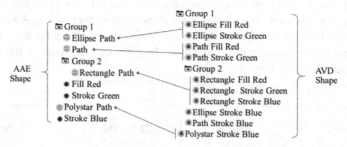

Fig. 2. Example of graphics objects rebuild corresponded to AVD format.

Finally, in the last stage we assemble obtained data into XML format. This XML represents a ready-to-go AVD asset.

Situationally, the results obtained after the four described stages may not be enough to produce fully correct assets. Information about some specific AAE features may be impossible to replicate in AVD.

A common case related to the mentioned issue is an export of animated paths that change their vertex count through a transition (Fig. 3a). From AAE we can extract information only about the initial and final states of a transition, while for Android it is unclear what happens between these states. It usually leads to an incorrect animation or even a crash on the Android side. We process such situations explicitly and insert some amount of intermediate states at the moments of path changes. Saving all the states allows making export correctly and keeps the animation smoothness.

One more case related to inability to replicate AAE animation in AVD happens, when transformation matrix is applied to recalculate new shape coordinates, e.g., 360° rotation about itself (Fig. 3b). The described case is managed similarly to the previous one.

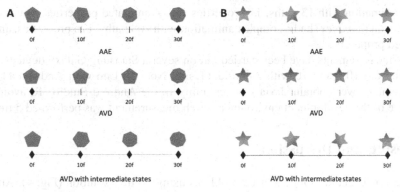

Fig. 3. Cases related to inability to replicate AAE animation in AVD.

4 Experiments

In order to assess the proposed approach, we surveyed on its pros and cons and compared it with Lottie's solution.

4.1 User Study

The user study examined different aspects of the participants' opinions about proposed approach and its comparison to the existed commonly used solutions for motion design development.

We involved 12 participants (9 male, 3 female). Participants were between 25 and 54 years old (avg. 34.2). To understand bottlenecks in motion design development process, we involved both designers (6 participants) and developers (6 participants). Creation of motion design was a direct duty for all the designers, so they were fully aware of the design development process. All the developers had regular tasks on developing animations for Android. Participants were not compensated.

Participants were briefed on how to use the proposed approach. We asked designers to explore and prepare ready-to-go assets with the proposed approach. Then, we asked developers to use those assets and reproduce animations in Android application. After both had enough time exploring the proposed approach all were invited to participate the online survey. Questions were grouped into two sub-categories: general section about motion design development and the section about proposed approach. On average it took the participants about 26 min to complete the questionnaire.

4.2 Performance Study

To assess performance of the proposed approach and compare it with Lottie's solution, we developed an Android application that can utilize AVD and JSON data. AVD data was produced with the proposed approach; JSON data was gotten with Lottie's solution. Android Studio 4.1 IDE was used to develop the application.

We prepared two compositions of different levels of complexity in the AAE CC2020 software. Both animations had 90 ms duration. The first composition (*simple*) had a simple animation with 13 paths, 11 properties, and 4 animated properties. The second composition (*complex*) had a complex animation with 208 paths, 176 properties, and 64 animated properties.

The measurements have been carried out on several Samsung Galaxy devices: S9+ with Android 10, Note 10 with Android 11, and Note 10 Lite with Android 11. All measurements were obtained via Profiler utility in the Android Studio. To avoid the influence of the development environment, each measurement was performed 5 times.

5 Results and Discussion

Both designers and developers faced problems using Lottie's solution (Fig. 4). Almost a half of the designers (43%) and a quarter of the developers (25%) expressed their disappointment with Lottie's feature set. Around a quarter of the participants are concerned about the use of extra dependencies (29% – designers and 25% – developers). The low performance of Lottie's solution bothers 14% of designers and 17% of developers. Although the designers hadn't mentioned the issues with maintenance of the resources obtained from Lottie's solution, 25% of developers mentioned this issue. The minority of participants (14% and 8% designers and developers, respectively) who took part in the survey did not meet problems using Lottie's solution.

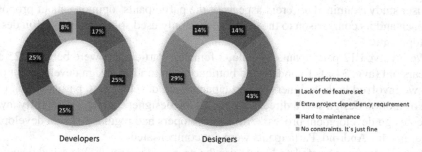

Fig. 4. Lottie's solution constraints.

Although Lottie's solution provides the possibility to get ready-to-go assets, those assets are not self-contained. Most participants (91%) noted that they additionally needed to use a video file to enhance understanding of the animation details. A lot of participants mentioned that they needed additional artifacts to clarify implementation for developers: PowerPoint presentation (50%), hand-off tools like ProtoPie or VI web guide (42%), text guide (33%), AAE composition (16%). It should be mentioned that participants preferred to use several additional artifacts with Lottie's assets (Fig. 5), which is accompanied by extra time costs.

Effectiveness assessment showed that most participants preferred our approach and thought that it saves time (92%) and simplifies the process (100%) of animation development (Fig. 6). A majority of the participants (67%) answered that prepared ready-to-go assets do not require an additional update or enhancement after being produced.

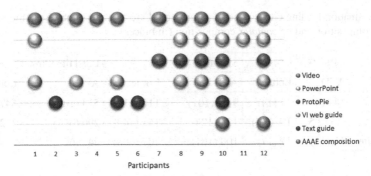

Fig. 5. Answers distribution on additionally required artifacts for motion design sharing.

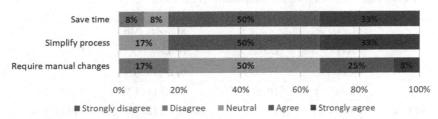

Fig. 6. Answers distribution on the effectiveness of the proposed approach.

The idea of the proposed approach was evaluated from negative to positive with a rating scale from −3 to +3 according to the User Experience Questionnaire [11]. All the questions got more positive responses neither negative (Fig. 7). The approach was evaluated as Supportive and Clear (the highest evaluation from all the participants). Only 1 out of 12 participants had doubts about the effectiveness, interest, and excitement.

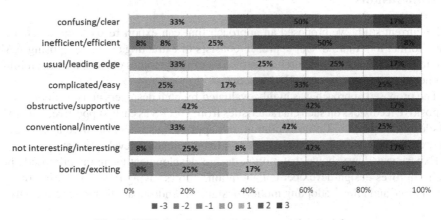

Fig. 7. UEQ-S evaluation of the proposed approach.

In the scope of performance assessment and comparison with Lottie's solution results of animation loading and playing are shown in Table 1 and Table 2, respectively.

Table 1. Animation loading comparison: data presented are average values for 5 measurement on *simple* composition and on *complex* composition (in braces).

	CPU, %		Memory, Mb		Load time, ms	
	AVD	Lottie	AVD	Lottie	AVD	Lottie
S9+	14 (14)	14 (14)	93.5 (101)	110 (117)	513 (700)	547 (549)
Note 10	0.5 (2.5)	1.5 (3.5)	122 (124)	151 (140)	290 (378)	302 (261)
Note 10 Lite	15 (11)	17 (17)	100 (101)	107 (108)	447 (628)	462 (463)

Table 2. Animation playing comparison: data presented are average values for 5 measurement on *simple* composition and on *complex* composition (in braces).

	CPU, %		Memory, Mb	
	AVD	Lottie	AVD	Lottie
S9+	7 (11)	12 (27)	67.5 (80.5)	79 (95.5)
Note 10	5.5 (7.5)	10.5 (13.5)	145.5 (148.5)	144 (156)
Note 10 Lite	8.5 (12)	13 (27)	101.5 (221)	119 (120.5)

Based on the obtained results, we can see that the proposed approach uses 13% less memory and 24% less CPU compared to Lottie's solution but requires 11% more time to complete the process on loading stage. In the playing stage our approach uses almost twice as less CPU resources but is almost equal in memory consumption.

6 Conclusions

In the current study we proposed an approach that can export ready-to-go assets in a native format for Android. Our approach consists of extracting and decomposing AAE data, rebuilding it into the hierarchical structure of the graphics objects, and assembling obtained data into ready-to-go AVD assets.

The proposed approach was highly evaluated by both designers and developers, and got positive feedbacks on such characteristics from UEQ-S as easy, supportive, effective, and clear. Compared to Lottie's solution, our approach uses almost twice as less CPU resources in the playing stage independently from animation level complexity.

Experiments have shown that motion design development using the proposed approach improves design-developer collaboration, allows saving time for sharing design information, and allows adopting motion design for Android application more easily.

References

1. Huhtala, J., et al.: Animated UI transitions and perception of time: a user study on animated effects on a mobile screen. In: Proceedings of the SIGCHI Conference on Human Factors in Computing Systems (CHI 2010), pp. 1339–1342. ACM, New York (2010). https://doi.org/10.1145/1753326.1753527
2. Morgan, H.: Motion Design and Its Impact on User Experience (2018). UXmatters. https://www.uxmatters.com/mt/archives/2018/11/motion-design-and-its-impact-on-user-experience.php. Accessed 19 Nov 2018
3. Harris, M.: Best animation software and apps for UI and UX design (2018). Digital Arts. https://www.digitalartsonline.co.uk/features/interactive-design/best-animation-software-apps-for-ui-ux-design/. Accessed 22 May 2018
4. Brown, J.M., Lindgaard, G., Biddle, R.: Joint implicit alignment work of interaction designers and software developers. In: Proceedings of the 7th Nordic Conference on Human-Computer Interaction Making Sense Through Design (NordiCHI 2012), pp. 693–702. ACM, New York (2012). https://doi.org/10.1145/2399016.2399121
5. Leiva, G., Maudet, N., Mackay, W., Beaudouin-Lafon, M.: Enact: reducing designer–developer breakdowns when prototyping custom interactions. ACM Trans. Comput.-Hum. Interact. **26**(3), 1–48 (2019). https://doi.org/10.1145/3310276
6. Maudet, N., Leiva, G., Beaudouin-Lafon, M., Mackay, W.: Design breakdowns: designer-developer gaps in representing and interpreting interactive systems. In: Proceedings of the 2017 ACM Conference on Computer Supported Cooperative Work and Social Computing, pp. 630–641. ACM, New York (2017). https://doi.org/10.1145/2998181.2998190
7. Bogachenko, A., et al.: All you need is web: visual interaction with no graphic background. In: Stephanidis, C., Antona, M. (eds.) HCII 2020. CCIS, vol. 1224, pp. 3–10. Springer, Cham (2020). https://doi.org/10.1007/978-3-030-50726-8_1
8. Steelkiwi Inc.: Lottie by Airbnb: Innovation or Limitation for Designers? (2019). https://uxplanet.org/lottie-by-airbnb-innovation-or-limitation-for-designers-11cc7666ea2c. Accessed 18 Jan 2019
9. Hidayat, T., Sungkowo, B.D.: Comparison of memory consumptive against the use of various image formats for app onboarding animation assets on Android with Lottie JSON. In: Proceedings of 2020 3rd International Conference on Computer and Informatics Engineering, IC2IE, Yogyakarta, pp. 376–381 (2020). https://doi.org/10.1109/IC2IE50715.2020.9274612
10. Creative Suite Developer Center: Adobe CEP APIs (2014). https://www.adobe.com/devnet/creativesuite/articles/adobe-cep-apis.html. Accessed 1 July 2014
11. Schrepp, M., Hinderks, A., Thomaschewski, J.: Design and evaluation of a short version of the user experience questionnaire (UEQ-S). Int. J. Interact. Multimed. Artif. Intell. 4(6), 103–108 (2017). https://doi.org/10.9781/ijimai.2017.09.001

UX Design, Education, and Cognition: An Exploration of a Metacognitive Systematic Model of Digital Interface to Mediate Knowledge Construction

Marília C. Galvão(✉), Emanuelle M. P. Simas(✉), Carla V. M. Marques(✉), and Claudia L. R. Motta(✉)

Universidade Federal do Rio de Janeiro, Rio de Janeiro, RJ 21941-916, Brazil
{mariliagalvao,ellesimas,carlaveronica,claudiam}@nce.ufrj.br

Abstract. User experience (UX) and User interface (UI) design, HCI and metacognition are starting to be explored subjects of academic studies and discussions. On the other hand, most of the researchers about these subjects does not focus on metacognition approaches. So, in this paper we present an exploratory study that covered the development of a metacognitive virtual learning tool that centralizes the student's cognition and learning structure as an object of observation when planning an interface that can a) be generalized to any content b) Optimize the user experience and C) Enhance the learning process. We highlight the contributions of the areas of Human Computer Interaction and User Experience design to help develop students' cognitive potential. Using design thinking as strategy, we are seeking to show that UX/UI design can contribute to a creative and logical introduction to contents, enriching students experience as a user, by awakening the understanding of their learning processes. In short, we believe that as the ways of contact with information are being changed it is important to society to explore different forms of helping to learn how to learn.

Keywords: UX design · UI design · HCI · Metacognition

1 Introduction

In the context of the pandemic caused by Sars-CoV-2, distance learning environments and virtual learning environments, are becoming necessities. Although, distance learning represents a new educational paradigm, where knowledge tends to be decentralized by the teacher and still allows for synchronous and asynchronous interaction and communication [1], the learning environments still present the same expository and conditioning pedagogical model as the classroom. Most of schools and universities had a digital migration and created their virtual environment and tools, this can mean an easier access to knowledge and a chance to let the students guide their way of learning how to learn, but with these opportunities and autonomy comes the fear of a poor learning. Therefore, this study search for ways to intervening in digital learning environments with HCI and UX/UI design with metacognition as foundation.

© Springer Nature Switzerland AG 2021
C. Stephanidis et al. (Eds.): HCII 2021, CCIS 1419, pp. 12–17, 2021.
https://doi.org/10.1007/978-3-030-78635-9_2

2 Theoretical Background

2.1 Metacognitive Design

With online education becoming more highlighted over the decades, design researchers like Kirsh [3] raise the question "As educators and designers, how can we create the conditions that will lead to better learning?". The researcher then suggests that one of the ways to optimize learning may be through the visual structures present in virtual teaching environments that make an important difference to facilitate the efficiency of cognition and metacognition, contributing to the construction of knowledge, critical and reflective thinking. This study explores on of the ways that design can contribute in the development of learning tools.

2.2 Theory of Objects

In his theory, Moles [7] inserts an object as a syntactic element involved in the phenomenological sphere and submitted to the logic of action, praxis and culture.

The consequence of the positioning of the element on the logic of action is the implication of a semantic system that qualifies and organizes objects in the existence of others that are also qualifiable.

Composing spaces and semantic intersections, objects can be graded according to the degree of belonging to the field of which it is part; it may also be singularly positioned closer or further from the object that represents the maximum valuation of belonging to such a space due to the sum of the qualities that the semantic belonging criterion postulates. Therefore, the system's consistency and coherence are verified in the stability of the distance valuation criterion and in the stable application of the criterion to the objects to be valued.

2.3 Graph Theory

Graph theory corresponds to the section of mathematical studies on discrete relationships and combinations [6]. The structure of a graph consists of vertices and edges, where the first corresponds to the finite sets of objects with correlational potential and the second the relations between the sets themselves [11].

Such a concept has application in areas of knowledge in addition to the exact ones. Fauconnier's theory of mental spaces [2], which plans [9] the semantic relations arising from the construction of meaning and the quality of ambiguities, as well as the syntactic tree resulting from the hierarchical decomposition of grammatical constituents (see Fig. 1) are examples of manifestation of theory in linguistics.

There are a wide range of possibilities for the construction of a graph. The graph above, defined as the tree graph, has the quality of connection and the absence of a cycle [5], that is, there are edges from any two of its vertices and the absence of closed circuits in the roots. At the first root, of less depth and of which all the branches they will originate in cascade, it is given degree zero, the second roots degree two and so on.

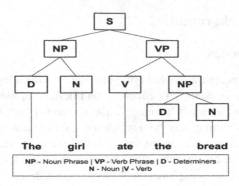

Fig. 1. Abstract syntax tree

2.4   Systemic Network: Decomposition and Hierarchization of Theory

The systemic network corresponds to the adequacy of theoretical knowledge to the logical-systemic structure. The principle of vertices and edges from graph theory (see Sect. 2.3) was used to trace the hierarchy of concepts, and the principle of Moles' pertinence (see Sect. 2.2), in this work materialized in theoretical objects, was applied in the verification of the theoretical consistency of the network.

The systemic decomposition of the theory resulted in a graph of the mapping of the object of knowledge as a conglomerate of interdependent relations and a visual arrangement of generalities and specificities. The figure below corresponds to the epistemic structure of the theory after decomposition (see Fig. 2).

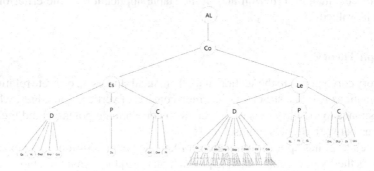

Fig. 2. Graph of epistemic decomposition

The graph of epistemic decomposition will differ according to the nature of the knowledge or decision making at each new node. In short, the network design comprises four stages: a) Selection and analysis of the theoretical set, b) Archive of the main domains (modules), c) Decomposition of the domains into subdomains (sub-modules) and d) Graphical realization of the hierarchy.

The analysis process of the theoretical set takes place in the grouping of reference materials. Following the analysis of the theoretical set, the registration of the modules materializes in the synthesis of the referential group carried out previously. Referential contents are reduced to unique markers (titles) that name the graph's nodes. Subsequently, the decomposition of modules into sub-modules corresponds to the theory's hierarchy process. The consistency of the network was verified in the existence of degrees of direct dependence on the more specific branches with respect to previous branches. Therefore, if a specific item exists simultaneously on two nodes, the network is rechecked to reduce possible conceptual deviations of magnitude.

3   Methods and Development

3.1   Discovery of Central Problems

This exploratory research began with the direct observation of speech therapy students during classes of cognitive psychology, according to Lakatos [4] direct observation is a type of activity that consists not only in seeing and hearing, but also in examining facts or phenomena that are desired studying. Thus, it was observed the interaction of students with the digital platform Activufrj, a learning supporting tool, used where students could find specialized reading materials about authors and theories.

We verify the students difficult to notice the connections between authors and theories, they also did not have a good experience while using the platform due to organization factors. Therefore, we propose to carry out an intervention started in the design of the community's HCI, UX and UI, investing in an approach that could benefit the students' cognitively and increase their satisfaction during navigation.

3.2   Process of Development and Testing

For the development of graphic intervention in the community that received speech therapy students, the cognitive strategy, design thinking based on the model proposed by Stanford University [10], and is divided into: empathize, define, ideate, prototype and test was used. During each phase, we could understand and point out the problem to be solved their issues on understanding the connection among psychologists, philosophers, theories, and their bad experience accessing the community, then led this problem to a logical solution using collaborative tool such as Trello to organize tasks to develop solutions, in the process of ideate we found that the most appropriate concept to create the UX/UI design intervention was using a mental model based on senior student knowledge/understanding of the subject leading to a tree graph (see Fig. 2.) with that, we arrived at a design prototype (see Fig. 3.) where we could apply at first, usability tests.

16   M. C. Galvão et al.

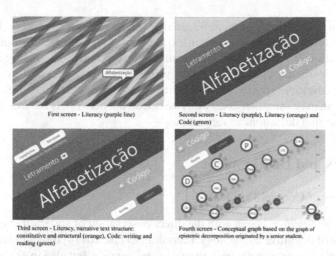

First screen - Literacy (purple line)

Second screen - Literacy (purple), Literacy (orange) and Code (green)

Third screen - Literacy, narrative text structure: constitutive and structural (orange), Code: writing and reading (green)

Fourth screen - Conceptual graph based on the graph of epistemic decomposition originated by a senior student.

Fig. 3. Design prototype for the community "Speech Therapy – Cognitive Psychology".

4   Results and Final Considerations

For the results of the usability test, five participants [8] interacted with the prototype and data was collected with the help of an online form (see Fig. 4.) created with Anvil, a free Python-based drag-and-drop web app builder. The online test had questions about the meaning of the images for the users, most of these users have no experience with speech therapy topics, it was intending to observe how they would rationalize the subjects with the help of the community design the experience.

The Table 1 show the answers related only to the first screen, most users the images were seen as something positive to interact with. This is a work in progress and the tests were about usability, only in a future and deeper investigation we will be able to track metacognition change in a quantitative way.

This study will continue to collect information to explore metacognition development through design. Our conclusion is that, we could observe the users felt joy and guidance when talked about the feeling of organization that the first screen transmits, they showed a rationalization about the image organization and it points out we are on a promising path.

Second screen of the test: Previous image of the prototype

Third screen of the test: question - What this image means to you?

Fig. 4.   Screens of the online form made with Anvil

Table 1. Slice of the answers to the online test about the first screen of the prototype

User ID	User thoughts about the first screen	Image name
[98929, 128556889]	It gives the idea of something creative and fun	First screen
[98929, 128965210]	The colors caught my attention the most, and it gives me a sense of organization	First screen
[98929, 129432827]	My first sensation when seeing the image was of joy, celebration, provoked by the colored diagonals that go in different directions	First screen
[98929, 138982816]	Lightness	First screen
[98929, 138983870]	The first sensation was of organization and cleanliness. The part that drew the most attention was the colors of the image, for being large and having vibrant colors on a more pastel background	First screen

References

1. Cabero Almenara, J., Carmen Llorente Cejudo, M.: Interaction in e-learning: use of tool, elements of analysis and educational possibilities. RIED **10**(2), 97–123 (2007). ISSN 1138-2783
2. Fauconnier, G.: Mappings in Thought and Language. 1st edn. Cambridge University Press, Australia (1997)
3. Kirsh, D.: Adapting the environment instead of oneself. Adapt. Behav. **4**(3/4), 415–452 (1996)
4. Lakatos, E.M., Marconi, M.A.: Metodologia do trabalho científico. 4 ed. Atlas, São Paulo (1992)
5. Lovász, L., Pelikáne, J., Vesztergombi, K.: Matemática Discreta, Rio de Janeiro SBM (2012)
6. Sanfilippo, A.: Graph theory. In: Brown, K. (ed.) Encyclopedia of Language & Liguistics, 2nd edn, pp. 140–142. Elsevier (2006)
7. Moles, A.A.: Teoria do Objeto - Edições tempo Brasileiro, RJ (1981)
8. NN/g Nielsen Norman Group. http://www.useit.com/alertbox/20000319.html. Accessed 15 Mar 2021
9. SISTEBIB. Universidade Federal do Amazonas. https://tede.ufam.edu.br/handle/tede/4788. Accessed 10 Mar 2021
10. Stanford.edu. https://web.stanford.edu/~mshanks/MichaelShanks/files/509554.pdf. Accessed 22 Mar 2021
11. Wallis, W.D.: A Beginner's Guide to Graph Teory. Birkhauser (2007)

Software Developers Are People, Too: Using Participatory Research in the Tech Industry

Ana F. Couvinhas[1]([✉]), André F. Pinto[1]([✉]), Denis A. Coelho[2]([✉]) [iD],
and Brad Paul[3]([✉])

[1] OutSystems, Algés, Portugal
{ana.couvinhas,andre.fernandes}@outsystems.com
[2] Jönköping University, Jönköping, Sweden
denis.coelho@ju.se
[3] WISCAP, Madison, USA
bpaul@wiscap.org

Abstract. This paper reports an ethnographic researcher's shift towards the tech industry while maintaining the purpose of spotting opportunities and problems. It must be emphasized that whether working with remote communities in far-flung corners of the world or sitting in a room full of software developers, the concept remains the same: it is all about the users. Ethnographic researchers may not live with software developers but are getting increasingly closer to them. This paper aims to explain how this is done, i.e., by using participatory methods, such as field diaries. The first author's initial realization of the full potential of diaries arose in Ethiopia and Mozambique, where efforts by institutions to help people often fail due to the lack of on-the-ground knowledge about the communities in which they operate. To address this, written and photo diaries were implemented so that community members could clearly express what is important in their everyday lives. In the current software company setting, we use the same method to understand what happens when users develop with our platform. The salient difference is that instead of receiving handwritten diaries and photos, we collect digital journals and screenshots from our users' experience. This enables moving towards a continuous research vision to identify new user needs timely and ensure we are always building the right thing. However, by adopting this and other proactive approaches for generative research, new challenges are emerging regarding the efficient collection and analysis of large amounts of qualitative information.

Keywords: Participatory research · Continuous research · Field diaries

1 Introduction

While fast-paced companies are finding that it is no longer enough to perform short-term UX research, continuous participatory user research in agile contexts is incredibly challenging. In this article, a parallel is drawn between human development field studies—namely in the Field Diaries Project—and those performed in the context of OutSystems,

C. Stephanidis et al. (Eds.): HCII 2021, CCIS 1419, pp. 18–24, 2021.
https://doi.org/10.1007/978-3-030-78635-9_3

a software company that created a low-code platform that allows businesses to develop, deploy, and manage enterprise applications.

As an ethnographic researcher, the first author's job focused on impacting 'real-world' environments. The Field Diaries Project started in highly remote areas of Mozambique at TechnoServe, a nonprofit organization that uses a business approach to reduce poverty. Then, it became an independent project that provided international research consulting services.

Whether researchers are working with remote communities in far-flung corners of the world or sitting in a room full of software developers, the concept remains the same: it's all about the users. So, this article builds on the first author's accumulated experience to explain how organizations can use participatory research methods, such as field diaries, to improve users' experience continuously, regardless of the research context.

2 Research Methods

This section concerns the research methodology, which follows a two-pronged approach. The reported research method is included in the autobiographical narrative inquiry subsection. The justification for adopting diaries as a research methodology when developing a low-code software platform is explained in the following subsections.

2.1 Autobiographical Narrative Inquiry

The methods used in the study reported in this paper support the implementation of a case study approach, with input from the first author's own experiences. Hence, the results comprise both autobiographical and observed elements. Autobiographical narrative inquiry [1], as used in the studies reported in this paper, locates the inquiry for both the author and the reader. It also allows the author to understand their relationship with the phenomenon under study [2, 3].

2.2 Reasons to Adopt Diaries as a Research Methodology

Often, organizations' efforts aimed at helping people fail due to the lack of on-the-ground knowledge and cultural beliefs about the communities in which they operate. To address this, the Field Diaries Project implemented written diaries so that community members could clearly express what is important in their everyday lives. That allowed researchers to identify community changes, whether big or small. Moreover, the Project provided research participants with cameras to capture everyday life through community photography. Frame by frame, they captured unconventional scenarios that outsiders would never be able to witness, from witch doctor rituals, household routines, and traditional dances to "farming spirits."

Currently, at the case company, the same method is used. Instead of receiving handwritten diaries and photos, the UX Research team receives digital journals and screenshots from the users depicting their experience. Then, researchers further explore user needs, concerns, and improvement suggestions with in-depth interviews.

So, regardless of the used method in a highly ethnographic context or digital company, the research methodologies share common aspects. At the case company, the research team increasingly embraced a participatory approach to deeply understand users' reality and allow them to shape the solutions.

By keeping diaries, the case company moves towards a continuous research vision to timely identify new user needs and ensure it is constantly building the right thing. With today's fast-paced environment, users' needs are changing often and quickly; therefore, it no longer makes sense to solely analyze telemetry data and perform short-term UX research. However, by adopting this and other proactive approaches for generative research, new challenges are emerging.

3 Challenges That Emerge From Continuous Research and How to Overcome Them

Continuous user research is much more challenging than short-term research, but it is definitely worth it. The three main challenges shared by the Field Diaries Project [4] and the case company while conducting continuous research were:

- Reaching research participants.
- Persuading them to collaborate with the organization continuously.
- Digesting the gathered information.

3.1 Reaching Research Participants

When working with highly remote communities in Africa, finding research participants is an adventure per se. Having a local research partner is crucial to learn the communities' social norms in advance and anticipate potentially uncomfortable conversations for the researcher.

It's also essential that the researcher knows in advance what their expected behavior should be. For example, in Mozambique's northern regions, an outsider shouldn't approach locals without first talking to the community leader, who is usually the spiritual leader. And to find the leader, the team needs precious help from the local partner, who will introduce the leader to the team.

When the research team receives their blessing to talk to locals, the leader also points out specific people who fit the target because they know everybody. To start nearing research participants, researchers can use one of the most effective ice-breakers and introduce themselves in the local dialect.

Getting research participants in extremely remote communities might take many hours because there's a need to build trust and empathy, which is deeply linked to the cultural setting in which the research will be performed.

At a software development company, reaching research participants is quite a different challenge, but there are some similarities in the process. At the case company, the low-code developers are the users who create the field diaries. So, the pool of potential research participants in the low-code context is much smaller. This is why a big part of our research participants are OutSystems Community members, mostly "Most Valuable Professionals" who often proactively provide snippets of valuable information.

Much like their work in remote African communities, researchers need to use a specific language to communicate with users. Although researchers don't need to learn how to introduce themselves in a participant's dialect, they need to know in advance the "low-code developers' language," that is, the basic technical jargon. Researchers often bring along technical colleagues who help them with this.

At the case company, researchers do not need to get blessings from the community spiritual leader. However, they should still take into account the social forces within the customers' companies (things like social norms, decision-making rules, and power dynamics). Researchers need to be aware of the company's different roles, how people interact and influence each other, and how we should approach different people to reach the targeted research participants.

In African communities, the best way to create a rapport with research participants was to dedicate a lot of time to informal settings. However, in the digital sector, participants tend to have tight schedules.

3.2 Persuading Research Participants to Collaborate With the Organization Continuously

In remote African communities, the researchers could not pay participants due to organizational policies. So, how did researchers keep them motivated for long periods of time? Surprisingly, researchers found that photography, strategic thinking, and status were the main reasons that kept participants motivated during the interactions with participants.

As the only ones with a photo camera in the community, research participants tended to create their own photography businesses by shooting social, familial, and religious events. Another thing that also motivated them to keep on writing diaries was that they had privileged access to research insights. So, they were aware of trends and small business opportunities with considerable potential within the community. In conclusion, understanding what kept research participants motivated was a surprising iterative process. It's vital that researchers organically identify what motivates users to keep their interest throughout the longitudinal research.

At the software development company, things are different. However, the sense of belonging and status also plays an integral part in keeping research participants motivated.

A large part of the research participants is OutSystems Community members. They use OutSystems products on a daily basis and are often available to share their thoughts, ideas for improvement, and dry-run new versions of the low-code platform. These research participants feel motivated to collaborate with researchers to have early access to new features, the privilege of being the first to explore them and suggest improvements. Also, research participants feel that they contribute to improving a tool that they use as part of their jobs: by helping the research team, the case company supports them in their work!

By being extremely active in the OutSystems Community and participating in continuous research initiatives, participants establish a privileged communication channel with OutSystems, which gives them status within that community—this is a similar process to that of research participants in Africa, who gain social recognition by being the voice of their communities.

Higher social recognition among the OutSystems Community means higher forum rankings and more badges, which leads to more professional opportunities as potential customers reach out to OutSystems partners and developers through the company's website. Also, being in a community where everyone is there to share their struggles, challenges and doubts means being part of a social group in which developers are motivated to help each other.

3.3 Digesting the Information Gathered

These participatory long-term research methods generate large amounts of qualitative data, making it much more challenging to digest than short-term research data. Often, UX researchers feel overwhelmed and struggle to make sense of all the gathered information.

In the Field Diaries, the written diaries were the core of our project, which allowed us to have dedicated staff to analyze and digitalize the information—the "Data Entry" team. One vital aspect was hiring computer literate people from the targeted community to interpret the writings' correct meaning and nuances—something an outsider couldn't do.

The Data Entry team translated and entered all the activities reported by the research participants in the system and the amount of time spent on each activity. Also, they registered community stories and other relevant information. Researchers often had meetings with the Data Entry team to align and validate if researchers analyzed the translated information correctly. Basically, researchers converted the qualitative data into storytelling snippets and measurable insights—for example, the amount of time a participant spent in a specific activity. Researchers clustered the information according to research themes after deconstructing the diaries and obtaining the information snippets in English.

At the software development company, diaries are one of the many techniques researchers use to collect information. They must digest it more quickly and efficiently than in the Field Diaries Project to feed the team with insights and keep the case company's agile environment running fast.

These diaries are essentially digital journals and screenshots in which research participants describe the experience they have with the product by providing written feedback on a few specific topics. These will allow teams to make informed decisions and identify unexpected issues.

Researchers compile the information from all research participants in a digital board, where snippets of information, thematic clusters, and thoughtful tags are the ways for successful information digestion.

For each research participant, researchers create a basic bio card and attribute a participant code. With the bio cards, researchers have an on-going list of anonymized bios that keeps growing and can be quickly and easily updated with new research participants or new diaries from existing participants.

Researchers then deconstruct the information that participants provide into small chunks of qualitative data and create a card for each snippet.

For quick traceability, the research team tags each card with the participant's code, geographic location, professional role, background, software proficiency, and other relevant tags for our analysis.

Finally, once researchers receive a new diary, they deconstruct it into small parts and distribute them on the board according to each piece of information's theme. Then, in every research sprint, researchers perform an affinity diagram analysis to update OutSystems teams with the latest insights.

Researchers also compare the research insights throughout time and in different scenarios. For example, they compare the experience of a novice OutSystems user with that of an expert user and analyze their software proficiency, agility, struggles, and so forth.

This is OutSystems' method to keep building knowledge about its users in a fast and consistent way, but this is a process that researchers are still iterating.

So, when drawing a parallel between the digestion of African diaries versus digital diaries, in both situations, there is the deconstruction of the diaries into snippets of information, thematic clustering, and data comparison.

4 Conclusion

Whether conducting continuous research in a remote community in Africa or a digital company, researchers face three common main challenges: reaching research participants, persuading them to collaborate with researchers continuously, and digesting the gathered information. To reach research participants, it is essential to: have a buddy, know the communities' social norms in advance, approach the right person to get access to target users, learn the basics of the local "dialect," and be conscious of the participants' time. To persuade participants to collaborate with researchers continuously, it is necessary to: promote a sense of belonging, enable ways for social recognition (status), and drive more business opportunities. Digesting the gathered information involves taking action to create participant bios (anonymous, with tags); deconstruct information into snippets; do thematic clustering; and compare data (target vs. control, before vs. after).

In sum, continuous user research is much more challenging than short-term research, but it is definitely worth it, as it enables a deep dive into users' needs and behaviors through time instead of at a single point in time. By keeping diaries, the case company moves towards a continuous research vision to timely identify new user needs and ensure that it is always building the right thing.

References

1. Clandinin, D.J., Connelly, F.M.: Narrative Inquiry: Experience and Story in Qualitative Research Jossey-Bass, San Francisco (2000)
2. Schaefer, L., Jean Clandinin, D.: Stories of sustaining: a narrative inquiry into the experiences of two beginning teachers. Learn. Landscapes 4(2), 275–295 (2011). https://doi.org/10.36510/learnland.v4i2.400

3. Schaefer, L.: Narrative inquiry for physical education pedagogy. Int. J. Pedagogies Learn. **8**(1), 18–26 (2013)
4. Couvinhas, A.F., Paul, B., Coelho, D.A.: The field diaries: an innovative participatory methodology. In: Proceedings 19th Triennial Congress of the IEA 2015, August, vol. 9, p. 14 (2015)

Where is the User in User-Centered Design?

Vera Fink[(⊠)] and Maximilian Eibl[(⊠)]

Technical University Chemnitz, Straße der Nationen 62, 09111 Chemnitz, Saxony, Germany
{vera.fink,maximilian.eibl}@informatik.tu-chemnitz.de

Abstract. If ISO [1] definitions are viewed through a "human" filter, the terms support only a system-side elimination. Is it more useful to develop solutions that enable people to achieve a goal, or to create well-being and positive experiences? In my thesis, I describe concrete examples from the ISO of how focus falls on the user.

The main point is to resolve the question between usability and user experience ("Can the methods work together?") and between the interests of project participants ("effective and efficient") and the interests of users ("positive user experiences"). Because of the malleable and imprecise (nondeterministic) human influence factor, there is a need for an empirical investigation in the form of an evaluation metric [2]. I write about the international standard ISO-9241 (guidelines for human-computer interactions), contributions from human-centered design, design thinking, and psychological needs. The question is: Are psychological needs a tool that can bring humans more into focus, and if so, how does this manifest itself in the design process?

Keywords: Human centered design · User experience · Psychological needs

1 Introduction

The product development process is very complex. In particular, it requires multidisciplinary or interdisciplinary visibility between development system architecture and the needs of a user. In addition to the systematic approach to software implementation, the user must be an essential factor [3].

In this article I compile the results of our workshops and present a research framework to discuss in the computer science community. I thereby focus on issues related to finding the user in the user-centered design process, like the one described by DIN EN ISO. Our research question is to make the user central. This can be achieved by considering the user experience with a focus on users' psychological needs and their influences, with the goal of improving the quality of life and well-being of people [4].

The standard DIN EN ISO 9241-210:2019 (referred to hereafter as ISO-210) describes a process for the development of usable and useful interactive systems in an industrial context, wherein the design process focuses on user requirements and requests. From the beginning of the development process, we know that hardware ergonomics is at the core of the health benefits provided by software ergonomics [5]. Software ergonomics

C. Stephanidis et al. (Eds.): HCII 2021, CCIS 1419, pp. 25–32, 2021.
https://doi.org/10.1007/978-3-030-78635-9_4

and the increasing prevalence of personal computers have led to computer-centered work-stations where, for the first time, users are actively involved in development, and which are meant to support them with user-friendly tools and concepts [3, 6]. The issues of user-friendliness seem not to change based on interdisciplinary basic sciences, like hardware ergonomics, occupational science, computer science, physiology, psychology, or the humanities, but remain rather as guidelines for health regulations in the workplace. These guidelines are structured according to precise instructions on what should not be done or what should be avoided (ISO), and how a system should be developed and designed in order to catch and allow as few user errors as possible during interaction [1]. While conducting workshops and doing research, I asked where users appear in processes and how they are involved.

In my search for the user in these processes, I examined the ISO standard more closely. Here it was apparent that the roles of stakeholders and users are tremendously important. Although an organization, represented by stakeholders who obtain client-specific systems, can directly influence design, user participation in evaluation is not required, only possible [ISO 210 p. 14 Chapter 5.3, second section]. This statement is in direct conflict with the title "users are involved in design and development." Corresponding comments from different sections underline another difference in the definition between shareholders and users. Definition 3.7 of human-centered design states that use of the term "human-centered" must also apply to shareholders, who would normally not be considered users. This is followed in Chapter 5.4 by a comment on the term "user-centered," which states that an evaluation must be carried out based on the user's perspective. The definitions of these terms, and their differences, lead one to the conclusion that it is not humans who are central, but rather the role of shareholders.

In addition, the objective perspective of the ISO, due to the abstract nature of the problem, leads to a loss of ideas from the beginning of the development process [7]. This situation creates an objective framework that can be easily measured, but within this framework it is difficult to thinking outside the box later in the development process.

The definition chapter provides another indication for what is central to the development process, according to the ISO. The word "human" appears in 4 of 18 definitions (22%). Even in the explanation for the term "human-centered design," Sect. 3.7, the word "human" does not appear except in the title [1]. This results in a variety of terms, such as system, product, service, development, maintenance, functionality, system operation, resources, technology, costs and, finally, organization. The word "system" is referred to a total of 30 times only in Chapter 3.

Section 3.11 clarifies the right of stakeholders to a system that must meet their requirements and expectations via the application of ISO aspects of system design; for example, by improving the identification and definition of functional requirements of the system, and increasing the likelihood that a product will be completed successfully on time and on budget, but not satisfaction. The ISO guidelines secure the final product, not the sensibilities of users. There is no evaluation section on how to test for user satisfaction.

Usability is another central point. Just as the definitions described in Chapter 2.2 reflect the process, the point is to consider only from the aspect of usability the requirements, user requests, and human factors (especially ergonomics), and how these can be used in such a way that they lead to increased effectiveness and efficiency in methods, knowledge, and described techniques. Only effectiveness and efficiency are no longer sufficient, and dark patterns are used to elicit emotion. Users are manipulated to not make decisions based on fear of loss; for example, cancelling a subscription [8].

2 Related Work Overview

One of the significant designs of the IoT (Internet of Things) through design thinking approaches, IDEO cards, and participatory design has been to create not the applications that designers think users want, but rather to engage participants to develop useful developments for themselves [9]. When users are involved in the drafting process, they become emotionally attached. This offers me, the user, the maximum benefit. But positive experiences with technology are mostly a side effect. The best result of Design Thinking is a well-designed application that is highly user-friendly but does not consciously evoke positive emotions. In the brainstorming phase, participatory design encourages emotions. This process is unsystematic because the emotionality and positive emotions are not in the foreground. You can work with the emotions that appear. The approach to a positive user experience by fulfilling psychological needs acts on the principle of consciously triggering emotions. Every human being has the same kinds of needs, but the expression and importance of those needs is individual.

We came to a similar result in the co-design workshop on our project on an assistive shopping robot in the supermarket (brief description of this procedure in Chapter 3) [10]. In the workshop, we had users develop a shopping robot themselves with the help of Lego®. The result was a higher level of acceptance of assistive shopping robots. We were able to confirm that participatory design encourages emotional involvement in the brainstorming phase.

In the research community, the value proposition for creating positive user experiences is sometimes questionable, as every developer and scientist today who comes into contact with human-computer interaction in any way implicitly wants to create a good, interactive product. They all want users to like, use, and recommend their applications. Does it make sense to look at the concepts of interaction that currently meet psychological needs, like connectedness, or to trigger and keep working on positive emotions like happiness [11]?

Marc Hassenzahl says that user experience design is first and foremost a dialogue with the user. Therefore, we go out and get to know the user, their behavior and their intention. The "Why?" is particularly important and can be unraveled and understood if you know the user's psychological needs. Experience is not the interaction with the product, but rather its application. It is a narrative that creates experiences, and which provides instructions that users follow based on their own motivation [12].

The view from the user's perspective enables us to describe novel technologies [13]. And value of inclusive design in contributing to the production of good, satisfying, responsible, socially sustainable, and commercially viable products [14]. We create positive experiences, and therefore positive technology [15].

3 Concept Approach

The "I-RobEka" project is developing an autonomous, mobile robot to be used as a shopping assistant. Part of this development was designing and testing a situationally adaptable interaction concept for to be used on tablet computers [10]. This framework is interesting for various scientific fields, as it has not yet been investigated in such a context. Therefore, we decided to create workshop frameworks where we engage in dialogue with users in order to gather knowledge and novel experiences in the field of robotics for human-computer interaction in the supermarket context.

3.1 Living-Lab

Living Lab [16] workshops help to bring in potential users and serve to reduce complexity. We created a Journey Map in our workshop [17], in which participants described their purchasing process, including their emotional states. In the third part of our workshop there was a visual stimulus: a 3D model of the robot made by the manufacturer and inserted into a picture of a supermarket, not an existing robot. This visual stimulus revealed many details about how the assistive robot should look, although it was only an artificial representation. Many workshop participants focused too much on the looks of the robot and criticized details. Almost all of them said that they would not use such a robot: "A nice idea, but not for me." Although it wasn't our focus, we recorded different opinions about the robot's appearance that varied widely. This puzzled us and led us to another question: If users are free to design a shopping robot, what would it look like? This is why we decided to hold an explorative co-design workshop where participants could build their own shopping robot.

3.2 Explorative Co-designed Workshops

Journey Map was a foundation for the following step. We asked the participants in the workshop to use the provided Lego® pieces or modeling clay to design a robot. This would help them overcome the problems they described at the end of the previous step. For the participants who preferred using Lego®, we offered a variety of pieces from the thematic sets "vehicles" and "creatures." This made it possible to attach eyes or other creature-like features to vehicles, or vice versa. In the next step, we asked a few questions to clarify certain aspects of the robot. As the last part, we asked the participants questions about their robot. We held three workshop sessions. Each session was structured in the same way (Living-Labs). The first session only had one participant, the second and third had two, respectively. Many of the younger generations had indicated that they would not use such assistance. Participants over 50 had a different opinion. We have adapted the workshop and set the age of the participants to 50+. The average age was 59.7. All the participants were female. Each participant received 30€ for his help [6]. Finally, we asked the participants questions about their robot, and each received €30 for their help and time. The users themselves came up with the ideas that we had already developed as visual stimulus in the Living Lab workshop. We realized that we understand the users better through the co-designed process. Through this workshop we have sharpened the focus on the psychological needs more [10].

4   Users as the Focus of UX

In this context, competence, security, autonomy, and connectedness can be psychological needs [18]. We want to use applications to consciously trigger positive emotions in users, and to systematize this process in order to prioritize emotionality and positive emotions [19]. Users are put in focus via their psychological needs. How well can humans assess these needs in the respective context of a product, and what does this assessment reveal? In order to analyze the effects of these needs on the design process, we have developed the following setting, as shown in Fig. 1 [20].

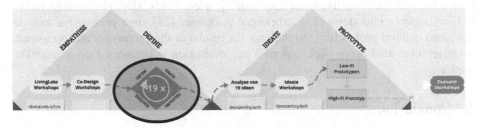

Fig. 1. Design process – study setting

In one semester in 2019, 71 students produced 19 independent prototypes ranging from low to high fidelity. The design phases were based on the classic design procedures. Figure 1 displays this sequence, divided into Empathize - Define - Ideate - Prototype. We then designed a joint prototype as a team, which we will compare after another semester (see Table 1).

Table 1. Exercise formation

Control group	Parameters
cpo1	Existing application with specification of psychological needs
cpo0	Existing application without specification of psychological needs
cpn1	Develop new applications with specification of psychological needs
cpn0	Develop new applications without specification of psychological needs

In a subsequent iteration loop, the 19 prototypes are assessed with a focus on psychological needs. There are a total of 4 control groups (cp). Two groups begin with no specification of these needs (0), and two others with specifications mixed with different levels of development (1). Two groups get the high-fidelity prototype from the first semester as a starting condition (o), and the two other groups start from scratch (n). See Table 1.

In the workshops that we conducted, we had the participants create their own journey maps, and we recorded all their statements. These statements give us an idea of the primary needs that should be met when shopping for groceries. Psychological needs

Fig. 2. Sequence of projects in control groups

were either assessed or ascertained in all groups. All groups have the same sequence of development processes (see Fig. 2).

In order to investigate or inquire about psychological needs, developers use user experience research methods like contextual inquiry, needs cards, UX concept exploration [21], experience interviews [22], experience categories [23], time perspective method [24], and cultural probes [25]. At the end, the results of the prototypes are compared: users are evaluated using click dummies and evaluation is performed using usability metrics.

5   Conclusion

The authors of [3] write that "Humanistic HCI" is a systematic and multifaceted series of humanistic contributions that are characterized by humanistic epistemology and methodological rigor. The contributions of the humanities are not always as visible as possible, and subject-specific disciplinary definitions often hinder collaboration between the humanities and HCI research.

The results of this semester setting provide answers as to how well psychological needs can be made a preliminary assumption in the respective context. What is the focus of psychological needs in the development process and what are the results? Do the results tell us how beginners (UX designers) can establish these needs before user research and then examine them with well-known methods [26]? These procedures in application development processes bring humans into focus. User experience is, at a minimum, just as important as usability. Software designers must understand psychological needs in order to work with them. This is what produces a useful framework for users. When designers can and want to use emotions in the context of the user's benevolent advocate, we refer to these as "white patterns."

References

1. DIN EN ISO Norm 9241-210 (2019)
2. Oulasvirta, A., Hornbæk, K.: HCI research as problem-solving. In: Proceedings of the 2016 CHI Conference on Human Factors in Computing Systems (CHI 2016), pp. 4956–4967. Association for Computing Machinery, New York (2016). https://doi.org/10.1145/2858036. 2858283
3. Butz, A., Krüger, A.: Human-Computer-Interaction. Library of Congress Cataloging-in-Publication Data. A CIP catalog record for this book has been applied for at the Library of Congress. De Gruyter Studium (2017). ISBN 978-3-11-047636-1
4. Calvo, R.A., Peters, D.: Positive Computing – Technology for Wellbeing and Human Potential. The MITT Press (2014). ISBN 978-0-262-02815-8

5. Vogel, O., Arnold, I., Chughtai, A., Kehrer, T.: Software Architecture - A Comprehensive Framework and Guide for Practitioners. Copyright © 2009 by Spektrum Akademischer Verlag, Heidelberg, Germany. Title of the German original: Software-Architektur. Grundlagen - Konzepte – Praxis (2009). ISBN 978-3-8274-1933-0
6. Sheldon, K.M., Elliot, A.J., Kim, Y., Kasser, T.: What is satisfying about satisfying events? Testing 10 candidate psychological needs. J. Pers. Soc. Psychol. **80**(2), 325–339 (2001). https://doi.org/10.1037//O022-3514.80.2.325
7. Rose, E.: Design as advocacy: using a human-centered approach to investigate the needs of vulnerable populations. J. Tech. Writing Commun. **46**(4), 427–445 (2016). https://doi.org/10.1177/0047281616653494
8. Leiser, M.: 'Dark Patterns': the case for regulatory pluralism, 16 July 2020. https://doi.org/10.31228/osf.io/ea5n2
9. Berger, A., Odom, W., Storz, M., Bischof, A., Kurze, A., Hornecker, E.: The inflatable cat: idiosyncratic ideation of smart objects for the home. In: Proceedings of the 2019 CHI Conference on Human Factors in Computing Systems (CHI 2019), Paper 401, pp. 1–12. Association for Computing Machinery, New York (2019). https://doi.org/10.1145/3290605.3300631
10. Fink, V., Börner, A., Eibl, M.: Living-lab and experimental workshops for design of I-RobEka assistive shopping robot: ELSI aspects with MEESTAR. In: Conference: Ro-Man the 29th IEEE International Conference on Robot & Human Interactive Communication, 31 August–04 September 2020 - VIRTUAL CONFERENCE (2020). https://doi.org/10.1109/RO-MAN 47096.2020.9223507
11. Hassenzahl, M., Eckoldt, K., Diefenbach, S., Laschke, M., Lenz, E., Kim, J.: Designing moments of meaning and pleasure. Experience design and happiness understanding experiences. Int. J. Des. **7**(3), 21–31 (2013)
12. Hassenzahl, M., Diefenbach, S., Göritz, A.: Needs, affect, and interactive products – facets of user experience. Interact. Comput. J. **22**(5), 353–362 (2010). https://doi.org/10.1016/j.intcom.2010.04.002
13. Dörrenbächer, J., Hassenzahl, M.: Changing perspective: a co-design approach to explore future possibilities of divergent hearing. In: CHI 2019, May Glasgow, Scotland, UK, Paper 29, 12 Pahers. ACM. New York (2019). https://doi.org/10.1145/3290605.3300259
14. Stephanidis, C., Antona, M. (eds.): UAHCI/HCII 2013, Part I. LNCS, vol. 8009, pp. 185–194. Springer, Heidelberg (2013)
15. Riva, G., Baños, R.M., Botella, C., Wiederhold, B.K., Gaggioli, A.: Positive technology: using interactive technologies to promote positive functioning. Cyberpsychol. Behav. Soc. Netw. **15**, 69–77 (2012). https://doi.org/10.1089/cyber.2011.0139
16. Living labs for innovation and development of information and communication technology: a literature review. Electron. J. Virtual Organ. Netw. **10** (2008). Special Issue on Living Labs
17. Customer journeys: a systematic literature review. J. Serv. Theory Pract. (2018)
18. Burmester, M., Zeiner, K.M., Laib, M., Perrino, C.H., Queßeleit, M.-L.: Experience design and positive design as an alternative to classical human factors approaches. In: INTERACT 2015 Adjunct Proceedings, pp. 153–160 (2015)
19. Desmet, P., Fokkinga, S.: Beyond Maslow's pyramid: introducing a typology of thirteen fundamental needs for human-centered design. Multimodal Technol. Interact. **4**, 38 (2020)
20. Fink, V., Eibl, M.: Wherein is the necessity and importance of changing human-computer interaction well-known design methods? In: Stephanidis, C., Antona, M. (eds.) HCII 2020. CCIS, vol. 1224, pp. 27–34. Springer, Cham (2020). https://doi.org/10.1007/978-3-030-50726-8_4
21. Desmet, P.M.A., Pohlmeyer, A.E.: Positive design: an introduction to design for subjective well-being. Int. J. Des. **7**(3), 5–10 (2013). http://www.ijdesign.org/index.php/IJDesign/article/viewFile/1666/587

22. Zeiner, K.M., Laib, M., Schippert, K., Burmester, M.: Das Erlebnisinterview – Methode zum Verständnis positiver Erlebnisse. In: Mensch und Computer 2016 – Usability Professionals (2016). https://doi.org/10.18420/muc2016-up-014

23. Zeiner, K., Henschel, J., Schippert, K., Haasler, K., Laib, M., Burmester, M.: Experience categories in specific contexts – creating positive experiences in smart kitchens. In: Marcus, A., Wang, W. (eds.) DUXU 2018. LNCS, vol. 10918, pp. 306–324. Springer, Cham (2018). https://doi.org/10.1007/978-3-319-91797-9_22

24. Perrino, C.H., Burmester, M.: Designing for time perspectives – Gestaltung der zeitlichen Dimension der UX. In: Mensch und Computer 2017 – Usability Professionals (MuC 2017), Regensburg, pp. 355–361 (2017). https://doi.org/10.18420/muc2017-up-0176

25. Krueger, A.E., Pollmann, K., Fronemann, N., Foucault, B.: Guided user research methods for experience design—a new approach to focus groups and cultural probes. Multimodal Technol. Interact. **4**, 43 (2020)

26. Hartson, R., Pyla, P.S.: The UX Book: Process and Guidelines for Ensuring a Quality User Experience. Elsevier (2012). ISBN 978-0-12-385241-0

Applying Stepped Task in Remote Unmoderated Test: A Case Report

Shushu He[✉]

Politecnico di Milano, Via Durando 38/A, 20158 Milan, Italy
shushu.he@polimi.it

Abstract. Internet firms have shared a common sense that agile user research is significant for agile developments. The unmoderated test, as one of the most commonly used qualitative approaches, has been widely adopted. Such an approach requires participants' trained skill of think aloud, and the remote unmoderated test platforms compensated for such a lack with their huge, trained user database. However, there is an inevasible bias that participants go for bonuses, thereby muck the tests or please the researcher. Would it reduce bias by innovatively applying stepped tasks in the remote unmoderated test? The research carries out pilot tests for validating the feasibility and identify the correct approach of applying stepped task in the situation of the remote unmoderated test. The user test of an online shopping platform is elaborated as a case study for validation of such an innovative approach. The research concludes that stepped tasks can be applied in remote unmoderated tests. However, the form of stepped task applied in remote unmoderated tests differs from the traditional moderated test which requires face-to-face communication between researcher and participants. To apply stepped task in the situations as remote usability test and unmoderated test, researchers need to 1) design tasks within a natural user journey and add connecting tasks which do not represent test objectives as to hide the test motivation from the participants; 2) observe user's natural behaviors at the beginning, and investigate user's motivations latter; 3) define stepped tasks' level of detail through piolet tests.

Keywords: Remote usability test · Unmoderated test · Stepped task · Think-aloud · User experience research

1 Introduction

The outbreak of COVID-19 lead to uncountable brick-and-mortar companies develop online businesses for opportunities for survival. In order to face the challenge of moving to e-commerce, the companies are demanding lean user tests to assist with agile development. Fortunately, many online user test platforms are mature to provide lean user testing services to these companies. However, the difficulty is that there are limited numbers of trained staff capable of carrying out user experience research in traditional brick-and-mortar companies.

User experience research derived from usability test which started to flourish in the 1970s. The usability test focuses on whether the user can effectively complete the

© Springer Nature Switzerland AG 2021
C. Stephanidis et al. (Eds.): HCII 2021, CCIS 1419, pp. 33–40, 2021.
https://doi.org/10.1007/978-3-030-78635-9_5

task through the interaction with the human-machine interface. Hix & Hartson (1993) and Nielsen (1994) elaborated three dimensions of usability: usefulness, interaction efficiency, and users' satisfaction [1, 2]. With the development of interaction design, the user test paradigm is expanding within the user experience research. According to the viewpoint of user experience research, user tests can be regarded as the research activities for investigating a certain product's usability, which could be a physical product or digital product. Putting user test in a general viewpoint, it should include qualitative and quantitative testing methods, involving various stages in the design from the early concept to the final evaluation and iteration in which moderated test and unmoderated test are the frequently used two, for the low cost, small sample size, low requirements of the test environment.

Both moderated tests and unmoderated tests require users to explain their thoughts while using it, which prefers users to be a little experienced using the think-aloud. There are many online user testing platforms nowadays providing a huge database with users experienced with think-aloud. User researchers can quickly recruit qualified participants through those online user testing platforms. This makes the lean user researches feasible. However, the online user testing platforms are embedded with inevitable bias led by the reward mechanism. The online testing platforms offer bonuses for stimulating users to participate in tests. Users are sometimes inclined to finish the tests as fast as possible to get rewarded but without reading the test introductions, which leads to useless samples. Even more, some users misunderstand that they can get positive reviews from the test posters only if they finish the tasks "correctly." Thus, these users try to guess the test's motivation to complete the task without "making mistakes." Users' motivations make the user test task design challenging because researchers have to hide the test purpose.

The research purpose of this paper is to find an online user testing method for making full use of the advantages of the online usability testing platform, meanwhile reducing the user testing bias caused by the platform's reward mechanism. In the following, the paper proposes an innovative online testing method: applying stepped tasks in the online unmoderated test to reduce the biases of online user testing platforms.

2   Unmoderated Test as a User Testing Approach

2.1   Think-Aloud Protocol

Think-aloud protocol, also known as think-out-loud, was introduced by Lewis and Mack in 1982 [3]. Nielson proposed to apply it in the usability test in his book Usability Engineering [2]. A typical user testing process via think-aloud is, firstly, the researcher provides the product or interface that needs to be tested and asks the participant to complete some designated tasks. While the participant interacts with the product or interface, the researcher shall remind the user to explain simultaneously what he/she thinks and feels. At the end of the test, the researcher summarizes the test findings through observation of users' behavior and user thoughts and produces design insights to guide the iteration of the product or prototype. Think-aloud applies to all stages of product development and design, as well as tangible and intangible products and prototypes [4, 5]. Think-aloud protocol has advantages as low-cost, short period of researcher training, small sample content, time-saving, thus, has been widely applied to the validation stage of agile development projects. However, it has a requirement of users' skill of using think-out-loud. If user lacks of experience of thinking while doing, he/she may concentrate too much on tackling the test tasks to explain his/her thoughts, which needs researchers always remind the user.

2.2 Moderated Test and Unmoderated Test

Moderated test is guided by a facilitator or moderator, and think-aloud is the main technic used by participants. The facilitator is an expert who has knowledge of the product being tested, as well as the knowledge of user experience research. The facilitator is in charge of assigning the tasks, guiding users, noting down users' behaviors and thoughts, and asking follow-up questions if it is needed [5]. One of the biggest advantages of moderated test is that the facilitator can adjust the test flow and questions according to the specific test situation real time. However, moderated test requires facilitators who are trained the interview and observation skills as to be exquisite to identify the design insights [6, 7]. Unmoderated test is very similar to moderated test, and the difference falls on the removal of facilitator's role, which makes the unmoderated test even leaner than moderated test. Researchers can publish several tests at the same time without training facilitators, and the data are collected in a short time. However, unmoderated test needs a sequence of fixed tasks assigned to users so that it has quite high requirement of the quality of the test protocol [6, 7]. If the user failed with thinking aloud, the sample would be invalid, and this led to a waste of the test cost.

3   Stepped Tasks Applied in User Tests: Case Study

3.1   Stepped Tasks Applied in On-Site Moderated Test

Stepped tasks derived from "scaffolding teaching" in pedagogy by breaking down a difficult question into several sub-questions with lower difficulties to assist students in achieving the educational goal [8–10]. In user tests, stepped tasks refer to related tasks aiming to achieve a final goal. The facilitator assigns a series of tasks to the participant [11]. The tasks are sequential, and the first task is the most summarized (i.e., sending a friendship request to your colleague on an App), and the last task should be the most detailed (i.e., please go to "My profile" page and find the "plus" button to send out a friendship request). The facilitator is in charge of choosing a certain stepped task according to the users' test performance. Adopting stepped tasks could be an appropriate strategy to deal with the problem that users are inclined to guess the test motivation since the starting tasks are general and highly summarized.

3.2   Advantages and Challenges of Applying Stepped Tasks in Online Unmoderated Test

Stepped tasks do not show the user testing goals initially but ask the user to do a very general task and reveal the test's goal in the later steps. If the online un-moderated tests could adopt the stepped tasks, the online user testing bias led by users' willingness to complete the tasks "perfectly" could be possibly reduced, as stepped tasks do not show the test goal directly at the beginning. However, the facilitator plays a key role in the on-site moderated test with stepped tasks. The challenge is how to carry out stepped tasks when the test is remoted and facilitator-free. This research proposes a strategy to apply stepped tasks into online unmoderated tests and eliminates the facilitator's role to enable the test flexibility and replicability.

3.3 The Case Study: The Unmoderated Test of L Brand's E-commerce Platform

This study shows an unmoderated test with the guidance of an eyeglasses seller's e-commerce platform's stepped task. It aims to verify the feasibility of applying stepped tasks in online user testing platforms without a facilitator. It also probes whether this innovative research strategy could reduce the test bias to a certain extend.

User Test Flow: As shown in Fig. 1, the online unmoderated test consists of 7 stages: define test questions, recruit participants, design test protocol, launch pilot test, launch regular test, analysis, and deliver design insights.

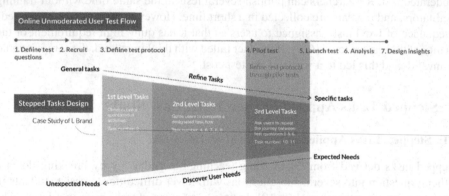

Fig. 1. The research process of applying stepped tasks in online unmoderated test.

Defining Test Questions: This test refers to the whole journey of how users configure their eyeglasses lenses on this website, including steps of browsing the pages, choose lens' brand, selecting lens' thickness, choosing lens' treatments, and add to shopping bag. Figure 2 shows screenshots of the key steps of this journey and the test questions embedded. Through the collaboration with the User Experience Design team and Product Team, this user test defined the following 6 test questions:

1) Do users have blocking issues in the spontaneous journey?
2) Users expect to apply vision insurance in which step of lens configuration?
3) If users think they have a heavy prescription, what kind of lenses are they going to choose?
4) Do users understand how to use the "learn more" button?

Fig. 2. Brand L's lens configurator and specific functions that need to be tested.

5) Do users understand "light-responsive treatment" includes a part of the "blue light treatment" function?

6) As shown in Fig. 2, test question 6, if users choose blue light treatment, the price of light-responsive treatment is $80.5; if users choose blue light treatment first, then, choose light-responsive treatment, the price turns to $127.17. Will users understand the change of the price?

Participants Recruiting: The research adopts Usertesting.com as the online test platform. Thanks to its huge user database, this test firstly screens users through demographics (i.e., the grade of Internet use, residence, mother tongue). Besides, there are 7 other screener questions in addition to further targeting the participants. The test recruited 15 desktop participants and 15 mobile users.

Define Test Protocol and Launch Pilot Tests: The key to define this test's test protocol is to rephrase test questions to several tasks to guide users to complete the test and speak out loud their thoughts without a facilitator's assistance. The tasks need to be written briefly, shortly, and precisely as much as possible to reduce participants' reading efforts and keep them concentrated. Moreover, the tasks should decorate the goal of the test by re-phrasing technics. For instance, this test's first level task avoided using the word "lenses" to prevent the participants from guessing that it is a test related to eyeglasses lenses and configuration.

Table 1. Stepped tasks applied in online unmoderated test protocol (final version).

Scenario: You are going to buy a pair of eyeglasses on the L website for the long-time reading and writing in front of screens

Tasks	Purpose
1. Please write down your prescription (written response)	Investigate whether users' mental model resonates with platform data
2. Please find a pair of eyeglasses that suit your need on this website, choose the lenses you need, then put the glasses in the shopping bag. Please remember to share your thoughts with us constantly. Please pause the recording to protect your privacy in case you need to type in your personal information	First level task: to observe users' spontaneous interactions with the interface
3. Did you use your vision insurance? If no, why didn't you use it? If yes, at which step did you fill your information? Did it meet your expectation?	Test question 2
4. Here's a new task. Please visit [link], once you are on the product detail page, please check the next task	Second level tasks: to guide participants to follow the designated test flow
5. Please choose the lens brand, and then move to the next task	Connecting question
6. Please choose the lens thickness, and then move to the next task	Test question 3
7. Could you tell what's the difference between classic anti-reflective lens treatment and premium anti-reflective lens treatment? (Verbal Response)	Test question 4
8. Please choose the blue light lenses	Third level tasks: to ask users to repeat a specific part of user journey, meanwhile, try to hide the test goal from them
9. Now you also want your lenses to have the ability to darken when exposed to sunlight. What would you choose?	
10. Which choice is the correct description below, and please share your reason with us (Multiple Choice) • Transition lens treatment costs $127.17 • Transition lens treatment costs $80.5 • It's more complicated than this, please explain	Test question 6
11. Based on your experience on this site, please mark the following sentence as true or false: "Light-responsive treatment also includes blue-light treatment." Please explain to us the reason. (Single Choice) • True • False	Test question 5
12. Please add this pair of eyeglasses to shopping bag and the test is finish. Would you like to share the final thoughts with us?	Ending question

For the first pilot test, there were 2 levels of stepped tasks, in which the first level includes Task No. 2 and the second level includes tasks No. 4 to 9. 1 desktop user and 1 mobile user were recruited for the first pilot test, and the result revealed that the test question 5 and 6 could be triggered only when users follow a specific flow; however, users' spontaneous interactions could not always touch these two questions. Therefore, the author refined the test protocol to add the third-level stepped tasks and ran the second round of pilot test. The result showed that test questions 5 and 6 should be shifted to ensure users could follow the specific flow. The third round of pilot verified the effectiveness of the test protocol (Table 1).

Transcript and Analysis: Usertesting Platform provides automatic transcript function that saves a lot of efforts from user experience researchers. Researchers can take notes about the key findings and mark them on the timeline. For the purpose of this case study, lean UX research to guide agile development, the test did not carry out triangulation and second transcription, verifying the test questions and provide design insights is sufficient.

Results: This test successfully guided the user to complete the tasks and verified the test questions. The results showed that the user did not encounter any blocking problems in the lens configuration process. The test results also suggested three points for further A/B tests:

1. Users did not know that they could log in vision insurance by only filling in the personal information.
2. Users couldn't tell the differences between different card contents. They had to use "learn more" button, but user expect to find clues on the cards in order to avoid jumping to another page (i.e., Classic & premium; Lens brand; Blue Light Treatment and Light-responsive Treatment).
3. Price and selections are confusing between Blue Light Treatment and Light-responsive Treatment.

4 Conclusion and Discussion

It is feasible to apply stepped tasks to online unmoderated tests. This strategy can contribute to reducing the online test bias led by the test platform reward mechanism by hiding the test goals at the beginning of the test. The combination of stepped task and online unmoderated test tool fastens the collection of samples, improves the quality of samples, and lessens the dependency of researchers' real-time in-person participation, making the user tests lean and easy to repeat. Stepped tasks are rather than a user testing technic, and it also leads to a strategic test protocol design. With the mind-set of stepped tasks, UX researchers can identify the appropriate level of task difficulty.

The challenge of applying stepped tasks to online unmoderated tests is the facilitator's absence that nobody could guide participants and select the appropriate task during the test.

This paper proposes a technic to guide the whole online unmoderated test, setting up a scenario close to the real use case. For instance, the test scenario description could be "you are going to gift your best friend for his birthday, and you have the budget of $120." The participant will very likely concentrate on the task of "buying a gift within $120," but not on guessing "which button on this page I am supposed to click?" Then, tasks are based on this gift-purchasing journey. As shown in the case study, the test protocol added some connecting questions which did not represent any research questions. Adding connecting questions contributes to making sense of the test flow and fuzz the test goal. This study also highly recommends careful pilot tests before the regular tests are launched. The levels of stepped tasks and the tasks within a certain level need to be refined and verified via rounds of pilot tests. The more general the task is, the more difficult for users to complete the task, but it could lead to some unexpected findings. The more specific the task is, the easier for users to get the test point. It could lead to validation of some expected usability issues.

References

1. Hix, D., Hartson, H.R.: Developing User Interfaces: Ensuring Usability through Product & Process. Wiley, Hoboken (1993)
2. Nielsen, J.: Usability Engineering. Morgan Kaufmann, Burlington (1994)
3. Lewis, C., Mack, R.: Learning to use a text processing system: evidence from "thinking aloud" protocols. In: Proceedings of the 1982 Conference on Human Factors in Computing Systems, pp. 387–392 (1982)
4. Van Someren, M.W., Barnard, Y.F., Sandberg, J.A.C.: The Think Aloud Method: A Practical Approach to Modelling Cognitive. AcademicPress, London (1994)
5. Olson, G.M., Duffy, S.A., Mack, R.L.: Thinking-out-loud as a method for studying real-time comprehension processes. In: New Methods in Reading Comprehension Research, pp. 253–286 (1984)
6. Bruun, A., Gull, P., Hofmeister, L., Stage, J.: Let your users do the testing: a comparison of three remote asynchronous usability testing methods. In: Proceedings of the SIGCHI Conference on Human Factors in Computing Systems, pp. 1619–1628 (2009)
7. Hertzum, M., Molich, R., Jacobsen, N.E.: What you get is what you see: revisiting the evaluator effect in usability tests. Behav. Inf. Technol. **33**, 144–162 (2014)
8. Sawyer, R.K.: The Cambridge Handbook of the Learning Sciences. Cambridge University Press, Cambridge (2005)
9. Verenikina, I.: Scaffolding and learning: its role in nurturing new learners (2008)
10. Klein, S., Leikin, R.: Opening mathematical problems for posing open mathematical tasks: what do teachers do and feel? Educ. Stud. Math. **105**(3), 349–365 (2020). https://doi.org/10.1007/s10649-020-09983-y
11. Pernice, K.: How to Maximize Insights in User Testing: Stepped User Tasks (2020)

Design for People, Design with People: The Complexities and Breakouts of Public Service Design in Practice

Wei-An Hsieh🆔 and Hsien-Hui Tang(✉)🆔

Department of Design, National Taiwan University of Science and Technology, Taipei, Taiwan
drhhtang@gapps.ntust.edu.tw

Abstract. Public service innovation for the underprivileged minority is challenging for meeting users' needs while avoiding compromising the rights of non-users. It also suffers from limited resources under considerations of proportionality and efficiency of public welfare. Commonly, to quickly respond to social needs, public sectors often take technology-oriented solutions instead of clarifying the underlying complexity. Lacking user-centered design, public services are often criticized for low usability and result in unsatisfaction and even more significant problems. Can service design, as a strategic method to counter issues with poorly defined parameters, non-binary solutions, help drive better public innovation?

Through a case study of EyeBus, the research purpose is to explore how service design enhanced the bus-riding experience for the visually impaired. The research objectives are (1) to clarify the complexities in the process of accessible public service design (2) to analyze how service design resolved the difficulties (3) to study how stakeholders' cooperation accelerated the practice of public services. The results of the research are (1) providing a case and principles of applying service design to public service innovation (2) promoting action plans for public sectors to encouraging more demand-oriented public service innovations. We hope that better practices of service design will drive more public good.

Keywords: Public service innovation · Service design · Visually impairment

1 Introduction

The number of the visually impaired in Taiwan has grown over 56000 until 2020, accounting for 0.2% of the country's population. Same as sighted people, the visually impaired have to go to work or school via public transportation. The bus is a preferred choice for the low ticket price and the significant bus routes among all public transports. However, it also can be dangerous for the unpredictable approaching time and location. Visually impaired passengers suffer from hailing buses in time, not mentioning finding bus doors in the few seconds buses stop by. Even though central and local governments in Taiwan have made attempts for accessible bus systems, few cases were of full implementation.

The contracting out pursuing cost-efficiency has led to the stagnation of public service innovation. The public sector tends to rely on technology-oriented solutions for

© Springer Nature Switzerland AG 2021
C. Stephanidis et al. (Eds.): HCII 2021, CCIS 1419, pp. 41–48, 2021.
https://doi.org/10.1007/978-3-030-78635-9_6

predictable and instant outcomes, ignoring public demands and thus caused complaints. Though the consensus of public-private collaboration has risen in recent years, conflicts exist among the multiple stakeholders. How can we design public services that satisfy stakeholders?

Service design as a strategic design method can deal with complex problems without clear boundaries and non-binary solutions (Prendeville and Bocken 2017). It is believed to unveil meta-questions (Sung 2020) that lie beneath the demands. Following the triple diamond process (Tang 2019), service designers solve problems by demand recognition, design iteration, and service validation.

The study is to first uncover the complexities of accessible public service innovation through literature review. Secondly, through a case study of EyeBus, we perform the strategies and results of service design approaches to improving the bus-riding experience. Last, we conducted semi-structured interviews to examine the challenges of demand-oriented solutions in practice.

2   The Complexities of Innovation in Accessible Transportation

Design Inclusively. WCAG (Web Content Accessibility Guidelines) addressed perceivable, operable, understandable, and robust as the four principles of accessible digital design. CABE (2006) put another four principles for accessible environment design: 1. Place people at the heart of the design process. 2. Acknowledges diversity and difference. 3. Offer choice where a single design solution cannot accommodate all users. 4. Provide for flexibility in use. In conclusion, accessibility designers should recognize diverse patterns of interaction and offer them with adjustable, consistent experience of service.

Deal with Interest Conflict Among the Public. Accessible public service designed for the specific ones may, on the contrary, threaten others' rights. (Chang and Yan 2011) The construction of tactile paving in Taiwan, as an example, has caused spinal injuries to wheelchair users (Liao 2008).

Avoid Reducing the Efficiency of the Public Transport System. People take the entire cost and time into consideration when choosing a means of transportation. Public transportation as a non-door-to-door service where the first-and-last mile exists between stations and households are less competitive to private vehicles.

Avoid Hardware Constructions. Taiwan is too densely populated to afford irreversible changes to the environment. Frequent public works may push people to private vehicles instead of the public transportation system. The Ministry of Transportation has recommended that public transportation should innovate based on the existing hardware system.

Ensure the Stability and Versatility of Solutions. Accessible public transportation as a service is a series of touchpoints related to each other (Stickdorn et al. 2018). Cases of bus-riding experience enhancement in Taiwan consisted of a single technology, which was unstable in the field. Since service gaps exist in every touchpoint may reduce usability or even availability, back-up experience design is vital in public service design. Besides, service planners should foresee the challenges of scaling up a solution to avoid costly redesigns in the future.

Reduce the Cost of Solutions. Public services are the ones provided for large numbers of citizens, in which there is a potentially significant market failure (Leinonkoski 2012). Therefore, the benefits of social innovations should be proven to overweigh the costs. Cases of bus-riding experience enhancement in Taiwan were unaffordable due to costly hardware constructions.

Convince Stakeholders to Commit to Innovation. The revenue of public transport companies constrained due to the fixed ticket price designated by the government. Hard to reach break-even points, companies lack the motivation to invest in innovations.

The complexities of accessible transport innovation were found through the case study of EyeBus, referring to varied domain knowledge, including public transport, public administration, and design. On the premise that multiple professions and stakeholders were involved in public services, solution providers should think holistically.

3   Service Design Methods to Overcome the Complexities

Service design originated in management is an approach to enhance the customer experience. It is expected as a strategic thinking tool to deal with wicked problems (Prendeville and Bocken 2017). Also, it is believed to re-think the relationships between public sectors and the citizens based on an equal interaction. (Cox et al. 2015). Stickdorn et al. (2018) suggested six principles in service design: human-centered, collaborative, iterative, sequential, real, and holistic.

EyeBus team proposed a service aiming to assist the blind to ride buses alone for work or school. EyeBus consisted of digital and physical touchpoints, including an app, bus telematics system, and boarding point. Visually impaired passengers could make bus reservations via the app and the bus telematics system. Boarding points represented tactile and visual hints where passengers and drivers met. Below were the strategies EyeBus made to counter the complexities of accessible public transport design.

Clarify User Needs. Given the different experiences of sighted and visually impaired people, the EyeBus team first applied shadowing, a research method observing detailed behaviors in the field to build empathy with visually impaired people and inclusive design principles for the solution. Secondly, the EyeBus team defined the target user and service goal with customer journey maps and persona matrix.

Survey for Opportunities. To help visually impaired passengers "hail" the buses in advance, the EyeBus team searched for existing touchpoints between passengers and bus drivers. Analyzing the six-channel service model proposed by Tang (2019), The EyeBus team chose well-developed technologies such as apps, bus telematics systems, and tactile hints among all the digital and physical touchpoints (Fig. 1).

Fig. 1. The six-channel analysis of existing bus-riding service

Propose with Graphics. The EyeBus team proposed their solution with a storyboard describing what users experience reserving a bus. Service blueprint as a graphical tool presenting how a service worked frontstage and backstage, the EyeBus team also introduced it to reach consensus among stakeholders.

Develop Prototypes and Iterate. Following the agile development principles, the Eye-Bus team validated the service feasibility with minimum viable products applying wizard of Oz. The EyeBus team invited visually impaired users to examine the app's usability, bus drivers to experience the degree of burden serving passengers, and O&M (orientation & mobility) instructors to evaluate the versability of boarding points (Fig. 2). Every iteration of the design was based on user feedback.

Fig. 2. The EyeBus team conducting tests with visually impaired users and O&M instructors.

Bridge the Gaps Between Touchpoints. Regarding that gaps in service touchpoints may cause poor experience, especially in multi-channel and cross-scenario services, the EyeBus team sketched back-up user flows instead of just proposing an ideal user journey. Moreover, they also had app hints matchable to physical environments, offering a sense of security for visually impaired users.

Validate the Feasibility of the Service. Upon the first launch of the service, the EyeBus team conducted a soft launch to examine its usability and feasibility. Facing the uncertainties in realities, they recorded every service gap with quantitative and qualitative research methods such as the G-S-M model for the next iteration (Fig. 3).

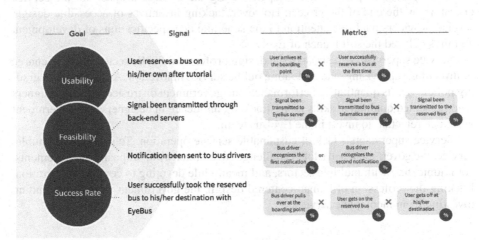

Fig. 3. The team applying the G-S-M model, a quantitative research method, to evaluate the usability and feasibility of EyeBus.

4   Challenges on Practicing a Demand-Oriented Solution

Multiple stakeholders are involved in EyeBus, including service receivers like visually impaired people and O&M instructors; service providers like bus corps and telematics system corps; service supervisors like central and local governments (Fig. 4). The EyeBus team put effort into managing stakeholder requirements during development. Through interviews among stakeholders, we summarized the underlying challenges to launch a demand-oriented solution as follows.

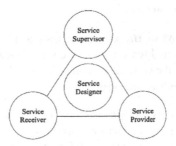

Fig. 4. The simplified stakeholders' map of public services

Service receivers – the low expectation of public interest. Though service receivers are the most benefited ones to EyeBus, they had already been disappointed at countless accessible attempts ending with nothing. Holding low expectations of public innovation, they tended to show a passive attitude of cooperation.

Service providers – ineffective collaboration among varied professions. Service providers played as partnered developers during the EyeBus project and the service operators by the end of the project. However, lacking incentives of accessible design, service providers paid less attention to the schedule and specifications of development and thus delayed the soft launch of EyeBus.

Service supervisors - distrust of the design profession. Public sectors were in charge of investing, supervising, and evaluating public service innovation. Accustomed to grading policies by its quantitative performance, the government distrusted service designers who presented qualitative skills more. Lacked confidence in designers, the government was once reluctant to invest in the EyeBus team.

Service supervisors - lack of sustainable service operation. To scale up the public service, the government had a lot of challenges to counter with: proposing procurements, communicating with multiple sectors, and meanwhile devoting to continuous iteration. Lacking the profession of human-centered design, the government would only end up investing in an incomplete service.

5   Final Remarks and Future Work

Prahalad and Ramaswamy (2004) proposed the DART model, which stood for the building blocks of co-creation: dialogue, access, risk assessment, and transparency. Several related attempts made by the EyeBus team were proved effective to break the barriers of collaboration. Stakeholders were convinced and thus willing to devote their recourse due to the actions below.

Make Strategies Visible. Inviting stakeholders to monthly meetings and making meeting minutes open to the public, the EyeBus team informed them of every consideration behind the decisions. Under frequent communication, the supervisors finally realized the importance of field tests and helped arranged bus stop constructions across departments.

> *"I was granted full access to your research, which helped me realize every effort you made under a decision. Feeling trustful of the team, I felt responsible for negotiating with the public sectors."*

Improve the Understanding of the Design Profession Among Stakeholders. The EyeBus proved the usability and feasibility of the service with quantitative and qualitative methods. Convinced by the credible research results, the government committed to expanding EyeBus to Taiwan's capital city.

> *"It wasn't until watching the POC (proof of concept) video did we realized that you were validating the feasibility of service instead of computer simulations. Since then, we changed our view of service design, believing that human-centered design research was crucial for presenting users' needs."*

Enhance the Empathy with Users Among Stakeholders. Quoting users' feedback, the EyeBus team proved the improvement of bus-riding experience among the past projects. Also, the EyeBus team invited stakeholders to field tests to help them get a clearer picture of users. With a deeper understanding of the visually impaired, the public sector became more observative on other related projects.

"I heard a lot of feedback from the visually impaired interviewee at your field test. Therefore, I felt brushed off when operators in other projects were submitting user feedbacks with mere 1-2 sentences."

Accelerate the Resource Leverage with Agile Development. The EyeBus team found the pivot of the seemingly exclusive relationship between service supervisors, providers, and receivers. They formed a cycle among stakeholders to introduce resources and accelerated it: (1) Service designers proposed and prototyped the solutions that overcame the recognized complexities. (2) Service designers verified and alternated the service by third-party users. (3) Service designers asked service supervisors and their cooperating companies for laboratory resources. (4) With an experimental environment closer to reality, service designers built prototypes with higher fidelity for the next iteration cycle.

In conclusion, we outlined the complexities of accessible transport design, which might be broadly interpreted as the ones of public service. Through the case study of EyeBus, we found out that professional service designers could play as the solution innovator and negotiator considering all stakeholders' needs. With service design tools and methods, designers were capable of and developing and examining service prototypes.

However, service design as a human-centered approach only specializes in proposing more feasible solutions. More challenges are to be solved during its implementation, especially after designers handing over the project to the responsible operators. To improve the demand-oriented public service, the public sector should help build iteration cycles by integrating resources across departments, introducing professional service validators, and systematically collecting user feedback. In this way, public service innovations can thrive and bring about the greater public interest. Lastly, the ones who put the solutions into practice and keep iterating for social needs are doing public service design.

References

Chang, H.H., Yan, S.G.: From charity toward civil rights: the development and challenges of the disability social welfare in Taiwan. Commun. Dev. J. Q. **133**, 402–416 (2011)

Cox, M.D., Green, L., Borodako, K., Sangiorgi, D.: Designing for public sector innovation in the UK: Design strategies for paradigm shifts. Foresight **17**(4), 332–348 (2015)

Leinonkoski, H.: Service design - An approach to better public services? A civil Servant's View. Working Papers (2012)

Liao, H.Y.: Manual of accessible facilities in buildings. Ministry of the Interior, Taipei (2008)

Prahalad, C.K., Ramaswamy, V.: Co-creating unique value with customers. Strategy Leadersh. **32**, 4–9 (2004)

Prendeville, S., Bocken, N.: Sustainable business models through service design. Procedia Manuf. **8**, 292–299 (2017)

Stickdorn, M., Hormess, M.E., Lawrence, A., Schneider, J.: This is Service Design Doing: Applying Service Design Thinking in the Real World. O'Reilly Media Inc., Sebastopol (2018)

Sung, S.H.: The Innovative Lessons of Thick Data - Anthropologist Among Industries. Reveal Books, Taipei (2020)

Tang, H.H.: The content of new service design (2019). https://medium.com/ditl/%E6%96%B0% E6%9C%8D%E5%8B%99%E8%A8%AD%E8%A8%88%E7%9A%84%E5%85%A7% E6%B6%B5-31f2319588a4

App Analysis with a Larger Than Usual Number of Usability Experts

Siva Ratna Kumari Narisetti[1]([⊠]) and Michael Twidale[1,2]

[1] Illinois Informatics Institute, University of Illinois at
Urbana-Champaign, Champaign, IL, USA
srn3@illinois.edu
[2] School of Information Sciences, University of Illinois at
Urbana-Champaign, Champaign, IL, USA

Abstract. Mobile app development and usage is booming in India; however, it is still in the early stages of adoption especially among the rural farming community. This research attempted to identify the usability problems of a selected agricultural mobile app, NaPanta, developed for Indian farmers. A twofold method was used to understand the usability and functionality of the app. Phase-1: the app was reviewed by experts (n = 18) using cognitive walkthrough and heuristic evaluation for usability and performance analyses. Phase-2: field studies with real users (n = 53) were conducted to compare and validate findings from the low-cost usability studies of phase-1. This paper discusses methods and findings of phase-1.

A mixed-methods approach was used to perform qualitative and quantitative data analysis. Thematic analysis and descriptive and inferential statistics were calculated. A total of 90 usability problems within 25 themes and two overarching categories were found. Lack of search functionality and lack of consistency topped the list.

This study also contributes to usability research by providing interesting insights on the number of experts required to identify most of the usability problems in comparison to the magic number 5. Results indicate our study required more than 5 participants to find 80% of the problems.

Keywords: Usability research · Agricultural mobile app · Mixed methods

1 Introduction

New methods of providing farmers and other rural stakeholders vital information to increase harvests and improve livelihoods and incomes are frequently created. However, availability and accessibility of this information at the necessary time is challenging in developing countries including India. With the rapid increase in mobile phone usage and the proliferation of smartphones and their vast libraries of applications, this offers app developers and researchers to develop and disseminate science-based information to farmers when they need it the most.

An agricultural app titled NaPanta [1] was selected for the study for its relevance and popularity. App developers often give more importance to the usability than the functionality of an app even though research has shown that one of the important and motivational

© Springer Nature Switzerland AG 2021
C. Stephanidis et al. (Eds.): HCII 2021, CCIS 1419, pp. 49–54, 2021.
https://doi.org/10.1007/978-3-030-78635-9_7

factors of using an agricultural app is accurate and timely information provided to the users [2, 3]. Hence, we conducted expert review of the selected app following cognitive walkthrough and heuristic evaluation methods to identify the usability and performance analyses.

In the following sections, we will discuss the methods and results.

2 Methods

2.1 Usability Inspection Methods

Cognitive Walkthrough for the Web [4] is an extension of Cognitive Walkthrough (CW) which tries to detect errors that occur when browsing and searching for information on a web site. For this study, the Cognitive Walkthrough for the Web (CWW) method was followed to perform the CW phase of the study. This is the most relevant CW extensions to our study. CWW was used to detect issues in a mobile application when browsing and searching through it for the information instead of on a web site. Browsing and searching the mobile application for the information were performed by experts for the tasks given by the researcher. The tasks for this purpose were developed based on the information needs of farmers identified in the previous literature on agriculture and rural development.

The heuristic evaluation (HE) method [5] is the widely used and most informal usability inspection method which involves having usability specialists and experts judge the usability of the user interface of the product/system by comparing with the established usability principles also known as heuristics. In this method, usability experts evaluate the interface to identify general usability issues based on the set of heuristics identified for that product, but not user specific issues.

There are many well-established heuristics proposed by usability scholars; the specific methods selected typically depends on the type of product being evaluated. A list of suitable heuristics was combined and selected from various proposed principles for evaluating a mobile application [6–9].

2.2 Research Setting and Data Collection

Cognitive Walkthrough and Heuristic Evaluation were used by a group of selected experts to evaluate the application. People with experience of evaluating and using mobile applications, designing interfaces, and with relevant educational exposure were recruited for the study. The determining factor was that they self-identified as having some expertise in usability. All the recruitment material including survey announcements and questions were approved by the University of Illinois Institutional Review Board (IRB). Experts were recruited through email and verbal announcements and snowball sampling (participants give recommendations of possibly interested participants).

All in-person usability studies were conducted at the University of Illinois Urbana-Champaign campus. Urbana-Champaign being a university town the study being conducted on campus, a majority of the participants were from the university community with others from relevant industries in the area. It turned out that some participants had never conducted usability studies but were familiar with the concepts from the courses learned in their degree program. Hence, we classified participants into two groups: expert participants and intermediate participants. Expert participants were people who had done usability studies and intermediate participants were those exposed to usability concepts and knowledge via classes and projects but who did not have any practical experience of conducting studies. With this classification criteria, we identified 9 participants as usability experts and 9 as intermediates out of a total of 18 participants.

A two-phase survey was used. The survey started with the researcher briefly explaining the survey process and taking consent from participants to participate in the study. Study procedure began by asking participants basic demographic questions such as age and profession or major, followed by the first phase; cognitive walkthrough.

In the cognitive walkthrough method, experts act as end-users to perform the tasks given by the researcher. Hence this phase starts with the researcher explaining the end-user's population of the app and tasks to be performed as given below:

- End-User Population: Rural Indian Farmers who usually have little or no experience in using smartphones or mobile applications.
- Tasks: The app under study, NaPanta, is an agricultural app whose main functionality is to disseminate required information to farmers. Hence the tasks will be to find information about general/identified information needs of the farmers.
- Guidance to perform the tasks: The app is already installed and activated with the local (Indian) mobile number. Hence participants would open the installed app directly and look for the information asked for in the given task.

The information needs were grouped into four stages of the agricultural life cycle including seed and cultivation varieties, disease and weed management, Market & Post-Harvest management, and Agriforum: an interactive chat forum.

In the heuristic evaluation phase, the heuristic principles selected were used to build the questions to test the app's interface for its usability and performance. Participants were asked to think aloud during the entire duration, and the sessions were audio-recorded. As the researcher asked questions to perform the tasks to find information, the participants were articulating their thoughts, ways of trying to find information, and comments on the app's interface. The researcher took notes while they were talking. Both the study notes and the audio recordings were used for the analysis.

3 Results and Analysis

3.1 Results

Study notes of the researcher and the audio recordings were used to develop the transcripts. Both quantitative and qualitative analysis were carried on the integrated data collected. First qualitative analysis was performed to identify themes, codes, and usability problems from the transcripts. Then descriptive statistics and inferential statistics such as t-test were performed on the average number of problems identified by two groups of participants: intermediate and experts to observe any differences between the two groups.

A hybrid approach of inductive and deductive coding and themes development was used. Some of the themes were taken from the previous study on apps analysis and some themes have emerged during the coding. The analysis started with multiple readings of the study notes (transcripts) to identify keywords and phrases. Relevant keywords and phrases were coded, and relevant codes were grouped into themes. A total of 90 usability problems were grouped into 25 themes.

From the top 10 problems identified by expert problems as given in Table 1, it can be observed that the major problems were associated with app-specific usability problems such as scattered information, lack of search functionality, and disorganized interface design. These problems can be addressed with a more careful design of the information architecture in the app.

Table 1. Top 10 problems identified by 7 or more participants.

Count	Usability problem	Theme
11	Information on seed dealers and seed varieties appeared at many different places	Information: Scattered
10	Some icons are towards the very bottom of the app	Visuals: Location
9	Text-based search: regular keyword search	Search
9	Found information when looking for something else	Missing connections
8	Un organized boxes on the home	Home screen
8	Too much information on the screen	Information: A lot
7	Lack of smooth flow	Ease of use
7	Alphabetical search: popping up as we type in dropdown	Search
7	Annoying frequent alerts	Visuals: Alerts

3.2 Analysis

The number of problems identified by each participant is shown in Fig. 1. The first bar in the figure indicates that participant 'E2': second expert participant found 34 usability problems and the fourth bar indicates that participant 'I8': eighth intermediate participant found 22 usability problems. Similarly, the number of problems identified by all expert and intermediate participants is shown below.

From the figure, it seems that there is a difference in the number of problems identified by intermediates and experts. To statistically examine this a t-test was performed on the average number of usability problems identified by two groups. The statistical test of means ($t = 2.8047$; $p = 0.017$) indicated a significant difference in the average number of problems reported by experts and intermediates.

Insights on the Number of Experts Required for the Usability Study. "How many participants are really enough?" is a question of concern for many researchers and professionals in the field of usability engineering. Many pioneers in the field conducted studies with varying numbers of users on different products and reported two different views. Some studies [10] identified that five number of participants are enough to get 80% to 95% of the usability problems while other studies [11] believed that more than five participants are needed to identify most of the problems. Yet there is no consensus on the sample size as it depends on various factors including size and properties of the product, type of the product, method of the usability study, skills and personalities of participants [12, 13].

This study with 18 participants (9 experts and 9 intermediates) identified a total of 90 usability problems in the app under study. As part of investigating how many participants would be enough to identify most of the problems, I used a random selection of 5 to

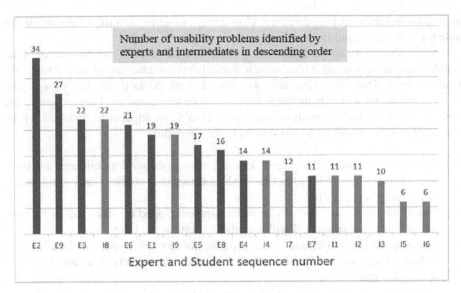

Fig. 1. Number of problems identified by experts and intermediate participants.

9 only experts and only intermediates to get insights on what percentage of problems would be identified by how many numbers of participants (Table 2.)

Table 2. All possible combinations of 9 choose number of participants and percentage of problems found.

No. of participants	Max%	Min%	Avg%
Experts			
5	74.44	46.67	63.19
6	76.67	57.78	69.31
7	78.89	64.44	73.51
8	81.1	73.33	78.44
9	82.2	82.2	82.2
Intermediates			
5	61.11	36.67	48.84
6	65.56	45.56	55.82
7	66.67	53.33	60.54
8	70	61.11	65.12
9	70	70	70

3.3 Discussion

In the first part of Table 2 on experts, the first row describes the maximum number of problems identified when 5 random participants from 9 expert participants for all combinations (9 choose 5 is 126) were selected. Similarly, the minimum and the average number of problems with a percentage of usability problems identified are given in the table for both expert and intermediate participants.

From Table 2, it can be noted that 8 experts could find around 80% of the total usability problems, and all 9 intermediate participants together found only 70% of the total problems. This study required more than 5 participants to identify most of the usability problems which is different to the number suggested by Turner, Lewis, and Nielsen. We think for our study to need more than 5 participants to find 80% of the usability problems could be due to various factors including:

1. The type of the product; our app under study was agricultural mobile app, and there were a few studies in this area that conducted usability studies hence the 5 magic number may not apply here.
2. Type of the study; our study examined an app developed for rural Indian farmers, and the study was conducted with usability experts in the USA.
3. Knowledge of the participants; inline with the above point, experts in the USA may not have domain knowledge about the content and functionality of an app developed for crop farmers.

This can conclude that there is no strict rule on the number of participants needed to identify most of the usability problems as it depends on the participant characteristics and the characteristics of the product under study.

References

1. NaPanta-Agriculture Crop Management App for Farmer - Apps on Google Play, https://play.google.com/store/apps/details?id=com.napanta.farmer.app. Accessed 17 Mar 2021
2. Patel, H., Patel, D.: Survey of android apps for the agriculture sector. Int. J. Inf. Sci. Tech. 6(1–2), 61–67 (2016)
3. Rana, S., Sontakki, B.S.: Mobile based agro advisory services (MAAS) in India: an assessment of their effectiveness. Hyderabad, India, 2017 (Report No. 234) (2017). Retrieved from ICAR-National Academy of Agricultural Research Management website. http://eprints.naarm.org.in/234/
4. Blackmon, M., Polson, P., Kitajima, M., Lewis, C.: Cognitive walkthrough for the Web. In: Proceedings of CHI, pp. 463–470 (2002)
5. Nielsen, J., Molich, R.: Heuristic evaluation of user interfaces. In: Proceedings of the SIGCHI Conference on Human Factors in Computing Systems, pp. 249–256. ACM (1990)
6. Nielsen, J.: Usability Engineering. Academic Press Inc., Cambridge (1994)
7. Gerhardt-Powals, J.: Cognitive engineering principles for enhancing human-computer performance. Int. J. Hum.-Comput. Interact. 8(2), 189–211 (1996)
8. Weinschenk, S., Barker, D.T.: Designing Effective Speech Interfaces, vol. 1. Wiley, New York (2000)
9. Inostroza, R., Rusu, C., Roncagliolo, S., Rusu, V., Collazos, C.A.: Developing SMASH: a set of smartphone' usability heuristics. Comput. Stand. Interfaces 43, 40–52 (2016)
10. Turner, C.W., Lewis, J.R., Nielsen, J.: Determining usability test sample size. Int. Encycl. Ergon. Hum. Factors 3(2), 3084–3088 (2006)
11. Lindgaard, G., Chattratichart, J.: Usability testing: what have we overlooked? In: Proceedings of the SIGCHI Conference on Human Factors in Computing Systems, pp. 1415–1424 (2007)
12. Alroobaea, R., Mayhew, P.J.: How many participants are really enough for usability studies? In: 2014 Science and Information Conference, pp. 48–56. IEEE (2014)
13. Demir, F., Parraci, W.: The more complex the less success in online library services: evaluating the user experience for international students. Issues Trends Educ. Technol. 6(2) (2018)

UX Researchers: Framing Brazilian's Perspectives

Fernando Nobre Cavalcante[1](✉) and Bruno Ribeiro[2](✉) [iD]

[1] The University of Campinas, Cidade Universitária Zeferino Vaz - Barão Geraldo, Campinas, SP 13083-970, Brazil
fnobre@unicamp.br
[2] Rio de Janeiro State University, R. São Francisco Xavier, 524 - Maracanã, Rio de Janeiro, RJ 20550-013, Brazil

Abstract. This paper explores the professional paradigms of integrating skills from Exact and Social Sciences, considering the phenomenon of datafication. It provides a comparative overview of UX workers' educational and professional backgrounds in the ICT industry in Brazil. The critical research hypothesis is that agile methodologies, primarily from the Exact Sciences, quantify these professionals' qualitative work. It applies a survey using a non-probability convenience sampling with professionals identified as UX Researcher on LinkedIn. The financial, e-commerce, and ICT services sectors are the ones that showed the highest adherence to the survey. Qualitative methods popularized in the discovery and validation stages of agile methods are primarily developed at short notice throughout the recruitment, planning, and analysis stages, underscoring the assumption of quantitative dominance. There is a clear dispersion about valuing time and empathy with agile methods among professionals with academic research experience. Cultural aspects and regional contexts continue to be methodological challenges for quantifying users' experiences, even if they sound like qualitative demands.

Keyword: Datafication · ICT workers · Triangulation · UX researcher · Experience · Public opinion

1 Introduction

In *The Structure of Scientific Revolutions*, which was first edited in 1962, Thomas Kuhn points out the paradigm shift that allowed the development of qualitative research in the philosophy of science [1]. Researchers began to see the need for the interpretative levels that the so-called hard sciences were beginning to value in a field of dispute. The development of the forms of human communication, along with the commercialization of inventions, considers a greater synergy between pure and applied sciences. Media history reveals the interest of Communication Studies and media professionals in processes, productions, and practices of innovations. When looking at it, one notes the political, corporate, and academic tensions, yet it opens a discussion for the different adherences to qualitative or quantitative methods. The profession of user experience researcher, newly

© Springer Nature Switzerland AG 2021
C. Stephanidis et al. (Eds.): HCII 2021, CCIS 1419, pp. 55–62, 2021.
https://doi.org/10.1007/978-3-030-78635-9_8

christened since the popularity of agile methods in the early 2000s, is equated by three words that deserve important considerations: experience, research, and user. This piece focuses on just one: the senses of the word experience.

Between the 1940s and 1960s, Paul Lazarsfeld set three agendas that would mark the quantification of communication studies: effects of public opinion, the role of mass media in politics, and advertising as a means to change attitudes and actions [2]. *The people's choice* was a methodological work to analyze the 1940 presidential election that would elect Franklin D. Roosevelt [3]. At that time, public opinion was synonymous with "user experience." Investments in innovation research in companies were not yet keeping up with the high competitiveness and the need for incremental differentiation. Decades later (1964–1985), Latin America, particularly Brazil, would live under authoritarian regimes and was already a potential consumer market for the American monopolies [4]. The support from President Getúlio Vargas during the first dictatorial cycle in Brazil, between 1937 and 1946, before the military regime, fomented the market to produce national content in radio broadcasting. Vargas made way for the popularization of television sets in the 1960s – the opening of the broadcasting sector to the private sector would later be a weapon against him [5]. The triad politics, elite, and innovators contextualize the abilities of communication professionals who, by opinion, paid attention to the so-called "experience." Indeed, the first academic institutes that came to professionalize journalism and advertising were founded in 1947 (Faculdade Cásper Líbero) and 1951 (Escola Superior de Propaganda e Marketing) located on Paulista Avenue in São Paulo – both schools formed by the national corporate coalition of the time. Only years later, while opposing dictatorial regimes, public universities become players in this ecosystem, taking particular interest in reception studies and French school [6] and Germanic critical studies.

Field disputes and networks of resistance were the contexts for Lazarsfeld's quantitative works not noticed in the Brazilian curricula of Media and Communication program, focusing on qualitative approaches. On the one hand, the interest in regional thinking on the qualitative studies of reception by Jesús Martín-Barbero and Eliseo Verón has turned Latin America toward the qualitative analyses of mediation [7] and mediatization [8, 9]. Moreover, the similar interests of Latin and European researchers in the effects of media on reception and socio-discursive studies began to drive interpretative methods and techniques to communication professionals [10–13]. On the other hand, Lazarsfeld's quantitative orientation, restricted in English-speaking countries, seems to have had a greater receptivity focused on the United States, about to develop Silicon Valley agile methods decades later.

This introduction presents a brief historical overview to contextualize the profession of user experience researchers, which has become popular in recent years. The empirical focus of user experience research (UXR) already promotes a debate about this profession's agendas, which has primarily focused on qualitative methods [14, 15]. However, the central question of this study expands the agenda of this growing profession in Brazil: are there ways to think about a "scientificization" of UXR? This study, still under review, presents some results of a supposed quantification of the qualitative doing that the profession requires. The key goal is to build a comparative research with Latin America on the relationship between i) professional background, ii) knowledge circulation, and iii) professional practice of UXR. Partnerships for translations and regional peculiarities to expand the research to other countries in Latin America are also expected.

2   Experience: The End of Public Opinion?

In *Die Träger der öffentlichen Meinung. Studien zur Soziologie der Öffentlichkeit*, Ernest Manheim (1933) initially problematizes the modern paradox of socialization. The Sociologist outlines how the transition from the 19th to the 20th century brought a new type of social relationship to issues of state sovereignty. He compels an apparatus of facts from the first three decades of the 1900s and how the current social model was collapsing, giving way to new forms of distribution in society. Manheim sticks to historical changes, passing through the rise of industrialization, the auto industry, capital and labor market, fashion and newspaper companies as means to underpin public opinion. Also, how it would directly affect the form of behavior and distribution of values in the society at that time. The 19th century not only affected people within society because the changes in the century also affected social consciousness, the Sociologist believed.

In this new consciousness, Sociology took root as an impression of a new fact that unfolded society from its special and prototypical form, almost in a comprehensive and total form of being and thought. Studying the specific meaning of using the expression "society and socialization," and how it was used, and what sense it has been interpreted over the centuries is the author's most significant feature in his book's first chapters.

Manheim projects these questions to the field of advertising, in this piece, highlighted as a lens to understand "experience." Just as society and the very concept of what society has changed according to the thinking of the time, so has the structure and how the structure of the term **publicity** is seen. The author focuses his analysis on objects of study, such as the notion of groups through brotherhoods and associations, the press, and the treatment of the set of information to an audience. This new modern category of public thought expresses the new way of reflecting the same political circumstances and a new life context in society. The Sociologist breaks down the evolution of advertising itself over time. With the creation of public institutions such as associations, parties, the media or "public thought", in this way advertising, in analogy to socialization (according to its special nonsense and prototypical forms to the way of being) has risen as a category.

Manheim's typology of public opinion allows describing types of authoritarian (qualitative), strategic (plural), and propagandistic (transcendental) communication and its addressing to the public. After all, his theory about the public opinion expressed in 1933 anticipates Jürgen Habermas' notion of the public sphere [16, 17] and can undoubtedly contribute to understanding the ideal types of group bonds: experiences. To do sociological research on the forms of publicity in groups affected by the groups mobilized by the evolution of the media has been the main interest in recent studies [18]. Methodologically, researching modalities of qualitative framing of advertising collections and, theoretically, combining Symbolic Interactionism with the Sociology of Knowledge.

In this sense, Ernest Manheim may be considered the first scholar to create a sociology of media, through a rigorously analytical communication model, in 1932. In the 1920s and early 1930s, researchers typically took a normative and culturally critical look at communication in society. The then despicable mass-circulation press, which used imagery strategies even more often, was considered sensationalist and culturally destructive. Sociologists criticized newspapers for polarizing public opinion to such an extent that it had made social consensus impossible. At the time, in Germany, the rising territory of the Nazi Party, the leading conservative positions were pronounced: the decline of the political culture in Germany, the rise of the Nazi Party, or the supposed threat of the Communists had to be faced with censorship of the press [19]. The topic "the press and public opinion" was discussed in a highly emotional way.

The public opinion understanding was quantified when the private opinion polling institutes took over the international and Latin markets. It became synonymous with mass opinion, with figures; the qualitative character of the fact that opinions arise in group links was forgotten. With the popularization of Lazarsfeld's works applied to the television industry and to electoral polls, the scenarios for quantifying the qualifiers were already being mapped out. Don Norman, in 1986, in the most relevant chapter of his book "User centered system design: New perspectives on human-computer interaction" did not address the experience issue [20]. Fourteen years after the publication of his canon work, he prioritized bringing academia and the market closer to the Human and Social Sciences, with the popularization of the Human-Centered Interaction era.

There are minor debates about the Latin character of qualitative research applied to market studies in UXR. Silicon methods are reproduced, ignoring the nuances of language and local knowledge. The subject, actor, agent, became a user quantified in clicks, so unimportant is that opinions are fostered in experiences in groups links. The agile methods, incorporated by Dr. Norman's consultancy and studies, dominated the current UXR literature, but opened loopholes for starting to prioritize qualitative research in the face of the consumer journeys datafication. Startup tools have become synonymous with research methods. An interview report went from the history of science to the story of an MVP – Minimum Viable Product. However, there is a great room for improvement in this market. With the employability of the tech sector and the demands for qualitative research in large corporations, adding to what Manuel Castells called the ultra-specialization of network companies, in this piece the matter of experience is raised, even though it is not, at this time, the main focus of investigation. The experiments will not be the end of public opinion, nor will they be subdued by the numbers and the success tutoring of monopolies. It is just the beginning of the group links frames of experiences.

3   The Triangulation of a Survey

The mediatization studies have highlighted the dominance of quantification in research that confronts big data [21]. The term datafication refers to the increasing digitization of media with software-based technology [22]. The differentiation of numerous media devices, the increasing connectivity of the space-time relationship, the start of business models underpinned by a media ubiquity, the rapid pace of innovation, and the increase in data processing and storage are the main characteristics of a deep mediatization [23]. The great call of datafication research is that the digital traces that the so-called big data quantify the sense of reality. Above all, the criticism, the need for support insights in theoretical foundations, and interpretation of the context are the great call of the studies of datafication.

The triangulation of research, in which observation leads the qualitative meeting with the quantitative stimulated in the currents that study the phenomena of deep mediatization, animates this article. With that in mind, the applied questionnaire was divided into five parts, highlighted in the dark gray colors of the images below. The Atlas.ti software program was used to create semantic networks between correlations of the questions (see Fig. 1).

The survey was undertaken by applying an online form by Typeform in March 2021. The non-probabilistic convenience sample included 92 professionals identified as UX Researchers on LinkedIn from various regions of Brazil. Following other surveys conducted by the area, the highest concentration of professionals was in the state of São Paulo (49.3%), followed by the states of Rio de Janeiro (13.7%) and Minas Gerais (9.6%).

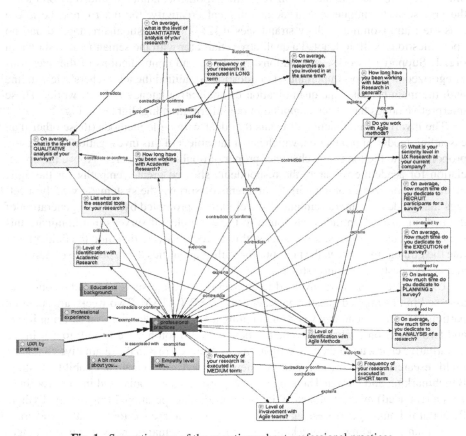

Fig. 1. Semantic map of the questions about professional practices.

Regarding academic training, all professionals have completed or are in the process of completing higher education. Among them, 40% hold a graduate specialist's degree, 16% a master's degree, and 4% a Ph.D. The major areas of training are the Humanities (Sociology, Social Communication, Advertising, and others), accounting for about 47.5%; followed by the area of Technology (Design, Engineering, Information Technology, and others), 38.1%; Business (Administration, Marketing, and others) and Agricultural Sciences (Agronomy), 1.4%.

Despite the humanistic background of most professionals, when asked about their adherence to academic research, the rate is 5.7 (on a 0 to 10 scale). In contrast, there is a greater willingness to other work methodologies, such as agile methods, which had an adhesion rate of 7.1 (on a 0 to 10 scale).

As for the work methodology, about 81.7% of the professionals use agile methods (Scrum, Lean, and others). There was also a high incidence of performing user research in short periods of time, about 91% of the professionals.

Quantification in this study does not refer to the statistical appeal developed with data, but to an objective nature, rather than an interpretive one; the regular, not the distinguishable; the neutral, not the engaged; the hypothetical, not the guided by premises; the precise in technique, not in methodological creativity; the macro, not the micro – as the Latin Communicology strand sees it [24]. The questionnaire applied had no open questions, still, it denoted a qualitative character with the semantic map shown in Fig. 1. Support networks, explanations, rebuttals, and contradictions of the questions categorized in the most important set of questions qualified the researchers' view in line with the main premise: the quantification of qualitative latency in UXR works. These interpretive nodes have been compiled in the information highlighted in Fig. 2.

The involvement depiction of teams that deal with agile methods (those other than cascading modes of production, which is not the object of this investigation) is inversely proportional to the long-term character proper of qualitative research. Above the appreciation for academic research, the respondents showed greater empathy for the agile methods themselves, common in the moments of sprints, the systematic weekly meetings that guide the "interdisciplinary" development promoted by the new generation of the tech industry. Contradictions found in the examples of surveys that dominate this sector: short term projects, carried out within a week. How to dive into the field, elaborate the ethnography, when the pressure for agility quantifies the experience of non-user actors? A question for future studies.

UXR professionals are involved in an average of three surveys simultaneously, as assessed in this applied questionnaire, entitled UXR LATAM. Two weeks are spent on participant recruitment, one week on planning a survey, three weeks on carrying it out, and two weeks on analyzing the data. They scored 6 (on a scale from 0 to 10) in the quantitative character of their investigations, as opposed to 8 in the qualitative character. Field research, Interview, In-depth interview, Forms/Questionnaires, Usability Testing, Benchmarking and Design Thinking are the main research tools used in their routines, with a (rounded) average of 5 each. Programming, Computational Linguistics, Python, R, Natural Language Processing figure as the least attractive tools (with an average lower than 2). Coding, eye-tracking and analysis of semantic networks had averages lower than 3. Regarding personal development, their main interests are topics around History, Consumer Behavior, Study, Professional Life (with a rounded average of 5, from 1 to 5); Sport is the topic of least interest, and the Numbers theme showed an average of 4. "Kanban", "Scrum", "Lean" and "X" were highlighted as the most dominant agile

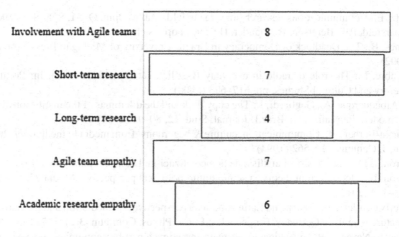

Fig. 2. Contradiction questions on the semantic map Average (0 to 10 scale).

methods in these companies. As for the seniority, most of the interviewees stated being at the levels of analyst (60%), specialist (26%), coordination (9%) and management (5%).

4   Conclusion

From Paul Lazarsfeld to Ernest Manheim, we have seen a polarization of quantitative and qualitative studies. The debates popularized by UXR consultancies fail to problematize a more interpretive sense of the term experience, which, in recent years, has been quantified in consumer journey clicks. It falls to the study to present a path for qualification in the elaboration of questionnaires that tend to have a broader, macro tone. Semantic networks of contradictions and endorsements, leading the researcher to more fluidly interpret questions that are numerically approachable is the proposal put forth. The user experience research profession in Brazil prevails in the financial sector and shows a growth potential as the vast majority of these professionals are still at less managerial levels in these companies. Agile methods seem to be synonymous with the professionalization of UXR, as much as the short-term research pressures. In this issue, it was pointed out the concern with the loss of the qualitative, interpretative and creative character in techniques such as ethnography, in-depth interviews, focus groups, among many others.

It is stressed that a better understanding of "experience" is only possible by investigating links in groups, far from the screens for interaction with digital goods. Longer deadlines for recruiting, carrying out and analyzing surveys are essential to maintain the qualitative character of experience investigations. *Frames of experience* can only be possible when one's natural environment is in focus.

References

1. Kuhn, T.S.: The Structure of Scientific Revolutions. University of Chicago press, Chicago (2012)

2. Katz, E.: Communications research since lazarsfeld. Public Opin. Q. **51**, S25–S45 (1987)
3. Lazarsfeld, P.F., Berelson, B., Gaudet, H.: The people's choice (1944)
4. Ames, B.: The Deadlock of Democracy in Brazil. University of Michigan Press, Ann Arbor (2002)
5. Calabre, L.: The role of radio in everyday Brazilian society (1923–1960). In: Portuguese Literary and Cultural Studies, pp. 617–623 (2000)
6. de Albuquerque, A., Gagliardi, J.: The copy desk and the dilemmas of the institutionalization of "modern journalism" in Brazil. Journal. Stud. **12**, 80–91 (2011)
7. Martin-Barbero, J.: Communication, culture & hegemony: from media to mediation//Review. Can. J. Commun. **19**, 562 (1994)
8. Verón, E.: Esquema para el análisis de la mediatización. Diálogos, pp. 9–16 (1997)
9. Verón, E.: Mediatization theory: a semio-anthropological perspective. Media. Commun. **21**, 163–174 (2014)
10. Averbeck-Lietz, S.: French and Latin American perspectives on mediation and mediatization: a lecture note from Germany. Empedocles: Eur. J. Philos. Commun. **3**(2), 177–195 (2011)
11. Fuentes Navarro, R.: Investigación y meta-investigación sobre comunicación en América Latina. MATRIZes, p. 13 (2019)
12. Scolari, C.A., Fernández, J.L., Rodríguez-Amat, J.R.: Mediatization (s): Theoretical Conversations between Europe and Latin America. Intellect Books (2020)
13. Daros, O.: French theoretical and methodological influences on Brazilian journalism research. Media Cult. Soc. 0163443721999936 (2021). https://doi.org/10.1177/0163443721999936
14. Robinson, J., Lanius, C., Weber, R.: The past, present, and future of UX empirical research. Commun. Design Q. Rev. **5**, 10–23 (2018)
15. Hassenzahl, M., Tractinsky, N.: User experience-a research agenda. Behav. Inf. Technol. **25**, 91–97 (2006)
16. Averbeck-Lietz, S.: Soziologie der Kommunikation: die Mediatisierung der Gesellschaft und die Theoriebildung der Klassiker. Walter de Gruyter GmbH & Co KG (2015)
17. Cavalcante, F.L.N.: Vínculos de ancoragens e enquadramentos temáticos: olhares itinerantes às interações midiatizadas em grupo. Tese (Doutorado em Estudos da Mídia), Universidade Federal do Rio Grande do Norte (2019)
18. Castells, M.: The Network Society A Cross-Cultural Perspective. Edward Elgar, Cheltenham (2004)
19. Averbeck, S.: Ernst Manheim (geb. 1900): Von der „Logik des konkreten Begriffs "zu „Functional Explanations ". In: Klingemann, C., Neumann, M., Rehberg, K.S., Srubar, I., Stölting, E. (eds.) Jahrbuch für Soziologiegeschichte 1995, pp 9–24. Springer, Heidelberg (1999). https://doi.org/10.1007/978-3-322-99766-1_1
20. Lindsay, P.H., Norman, D.A.: Human Information Processing: An Introduction to Psychology. Academic Press, Cambridge (2013)
21. Couldry, N., Hepp, A.: The Mediated Construction of Reality. Wiley, Hoboken (2018)
22. Karanasios, S., Thakker, D., Lau, L., et al.: Making sense of digital traces: an activity theory driven ontological approach. J. Am. Soc. Inform. Sci. Technol. **64**, 2452–2467 (2013)
23. Hepp, A.: Deep Mediatization: Key Ideas in Media & Cultural Studies. Routledge, London (2019)
24. Orozco, G., González, R.: Una coartada metodológica: abordajes cualitativos en la investigación en comunicación, medios y audiencias. Tintable (2012)

A Novel Experimental Equipment and Methods Using an Online Video Conference Tool to Collect Human Subjects Data Without Physical Interaction

Hyunjoo Park, Hyunjae Park, and Sang-Hwan Kim[✉]

Department of Industrial and Manufacturing Systems Engineering,
University of Michigan-Dearborn, Dearborn, MI 48128, USA
{jooo,jeee}@umich.edu, dysart@umcih.edu

Abstract. There have been suggestions of remote usability test and experiment methods to collect human performance data while interacting with prototypes. The pandemic caused by COVID-19 has increased the necessity of remote testing methods due to constraints on interacting with participants in the same location with physical contacts. The present study introduces a convenient and effective remote experiment method using a commercial video conference application. While an experimental prototype is running in an experimenter's computer, a participant in another place can access and manipulate the prototype to complete given experimental tasks using the remote-control functions in conference application. A case study to investigate the effects of text features in vehicle infotainment systems on driver's performance validated the utility of the suggesting method. Even though the method includes limitations compared to conventional lab experiments, the advantage seems overwhelming to the disadvantages when the remote data collection experiment is inevitably required. It is expected that the suggested method can be used with some modifications based on context of each experiment.

Keywords: Remote experiment · Human performance data · Video conference

1 Introduction

1.1 Hardship in Collecting Data from Experiment

Due to COVID-19, there have been substantial changes in people's lives including limited in-person contact. It is expected that even after COVID-19 is terminated a number of aspects of our lives will not be the same as before and rather transform into new ways of life. These changes brought a lot of constraints on human-computer interaction or human factors research as well. Particularly, it might be inconvenient or somewhat infeasible to collect human performance data through physical contact with participants in usability test or lab experiment under the pandemic circumstances due to the policy that strongly restricts the physical contact. In order to address this constraint, other experimental methods without physical contact with participants are required.

© Springer Nature Switzerland AG 2021
C. Stephanidis et al. (Eds.): HCII 2021, CCIS 1419, pp. 63–66, 2021.
https://doi.org/10.1007/978-3-030-78635-9_9

1.2   Remote Evaluation Methods

Before the constraints of the pandemic, several usability evaluation methods were introduced and used to collect data without physical interaction with participants. For example, Brush et al. demonstrated a remote usability test method. In their study, each participant had to visit the lab to install an experimental prototype in their own computer and data including verbal protocol was collected remotely though phone call [1]. Interestingly, they found no significant differences between in-site and remote test as well as the fact that most participants preferred the remote experiment. Tulis et al. used a web environment for the participant to participate the test in their own place using web browsers [2]. However, there were limitations in data collection due to infeasibility of real-time interaction between experimenter and participant. Andresen et al. conducted a study to compare different testing methods including lab testing, remote synchronous testing, remote asynchronous expert testing, and remote asynchronous user testing [3]. In their remote test methods, videos of participants' face and screen were recorded along with manual data collection.

Even though there have been many successful instances of remote evaluation methods, there are still problems in the remote data collection methods in the previous studies compared to actual experiment in a lab environment, including: 1) the participants should have the experimental equipment or prototype in own place or should receive from experimenter; 2) it is hard to instruct experimental tasks as well as to monitor the participant performance in real time; 3) types of tasks that the participants are limited; and 4) the types and quality of performance measures (e.g., reaction time, attention movement, etc.) are also limited.

In order to address this constraint from the Pandemic and historical remote test methods, this study proposes an experimental methodology in collecting data through synchronized remote experiments in a simple way. Since a decent video conference software supports remote control feature, it can be used for remote experiment. That is, while an experimental prototype is running in experimenter's computer, participants can manipulate the prototype using the remote-control functions in their own place rather than in a lab. A case study conducted using the method may validate its utility and demonstrate more detailed ideas.

2   Case Study: Investigating Legibility in Vehicle Interface Using Synchronized Remote Experiment

The original purpose of the study was to investigate effective font faces and line spacing for in-vehicle infotainment display by assessing legibility and satisfaction of drivers in terms of driving safety. Instead of inviting participants to the lab to conduct an experiment with driving tasks by using a driving simulator, an experimental method was used, allowing participants to remotely complete experimental tasks at their residence. The experimental data was collected using a commercial video conference application which provides remote control feature.

That is, the experimental task prototype was executed on the experimenter's computer and a participant used the remote-control function during the online conference in order to perform the given task, including mouse cursor control and keystrokes. Participants' performance data was recorded in the prototype application on the experimenter's computer and the video files of participants' face including eye movement and reactions recorded by the video conference application. Figure 1 illustrates general structure of the experimental setup and feature of the outputs.

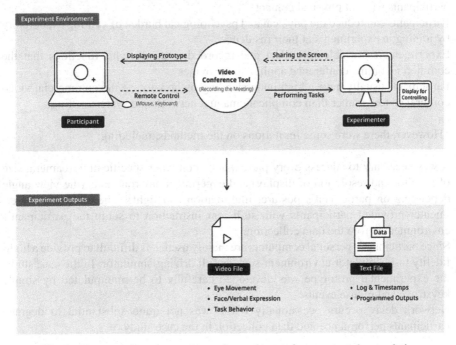

Fig. 1. Conceptual structure of experimental setup for remote task completion

As shown in Fig. 1. A Java-based driving task simulation software was presented in experimenter's computer (i.e., host of the video conference), which includes a primary tracking task and a secondary information acquisition task. During the experiment, a participant was watching the simulator as well as complete the tracking task using keyboard or mouse in his/her own computer. The keyboard or mouse event signals were transmitted to experimenter's computer through remote control functions in the video conference tool. Then the experimenter's computer runs based on participants' manipulations and designated output files were recorded in experimenter's computer according to the program (e.g., tacking performance such as distance to target along with the time stamps). Since the participant's computer has video camera, the participant's face could be recorded in a video file in a cloud or experimenter's local computer, and this was used to analyze participant's eye (attention) movement profile. In addition to this, participant's task completion behavior (e.g., cursor movement) was video recorded for further analysis. All experiment were successfully completed, and viable performance data were collected without inviting the participant to the experiment place.

3 Discussion and Conclusion

Based on the case study, it was possible to confirm the advantages of the remote experiment as followings:

- Empirical research could be conducted while communicating non-face-to-face with participants without physical contact
- Participants can reduce the physical and psychological burden of visiting a laboratory by joining in experiments at their residence
- Experimenters are able to collect and record data easily with functions that the commercial online conference application provides
- Participants usually have a high understanding on how to use the commercial video conference tool, rather than complicate manual network and system setting.

However, there were some limitations on the methods, including:

- It was necessary to address every participant's computer specification (camera, size of monitor and resolution of display) and experiment environments (the view angle depending on participant's posture, illumination and light). Therefore, the experimenter provided participants with sufficient instruction to setup the participant's environment before the data collection.
- Since participant's personal computers are mainly used, it is difficult to provide a high-fidelity task simulator environment such as full driving simulator. In the case study, the experimental prototype was developed carefully to be manipulated by simple keystroke and mouse events.
- Network delay occurs occasionally but it was not quite substantial to degrade participants performance and data collection in the case study.

Despite these some shortcomings, the experiment in the case study has been conducted successfully using the method because it seemed that the advantages in the current situation are overwhelming.

This experimental method can be adjusted according to the type or purpose of each of other relevant experiments in future. It is also expected that the method can be actively utilized in various ways as a non-face-to-face data collection method that overcomes physical experimental limitations.

References

1. Brush, A.J.B, Ames, M., Davis, J.: A comparison of synchronous remote and local usability studies for an expert interface. In: Extended Abstracts of the 2004 Conference on Human Factors and Computing Systems - CHI 2004 (2004). https://doi.org/10.1145/985921.986018
2. Tom, T., Stan, F., Michelle, M., Carrie, C., Marguerite B.: An empirical comparison of lab and remote usability testing of web sites (2002)
3. Andreasen MS, Nielsen HV, Schrøder SO, Stage J, What happened to remote usability testing? In: Proceedings of the SIGCHI Conference on Human Factors in Computing Systems - CHI 2007 (2007). https://doi.org/10.1145/1240624.1240838

Taking the Next Step Towards Convergence of Design and HCI: Theories, Principles, Methods

Dagmar Steffen[✉]

School of Art and Design, Lucerne University of Applied
Sciences and Arts, Lucerne, Switzerland
dagmar.steffen@hslu.ch

Abstract. The current digital transformation of the world of things with more and more hybrid, interconnected artifacts leads to a convergence of the different disciplines involved in this development. A close transdisciplinary collaboration of design, computer science, environmental and cognitive psychology requires an integration of the disciplines' knowledge bases. To this end, the article highlights selected theories, principles, and methods of product design and human-computer interaction, their parallel yet time-delayed development, and the existing overlaps. Among other things, it shows that the semiotics established in product design has so far only been superficially received in HCI. An integration of semiotic or semantic theory and a human-centered design approach is proposed to address current challenges of digital transformation and hybrid artifacts: such as the invisibility dilemma and the control dilemma posed by AI, as well as issues of sustainability inherent in the hybrid artefacts of the Internet of Things.

Keywords: Internet of Things · Design theory · Product semantics

1 Introduction

The current transformation of conventional products into hybrid, networked artifacts represents a qualitative leap that challenges the distinction between 'digital' and 'analog', 'material' and 'immaterial' [40, 41, 44]. The development, design and implementation of these hybrid artifacts is an interdisciplinary task, in which various professions – product-, graphic-, interaction-, and user experience design, engineering and computer science – are involved. These disciplines have different roots, their own thought leaders, constituent discourses, specialized theories and methods [37]. Due to its much longer history, design today has a broad foundation of coexisting and complementary theoretical approaches, methods, and a humanistic philosophical stance. In contrast to design, the field of HCI is not only younger, but much more determined by technical rationalism and pragmatic interests [3, 4]. Accordingly, the development of theoretical foundations was primarily directed towards guidelines, principles, and methods aimed at ensuring the usefulness and usability of computer programs and websites.

© Springer Nature Switzerland AG 2021
C. Stephanidis et al. (Eds.): HCII 2021, CCIS 1419, pp. 67–74, 2021.
https://doi.org/10.1007/978-3-030-78635-9_10

On the whole, a parallel but temporally staggered development of the theories and methods of design and HCI can be noted, where HCI has often caught up with what was already state of the art in the field of design. At the same time, there are also bodies of knowledge and methods that have so far been used almost exclusively in one of the fields, despite the fact that their application would also be beneficial for the other fields involved in product development.

Taking into consideration the current progress and dissemination of hybrid artifacts, artificial intelligence (AI), and machine learning, this preliminary study will argue for a further integration and advancement of existing theories, principles, and methods from design, HCI and user experience as well as a stronger involvement of designers and design researchers at an early stage of product development.

Since design has historically played a key role in socio-cultural innovations and the embedding of new technologies in the everyday life of people [5, 40, 48], the question arises as to how design, in interdisciplinary collaboration with computer science, cognitive psychology and environmental psychology, among others, can help shape the digital transformation of artifacts in a human-centered and sustainable way. In this context, the discipline not only has a responsibility, but also a special competence, since design has always been an integrative activity that brings together knowledge and competences from different fields – from the natural sciences, engineering, humanities and social sciences – for practical purposes [6, 15] and is able to act competently in this inter- and transdisciplinary field of tension.

1.1 State of the Art of Convergence of Design and HCI

In the last few decades numerous practitioners and researchers have worked to bring theories, processes, and methods of design and designerly ways of thinking and acting to computer science to humanize and improve the interaction between people and computers [14, 45]. Frequently a development was repeated in the field of HCI that had already taken place decades earlier in the field of product design.

One of the most important developments was a paradigm shift in both disciplines which can be briefly described as "from function to meaning" [7]. While modern design and its theoretical principles were mainly focused on requirements of practical product usage and industrial mass production, in the course of the 1970s semantic and symbolic product qualities and the related emotional bond moved to the fore in order to meet the hitherto neglected psychological needs of users [18]. About thirty years later, with the public accessibility of the Internet and dissemination of digital devises the nascent field of interface and interaction design experienced the same development stages: from function, usefulness, and usability to 'user experience' [34], 'hedonic qualities' [12, 22], and 'emotional design' [35]. Unaware of the already existing body of knowledge in product design, particularly with regard to design semantics and semiotics, the HCI-community started over again developing or adapting theoretical terms and models in order to guide interface- and interaction design practice. Although not exhaustive, a number of overlaps between theories, concepts and methods of design and HCI should be mentioned:

Workflow. Oswald [37] recalled that the labor- and time-saving working processes and a reduction of the walking routes in the Frankfurt kitchen, developed by Margarete Schütte-Lihotzky in 1926, was an early predecessor of workflow and process design, which are currently embraced by usability engineering.

Semiotics/Theory of Product Language. Oberquelle [36], who dealt with design issues in HCI, had early on pointed out the relevance of semiotics for user-centered HCI. Yet, in the existing HCI literature, semiotics has been referred to almost only in the context of computer-generated art and 'aesthetic computing' [32], the graphic design of websites [1, 11, 46, 52], or very generally to the communicative and interactive nature of digital objects [cf. 2, 9].

Semantic Differential. The method of the Semantic Differential borrowed from psychology was introduced to product design or rather the so-called 'theory of product language' by Gros [19] to investigate product's impression (look & feel) on beholders and target groups. At a later time Hassenzahl, Burmester, and Koller [23] applied this method for measuring the hedonic and pragmatic quality of websites and interactive applications as perceived by users.

Product Personality/Persona. Gros [20] used the concept of persona or as he put it product personality within the theory of product language for the embodiment of product's expression or – seen from another angle – characterization of product's target group. Later Cooper [10] suggested that computer scientists could use personas to get a more realistic idea of the users of their software applications.

Affordance/Indication Sign. The term affordance, which goes back to the psychologist Gibson [17], was introduced into the fields of design and HCI by Norman [33] and Krippendorff [29, 30]. The term refers to the fact that, depending on specific properties, an artifact invites to use it for certain purposes and in a certain way. However, the concept of the so-called indication sign [13], which has its roots in the philosophy of Langer [31], is a key concept in the theory of product language that comprises the scope of the aforementioned affordances and even goes beyond this; in addition, they communicate product's properties such as performance, quality standard, technical status, etc.

Metaphors. The invention of the desktop metaphor by Kay and its application to the Apple interface, including numerous other icons, contributed decisively to the easy readability and intuitive usability of the PC. Notwithstanding metaphors referring to historical forms, engineering or nature, were early on also applied to housing design of electronic devices to make the functions and operation of a 'black box' filled with technical components understandable and easily accessible [8]. At present, the metaphor design approach is used only sporadically for smart products, e.g., humanoid robots or Sony's robotic dog 'Aibo'.

Pattern Language. In 1977, Alexander and colleagues developed the concept of a so-called pattern language by systematically showing exemplary solution patterns for more than 250 general problems, which are transferable to comparable applications. This approach took on a new relevance in interface design, where developers quickly arrive at good design solutions by resorting to predefined patterns [7, 11, 21].

2 Challenges in Development and Design of Hybrid Artifacts

The digital transformation of the world of things brings about a fundamental change in the relationship of people and objects, since smart objects develop a life of their own. At the same time, they currently still look much the same as their dumb predecessors. The design of virtual assistants like Google Nest or Google Home mini, to name a few, is still based on the outdated functionalist doctrine of the so-called Good Design, according to which less is more. As is often the case when new technologies are introduced, they are initially stuck with the old patterns. Thus, an in-depth analysis of ten voice assistants and social robots (including Amazon's Alexa, Google Home, and Jibo) in terms of physical appearance, input and output modalities, feedback systems, and discoverability of functions concludes that the materialization of AI functions into tangible objects is still deficient. Even basic principles of interaction design have not been sufficiently considered [47]. Two of the most important challenges of smart assistants' design are addressed below.

2.1 Control Dilemma

The control dilemma arises from the fact that on the one hand, smart assistants such as the smartphone are assigned certain tasks that they are supposed to manage independently to relieve users by reducing cognitive load [51]. But on the other hand, it is annoying when the assistants initiate undesirable actions or when their activities are not transparently traceable [28]. In both cases, users can feel unpleasantly surprised, ignored, or even patronized by the smartness of hybrid artifacts.

2.2 Invisibility Dilemma

The invisibility dilemma is at least equally problematic: When smartness is seamlessly integrated into Good Design-style voice assistants, supposedly familiar everyday objects such as consumer electronics, or the built environment this new quality of the artifacts is not apparent to people. Therefore, people have no opportunity to adjust their expectations and behavior accordingly. However, in the context of product categories, such as household appliances or automobiles, designers had repeatedly advocated that hiding advanced technology, new materials or ideas in an old design does not make sense. There is a widespread consensus that groundbreaking products should clearly show their innovative character, so that users can perceive the added value [27, 42]. There are strong reasons to demand this from smart products as well, especially if the devices encroach on users' privacy and affect data security. An AI iconography, a set of visual signs or rather small icons that communicate various key factors of AI functions and operations to stakeholders, as suggested by Pilling et al. [38], is at least one possible semiotic approach to resolve this dilemma.

2.3 Interplay Between Hardware, Software and Interface

To this day, at least a few computer scientists consider the hardware of hybrid artifacts merely as a so-called 'form factor' [39] that lies outside of one's own field of expertise and does not need to be taken into account. However, separate development and design of hardware, software, interface and interaction is problematic, especially for new products. The importance of a holistic approach can be exemplified by Apple's products, in which all components always form a unique symbiosis: Starting with the intuitive operation of the graphical user interfaces and touchscreens, the design language of the housings, to the innovative handling of materials, construction and manufacturing techniques [2, 43].

Furthermore, it is supported by so-called digital materialism studies, which reject the dualism between nature and culture, mind and matter and seeks to mediate between natural science, the arts, and environmental ethics [41]. To this end, it is necessary, for example, to scrutinize and uncover concrete connections between for instance the materiality of the touchscreen, operating gestures, and the perception of the media content by people [50].

3 Next Step of Cooperation and Integration of Design and HCI

As has been shown issues around sensual perception, communication and interpretation of hybrid artifacts by users are crucial. Like any other product, hybrid artifacts are perceived as signs, and their use and operation are guided by users' interpretation of signs inscribed in the artifact. In fact, various terms and concepts of product design semantics have already been redeveloped or borrowed by HCI to catch up. However, since these terms and concepts have not yet been systematically related to each other, and since a consistent semiotic perspective on the subject matter is also missing so far, this is suggested for further research.

Furthermore, a design semiotics approach can be used to deal with relevant and so far neglected issues, just to mention sustainability concerns. In her analysis of the interface design of technical devices, Weber [49] raised the question of why users of consumer electronics, for example, "receive visual feedback on volume or performance, while feedback on energy consumption is still lacking". Since the increasing energy consumption associated with the digital transformation is highly relevant, but at the same time massively underestimated [24], this consumption should also be made perceptible – as well as the before mentioned equally invisible AI of hybrid artifacts.

However, whether users perceive hybrid artifacts as such, whether they develop a basic understanding of smartness, whether they can perform only certain predefined tasks, or whether they are also able to use them in accordance with situationally deviating individual needs and purposes is a crucial question – and at the same time a huge challenge for design in the broadest sense [16]. How hybrid artifacts are received by the users, which 'technology emotions' [25] are triggered and how an innovative technology is ultimately accepted, depends much on a holistic human-centered design approach. As Junginger [26] has pointed out, a human-centered design approach goes beyond user-centered design as it is currently understood and practiced in the field of HCI. While user-centered design only focuses on a person's immediate experience with a particular product or service, the human-centered design approach takes a systemic perspective that strives to create and realize new opportunities for desirable relationships and interactions between people, products or services, and their living environments. This means that human-centered design addresses not only issues such as interactions between hybrid artifacts and users, but also includes artifacts' consequences on society and the environment. Thus, design should not only be seen as a service provider when it comes to adapting technology to user needs and making applications usable and enjoyable. Design, understood as a holistic, human-centered approach, should already be involved in negotiating which technical functions and hybrid artefacts are really desirable and should be further developed. The challenge lies not only in the design of the hybrid artifacts, but in the design of the technology itself. Or as Geiger [16] put it in a nutshell: "Technology design is much more than the design of beautiful product housings and easy-to-use surfaces. Because it raises the question of power: Who rules over whom – man over technology or vice versa?".

Acknowledgements. This preliminary study has been supported by the Interdisciplinary Cluster (ITC) 'Digital Transformation of the working world' co-headed by Simone Gretler and Rolf Kamps at the Lucerne University of Applied Sciences and Arts. I would like to address thanks to my colleagues Clemens Nieke, Marcel Uhr and Thilo Schwer for many fruitful discussions within this study.

References

1. Allanwood, G., Beare, P.: User Experience Design: Creating Designs Users Really Love. Fairchild Books, London (2015)
2. Antonelli, P., et al.: Talk to Me: Design and the Communication Between People and Objects. Museum of Modern Art, New York (2011)
3. Auernhammer, J.: Human-centered AI: different human-centered design practices in the design and research of ethical AI. In: Proceedings of DRS 2020, Design Research Society Conference, Brisbane, vol. 3, pp. 1315–1333 (2020)
4. Baranauskas, M.C.C., Bonacin, R.: Design – indicating through signs. Des. Issues 24(3), 30–45 (2008)
5. Bonsiepe, G.: Interface – An Approach to Design. Jan van Eyck Academy, Maastrich (1999)
6. Buchanan, R.: Design research and the new learning. Des. Issues 17(4), 3–23 (2001)
7. Bürdek, B.E.: From function to meaning: in the long run everything is design. In: Vidal, F. (ed.) Ernst Bloch und das Bauhaus: gestern und heute, pp. 151–174. Talheimer, Mössingen-Talheim (2008)
8. Bürdek, B.E.: Design. History, Theory and Practice of Product Design. Birkhäuser, Basel (2015)
9. Buurman, G.M. (ed.): Total Interaction. Theory and Practice of a New Paradigm for the Design Disciplines. Birkhäuser, Basel (2005)
10. Cooper, A.: The Inmates are Running the Asylum. Macmillan Computer Publishing, Indianapolis (1999)
11. Cooper, A., Reimann, R., Cronin, D.: About Face. Interface und Interaction Design. Wiley, Indianapolis (2007)
12. Diefenbach, S., Hassenzahl, M.: Psychologie in der nutzerzentrierten Produktgestaltung Mensch-Technik-Interaktion-Erlebnis. Springer, Berlin (2017). https://doi.org/10.1007/978-3-662-53026-9
13. Fischer, R., Mikosch, G.: Grundlagen einer Theorie der Produktsprache, Anzeichenfunktionen (1984). Reprint in: Schwer, T., Vöckler, K. (eds.): Der Offenbacher Ansatz. Zur Theorie der Produktsprache, pp. 123–183. Transcript, Bielefeld (2021). https://www.transcript-verlag.de/978-3-8376-5569-8/der-offenbacher-ansatz/. Accessed 26 Mar 2021

14. Forlizzi, J., Zimmermann, J., Evenson, S.: Crafting a place for interaction design research in HCI. Des. Issues **24**(3), 20–29 (2008)
15. Friedman, K.: Design knowledge: context, content and continuity. In: Durling, D., Friedman, K. (eds.). Doctoral Education in Design. Foundations for the Future. Proceedings of the Conference in La Clusaz, pp. 5–16. Staffordshire University Press, Stoke-on-Trend (2000)
16. Geiger, A.: Andersmöglichsein. Zur Ästhetik des Designs. Transcript, Bielefeld (2018)
17. Gibson, J.J.: The Ecological Approach to Visual Perception. Houghton Mifflin, New York (1979)
18. Gros, J.: Dialektik der Gestaltung (1971). Reprint in: Schwer, T., Vöckler, K. (eds.): Der Offenbacher Ansatz, pp. 38–65. Reference as above, [13]
19. Gros, J.: Grundlagen einer Theorie der Produktsprache, Einführung (1983). Reprint in: Schwer, T., Vöckler, K. (eds.): Der Offenbacher Ansatz, pp. 88–122. Reference as above, [13]
20. Gros, J.: Grundlagen einer Theorie der Produktsprache, Symbolfunktionen (1987). Reprint in: Schwer, T., Vöckler, K. (eds.): Der Offenbacher Ansatz, pp. 184–207. Reference as above [13].
21. Guder, F.: Gestaltungsmuster – Algorithmen des Design, in: Denzinger, J. (ed.): Das Design digitaler Produkte, pp. 108–113. Birkhäuser, Basel (2018)
22. Hassenzahl, M., Platz, A., Burmester, M., Lehner, K.: Hedonic and ergonomic quality aspects determine software's appeal. In: Conference Proceedings Human Factors in Computing Systems CHI. pp. 201–206. The Hague (2000)
23. Hassenzahl, M., Burmester, M., Koller, F.: AttrakDiff: Ein Fragebogen zur Messung wahrgenommener hedonischer und pragmatischer Qualität. In: Ziegler, J., Szwillus, G. (eds.) Mensch & Computer. Interaktion in Bewegung, pp. 187–196. Vieweg+Teubner, Wiesbaden (2003). https://doi.org/10.1007/978-3-322-80058-9_19
24. Hessler, M.: Society – technology – people. Interview with Prof. Martina Heßler. Bundesinstitut für Berufsbildung (BIBB) (2019). https://www.youtube.com/watch?v=1JzeB1jyiAA&t=655s. Accessed 26 Mar 2021
25. Hessler, M. (ed.): Technikemotionen. Ferdinand Schöningh. Paderborn (2020)
26. Junginger, S.: Transforming Public Services by Design: Re-orienting Policies, Organizations and Services Around People. Routledge, London (2017)
27. Karjalainen, T.M.: Semantic transformation in design. Communicating strategic brand identity through product design references. Publication series University of Art and Design Helsinki (2004)
28. Kranz, M., Holleis, P., Schmidt, A.: Embedded interaction: Interacting with the Internet of things. IEEE Internet Comput. **14**(2), 46–53 (2010). https://doi.org/10.1109/MIC.2009.141
29. Krippendorff, K.: On the essential contexts of artifacts or on the proposition that "Design is making sense (of things)." Des. Issues **5**(2), 9–39 (1989)
30. Krippendorff, K.: The semantic turn. A new foundation for design. Taylor & Francis, Boca Raton (2006)
31. Langer, S.K.: Philosophy in a New Key. A Study in the Symbolism of Reason, Rite, and Art. Harvard University Press, Cambridge (1942)
32. Nake, F., Grabowski, S.: The interface as sign an as aesthetic event. In: Fishwick, P. (ed.) Aesthetic Computing, 53–69. MIT Press, Cambridge (2006)
33. Norman, D.A.: The Psychology of Everyday Things. Basic Books, New York (1988)
34. Norman D.A., Miller, J., Henderson, A.: What you see, some of what's in the future, and how we go about doing it: HI at Apple Computer. In: Proceedings of CHI 1995 Conference Companion on Human Factors in Computing Systems, Denver, Co (1995)
35. Norman, D.A.: Emotional Design. Why We Love (or Hate) Everyday Things. Basic Books, New York (2004)

36. Oberquelle, H.: Benutzergerechte MCI in einer dynamischen Welt – Eine Gestaltungsaufgabe. In: Hellige, H.D. (ed.) Mensch-Computer-Interface. Zur Geschichte und Zukunft der Computerbedienung, pp. 157–172. Transcript, Bielefeld (2008)
37. Oswald, D.: Towards a redefinition of product design and product design education. In: Proceedings of the International Conference on Engineering and Product Design Education. (E&PDE) Trondheim (2010)
38. Pilling, F., Akmal, H., Gradinar, A., Lindley, J., Coulton, P.: Legible AI by design: design research to frame, design, empirically test and evaluate AI iconography. In: Botta, M., Junginger, S. (eds.) Proceedings Swiss Design Network (SDN) Symposium 2021, Design as common good, pp. 548–565 (2021). https://designascommongood.ch/Design-as-Common-Good-Proceedings-Open.pdf. Accessed 26 Mar 2021
39. Preim, B., Dachselt, R.: Interaktive Systeme. User Interface Engineering, 3D-Interaktion, Natural User Interfaces, 2nd edn. Springer, Berlin (2015). https://doi.org/10.1007/978-3-642-45247-5
40. Redström, J., Wiltse, H.: Changing Things. The Future of Objects in a Digital World. Bloomsbury, London (2019)
41. Reichert, R., Richterich, P., Abend, P., Fuchs, M., Wenz, K. (eds.): Digital Culture & Society, Digital Material/ism, 1(1). Transcript, Bielefeld (2015). http://digicults.org/issues/digital-materialism. Accessed 26 Mar 2021
42. Roy, R.: Case studies of creativity in innovative product development. Des. Stud. **14**(4), 423–443 (1993)
43. Schulze, S., Grätz, I. (eds.): Apple Design. Hatje Cantz, Ostfildern (2011).
44. Selle, G.: Ding, Halb-Ding, Nicht-Ding, In-Ding, Über-Ding. Über sichtbares und unsichtbares Design. In: Gleiter, J.H. (ed.) Symptom Design. Vom Zeigen und Sich-Zeigen der Dinge, 39–66. Transcript, Bielefeld (2014)
45. Shneiderman, B., Plaisant, C., Cohen, M., Jacobs, S., Elmqvist, N.: Designing the User Interface: Strategies for Effective Human-Computer Interaction, 6th edn. Pearson, Boston (2018)
46. Sieckenius de Souza, C.: Semiotics. In: Interaction Design Foundation (ed.) The Encyclopedia of Human-Computer Interaction, 2nd edn. https://www.interaction-design.org/literature/book/the-encyclopedia-of-human-computer-interaction-2nd-ed/semiotics. Accessed 26 Mar 2021
47. Spallazzo, D., Sciannamé, M.; Ceconello, M.: The domestic shape of AI: a reflection on virtual assistants. In: 11th Proceedings of Design and Semantics of Form and Movement International Conference (DeSForM) MIT Boston, pp. 52–59. Scopus, Cambridge (2019)
48. Steffen, D.: Design semantics of innovation. In: Vihma, S. (ed.) Design Semiotics in Use, pp. 82–110. Publication Series Aalto University, School of Art and Design Helsinki (2010)
49. Weber, H.: Blackboxing? Zur Vermittlung von Konsumtechniken über Gehäuse- und Schnittstellendesign. In: Bartz, C., Kaerlein, T., Miggelbrink, M., Neubert, C. (eds.) Gehäuse: Mediale Einkapselungen, pp. 115–136. Wilhelm Fink, Paderborn (2017)
50. Werning, S.: Swipe to unlock. How the materiality of the touchscreen frames media use and corresponding perceptions of media content. In: Reichert, R., et al. (eds.) pp. 55–72. (reference as above 41). http://digicults.org/issues/digital-materialism. Accessed 26 Mar 2021
51. Wölfel, M.: Der smarte Assistent. In: Ruf, O. (ed.) Smartphone-Ästhetik. Zur Philosophie und Gestaltung mobiler Medien, pp. 268–288. Transcript, Bielefeld (2018)
52. Wood, D.: Interface Design: An Introduction to Visual Communication in UI Design. Fairchild Books, Bloomsbury (2014)

Social Connectedness and Online Design Education Outcome: A Relationship Model

Christy Vivek Gogu[✉] and Jyoti Kumar

Indian Institute of Technology Delhi, New Delhi, India

Abstract. Ample research has been done to argue the positive effects of Social Connectedness in people, especially in student communities. Recently, internet communities have emerged as a form of social network, and online social networking sites have rapidly expanded [1, 2]. With increase in internet connectivity and know-how, the need for online learning is rising. Literature reports the importance of social connectedness in making learning wholesome and effective, both in the online and face-to-face scenario [3, 4]. This paper reports a section of the author's doctoral research, wherein a relationship model was developed depicting the impact of learning experience on various aspects of design education and ultimately its outcome. This model provides a theoretical framework for this research that focuses mainly on social connectedness amongst design students and instructors and exploring its possible effects on the learnability of empathic design skill and motivations. It is proposed that an intentional learning experience improves social connectedness amongst design student communities, making them more socially connected designers capable of generating socially connected designs. The model connects various components of design education, such as course content/pedagogical style, teamwork/collaboration, learnability, creative ideation and motivation, online platform, etc. to the student's perceived social connectedness which is already a product of various influences like family, culture, personality, etc. The paper submits that all these components together help in the development of a socially connected designer with greater levels of user empathy, collaborative abilities, team communication abilities, cultural sensitivity, etc.

Keywords: Social connectedness · Learning experience · Virtual learning · Design pedagogy

1 Introduction

According to Laffey, G. Lin, & Y. Lin, (2006) [5], education and various learning interactions, whether traditional face to face or online, to be social practices. In-depth and meaningful interpersonal relationships are known to elevate one's performance in academic life [6]. Literature argues the positive effects of social connectedness (SC) in people groups, student communities in particular. More recently, internet communities have emerged as a form of social network and online social networking sites have rapidly expanded [1]. It is argued that SC makes learning wholesome and effective, both in online and traditional scenarios [3, 4]. Social learning theorists claim that successful learning

© Springer Nature Switzerland AG 2021
C. Stephanidis et al. (Eds.): HCII 2021, CCIS 1419, pp. 75–81, 2021.
https://doi.org/10.1007/978-3-030-78635-9_11

takes place in an environment where individuals can construct ideas, culture, histories, and meaning based on ongoing social interactions and collaborative functioning [7].

As part of the author's doctoral research, a relationship model has been developed to understand and depict the scope of influence of learning experience on various aspects of design education and ultimately its outcome. The model connects various components of design education, as discussed in the sections that follow, to the student's perceived social connectedness which is already a product of various influences like family, culture, personality, etc. This model provides a theoretical framework for this research focusing primarily on social connectedness amongst design students and instructors and exploring its possible effects on the learnability of empathic design skill and motivations.

2   Elements of the Relationship Model

A multitude of factors impact a design student's perceived social connectedness, we argue that one of these is the learning environment experience. Further, a student's perceived SC influences the way they interact with other students and their instructors, apart from other learning interactions. In the following sections, we discuss some of the components of design education that assist in developing problem solving and creative aptitude of a design student. We also look at perceived social connectedness as a product of various influences like family, culture, personality, etc.

2.1   Social Connectedness

Social connectedness has been used in many different contexts including mental health and wellbeing, social behavior, community development, student motivations, community health and attitudes. It is also seen as a product of cultural influences, family background and personality type [8, 9]. Van Bel, et al. arrived at the concept of Social Connectedness. They define social connectedness as 'a short-term experience of belonging and relatedness, based on quantitative and qualitative social appraisals, and relationship salience' [10]. Literature suggests that many ethnic minority elders strongly believe that family is responsible for providing emotional and social support [11]. This reliance on the family often leads to a reluctance to grow one's social network outside of the family context, even when feeling lonely and isolated [12].

Online Social Connectedness.   Recently, Internet communities have emerged as a form of social network, and online social networking sites have rapidly expanded [1, 2]. The current growth of online social interaction highlights the importance of examining social implications associated with online activity [13]. While prior research provides insight into the online experience and emphasizes the potential benefits of online activity such as positive psychological outcomes, particularly for those who are unable to connect face-to-face [14], this research aims to focus on the possibility of improving perceived social connectedness amongst design student communities, both online and face to face. In online education, it is argued that the extent to which students in distance education courses feel socially connected is frequently cited as a key factor in online course success [15]. While much work has been done in the humanities field with regards to perceived connectedness and its benefits, this model was developed to assist research focusing mainly on social connectedness amongst design students and instructors and exploring its possible effects on the learnability of empathic design skill and motivations.

Social Connectedness in Education. Social learning theorists claim that collaborative learning environments, where students develop and engage in networks of communication as they work towards achieving learning goals leads to successful learning [7].

Coming to online learning environments, participants are known to try and adapt to the new social environment and proceed in processing any social information available [16]. Kreijns et al. (2004) [17] indicate that the effectiveness of online group learning is dependent on these social interactions that students engage in. Although students find it is easier to connect socially and make friends with others in traditional face to face class settings, they realize the importance of connecting socially in virtual classroom settings as well [18]. Research also suggests a positive correlation between healthy interpersonal relationships and academic output [19].

Social Connectedness in Design Education. Empathy is an important trait for a designer. Understanding the user and their experience has a central place in user-centred design [20]. Research shows that social connectedness can enhance empathy (and vice versa) towards strangers and therefore can be learnt. In a study by Hutcherson, et al. (2008) [21], the authors used a brief loving-kindness meditation exercise to examine whether social connection could be created toward strangers in a controlled laboratory context. The results suggested that this easily implemented technique may help to increase social connectedness and decrease social isolation.

Therefore, a design learning environment that promotes perceived social connectedness can aid future designers to be trained in developing empathy that is essential for a more user-centred approach to designing. In this study, we posit that students experiencing higher levels of perceived connectedness are better able to collaborate in design projects, understand the user better and therefore become more empathic designers.

2.2 Social Interaction

Literature shows a strong correlation between felt social connectedness and levels of social interaction. The instructor is known to play an important role in helping students develop feelings of connectedness in online courses. This interaction could mitigate feelings of isolation among students in online learning environments and positively impact the student dropout rate. Developing a sense of community and connectedness can be achieved with the incorporation of social media into educational settings, institutions, and facilitators alike are encouraged to explore how technology such as Instagram and Vine might be used to help in this area [22].

2.3 Collaboration and Teamwork

Literature identifies creative learning as a process of collaborative and purposeful activity [23]. It stresses the importance of creative networks, communications, teamwork, and self-determination that generates innovation, curiosity, initiative, imagination and invention amongst students [24].

2.4 Learnability and Motivation

A learning environment is an atmosphere of a classroom that influences the interactions between instructor and students [25]. Free communication, cooperation and trusting each other are components of a good learning environment that emphasizes positive relationships, initiative, investigative and creative learning [26].

2.5 Creative Ideation

Creativity is a core skill of a student that transforms them from a learner to an innovator [27]. Creativity arises from the fact that individuals work together as a team and are supported by the environment [28]. Creative ideation techniques are one of the main building blocks of design education.

2.6 Student Motivation

In a meta-analysis conducted on the role that psychosocial factors play in determining college performance and persistence, they found that performance-based and goal-based motivation constructs were predictive of both academic performance and persistence [29]. They also found that social connectedness constructs were predictive of persistence after controlling for academic preparation.

2.7 Socially Connected Designer

The term 'socially connected designer' has been coined by the authors for the purpose of their research work. The model suggests that a socially connected designer exhibits high user empathy, collaborative abilities, team communication, cultural sensitivity and stakeholder understanding, while further study is required to ascertain these traits.

3 Relationship Model

With the premise of the literature supporting the above-mentioned components in design education, a relationship model was developed to guide the course of the wider research and plan the various stages of observation, experiment and intervention. In this model, we posit that an intentional learning environment experience can positively influence the students' perceived social connectedness, resulting in their increased levels of class interaction and group work. This in turn, equips them to collaborate better in design projects, resulting in their increased learnability, ideation and motivation. This results in an increased understanding of the user, making them more socially connected designers who display greater user empathy, collaborative abilities, team communication, cultural sensitivity and stakeholder understanding.

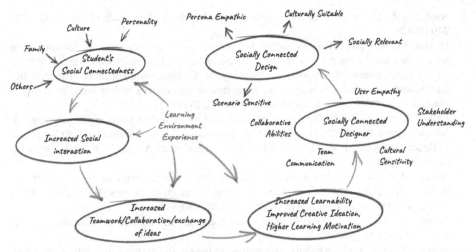

Fig. 1. Relationship model showing the relationship between social connectedness and design education outcome.

Therefore, a design learning environment that promotes perceived social connectedness can aid future designers to be collaborative and empathic, traits that are essential for a more user-centred approach to designing and enable them to be more socially motivated and relevant in their design career journey.

The relationship between the various components discussed in Sect. 2, is depicted in Fig. 1, and as shown, the learning environment experience plays a vital role in multiple stages and therefore, has the capacity to influence the perceived social connectedness of a design student over the course of their learning journey. While there are possibilities of overlapping of the various components at different points in the student learning process, this relationship model, helps to look at each segregated component individually in order to study the impact of learning environment experience on each of the components in detail.

The authors understand that though there may be other components, such as course content, cultural settings, instructor and student personalities, etc. for the purview of this research, only these components are taking into consideration.

The model identifies all these components as together assisting in the development of a socially connected designer with greater levels of user empathy, collaborative abilities, team communication abilities, cultural sensitivity, etc. We propose that an intentional learning experience improves social connectedness amongst design student communities, making them more socially connected designers capable of generating socially connected designs.

References

1. Boyd, D.M., Ellison, N.B.: Social network sites: definition, history and scholarship. J. Comput.-Mediat. Commun. **13**, 210–230 (2008)

2. Nadkarni, A., Hofmann, S.G.: Why do people use Facebook? Pers. Individ. Differ. **52**, 243–249 (2012)
3. Drouin, M., Vartanian, L.R.: Students' feelings of and desire for sense of community in face-to-face and online courses. Indiana University-Purdue University Fort Wayne (2010)
4. Green, T., Hoffmann, M., Donovan, L., Phuntsog, N.: Cultural communication characteristics and student connectedness in an online environment: perceptions and preferences of online graduate students. Int. J. e-learn. Distance Educ. **32**(2) (2017)
5. Laffey, J., Lin, G.Y. Lin, Y.: Assessing social ability in online learning environments. J. Interact. Learn. Res. **17**(2), 163–177 (2006). Association for the Advancement of Computing in Education (AACE), Waynesville, NC (2006). Accessed 23 August 2020. https://www.lea rntechlib.org/primary/p/5981/
6. Allen, J., Robbins, SB., Casillas, A., Oh, I.S. Third-year college retention and transfer: effects of academic performance, motivation, and social connectedness. Res. High. Educ. **49**(7), 647–664 (2008). https://doi.org/10.1007/s11162-008-9098-3
7. Brown, J.S., Collins, A., Duguid, P.: Situated cognition and the culture of learning. Educ. Res. **18**(1), 32–42 (1989)
8. Satici, S.A., et al.: Linking social connectedness to loneliness: the mediating role of subjective happiness. Pers. Individ. Differ. **97**, 306-310 (2015)
9. Yoon, E., Lee, R.M.: Importance of social connectedness as a moderator in Korean immigrants' subjective well-being. Asian Am. J. Psychol. **2**, 93–105 (2010)
10. Van Bel, D.T., Smolders, K.C.H.J., IJsselsteijn, W.A., de Kort, Y.: Social connectedness: concept and measurement. Intell. Environ. **2**, 67–74 (2009). https://doi.org/10.3233/978-1-60750-034-6-67
11. Schwartz, S.: The applicability of familism to diverse ethnic groups: a preliminary study. J. Soc. Psychol. **147**, 101–118 (2007). https://doi.org/10.3200/SOCP.147.2.101-118
12. Diaz, L.G., Savundranayagam, M.Y., Kloseck, M., Fitz-simmons, D.: The role of cultural and family values on social connectedness and loneliness among ethnic minority elders. Clin. Gerontol. **42**(1), 114–126 (2019). https://doi.org/10.1080/07317115.2017.1395377
13. Sheldon, K.M., Abad, N., Hinsch, C.: A two process view of Facebook use and relatedness need-satisfaction: disconnection drives use and connection rewards it. J. Pers. Soc. Psychol. **100**, 766–775 (2011)
14. Grieve, R., Indian, M., Witteveen, K., Tolan, G.A., Marrington, J.: Face-to-face or Facebook: can social connectedness be derived online? Comput. Hum. Behav. **29**(3), 604–609 (2013)
15. DiRamio, D., Wolverton, M.: Integrating learning communities and distance education: possibility or pipedream? Innov. High. Educ. **31**, 99–113 (2006). https://doi.org/10.1007/s10755-006-9011-y
16. Culnan, J.J., Markus, M.L.: Information technologies. In: Jablin, F.M., et al. (eds.) Handbook of Organizational Communication: An Interdisciplinary Perspective, pp. 420–443. Sage, Newbury Park (1987)
17. Kreijns, K.M., Kirschner, P.A., Jochems, W., van Buuren, H.: Determining sociability, social space, and social presence in (a)synchronous collaborative groups. Cyber Psychol. Behav. **7**(2), 155–172 (2004)
18. Glisan, E., Trainin, G.: Online Community and Connectedness A Pilot Study. University of Nebraska/Lincoln. Spring 2006 (2006)
19. Morrison, E.F., Rimm-Kauffman, S., Pianta, R.C.: A longitudinal study of mother-child interactions at school entry and social and academic outcomes in middle school. J. Sch. Psychol. **41**(3), 185–200 (2003)
20. Koskinen, I., Battarbee, K.: Introduction to user experience and empathic design. In: Koskinen, I., Battarbee, K., Mattelmäki, T. (eds.) Empathic Design, User Experience in Product Design, pp. 37–50. IT Press, Helsinki (2003)

21. Hutcherson, C.A., Seppala, E.M., Gross, J.J.: Loving-kindness meditation increases social connectedness. Emotion **8**(5), 720–724 (2008). https://doi.org/10.1037/a0013237
22. Zimmerman, T., Nimon, K.: The online student connectedness survey: evidence of initial construct validity. Int. Rev. Res. Open Distance Learn. **18**(3), 25–46 (2017). https://doi.org/10.19173/irrodl.v18i3.2484
23. McWilliam, E., Dawson, S.: Teaching for creativity: towards sustainable and replicable pedagogical practice. High. Educ. **56**, 633–643 (2008)
24. Sternberg, R.: Making creativity the centrepiece of higher education, paper presented at the creativity or conformity? Building cultures of creativity in higher education. University of Wales Institute, Cardiff. 8–10 January 2007
25. Greenhow, C., Peppler, K.A., Solomou, M.J.: Building creativity: collaborative learning and creativity in social media environments (2011)
26. Peterson, R.E., Harrison III, H.L.J.T., Teacher, E.: The created environment: an assessment tool for technology education teachers. Technol. Eng. Teach. **64**(6), 7 (2005)
27. Songkram, N.: Creating Innovation: Changed Learners to Innovators. Chulalongkorn University Press, Bangkok (2013)
28. Anderson, N., Potočnik, K., Zhou, J.: Innovation and creativity in organizations: a state-of-the-science review, prospective commentary, and guiding framework. J. Manage. **40**(5), 1297–1333 (2014)
29. Robbins, S.B., Lauver, K., Le, H., Davis, D., Langley, R., Carlstrom, A.: Do psychosocial and study skill factors predict college outcomes? A Meta-Anal. Psychol. Bull. **130**(2), 261–288 (2004). https://doi.org/10.1037/0033-2909.130.2.261. PMID: 14979772

The Foundation, Trend and Frontier of Service Design Research in English Literature

Ya-Wei Zhang[✉] and Wei Ding

East China University of Science and Technology, Shanghai 200237, China

Abstract. Having a deep insight of the international research progress in the field of service design is an inevitable requirement for the further development of service design industry. Based on 401 English articles on service design from the core collection database of Web of Science from 1999 to 2019, with the help of CiteSpace software, the research foundation, trend and frontier of service design are visually analyzed. The study found that: ① The research topics of service design cover a wide range of fields. They mainly falls into three groups: the origin of service design, the logic and method of service design, and the relationship between service design, enterprise and society. The logic and method of service design is the longest and most active knowledge group among them; ② From 2002 to 2011, the relationship between service design and perceived service quality is the frontier of research. From 2008 to 2014, the concept and application of service-oriented architecture is the frontier of research.

Keywords: Service design · Citespace · Knowledge groups · Evolution path · Research frontier

1 Introduction

Gone through the stages of product economy and information economy, the industrial paradigm now enters the stage of service economy. The paradigm of service economy breaks the limitation of traditional thinking and emphasizes to improve user experience and product value by creating excellent services. In line with this new industry paradigm, service design as a new design thinking came into being. In 1994, the British Standards Institution issued the world's first service design management guidelines (BS7000-3 1994), scholars then began to study service design in depth [1]. Service design research conforms to the trend of the times. Having a deep insight of the international progress in the field of service design is an inevitable requirement for the further development of service design industry. For this reason, this paper uses CiteSpace visual analysis software to explore the knowledge base, evolution trend and research frontier in the field of service design in English core database.

2 Data Collection

The articles analyzed in this paper come from three citation indexes in the core collection database of "Web of Science", namely SCI-Expanded, SSCI and CPCI-S. The search

© Springer Nature Switzerland AG 2021
C. Stephanidis et al. (Eds.): HCII 2021, CCIS 1419, pp. 82–89, 2021.
https://doi.org/10.1007/978-3-030-78635-9_12

time is August 1, 2019, the search term is limited to the "Title" field, and the search term is "service design" or "service-oriented design". The language is English. The literature types are Proceedings Paper and Article, and the time span is from January 1999 to 2019. 401 articles were obtained after manual deletion.

Base on the changing number of annual published articles, service design research are divided into four stages: The first stage is 1999–2003, which is the embryonic stage. Service design research articles began to appear. The number of annual publications was less than 10 in this stage; The second stage is 2004–2014, which is the start-up stage. In this stage, the research enthusiasm gradually increased, with the annual number mostly more than 10. The annual number of papers showed a tortuous rise. The third is 2015–2017, which is the rising stage. In this stage, the number of published papers increased rapidly, reaching the peak of 56 in 2017; The fourth is 2018 which is the adjustment period. In 2018, the total number of published papers dropped to 33. The data of 2019 only collected till July, so no analysis is made here.

3   Metrological Analysis of English Articles on Service Design

3.1   Knowledge Groups

By drawing the network map of literature co-citation, this paper tries to identify the knowledge groups existing in international service design research. In Fig. 1, one node represents one document. The bigger the node is, the more times the document is cited. The thicker the connection between nodes, the closer the relationship between documents. As shown in Fig. 1, there are three main clusters in the service design cited network. That means the research of service design can be divided into three knowledge groups. Based on the detailed information further abstracted from Fig. 1, those three groups are named: the origin of service design problems, the logic and methods of service design, and the relationship between service design, enterprises and society (Table 1).

#C1 Knowledge group is about the origin of service design. In this group, the first cited article appeared in 2002. In this group, the centrality is generally not high, the relationship with other clustering nodes is weak, and there is no obvious branch. As the earliest cluster, this knowledge group mainly discusses the problem of "what is service design". In 2000, Edvardsson used the survey data of Swedish customer satisfaction index and the performance data of competitive industries to study the logical differences between services and products in terms of customer satisfaction and loyalty, which triggered academic discussion on the relationship between intangible services and tangible products [2]. In 2002, Goldstem and other scholars think critically about what is service design and how to apply the service concept to service planning and service recovery design process [3]. The most cited and central paper in the cluster is Goldstem's *The Service Concept: the Missing Link in Service Design Research?* in the Journal of operations management, and there are some node articles around it.

#C2 knowledge group focuses on the logic and methods of service design. As it is shown in Fig. 1, #C2 knowledge group is the largest knowledge group in the whole service design research field, with the longest time span and the biggest centrality average value. In 2004, Vargo [4] put forward the theory of service oriented logic for the first time.

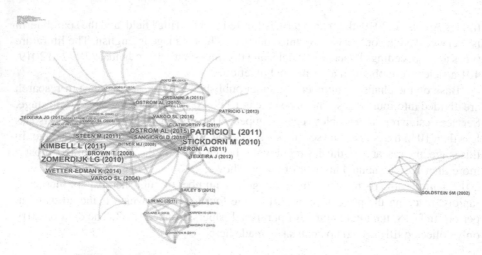

Fig. 1. Co-cited network map of English documents on service design

He suggested replacing the traditional product-oriented logic with a brand-new service-oriented logic, focusing on the relationship between service providers and consumers, other supply and value chain stakeholders, creating value together through continuous interaction, and emphasizing the transformation from producing tangible products to providing intangible services. Once the theory was put forward, it aroused widespread concern and discussion in management and business circles. The article with the highest centrality in this cluster (and also in all of the clusters) is *Designing for Service as One Way of Designing Services* written by Kimbell published in the International Journal of Design, focusing on the core idea of service-oriented logic. There are obvious settlements around this article, which shows that scholars have carried out follow-up research around the service-oriented logic, and have gained some achievement [5–8]. Scholars apply service-oriented logic to different industries and types of supply chain, forming a new research horizon. The branch attaches importance to interdisciplinary research and emphasizes the innovation of service design methods by integrating methods and tools of different disciplines, such as ethnography, management, system design and interaction design [9]. Stickdorm [10], Patricio [11], and Ostrom [12] and other scholars have proposed that interdisciplinary research is the breakthrough point of service design method innovation. The branch of service design method is a powerful supplement to service design practice.

#C3 Knowledge Group mainly studies the relationship between service design, enterprises and society. This clustering network appeares late. It mainly focuses on the impact of service design on business and society, as well as the impact of business and society on service design, the responsibility and ethics of service designers [13–16]. The centrality of the nodes in this knowledge group is not high, which shows that this research field has not attracted wide attention at present.

Table 1. List of important node documents

Author	Time	Title	Publication
#C1 Knowledge Group		Origin of service design	First cited in 2002
Edvardsson BO	2000	The effects of satisfaction and loyalty on profits and growth: Products versus services	*Total Quality Management*
Goldstem	2002	The service concept: the missing link in service design research?	*Journal of Operations Management*
Henver AR	2004	Design science in is research	*MIS Quarterly*
#C2 Knowledge Group		Logic and Method of Service Design	First cited in 2004
Vargo SL	2004	Evolving to a New Dominant Logic for Marketing	*Journal of Marketing*
Stickdorm	2010	This is Service Design Thinking: Basics, Tools, Cases	*This is Service Design Thinking: Basics, Tools, Cases*
Zomerdijk LG	2010	Service Design for Experience-Centric Services	*Journal of Service Research*
Patricio L	2011	Multilevel Service Design: From Customer Value Constellation to Service Experience Blueprining	*Journal of Service Research*
Kimbell L	2011	Designing for Service as One Way of Designing Services	*International Journal of Design*
Wetter-Edman K	2014	Design for Value Co-Creation: Exploring Synergies Between Design for Service and Service Logic	*Service Science*
Ostrom AL	2015	Sevice Research Priorities in a Rapidly Changing Context	*Journal of Service Research*
Vargo SL	2016	Institutions and axioms: an extension and update of service-dominant logic	*Journal of the Academy of Marketing Science*
#C3 Knowledge Group		The relationship between service design, enterprise and society	First cited in 2011
Lin MC	2011	Service Design and Change of Systems: Human-Centered Approaches to Implementing and Spreading Service Design	*International Journal of Design*
Bailey S	2012	Embedding service design: The long and the short of it	*Proceedings of the 3rd Nordic Conference on Service Design and Service Innovation*
Polaine A	2013	Orange: A Service Design Case Study	*Design Management Review*
Sangiorgi D	2015	Emerging Issues in Service Design	*The Design Journal*

3.2   The Evolution Path of Service Design Research Topics

Key words are the concentration and refinement of documents, which can reflect the research perspectives and methods. In this paper, keyword co-occurrence network is used to study the research hotspots and development trends in the field of service design. Keep the time span unchanged, select Node Types as "Keyword", and get the keyword co-occurrence map in the field of international service design research after running the software. As shown in Fig. 2, the network includes 88 nodes and 216 connections.

Based on the stage division in the previous part of the article, the high-frequency keywords are analyzed. Table 2 lists the keywords with frequency of 5 times or more. The more frequent, the more important the keyword is. If the centrality of a keyword exceeds 0.1, it means that there are a lot of researches around the keyword, and the keyword is important. As the search term in this paper contains "service design", "service design" and "design" are removed from the following high-frequency words.

Fig. 2. Co-occurrence map of keywords in English documents of service design

Table 2. List of high-frequency keywords

Time quantum	Year	High frequency keywords	Frequency	Centrality
1999–2003	1999			
		—	—	—
	—	—	—	—
	2002	Quality	20	0.18
	2003			
		—	—	—
2004–2014	2004	Service engineering	Six	0
		—	—	—
	—	—	—	—
	2008	Management	17	0.04
	2008	Model	13	0.25
	2008	SOA	10	0.12
	2008	Science	Seven	0.01
	2009	System	25	0.06
		—	—	—
	—	—	—	—
	2014	Innovation	19	0.13
2015–2019	2015	Experience	13	0.12
	2016	Product	Eight	0.12
	2016	Dominant logic	Five	0.03
	2016	Framework	Five	0.02
		—	—	—
	—	—	—	—
	2019			
		—	—	—

(1) In the embryonic stage of 1999–2003, the related research articles were few, the theoretical research results were weak, and only one high-frequency word "Quality" appeared. "How to use service design to promote enterprise management and improve the quality of customer experience" is the research focus at this stage.

(2) During the start-up stage from 2004 to 2014, the number of research papers on service design increases significantly. In this stage, there are many high-frequency words with high centrality, which are "service engineering", "management", "model", "SOA", "science", "system" and "innovation". Service-oriented logic is the research hotspot in this stage. Service-oriented logic has gone deep into the research field of service innovation, and has been applied to specific cases. Service-oriented logic refers that the business and management modes of enterprises have changed. With the assistance of information technology, enterprises and customers now create value together through resource sharing and integration. Service-oriented architecture (SOA) is one of the effective ways to realize the sharing, integration and application of information resources.

(3) In the rising stage from 2015 to 2017, the high-frequency words are "experience", "product", "dominant logic" and "framework", and their centralities are generally high. This shows that the research of service design is further deepened on the basis of the original theory. In the rising stage, the research on service-oriented logic is still active. SOA conforms to the situation, continuously improves the user experience and enterprise value through the continuous improvement of the interaction process of product service design. In 2018 and beyond, the number of keywords is abundant, but there is no keyword with frequency larger than 5 times, which indicates that the research topic of service design has entered the branch expansion stage.

3.3 Overview of Research Frontiers at Different Stages

Burst Terms which are extracted from keywords show the sudden changes in the research field, and present the research frontiers at different stages. The burst terms on service design are listed below (Table 3). There are two burst terms in the field of service design. "Quality" is the burst term from 2002 to 2011. The relationship between service design and public perceived service "quality" is the research frontier during those years. "SOA" is the burst term from 2008 to 2014. SOA management, mode, system, SOA and innovation are the research frontiers in this period.

Table 3. Burst terms of service design research

Burst terms	Strength	Start year	End year	1999-2019
Quality	4.3448	2002	2011	___ ___ _ ▬▬ ▬▬ ▬▬ ▬▬ ▬▬ ▬▬ ▬▬ ___ ___ ___ ___ ___
SOA	4.3198	2008	2014	___ ___ ___ ___ ___ ___ ___ ▬▬ ▬▬ ▬▬ ▬▬ ▬▬ ___ ___ ___

4 Conclusion

Through the analysis of the changing number of annual English papers on service design, we find that there are four research stages in the field of service design (embryonic stage, start-up stage, rising stage and adjustment stage); With the help of article co-citation network map, three knowledge groups in this field were found out(the origin of service design problem, the logic and method of service design, the relationship between service design and enterprise and society); According to the co-occurrence map of keywords, the research keywords and the evolution path of service design research in different periods from 1999 to 2019 are extracted; By sorting out the burst terms, we get the research frontier (Quality and SOA) at different stages in the field of service design research.

In 2004, Vargo replaced the traditional product-oriented logic with a brand-new service-oriented logic, which triggered a great change in the design industry. In today's rapidly changing environment, the new breakthrough in thinking logic with pioneering significance is still waiting to be explored. The disadvantage of this paper is that it only analyzes the articles in the Web of Science database, and may miss some important documents in other databases. This deficiency needs to be improved by follow-up researchers.

References

1. Moultrie, J., Livesey, F.: Measuring design investment in firms: conceptual foundations and exploratory UK survey. Res. Policy **43**(3), 570–587 (2014)
2. Edvardsson, B., Johnson, M.D., Gustafsson, A., et al.: The effects of satisfaction and loyalty on profits and growth: products versus services. Total Qual. Manage. **11**(7), 917–927 (2000)
3. Goldstein, S.M., Johnston, R., Duffy, J., et al.: The service concept: the missing link in service design research? J. Oper. Manag. **20**(2), 121–134 (2002)
4. Vargo, S., Lusch, R.: Evolving to a new dominant logic for marketing. J. Mark. **68**, 1–17 (2004)
5. Zomerdijk, L.G., Voss, C.: Service design for experience-centric services. J. Serv. Res. **13**(1), 67–82 (2010)
6. Kimbell, L.: Designing for service as one way of designing services. Int. J. Des. **5**(2), 41–52 (2011)
7. Wetter-Edman, K., Sangiorgi, D., Edvardsson, B., et al.: Design for value co-creation: exploring synergies between design for service and service logic. Serv. Sci. **6**(2), 106–121 (2014)
8. Vargo, S.L., Lusch, R.F.: Institutions and axioms: an extension and update of service-dominant logic. J. Acad. Mark. Sci. **44**(1), 5–23 (2016)
9. Hu, F., Sato, K., Zhou, K., et al.: Meaningful experience in service design: case study of SAPAD framework application. In: Peruzzini, M., Pellicciari, M., Bil, C., Stjepandic, J., Wognum, N., (eds.) Transdisciplinary Engineering Methods for Social Innovation of Industry 4.0, pp. 526–535. IOS Press, Netherlands (2018)
10. Stickdorn, M., Schneider, J., Andrews, K., et al.: This is service design thinking: Basics, tools, cases, vol. 1. BIS Publishers, Amsterdam (2011)
11. Patricio, L., Fisk, R.P., Cunha, J.F.E., et al.: Multilevel service design: from customer value constellation to service experience blueprinting. J. Serv. Res. **14**(2), 180–200 (2011)
12. Ostrom, A.L., Parasuraman, A., Bowen, D.E., et al.: Service research priorities in a rapidly changing context. J. Serv. Res. **18**(2), 127–159 (2015)

13. Lin, M.C., Hughes, B.L., Katica, M.K., et al.: Service design and change of systems: human-centered approaches to implementing and spreading service design. Int. J. Des. **5**(2), 73–86 (2011)
14. Aier, S., Gleichauf, B.: Towards a sophisticated understanding of service design for enterprise architecture. In: International Conference on Service-Oriented Computing, pp. 316–326 (2008)
15. Sangiorgi, D., Junginger, S.J.D.J.: Emerging issues in service design. Des. J. **18**(2), 165–170 (2015)
16. Polaine, A., Løvlie, L., Reason, B.O.: A service design case study. Des. Manage. Rev. **24**(3), 48–49 (2013)

Perceptual, Cognitive and Psychophisiological Aspects of Interaction

Accelerometer-Based Estimation of the User Interest While Viewing Content on Smartphones Considering Viewing Conditions

Chisato Amada[1]([✉]), Tota Mizuno[1], Yu Matsumoto[1], Kazuyuki Mito[1],
Naoaki Itakura[1], Taiyo Nakashima[2], and Takeshi Hanada[2]

[1] The University of Electro-Communications, 1-5-1, Chofu-gaoka Chofu-shi, Tokyo, Japan
`a2030008@edu.cc.uec.ac.jp`
[2] Coamix Inc., Kichijoji Jizo Building, 1-9-9, Kichijoji-Minamimachi, Musashino-shi,
Tokyo, Japan

Abstract. With the abundant availability of digital content, people have been facing difficulty finding what they prefer. Several recommendation systems have been developed, but conventional ones are primarily based on purchase and browsing histories, which do not reflect user evaluation. This study focuses on analyzing invisible and feeble physiological tremors to reflect user evaluation. One factor affecting physiological tremors is said to be psychological change. In our earlier study, the acceleration data while reading comic books on a smartphone were collected using the 3D accelerometer of a smartphone. Consequently, it was suggested that the more interesting a story becomes, the less the people move. In this study, we attempted to relatively evaluate the acceleration data while reading and estimate the user interest with no limit on postures. The acceleration data of six subjects while not reading and while reading comic books on a smartphone were collected using the 3D accelerometer of a smartphone. They read comic books in both sitting and standing postures. As a result of performing fast Fourier transforms, the data while reading comic books obtained the bigger peak amplitude than the data while not reading. In addition, the amplitude integral value of interesting pages became smaller than that of less interesting pages. On an average, the rate was 84.9%. These results suggested that viewing content on a smartphone affected the amplitude of physiological tremors, and people moved less while reading interesting pages.

Keywords: Evaluation of psychological state · Physiological tremor · Accelerometer · Recommendation system

1 Introduction

Recently, digital devices have become popular, and they allow people to access abundant digital content. However, this abundance of content often makes it difficult for people to find what they prefer. Conventional recommendation systems are primarily based on the purchase and browsing history, which do not reflect user evaluation. Therefore, the

© Springer Nature Switzerland AG 2021
C. Stephanidis et al. (Eds.): HCII 2021, CCIS 1419, pp. 93–98, 2021.
https://doi.org/10.1007/978-3-030-78635-9_13

need for novel recommendation systems that can effectively reflect user evaluation has increased.

Bio-signals are one of the parameters that reflect user evaluation. Matsui et al. estimated user interest using an eye-tracking system [1], and Yukawa et al. used a web camera and image processing technology [2]. However, such devices are expensive, and it is not easy to apply these technologies on a large scale. On the other hand, a significant number of people use smart devices such as smartphones. These devices have built-in sensors such as accelerometers or gyroscopes. Using these sensors to evaluate the user interest leads to the design of a new system that can be widely utilized.

Yan [3] estimated user interest using the 3D accelerometer of a smartphone. He performed fast Fourier transform (FFT) on the acceleration data while subjects viewed tweets and compared the results with the self-evaluations of their interest. He observed that the distribution of frequency components tended to spread for the less interesting images. Therefore, it was suggested that the smartphone acceleration data could effectively estimate the user interest. However, Yan did not consider the subjects' posture. As the acceleration data changes as a result of holding a smartphone, it is necessary to obtain an approach to measure the acceleration that is unaffected by the posture.

Invisible and feeble physiological tremors are bio-signals, and one factor affecting these tremors is psychological change [4]. However, as physiological tremors are generally measured by fixing joints and wearing a light accelerometer, it is difficult to measure them while simply holding a device. Therefore, in our earlier study [5], we proposed a method to measure the acceleration data that includes physiological tremors without being affected by postures by using accelerometers of a smartphone and smartwatch. The results suggest that the proposed method can be used to estimate the user interest. However, there were certain concerns. First, the acquisition data was not evaluated relatively. Second, a page-by-page analysis was not performed. Finally, a limit was set on the posture while reading comic books.

In this study, we attempted to acquire the acceleration data while not reading and while reading and track interest changes by page. In addition, we examined whether it was possible to estimate the user interest using only a smartphone in different postures.

2 Analysis Methodology

The accelerometer measures three values, from the x-axis, y-axis, and z-axis. Because the acceleration data include the gravitational component, the active component was extracted by dividing the instantaneous values of acceleration (see Fig. 1) into gravitational and active components (see Fig. 2). The gravity direction value was obtained from the sum of each active component of the axis.

We performed FFT on the gravitational active component and a page-by-page analysis using a band-pass filter. When performing FFT, the number of sampling points was 512 such that the resolution was approximately 0.1 Hz. Moreover, to get closer to the true value, 50% overlap was applied, and the ensemble average was obtained. The band-pass filter was applied to the frequency band of the peak amplitude obtained from the FFT results.

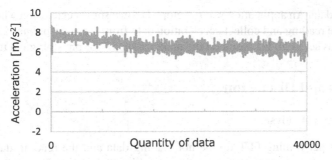

Fig. 1. Instantaneous values of acceleration

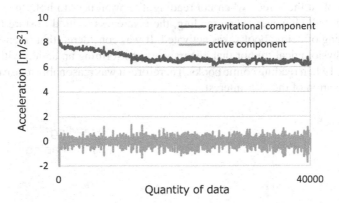

Fig. 2. Gravitational and active components

3 Experiment

3.1 Procedure

Six subjects participated in this experiment. We set both sitting and standing as reading postures. In each posture condition, first, the subjects remained in the position for approximately 3 min, and the present five psychological states (comfortable, sleepy, surprised, sad, and angry) were evaluated. Then, they began to read the comic books. We prepared four different types of comic books, and they read the comic books in any order they wanted. They read the same comic book in the standing condition. We did not instruct about the posture while reading; therefore, the subjects read comic books in any posture they wanted. In addition, we recorded subjects' postures using a web camera. After reading, they self-evaluated their psychological state at that time and the story they had just read. Moreover, they evaluated their interest in each page on three levels (very interesting, interesting, and so-so).

3.2 Measurement

Because the results of our earlier study [5] suggested that it was possible to estimate the user interest using only a smartphone, we used only a smartphone to collect the acceleration data. An application was developed to measure acceleration while not reading and while reading and collect acceleration data from the smartphone. The sampling frequency was set to 50 Hz based on the main frequency of physiological tremor.

4   Results and Discussion

4.1   Frequency Analysis

The result of performing FFT on the not reading data and the reading data is shown in Fig. 3. The amplitude peak for reading was bigger than that for not reading. This tendency was observed in all subjects irrespective of the posture condition. As there was no need to look at the screen when not reading, the awareness to hold the smartphone was not activated. However, when reading, the awareness to hold posture to facilitate an easy reading of comic books was activated. It was considered that intention tremor, which is a physiological tremor that occurs when performing an action with intention, was generated when reading comic books. Therefore, it was reasonable to use the reading data for evaluation of the user interest.

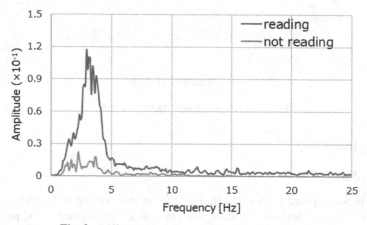

Fig. 3. Difference between not reading and reading

Next, we performed FFT on the time series data. In some data, the amplitude tended to decrease as the number of pages that showed interest increased. Therefore, FFT was performed separately for the pages that showed interest and those that did not. One example is shown in Fig. 4. The amplitudes of the pages that showed interest were smaller than those of the pages that showed no interest. Considering the fact that the frequency band of the amplitude peak varies from subject to subject, we calculated the percentage of pages that showed a less integral value of amplitude than the pages that showed more interest in two frequency bands, 3–5 Hz and 3–20 Hz. Consequently, the average of all subjects was 78.1% for 3–5 Hz and 84.9% for 3–20 Hz. These results suggested that people moved less while reading interesting pages.

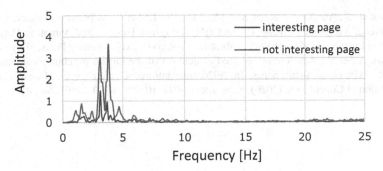

Fig. 4. Difference between interesting page and not interesting page

4.2 Page-By-Page Analysis

As a result of calculating the average squared value of the band-pass filter for each page, for one subject, the works with less interest had smaller fluctuations in the squared value. However, for other subject, there was a similar level of fluctuation irrespective of the interest level. No common tendency was observed among all subjects. By checking the images of the web camera, it was observed that the squared value increased when the way to hold the smartphone changed or the posture moved voluntarily. Therefore, it was suggested that it was difficult to estimate the user interest for each page using only the acceleration data of smartphones.

5 Conclusion

As a result of performing FFT, it was suggested that viewing content on a smartphone affected the amplitude of physiological tremors, and people moved less while reading interesting pages. Furthermore, the posture during reading significantly affected physiological tremors, and the way to estimate the user interest using only the acceleration data of the smartphone was considered to be limited.

For future work, we will examine a way to estimate the user interest using our proposed method [5] that takes the difference between the acceleration data of a smartphone and a smartwatch, thereby reducing the influence of the posture.

References

1. Ken, M., Mutsumi, S., Pao, S., Wataru, K.: Preliminary analysis on correlation of comic reading time and comic components. In: 2013 International Workshop on Smart Info-Media Systems in Asia (2013)
2. Kazuhide, Y., Masanori, M., Kazunori, I., Koji, U., Shigeo, K.: An approach to provide services to estimate degree of interest. J. Inf. Process. Soc. Jpn **1**, 12–21 (2011)
3. Yan, H.: Yuza no Furumai ni Motoduku Kyomi Suitei ni Yoru Kontentsu Etsuran Shien Shuhou ni Kansuru Kenkyu (A Study of Support Methods for Watching Content Based on User Behavior). Kyushu University Institutional Repository, Fukuoka (2016)

4. Kazuyoshi, S., Yutaka, S., Kazuyuki, M., Masato, T.: Seitai no Furue to Shindo Chikaku. Mechanical Vibration no Kino Hyouka (Physiological Tremors and Vibration Perception. Function Evaluation of Mechanical Vibration). Tokyo Denki University Press, Tokyo (2009)
5. Chisato, A., et al.: Accelerometer-based evaluation of the human psychological state while viewing content on smartphones. In: 2020 International Conference on Human-Computer Interaction in Copenhagen (2020). https://doi.org/10.1007/978-3-030-50726-8_41

Handgrip Force Sensor to Measure Mental Workload

Carlos Arce-Lopera(✉) , Rafael Ospina, and Juan Madrid

Universidad Icesi, 760046 Cali, Colombia
caarce@icesi.edu.co

Abstract. Mental workload is closely related to changes in performance during a task. For example, performance declines when the mental workload is too high or too low. Also, numerous factors can influence mental workload making it difficult to measure precisely. There have been several operational definitions of mental workload using psychophysiological measures. However, they are cumbersome limiting their application in natural situations. Here, we present a handgrip force sensor designed to be used as a tool for measuring the mental workload of a task. The system is based on force-sensitive resistors placed on the hand fingers. Preliminary experimental results showed that our system can identify accurately the changes in mental workload by association with handgrip force patterns.

Keywords: Mental workload · Handgrip force · NASA TLX

1 Introduction

Measuring mental workload can quantify the cost of performing tasks and help to predict operator and system performance [1]. The usual biometric signals related to the psychophysiological measurement of the workload are electrocardiogram, electromyogram, galvanic skin response, and respiratory signals [2–4]. From those signals, the electrocardiogram and the galvanic skin response have been found to be more accurate to analyze and predict changes in workload associated with the decline of task performance [3]. However, the installation of such sensors is cumbersome limiting their application in natural situations.

An alternative is to measure the handgrip force as a mental workload indicator. Indeed, different researches suggested the existence of the correlation between mental workload and handgrip force [5–7]. Measuring the handgrip force could be a useful tool to apply in daily tasks where the user has to hold an object such as when driving, playing sports, holding a mouse in the office, playing musical instruments, among others.

© Springer Nature Switzerland AG 2021
C. Stephanidis et al. (Eds.): HCII 2021, CCIS 1419, pp. 99–103, 2021.
https://doi.org/10.1007/978-3-030-78635-9_14

2 Method

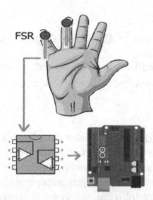

Fig. 1. Handgrip force acquisition system.

The handgrip force was measured using a system with four force-sensitive resistors (FSR). The system is based on FSRs placed on two fingers in each participant's hands (See Fig. 1). Participants wore the sensor while manipulating a Bluetooth gamepad controller linked to a mobile device. They were asked to play a mobile game while their handgrip force patterns were recorded. Different game settings with several levels of difficulty and mental workload were designed inside the game. To generate tasks with different mental workload, two sets of mathematical questions designed with basic and advanced operations were used. Also, to create a naturalistic and controllable scenario, video games were used as a method to test the correlation between task performance, mental workload, and physiological signals [8, 9]. The following test protocol was applied to 5 participants: 2 women and 3 men with an age range from 23 to 28 years old.

2.1 Test Protocol

1. The participant played a scenario without sensors. This step was included to accustom the subject with the task and to record the way they handled the interface with their hands.
2. Two sensors are placed in both hands depending on how the participant held the control (See Fig. 2).
3. Two reference levels of pressure are recorded when handling the control: the highest when pressing as strong as possible and the lowest when pressing as light as needed to handle the control. This step served as calibration for the sensor.
4. The participant played a scenario (low difficulty) while solving simultaneously basic mathematical questions. In the end, the Nasa TLX is applied.
5. The participant played a scenario (high difficulty) while solving advanced mathematical questions in parallel. In the end, a Nasa TLX is applied.
6. Steps 4 and 5 are recorded as tasks 1 and 2, respectively.

Fig. 2. Participant during experimental task. Left image shows the back of the controller where the sensors are visible. Right image shows the participant's point of view.

After task completion, NASA's Task Load Index Test (TLX) was administered to obtain a subjective mental workload measure. Previous research showed that different levels of mental workload provoke different intensities of the handgrip force [7]. However, the expected results could be modified by external factors. In fact, personal emotions and motivation could modify the user grip force. Thus, in step 1, participants were told to fully focus on the experimental task. Also, to isolate external factors, in the first step of the protocol, the experiment was explained with great calm, trying to bring tranquility to the participant.

3   Results

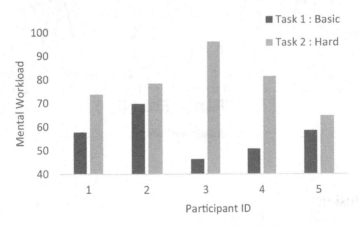

Fig. 3. Mental workload per user and task.

Subjective mental workload, rated using the Nasa TLX, was significantly different ($t(4) = -2.8$; $p < 0.05$) between task 1 (mean = 56.5; SD = 8.8) and task 2 (mean = 78.8; SD = 11.5). Figure 3 shows the mental workload for each subject and task.

For the handgrip force sensor, the recorded signal was calibrated and normalized using the results of step 3 in the test protocol. Subsequently, the four moments about the mean of the signal and the number of events where the user pressed continuously at least for one second were calculated. Using those features as explanatory variables and mental workload as the dependent variable, a multiple regression analysis was computed. The best model showed that the mean, skew and kurtosis of the handgrip force signal explained 86.8% of the variance of workload (R2 = 0.87, F (3, 5) = 11.01, p = 0.01).

On the other hand, to detect frequency patterns on the handgrip force signal, a frequency domain analysis was carried out for each user. Results revealed that most of the subjects used a higher force grip when playing the hard level. However, the magnitude of different frequency components was higher for the basic level. This result may suggest that higher mental workload can be associated with loss of attention in handgrip force (See Fig. 4).

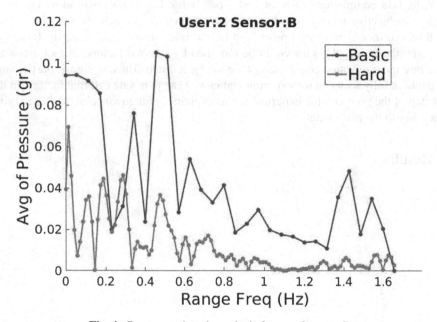

Fig. 4. Frequency domain analysis for user 2 sensor B

4   Conclusion

There are some indicators in previous research showing that handgrip force has different behavior when the mental workload changes. Our results support these research findings by showing that handgrip force tends to be higher and constant in frequency when the workload increases. On the other hand, in a low mental workload situation, subjects tend to have lower force in the grip but in higher frequency time intervals. Moreover, a statistical model revealed that global statistical variables of the handgrip force sensor signals explained 87% of the variance of the mental workload. These results are promising first steps to enable the construction of mental workload sensitive wearable sensors that do not interfere with natural interactions with objects. Future work will focus on experimental replication favoring ergonomic requirements for different types of tool grip and tasks.

Finally, our handgrip force sensor showed a significant correlation between the variables mean, skew, and kurtosis and the variance of mental workload. However, the positioning of the sensors remained a difficult challenge in the physiological measurement. Future work should test the system using sensors in all the hand fingers.

References

1. Cain, B.: A Review of the Mental Workload Literature. Presented at the Defence Research and Development Canada Toronto Human System Integration Section; 2007. Report No.: RTO-TRHFM-121-Part-II. Contract No. (2007)
2. Healey, J.A., Picard, R.W.: Detecting stress during real-world driving tasks using physiological sensors. Trans. Intell. Transport. Syst. 6, 156–166 (2005). https://doi.org/10.1109/TITS.2005.848368
3. Mohanavelu, K., Lamshe, R., Poonguzhali, S., Adalarasu, K., Jagannath, M.: Assessment of human fatigue during physical performance using physiological signals: a review. Biomed. Pharmacol. J. 10, 1887–1896 (2017)
4. Mundell, L.C.: Predicting performance using galvanic skin response (2016). https://dspace.mit.edu/handle/1721.1/105086
5. Baronti, F., Lenzi, F., Roncella, R., Saletti, R.: Distributed sensor for steering wheel rip force measurement in driver fatigue detection. In: Automation Test in Europe Conference Exhibition 2009 Design, pp. 894–897 (2009). https://doi.org/10.1109/DATE.2009.5090790
6. Parzer, P., et al.: FlexTiles: a flexible, stretchable, formable, pressure-sensitive, tactile input sensor. In: Proceedings of the 2016 CHI Conference Extended Abstracts on Human Factors in Computing Systems, pp. 3754–3757. ACM, New York (2016). https://doi.org/10.1145/2851581.2890253
7. Wagner, M., Sahar, Y., Elbaum, T., Botzer, A., Berliner, E.: Grip force as a measure of stress in aviation. Int. J. Aviat. Psychol. 25, 157–170 (2015). https://doi.org/10.1080/10508414.2015.1162632
8. Noraziah, A., Abdullah, M.A.S., Aqtar, N., Fakhreldin, M.A.I., Wahab, M.N.A.: Greenvec game for skin conductivity level (SCL) biofeedback performance simulator using galvanic skin response (GSR) sensor. Int. J. Softw. Eng. Comput. Syst. 1, 41–53 (2015)
9. Soares, R.T., Sarmanho, E., Miura, M., Barros, T., Jacobi, R., Castanho, C.: Biofeedback sensors in electronic games: a practical evaluation. In: 2017 16th Brazilian Symposium on Computer Games and Digital Entertainment (SBGames), pp. 56–65 (2017). https://doi.org/10.1109/SBGames.2017.00015

Using Abstract Icon Systems in the Digital Divide Era: Are Users Icon Blind?

Antonio Capobianco[1]([⊠]), Karim Chibout[1], Pegdwinde Kontiebo[2], and David Cazier[1]

[1] University of Strasbourg, Strasbourg, France
{a.capobianco,karim.chibout,david.cazier}@unistra.fr
[2] University of Lille, Lille, France
pegdwinde.kontiebo.etu@univ-lille.fr

Abstract. We tackle the digital divide issue from the user experience point of view. Our study aim at obtaining information on the impact of UI/UX design choices on the participants' achievement strategies. In that prospect, we asked voluntary participants receiving social benefits at a social action center to perform typical account management tasks on two French administration websites. Then we analyzed their visual exploration strategies.

The results of this preliminary study suggest that highly symbolic pictographic representations are ignored by users in a situation of digital precariousness. They spend a large amount of time looking through the textual content to find indications, submenus or links to navigate rather than exploiting the shorthand access provided through the abstract icon system. These ergonomic choices constitute an additional barrier to the use of these technologies by fragile users.

Keywords: Digital divide · Illectronism · Eye-tracking studies · UX/UI design · User experience

1 About Digital Divide and Digital Literacy

In this study, we seek to identify and measure the difficulties encountered by users in situation of illectronism (or digital incapacity) when they use web interfaces for administrative procedures. We aim to achieve two complementary objectives. On one hand, to improve web interfaces in their ergonomic aspects so that they take into account the specific characteristics of people involved. On the other hand, to train these individuals (at a minimal level) on Information Technologies (IT) tools that take an ever-increasing importance in their everyday lives. We are indeed living in an e-permeated society in which digital technology becomes omnipresent, and even pervasive [1] to such an extent that almost all of our social, professional and leisure activities depend on it.

In this regard, digital skills are identified as *survival skills* [2] if people do not want to find themselves 'outside the world', victims of a digital divide. Originally, the concept of *digital divide* [3] referred to the divide between people with access to new technologies (smartphones, computers, Internet) and those without it. Since **hardware access problems** have almost disappeared, a *second level digital divide* [4] was revealed; linked

© Springer Nature Switzerland AG 2021
C. Stephanidis et al. (Eds.): HCII 2021, CCIS 1419, pp. 104–110, 2021.
https://doi.org/10.1007/978-3-030-78635-9_15

to **software accessibility** issues and *digital literacy* [5], i.e. the ability to understand and use multiple information reachable through digital tools. Subsequently, the concept became more complex in its definition and terms associated with it increased [6]: *eLiteracy, e-Skills, computer literacy, ICT literacy, 21st century literacy/ies, etc.* The plural form *literacies,* sometimes used (for example in [7]), emphasizes both the richness and the vagueness conveyed by this notion. In the light of literature, it generally presents blurred outlines. Thus, in some studies, it is related to a **component** of a wider field of skills (called for example *transliteracy* [9]) which makes possible to create and process information through various media or interact in rich and complex environments. Whilst other authors give it the status of **central category** to which other literacies/skills will be attached. Aviram and Eshet-Alkalai [8] suggest a set of specific literacies united under this generic term: among them we can find photo-visual literacy, branching literacy, or information literacy, etc. Lower-level skills can be grouped into minimum criteria such as information literacy, media literacy, and digital citizenship [9] or fall into key nested categories [10]: cognitive (information literacy, linguistics, photo-visual, etc.), technical and socio-emotional.

Finally, digital literacy is also understood even more broadly as a set of *social practices* [11]. Here, interacting with IT environments become fully part of **the digital culture** that appeared at the start of the 21st century and which, according to Prensky [12], is assimilated more simply and more quickly by the generations born with these technologies (*digital natives*) than by previous generations (*digital immigrants*). The new culture generates its share of exclusion: according to INSEE (French National Institute of Statistics and Economic Studies) [13], illectronism affects 17% of the French population. These persons are for example unable to perform, without help, online administrative procedures while the dematerialization of public services became standard. These persons must at all costs acquire skills in the use of digital tools (online information search, email communication, knowledge and use of operating systems, etc.) to have effective access to these services and prevent the loss of their social rights and benefits.

With the new media, we are facing an unprecedented situation of **deculturation** of the elderly and/or precarious people. A *digital resocialization* [14] is needed to maintain their full citizenship. In this social context, a lot of studies focused on the factors of acquisition/non-acquisition of digital skills (cf. the synthetic review by Scheerder & al. [15]). These studies highlighted several types of interacting factors: economic (income level, socio-professional category, etc.), socio-demographic (age, sex, environment of life, etc.), cultural (ethnicity, Internet use language, etc.) and individual events (state of health, personality, interest…) to name only the main ones.

Conversely, the question of interfaces (complexity, incompatibility) as source of rejection of ICTs or as source of difficulties in their use is poorly addressed. Note, however, the study of Castilla et al. [16] produced on a virtual social network (called *Butler*) dedicated to learning digital literacy skills for the elderly. The results show, for example, greater ease of use when browsing is done in a linear fashion – *i.e.*, closer to the mental model of this category of users as it fits to the usual way of reading old media like newspapers or magazines. On the opposite, the hypertext structure, specific to websites, tends to confuse elderly populations, specifically because it requires more cognitive resources.

Building up on this approach, we propose to study the causes of the digital divide from a user experience point of view by measuring the impact of UI/UX design choices on the websites of two French administration: the *Allocation Familiales* (CAF: Family allowance fund) [17] and *Pôle Emploi* (job seekers national services) [18]. In this perspective, we led an experimental research with voluntary participants of a regional social center. The main objective of our work is to propose a set of working design and training solutions to ease the use of Internet services for administrative procedures for people suffering from the *digital divide*.

2   Experimental Procedure

In order to better understand the encountered difficulties, we decided to study the visual exploration strategies of people suffering from the *digital divide i.e.*, with a low level of digital literacy, on public services websites to which they must resort on a regular basis (job search, periodic updates of their administrative situation in order to obtain social benefits, etc.)

2.1   Participants

We recruited 9 people (4 women and 5 men) corresponding to our target audience among the users of the Bischwiller Social and Family Action Center (CASF) [19] to participate in our study. Six were between 25 and 34 years old, 2 between 35 and 54 years old and 1 between 55 and 64 years old. Their level of academic education, according to the Unesco ISCED 2011 ranking [20], was for 8 of them level 3 (high school) and 1 level 4 (Post-secondary non-tertiary education). As each of them benefit from the tutoring of the CASF regarding their use of state digital services, they can all be considered as suffering from the digital divide.

We asked two CASF coaches to assign each participant an evaluation of their level of digital literacy, based on the participants' previous known experiences with the selected sites. The evaluation was carried out on a 7-level Likert scale ranging from 1 (follow – the participants have no autonomy whatsoever in performing the tasks) to 7 (set strategy, inspire, mobilize – the participants are able to teach other participants how to use the web services) to correspond to the levels of digital competence identified by the SFIA benchmark [27]. The average level observed was 3.5 with values ranging from 1 (follow) to 5 (apply – the participant is sufficiently autonomous to be able to perform the action alone).

After learning about the objectives of the study and the course of the experimental session, participants were asked to sign a consent form and were then seated at the experimental station. This consisted of a laptop computer equipped with a measuring device from the TEA company [21]: a TEA Captiv T-Sens GSR electrodermal activity sensor and an Eyetech VT3 Mini eye tracker. The data was processed using the TEA Captiv labs software. The two web sites chosen for our work were the *CAF* website [17] and the *Pôle Emploi* website [18]. Before validating this choice, we asked 4 UI/UX designers to assess the quality of the interfaces of these sites. Our goal here was to confirm that these websites did not have design issues that might disqualify them from our work. The consulted experts did not identify any major ergonomic problem. The main results of this evaluation are presented in Table 1.

Table 1. Expert evaluations of the chosen websites.

	https://www.caf.fr/	https://www.pole-emploi.fr
Strong points	Color consistency; Visibility of elements of interest; Well-organized page; Adapted and readable typology; Consistency of icons	Color consistency; Icons visibility; Page hierarchy and organization
Weak points	Low contrasts; Information density; Complex menu	Low contrasts; Low significance of some abstract icons

Participants were invited to carry out tasks specific to the platform consulted. For the CAF website they were asked to connect to their users' accounts and update their quarterly declaration or to retrieve a certificate of entitlement. For the *Pôle Emploi* website, they were asked to connect to their users' accounts and to declare a monthly activity situation and/or consult a job offer and/or update their resume.

The entire experimental procedure was carried out in accordance with the ethical rules required: each participant was informed of the objectives of our research, of their legal rights regarding the data collected and how the collected data would be used. All the data has been anonymized before the analysis.

2.2 Analysis Procedure

In order to highlight visual exploration strategies, the web pages consulted were divided into Areas Of Interest (AOI) identifying the different functional categories of the interactive components. To do so, we have developed an AOI taxonomy based on the classification of Romero et al. [22]. In order to simplify the analysis, we identified two main categories of interactive elements: *text-based* and *icon-based* interactive elements.

A *text-based interactive element* relies primarily on textual content to convey information about their functionality. It may be imperative control elements such as hyperlinks, menus or buttons [22]. An *icon-based interactive element* – in our study, it was always a button - has a semantics that is mainly conveyed by a pictographic element. In the studied websites, the icons that convey this information use a high level of abstraction of the corresponding functionality and can be qualified as *abstract icons* according to the classification proposed by Kim et al. [23]. We finally retained 5 AOI categories during our analyzes: *Icon-based button*, *Text-based button*, *Text entry controls*, *Menu*, *Hyperlink*. We compared, for these 5 AOI categories, a measure of *attractiveness* and a measure of *interest*. The *attractiveness – i.e.,* the intrinsic capacity of the interactive element to capture the users' attention - is given by the time elapsed before the first ocular fixation on the AOI. The *interest – i.e.,* the intrinsic capacity of the interactive element to maintain the users' attention - is given by the time spent on the AOI.

We also considered the *arousal* measure which is an indicator of the emotional response to the perceived visual stimulus. This measurement, derived from the skin conductance measurement from the GSR sensor, is provided by the Captiv Labs software from TEA [21]. While the subjective value of this physiological measurement is difficult to interpret, as it can be correlated with a positive or negative emotion depending on the context, we chose to interpret a high arousal measure as an indicator of recognition of the considered element. Indeed, arousal is an indicator of the existence of an emotional response. Whether the emotion is positive or negative, it indicates a recognition of AOI either as responding to the objective (manifestation of a positive emotion such as attraction) or as not responding to the objective (manifestation of a negative emotion such as frustration or stress). Either way, this means that the element's semantics could be interpreted by the person.

3   Results and Discussion

In some cases, the AOIs were never spotted by the participants during their exploration of the corresponding website. We observe that the *Icon-based buttons* are the more frequently ignored interactive elements (16 occurrences for the overall experiment) (see Fig. 2A). This result gives a first insight indicating that this type of AOI might be considered as being of poor relevance by the participants. Since the given *attraction* and *interest* measures were always 0, which have a significant impact on the calculated statistics, and to avoid introducing bias into our quantitative analysis, we removed these data from our subsequent analysis.

Fig. 1. Some AOI's identified on the websites. On the left, two examples of *text-based interactive elements*. On the right, two examples of *Icon-based interactive elements*.

After removing these occurrences, we analyzed the measure of *attraction*, namely the time elapsed on the screen before the first fixation on the AOI. The *Icon-based buttons* are the interactive elements that are seen the latest, with a great variability between the different measures (median = 28.2, IQR = 58.8, cf. Fig. 1B), followed by the *Text-based buttons* (median = 12.4, IQR = 20.8). This indicates that text-based elements attract attention more rapidly that icon-based elements, with a stronger appeal for written text rather than interaction widgets such as buttons.

The measure of *interest* (Fig. 1C) indicates that the time spent on the buttons, whether they are *text-based* (median = 4.75, IQR = 6.127) or *icon-based* (median = 4.6, IQR = 17.2) is low when compared to other interactive elements. This result is consistent if we assume that the amount of information provided by these AOIs is quite small and does not necessarily require prolonged attention to extract useful information. In contrast, the greater variability in the measurements suggests that *image-based* buttons are more difficult to understand than *text-based* buttons. This interpretation also seems to be confirmed by the results observed for the *arousal* (Fig. 1D). Arousal values are nigh to zero for *icon-based* buttons (median = 0, IQR = 0), while they are higher for *text-based* buttons (median = 4.85, IQR = 52.97). According to our interpretation, this would mean that *text-based* buttons are recognized for their functional role on the page, but *icon-based* buttons are not. All these results suggest that icon-based interactive elements are not recognized for their functionalities, if not purely ignored by the users with low digital literacy. Icon based buttons are seen less often than other elements. In addition, they are generally perceived later, and arouse less interest among users.

Overall, these results highlight that pictographic elements with a high level of abstraction are of little interest to users with low digital literacy, which phenomenon we refer to as *icon blindness*. This is quite interesting, given the fact that current trends in web design and in user-interface design in general tend towards more and more abstract representations of functionalities.

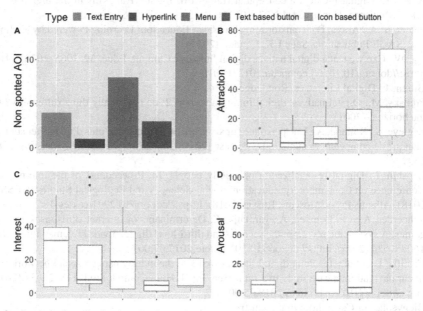

Fig. 2. Statistical analysis. **A.** *Number of non-spotted AOIs* for the 5 categories. **B.** *Attraction measure:* time (in s) before first fixation on AOI. **C.** *Interest measure:* time (in % of the overall time spent on the website page) spent on AOI. **D.** *Arousal:* percentage of max arousal value.

This *icon blindness* phenomena appears as a potentially important factor in the comprehension of the ongoing digital divide. It argues for further exploring explanation factors within the UI/UX and cognitive fields that have been scarcely studied and may explain the appearance and persistence of a *second level digital divide* [4, 10, 16]. If our results are confirmed by further research, they could have an important impact on the design choices one should make to address to people with low digital skills. We are planning on realizing a second analysis, with a larger number of participants, to consolidate these first outcomes of our exploratory work.

References

1. Punagin, S., Arya, A.: Privacy in the age of pervasive internet and big data analytics challenges and opportunities. IJMECS **7**, 36–47 (2015)
2. Eshet-Alkalai, Y.: Digital literacy: a conceptual framework for survival skills in the digital era. J. Educ. Multimed. Hypermed. **13**(1), 93–106 (2004)
3. Peña-López, I.: Falling through the net: Defining the digital divide (1999)
4. Hargittai, E.: Second-level digital divide: mapping differences in people's online skills. arXiv preprint cs/0109068 (2001)
5. Gilster, P., Glister, P.: Digital Literacy. Wiley Computer Pub, New York (1997)
6. Gallardo-Echenique, E.E., de Oliveira, J.M., Marqués-Molias, L., Esteve-Mon, F.: Digital competence in the knowledge. Society **11**, 17 (2015)
7. Wheeler, S.: Digital literacies for engagement in emerging online cultures, vol. 12 (2012)
8. Eshet, Y.: Digital literacy: a conceptual framework for survival skills in the digital era. J. Educ. Multimed. Hypermed. **13**, 93–106 (2004)
9. Peters, M.A., Araya, D.: Transforming American Education: Learning Powered by Technology. SAGE Publications Sage UK, London (2011)
10. Ng, W.: Can we teach digital natives digital literacy? Comput. Educ. **59**, 1065–1078 (2012). https://doi.org/10.1016/j.compedu.2012.04.016
11. Gillen, J.: Digital Literacies. Routledge (2014)
12. Prensky, M.: Digital natives, digital immigrants part 2: do they really think differently? On the horizon. (2001)
13. Legleye, S., Rolland, A.: Une personne sur six n'utilise pas Internet, plus d'un usager sur trois manque de compétences numériques de base (2019). https://www.insee.fr/fr/statistiques/4241397
14. Lapshin, I.: Digital resocialization of elderly people. In: Proceedings of the International Conference on Contemporary Education, Social Sciences and Ecological Studies (CESSES 2018). Atlantis Press, Moscow, Russia (2018). https://doi.org/10.2991/cesses-18.2018.217
15. Scheerder, A., van Deursen, A., van Dijk, J.: Determinants of Internet skills, uses and outcomes. A systematic review of the second- and third-level digital divide. Telemat. Inform. **34**, 1607–1624 (2017). https://doi.org/10.1016/j.tele.2017.07.007
16. Castilla, D., et al.: Teaching digital literacy skills to the elderly using a social network with linear navigation: a case study in a rural area. Int. J. Hum Comput Stud. **118**, 24–37 (2018). https://doi.org/10.1016/j.ijhcs.2018.05.009
17. Bienvenue sur Caf.fr. http://www.caf.fr/
18. https://www.pole-emploi.fr/, https://www.pole-emploi.fr/accueil/
19. CASF. https://casfbischwiller.centres-sociaux.fr/
20. UNESCO Institute for: International standard classification of education: ISCED 2011. UNESCO Institute for Statistics Montreal (2012)
21. TEA - Measurement and analysis of Human Behavior. https://www.teaergo.com/. Accessed 17 Mar 2021
22. Romero, R., Díez, D., Montero, S., Díaz, P., Aedo, I.: Towards a Systematic Development of RIAs: Taxonomy for classifying Rich-User-Interface Components, vol. 14 (2011)
23. Kim, J.H., Lee, K.P.: Cultural difference and mobile phone interface design: icon recognition according to level of abstraction. In: Proceedings of the 7th International Conference on Human Computer Interaction with Mobile Devices & Services, pp. 307–310 (2005)

Impact of Viewing Distance to Virtual Screen upon Kraepelin-Task Performance and Its Psychological Fatigue

Makio Ishihara[1(✉)] and Yukio Ishihara[2]

[1] Fukuoka Institute of Technology, Fukuoka 811-0295, Japan
m-ishihara@fit.ac.jp
[2] Shimane University, Shimane 690-8504, Japan
iyukio@ipc.shimane-u.ac.jp
https://www.fit.ac.jp/~m-ishihara/Lab/

Abstract. This manuscript discusses an impact of viewing distances to a virtual screen in an immersive environment upon psychological fatigue by assessing calculation performance of Kraepelin test. The viewing distance can be adjusted from 0.5 m to 128 m. The result shows that there is a certain tendency to alleviate psychological fatigue at the furthest viewing distance.

Keywords: Task performance · Kraepelin-task · Viewing distance · Virtual display

1 Introduction

The VDT syndrome is a symptom that is caused by extensive use of eyes for long hours and pains in the neck or shoulders due to sitting at desks for long periods of time, and physiological stress that stems from monotonous and continuous work requiring no errors etc.

To deal with the VDT syndrome, A. Uetake et al. [4] discussed an evaluation method of eye fatigue during VDT tasks. They found that eye fatigue is expressed as a function of pupil diameter and focusing strength. T. Katayama et al. [2] investigated the impact of color patterns displayed on a screen on work performance and fatigue. They found that an appropriate contrast between characters and background tends to alleviate much more fatigue. Y. Kato et al. [3] built a posture feedback neck band to alleviate pain in the neck and shoulders. The users wear the band on their neck and the band rings an alarm when their posture becomes misaligned during VDT tasks.

In regard to human ergonomics, international standards of ISO9241-303 specify requirements for output devices, especially for electronic visual displays. It says for example that the viewing distance, which refers to the physical distance between the surface of the computer screen and the user's eyes, should be 30 to 40 cm for children and young people, and more than 40 cm for adults and older

© Springer Nature Switzerland AG 2021
C. Stephanidis et al. (Eds.): HCII 2021, CCIS 1419, pp. 111–118, 2021.
https://doi.org/10.1007/978-3-030-78635-9_16

Fig. 1. Screenshot of the HMD view.

people. Though a lot of approaches and efforts from various points of view have been made to address VDT syndrome over the years, it still remains a problem for many office workers.

As mentioned, optimal viewing distances have been discussed often from the side of human ergonomics but not task performance. Previously, the authors [1] showed that long viewing distances to a computer screen could improve performance of mouse manipulation in terms of speed and accuracy. In their study, two experiments of tapping and tracing tasks (ISO9241) were conducted for three viewing distances of 0.5 m, 32 m and 128 m from a virtual computer screen in an immersive virtual space provided by an HMD. This study aims to cover discussion about the impact of those viewing distances on psychological fatigue by including a calculation task of Kraepelin test.

2   A HMD-Based Virtual Display Environment

The system consists of a HMD device of HTC Vive Pro and a high-end host computer of Dell Alienware. The HMD is connected to the host computer and the host computer runs Unity (2019.1.14f1) to compose a virtual space where a virtual computer screen is placed. Figure 1 shows a screenshot of the HMD view which the user sees in. There is a virtual computer screen in that view and the user manipulates the contents on it. The contents on the virtual computer screen come from the host computer and all the input made on the virtual computer screen like mouse clicks and drags, goes back to the host computer to update the contents. The user can adjust its viewing distance in real time with a Vive trackpad. The viewing distance can be adjusted between 0.5 m and 128 m.

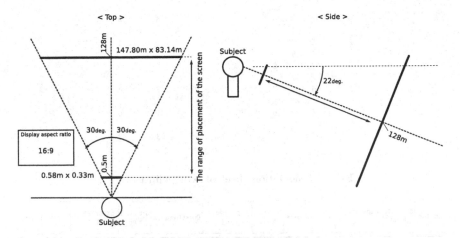

Fig. 2. Experiment design.

3   Experiment on Calculation Performance

The aim of this experiment is to evaluate an impact of viewing distances on calculation performance. Figure 2 shows the design of the experiment. The left diagram shows the top view and the user sees a virtual computer screen just in front of him/her. The virtual computer screen is enlarged with a constant horizontal FOV of 60 degrees as the viewing distance becomes long. The user perceives a small screen at the short viewing distance and does a large screen at the long distance. The right diagram shows the side view and the virtual computer screen is placed along a line at the angular position of 22° below the eye level according to ergonomics of human system interaction in ISO9241. Three constant viewing distances of 0.5 m, 32.0 m and 128.0 m are given for each subject to perform the given task. The three constant viewing distances are referred to as Near, Middle and Far, respectively.

3.1   Tasks and Subjects

Each subject is asked to perform Kraepelin test at each condition:Near, Middle and Far. Kraepelin test measures accuracy and speed of addition of a 1-digit number to a 1-digit number. Figure 3 shows a look of Kraepelin test and the subjects are asked to add a number to the adjacent number from left to right and answer the first digit of the obtained value as many and correctly as possible in 15 min. During the test, the elapsed time, the count of total answers and correct ones for measuring calculation performance, and a sequence of heart beats for measuring psychological fatigue are measured. Before and after the test, a flicker perception threshold or FPT is obtained for measuring psychological fatigue as well. For measuring physical fatigue, they are asked to fill out a questionnaire defined in ISO9241 after the test.

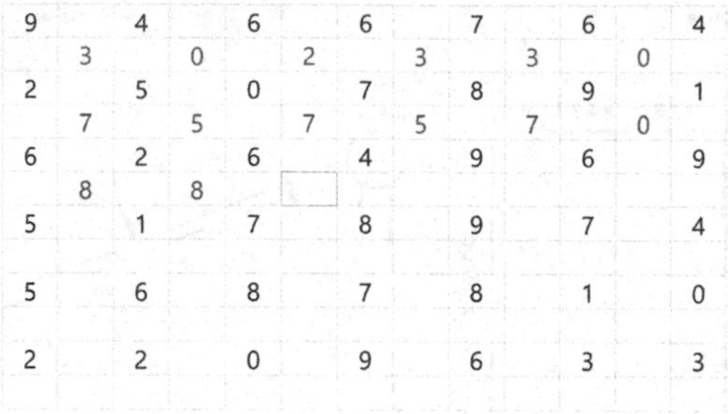

```
9     4     6     6     7     6     4
   3     0     2     3     3     0
2     5     0     7     8     9     1
   7     5     7     5     7     0
6     2     6     4     9     6     9
   8     8    [ ]
5     1     7     8     9     7     4

5     6     8     7     8     1     0

2     2     0     9     6     3     3
```

Fig. 3. Calculation sheet of Kraepelin test.

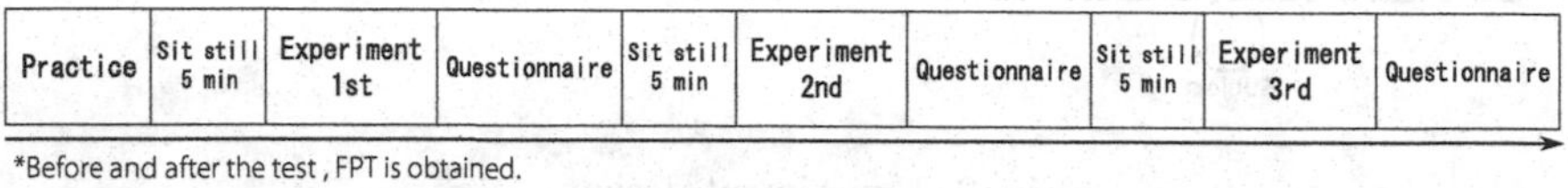

Practice	Sit still 5 min	Experiment 1st	Questionnaire	Sit still 5 min	Experiment 2nd	Questionnaire	Sit still 5 min	Experiment 3rd	Questionnaire

*Before and after the test , FPT is obtained.

Fig. 4. Procedure of the experiment.

There are 14 subjects aged from 21 to 24. They are students from a course of computer science and engineer in our university and all are right-handed and have experience with manipulating a computer mouse. They also have good eyesight.

3.2   Experiment Procedure

Figure 4 shows a procedure of the experiment. The subject has a practice time to become familiar with the test before it begins. After that, he/she sits still for 5 min then starts the test at one of the conditions of Near, Middle and Far, and fills out a questionnaire about his/her physical fatigue. He/she sits still for another 5 min then starts the task again at the other condition and fills out the questionnaire. The order of conditions between Near, Middle and Far is balanced among subjects to remove order effects. Each subject performs one trial at each condition, resulting in

$$14 \text{ subjects} \times 3 \text{ conditions} \times 1 \text{ trial} = 42 \text{ trials in total.} \qquad (1)$$

3.3   Results

Figure 5 shows the speed of calculation. The horizontal axis shows the three conditions of Near, Middle and Far, and the vertical one does the total number of answers among subjects on average at each condition and the corresponding standard deviation. From the figure, there seems not to be a relation between those conditions and the speed of calculation. Figure 6 shows the performance of calculation. The horizontal axis is the same with Fig. 5 and the vertical one shows

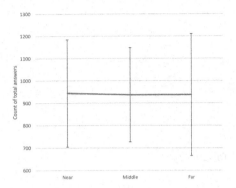

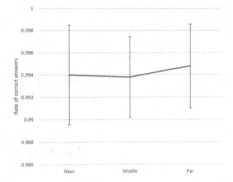

Fig. 5. Speed of calculation defined as the total number of answers among subjects on average at each condition and the corresponding standard deviation.

Fig. 6. Performance of calculation defined as the percentage of the number of correct answers for the total one among subjects on average at each condition.

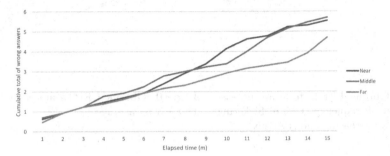

Fig. 7. Cumulative total of wrong answers per minute.

the percentage of the number of correct answers for the total one among subjects on average at each condition. From the figure, there is a certain increase in the percentage at the Far condition. Figure 7 shows the temporal performance of calculation. The horizontal axis shows the elapsed time in minute and the vertical one does the cumulative total number of wrong answers. From the figure, there seems a tendency to hold calculation performance at the latter half of the test.

Figure 8 shows physical fatigue. The horizontal axis shows the conditions and the vertical one does the questionnaire score among subjects on average at each condition. From the figure, physical fatigue tends to be alleviated at the farthest viewing distance except for the eyes.

Figure 9 and Fig. 10 show psychological fatigue, and they are obtained from Flicker test. The Flicker test provides a subjective indicator of the psychological fatigue by asking the subject to see a light switching between on and off fast, and judge the timing of transition between continuous perception of the light and intermittent one. The timing is measured as the number of counts of flickering light per section and it is called Flicker Perception Threshold or FPT. FPT holds

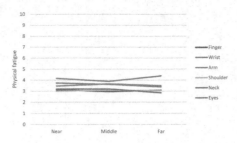

Fig. 8. Physical fatigue.

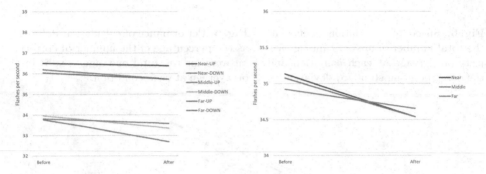

Fig. 9. Obtained FPTs from an increasing order of frequency (UP) of flickering light or a decreasing one (DOWN).

Fig. 10. Obtained FPTs among UP and DOWN on average.

comparatively high when the psychological fatigue is low or vice versa. Generally, FPT differs when it is measured from an increasing order of frequency (UP) of flickering light or a decreasing one (DOWN), and the FPT obtained from UP is often larger than the one from DOWN. Figure 9 is a pair of FPTs obtained from UP and DOWM among subjects on average before and after the test for each condition. From the figure, validity of the test is confirmed. Figure 10 shows FPTs among subjects over UP and DOWN on average before and after the test for each condition. From the figure, psychological fatigue becomes large after the test in comparison with the one before it for all the conditions. The amount of increase of psychological fatigue holds the smallest for the farthest condition.

Figure 11 and Fig. 12 show psychological fatigue as well, and they are obtained from the subject's heart rate (RRI). By carrying out a spectral analysis of the given RRI sequence, the ratio of LF (the spectral integration at 0.05 to 0.15 Hz) to HF (the spectral integration at 0.15 to 0.40 Hz) is used to express an index of psychological fatigue: relax (0.0∼0.8) and high psychological fatigue (2.0∼5.0) according to Fatigue Science Laboratory Inc. A moving window of 5 min is employed to carry out the analysis and observe changes of the index of LF/HF per second through the test. Figure 11 is a list of graphs showing the change of the index over the test for each of 6 subjects. The data of RRIs from

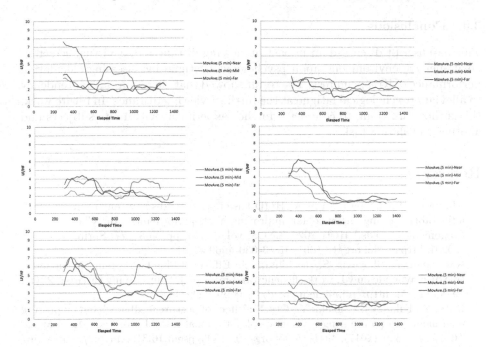

Fig. 11. Temporal change in LF/HF obtained from 6 subjects. The data from the left 8 subjects was corrupted due to the device failure.

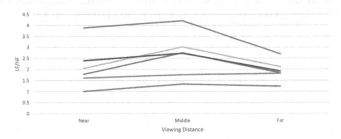

Fig. 12. Average of LF/HF at each condition.

the left 8 subjects was corrupted due to the device failure. The horizontal axis is the elapsed time in second and the vertical one the index of LF/HF for each condition of Near, Middle and Far. From those graphs, psychological fatigue tends to be alleviated at the farthest viewing distance.

Figure 12 is a graph showing the index of LF/HF over the test on average at each condition for each subject. The horizontal axis shows the conditions and the vertical one does the index of LF/HF. From the graph, the amount of alleviation of psychological fatigue tends to vary depending on subjects.

3.4   Conclusions

This manuscript discussed an impact of viewing distances to a virtual screen in an immersive environment upon psychological fatigue by assessing calculation performance of Kraepelin test. The result showed that there is a certain tendency to alleviate psychological fatigue at the furthest viewing distance. In future work, the authors are going to conduct a further experiment with more subjects and another calculation task.

References

1. Ishihara, M., Ishihara, Y.: A HMD-based virtual display environment with adjustable viewing distance for improving task performance. In: Chen, J.Y.C., Fragomeni, G. (eds.) HCII 2020. LNCS, vol. 12190, pp. 468–477. Springer, Cham (2020). https://doi.org/10.1007/978-3-030-49695-1_31
2. Katayama, T., Shoyama, S., Tochihara, Y.: Effects of blue background in the negative display mode on vdt work efficiency and fatigue. J. Hum. Living Environ. 22(1), 29–38 (2015). http://ci.nii.ac.jp/naid/110009973299/en/
3. Kato, Y., Fukuda, S., Suzuki, Y., Ota, S.: Effect of posture feedback band on posture alignment and pain during a visual display terminal task. J. Jpn. Soc. Exp. Mech. 16(4), 315–319 (2017). https://doi.org/10.11395/jjsem.16.315. http://ci.nii.ac.jp/naid/130005300060/en/
4. Uetake, A., Otsuka, M., Takasawa, Y., Murata, A.: On evaluation index for visual fatigue induced during a vdt task. Trans. Inst. Electron., Inf. Commun. Eng. A 83(12), 1521–1529 (2000). http://ci.nii.ac.jp/naid/110003313913/en/

Physiological Correlates of Time Stress During Game Play

Daniel H. Lee(✉) and Tzyy-Ping Jung

Institute for Neural Computation, University of California San Diego,
9500 Gilman Dr, La Jolla, CA 92093, USA
tpjung@ucsd.edu

Abstract. The objective of this study is to develop and use a virtual reality game as a tool to assess the effects of realistic stress on the behavioral and physiological responses of participants. The game is based on a popular Steam game called Keep Talking Nobody Explodes, where the players collaborate to defuse a bomb. Varying levels of difficulties in solving a puzzle and time pressures will result in different stress levels that can be measured in terms of errors, response times, and other physiological measurements. The game was developed using 3D programming tools including Blender and a virtual reality development kit (VRTK). To measure response times accurately, we added LSL (Lab Stream Layer) Markers to collect and synchronize physiological signals, behavioral data, and the timing of game events. We recorded Electrocardiogram (ECG) data during gameplay to assess heart rate and heart-rate variability (HRV) that have been shown as reliable indicators of stress. Our empirical results showed that heart rate increased significantly while HRV reduced significantly when the participants under high stress, which are consistent with the prior mainstream stress research. This VR game framework is publicly available in GitHub and allows researchers to measure and synchronize other physiological signals such as electroencephalogram, electromyogram, and pupillometry.

Keywords: Virtual reality · Stress · Heart rate · Heart rate variability

1 Introduction

Various real-life stress can induce homeostatic changes in human behavior, brain, and body. For instance, associations have been reported between achievement on tests of memory and attention and the experience of everyday minor stressful events [11,14]. To modify the amount of stress that a person has, researchers have been relying on manipulating the various factors of their subjects' lives, such as their sleep quality and workload. However, it is unrealistic to control every aspect of the subjects' lives, and they may always be more or less stressed than the researchers think they are, varying the data from the experiment. Furthermore, stress research to date centers on simplified stimulus-response paradigms

© Springer Nature Switzerland AG 2021
C. Stephanidis et al. (Eds.): HCII 2021, CCIS 1419, pp. 119–126, 2021.
https://doi.org/10.1007/978-3-030-78635-9_17

conducted in highly controlled environments that do not resemble authentic settings, where real-life stress typically takes place. We propose developing a controlled virtual-reality (VR) environment that can allow for greater control over the subjects' stress and performance when completing tasks [2]. These types of games are known as games with a purpose (GWAP). They are tools for helping scientists perform experiments and collect data [8].

This study modified a popular VR game, Keep Talking and Nobody Explodes [6], to test participants in a controlled environment. Keep Talking Nobody Explodes is a VR game where one player disarms a bomb while communicating with another player, a bomb-defusing expert, who has the bomb defusing instructions. The modules or puzzles for disarming the bomb include certain wires that must be cut, buttons that must be pressed at certain times, and keypads that must be pressed in a certain order. The player will need a VR headset (e.g. Oculus or HTC Vive) and controllers to play the game. Only the player can see the puzzles and bomb in VR, while the bomb-defusing expert can only check a manual to find instructions to solve the puzzles. The player and the bomb-defusing expert must communicate effectively to defuse the bomb.

2   Methodology

To create a controlled environment where researchers can measure the performance of a task and manipulate how well the subject performs, we designed a VR game based on the game Keep Talking and Nobody Explodes [6], which measures the subjects' reaction times, communication times, and precision and recall of tasks. There are multiple levels of difficulty expressed in more puzzles (modules) and less time to solve them. There are many ways to measure stress and among those one of the most widely studied methods is to measure heart rate (HR) and Heart-Rate Variability (HRV) derived from ECG recordings [7]. We developed a simple framework where we can record the ECG signals while subjects playing the game under varying stress conditions, which are synchronized with the start and end times of game modules or events within the game. The event markers are created by the Lab Streaming Layer (LSL), a recording and annotation software [15] that synchronizes the recorded signals with events during the game.

In our version of the game, we implemented the following five types of game modules: Wires, Keypad, Simon Says, Button and Venting Gas, and each with a timer. The timer was implemented using the Unity time.time function. For the Wire module (shown in the top left, top right, and two in the middle right of Fig. 1), the player is required to cut a certain wire based on the color of the wires and how many there are. For the Keypad module (shown at the bottom right), the player must press the keypad in a certain order depending on the symbols displayed on the keypad. For the Simon Says module (shown in the top and bottom middle), the player must press the buttons in a certain order based on which button is blinking. For the Button module (shown in the leftmost middle row), the player must press the button at a certain time to solve it. The Venting

Gas module, in the bottom left, is a "needy module" that captures the player's attention and causes more stress. The entire description of the game, the design of the modules, and the implementation of the tools such as the lab stream layer details can be found in the full paper at [9].

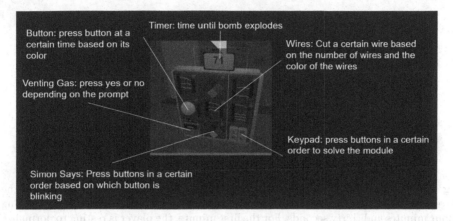

Fig. 1. An image of the bomb in the VR game. The top left, right and middle portions of the bomb are the wire modules. The top middle and bottom middle modules are the Simon Says modules. The module in the bottom right is the keypad module, the module in the middle left is the button module, and the module in the bottom left is the venting gas module.

2.1   Recording and Analyzing Electrocardiogram Data

The goal of this pilot study was to explore how the physiological responses of healthy individuals relate to the variability in time stress. To this end, we recorded the event markers, the players' ECG, and their behavioral data under three conditions: stressful (hard), non-stressful (easy), and resting conditions. The stressful (hard) condition required the player to solve a puzzle module in twenty seconds, while the non-stressful (easy) condition allowed the player to solve a puzzle module in two minutes, and the resting condition allowed the player to take a break for one minute between two modules. In each experiment, the participants played four hard sessions, four easy sessions, and eight resting sessions. The easy and hard sessions were played in random sequence in the experiment. Two healthy individuals participated in this pilot study, resulting in the ECG signal data for a total of eight hard, eight easy, and 16 resting sessions. This study used a wearable ECG device called *Heartypatch* and its recording software [5] to record the ECG data during game play. Figure 2 shows the ECG data synchronized with event markers from the game, revealing the various levels of ECG signals depending on how stressful the player was at key points in the game. This study focuses on two physiological responses of our participants:

HR and HRV. HRV is the fluctuation in the time intervals between adjacent heartbeats [12]. To calculate HRV, we first find the time intervals between the consecutive heartbeats using the findpeaks function in MATLAB.

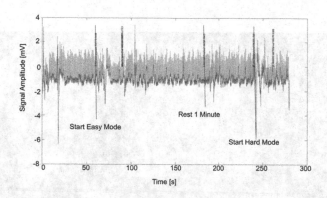

Fig. 2. We recorded the ECG of the player using the HeartyPatch sensor while the player was playing the game, and overlaid it with the event markers. The total recording is four minutes and thirty seconds. For the first minute, the player is resting to normalize their heartbeat. Afterward, for two minutes the player is playing the non-stressful version of the game (easy mode). The player then takes a minute rest and starts the stressful version of the game for twenty seconds (hard mode).

3   Experimental Results

After collecting the data through LSL from our experiment, we split the data using the event markers from the game. We identified which sections of the ECG data correspond to easy, hard, or resting sessions. We then analyzed the data from the separated and categorized (easy, hard, or resting) sessions to find the average heart rate and HRV values for the easy, hard, or resting conditions using MATLAB. Figure 3 shows the average heart-rate values under the three (resting, hard, and easy) conditions. The hard (stressful) sessions have the highest average heart rate of 96 bpm. The resting and easy (non-stressful) sessions have average heart rates of 84 and 82 bpm, respectively. The difference between the average heart rates of easy and resting sessions is small, but the error bar for the easy sessions is larger, indicating that the variation of heart rates in the easy sessions is larger.

Figure 4 shows the average HRV in milliseconds, along with error bars, under the three (resting, hard, and easy) conditions. As shown in the bar graph, the average HRV value under the stressful (hard) condition is around 30 milliseconds while those under the non-stressful (easy) and resting conditions are around 40 milliseconds and 50 milliseconds, respectively. Thus the difference between the average HRV values of the resting and easy conditions is around ten milliseconds,

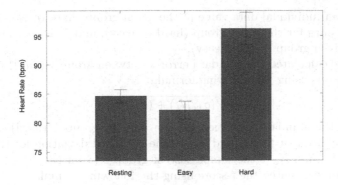

Fig. 3. This figure shows the average heart rates in beats per minute for two subjects for the 16 resting sessions, eight easy (non-stressful) sessions, and eight hard (stressful) sessions. The error bars denote the variations in the heart rates within the resting, easy and hard sessions.

and the difference between those under the easy and hard conditions is also ten milliseconds, which makes the difference between the average HRV values under hard and resting conditions to be about 20 milliseconds. We also note that the average HRV value under the stressful (hard) condition is the lowest.

We used statistical tests to examine if the differences in HRV between conditions are statistically significant. To calculate statistical significance, we determined the null hypothesis and an alternate hypothesis. Since the level of statistical significance is often expressed as a p-value between zero and one, we calculated p-value to show that our results are statistically significant. Typically, a p-value less than 0.05 is considered statistically significant. We thus used a one-tailed hypothesis with a significance level of 0.05.

To calculate the p-values, we first calculated the standard deviation for both sets of data under the statistical comparison. Then, we calculated the t-score and the degrees of freedom using the number of samples in each data set [13]. Finally, we used a p-value calculator to find the p-value using the t-score and the degrees of freedom [3].

For example, to find the p-value between hard (group 1) and easy (group 2) sessions, we used the following steps:

First, we determined the null hypothesis and the alternative hypothesis as follows: The null hypothesis: "There is no significant difference in the data sets (HRV values) of group 1 (hard sessions) and group 2 (easy sessions)." The alternative hypothesis: "There is a significant difference in the data sets (HRV values) of group 1 (hard sessions) and group 2 (easy sessions)."

Second, we calculated the standard deviation σ of the HRV values (data sets) for the hard sessions and easy sessions using the following formula:

$$\sigma = \sqrt{(\sum_{i=1}^{N} (x_i - \mu)^2)/(N-1)}, \tag{1}$$

where x_i is an individual data value in the given group (hard or easy), μ is the mean of the data for the given group (hard or easy), and N is the total sample size of the given group (hard or easy).

Third, we calculated the standard error s between group 1 (hard) and group 2 (easy) sessions using the following formula:

$$s = \sqrt{(\sigma_1/N_1) + (\sigma_2/N_2)}, \tag{2}$$

where σ_1 is the standard deviation for the data in group 1 (hard), N_1 is the sample size of group 1 (8 for hard), σ_2 is the standard deviation for the data in group 2 (easy), and N_2 is the sample size of group 2 (8 for easy).

Fourth, we calculated the t-score using the following formula:

$$t = |\mu_1 - \mu_2|/s, \tag{3}$$

where μ_1 is the mean of the data for group 1 (hard), μ_2 is the mean of the data for group 2 (easy), and s is the standard error between group 1 and group 2.

Next, we calculated the degrees of freedom d using the following formula:

$$d = N_1 + N_2 - 2, \tag{4}$$

where N_1 is the sample size of group 1 (8 for hard), and N_2 is the sample size of group 2 (8 for easy).

Finally, we used the p-value calculator [3] to find the p-value based on the t-score and the degrees of freedom d.

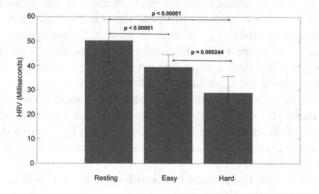

Fig. 4. This figure shows the average HRV values under three conditions for two subjects. The statistical testings show that the HRV differences in the resting vs hard, resting vs easy, and easy vs hard are all significant.

As shown in Fig. 4, the p-value for the null hypothesis that there is no significant difference between the average HRV values in hard and easy sessions is $p = 0.00244$, which is less than the significance level of 0.05, indicating the difference between these values is statistically significant and unlikely to happen by chance. The HRV differences between resting and hard groups and between resting and easy groups are also statistically significant since their p-value is much less than 0.05 ($p < 0.00001$).

3.1 Comparison with Other Results on HRV Under Stressful Conditions

We compared our findings of the lower HRV values under stress to prior work such as [1], which analyzed the influences on HRV Values in athletes, and [7], which analyzed the relationship between HRV and regional cerebral blood flow. Both studies showed that stress in athletes and higher blood flow was correlated with lower HRV values.

In the study [10], researchers evaluated the effect of real-life stress on the cardiac response of the subjects. They concluded that stress increases arterial pressure and impairs cardiovascular homeostasis.

Furthermore, in another study [16], participants performed tasks that either had a physical, mental, or combined load, while their HRV was measured. The study concluded that HRV is affected by changes in physical or mental states, and they were also able to differentiate between resting, physical and mental conditions through the characteristics of HRV.

Researchers surveyed London-based civil servants (aged from 35 to 55) [4] to evaluate the stress levels due to their work. They reported correlations between high work stress, low physical activity, poor diet, and most importantly low HRV.

4 Conclusions and Next Steps

In conclusion, we created a VR GWAP framework based on the game "Keep Talking and Nobody Explodes" intending to relate physiological data and stress levels. The framework includes event markers so that the physiological, behavioral, and audio data streams and events in the game are totally synchronized. We used ECG to show how this GWAP can be used to assess the physiological correlates of time stress. The empirical results were consistent with those reported in prior studies that the HRV values decrease with increasing levels of stress [4, 7, 12, 16].

Our game is meant to be a framework for experimentation so that other researchers can add more tools or sensors. We used ECG to measure HR AND HRV as they are known to be correlated with stress. However, this framework can be extended to other modalities such as electroencephalogram (EEG) to measure brain activities that are correlated with stress, or eye gaze/pupillometry to find other physiological correlates of stress. This framework also allows a thorough investigation into the speech characteristics of players under stress, for example, to extract features such as pitch or loudness. We believe that this framework can facilitate further research on the associations between physiological signals and stress (and other mental and cognitive states).

Acknowledgment. This work was supported in part by grants from US NSF (CBET-1935860, NCS-1734883, IP-1719130, and SMA-1540943) and US Army Research Lab STRONG Program to TPJ. The authors want to thank Robin Xu for helping with the VR game code and Kuanjung Chiang for helping with the data analysis.

References

1. Aubert, A., Seps, B., Beckers, F.: Heart rate variability in athletes. Sports Med. **33**, 889–919 (2003). https://doi.org/10.2165/00007256-200333120-00003
2. Bailenson, J.: Experience On Demand: What Virtual Reality Is, How It Works, and What It Can Do. W.W. Norton & Company, New York (2019)
3. Social Science Statistics (2002). https://www.socscistatistics.com/pvalues/tdistribution.aspxr
4. Chandola, T., et al.: Work stress and coronary heart disease: what are the mechanisms? Eur. Heart J. **29**(5), 640–648 (2008). https://doi.org/10.1093/eurheartj/ehm584
5. Chiang, K.: Heartypatch (2020). https://github.com/q89123003/HeartyPatch
6. Games, S.C.: Keep Talking and Nobody Explodes (2015).https://keeptalkinggame.com/
7. Kim, H.G., Cheon, E.J., Bai, D.S., Lee, Y.H., Koo, B.H.: Stress and heart rate variability: a meta-analysis and review of the literature. Psychiatry Invest. **15**(3), 235–245 (2018). https://doi.org/10.30773/pi.2017.08.17
8. Lance, B.: Towards Serious Games for Improved BCI. http://liinc.bme.columbia.edu/publications/towards-serious-games-for-improved-bci/
9. Lee, D.H., Jung, T.P.: A Virtual Reality Game as a Tool to Assess Physiological Correlations of Stress. arXiv e-prints arXiv:2009.14421 (2020)
10. Lucini, D., Norbiato, G., Clerici, M., Pagani, M.: Hemodynamic and autonomic adjustments to real life stress conditions in humans. Hypertension **39**, 184–188 (2002)
11. Neupert, S., Almeida, D., Mroczek, D., Spiro, A.: Daily stressors and memory failures in a naturalistic setting: Findings from the va normative aging study. Psychol. Aging **21**(2), 424–429 (2006). https://doi.org/10.1037/0882-7974.21.2.424
12. Shaffer, F., Ginsberg, J.: An overview of heart rate variability metrics and norms. Frontiers in Public Health 5(258) (2017). https://doi.org/10.3389/fpubh.2017.00258
13. How to Calculate Statistical Significance (Plus What It Is and Why It's Important) (2020). https://www.indeed.com/career-advice/career-development/how-to-calculate-statistical-significance
14. Stawski, R.S., Mogle, J., Sliwinski, M.J.: Intraindividual Coupling of Daily Stressors and Cognitive Interference in Old Age. J. Gerontol.: Ser. B 66B(1), i121–i129 (2011). https://doi.org/10.1093/geronb/gbr012
15. Lab Streaming Layer (2018). https://github.com/sccn/labstreaminglayer
16. Taelman, J., Vandeput, S., Gligorijevic, I., Spaepen, A., Van Huffel, S.: Timefrequency heart rate variability characteristics of young adults during physical, mental and combined stress in laboratory environment. In: Conference Proceedings IEEE Engineering in Medicine and Biology Society, pp. 1973–1976 (2011). https://doi.org/10.2165/00007256-200333120-00003

Measuring the Apparent Movement Perception Thresholds of Kinetic Forms with Surface Lines and Forms of Various Color Combinations

Chih-Wei Lin[1,2]([✉]), Lan-Ling Huang[1,2], Chi-Meng Liao[1,2], and Hsiwen Fan[3]

[1] Fujian University of Technology, Fuzhou 350118, Fujian, China
copy1.copy2@msa.hinet.net
[2] Design Innovation Research Center of Humanities and Social Sciences Research Base of Colleges and Universities in Fujian Province, Fuzhou 350118, Fujian, China
[3] Chiba University, Chiba 263-8522, Chiba, Japan

Abstract. In this study, lines and forms of various color combinations and with eight different color visibility rankings were examined with regard to their rotational speed thresholds. Whether they influenced the visual illusion effects of kinetic forms and participants' perception and judgment of apparent movement was explored, as were the causal relationships between color visibility ranking, rotational speed, and apparent movement. The method of adjustment in psychophysics was used in the experiment, which revealed relationships between the color combinations and rotational speed, the upper and lower absolute thresholds of illusory motion and the speed threshold range, and participants' perception and judgment of apparent movement. The optimal kinetic illusion effect and apparent movement perception effect were obtained under the combination of the black figure and white background.

Keywords: Motion form · Motion perception · Motion illusion

1 Introduction

The kinetic illusion effect, kinetic perception effect, and pattern performance displayed by kinetic forms originate from the combination of various form elements and their interaction with rotational motion. The combination of various kinetic form elements produces kinetic illusion effects, kinetic perception effects, and pattern presentation with different forms and levels. Thus, in this study, lines and forms of various color combinations and with different color visibility rankings were experimentally examined under rotational movement. The observed kinetic illusion effects and pattern presentation were used to discuss the kinetic perception involved in order to understand the relationships between kinetic forms and kinetic perception.

2 Kinetic Perception Effects and Pattern Presentation of Apparent Movement

The visual masking effect is present in apparent movement; moreover, any stimuli involved must be continuous. Although the stimulus that triggers motion perception

© Springer Nature Switzerland AG 2021
C. Stephanidis et al. (Eds.): HCII 2021, CCIS 1419, pp. 127–132, 2021.
https://doi.org/10.1007/978-3-030-78635-9_18

remains stationary, an illusion of movement can be driven by actual moving objects. Regarding the experimental samples, continuous spiral lines were used as the apparent movement stimulus. The visual masking effect was induced by the visual interference phenomenon of the rotation generated by the stimulus, which created illusions in a manner similar to the visual effect principle of apparent movement. The kinetic perception effect and patterns of continuous motion were observed under the rotation of the continuous lines.

3 Experimental Design and Samples

The method of adjustment used in psychophysics to measure absolute thresholds was applied in the experiment, which followed a within-subjects design. The equipment was a digital variable-frequency wireless control system that was connected to a computer for operation and monitoring. The 32 participants were recruited through judgmental sampling, a nonprobability sampling technique. The samples comprised eight sets of lines and forms of various color combinations; the sets exhibited the highest levels of color visibility according to a ranking performed in advance. Each line was 10 mm in width and set at an angle of 15°[1]. The observation distance was 1 m. The cone height was 25 cm [2–4], and the cone width was 12 cm [5] (Table 1).

Table 1. Eight color graphic and cylinder (triangular pyramid)

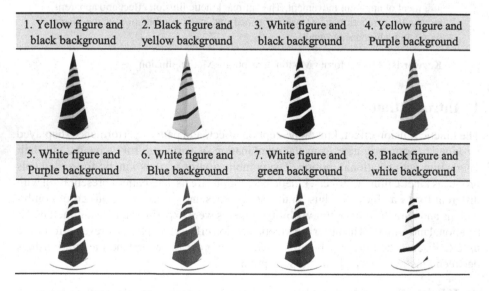

1. Yellow figure and black background	2. Black figure and yellow background	3. White figure and black background	4. Yellow figure and Purple background
5. White figure and Purple background	6. White figure and Blue background	7. White figure and green background	8. Black figure and white background

4 Results and Discussion

4.1 Experimental Results

The lower absolute threshold of the black figure and white background combination of lines and forms appeared first (black figure and white background combination: 41.563 < 46.25 < 48.625 < 50.844 < 52.719 < 54.688 < 54.938 < 56.156 rpm). Its upper absolute threshold did not remain the highest throughout the experiment (67.063 > 66.531 > 65.719 > 65.219 > black figure and white background combination: 64.375 > 64.313 > 63.156 > 62.875 rpm). However, the rotational speed differences of the eight sets of color combinations were extremely small. The highest speed thresholds indicated the longest kinetic illusion time and the optimal effect (black figure and white background combination: 22.812 > 16.625 > 14.531 > 13.469 > 12.5 > 11.593 > 11.031 > 10.907 rpm). Overall, the combination of the black figure and white background in apparent movement exhibited the optimal kinetic illusion effect and apparent movement perception effect (Table 2, Fig. 1).

Table 2. Rotating speed thresholds of apparent movement for the eight types of color graphics (rpm)

Type of color graphic	Perception threshold			Mean
1. Yellow figure and black background	Upper AT	Speed threshold	10.907	67.063
	Lower AT			56.156
2. Black figure and yellow background	Upper AT	Speed threshold	11.593	66.531
	Lower AT			54.938
3. White figure and black background	Upper AT	Speed threshold	11.031	65.719
	Lower AT			54.688
4. Yellow figure and Purple background	Upper AT	Speed threshold	12.5	65.219
	Lower AT			52.719
5. White figure and Purple background	Upper AT	Speed threshold	13.469	64.313
	Lower AT			50.844
6. White figure and Blue background	Upper AT	Speed threshold	14.531	63.156
	Lower AT			48.625
7. White figure and green background	Upper AT	Speed threshold	16.625	62.875
	Lower AT			46.250
8. Black figure and white background	Upper AT	Speed threshold	22.812	64.375
	Lower AT			41.563

AT = absolute threshold

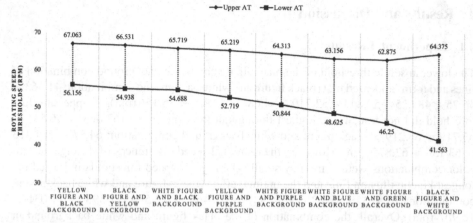

Fig. 1. Run chart in the thresholds of apparent movement in eight color graphics (rpm)

4.2 Relationships Between Color Visibility Ranking, Rotational Speed, and Apparent Movement

In the lower absolute threshold interval (41.563 to 56.156 rpm), the lower the color visibility ranking was, the lower the lower absolute threshold became. The color visibility ranking and the time of the perceived absolute threshold were negatively correlated. The lower absolute threshold value of the black figure and white background combination (41.563 rpm) appeared earlier—that is, the participants perceived apparent movement under this combination the fastest. Conversely, the higher the color visibility ranking, the higher the lower absolute threshold. The lower absolute threshold value of the yellow figure and black background combination (56.156 rpm) appeared later; this involved a negative correlation. In other words, the participants perceived apparent movement under this combination the slowest.

Regarding the upper absolute threshold interval (62.875 to 67.063 rpm), the lower the color visibility ranking, the lower the upper absolute threshold. The color visibility ranking and the time of the perceived upper absolute threshold were negatively correlated. The upper absolute threshold of the white figure and green background combination (62.875 rpm) appeared earlier, meaning that the participants did not perceive apparent movement under this combination. Conversely, the higher the color visibility ranking, the higher the upper absolute threshold. Under the negative correlation, the upper absolute threshold of the yellow figure and black background combination (67.063 rpm) appeared later, meaning that the participants were able to perceive apparent movement under this combination.

Regarding the range of the speed threshold, the lower the color visibility ranking was, the wider the range became; that is, the lower the ranking was, the longer the kinetic illusion time became and the better the effect was. Negative correlations were noted between the color visibility ranking, kinetic illusion time, and kinetic illusion effect. The range of the speed threshold was the greatest under the black figure and white background combination (22.812 rpm); in other words, the kinetic illusion time of the was the longest under this combination, with the optimal effect. Conversely, the

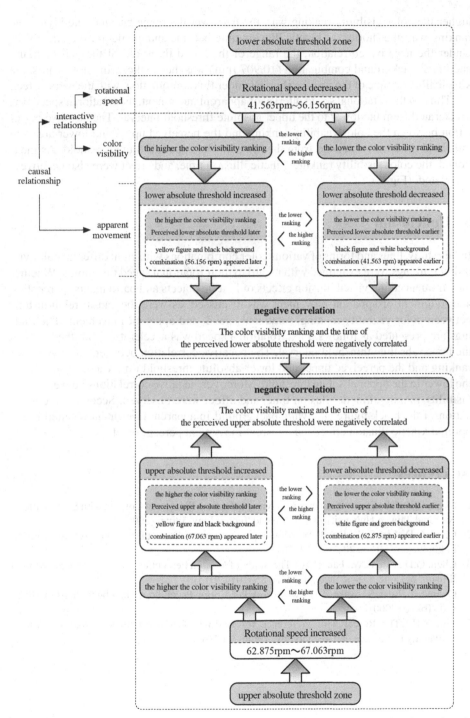

Fig. 2. Interactive and causal relationships among color visibility ranking, rotational speed, and apparent movement

higher the color visibility ranking was, the narrower the range became; the higher the ranking was, the shorter the kinetic illusion time became and the poorer the effect was. Under the negative correlation, the range of the speed threshold of the yellow figure and black background combination (10.907 rpm) was the smallest. In other words, the kinetic illusion time of the was the shortest under this combination, with the worst effect.

Thus, in the rotational speed interval of apparent movement, the rotational speed was accelerated from the lower to the upper absolute threshold interval. The negative correlation between the color visibility ranking and the perceived upper and lower absolute threshold time, was extended from the lower to the upper absolute threshold. As mentioned, the color visibility ranking, kinetic illusion time, and effect were also negatively correlated. (Fig. 2).

5 Conclusion

In this study, lines and forms of various color combinations with eight different color visibility rankings were examined with regard to their rotational speed thresholds. Whether they influenced the visual illusion effects of kinetic objects and participants' perception and judgment of apparent movement was discussed, as were the causal relationships between color visibility ranking, rotational speed, and apparent movement. The findings are presented as follows. First, rotational speed was accelerated from the lower to the upper absolute threshold interval. The negative correlation between color visibility ranking and the perceived upper and lower absolute threshold time was extended from the lower to the upper absolute threshold. Moreover, negative correlations between color visibility ranking, kinetic illusion time, and effect were observed. Second, the combination of the black figure and white background in apparent movement resulted in the optimal kinetic illusion effect and apparent movement perception effect.

References

1. Chen, G.D.: The Study of Kinetic Art Dynamic Optical Illusion on Column with Spiral Pattern. National Taiwan University of Science and Technology, Taipei (2008)
2. Chen, G.D., Lin, C.W., Fan, H.W.: Motion perception on column of rotational dynamic illusion in kinetic art. J. Des. **20**(3), 1–19 (2015)
3. Chen, G.D., Lin, C.W., Fan, H.W.: The Study of Motion Perception On the Rotational Motion Illusion of Cone. J. Sci. Technol. **24**(1), 85–101 (2015)
4. Oyama, T., Imai, S., Wake, T.: New Sensory Perception Psychology Handbook. Seishin Shobo Ltd, Tokyo (2000)
5. Liu, Y.H.: The Research of Preference for Ratio of Geometry Shapes. National Yunlin University of Science and Technology, Yunlin (2010)

Summary on the Situation Awareness Requirement Analysis Method of Civil Aircraft Cockpit for the Flight Crew

Xianchao Ma, Xianxue Li[✉], and Tingying Song

Shanghai Aircraft Design and Research Institute, No. 5188 JinKe Road, PuDong New District, Shanghai 201210, China
lixianxue@comac.cc

Abstract. Flight crew's situation awareness is very important for them to fulfill the flight mission. In this paper, aspects that impact flight crew's situation awareness is introduced which include the pilot's psychology, physiology, knowledge and skill, attention distribution, and surrounding environment.

Keywords: Flight crew · Situation awareness · Civil aircraft

1 Introduction

Flight is a very complicated activity under the control of flight crew members. Flight crew's good situation awareness during fight especially under emergency or abnormal conditions can help deal with these problem and is the key to ensure flight safety.

In the subject of human factor, situation awareness is used to describe the level of understanding of the operator's environment. Situation awareness focuses on how to be fully acknowledged of what is happening and take correct actions to complete the tasks flight crew situation awareness refers to the sum of the elements that the flight crew need to know to complete the task.

2 Level of Situation Awareness

Situation awareness is divided into three levels: perception, understanding, and prediction. Good situation awareness can help the flight crew to fulfill these three work and any problems will make the flight crew lose good situation awareness. The flight crew need to know what has happened, what is happening and what will happen. The flight crew's situation awareness is directly related to flight safety, the higher the situation awareness, the safer the flight mission. So the cockpit shall be designed to supply enough situation awareness for the flight crew to help them make timely and correct actions flight crew's situation awareness can be effected by the following three aspects:

The first aspect is each flight crew member's personal situation awareness. Everyone's situation awareness is independent and also is part of the cockpit group situation awareness, it will make an impact on the group situation awareness.

© Springer Nature Switzerland AG 2021
C. Stephanidis et al. (Eds.): HCII 2021, CCIS 1419, pp. 133–136, 2021.
https://doi.org/10.1007/978-3-030-78635-9_19

The second aspect is the information exchange among the flight crew members and the level they understand each other. Information exchange is the basis of generating group situation awareness, and whether the flight crew members can accurately understand each other's intentions will directly determine whether a good group situation awareness can be established.

The third aspect is other factors that may make important effect on the situation awareness such as the captain's leadership arts or each pilot's character.

3 Influence Aspects

The above three aspects will effect the perception, understanding, and prediction of pilots from different angles. These aspects are influenced by the pilot's psychology, physiology, knowledge and skill, attention distribution, and surrounding environment.

(1) **Psychological situation.**
Conformity. In psychology, conformity refers to the phenomenon that individual ideas, cognition, and behavior are influenced by group pressure and tend to the majority opinion. When a flight instructor or pilot with much flight experience acts as a co-pilot, his/her opinion can affect the captain's behavior even though the opinion is not correct.
Bad emotions. Bad emotions such as complacency, impatience, paralysis, excessive tension, fear can easily decrease the pilot's ability of handling external information, thus adversely affecting the flight safety.

(2) **Physiological state.**
The pilots may perform the flight missions during different weather or special conditions which requires them keep in good health. If their vision, hearing, and other physical functions do not meet the flight requirements, it is impossible to accurately and quickly understand the situation during flight, nor can the pilot make the correct judgment and response, so that there will be a flight accident.

(3) **Knowledge skills.**
The knowledge structure of pilots is divided into flight theory knowledge and flight practice knowledge. Only by reserving enough knowledge, the pilot can deal with emergency situations when the situation changes.

(4) **Attention distribution.**
Attention distribution is to assign attention to different objects when two or more activities are carried out simultaneously. Attention distribution is a necessary condition to improve work efficiency. As a pilot, his attention may shift from external weather to crew instrumentation, to ATC, to other crew members or cabin crew. Of course, external factors, such as noise, lighting, vibration, odor, may also attract his attention. However, attention distribution is mainly driven by the thinking pattern in the situation at that time. If one does not prepared enough, he may miss out some key tips that lead to distraction and finally it will lead to a wrong understanding of the situation.

(5) **Surrounding environmental factors.**

The surrounding environmental factors refer to the external environment which is not affected by the personal psychological condition, such as the contents of the instrument display and the flight information collected by visual measurement, such as thunderstorms and ice. All the environment factors can affect the pilots' judgment and decision.

4   Situation Awareness Analysis Procedure

The general flight crew situation awareness analysis procedure is as Fig. 1.

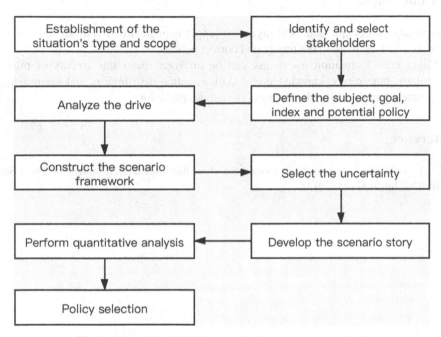

Fig. 1. Procedure of flight crew situation awareness analysis

The detail procedures are as follows:

1. Identify and select stakeholders: the stakeholders of flight mission are pilots, manufacturer and the airline company.
2. Define the subject, goal, index and potential policy: Different flight mission need be analyzed under different subject and goals, for example alerting information should be concerned when the flight crew alerting system is to be analyzed. The potential policy includes relative law and regulations.
3. Analyze the drive: drive from society, technology, economy, environment and politics need to be analyzed. Drive related to flight mission is mainly technology drive (technical capability of aircraft system design) and environment drive (weather during flight).

4. Select the uncertainty: analyze each drive, consider their uncertainty degree and the impact on the future.
5. Construct the scenario framework: construct the scenario framework based on the critical uncertainty such as flight environment, weather and the aircraft status.
6. Develop the scenario story: According to the flight phase, complete a detailed and convincing scenario description which can reflect the drive and uncertainty factors.
7. Perform quantitative analysis: Describe the scenario story based on quantitative information.
8. Policy selection: select relative policy and regulations.

5 Conclusions

In summary, the cockpit shall be designed to supply enough situation awareness for the flight crew to help them make timely and correct actions.

Flight crew's situation awareness can be analyzed from the aspects of pilot's psychology, physiology, knowledge and skill, attention distribution, and surrounding environment based on situation awareness analysis procedure.

Reference

1. Li, T.: Influence factors analysis about the cockpit flight situational awareness. China Sci. Technol. Inf. **9**, 47–48 (2012)

Pointedness of an Image: Measuring How Pointy an Image is Perceived

Chihaya Matsuhira[1]([✉]), Marc A. Kastner[2], Ichiro Ide[1,3],
Yasutomo Kawanishi[1], Takatsugu Hirayama[4], Keisuke Doman[5],
Daisuke Deguchi[1], and Hiroshi Murase[1]

[1] Graduate School of Informatics, Nagoya University, Nagoya, Aichi, Japan
matsuhirac@murase.is.i.nagoya-u.ac.jp,ddeguchi@nagoya-u.jp,
{ide,kawanishi,murase}@i.nagoya-u.ac.jp
[2] National Institute of Informatics, Tokyo, Japan
mkastner@nii.ac.jp
[3] Mathmatical and Data Science Center, Nagoya University, Nagoya, Aichi, Japan
[4] Institute of Innovation for Future Society, Nagoya University, Nagoya, Aichi, Japan
takatsugu.hirayamae@nagoya-u.jp
[5] School of Engineering, Chukyo University, Toyota, Aichi, Japan
kdoman@sist.chukyo-u.ac.jp

Abstract. For computers to understand human perception, metrics that can capture human perception well are important. However, there are few metrics that characterize the visual perception of humans towards images. Therefore, in this paper, we propose a novel concept and a metric of *pointedness* of an image, which describes how pointy an image is perceived. The algorithm is inspired by the Features from Accelerated Segment Test (FAST) algorithm for corner detection which looks on the number of continuous neighboring darker pixels surrounding each pixel. We assume that this number would be proportional to the perceived *pointedness* in the region around the pixel. We evaluated our method towards how well it could capture the human perception of images. To compare the method with similar metrics that describe shapes, we prepared silhouette images of both artificial shapes and natural objects. The results showed that the proposed method gave nearly equivalent perceptual performance to other metrics and also worked in a larger variety of images.

Keywords: Human perception · Pointedness · Measurement

1 Introduction

Understanding human perception by computers requires appropriate metrics that can capture human perception well. Despite this fact, there are few metrics that characterize the visual perception of images.

A psychological study [12] has suggested that our vision system uses shape information as one of the basic visual features. In this context, in this paper,

© Springer Nature Switzerland AG 2021
C. Stephanidis et al. (Eds.): HCII 2021, CCIS 1419, pp. 137–144, 2021.
https://doi.org/10.1007/978-3-030-78635-9_20

we introduce a novel concept and a metric of *pointedness* of an image, which we define as "How pointy an image is perceived by humans." For example, a photo of a pineapple would be intuitively perceived more pointy than that of an orange because we think of a pineapple as a more pointy, or thorny object than an orange. Thus, the *pointedness* of the former image should be higher than the latter.

There are several studies that have proposed metrics to measure the concepts of *circularity* [1,4], *roundness* [6], or *compactness* [2]. Since they are designed to describe shapes for use in applications like 3D editing, they do not necessarily match human perception well. Thus, we aim to solve this limitation and propose a metric designed to describe human perception foremost. Besides, these metrics measure those concepts only from binary images that basically contain one or several shapes.

In our proposed method to measure *pointedness*, we take advantage of a classical method of Features from the Accelerated Segment Test (FAST) corner detection algorithm [9], which first calculates a simple intensity comparison for each pixel in an image. While a single corner in an image may be perceived pointy, the algorithm does not calculate a *pointedness* score. Therefore, we extend the intensity comparison part of the FAST algorithm to calculate a feature map, and process it further to obtain a *pointedness* score for an image.

Our main contributions are:

- Introducing the concept of *pointedness* of an image which describes how pointy the image is perceived by humans.
- Developing a method to calculate the *pointedness* of an arbitrary gray-scale image.
- Performing a subjective analysis of visual perception of depicted shapes with regard to the *pointedness*.

2   Related Work

2.1   Human Perception Towards Shapes

Psychological studies delve into how the human visual system perceives the world around us. Prominently, Gestalt psychology [7] started research on shapes and visual perception. Following, a study by Treisman et al. [12] proposed a theory of visual attention suggesting that our vision focuses on several specific features including information of colors, orientations, and shapes at the preattentive stage of the recognition of an object. Furthermore, a recent study by Huang et al. [5] also proved that preattentive shape features can be explained by three basic dimensions of segmentability, compactness, and spikiness.

These studies suggest that how pointy or round a shape is plays an important role in our visual perception.

2.2   Metrics Describing Shapes

There are metrics related to our study, such as *circularity* [1,4], *roundness* [6], or *compactness* [2]. Strictly speaking, these three terms are defined as different

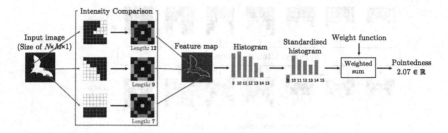

Fig. 1. Process flow of the proposed method. From an input image, we first calculate a feature map, where each pixel represents the number of continuous surrounding darker pixels. Next, we determine a histogram for the high intensity values. After standardizing the resulting histogram, we obtain the *pointedness* of an input image by calculating the weighted sum of the histogram.

concepts. However, they are often considered to represent the same concept in a 2D Euclidean space: "How close the shape is to a circle" [10]. Although those definitions are not unique and vary from paper to paper [10], the most common definition is

$$\text{Circularity} = \frac{4\pi\text{Area}}{\text{Perimeter}^2}, \tag{1}$$

where Area is the area and Perimeter is the perimeter of a target shape. This measurement ranges from 0 to 1, and equals 1 if and only if the shape is a circle.

Because of this definition, *circularity* is mostly designed to work on contours or silhouettes. Our proposed metric of *pointedness*, in contrast, is designed to work on gray-scale images in order to tackle this limitation.

2.3 FAST Algorithm

Features from Accelerated Segment Test (FAST) [9] is an algorithm used for corner detection. The core idea is a circle-wise intensity comparison. First, intensities of 16 circle-wise pixels around a target pixel p are compared with an intensity of p, and then each of the surrounding 16 pixels are classified by a threshold into three categories: darker, brighter, and similar. Next, the numbers of continuous darker/brighter pixels are counted respectively and the decision whether p is a corner or not is made according to those numbers.

3 Pointedness Calculation

In this paper, we propose a novel method that measures the introduced concept of *pointedness* from an input gray-scale image. We expect that foreground objects have high intensity and the background has low intensity. The process flow of the method is illustrated in Fig. 1.

First, we obtain a feature map from an input image, which describes the degree of *pointedness* for each pixel in an image. Here, we utilize the idea of

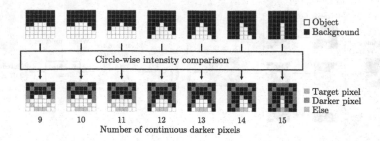

Fig. 2. Examples of regions with a large number of continuous darker pixels. This approximates the *pointedness* at the pixel.

a circle-wise intensity comparison in the FAST algorithm. In detail, for each neighboring pixel p_s surrounding a target pixel p, if the intensity of p_s is less than the intensity of p minus a threshold t, p_s is classified as a darker pixel. Then, we assume that the number of continuous darker pixels surrounding each pixel can be used for the calculation of a *pointedness* score for the region. For example, if the number of darker pixels is high, the shape around the point would be perceived pointy, while if it is low, it would be perceived less pointy. Examples of this idea are shown in Fig. 2. We obtain a feature map of which each pixel denotes the number of surrounding darker pixels at the point. A region around the pixel where the number of darker pixels is eight, has a flat contour, while one where the number of darker pixels is less than eight, has a dented contour. According to findings in psychological research [5], something is perceived pointy by humans if we expect a potential danger of grasping it. Therefore, in this study, we do not treat a dented contour as pointy, and we assume that only a value between nine and fifteen has influence on the *pointedness* of an image.

Next, by counting the values between nine and fifteen in the feature map, we obtain a histogram with seven bins. If x_n is defined as the occurrence of pixels with a value of n, the value of the n-th bin, y_n, is described as

$$y_n = \frac{x_n}{\sum_{n \in \{9,\ldots,15\}} x_n}. \tag{2}$$

Let Y_n be a random variable that represents the probability of y_n. We here assume Y_n to have a normal distribution denoted as $Y_n \sim \mathcal{N}(\mu_n, \sigma_n^2)$.

Then, in order to obtain a standardized normal distribution, we standardize Y_n for every n, obtaining a standardized histogram. Each bin of the histogram is described as a variable $\frac{Y_n - \hat{\mu}_n}{\hat{\sigma}_n}$, where $\hat{\mu}_n$ and $\hat{\sigma}_n$ are estimated values of μ_n and σ_n calculated as,

$$\hat{\mu}_n = \frac{1}{n} \sum_{i=1}^{m} y_{ni}, \quad \hat{\sigma}_n = \frac{\Gamma(\frac{n-1}{2})}{\Gamma(\frac{n}{2})} \sqrt{\frac{1}{2} \sum_{i=1}^{m} (y_{ni} - \hat{\mu}_n)^2}, \tag{3}$$

where y_{ni} is an observed value taken from Y_n of the i-th image and $\Gamma(x)$ is the gamma function.

(a) Experiment 1: Artificial shapes (b) Experiment 2: Natural shapes

Fig. 3. Datasets used in each of the experiments.

Lastly, because the relationship between the number of darker pixels and the *pointedness* is not necessarily linear, we calculate a weighted sum to obtain the *pointedness* score P for an image, formulated as

$$P = \sum_{n \in \{9,\ldots,15\}} \text{hist}(n)w(n) = \sum_{n \in \{9,\ldots,15\}} \left(\frac{y_n - \hat{\mu}_n}{\hat{\sigma}_n} \right) w(n), \tag{4}$$

where $\text{hist}(n)$ represents the frequency of the n-th bin of the standardized histogram, and w represents a manually designed weight function for each bin. The weight function should be a monotonically increasing function that maps an interval of $[9, 15]$ to $[0, 1]$. In this way, it can give a corresponding weight for each number of darker pixels.

The obtained score P is in the range of $(-\infty, +\infty)$, and this value is expected to be proportional to human perception towards *pointedness*. For the case where P should be finite, we can obtain the score in the range of $(0, 1)$ by applying a sigmoid function to P obtained by Eq. 4 that is defined as

$$\text{sigmoid}(x) = \frac{1}{1 + e^{-x}}. \tag{5}$$

4 Evaluations on Binary Images of Shapes

We conducted two subjective experiments to evaluate how well the proposed method can capture the human perception towards the proposed concept of *pointedness*. Although our method can be applied to arbitrary gray-scale images, we chose binary images in these experiments for the comparison with the related metric of *circularity* [10]. Each experiment used 12 images of 128×128 pixels which are shown in Fig. 3. In the first experiment, we prepared binary images each of which contains an artificial shape. These shapes were created by distorting radial frequency patterns [13], which are defined by deformations of circles through sinusoidal modulation of the radius in polar coordinates. In the second experiment, we selected silhouette images of more natural objects from the MPEG-7 Core Experiment CE Shape 1 Dataset [8]. We separated the experiments in this way because we assumed that the human responses to those images might differ depending on whether the images were familiar or unfamiliar to them.

Table 1. Subjective evaluation of two experiments. Each entry shows the Pearson's correlation between the scores determined by the metric and the scale obtained in a user study.

Type	Method	Weighting	Experiment 1 (Full dataset)	Experiment 2 (Full dataset)	(w/o Lizard)
Comparative	$-$Circularity	—	0.859	0.632	0.514
	Circularity^{-1}	—	**0.919**	**0.772**	0.494
Proposed	Pointedness w/o sigmoid	$a = 0.5$	0.844	0.627	0.611
		$a = 1.0$	0.830	0.651	0.586
		$a = 2.0$	0.782	0.683	0.542
	Pointedness w/ sigmoid	$a = 0.5$	**0.919**	0.673	**0.639**
		$a = 1.0$	0.904	0.664	0.596
		$a = 2.0$	0.853	0.664	0.541

In both experiments, the same eight Japanese participants in their twenties conducted the survey. We showed the participants a randomly selected pair of images. Then, we asked them to choose intuitively which image looked more pointy. No more instruction was given in the process. After the participants answered for all the $_{12}C_2 = 66$ pairs of images, we obtained the ground truth scales in the range of $[0,1]$ by applying Thurstone's paired comparison method [11] to the $_{12}C_2 \times 8 = 528$ answers.

The results of the two experiments are shown in Table 1. As a metric, we measured Pearson's correlation between the ground truth scale and the calculated *pointedness*. As a weight function for the calculation of *pointedness*, we prepared a simple function with a hyper-parameter a, which is defined as

$$w_a(n) = \left(\frac{n-8}{7}\right)^a \quad (9 \le n \le 15). \tag{6}$$

As comparative methods, we used a *circularity* measurement defined by Eq. 1. Since this measurement is thought to measure the opposite concept of our *pointedness*, we calculated $-$Circularity and Circularity^{-1} instead.

We can observe that the proposed method gives nearly equivalent correlations to *circularity* in both of the experiments. However, the correlation 0.772 given by the inverse of *circularity* in the second experiment appears surprisingly large. To analyze this, we plotted the calculated *pointednesses* and the inverse of *circularity* values in Fig. 4. Here, we used the sigmoid function and the weight function with $a = 0.5$ for the calculation of *pointedness*. From this, we found that the image of "lizard" had a strong impact on the calculation of the correlation in the second experiment because its ground truth was much higher than the others. Therefore, we performed the second experiment without using the "lizard" image, where the results were closer to the expected correlations. From these, we recognized one limitation of our method that the calculated *pointedness* mainly focuses on some specific pointy points in an image, not the whole shape as we humans do, resulting in few differences among relatively pointy images (e.g. "chicken", "bat", and "lizard").

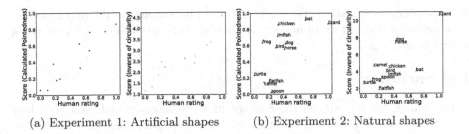

(a) Experiment 1: Artificial shapes   (b) Experiment 2: Natural shapes

Fig. 4. Scatterplot of the calculated *pointednesses* (left) and inverse of *circularity* values (right) for images used in each of the experiments.

Low pointedness   High pointedness

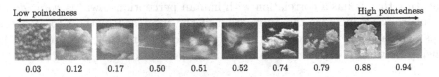

0.03   0.12   0.17   0.50   0.51   0.52   0.74   0.79   0.88   0.94

Fig. 5. Example of cloud images and their *pointednesses* calculated by our method.

5 Application to More General Images

Pointedness can be measured from arbitrary gray-scale images with our method. Therefore, we applied our method to several images of clouds since those images seemed to suit our method well. We selected 10 images from Flickr[1], which captured one or more clouds clearly in the center of the images. Then, we sorted those images according to our *pointedness* metric.

The result is shown in Fig. 5. Here, we set the threshold $t = 10$, a relatively low value, so that our method can consider the texture patterns of the surface of the clouds for the *pointedness* calculation. We then calculated gray-scale images and resized them to 512×512 pixels. Here, we chose a weight function with $a = 0.5$.

From Fig. 5, we confirmed that the broad tendency of the calculated *pointednesses* matches our perception, although the order and the rating might vary from person to person.

The application to arbitrary images is a very difficult task. We recognize that our current method mainly focuses on contours of shapes in an image and thus in the next step, we need to consider pointy features of objects which do not appear as contour information. However, the subjective evaluation conducted in Sect. 4 showed that our proposed method could capture *pointedness* reasonably well. Furthermore, our method could also measure *pointedness* of a sub-region of an image by applying a mask to a feature map.

Our method is designed to capture human perception. Thus, the main application of our method is to investigate and analyze psychological phenomena around human vision such as sound symbolism [7] and synesthesia [3] based

---

[1] https://www.flickr.com/.

on data-mining approaches. Quantifying those phenomena would give meaningful insights for computers to understand human perception in vision-processing related tasks.

6 Conclusion

In this paper, we introduced the concept of *pointedness*, which describes how pointy an image is perceived by humans. Moreover, we proposed a method to measure the *pointedness* from an arbitrary gray-scale image. We conducted two experiments to investigate how well our method can capture human perception towards binary images, and confirmed that our method gives a high correlation, indicating that it has a correlation with human perception towards *pointedness*.

Future work includes the application of the proposed method to attention maps generated by deep learning models in order to further analyze the relationship between computer vision and human perception.

Acknowledgements. This work was partly supported by MEXT grant-in-aid for Scientific Research (16H02846), Microsoft Research CORE-16 program, and a joint research project with NII, Japan.

References

1. Bottema, M.J.: Circularity of objects in images. In: Proceedings of the 2000 IEEE International Conference on Acoustics, Speech, and Signal Processing, vol. 4, pp. 2247–2250 (2000)
2. Bribiesca, E.: Measuring 2-D shape compactness using the contact perimeter. Comput. & Math. App. **33**(11), 1–9 (1997)
3. Cytowic, R.E.: The Man Who Tasted Shapes. MIT Press, Cambridge, MA, USA (1998)
4. Haralick, R.: A measure for circularity of digital figures. IEEE Trans. Sys., Man, Cybern. **4**, 394–396 (1974)
5. Huang, L.: Space of preattentive shape features. J. Vis. **20**(4), 10 (2020)
6. Jain, A.K.: Fundamentals of Digital Image Processing. Prentice-Hall, Upper Saddle River, NJ, USA (1989)
7. Köhler, W.: Gestalt Psychology. H. Liveright, New York, NY, USA (1929)
8. Latecki, L.J., Lakamper, R., Eckhardt, T.: Shape descriptors for non-rigid shapes with a single closed contour. In: Proceedings of the 2000 IEEE International Conference on Computer Vision and Pattern Recognition, vol. 1, pp. 424–429 (2000)
9. Rosten, Ed, Drummond, T.: Machine learning for high-speed corner detection. In: Leonardis, A., Bischof, H., Pinz, A. (eds.) ECCV 2006. LNCS, vol. 3951, pp. 430–443. Springer, Heidelberg (2006). https://doi.org/10.1007/11744023_34
10. Santiago-Montero, R., Bribiesca, E., Santiago, R.: State of the art of compactness and circularity measures. Int. Math. Forum **4**, 1305–1335 (2009)
11. Thurstone, L.L.: The method of paired comparisons for social values. J. Abnorm. Psychol. **21**(4), 384–400 (1927)
12. Treisman, A.M., Gelade, G.: A feature-integration theory of attention. Cognit. Psychol. **12**(1), 97–136 (1980)
13. Wilkinson, F., Wilson, H.R., Habak, C.: Detection and recognition of radial frequency patterns. Vis. Res. **38**(22), 3555–3568 (1998)

Modulation of Olfactory Perception by Presenting Heat Sensation: Effects of Different Methods on Degree of Olfactory Perception Modulation

Yoshihiro Okamoto$^{(\boxtimes)}$ ⓘ, Haruka Matsukura ⓘ, and Kosuke Sato ⓘ

Osaka University, Osaka 5608531, Japan
okamoto@sens.sys.es.osaka-u.ac.jp,
{haruka.matsu,sato}@sys.es.osaka-u.ac.jp

Abstract. Olfaction is notorious as a vague and ambiguous sense. Some researches proposed a method that takes advantage of the feature to present more kinds of odors than the actual number of fragrances. However, it is still unclear what kind of factors affect the optimization of olfactory modulation. This paper investigated the effect of differences in methods to present heat sensation including presentation setups, areas, and positions of heat sensation. The heat sensation is stimulated by air flow and metal contact with a fan heater or a Peltier device. The heat sensation is presented to either apex of nose, philtrum, left cheek, or right cheek. In the experiment, the subjects were instructed to answer the scores to the odor of R-(+)-limonene and the odorless air presented with heat sensation compared to the odor impressions at room temperature by Likert scale questionnaire for the 8 adjective pairs. The experimental results suggested that the perceived odor impressions of R-(+)-limonene differed strongly depending on the presentation methods other than the presented temperature and humidity. In particular, presenting in a large area around the nose are considered more capable of modulating odor perception than the other methods.

Keywords: Olfaction · Heat sensation · Perceptual modulation

1 Introduction

Scents can be used to reduce stress and stabilize the mind [1]. It is also possible to enhance the sense of presence and immersion during the virtual reality (VR) experience [2] by presenting scents in conjunction with visual and audio information. The devices to present scents in VR systems are called olfactory displays. There are some researches in which methods to present more kinds of odors than the originally prepared elemental fragrances by mixing them in different rations

This work was supported by JSPS KAKENHI Grant Number 19K14947.

were proposed [3,4]. However, a set of primary odors which can produce arbitrary odors has not yet established in olfaction, while the three primary colors are identified in vision. In order to present a wide variety of odors, it is necessary to prepare a large number of fragrances in advance. There are some olfactory displays [5,6], which can hold only several kinds of odor cartridge in them. That leads to increasing in the size of olfactory displays.

Olfaction is notorious as a vague and ambiguous sense [7,8]. A research proposed a method that takes advantage of the feature to present more kinds of odors than the actual number of fragrances set in an olfactory display [9]. It has also been reported that olfaction is affected by temperature and humidity [10]. In our previous work [11] exploring other modalities to modulate olfactory perception, we reported a device that presents temperature and humidity-controlled air to a small region onto the user's face in conjunction with odor. The experimental results suggested that olfactory perception can be modulated only by controlling temperature and humidity on a small region of user's face. Nevertheless, the area and position to present thermal and humidity sensation were not investigated. In other words, it is unclear what kind of factors affects the optimization of modulation of olfactory perception. In this paper, we investigates how olfactory perception is affected by difference in methods to present heat sensation, including presentation setups, areas, and positions of heat sensation (Fig. 1).

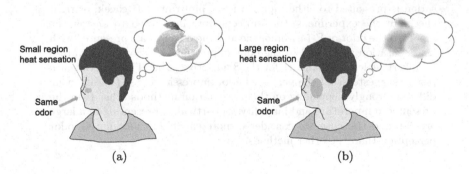

Small region
heat sensation

Same
odor

Large region
heat sensation

Same
odor

(a)   (b)

Fig. 1. Modulation of odor impressions by heat sensation. (a) To present heat sensation to a small region. (b) To present heat sensation to a large region.

2   Experimental Setups

We built two types of experimental setups that can adjust the area and position of heat sensation presentation. One is the setup using a fan heater (hereinafter called "FH setup"), and the other is the setup using a Peltier device (hereinafter called "PD setup"). FH setup is shown in Fig. 2. FH setup consists of a blower fan (San Ace B97 9BMB24P2K01, SANYO DENKI), a heater (HMA400F-1,

ORIENTAL MOTOR), a wind mask, and a tube for odor presentation. The wind mask is made of a A4 cardboard punched with a hole. Warm air is generated by passing the air blowing from the fan outlet through the heater. The warm air is presented to a limited area onto the subject's face by letting the air pass through the hole of the wind mask. By changing the diameter of the hole, the area of heat sensation is changed. The odor presentation tube is made of a silicone rubber. The subject sniffs an odor by bringing the tip of the tube close to the nose with the hand.

Figure 3 shows PD setup. It consists of an aluminum block, a Peltier device (TEC1-12706), and a tube for odor presentation. The Peltier device is of size 40×40 mm and is bonded to a face of the aluminum block with thermally conductive glue. The temperature of the Peltier device is controlled by referring to the value of a temperature sensor attached to the aluminum block's surface. In order to compare the heat sensation, the subject puts an instructed region of the face onto the opposite face of the aluminium block to the face on which the Peltier device was attached.

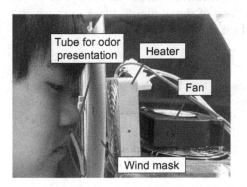

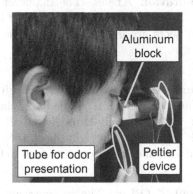

Fig. 2. Presentation setup to present heat sensation with a fan heater (FH setup)

Fig. 3. Presentation setup to present heat sensation with a Peltier device (PD setup)

3   Human Subject Experiments

We conducted human subject experiments to investigate the effects of difference in the methods to present heat sensation on the odor's impressions. In this experiment, the difference of the presentation setups, the presentation areas, and the presentation positions was compared. The subjects were 5 male university students (the age range is 21 to 25 years old).

3.1 Conditions

In this experiments, there were 16 different ways to present heat sensation: combinations of two types of presentation setups, two types of presentation areas (Fig. 4(a)), and four types of presentation positions (Fig. 4(b)). Also, odorless air and air containing limonene vapor were presented to the subjects.

Setups. FH setup and PD setup were used as the presenting setup conditions. For each FD and PD setup, two systems with the same configuration were prepared at the same time. One of the two system was temperature-controlled, and the other system was not. The system with temperature control presented heat sensation at 37.0 °C, and the system without temperature control presented at the room temperature (20.7 °C).The subjects were asked to compare the odor impressions of the systems with and without temperature control by moving their head by turns.

Presentation Areas. The diameter of presentation areas in FH setup were either 10 mm or 20 mm. Each side of the face of the alminum block onto which the subjects are instructed to put their face in order to feel was either 10 mm or 20 mm.

Presentation Positions. The positions of the heat sensation presentation were at four different positions on the face: the apex of the nose (hereinafter called "AN"), the philtrum (hereinafter called "P"), the left cheek (hereinafter called "LC") and the right cheek (hereinafter called "RC"). The subjects were instructed which position were used to feel the heat sensation in each experiment.

Presented Odor. The presentation odor were generated by passing the air into liquid of (R)-(+)-limonene (hereinafter called "limonene"). Limonene is a chemical found in citrus fruits and is widely used as air freshener fragrance. For purpose of comparison, experiments using odorless air were also conducted. The odorless air means the air in the experimental room that was not subjected to any particular manipulation.

3.2 Procedures

The subjects were presented with the heat sensation by the system without temperature control and then presented heat sensation by the device with temperature control. Then, the subjects answered the odor impressions perceived by the device with temperature control based on the odor impressions perceived by the device without temperature control. The subjects answered on 7-point Likert scale questionnaire from −3 to 3 for the 8 adjective pairs shown in Table 1.

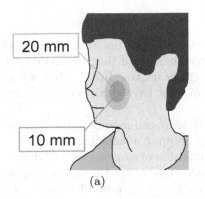 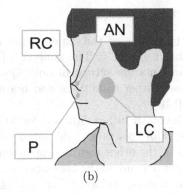

(a)   (b)

Fig. 4. Conditions of the presentation of heat sensation. (a) The example of presentation areas. A small circle means presenting heat sensation to 10 mm, and a large circle means to present heat sensation to 20 mm. (b) The positions of the presentation of heat sensation. "AN" means the apex of nose, "P" means the philtrim, "LC" means the left cheek, and "RC" means the right cheek.

Table 1. Likert scale questionnaire used in the experiments. The subjects were instructed to answer scores to the impression of the odor presented with temperature control compared to the odor presentation without temperature control.

Questions			
Q1.	Clear (-3)–Vague (3)	Q5.	Heavy (-3)–Light (3)
Q2.	Clean (-3)–Dirty (3)	Q6.	Relaxing (-3)–Stimulating (3)
Q3.	Sober (-3)–Flashy (3)	Q7.	Simple (-3)–Complex (3)
Q4.	Fresh (-3)–Old (3)	Q8.	Weak (-3)–Strong (3)

The subjects were allowed to sniff the odor as long as they wanted. To control the order effect, we adjusted the orders of the heat sensation (with and without temperature control), presentation areas (10 mm and 20 mm), presentation positions (AN, P, LC and RC) and air (with and without odor) presented to each subject. However, all the experiments using FH setup were conducted before those using PD setup in this time.

4   Results and Discussions

For the results of odorless air and air including limonene vapor, three-way ANOVA with presentation setups, presentation areas, and presentation positions as factors was conducted. Also, Bonferroni's multiple comparison test was applied to compare the presentation positions for the results that showed significant difference or significant trend.

4.1 Odorless Air

For the results of the experiments using odorless air, one of each main effect
are shown in Fig. 5. The analysis of the results showed that the main effect of
the presentation setups in only Q8 had significant trend($p < 0.10$), while the
effects of other conditions and questions did not have statistically significance
($p > 0.10$).

The result in Fig. 5(a) suggests that FH setup can modulate the impressions
of the odor to weaker, compared with PD setup. No significant difference was
found in the other results, suggesting modulation of impressions of odorless air
does not depend on the presentation methods. In addition, the averages of almost
all the results, including Fig. 5(b) and Fig. 5(c), were around zero, suggesting
that the impressions of odorless air does not change significantly when higher
temperature is presented onto the face.

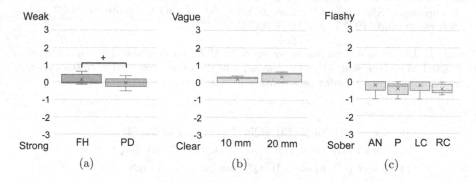

Fig. 5. Some results of experiments using odorless air ($+$:$p < 0.10$). (a) Comparison of presentation setups. (b) Comparison of presentation areas. (c) Comparison of
presentation positions.

4.2 Air Including Limonene Vapor

For the results of the experiments using limonene, the all results of the main
effects and interactions which are found to be significance ($p < 0.05$) or significant trend ($p < 0.10$) are shown in Fig. 6.

Figures 6(a), 6(b) and 6(c) suggest that the odor impression can be modulated depending on the presentation setups. Also, it suggests that PD setup can
give dirtier and heavier impressions than FH setup. In particular, for Fig. 6(a),
the average of PD setup is shifted to one (Likert scale), while the average of FH
setup is close to zero, suggesting that the PD can modulate the odor impressions
more than FH setup.

Figures 6(d) and 6(e) suggest that the odor impressions are modulated
depending on the presentation areas. In particular, for Fig. 6(d), the average
of 20 mm is above zero, while the average of 10 mm is almost zero. Therefore, it

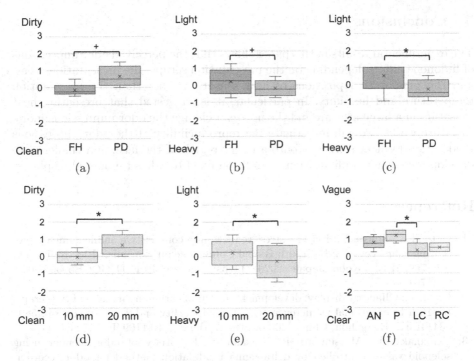

Fig. 6. Some results of experiments using limonene (*:$p < 0.05$, +:$p < 0.10$). (a) Comparison of presentation setups when hole diameter of wind mask and each side of the block face were 20 mm. (b) Comparison of presentation setups when hole diameter of wind mask and each side of the block face were 10 mm. (c) Comparison of presentation setups when heat sensation was presented to AN. (d) Comparison of presentation areas when PD setup was used. (e) Comparison of presentation areas when FH setup was used. (f) Comparison of presentation positions.

suggests that the larger the presentation area is, the more the odor perception can be modulated.

Figure 6(f) suggests that the odor impression were modulated depending on the presentation positions. Also, it suggests that P can give a vaguer impression than LC. In particular, the average of the nose area (AN and P) is above zero, while the average of the cheek area (LC and RC) is around zero. Therefore, it suggests that the presentation around the nose can modulate the odor impressions more than the presentation around the cheek.

In other words, it is suggested that presenting heat sensation in a large area around the nose with PD setup can modulate the odor impressions the most among the other conditions used in this experiments. For the odor of limonene, the impression can be modulated to vaguer and dirtier with the above conditions compared with the room temperature.

5   Conclusions

The experimental results in this paper shows that the perceived odor impressions of limonene differs depending on the presentation setups, the presentation areas, and the presentation positions of heat sensation other than the presentation temperature and humidity. In particular, it is suggested that presenting heat sensation in a large area around the nose can change the odor impressions more. In future works, we will investigate the reproducibility of the odor impressions modulation by heat sensation onto a larger region of the face, and challenge to develop a compact configuration so as to be fixed to a head mounted display.

References

1. Goto, T., Shibuya, Y.: Player's stress reduction in competitive online game by presenting calm scent. In: IEEE 9th Global Conference on Consumer Electronics, pp. 756–760. IEEE, Kobe, Japan (2020). https://doi.org/10.1109/GCCE50665.2020.9291764
2. Chen, Y.: Olfactory display: development and application in virtual reality therapy. In: 16th International Conference on Artificial Reality and Telexistence, pp. 580–584. IEEE, Hangzhou, China (2006). https://doi.org/10.1109/ICAT.2006.95
3. Yamanaka, T., Matsumoto, R., Nakamoto, T.: Study of odor blender using solenoid valves controlled by delta-sigma modulation method for odor recorder. Sens. Actuators, B Chem. **87**(3), 457–463 (2002). https://doi.org/10.1016/S0925-4005(02)00300-3
4. Nakamoto, T., Minh, H. P. D.: Improvement of olfactory display using solenoid valves. In: IEEE Virtual Reality Conference, pp. 179–186 (2007). https://doi.org/10.1109/VR.2007.352479
5. Aroma Shooter. https://aromajoin.com/products/aroma-shooter. Accessed 16 March 2021
6. VAQSO VR. https://vaqso.com. Accessed 16 March 2021
7. Cain, W.S.: To know with the nose: Keys to odor identification. Science **203**(4379), 467–470 (1979). https://doi.org/10.1126/science.760202
8. Morrot, G., Brochet, F., Dubourdieu, D.: The color of odors. Brain Lang. **79**(2), 309–320 (2001). https://doi.org/10.1006/brln.2001.2493
9. Numbu, A., Narumi, T., Nishimura, K., Tanikawa, T., Hirose, M.: Visual-olfactory display sensory map. In: IEEE Virtual Reality Conference, pp. 39–42. IEEE, Boston, MA, USA (2010). https://doi.org/10.1109/VR.2010.5444817
10. Kuehn, M., Welsch, H., Zahnert, T., Hummel, T.: Changes of pressure and humidity affect olfactory function. Eur. Arch. Otorhinolaryngol. **265**, 299–302 (2008). https://doi.org/10.1007/s00405-007-0446-2
11. Fujino, Y. Matsukura, H., Iwai, D., Sato, K.: Odor modulation by warming/cooling nose based on cross-modal effect. In: IEEE Conference on Virtual Reality and 3D User Interfaces, pp. 929–930. IEEE, Osaka, Japan (2019). https://doi.org/10.1109/VR.2019.8797727

Exploring People's Hue Ranking Ability Across the Color Ring: Taking the Categorization Effect into Consideration

Han Qiao[1,2], Jingyu Zhang[1,2(✉)], and Mengdi Liu[3]

[1] Institute of Psychology, Chinese Academy of Sciences, Beijing, China
zhangjingyu@psych.ac.cn
[2] Department of Psychology, University of Chinese Academy of Sciences, Beijing, China
[3] Consumer BG Software Human Factor Research and UX Innovation Department, Huawei Device Co. Ltd, Shenzhen, China

Abstract. HCI specialists are fully aware that effective use of color can enhance interaction design. Therefore a precise mapping between colors' physical attributes and human perception is needed. Whereas the CIELch color space is a useful mapping, we sought to examine whether the existence of the category perception effect suggested some further amendment should be made. We used the paradigm adapted from the Portal color sort test (PCST) and recruited 101 undergraduate students to test our hypothesis. We found that participants' ability to order the hue correctly increased as color categories increased. Future research should consider the color categorization effect in color space modeling. Practitioners should consider this categorization effect when choosing hues to represent order.

Keywords: Uniform color space · Category effect · Interface design

1 Introduction

HCI specialists are fully aware that effective use of color can enhance interaction design. Color is used to call attention to items, signal users, and improve display aesthetics. Using color effectively and tastefully is often beyond the scientific community's abilities, application programmers and the wider public [1, 2]. A precise mapping between colors' physical attributes and human perception is needed not only for the convenience of designers and ordinary users but also for understanding the link between the physical world and the psychological world.

1.1 Color Categorization

In everyday life, we do not communicate colors in hue, lightness and saturation. Instead, we use the color term to indicate an extensive range of different colors. The typical color terms are black, white, gray, pink, red, orange, yellow, green, blue, purple, and brown, but the terms are different across languages. Here, we focus on the effects of color categorization on color perception.

C. Stephanidis et al. (Eds.): HCII 2021, CCIS 1419, pp. 153–157, 2021.
https://doi.org/10.1007/978-3-030-78635-9_22

1.2 Category Effects on Color Perception

Color vision has long been the prime example of categorical perception [6]. According to the idea of categorical perception, pairs of otherwise equidistant colors are perceived as more different when they belong to two different categories than when they belong to the same category. Such effects on the perception of color difference that are specific to categories are called category effects. Category effects can be observed through reaction time difference of judging whether given paired colors are from the same or different categories. Daoutis, Pilling, and Davies [7] also confirmed such effects through 3 color search experiments. Results showed that when the target and distractors fell within the same category, the search was difficult. When they fell within three distinct categories, response times and search slopes were significantly reduced. Recently, Witzel and Gegenfurtner [8] further investigated categorical facilitation, measured response time and error rates, controlling sensitivity by using colors that were equally discriminable according to empirically measured thresholds. Robust categorical facilitation occurred for pink, orange, yellow, green and purple.

1.3 Uniform Color Space

A lot of work has been done here to develop perceptually uniform color space [3–5, 9], such as CIELAB, NCS, but till now, no color space is perfectly matched with human perception, especially for perceived hue compared with two other attributes, saturation and lightness. For instance, for CIELAB, the cyan-blue to the blue-purple region is the least uniform, whereas, for Nayatani's space, the red region shows the least uniformity. Two reasons may mainly cause the difficulty to build up hue-based uniform color space. One reason is that hue varies from saturation and lightness [3]. The other reason is that the category perception effect [6–8, 10] suggests some further amendments should be made. Still, few studies have thoroughly investigated this effect on existed color models.

In this study, we sought to examine whether the ability to order the hue correctly holds constant across the color ring or increases as color categories increases.

2 Method

2.1 Participants

One hundred and four Chinese undergraduate students participated in this study. Their mean age was 21.5($SD = 2.3$), ranging from 18 to 29. 40.4% were male.

2.2 Experiment Design

We used the paradigm adapted from the Portal color sort test (PCST) [11], which is a simple test used for clinical testing color sensitivity. In this study, we intended to utilize this paradigm to measure whether participants' color ranking ability was constant across when the number of color categories was different. We conducted a within-subject design. The independent variable was the number of categories, and the dependent variable was the ranking error score. We controlled the lightness, chroma of all the colors, the physical distance of colors both within categories and between categories, and the lightness, chroma, hue of background color.

2.3 Experiment Stimuli

All the colors we chose from the CIE LCh color space, which is known as a uniform color space. We set the background color to Lightness 100, Chroma 0, Hue 153, and also controlled the Lightness 60, Chroma 80 of all the colors we used. There were four color sets from the color ring (0–90, 90–180,180–270, 270–360). Each color set consisted of eleven hues spaced 10° apart, in which the two ends were fixed while the remaining nine hues were presented in random order. Whereas color set 270–360 contains three color categories (pink, purple and blue), the other color sets only contain two color categories. Each color set was in one interface, and four color sets would appear randomly (Fig. 1). We designed an application to achieve the whole procedure and used a mobile phone to perform our experiment.

2.4 Procedure

Participants first read and signed a written informed consent form. Then they were introduced instructions of the experiment and performed one practice to familiarize the operations of the experiment. After that, they started the formal experiment. They should move the position of nine hues to match the chromatographic order of four color sets one by one as soon as possible. Participants' ranking results were logged automatically through our application, and the error score of each color set was also calculated for each participant based on the methods from Melamud, Simpson, & Traboulsi [11].

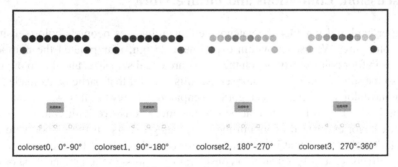

Fig. 1. Experimental stimulus interface across four color sets

3 Results

We removed three participants' data from the analysis because their ranking scores were over three standard deviations above the average.

The results of repeated measures analysis of variance (ANOVA) showed that the sorting error scores were significantly different across the four color sets, $F(2.49, 249.29)$ = 4.13, p = .011, η^2 = .040. Post-hoc analysis showed that the errors made in color set 270–360 (M = 15.17, SE = .39) were significantly less than that of color set 90–180 (M = 17.37, SE = .68) and 180–270 (M = 17.54, SE = .52), which proved our hypothesis that people were more able to rank the hue according to the chromatographic order. It suggested that people were more sensitive to inter-category differences than intra-category differences (Fig. 2).

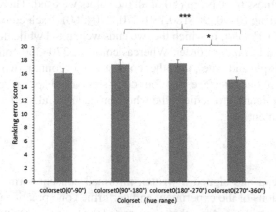

Fig. 2. Experimental results of repeated measures analysis of variance (Note: * p < 0.5, *** p < .001)

4   Discussion, Limitations and Future Work

This paper explored whether the category effect influences people's color sensitivity on the color ring. We used a within experiment design, manipulated the number of categories in four color sets of which the colors are equal step size, and the color counts were also the same within each color set. Results showed that participants made fewer errors in the color set with more categories compared with fewer ones, which confirmed our hypothesis. The is because that people are more sensitive with colors belong to different categories instead of within the same category. As all the colors were from the CIELCh color space that is known as a uniform color space, it is indicated that the category effects should be taken into consideration, and some amendments should be made towards uniform modeling.

There are some limitations that should be mentioned here. First, we only chose the color ring from the specific saturation and lightness; whether the results could be extended to other saturation and lightness needs further experiments. Second, as color categories are impacted by languages and culture [12], whether the results could be generalized to other culture and language using district also call for further experiments.

Future researchers could explore this study's generalization across different tasks and more colors with other saturation and lightness. Researchers in the field of building metrics of color space might take the color categorization effect into account. Practitioners should also pay attention to this effect when choosing hues to represent order.

References

1. Meier, B.J.: ACE: a color expert system for user interface design. In: Proceedings of the 1st Annual ACM SIGGRAPH Symposium on User Interface Software, pp. 117–128, January 1988
2. Crameri, F., Shephard, G.E., Heron, P.J.: The misuse of color in science communication. Nat. Commun. **11**, 5444 (2020). https://doi.org/10.1038/s41467-020-19160-7
3. Ebner, F., Fairchild, M.D.: Finding constant hue surfaces in color space. In: Color Imaging: Device-Independent Color, Color Hardcopy, and Graphic Arts III, vol. 3300, pp. 107–117. International Society for Optics and Photonics, January 1998
4. Kalvin, A.D., Rogowitz, B.E., Pelah, A., Cohen, A.: Building perceptual color maps for visualizing interval data. In: Human Vision and Electronic Imaging V, vol. 3959, pp. 323–335. International Society for Optics and Photonics, June 2000
5. Safdar, M., Cui, G., Kim, Y.J., Luo, M.R.: Perceptually uniform color space for image signals including high dynamic range and wide gamut. Opt. Express **25**(13), 15131–15151 (2017)
6. Bornstein, M.H., Korda, N.O.: Discrimination and matching within and between hues measured by reaction times: some implications for categorical perception and levels of information processing. Psychol. Res. **46**(3), 207–222 (1984)
7. Daoutis, C.A., Pilling, M., Davies, I.R.: Categorical effects in visual search for color. Vis. Cogn. **14**(2), 217–240 (2006)
8. Witzel, C., Gegenfurtner, K.R.: Categorical facilitation with equally discriminable colors. J. Vis. **15**(8), 22 (2015)
9. Gravesen, J.: The metric of color space. Gr. Models **82**, 77–86 (2015)
10. Maule, J., Witzel, C., Franklin, A.: Getting the gist of multiple hues: metric and categorical effects on ensemble perception of hue. JOSA A **31**(4), A93–A102 (2014)
11. Melamud, A., Simpson, E., Traboulsi, E.I.: Introducing a new computer-based test for the clinical evaluation of color discrimination. Am. J. Ophthalmol. **142**(6), 953–960 (2006)
12. Regier, T., Kay, P.: Language, thought, and color: whorf was half right. Trends Cogn. Sci. **13**(10), 439–446 (2009)

Effectiveness of Self-customized Refresher and Just-In-Time-Training for Mechanical Repair Task Performance

Christopher Stevens⊙, John Karasinski⁽✉⁾⊙, Kimberly Jenks⊙,
Sarah O'Meara⊙, Savannah Buchner⊙, Tanisha Potnis, Ryan Rocha,
and Stephen Robinson

University of California, Davis, Davis, CA 95616, USA
karasinski@ucdavis.edu

Abstract. Future space exploration missions are expected to increase in duration with timelines as long as three years. Applying the current training paradigm to support longer duration missions reveals a substantial skill decay risk and an untenable training to mission ratio. The aim of this research is to address these issues by investigating customized interventions applied immediately before task execution for both previously trained and novel tasks. For previously trained tasks, we investigated the efficacy of self-made refresher videos, which are customized by the individual, versus the standard practice of simply reviewing task procedures. For novel tasks, we investigated the efficacy of customizable procedures versus standard procedures when used for just-in-time training. Two experiments were performed investigating the effectiveness of these interventions. The results were not statistically significant, but they suggest that there may be benefits to the interventions. Further research is required to quantify the results of the customizations and provide recommendations for training practices more accurately.

Keywords: Human performance · Procedures · Refresher training

1 Introduction

Future space exploration missions are expected to increase in duration with timelines stretching up to three years. Currently, astronauts train on the ground for up to 18 months prior to embarking on a six-month mission aboard the International Space Station (ISS) [1]. This training paradigm can result in skill decay due to the elapsed time between training on the ground and application onboard the ISS. To mitigate skill decay, procedures are reviewed onboard the ISS prior to attempting significant tasks [9]. However, this paradigm poses two significant challenges for long duration missions: 1) the ratio for ground preparation to flight time is not sustainable, and 2) increased elapsed time since ground training will

© Springer Nature Switzerland AG 2021
C. Stephanidis et al. (Eds.): HCII 2021, CCIS 1419, pp. 158–165, 2021.
https://doi.org/10.1007/978-3-030-78635-9_23

likely result in greater skill decay. Astronauts on long-duration missions are certain to be faced with critical and complex tasks for which they either have not recently trained or have never been trained to complete [4]. In addition, in-flight crew hours are among the most precious of resources in human spaceflight, so onboard training efficiency is of prime importance. The field of training research is extensive but is less mature for the unique environment of microgravity and high-risk nature of human spaceflight [14].

Highly skilled occupations, such as aviation, medicine, and spaceflight, require extensive training to perform complex, critical tasks. Over time, the efficacy of the training decreases as learners begin to forget their early training and their learned skills decay [15]. Post-training skill decay for complex systems has been extensively investigated, and research has shown that deviations from established procedures can have catastrophic consequences [16]. Skill decay may be mitigated by implementing refresher training (i.e., training that reviews a previously learned skill). Nishiyama et al. found that a 15-minute refresher CPR course positively affected the skills evaluation one year after the initial training [10]. For untrained, critical tasks, training immediately prior to execution, also called just-in-time training (JITT), may be necessary. JITT refers to preparing an astronaut to conduct complex and critical tasks during a mission, usually only hours or minutes before the task must be conducted. This can be especially relevant in long duration missions, where there may be no onboard expert, real-time communication with mission control is unavailable, or there's little time to solve an emergency issue [5].

We conducted two human subject studies to investigate the effectiveness of refresher training and JITT. The choice of an evaluation task has implications for the interpretation and application of results from training experiments [16]. We considered the most critical onboard events that could challenge a long-duration crew with the criterion that there must be time for onboard refresher crew training to occur, and we selected component replacement in a critical, complex fluid/electrical/mechanical system. The task selected was carburetor inspection for a small generator (Honda EU 2000i) as analog for spaceflight hardware (see Fig. 1a). For this task, participants had to disassemble a generator and inspect the float valve tip within the generator's carburetor. We developed a flight-like procedure for the task, used in both studies, that participants followed in training and during task execution.

The selection of a critical repair task led us to focus on three areas of performance: time, conformance to procedures, and cognitive margin. These three areas allowed us to investigate participant efficiency and accuracy, and their associated workload while completing the task. Task completion time is used in a variety of performance analyses across a range of disciplines. It has been used as an objective metric to evaluate surgical skill [3], industrial maintenance and assembly [16], and car service maintenance [2]. In these studies, lower completion time is associated with higher levels of experience and/or higher levels of performance on the task under evaluation.

Deviation from procedures involving complex, critical systems can have catastrophic consequences. Rashid et al. performed root cause analysis on 58 maintenance related helicopter safety occurrences and identified "Incorrect Installation/Assembly" or "Part(s)/material omitted at installation/assembly" as the cause of 25.88% of the occurrences [12]. Additionally, maintainer procedural mistakes were specifically identified as contributing factors for several incidents in the same sample [13]. Similar to helicopter maintenance, procedural mistakes during a complex repair on a space vehicle can lead to severe outcomes. We measured deviation from procedures for the refresher experiment by classifying participant's actions in the context of procedural steps. Each action was analyzed in terms of execution (did the subject perform the step correctly), order (did the step occur in the correct procedural order), and completeness (did the subject complete the full step or just a part). We used the percentage of actions categorized as correct to measure subject accuracy.

Analyzing workload as an additional metric allows for a more complete investigation of task-performance than time (efficiency) and conformance to procedures (accuracy) alone. Humans have a limited ability to process and respond to information [11]. According to O'Donnell and Eggemeier, workload is defined as the "portion of the operator's limited capacity actually required to perform a particular task" [11]. As the workload required by a primary task increases, the capacity for secondary tasks decreases. Lowenthal et al. showed that measuring secondary task performance provided the ability to discriminate between similar levels of primary task performance [8]. For the refresher experiment, we measured workload with a secondary task, and for the JITT experiment we used the NASA-TLX [6,7]. We recruited participants from the University of California, Davis engineering student population to participate in two experiments investigating the effectiveness of customized training materials applied to refresher and just-in-time training prior to the execution of a mechanical maintenance and inspection task. We compared standard procedure review to 1) self-made videos for refresher training and 2) customizable procedures.

2   Refresher Training Experiment

In the refresher training experiment, we investigated changes in task performance of participants after a six-month break following an initial training. Based on anecdotal evidence from astronauts, we hypothesized that self-made videos would allow participants to maintain higher levels of performance than the current practice of only reviewing procedures. We designed a three-stage experiment to test our hypothesis. In Stage 1, we recruited participants from the engineering student population and screened them for mechanical aptitude and prior knowledge. In Stage 2, we trained participants to complete a mechanical repair task and then evaluated their performance. After their evaluation, participants in the treatment group each created a 5-minute refresher video. Alternatively, participants in the control group watched a standardized training video. Six months later, participants returned for Stage 3. During Stage 3, participants completed the same evaluation given in Stage 2 after a brief review of available materials. During the 7-minute review period, participants in the control group reviewed procedures, and participants in the treatment group reviewed their self-made refresher videos and procedures. Performance metrics included completion time, correct steps, and cognitive margin measured by response time to a secondary two-choice task. For improved granularity, completion time metrics included the overall task completion time, as well as the completion time for 19 distinct subtasks (i.e., groupings of procedure steps). We evaluated participant performance using percent change from pre-break to post-break to remove potential sources of uncontrolled variance due to differences between participants. We conducted one-way ANOVAs to analyze the effect of group on the percent change in task time $(F(1, 12) = 1.16, p = 0.30)$, percent change in correct steps $(F(1, 12) = 1.72, p = 0.21)$, and the percent change in secondary task average response time $(F(1, 12) = 3.58, p = 0.08)$. The main effect of group was not significant for any of the measured metrics, suggesting that the self-customized refresher videos did not influence participant performance or workload. To further investigate how the refresher videos may have influenced the participants, we conducted a two-way ANOVA on the percent change in subtask time with one between variable (participant group) and one within variable (subtask), using Satterthwaite's method to adjust the degrees of freedom when participants did not complete a subtask. The main effect of group was not significant $(F(2, 23.31) = 0.38, p = 0.69)$, nor was the main effect of subtask $(F(18, 191.15) = 1.52, p = 0.09)$, and the interaction effect between group and subtask was also not significant $(F(30, 193.13) = 0.63, p = 0.93)$.

The hypothesis that self-made videos will be highly effective compared to the current practice of procedure review was not conclusively supported by the data collected during the experiment. Some of the primary benefits of the refresher video are the ability for participants to add additional information about the execution of the task to the procedure and to demonstrate actions. When completing subtask 8 post-break, 5 out of 6 participants in the treatment group applied a skill that was taught in training and not found in the procedure, compared to only half of the participants in the control group. Application of a previously learned skill lends support to the idea that the self-made refresher video can be helpful by supplying supplemental information that is not contained in the procedure.

3   Just-In-Time Training Experiment

In the just-in-time-training (JITT) experiment, we studied the effects of self-customization of procedures for JITT in a complex-system repair task. As in the refresher training experiment, participants in this experiment completed a float valve inspection of a Honda generator, however, they used electronic versions of the procedures.

Twenty new participants from the engineering student population were randomly assigned into two different groups (N = 10 per group) for the experiment, which differed in that only the treatment group could self-customize by expanding the procedures. The procedures were designed such that each step had several sublevels of detail (see Fig. 1b). The lower the sublevel, the more detail and instructions were provided on how to perform that task. The treatment (expandable) group could expand the procedures as they saw fit, allowing them to customize their procedure to the degree of information they desired. If they felt they could perform a step without additional clarification, however, then they were not required to expand and read more detailed information. If, however, more information was needed, participants had the option to expand and view more detailed information. The control (static) group had no ability to customize their procedures and were instead provided the fully expanded version.

To familiarize participants with the procedure software and tool usage, skills training was completed before the critical task. During skills training, participants were evaluated to ensure that they met a basic proficiency with the tools, and to affirm that they were using the procedures software correctly. After completing skills training, participants began the critical task. After completing the critical task, participants answered questionnaires to assess their subjective cognitive workload with the NASA-TLX.

The primary objective of the experiment was to measure differences in performance via task completion time and subjective cognitive workload between the two groups. The primary null hypothesis to be tested was "the ability to self-customize procedures has no effect on participant performance or workload." We conducted one-way ANOVAs with one between-participants variable (participant group) on the task completion time and the NASA-TLX workload score. We also conducted a two-way ANOVA to investigate if completion time was correlated with subjective workload, and to investigate if there was an interaction effect between the groups. We hypothesized that when compared to the static group, participants that were able to self-customize (the expandable group) would:

1. Complete the critical task more quickly, as they were not required to review detailed procedures for tasks where they did not require additional assistance.
2. Report the same subjective workload, as they could self-customize the procedure to their personal needs.

We hypothesized these effects under the assumption that participants will be better able to take advantage of their existing skills. Participants in the control group would be required to read and complete each step, even if they do not require the additional details of instruction that was provided by the expanded procedures. By not expanding the procedure to a more detailed level, participants in the treatment group should be able to complete the task more quickly. Additionally, participants in the control group may become frustrated with over detailed procedures, causing them to not read as carefully, which may result in an increased number of errors. We expect workload indicated by the NASA-TLX to remain roughly the same, as the additional workload of interacting with the procedures is minimal.

Our first hypothesis, that the self-customizable procedures would decrease task execution time, was not supported, and the one-way ANOVAs was not

- 2.4.   Detach the Fuel Tube from the left side and place open end into the Gasoline Container.

    - 2.4.1.   The left side of the Fuel Tube is indicated by the red spacer. Disengage the tension clamp and remove the Fuel Tube from the fitting.

        2.4.1.1.   Remove the tension clamp by pushing both of the tabs on the clamp toward one another using Pliers. Hold the tabs with the Pliers while pulling the clamp off of the fitting and up the tube.

        2.4.1.2.   Once the tension clamp is disengaged, pry the Fuel Tube from the fitting using a Flat Head Screwdriver.

    2.4.2.   Let the removed end of the Fuel Tube rest in the Gasoline Container.

(a)   (b)

Fig. 1. (a) A participant completes a carburetor inspection of a Honda Generator. (b) A section of customizable procedures fully expanded. Dashes indicate where steps could be expanded or collapsed.

statistically significant ($F(1, 18) = 0.28, p = 0.60$). The one-way ANOVA for subjective workload was also not significant ($F(1, 18) = 0.09, p = 0.76$), however, indicating that the expandable group did not incur additional cognitive loads compared to the static group, supporting our second hypothesis. The results of our two-way ANOVA indicated that there was no difference between groups ($F(1, 16) = 0.23, p = 0.64$), but that completion task time was significantly higher for subjects that reported higher subjective workload ($F(1, 16) = 5.13, p = 0.04$), though there was a significant interaction effect between groups ($F(1, 16) = 5.41, p = 0.03$). From further investigation of the interaction effect, we found that only participants in the static group reported higher cognitive workload when their completion time increased. Compared to the static group, the expandable group reported the same workload regardless of their completion time. This may indicate that those participants that struggled with the static procedure then required more time and had a higher associated cognitive load, while the expandable procedure was better suited for those with less mechanical repair ability. One benefit of the expandable procedure may be that it acts as an equalizer, allowing participants with a variety of skill levels to perform at the same level without increasing their subjective workload levels.

4   Discussion

We investigated the impact of customized training interventions on performance for a complex mechanical repair task. The practice of reviewing self-made refresher videos was not shown to have a statistically significant effect compared to the practice of reviewing procedures prior to task execution. However, the application of learned skills and participant feedback via questionnaires in the refresher training experiment suggests that self-made videos can be a useful addition to refresher training. Insufficient information may have prevented participants from creating the most effective videos. Errors unrecognized by the participant were not addressed in videos and participants may lack the ability to predict what they will forget during the break. Additional information about common errors or the participant's relative performance would likely have led to more effective videos and better performance.

In our second experiment, we investigated whether the ability to self-customize procedures, which allowed participants to expand procedures to show additional levels of details as desired, could effectively improve JITT and performance for task naïve participants. We found that workload did not increase when using expandable procedures, but that the completion time was also not reduced. This may be because participants expand procedures even when they do not need additional help, checking to see if they truly understand the task that needed to be completed. Further research into expandable procedures should identify automated means of measuring if procedures are being completed accurately, rather than simply the amount of time they require to complete.

The results indicated some effects of the refresher training on the performance metrics, but there were less differences for the JITT study. Both studies may benefit from increased participant number, different customization strategies, and increased guidance for self-customization. Future work may include an adaptive procedure display based on performance and perceived cognitive workload or testing customization strategies on experts, who bring experience and unique approaches to tasks.

References

1. Aguzzi, M., Bosca, R., Müllerschkowski, U.: Astronaut training in view of the future: a Columbus payload instructor perspective. Acta Astronaut. **66**(3–4), 401–407 (2010). https://doi.org/10.1016/j.actaastro.2009.07.022, https://linkinghub.elsevier.com/retrieve/pii/S0094576509003671
2. Borsci, S., Lawson, G., Broome, S.: Empirical evidence, evaluation criteria and challenges for the effectiveness of virtual and mixed reality tools for training operators of car service maintenance. Comput. Ind. **67**, 17–26 (2015). https://doi.org/10.1016/j.compind.2014.12.002, https://linkinghub.elsevier.com/retrieve/pii/S0166361514002073
3. D'Angelo, A.L.D., et al.: Idle time: an underdeveloped performance metric for assessing surgical skill. Am. J. Surg. **209**(4), 645–651 (Apr 2015). https://doi.org/10.1016/j.amjsurg.2014.12.013, https://linkinghub.elsevier.com/retrieve/pii/S0002961015000045
4. Doarn, C.R., Williams, R.S., Nicogossian, A.E., Polk, J.D.: Training in space medicine. In: Nicogossian, A.E., Williams, R.S., Huntoon, C.L., Doarn, C.R., Polk, J.D., Schneider, V.S. (eds.) Space Physiology and Medicine, pp. 463–477. Springer, New York, New York, NY (2016). https://doi.org/10.1007/978-1-4939-6652-3_18, http://link.springer.com/10.1007/978-1-4939-6652-3_18
5. Foale, C.M., et al.: Diagnostic instrumentation aboard iss: just-in-time training for non-physician crew-members. Aviat. Space Environ. Med. **76**(6), 594–598 (2005)
6. Hart, S.G.: Nasa-task load index (NASA-TLX); 20 years later. In: Proceedings of the Human Factors and Ergonomics Society Annual Meeting vol. 50, no. 9, pp. 904–908 (October 2006). https://doi.org/10.1177/154193120605000909, http://journals.sagepub.com/doi/10.1177/154193120605000909

7. Hart, S.G., Staveland, L.E.: Development of NASA-TLX (Task Load Index): results of empirical and theoretical re-search. In: Advances in Psychology, vol. 52, pp. 139–183. Elsevier (1988). https://doi.org/10.1016/S0166-4115(08)62386-9, https://linkinghub.elsevier.com/retrieve/pii/S0166411508623869

8. Lowenthal, C., Liu, A., Natapoff, A., Oman, C.: Effect of sleepiness on performance and workload during space robotics tasks. In: Aviation, Space and Environmental Medicine, vol. 35, pp. A79-A79 (2012)

9. National Aeronautics and Space Administration: International Space Station Timelines (April 2014). http://www.nasa.gov/content/international-space-station-timelines-april-2014

10. Nishiyama, C., et al.: Effectiveness of simplified 15-min refresher BLS training program: a randomized controlled trial. Resuscitation **90**, 56–60 (May 2015). https://doi.org/10.1016/j.resuscitation.2015.02.015, https://linkinghub.elsevier.com/retrieve/pii/S0300957215000829

11. O'Donnell, R.D., Eggemeier, F.T.: Workload assessment methodology. In: Boff, K.R., Kaufman, L., Thomas, J.P. (eds.) Handbook of Perception and Human Performance: vol. 2. Cognitive Processes and Performance, chap. 42, pp. 42-1. Wiley-Interscience (1984)

12. Rashid, H.S.J., Place, C.S., Braithwaite, G.R.: Investigating the investigations: a retrospective study in the aviation maintenance error causation. Cogn. Technol. Work **15**(2), 171–188 (2013). https://doi.org/10.1007/s10111-011-0210-7, http://link.springer.com/10.1007/s10111-011-0210-7

13. Rashid, H., Place, C., Braithwaite, G.: Helicopter maintenance error analysis: beyond the third order of the HFACS-ME. Int. J. Ind. Ergon.**40**(6), 636–647 (2010). https://doi.org/10.1016/j.ergon.2010.04.005, https://linkinghub.elsevier.com/retrieve/pii/S0169814110000478

14. Salas, E., Cannon-Bowers, J.A.: The science of training: a decade of progress. Annu. Rev. Psychol. **52**(1), 471–499 (2001). https://doi.org/10.1146/annurev.psych.52.1.471, http://www.annualreviews.org/doi/10.1146/annurev.psych.52.1.471

15. Wang, X., Day, E.A., Kowollik, V., Schuelke, M.J., Hughes, M.G.: Factors influencing knowledge and skill decay after training: a meta-analysis. In: Individual and team skill decay: The science and implications for practice., pp. 68–116. Applied psychology series., Routledge/Taylor & Francis Group, New York, NY, US (2013)

16. Webel, S., Bockholt, U., Engelke, T., Gavish, N., Olbrich, M., Preusche, C.: An augmented reality training platform for assembly and maintenance skills. Robot. Auton. Syst. **61**(4), 398–403 (2013). https://doi.org/10.1016/j.robot.2012.09.013, https://linkinghub.elsevier.com/retrieve/pii/S0921889012001674

Research on Rationality of Safety Sign Location Setting Based on Visual Search Performance

Guilei Sun[✉], Yiyang Hu, Qi Yang, Junyu Zhou, and Yujie Yin

School of Safety Engineering, China University of Labor Relations, Beijing 100048, China
sunguilei@culr.edu.cn

Abstract. To research the rationality of the location of safety signs, the safety signs were set at different positions and heights in the corridor. 30 subjects were invited to attend the experiment. Tobii eye tracker was used to record eye movement data which could reflect the distribution of subjects' attention in two research experiments. The fixation duration of subjects on the signs in the corridor was taken as the evaluation index for drawing attention. SPSS was used to analyze the data from the eye tracker. The results indicate that there was no significant correlation between the eye height and the fixation duration to safety signs at different positions. The safety signs should be set at about 1.25m, and it could be paid more attention to post them on the wall without other disturbances. As the signs of emergency evacuation that should be set low, it is more reasonable to set them on the ground than on the walls. Therefore, the location setting of the safety signs have very important influence on visual search performance.

Keywords: Safety signs · Location setting · Eye movement characteristics · Fixation duration · Ocular height

1 Introduction

Safety signs play an important role in safety. The effect of safety signs is affected by many factors. Jun et al. [1] found that different safety signs have significant differences in human neural response and behavior. Lara et al. [2] found that effect of safety signs existed in virtual environments on middle-aged workers. Yunzeng et al. [3] discovered the limitations of safety signs for multicultural workers when studying the development direction of the digital safety sign system. Rong et al. [4] researched specific design and application schemes for improving the role of safety signs in low-level lighting areas in passenger ship corridors, stairways and doors. Jeong [5] improved the design of the visibility and legibility of railway safety signs. Yu et al. [6] researched and designed the safety signs of the coal tunnel driving face. Jingpeng [7] analyzed the factors that affect the effectiveness of the safety sign design from the individual characteristics of the person and the characteristics of the safety sign itself. However, there are few studies on the position setting of safety signs. In China, the national standards, *GB 15630 Requirements for the Setting of Fire Safety Signs* [8] and *GB 2894 Safety Signs and Guidelines for Their Use* [9], do not specify the specific height and position of the safety signs. The research

C. Stephanidis et al. (Eds.): HCII 2021, CCIS 1419, pp. 166–174, 2021.
https://doi.org/10.1007/978-3-030-78635-9_24

on the rationality of the position and height of the safety signs can enable people to avoid accidental dangers in advance, therefore, it is important to have a research on safety signs location.

There are many factors that affect people's attention, and eye trackers are one of the most used equipment on studying the attention. Yohana et al. [10] studied the comprehensibility of symbol safety signs through eye tracker and EEG. Na et al. [11] used the eye tracking function of the eye trackers to find the most suitable subway safety sign color. Shuicheng et al. [12] used eye trackers to study the significance of coal mine safety signs. To find the best position of the safety signs, it is necessary to consider the distribution of personnel's attention from the perspective of human factors such as fixation duration and saccade time.

2 Experiments

2.1 Subjects and Equipment

30 subjects aged 20–25 with a height in the range of 155cm-185cm and a male to female ratio of 1:1, were selected for this experiment. To avoid the influence on the test results, the subjects, who were required to be no severe astigmatism, were voluntarily attending the experiment, and following the test instructions to complete the test. Tobii glasses is used in this studying which can automatically determine the subjects fixation position in a natural state within 17 μs (60 Hz), and accurately test the subject's response to the displayed signs, and the subject's unintentional response record his eye movement data.

2.2 Experimental Design

To ensure the scientific, authenticity and persuasiveness of the experimental results, attention is the single factor for the studying and the experimental environment is required to be well-lit and quiet. Evacuation Signs were used to carry out the rationality experiment of the safety signs position and warning signs were used to carry out the rationality experiment of the heght setting of safety signs (Fig. 1).

Fig. 1. Signs for safety evacuation and warning signs

2.3 Experimental Scene Design

The experiment location is an unfamiliar circular corridor to the subjects. The corridor is divided into two parts, and the signs set at different positions is numbered: signs 1 to 8 are used for evacuation signs to study the rationality of the position of safety signs, and signs A to E are used for warning signs to study the rationality of the height setting of safety signs. The specific settings are shown in Fig. 2.

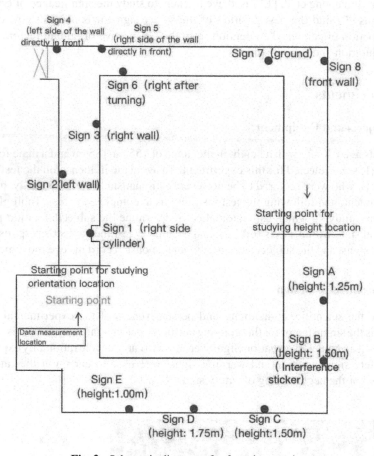

Fig. 2. Schematic diagram of safety signs setting

Design for Position Research. Using the control variable method to form five groups of control groups for the signs set in different positions, as shown in Table 1:

Table 1. Signs design research position

Group	Sign number and the corresponding position	
1	Sign 1 (right side cylinder)	Sign 3 (right side wall)
2	Sign 2 (left wall)	Sign 3 (right side wall)
3	Sign 4 (left side of the wall directly in front)	Sign 5 (right side of the wall directly in front)
4	Sign 3 (right after non-turning)	Sign 6 (right after turning)
5	Sign 7 (ground)	Sign 8 (front wall)

Design for Height Research. Controlling variable method is used to consider the length of the signs itself, four sets of signs with different heights in the height range of 1.00 m–1.75 m form two sets of control groups, as shown in Table 2:

Table 2. Signs design for height research

Group	Sign letter and the corresponding height			
a	Sign A(1.25m)	Sign C(1.50m)	Sign D(1.75m)	Sign E(1.00m)
b	Sign C(1.50m)		Sign B (with interference on the wall at 1.50m)	

3 Data Analysis

3.1 Data Export

According to the research of Tian et al. [12] on the significance of coal mine safety signs and Zhaofei et al. [13] on the significance of safety signs in different fonts, the fixation duration of the subject on the signs was used as the standard for analyzing the significance of the signs. Based on the research settings, the longer the fixation duration on the sign, the more rationality the position of the sign is set. Therefore, the fixation duration at different signs is exported after the experiment.

3.2 Parameter Analysis

Eye Height Data Analysis. The normality of the eye height and the fixation duration on each sign is checked with S-W test, and the results are shown in Table 3. 0.05 is chosen as the significance level. According to the results, the significance(P) of the fixation duration on the sign is less than 0.05, so the eye height data conforms to the normal distribution while the fixation duration on the signs does not conform. Spearman

Table 3. Data normality test and correlation coefficient between sign and eye height

Data	Sig.(P)	Correlation coefficient between sign and eye height
Eye height	0.812	—
1	0.000	−0.049
2	0.000	−0.170
3	0.000	−0.228
4	0.000	0.008
5	0.002	0.118
6	0.000	0.228
7	0.000	0.243
8	0.003	0.087
A	0.000	0.015
B	0.000	−0.043
C	0.000	−0.110
D	0.000	0.045
E	0.000	−0.064

correlation analysis was carried out on the eye height and the fixation duration to different signs, and the results were summarized in Table 3.

The results showed that the absolute value of the correlation coefficient between the fixation duration on each sign and eye height is less than 0.3. Therefore, there is no significant correlation between the eye height and fixation duration, which means that the eye height will not affect the subject's fixation time on the sign.

Parameter Analysis for Position. The average fixation duration of the subjects on each sign position in shown in Fig. 3. It can be known that the difference of the average fixation duration is large, sign 7 is given the longest fixation duration while sign 6 is given the least. It indicates that the position has great influence on the fixation duration. S-W normality test are shown in Table 4. The normality test shows that the average fixation duration does not conform to the normal distribution. Therefore, the K related sample test in the non-parametric test is continued, the results is shown in Table 5, which indicate that the difference between the data samples is statistically significant.

Based on the above analysis, the five groups (in Table 1) can be discussed as follows:

1. Group 1: sign 1 (right side cylinder) is easier to attract subjects' attention than sign 3 (right side wall).
2. Group 2: sign 2 (wall on the left) is easier to attract subjects' attention than sign 3 (wall on the right).
3. (3) Group 3: sign 4 (on the left side of the wall directly in front) is easier to attract subjects' attention than sign 5 (on the right side of the wall in front of it).

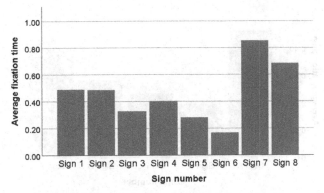

Fig. 3. The fixation duration on different position signs

Table 4. Normality test for average fixation duration

Sign number	Statistics	Sig.(P)
1	0.631	0.000
2	0.699	0.000
3	0.655	0.000
4	0.753	0.000
5	0.875	0.002
6	0.634	0.000
7	0.820	0.000
8	0.873	0.002

Table 5. K related sample test for position

Subjects	Test statistics
Number of cases	240
Bangla	220.417
Degree of freedom	1
Progressive sig. (P)	0.000

4. (4) Group 4: sign 3 (right after not turning) is easier to attract subjects' attention than Sign 6 (right after turning).
5. (5) Group 5: sign 7 (ground) is easier to attract subjects' attention than sign 8 (front wall).

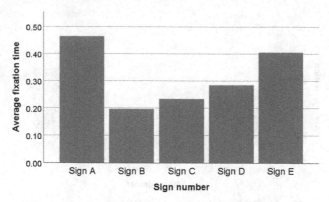

Fig. 4. The average fixation time on different height signs

Parameter Analysis for Height
The average fixation duration of the subjects on the signs of each height are shown in Fig. 4. The biggest different is between sign A and sign B. The results of normality test with S-W test are shown in Table 6. The significance(P) shown in the table does not conform to the normal distribution. K related sample test is used and the results are shown in Table 7. It can be seen from the results that the difference between the data samples is statistically significant.

Table 6. Average fixation duration and normality test

Sign number	Statistics	Degree of freedom	Significance(P)
A	0.716	30	0.000
B	0.741	30	0.000
C	0.671	30	0.000
D	0.677	30	0.000
E	0.624	30	0.000

Table 7. K related sample test for height

Subject	Test statistics
Number of cases	150
Bangla	150.000
Degree of freedom	1
Progressive significance (P)	0.000

Based on the above analysis, the two groups (in Table 2) are discussed:

1. Group a: the attention being attracted from most to least: Sign A (1.25m) > Sign E (1.00m) > Sign D (1.75m) > Sign C (1.50m);
2. Group b: Sign C (1.50m) is easier to attract people's attention than sign B (with interference on the wall at 1.50m).

4 Conclusions

When the position or height of the sign is more likely to attract people's attention, it means that is more prominent and more rationality.

Through the experiment and the processing and analysis of the experimental results, conclusions on the location of the safety sign are showing as follows:

1) There is no significant correlation between the eye height and the fixation duration on the safety signs at different positions;
2) It will draw more attention for safety signs to be placed on a protruding cylindrical surface than on a normal wall. Safety signs to be placed on the left or left front wall will draw more attention than to be placed on the right or right front wall. Safety signs to be placed before turning are more rationality than after turning. Safety signs as emergency evacuation signs is more rationality to be set on the ground than on the wall.
3) In the height range of 1.00 m–1.75 m, it is rationality to set the safety signs on the wall with no interference objects around 1.25m.

Acknowledgments. The presented work has been supported by General project of China University of Labor Relations (21XYJS012).

References

1. Jun, B., Huijian, F., Jia, J.: Are we sensitive to different types of safety signs? Evidence from ERPs. Psychology Research and Behavior Management 2020 (default), pp. 496–505 (2020).
2. Lara, R., Emilia, D., Francisco, R.: Research on workplace safety sign compliance: validation of a virtual environment prototype. Procedia Manufact. **3**, 6599–6606 (2015)
3. 김윤중., 김후성.:A study on safety signage system design for reduction of industrial accidents in construction site. considering work environment of multicultural workers. J. Korean Soc. Des. Cult. **24**(1), 105–117 (2018)
4. Rong, X., Jianye, Z.: Passenger ship low-level lighting and related safety signs design. Ship Ocean Eng. **49**(5), 1671–7953 (2020)
5. Jeong, J.G., Bang, M.S., Kang, H.S., Jeong, H.I.: A study on the improvement of the railway safety sign for enhancing visibility and legibility. J. Korean Soc. Saf. **31**(5), 171–176 (2016)
6. Yu, A., Dan, L.: Research on safety signs of coal road driving face. Saf. Coal Mines **47**(8), 21 (2016)
7. Jingpeng, Y.: Empirical Research on the Influencing Factors of Safety Sign. Zhejiang University, Hangzhou (2009)
8. Tianjin Fire Research Institute of Ministry of the Public Security. Empirical Research on the Influencing Factors of Safety Sign. State Bureau of Technical Supervision, Beijing (1995)

9. Beijing Municipal Institute of Labour Protection., Beijing Institute of Optoelectronic Technology.: Safety signs and guidelines for their use. General Administration of quality supervision, inspection and Quarantine of the people's Republic of China; China National Standardization Administration Committee, Beijing (2008)
10. Yohana, S., Shuping, X.: Correction to: eye movements and brain oscillations to symbolic safety signs with different comprehensibility. J. Physiol. Anthropol. **37**(1), 30 (2018)
11. Na, C., Ming, Z., Kun, G.: The physiological experimental study on the effect of different color of safety signs on a virtual subway fire escape—an exploratory case study of zijing mountain subway station. Int. J. Environ. Res. Public Health **17**(16), 5903 (2020)
12. Shuicheng, T., Ying, C., Yuan, Z.: Eye movement analysis of location setting on the significant influence of coal mine safety signs. J. Xi'an Univ. Sci. Technol. **37**(5), 1672–9315 (2017)
13. Zhaofei, L., Guoxun, J., Kun, Z.: Children's eye movement characteristics of warning signs with different shapes. J. Saf. Environ. **15**(5), 1009–6094 (2015)

Research on Evaluating the Workload of Apron Controllers Based on DORATASK Model

Qunyu Xu[1($\boxtimes$)], Dongxi Xiao[2], Qi Ying[1], Mei Rong[1], and Chuanjun Tang[2]

[1] China Academy of Civil Aviation Science and Technology, 24 BeiLi XiBaHe, Chaoyang District, Beijing 100028, China
{xuqy,yingqi,rongmei}@mail.castc.org.cn

[2] Beijing Capital International Airport Co., Ltd., 09 SiWei Rd, Shunyi District, Beijing 100621, China
{xiaodx,tangcj}@bcia.com.cn

Abstract. With the rapid development of air transport industry, implementing the independent apron control has become an urgent need for the large-scale airports in China. Apron controllers are very important to the apron control for their dominant roles in commanding, monitoring and coordinating aircraft apron operations at airport. To ensure the safety of apron operation and improve the operational efficiency of the apron control, it is necessary to scientifically evaluate the workload of apron controllers and reasonably arrange the required controller positions. There has two people from the apron control: the controller and the coordinator. This paper focuses on analyzing the controller's workload. The observable tasks performed by apron controllers could be mainly composed of 3 parts: standard communications with pilots, including issuing commands and monitoring pilots repeat commands; electronic strip system operations, such as manually using keyboard and mouse; and the telephone coordination to solve problem when an aircraft is facing an actual or potential conflict. In this paper, actual flight data from July 1st to August 31st, 2020 at Beijing Capital International Airport is firstly analyzed to determine the peak and valley traffic hours, and then based on field observation and time collection for measuring those observable tasks for the controllers at those peaks and valleys, the average time required for the controllers to command a single flight is obtained. Then the total task load of the controllers is calculated by using DORATASK model, which considers the observable, non-observable and recovery tasks. With the calculated workload and required positions for apron controllers, comparative analysis is conducted. Experiment results show that the proposed model is applicable and is very in good consistency with practical operations at airport.

Keywords: Apron control · Apron controller · Controller workload · Controller positions · DORATASK model · Workload evaluation

1 Introduction

With the rapid development of China's air transport industry, the airport traffic volume and support sorties have increased significantly. In order to solve the problem of increasing airport taxiing conflict and low operational efficiency of the traditional air traffic control (ATC) tower control for aircraft apron operations, implementing the independent apron control has become an urgent need for the large-scale airport in China [1]. The Civil Aviation Administration of China (CAAC) initiated the transfer of the apron control in 2013 [2] and issued the overall plan for aircraft apron control in 2018 to accelerate the transfer of aircraft apron control in high-density airports [3].

The apron controllers are very important to the apron control for their dominant roles in commanding, monitoring and coordinating aircraft apron operations [4, 5] at airports. To ensure safety of apron operations and improve the operational efficiency of the apron control, it is necessary to scientifically evaluate the workload of apron controllers and reasonably arrange the required controller positions.

There has two people from the apron control: the controller and the coordinator. This paper focuses on analyzing the controller's workload. Although there has much works on ATC controller workload [6, 7], few works directly on the apron controller. A new workload model for apron controllers is proposed in Sect. 2, and workload evaluation is made in Sect. 3. Conclusion and future work are given in Sect. 4.

2 Workload Modelling of Apron Controllers

2.1 DORATASK Model

The DORATASK model is widely used for task assessment and workload analysis. This model was first used by the United Kingdom Operational Research and Analysis Bureau to estimate ATC sector capacity (DORA Interim Report 8818), for terminal sectors (DORA Interim Report 8916) and to calibrate a simulated model for two route sectors of the London ACC (DORA Report 8927) [8, 9].

In this model, workload is calculated by adding up time it takes the controller to perform all the necessary tasks, including three main types: the observable tasks, the non-observable tasks, and the recovery tasks.

The observable tasks are routine tasks performed by controller, such as standard communications, filling out flight process strips, and those tasks aimed at solving conflicts when an aircraft is facing an actual or potential conflict. These tasks can be recorded and timed by observers. The non-observable tasks are mental tasks carried out by controller, such as screen monitoring, flight identification, comparing progress sheet and those mental tasks required to identify aircraft or forecast conflicts. These tasks cannot be actually recorded and timed. In addition, the model considers that the controller needs a time for recovery, which is the third category, the recovery tasks. The sum of these three types of tasks is the controller's total workload.

2.2 DORATASK Based Workload Model for Apron Controllers

To better apply the DORATASK model to the apron controllers workload, field observation is firstly conducted in actual apron control tower at Beijing Capital International Airport (BCIA). The specific tasks performed by apron controllers when commanding the arrival, departure and tug traffic are analyzed carefully in this study. For instance, apron controllers will conduct 10-step processes for an arrival flight, including identifying the flight, communication for flight reception, inquiring about availability of planned parking space, identifying the aircraft operational conditions, issuing aircraft taxing instructions, filling out flight process strips by using keyboard and mouse, both radar and visual screen monitoring, and telephone coordination with others for problem solving when an aircraft is facing an actual or potential conflict. There have 12-step processes for commanding an departure flight and 9-step for a tug.

Considering these processes are crossing randomly when commanding the arrival, departure and tug traffic, to facilitate the time collection, the observable task will be analyzed as a whole, irrespective of what kind of flights are under command. Based on summarized analysis, the observable tasks performed by the apron controller could be mainly composed of 3 parts: standard communications with the pilots, including issuing the commands and monitoring pilots repeat commands; electronic strip system operation, such as using keyboard and mouse to fill out flight process strips; and the telephone coordination with personnel working in other departments for problem solving when an aircraft is facing an actual or potential conflict.

With the use of DORATASK model, the workload of apron controllers can be classified into following 3 categories [6] as shown in Table 1.

Table 1. Task classification of apron controllers based on DORATASK model

Observable task	Non-observable task	Recovery task
1. Stand communications WL_{C11} 2. Electronic strip operation WL_{C12} 3. Telephone coordination WL_{C13}	WL_{C2}: Mental tasks, e.g. screen monitoring, identifying aircraft or forecast conflicts	WL_{C3}: time needed for recovery

The apron controller workload WL_C could be established as:

$$WL_C = \frac{WL_{C1} + WL_{C2} + WL_{C3}}{\Delta t} = \frac{\sum_{i=1}^{3} WL_{Ci}}{\Delta t} \qquad (1)$$

Where Δt is the unit time and is defined as 1 h in this paper.

According to the DORATASK model, the observable workload should account for about 50% of the total workload, i.e. the total workload is about 2 times of the observable workload. Therefore, the apron controller workload could be simplified as.

$$WL_C = \frac{2 \times WL_{C1}}{\Delta t} = \frac{2 \times \sum_{i=1}^{3} WL_{C1i}}{\Delta t} \qquad (2)$$

2.3 Workload Analysis for Apron Controllers

The specific steps for analyzing the apron controller workload are as follows:

(1) Obtain the average times that apron controller spent on standard communications, electronic strip operation, and telephone coordination, while commanding a single flight in each unit time, which are defined as T_{C11}, T_{C12}, and T_{C13}, respectively. According to the DORATASK model, the observable workload should account for about 50% of the total workload, therefore, the average total workload of apron controllers to command a single flight in each unit time is

$$T_C = 2 \times (T_{C11} + T_{C12} + T_{C13}) \tag{3}$$

(2) Count the total number of flights in each unit time, including the arrival, departure and tug traffic, which are defined as N_A, N_D, and N_T, respectively. Therefore, the total number of flights required for apron controllers to command in each unit time is

$$N_C = N_A + N_D + N_T \tag{4}$$

(3) Calculate the total workload of apron controllers in each unit time as

$$WL_C = T_C \times N_C = (2 \times (T_{C11} + T_{C12} + T_{C13})) \times (N_A + N_D + N_T) \tag{5}$$

(4) Calculate the maximum workload that one apron controller could accept in each unit time. Considering the DORATASK model concluded that the average workload task of the controller must be less than 80%, in this paper, the maximum workload of the apron controller in each unit time is given as

$$WL_{Max} = 3600s \times 80\% = 2880s \tag{6}$$

(5) Calculate the number of people required working at apron controller positions as

$$P_C = Ceil\left(WL_C / WL_{Max}\right) \tag{7}$$

(6) Calculate the maximum number of flights that one apron controller could command in each unit time as:

$$N_{Max} = Floor\left(WL_{Max} / T_C\right) \tag{8}$$

3 Workload Evaluation for Apron Controllers

3.1 Data Collection and Processing

Based on actual flight data including the arrival, departure, and tug traffic, from July 1st to August 31st, 2020, provided by the BCIA Apron Control Department, the number of hourly flights in July and August is firstly analyzed to determine the peak and valley traffic hours, as shown in Table 2.

Table 2. Peak and valley traffic hours at Beijing capital international airport

Time periods		Average flight numbers in July 2020	Average flight numbers in August 2020
Valley Hour	06:00–07:00	12	20
Peak Hour	08:00–09:00	25	42
	14:00–15:00	35	42
	18:00–19:00	30	40
	21:00–22:00	25	38

Then, by referencing the BICA apron controller's practical experiences combined with the data in Table 2, the time periods for sampling data collection are selected. At these selected time periods, data collection for N_C, T_{C11}, T_{C12}, and T_{C13} is carried out and Table 3 shows an example of those collected average values in second.

In this paper, through statistical analysis, the average total observable task required for apron controllers to command a single flight in each unit time is calculated as T_{C1} = 47.6446s.

Table 3. Average time required for apron controllers to command a single flight

Selected time periods	N_C	T_{C11}	T_{C12}	T_{C13}
06:00–07:00	28	38.46	3.85	9
07:00–08:00	32	38.84	3.78	9
08:00–09:00	20	34.45	3.50	32
13:00–14:00	34	29.94	3.47	11.5
14:00–15:00	31	31.19	3.35	23.3
17:00–18:00	43	31.09	3.23	10.33
18:00–19:00	43	31.86	3.28	17.25
20:00–21:00	47	32.74	3.21	12.57
21:00–22:00	25	21.52	2.64	7.5

3.2 Data Evaluation

In this section, to verify the applicability of the proposed model, comparative analysis is conducted by comparing the calculated number of controller positions by the model with the actual number of controller positions at BCIA.

The busiest day in each month, July 26 and August 30, 2020, are selected for data evaluation. By using actual hourly flight numbers N_C and the T_C calculated in Sect. 3.1, the number of required controller positions could be calculated following formula 8, and compared with actual number of controller positions, as shown in Table 4.

Table 4. Comparison analysis for July 26 and August 30, 2020

Time periods	July 26, 2020			Controller positions		August 30, 2020			Controller positions	
	N_A	N_D	N_T	Model	Actual	N_A	N_D	N_T	Model	Actual
06:00–07:00	1	12	3	1	1	2	17	4	1	1
07:00–08:00	0	18	6	1	1	0	33	9	2	2
08:00–09:00	4	24	8	2	2	6	28	6	2	2
09:00–10:00	6	16	7	1	1	10	21	4	2	2
10:00–11:00	10	9	3	1	1	21	11	1	2	2
11:00–12:00	16	13	0	1	1	22	13	0	2	2
12:00–13:00	15	13	0	1	1	17	20	0	2	2
13:00–14:00	20	9	1	1	1	21	19	1	2	2
14:00–15:00	17	32	2	2	2	25	12	0	2	2
15:00–16:00	11	9	3	1	1	21	23	1	2	2
16:00–17:00	13	17	2	2	1	18	22	1	2	2
17:00–18:00	15	12	5	2	1	22	28	2	2	2
18:00–19:00	22	16	2	2	2	22	20	2	2	2
19:00–20:00	11	10	9	1	1	17	14	0	2	1
20:00–21:00	13	9	8	1	1	16	20	4	2	2
21:00–22:00	22	4	4	1	1	25	6	6	2	2
22:00–23:00	15	4	6	1	1	26	8	5	2	2
23:00–00:00	19	5	5	1	1	20	4	5	1	1

With formula 8, the maximum number of flights that one apron controller could command in each unit time N_{Max} is 30. From the Table 4, it could be seen that the proposed model is well applicable to actual conditions, while there still exists a few mismatches, where it could be found that those flight numbers are around 30. Therefore, there still need to be studied working on determining the P_C and N_{Max}.

4 Conclusion and Future Work

In this paper, actual flight data from July 1st to August 31st, 2020 at Beijing Capital International Airport is firstly analyzed to determine the peak and valley traffic hours, and then based on field observation and time collection for measuring those observable tasks for apron controllers at those peaks and valleys, the average time required for apron controllers to command a single flight is obtained. Then the total task load of apron controllers is calculated by using DORATASK model, which considers the observable, the non-observable and recovery tasks. With the calculated required positions for apron controllers, comparative analysis is conducted with the actual numbers to verify the applicability of the proposed model. Experiment results show that the proposed model is well applicable and is very in good consistency with practical operations at BICA.

Future work will add the subjective workload evaluation [10] for experiments comparison. Investigating the relations between the number of flights commanded by apron controllers and their subjective workload fatigues, and studying whether it is necessary to adjust the proposed model output or adjust BICA current position arrangement, will be further conducted to better scientifically evaluate the workload of apron controllers and reasonably arrange the required controller positions.

References

1. Yao, L.: Airport apron operation management related issues research. Mod. Manag. **8**(4), 395–399 (2018). (In Chinese)
2. CAAC, Notice of promoting the transfer of aircraft apron operation management to airport management organization, 22 Aug 2013. (In Chinese)
3. CAAC, Overall plan for aircraft apron control handover, 25 April 2018. (In Chinese)
4. National Academies of Sciences, Engineering, and Medicine. Airport Apron Management and Control Programs, The National Academies Press, Washington, DC (2012)
5. A Day in the Life of an Apron Controller, Future Airport talks to Dieter Strehl, apron controller at Munich Airport. https://www.airport-technology.com/features/feature114087. Accessed 20 Jan 2021
6. ICAO Doc 9426, Air Traffic Service Planning Manual
7. Xin, H., Xuebo, L.: The research on the workload of tower controllers and the equipment of control positions. J. Changzhou Inst. Technol. **26**(6), 17–20 (2013). (In Chinese)
8. Roberto, A.J.: Guide for the application of a common methodology to estimate airport and ATC sector capacity for the SAM region, ICAO RLA/06/901 (2009)
9. Richmond, G.C.: The DORATASK methodology for sector capacity assessment: an Interim description of its adaptation to terminal control (TMA) Sectors. In: DORA Report 8916. Civil Aviation Authority, London (1989)
10. NASA, NASA-Task Load Index (TLX)

A Study of the Impact of Changes in Software Interface Design Elements on Visual Fatigue

Jinyao Zhang, Zhengyu Wang[✉], Meiyu Zhou, Yajing Xu, Lu Zhong, Hanwen Du, Li Wang, and Yibing Wu

School of Art Design and Media, East China University of Science and Technology, No. 130, Meilong Road, Xuhui District, Shanghai, People's Republic of China

Abstract. With the advent of the paperless era, electronic working devices have become the norm, and people are increasingly relying on software in mobile phones and computers to process their work. Long hours of reading and searching, as well as the use of different character sizes, line spacing, color values, and the chroma of the software interface, can have an impact on visual fatigue. Long-term visual fatigue can lead to myopia, red eye, and glaucoma, which can cause health problems and reduce productivity. Therefore, interface design is of paramount importance to the software workforce. At present, most of the experimental literature focuses on the relationship between the physical properties of computers or mobile phones and visual fatigue. The study, which collected research literature from 2010–2020, examined the impact of software interface design elements on visual fatigue. We divide the interface design elements into text, color and graphics, and classify the literature according to the categories of interface elements to explore the changing patterns and trends of research themes and methods over time. This study provides a methodological basis for the future study of visual fatigue-related interface design and puts forward some suggestions for future research directions.

Keywords: Visual fatigue · User interfaces · Interface design · Visual perception · Information interaction

1 Introduction

As the number and variety of computer and mobile phone software increase, the frequency and length of interactions with the soft interface in daily life, work and entertainment are rapidly increasing. Long-term focus on the software interface can lead to visual fatigue and a host of problems. Existing research has found that text, color and graphics are associated with visual fatigue in interface design. The appropriate use of interface design elements can reduce visual fatigue, while inappropriate use can accelerate the onset of visual fatigue, increase the level of visual fatigue and even lead to eye disease. The study of visual fatigue is increasing every year all over the world, but it is mainly focused on the impact of physical properties of software interface display devices or user environments on visual fatigue. Not much research has been conducted

© Springer Nature Switzerland AG 2021
C. Stephanidis et al. (Eds.): HCII 2021, CCIS 1419, pp. 182–188, 2021.
https://doi.org/10.1007/978-3-030-78635-9_26

on the effects of software interface design elements on visual fatigue. Therefore, from the current research on the influence of interface design on visual fatigue, the following two questions are proposed: 1) Which interface design elements are currently the focus of visual fatigue research; 2) What methods are available to detect the incidence of visual fatigue and how to measure the degree of eye fatigue? We look forward to providing direction and methodological basis for future experimental research in this field.

2 Statistics and Analysis

2.1 Research Themes

Over time, research themes have become more specific, ranging from whether software interface design causes visual fatigue to specific elements that cause visual fatigue. With the continuous upgrading of user requirements, the research on software interface design has made progress.

Autogenic factors are the result of differences between individuals or of individuals themselves changing over time. If the user has eye disease, physical discomfort, psychological pressure, etc., visual fatigue will be increased to some extent. These conditions are difficult to change by design. Therefore, scholars pay more attention to the design elements related to software interface, such as text (character size, line spacing, text layout, etc.), color (color values, chroma, contrast polarity, etc.), and graphics (graphic shapes, etc.).

After comparing and evaluating the literature on the effects of interfaces on visual fatigue over the past 10 years, we selected 11 papers related to interface design elements [1–11], which are summarized in the figure below (see Fig. 1).

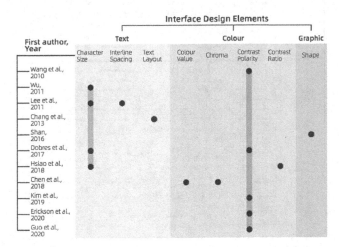

Fig. 1. Correlation between theme change and time in studies on the effect of interface design elements on visual fatigue.

As can be seen from Fig. 1, since 2010, the main research theme of interface design around visual fatigue has been textual and color elements, while most of the early research

184   J. Zhang et al.

has focused on textual elements. In recent years, colour elements have been the major research themes. In the study of textual elements, the effect of character size on visual fatigue is the main content. The effect of contrast polarity on visual fatigue has received major attention in studies on color elements. Research on graphic elements is rare, with only one study on the use of shape rule in web design retrieved between 2010 and 2020. The study did not conduct an experimental study, nor did it specify the effect of graphic use on visual fatigue.

At present, the effect of graphic elements on visual fatigue is seldom studied in interface design, which may be a worth-concerning theme for future research.

2.2 Research Methods

To date, research on the effects of changes in software interface elements on user visual fatigue has used several methods to assess and measure visual fatigue. After analyzing the studies mentioned above, the research methods used in the 10 papers were collected [1–4, 6–11] (one paper was removed because no experimental study was conducted). The methods were classified into three categories according to their characteristics: task measurement, physiological measurement, and subjective assessment. In the papers collected, statistics on the number of occurrences of the three methods are shown in the figure below (see Fig. 2).

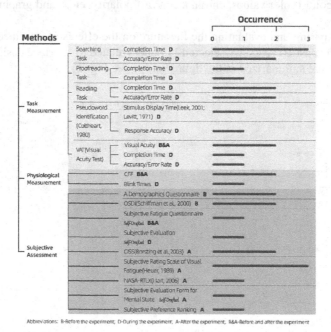

Fig. 2. Statistics and classification of visual fatigue detection methods in studies of the impact of interface design on visual fatigue.

As can be seen in Fig. 2, subjective assessment and task measurement are the most commonly used methods to study the effect of interface design elements on visual fatigue.

Questionnaires are mostly used for subjective assessment. Different questionnaires are used at different stages of the experiment. For example, demographic questionnaires and OSDI were used before the start of the experiment to assess the level of visual fatigue of the subjects in the pre-experimental phase. The subjective fatigue questionnaire, proposed by Guo [11], was used before and after the experiment. By comparing the results of the questionnaire, we can evaluate the degree of visual fatigue of subjects after the experiment. The Subjective evaluation method proposed by Chen [8] evaluated the effects of three colors (each color with nine different combinations of color values and chroma) on visual fatigue. After the user gazed at each combination, the subjective evaluation was performed to collect the user's subjective perception of eyestrain. In addition to the above questionnaires, we collect five subjective assessment questionnaires or methods used after the experiment, among which the subjective rating scale of the visual fatigue questionnaire [12] was the most common one. This questionnaire is a rating scale with six items to collect subjective rating of visual fatigue: (1) "I have difficulties in Seeing"; (2) "I have a strange feeling around the eyes"; (3) "My eyes feel tired"; (4) "I feel numb"; (5) "I have a headache"; (6) "I feel dizzy looking at the screen." Each item was rated on a 10-point scale for severity of discomfort, with "1" representing "not at all" and "10" representing "very much".

Task measurement can be divided into searching tasks, proofreading tasks, reading tasks, pseudo-word recognition task, and visual acuity test(VAT). Searching and reading tasks are the most common tasks and are measured with the indicators of completion time and accuracy.

Studies using physiological measurement methods are not very common and are limited to Critical Flash Fusion Frequency (CFFF) and blink times statistics. CFFF, also known as Critical Flash Fusion (CFF), is the minimum frequency of a stimulus that is just capable of eliciting the sensation of flash fusion. It expresses the limitations of the visual system's ability to discriminate over time and reflects the extent to which people can distinguish flashbacks. It has been found that visual fatigue causes a significant decrease in flash fusion frequency values. The method of calculating the flashing time is to compare the differences of the flash time caused by different interface design elements. The more blinks, the more severe the visual fatigue.

In summary, the subjective evaluation methods mostly take the form of questionnaires. However, subjective qualitative methods have the limitations, as their results may also be influenced by the subject's emotions. Physiological measurement methods focus on changes in physiological signals and provide a more objective assessment of fatigue states. The task measurement method is mainly used to detect visual performance and visual fatigue at the same time. The measurement accuracy and completion time are the main measurement indexes. However, visual fatigue is not the only factor in the deterioration of visual performance. Therefore, the task measurement method cannot directly detect visual fatigue, but requires the use of physiological measurement and subjective assessment methods to assist in the detection of visual fatigue. Most articles tend to use more than one method to ensure the accuracy of the measurement results.

To explore the regularity of research methods over time, we summarize the methods used in the 10 articles in chronological order in the figure below [1–4, 6–11] (one article has been removed because no experimental study was conducted) (see Fig. 3).

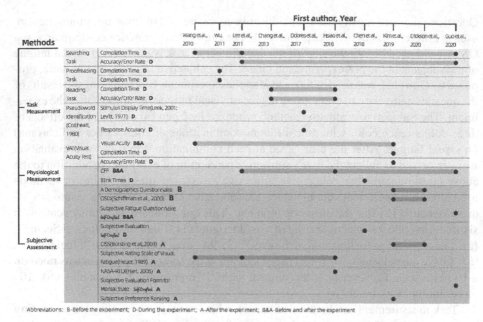

Fig. 3. Correlation between changes in visual fatigue detection methods and time in studies of the impact of interface design on visual fatigue.

As shown in Fig. 3, over time, the high-frequency methods used in the studies have changed from task measurement methods to physiological measurement and subjective assessment methods, with a tendency to apply a combination of methods. Early studies tended to use searching, proofreading, and reading tasks, supplemented by the subjective rating scale of visual fatigue questionnaire [12], visual acuity test, or the CFF. In recent years, studies tend to combine physiological measurement and subjective assessment, and propose new subjective assessment scales.

3   Conclusion

By categorizing and summarizing the literature on the impact of the software interface design elements on users' visual fatigue, this study outlines and classifies the research themes and methods. We find that the number of articles related to visual fatigue has increased significantly since 2011, entering a period of rapid growth, but some common problems need further breakthroughs: (1) In terms of research themes, existing research focuses on two interface design elements, text, and color, while the effect of graphic elements on visual fatigue is seldom studied. Much of the current research focuses on a single type of element rather than a combination of multiple elements; (2) In terms of research methods, task measurement and subjective assessment methods are more common and diverse. Physiological measurement methods, on the other hand, are less diverse and less frequently used.

This study shows that more and more research has been conducted on studies on interface design concerning visual fatigue, with a gradual enrichment of research themes and a diversification of research methods. It is worth mentioning that the interface presentation carriers used by scholars have evolved from early electronic paper and LCD screens to head-mounted display (HMD). Currently, scholars have studied the effects of 2D and 3D baseball game interface on visual fatigue and found that 3D HMD game interface causes higher visual fatigue [13]. Therefore, the effect of 3D interface on user visual fatigue may be the future research direction.

Due to the complexity of the elements influencing visual fatigue, the themes and methods in this area still need to be further explored and deepened. We believe that future research themes can focus on the relationship between graphic elements of interface design and visual fatigue, and combine two or three elements to study their effects on visual fatigue. Future research methods can increase the use of physiological measurement methods, and draw lessons from other visual fatigue research fields, such as eye movement parameters, pulse signals, ECG, etc., to improve the objectivity and reliability of research results.

References

1. Wang, A.H., Kuo, H.T., Huang, S.: Effects of polarity and ambient illuminance on the searching performance and visual fatigue for various aged users. IEEE (2010)
2. Wu, H.-C.: Electronic paper display preferred viewing distance and character size for different age groups. Ergonomics **54**(9), 806–814 (2011)
3. Dsl, A., et al.: Effect of light source, ambient illumination, character size and interline spacing on visual performance and visual fatigue with electronic paper displays. Displays **32**(1), 1–7 (2011)
4. Chang, W.-T., Shih, L.-H., Chiang, Z., Huang, K.-C.: On the reading performance of text layout, switch position, topic of text, and luminance contrast for chinese e-books interface design. In: Yamamoto, S. (ed.) HIMI 2013. LNCS, vol. 8016, pp. 567–575. Springer, Heidelberg (2013). https://doi.org/10.1007/978-3-642-39209-2_63
5. Shan, Y.: The application of shape rule in web page design. In: 2016 6th International Conference on Machinery, Materials, Environment, Biotechnology and Computer (MMEBC 2016) (2016)
6. Dobres, J., Chahine, N., Reimer, B.: Effects of ambient illumination, contrast polarity, and letter size on text legibility under glance-like reading. Appl. Ergon. **60**, 68–73 (2017)
7. Hsiao, C.Y., et al.: Usability evaluation of monocular optical head-mounted displays on reading tasks. J. Ambient Intell. Hum. Comput. 1 (2018)
8. Chen, C.C., Huang, Y.Y.: Exploring the effect of color on the gaze input interface. In: International Conference on Applied System Invention (2018)
9. Kim, K., et al.: Effects of dark mode on visual fatigue and acuity in optical see-through head-mounted displays. In: Symposium on Spatial User Interaction (2019)
10. Erickson, A., et al.: Effects of dark mode graphics on visual acuity and fatigue with virtual reality head-mounted displays. In: 2020 IEEE Conference on Virtual Reality and 3D User Interfaces (VR). IEEE (2020)
11. Guo, C., et al.: Study on the effect of different color schemes of form on visual fatigue. In: 2020 IEEE International Conference on Artificial Intelligence and Computer Applications (ICAICA). IEEE (2020)

12. Heuer, H., et al.: Rest position of the eyes and its effect on viewing distance and visual fatigue in computer display work. Z Exp Angew Psychol. **36**(4), 538–566 (1989)
13. Lin, P.H., Chang, C.N.: Effects of display interface, operation time, and speed on signal detection theory, visual fatigue, and presence: an example of 3D baseball games. J. Technol. **32**(3), 219–226 (2017)

Designing for Children

Social Presence in Evaluations for a Humanoid Robot and Its Effect on Children-Robot Relationship

Yi-Chen Chen[1,3,4], Edwinn Gamborino[2,3,4], Li-Chen Fu[2,3,4], Hsiu-Ping Yueh[1,4,5], and Su-Ling Yeh[1,3,4,6]($\boxtimes$)

[1] Department of Psychology, National Taiwan University, Taipei, Taiwan
suling@ntu.edu.tw
[2] Department of Electrical Engineering and Department of Computer Science and Information Engineering, National Taiwan University, Taipei, Taiwan
[3] MOST Joint Research Center for AI Technology and All Vista Healthcare, Taipei, Taiwan
[4] Center for Artificial Intelligence and Advanced Robotics, National Taiwan University, Taipei, Taiwan
[5] Department of Bio-Industry Communication and Development, National Taiwan University, Taipei, Taiwan
[6] Graduate Institute of Brain and Mind Sciences, National Taiwan University, Taipei, Taiwan

Abstract. As children are at a critical stage in their lives in developing and practicing social skills, they tend to imagine objects as interactive agents. For example, even a toy dinosaur can be perceived as affable and more as a social entity, namely, with a strong social presence (SP). This study investigated whether perceived SP changes (measured using the SP questionnaire) as children interacted with a robot. Furthermore, we investigated how SP modulated children-robot relationships and children's overall attitudes towards robots. Children aged 6–12 interacted with a companion robot, RoBoHoN, for short intervals. Attitude evaluations were completed at three-time points: prior-, mid-, and post-interaction. SP and rapport with RoBoHoN were measured and compared mid-and post-interaction, while attitudes towards the robot were tested prior- and post-interaction. The results showed a stronger intention to use robots before interaction correlated with higher SP scores with RoBoHoN. As SP level was stable across mid- and post-interaction, we analyzed SP as a between-groups factor to compare attitude evaluations among children who rated RoBoHoN with higher versus lower SP scores. The high SP group found RoBoHoN to be more likable and playing with it as more enjoyable, but the effect on rapport level was marginal. The Implicit Association Task revealed no bias towards robots among children in both groups. This study shows SP's positive effect on children-robot interaction and highlights the importance of SP in designing social companion robots for children.

Keywords: Children-robot interaction · Social presence · Robots acceptance · Negative attitude towards robots · Implicit association task

© Springer Nature Switzerland AG 2021
C. Stephanidis et al. (Eds.): HCII 2021, CCIS 1419, pp. 191–199, 2021.
https://doi.org/10.1007/978-3-030-78635-9_27

1 Introduction

Perceived sociality is fundamental to initiating and sustaining the entire process of child-robot interaction. Children who are still developing and practicing their social skills tend to imagine objects as interactive agents, namely, with strong social presence (SP). Perceived SP is defined as the degree to which a person is perceived as a "real person" in mediated communication [1]. Children who perceived stronger SP to a pet robot produce more engaging activities like petting and grooming and reciprocity actions such as teaching new skills and demanding attention [2]. In the learning context, the robot's tutoring experiences often exceed computer-based tutoring systems' effectiveness [3]. Therefore, investigating perceived SP can be the first step in promoting robot usage to the children population.

Breazeal [4] argues that robots' social abilities are among the significant determinants for accepting and using robots. Chien [5] showed that interacting with a socially assistive robot can increase older adults' acceptance despite their initially lower curiosity towards robots. In the same vein, perceived SP is positively associated with the increased intention to use the robot in older adults [6]. These results imply that among users with less familiarity with technology (i.e., older adults), SP could facilitate the intention to use the robot and lead to positive human-robot relationships. However, unlike adults who have witnessed the recent decades' dramatic advances of technology and need interaction before developing acceptance, children are born in this digital era. Therefore, children may be intrinsically more accepting towards robots, rendering prior exposure to a robot unnecessary. It is likely that children's overall acceptance of robots could directly impact the perceived SP.

Not only is higher SP related to greater enjoyment [6, 7], but a stronger SP is also linked to greater attraction [8]. Although SP seems like a determinant for various positive attitudes towards robots, it does not eliminate all concerns towards interacting with robots. For instance, robots with higher social abilities were found to elicit more ambivalent attitudes from participants: being viewed as allies and enemies simultaneously [9]. Similarly, attitudinal ambivalence can be found between explicit and implicit measures of attitudes. While negative attitudes towards robots can be reduced by interaction experience, implicit negative attitudes remain significant in older adults [5]. These results underscore that attitudes towards robots are multi-dimensional rather than bipolar. As few studies have focused on children's attitudes towards robots, it is crucial to include positive and negative aspects, and behavioral measures in addition to questionnaires to examine SP's effect on children's attitudes towards robots.

Since SP can profoundly influence attitudes that develop later, its stability plays a crucial role in designing social robots. In a previous study [10], children's perceived SP decreases the most after five weeks of interaction in a chess game context. As most studies assessed SP after only one interaction, results may be confounded by novelty, which has been shown to influence positive evaluations in children's study [11]. Alternatively, preconceptions of a robot's capabilities would be overridden as children become more familiar with the robot. As such, unmet expectations could lower SP and robot likability. The above demonstrates the necessity to revisit SP through repeated measures to fortify previous claims of its effect on attitudes. Thus, our goals are to explore: 1) whether SP remains stable across short but intense interaction sessions, 2) could acceptance to robots predetermine perceived SP, 3) how does SP modulate children-robot interaction, and 4) children's overall attitudes towards robots.

2 Method

2.1 Apparatus

A small humanoid robot, RoBoHoN, developed by Sharp Corporation, was introduced to interact with children participants. In contrast to most studies using the Wizard-of-Oz implementation, we programmed the RoBoHoN system with basic Natural Language Processing (NLP) capabilities that can execute behaviors autonomously (*see details in* [12]). For example, the robot can generate different replies depending on users' responses to questions like "Would you like to hear a funny joke?". Also, expected replies were predefined (e.g., answers to a riddle, name, and gender) and used in the robot's utterances in the subsequent interactions. In this study, RoBoHoN could initiate four actions: dancing, playing short videos, telling jokes, and chatting.

2.2 Procedure

After confirming and agreeing with the experiment content, the children's parents completed the consent form, and experimental procedures were explained to the children. Interaction sessions were split into 5 to 10-min intervals for a total of 30 min due to limited time slot, and interaction intervals were divided among four days. Three parallel groups of experiments were also running simulatenously. Participants chatted freely with RoBoHoN during each interaction, and the robot would perform actions according to participants' responses (*see* Apparatus). Evaluations were collected at three time points during the series of interactions: 1) before participants had made contact with RoBoHoN, 2) at the midpoint of interaction sessions with approximately 15 min of accumulated interaction, and 3) after all interaction sessions with 30 min of accumulated interaction. Participants were informed that they could stop the interaction whenever they felt uncomfortable or bored.

2.3 Participants

Nineteen children (ages from 6–12) were recruited from a five-day robotics/programming workshop held by the Computer and Information Networking Center at National Taiwan University, Taiwan. Five children failed to complete the experiment (requested to end the interaction, absence, unable to understand the task); thus, 14 participants (4 female, age $= 10.79 \pm 1.12$) remained for further analyses.

2.4 Measurements

Self-reported questionnaires were used to measure the impression of the robot. Participants rated their perception of RoBoHoN by using the social presence questionnaire (5 items, mid-interaction: $\alpha = .86$; post-interaction: $\alpha = .83$) [2], perceived enjoyment questionnaire (5 items, mid-interaction:$\alpha = .86$) [13], likability ratings (4 items, mid-interaction: mid-interaction:$\alpha = .73$) [14], and Human-Agent Rapport Questionnaire (HARQ) (14 Items, mid-interaction: $\alpha = .90$; post-interaction: $\alpha = .83$) [15].

In terms of general attitudes towards robots, the questionnaire-based measurements include the 1) acceptance towards technology scale [16], where items were adopted by a previous study that examined the acceptance towards robots (perceived usefulness, PU (4 items, $\alpha = .77$), perceived ease of use, PEU[1] (4 items, pre-interaction: $\alpha = -.11$), and intention to use, IU (2 items, pre-interaction: $\alpha = .79$) [5]), 2) state curiosity (3 items, pre-interaction: $\alpha = .83$) [5]), and 3) the negative attitudes towards robots scale (NARS) (future/social influence, FSI[2] (3 items, pre-interaction:$\alpha = .57$, post-interaction:$\alpha = .53$), relational attitudes, RA (5 items, pre-interaction:$\alpha = .62$, post-interaction: $\alpha = .75$), and actual interactions and situations, AIS[3] (3 items, pre-interaction:$\alpha = .17$, post-interaction:$\alpha = .81$) [17].

Implicit attitudes towards robots was assessed using the adapted version of the implicit association test (IAT) after interaction [5]. The IAT measures an individual's automatic associations of two target concepts (e.g., robot vs. human) along an attribute dimension (e.g., negative vs. positive emotional words) by the reaction time while pairing concepts to attributes. Participants were instructed to respond as fast and accurately as possible to the presented associations (further details for experimental stimuli and design refer to [5]). *Cohen's d* was calculated as the index of implicit attitude towards robots, named as D1 score[4]. Higher D1 scores represent better efficiency in associating robots with negative evaluations; in other words, a more robust negative attitude towards robots relative to humans.

3 Results

3.1 Perceived Social Presence was Stable Across Interactions

We compared attitude evaluations among children who rated RoBoHoN with higher versus lower SP scores (Low SP: M = 15.3, High SP: M = 22). Results of analysis of variance (ANOVA) (between-subject factor: High vs. Low SP group; within-subject factor: mid- vs. post-interaction) showed no interaction effect $F(1, 12) = 1.33, p = .27$, $\eta_p^2 = .10$. Moreover, the main effect of time was not significant $F(1, 12) = .85, p = .37$, $\eta_p^2 = .07$, indicating no differences between mid- or post-interactions for both groups of children. An independent-samples t-test was calculated to ensure that age did not differ between the two groups (Low SP: M = 11.14, SD = 0.9; High SP: M = 10.43, SD =

---

[1] The negative Cronbach's alpha value in PEU subscale indicates a heterogenous consistency, thus the PEU factor will be precluded from the further analyses.

[2] The following item in NARS were excluded from analyses due to low internal consistency (in FSI): "I feel that if I depend on robots too much, something bad might happen".

[3] The low Cronbach's alpha value in pre-interaction AIS subscale indicates a poor internal consistency, thus the AIS factor will be precluded from the further analyses.

[4] D1 score was calculated by subtracting the mean reaction time of the congruent stage from the incongruent stage and divided by the difference with the combined standard deviation of these two critical stages.

1.27; $t(12) = 1.21, p = .25$). As SP was stable across interactive sessions, SP assessed at mid-interaction, representing first impressions towards the robot, thus serves as the main factor in the following analyses.

3.2 Higher Intention to Use Robot Correlated with Higher SP After the First-Time Interaction

Results of Pearson's correlation analyses indicated that, among all the attitudes towards robots, IU in the TAM ($r = .74, p = .002$) was the only factor positively associated with SP before interaction. Others showed no correlation with SP: PU in the TAM ($r = .065$, $p = .83$), state curiosity ($r = .42, p = .08$), the subscales in NARS, FSI ($r = -.17, p = .57$), and RA ($r = -.42, p = .14$).

3.3 Higher SP Corresponded to Better Impressions of the Robot

Independent-samples t-tests were performed to investigate whether differences in SP reflect a better interactive experience with RoBoHoN. Subjective rating of likability was higher in the High SP group than that of the Low SP group. The level of enjoyment in the High SP group was also rated higher than that of the Low SP group (Table 1).

Table 1. Results of independent-samples t-test examining impressions on RoBoHoN

	Low SP		High SP		df	t-value
	M	SD	M	SD		
Likability	5.54	0.92	6.71	0.30	7.3	3.2^*
Enjoyment	5.69	0.81	6.8	0.22	6.8	3.7^{**}

$^*p < .05.$ $^{**}p < .01.$

3.4 Rapport Increased After Interactions Regardless of SP

To investigate how SP affected rapport between children and RoBoHoN after the series of interactions, a two-way mixed ANOVA (within-subject factor: mid- vs. post-interaction; between-subject factor: Low vs. High SP group) was performed (Table 2 shows descriptive values). The main effect of interacting experience was found, $F(1, 12) = 9.67, p = .009, \eta_p^2 = .45$, indicating that the level of rapport increased after a series of interactions. Rapport was rated marginally higher in the high SP group compared to low SP group ($F(1, 12) = 4.69, p = .051, \eta_p^2 = 0.28$). However, no interaction was found between interacting experiences and the SP group ($F(1, 12) = 0.23, p = .64, \eta_p^2 = 0.02$).

3.5 Higher SP Corresponded to Lower Negative Relational Attitudes to Robots

Mixed ANOVAs were performed on the subscales of NARS. The main effect of SP was found in the RA subscale, $F(1, 12) = 5.81, p = .033, \eta_p^2 = 0.33$: Children in the High SP group expressed less RA compared to those of the Low SP group (Fig. 1). No other effects were significant ($ps < .05$).

Table 2. Descriptive values for rapport as a function of a 2 (interaction) × 2 (group) design

Interaction	Group			
	Low SP		High SP	
	M	SD	M	SD
Mid-	3.39	0.31	3.72	0.27
Post-	3.76	0.46	4.23	0.63

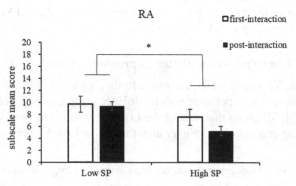

Fig. 1. Results of the RA subscale in the NARS. The relational attitude (RA) towards robots was lower in the High SP group regardless of the interactive experiences. Error bars represent one standard error from the mean.

3.6 No Implicit Bias Towards Robots

An independent-samples t-test showed that there was no difference in the D1 scores between the Low SP (M = 0.27, SD = 0.38) and High SP group (M = 0.23, SD = 0.48), $t(12) = 0.18$, $p = .86$. The one-sample t-test further revealed that the D1 score in both the Low ($t(6) = 1.85$, $p = .11$) and High SP ($t(6) = 1.24$, $p = .26$) group did not significantly differ from zero. These results indicated that regardless of the level of perceived SP, children did not express implicit biases towards robots.

4 Discussion, Limitations, and Future Work

The present work investigated the effect of a robot's SP and children's interactive experiences on the children-robot relationship and children's general attitudes towards robots. Our study showed that the perceived SP of an interactive social robot did not decay in short and intensive interaction sessions. SP has been shown to decline drastically after a 5-week interaction [10]. The relatively stable SP in this study could be due to the short time interval (i.e., three days). Alternatively, the improved social abilities of RoBoHoN compared with other robots equipped with only emotional gestures could also account for this effect. Future studies should consider the embedded social ability of robots when examining the temporal effect of SP. Our findings suggest that SP has positively affected the robot's evaluation, including its likability and interaction enjoyment. However, SP has only a marginal effect on rapport level, where interaction experience has a more significant impact. Since the development of relationships is a slow process, and frequency of interaction can be a critical factor in children's perception of friendship [18], this suggests that SP's positive effects are impression-wise; actual interaction plays a prominent role in increasing perceived closeness.

Among the NARS subscales, anxiety of having a relationship with robots decreased in children with higher perceived SP. Unlike adults who find robots that simulate human social ability unnerving [19], children seem less troubled by a robot's social ability. Instead, they found fewer concerns of relationship-building after interacting with a robot with high SP. Interestingly, children do not have an implicit bias towards robots as adults do [5]. Regardless of their perceived level of SP, children did not tend to associate negative emotions with robots. The phenomenon echos with our conjecture that children in this generation have a more liberal acceptance of robots than adults do.

As SP is shown to be critical in influencing users' decision to accept social robots [7], our study showed that the overall acceptance towards robots before actual contact could also have a facilitative effect on SP. Specifically, the intention to use robots affects how sociable a robot would be to children. According to the technology acceptance model, enjoyment is the intrinsic motivation of using technology [7]. Therefore, for children, SP of robots may increase as a function of individual differences in pleasure-seeking. State curiosity towards robots and NARS showed no correlation to SP, which further highlights that attitudes based on practical concerns (e.g., information selection, future direction, etc.) are not the primary factor for shaping the perception of SP.

A major limitation of this study is the selection of the samples. Since all participants were recruited from a robot programming camp, they may have higher acceptance of robots or better familiarity with robotic technology. Thus the differential effects between SP groups may be less prominent. Moreover, part of the questionnaire-based attitude tasks' subscales did not have consistent reliability (i.e., the PEU in TAM and the FSI and AIS in NARS), probably due to the relatively complex wording that was designed for adults. This highlights the need for studies that develop/construct attitudinal scales to assess acceptance and negative attitude of robots specifically for children.

5 Conclusions

This study provides important implications for children-robot interactions. Based on the present results, perceived SP positively affects impressions towards robots, which further reduces anxiety in relationship-building with robots in general. Furthermore, the lack of an implicit bias to robots underscores the distinctiveness of children users from adult users. To promote childern's use of robots, robotic designers should consider enhancing the perceived SP of robots through increasing the intention to use robots, which may lead to a more positive attitudes towards robots.

References

1. Short, J., Williams, E., Christie, B.: The Social Psychology of Telecommunications. Wiley, Toronto, London, New York (1976)

2. Heerink, M., et al.: A field study with primary school children on perception of social presence and interactive behavior with a pet robot. In: 2012 IEEE RO-MAN: The 21st IEEE International Symposium on Robot and Human Interactive Communication, pp. 1045–1050, September 2012. https://doi.org/10.1109/roman.2012.6343887

3. Janssen, J.B., van der Wal, C.C., Neerincx, M.A., Looije, R.: Motivating children to learn arithmetic with an adaptive robot game. In: Mutlu, B., Bartneck, C., Ham, J., Evers, V., Kanda, T. (eds.) ICSR 2011. LNCS (LNAI), vol. 7072, pp. 153–162. Springer, Heidelberg (2011). https://doi.org/10.1007/978-3-642-25504-5_16

4. Breazeal, C.: Toward sociable robots. Rob. Auton. Syst. **42**(3–4), 167–175 (2003). https://doi.org/10.1016/S0921-8890(02)00373-1

5. Chien, S.-E., et al.: Age difference in perceived ease of use, curiosity, and implicit negative attitude toward robots. ACM Trans. Hum.-Robot Interact. **8**(2), 9 (2019)

6. Heerink, M., Kröse, B., Evers, V., Wielinga, B.: The influence of social presence on enjoyment and intention to use of a robot and screen agent by elderly users. In: Proceedings of the 17th IEEE International Symposium on Robot and Human Interactive Communication. Technische Universität München, Munich, Germany (2008). https://doi.org/10.1109/roman.2008.4600748

7. Shin, D.H., Choo, H.: Modeling the acceptance of socially interactive robotics: social presence in human-robot interaction. Interact. Stud. **12**(3), 430–460 (2011). https://doi.org/10.1075/is.12.3.04shi

8. Lee, K.M., Peng, W., Jin, S.A., Yan, C.: Can robots manifest personality?: An empirical test of personality recognition, social responses, and social presence in human-robot interaction. J. Commun. **56**(4), 754–772 (2006). https://doi.org/10.1111/j.1460-2466.2006.00318.x

9. Dang, J., Liu, L.: Robots are friends as well as foes: ambivalent attitudes toward mindful and mindless AI robots in the United States and China. Comput. Human Behav. **115**, 106612 (2021). https://doi.org/10.1016/j.chb.2020.106612

10. Leite, I., Martinho, C., Pereira, A., Paiva, A.: As time goes by: long-term evaluation of social presence in robotic companions. In: Proceedings - IEEE International Symposium on Robot and Human Interactive Communication, pp. 669–674 (2009). https://doi.org/10.1109/roman.2009.5326256

11. Kanda, T., Shimada, M., Koizumi, S.: Children learning with a social robot. In: 2012 7th ACM/IEEE International Conference on Human-Robot Interaction (HRI), pp. 351–358 (2012)

12. Gamborino, E., Yueh, H.-P., Lin, W., Yeh, S.-L., Fu, L.-C.: Mood estimation as a social profile predictor in an autonomous, multi-session, emotional support robot for children. In: 2019 28th IEEE International Conference on Robot and Human Interactive Communication (RO-MAN), pp. 1–6, October 2019. https://doi.org/10.1109/ro-man46459.2019.8956460

13. Heerink, M., Kröse, B., Evers, V., Wielinga, B.: Assessing acceptance of assistive social agent technology by older adults: the almere model. Int. J. Soc. Robot. **2**(4), 361–375 (2010). https://doi.org/10.1007/s12369-010-0068-5

14. Bartneck, C., Kanda, T., Ishiguro, H., Hagita, N.: Is the uncanny valley an uncanny cliff? In: RO-MAN 2007-The 16th IEEE International Symposium on Robot and Human Interactive Communication, pp. 368–373 (2007)

15. Cerekovic, A., Aran, O., Gatica-Perez, D.: Rapport with virtual agents: what do human social cues and personality explain? IEEE Trans. Affect. Comput. **8**(3), 382–395 (2017). https://doi.org/10.1109/TAFFC.2016.2545650

16. Venkatesh, V., Davis, F.D.: A theoretical extension of the technology acceptance model: four longitudinal field studies. Manage. Sci. **46**(2), 186–204 (2000)

17. Syrdal, D.S., Dautenhahn, K., Koay, K.L., Walters, M.L.: The negative attitudes towards robots scale and reactions to robot behaviour in a live human-robot interaction study (2009)

18. Newcomb, A.F., Bagwell, C.L.: Children's friendship relations: a meta-analytic review. Psychol. Bull. **117**(2), 306–347 (1995). https://doi.org/10.1037/0033-2909.117.2.306
19. Gray, K., Wegner, D.M.: Feeling robots and human zombies: mind perception and the uncanny valley. Cognition **125**(1), 125–130 (2012). https://doi.org/10.1016/j.cognition.2012.06.007

Research and Design of Children's Household Nebulizer Requirements Based on Kano Model

Tianhong Fang$^{(\boxtimes)}$ and Yiwen Han

School of Art Design and Media, East China University of Science and Technology,
Shanghai 200237, China

Abstract. With the intensification of air pollution, the probability of children suffering from respiratory diseases has greatly increased. More and more people are performing nebulization therapy at home. The purpose of this article is to understand the perceptual needs of parents when choosing household nebulizers for preschool children, so that children can complete the treatment more comfortably. The Kano model is used to analyze the functional requirements of non-autonomous children's parents for children's household nebulizers, and obtain the priority of requirements, then establish the appearance semantic space based on Kansei engineering, and use factor analysis to obtain the appearance perceptual needs. Finally, a reference design of functional and appearance is proposed for the design of children's household nebulizers. This article combines the Kano model with Kansei engineering to obtain the functional requirements and appearance requirements of parents for children's household nebulizers, and verify them through design practice. It can provide reference for the design of children's household nebulizers in the future.

Keywords: Kano model · Children · Household nebulizer · Kansei engineering

1 Introduction

In recent years, as air pollution caused by haze has increased, the prevalence of chronic diseases among children is gradually increasing. At present, there are about 6 million children with asthma in China, and it is increasing at a rate of 20%–50% every ten years. An epidemiological survey in China in 2013 showed that the prevalence of asthma among children aged from 0 to 14 in cities was 3.02%, and the prevalence of all age groups showed an upward trend [1].

As the most direct treatment for asthma, nebulizers are gradually replacing drugs and injections. With the rise of home medical products, household nebulizers have gradually entered people's homes with their convenience and efficiency. Treatment at home is not only more convenient, but also avoids cross-infection. However, due to the low penetration rate of nebulizers in the domestic market, there are few designs of household nebulizers for children. In addition, products need to meet the perceptual needs of users while meeting functional requirements.

Therefore, this article is based on perceptual engineering and Kano model, taking parents of non-autonomous children as the research object, analyzing parents' perceptual needs for nebulizers in the process of treating children and purchasing products.

© Springer Nature Switzerland AG 2021
C. Stephanidis et al. (Eds.): HCII 2021, CCIS 1419, pp. 200–207, 2021.
https://doi.org/10.1007/978-3-030-78635-9_28

2   Methods

2.1   Kansei Engineering

Kansei Engineering was proposed by the Japanese scholar Yamamoto Kenichi. Through perceptual engineering, users' perceptual needs for products can be transformed into product morphological design elements. Measurement methods are divided into psychological measurement methods and physiological measurement methods. At present, the semantic difference method is a commonly used psychological measurement method to measure emotion. On the basis of traditional engineering methods to solve product design problems, Kansei Engineering incorporates the emotional needs of users to make products more in line with user preferences.

2.2   Application of Kano Model in Kansei Engineering

In addition to the perceptual appearance research of the product, the functional requirements of the product itself need to be discussed, so the Kano model is mentioned here. The Kano model was announced by Tokyo Institute of Technology professor Noriaki Kano at the Japan Quality Management Conference in 1982 [5]. By analyzing the degree of user satisfaction with the product, the product functions are classified to determine the priority in the product realization process. The Kano model divides user needs into five categories: basic needs, expected needs, exciting needs, indifferent needs, and reverse needs. Its evaluation mode is to directly ask users about their overall satisfaction with the product when a certain factor is present or missing.

The combination of Kansei Engineering and Kano model has been involved in many fields. Guoqiang Chen et al. combined Kano model with Kansei Engineering, through principal component analysis combined with multiple linear regression, explored the relationship between user's perceptual needs and product design, and took public bicycles as an example to merge product features into basic types and expectations and excitement [5]. Bao Zhang et al. planned the CMF design process and completed the CMF design of the Bluetooth speaker based on the perceptual engineering and KANO model [7]. However, there is still few research in the field of home medical products, most of which are for general medical patients and doctors, and there is a lack of research for children.

This article hopes that through the research of Kansei Engineering and Kano model, we can get a more comprehensive understanding of parents' perceptual needs for the functional and appearance of children's household nebulizers. Then we can design products that meet the overall needs of parents, help parents and children successfully complete parental treatment. The research process is shown in Fig. 1.

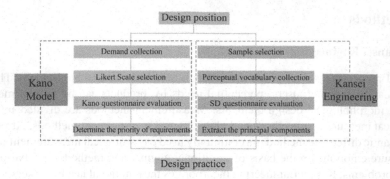

Fig. 1. Study process.

3 Perceptual Research on Children's Household Nebulizers

The household nebulizer is used as a daily treatment instrument, mainly to provide nebulization treatment for patients. Because of their particularity, children need targeted designs. According to the research of early childhood psychology and emotional characteristics, it can be found that children aged 3 to 6 are in a period of rapid growth and fluctuation of emotional development. From the age of 3, children initially form self-awareness and have an objective understanding of emotional state. Children's emotions at the age of 6 have developed to become more comprehensive, and children from 7 to 8 years old are generally able to view emotions rationally. Therefore, this product is mainly designed for children between 3 and 6 years old.

However, due to the particularity of the separation between actual users and purchasers of children's products, and children aged 0 to 6 are non-autonomous children, the decision-making power is dominated by parents [9]. Therefore, the needs of parents must be fully considered. As a purchaser, if the product cannot meet the needs of the parent, it will be difficult for the product to reach the child. So the main research objects of this article are parents of children aged 3 to 6. And break down the needs of parents into functional needs and perceptual appearance needs.

3.1 Acquisition of Product Functional Requirements

The basic function of a nebulizer is to perform nebulization therapy, but due to the particularity of children, their physical and psychological characteristics need to be considered. Therefore, parents have different needs for different functions when they treat and purchase products for children. In this paper, Kano model is used to determine the functional requirement level of children's household nebulizers.

Demand Collection. First of all, through the literature, the Internet, and user surveys, we understand the main issues that parents are concerned about in the process of nebulization treatment for children. According to the problems in use, the situation analysis method is adopted, and the user needs are improved through discussions with related users and designers, as shown in Table 1.

Table 1. The initial user needs of children's household nebulizers.

No.	User needs	No.	User needs
1	Suitable mask	8	Easy to clean
2	Soft mask edges	9	Adjustable fog
3	Low machine noise	10	Fun
4	Small size	11	Interactivity
5	Portable	12	Easy to charge
6	Good-looking	13	Gameplay
7	Durable		

Likert Scale Selection. In order to ensure the accuracy of the selected user requirements, the 13 user requirements were tested. Design a questionnaire through the Likert scale method to evaluate the importance of each original requirement. The importance is assigned 5 points, 4 points, 3 points, 2 points, and 1 point respectively from high to low. And select 100 respondents to conduct a questionnaire survey. In order to ensure the accuracy of the experiment, the interviewees all had a certain understanding of children's household nebulizers. The questionnaire data was analyzed by SPSS software, and the reliability analysis was performed using Kronbach's alpha coefficient. The skewness coefficient and the total correlation coefficient CITC of the corrected terms are used as the test standard to screen user needs.

The absolute values of the skewness coefficients of requirements 4, 7, 8, and 9 are greater than 0.7, which does not meet the standard of skewness test. The corrected item of requirement 4 has a total correlation coefficient CITC < 0.3, and the Cronbach alpha coefficient after deletion is higher than the original, which does not meet the test standard of homogeneity test. Therefore, by excluding the unsatisfactory requirements and the low average requirements, the first seven requirements are selected, which are "Suitable mask", "Soft mask edges", "Good-looking", "Durable", "Easy to clean", "Adjustable fog", "Fun".

Kano Model Analysis. Design the KANO questionnaire according to 7 requirements. The questionnaire level is divided into satisfactory, as it should be, indifferent, acceptable, and dissatisfied. The survey is completed by the subjects' positive and negative evaluation of a certain characteristic of the product. Take "**Suitable mask**" as an example. Ask "what do you think when the mask is suitable?" "how do you feel when the mask isn't suitable?" for the subjects to evaluate.

86 parents of children who know about nebulizers were selected to conduct a questionnaire survey. The results of the questionnaire are classified by the KANO model demand classification evaluation form. Get the KANO category and Better-Worse coefficient corresponding to each demand. The calculation formula of Better-Worse coefficient is as follows:

$$SI = (A + O)/(A + O + M + I) \tag{1}$$

$$DSI = -1 \times (O + M)/(A + O + M + I) \tag{2}$$

Among them, M means necessary demand; O means desired demand; A means charm demand; R means that customers do not need this quality characteristic, or even dislike the quality characteristic; I means no difference demand; Q means questionable result. SI stands for satisfactory influence factor; DSI stands for unsatisfactory influence factor.

Draw a sensitivity matrix (see Fig. 2) based on the Better-Worse coefficient to determine the priority of demand improvement. According to the Better-Worse analysis chart, it can be found that the expected attributes include "suitable mask", and the attractive attributes include "Fun', "good-looking", "Adjustable fog" and "soft mask edges". Therefore, this article mainly focuses on expectations. And the demand of charm is used as a reference for the functional design of children's household nebulizers.

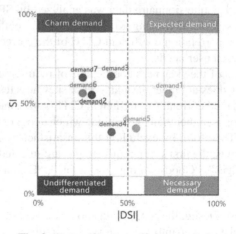

Fig. 2. Better-Worse coefficient analysis.

3.2 Acquisition of Product Appearance Requirements

In addition to the analysis of functional requirements, this article also uses Kansei engineering to obtain product appearance requirements, so as to have a more comprehensive understanding of users' needs for children's household nebulizers, and design products according to their functional and appearance requirements.

Sample Selection. A large number of samples of children's household nebulizers of different shapes have been searched from the market and websites. Through classification and screening by design professionals, 32 product samples were obtained by excluding pictures with similar shapes and low picture quality. They were grouped, classified and merged, using expert evaluation and card sorting methods, and finally got the 8 most representative samples, with lowercase letters as their order (see Fig. 3).

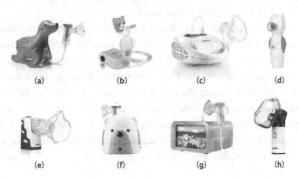

Fig. 3. Product sample selection.

Perceptual Vocabulary Collection. A large number of perceptual vocabularies related to children's household nebulizers have been searched through the Internet, books, interviews, etc. 40 perceptual words about children's nebulizers were obtained through preliminary screening.

Relying on the experience and knowledge of the relevant designers, the simplification and screening were carried out, the synonyms were reduced, the derogatory words were removed, the clustering was collected, and the 8 groups of adjectives that constitute the morphological feature space for Y_i were sorted and saved (see Table 2).

Table 2. Perceptual word pair.

No.	Word pair	No.	Word pair	No.	Word pair
Y_1	Dangerous-Safe	Y_4	Indifferent-Kind	Y_{10}	Industrial-Cute
Y_2	Amateur-Professional	Y_8	Bulky-Small	Y_{11}	Traditional-Interesting
Y_3	Complicated-Simple	Y_9	Geometric-Round		

Date Analysis. Combine the representative samples selected above to make a corresponding questionnaire for perceptual image vocabulary. 120 parents (60 males and 60 females) were selected, and the representative samples were evaluated and scored through the semantic difference scale. In order to reduce experimental errors, the interviewed parents all have college education or above, and have a certain understanding of children's household nebulizers.

The evaluation scale of the semantic difference scale is divided into 7 levels. After clarifying the meaning of each number, the parents start scoring.

Sort 120 questionnaires, sum each pair of perceptual words in each sample and calculate the average. Import the obtained data into SPSS software, and perform dimensionality reduction processing on the data through factor analysis. The explanation of the total variance shows that the children's household nebulizers are greatly affected by two components, which are component 1 and component 2, and the two components account for 87.524% of the overall proportion.

At the same time, the gravel map shows that there are two components with eigenvalues ≥ 1. The slope of the curve tends to be flat from the first inflection point, so it is verified that the method is feasible and it is reasonable to extract two factors.

The component matrix is obtained by the principal component extraction method. Here, the factors with load larger than 0.8 are selected, and the factors with smaller weights are excluded to analyze the main influencing factors of each component. There are Y_1, Y_2, Y_3 in component 1, and Y_6 in component 2. Therefore, it can be concluded that parents' perceptual needs for the appearance of children's household nebulizers are "safe", "professional", "simple" and "mellow".

4   Design of Children's Household Nebulizers

Based on the above-obtained functions and perceptual appearance requirements, the children's household atomizer concept has been designed as follow (see Fig. 4). The design scheme is obtained through 3D modeling and rendering.

Fig. 4. Product sample selection.

In the product function, a button for adjusting the amount of fog is integrated, and the current amount of fog is displayed by lighting. The edge of the mask is transformed into soft silicone, which can not only fit the face, but also achieve a soft effect. An underwater ring device is added to the body. The pressure sensor under the device can be triggered by the child's breath, and small bubbles can be squeezed upwards. The small bubbles can drive the ring in the tank to swim. The pillar in the center of the tank provides the ring set in, so as to realize a fun interaction between children and the machine. In addition, it is equipped with a peak flow meter to detect the current condition of children and make real-time medical records.

In the appearance of the product, the round shape is adopted, and the curve fits the grip of the child's upper hand and is not easy to slip off. In terms of color, white with professional colors is used, and warm colors with a sense of security are incorporated.

5 Conclusion

In order to make up for the lack of research on children's household nebulizers in the market, this article takes parents of involuntary children as the research object, and analyzes parents' perceptual needs for nebulizers in the process of treating children and purchasing products. The Kano model is used to analyze the functional requirements of non-autonomous children's parents for children's household nebulizers, and then establish the appearance semantic space based on perceptual engineering, and use factor analysis to obtain the appearance perceptual requirements. Through the above analysis, the functional and appearance perceptual requirements are obtained, so as to carry out the design practice of children's household nebulizers, and provide references for the design of children's household nebulizers.

References

1. National Children's Asthma Prevention and Control Cooperative Group: The third epidemiological survey of childhood asthma in Chinese cities. Chin. J. Pediatr. **51**(10), 729735 (2013)
2. Larson, I.A., Rodean, J., Richardson, T., Bergman, D., Morehous, J., Colvin, J.D.: Agreement of provider and parent perceptions of complex care medical homes after a care management intervention. J. Pediatr. Health Care **35**(1), 91–98 (2021)
3. Xi, X., Sun, W.: Design of home medical equipment products based on data from Tmall Medical Museum. Sci. Technol. Innov. Appl. **33**, 39–40 (2015)
4. Chen, G., Jiang, N., Zhang, P., Liu, Y.: Study on the modeling design of children's companion robot based on perceptual engineering. Packag. Eng. 1–8 (2020)
5. Chen, G., Shi, H., Zhang, F.: Innovative design of smart watches based on TRIZ and Kano models. Packag. Eng. **37**(16), 83–86 (2016)
6. Xiaoyun, X., Xie, Q., Zhang, S.: Children's participatory smart product design method using kansei engineering. Packag. Eng. **40**(18), 129–134 (2019)
7. Zhang, B., Hu, A., Zhang, D.: Research on CMF design method of bluetooth speaker based on kansei engineering. Packag. Eng. 1–8 (2020)
8. Tian, Z., Che, J., Li, J., Zhang, L.: Study on bicycle modeling requirements based on kansei engineering and kano model. Mach. Des. **34**(5), 113–118 (2017)

Maybe I Can Help? Google as a Translator and Facilitator for an Inter-lingual Children's Chat Application

Dev Raj Lamichhane(✉), Janet C. Read, and Zixi You

University of Central Lancashire, Preston PR1 2HE, UK
drlamichhane1@uclan.ac.uk

Abstract. In this paper, we describe the calculation of accuracy and understandability of the Google translations of 15 Nepalese and 22 English letters written by children. The accuracy of the translation is calculated using a Minimum String Distance algorithm comparing with the correct translation. For the Understandability calculation, 92 English and 36 Nepalese children participated in an activity that ascertained this. We found out that most of the translated texts are understandable even if they are not accurate. In the paper, we also unpick how Google Translate loses some information during translation and we discuss its effect on the understandability. We also explore the creativeness of children when they were trying to understand some unclear translations.

Keywords: Google translate · Accuracy · Understandability · Minimum string distance · Cross cultural chat

1 Background and Related Research

This paper reports work from a larger project where a digital pen pal application, 'Digipal', is being developed for children from different countries to chat with each other, make friends, and learn about each other's lifestyles and culture. The idea is similar to the old school pen pal letter exchange activity. A core question is: which language should children use in the app during chatting? One solution would be to ask all the children to talk in English, however, this would give children with better English knowledge some advantage, and we cannot expect that every child can write in English. Furthermore, from a sociolinguistic perspective, one of the most important ways to protect local languages (variation), especially those in danger of elimination, is to encourage the younger generation to use local language in their communication. Thus, one of the major aims of our project is to create a method where children can communicate in their own language and in so doing can promote the idea that all languages are equal. To make this happen, we need to integrate some type of translation software within the application to translate the children's letters, or at least to facilitate the inter-lingual communication.

From the time when there were no programs or software to do translation (i.e. human translator being the only solution), translation technology has evolved from word based to phrase based, then to statistical and memory based translation to neural

C. Stephanidis et al. (Eds.): HCII 2021, CCIS 1419, pp. 208–215, 2021.
https://doi.org/10.1007/978-3-030-78635-9_29

translation [6]. With the advent of AI and neural networks translation, software has been able to become highly available and adaptive. Google Translate (GT) is the most used translation engine in the world; first introduced in 2006, it is a web-based machine translation service which currently translates between more than 100 different languages. In 2016 Google enhanced its product by adding neural machine translation, [2], which uses deep learning techniques and example-based machine translation to translate the whole sentence with better accuracy with the help of end to end artificial neural networks. For every translation, Google looks for the pattern in millions of examples and decides which words to choose and how to arrange them. GT learns from millions of examples that makes it more accurate day by day. Google Translate is the most popular and frequently used translation software, and it is easy to implement within applications.

Google Translate has been evaluated in a range of academic papers, but these have primarily been with adult text. Examples include evaluations of the effectiveness of Google Translate for English into Bahasa [10], and from English into Arabic [7]. Translation using Google is sometimes inaccurate and can be misleading, it can sometimes change the meaning of whole text. It has been shown in studies that the full equivalence of translations between languages is very rare [4]. When technical terms are translated, there is a high risk of mistranslation and misunderstanding as shown in a study looking at translation in the context of accounting where back translation was used to check accuracy [3]. In another study, Groves and Mundt, [5], recruited some students whose first language was not English and asked them to complete their assignment in their first language which was later translated to English using Google Translate. They found that the translated English text had many grammatical errors. Van Rensberg et al., [11], translated 6 different texts from Afrikaans to English and vice-versa using Google Translate and concluded that the translation system needed a lot of improvements in their quality. Researchers also looked at the translation between English and Arabic. ElShiekh, [1], analysed the results from the translation and found out the translation had similar sort of errors such as identifying Arabic vowels, struggling with long and complex sentences etc.

With its use being widespread, the average reader can generally make sense of a translation from Google as long as he or she has some idea of the context. Therefore, to evaluate the role Google Translate plays in non-critical applications, whilst accuracy might be sub-optimal, understandability matters. For example, if a sentence which originally reads '*I have mum, dad and sister in my family*' is translated by Google into '*I have mum, dad, sister, my family*'; it may not be 100% accurate but a reader could look at the translated text and probably understand what the writer wanted to say, i.e., it is understandable. When children come across translated text, compared with adults, they have less knowledge of their own language to make the adjustments that might be needed in order to make sense of the text. For these reasons, a study of how children make sense of translated text is timely.

2 Study

2.1 The Data Set

Our study sought to look at the accuracy and understandability of children's text that had been translated using Google Translate. Our data set was built by asking Nepalese children and English children to write short letters to one another. This took place in schools in the two countries and resulted in 15 Nepalese letters (Ns) and 22 English letters (Es). Each letter was then processed as follows:

The Ns were labelled as N1, N,... to N15. These were translated into English by a bilingual - taken as the correct translations (CTNs) and named CTN1, CTN2...etc. Then they were translated into English using Google Translate to give us GTNs individually GTN1, GTN2, etc. A similar approach was used for all the English letters E1, E2,... E22 to get correctly translated letters in Nepalese CTE1, CTE2,... etc., and Google translated letters in Nepalese GTEs individually GTE1, GTE2,... etc.

2.2 Calculating Translation Accuracy

We chose to calculate accuracy by comparing the Google translated text with a 'correct translation' done by a fluent bilingual. We applied the Levenstein string distance at a character level to line up the two texts that were being compared and then calculated an error rate based on the number of insertions, deletions or replacements needed to transform one string to another [9]. We used the equation from [12] and modified it for our purposes to calculate translation Error Rate (ER) and Accuracy (A) as shown:

$$ER = (MSD\,(GTx, CTx)/max\,(|GTx|, |CTx|)) \times 100 \tag{1}$$

$$A = (100 - ER)\% \tag{2}$$

Here, MSD (GT, CT) is the number of edit distances needed to convert GT into CT.

$|GTx|$ = *Number of characters in GTx.*
$|CTx|$ = *Number of characters in CTx.*

For example, for a Nepalese letter:

N = पुरयि साथी, नमस्ते, मलाई यहाँ सांचै छ।
GTN = Dear friend, Hello, I am really here.
CTN = Dear friend, Hello, I am fine here.
|GTN| = 37.
|CTN| = 35.

The difference between GTN and CTN are the words '*really*' and '*fine*'. To convert GTN into CTN, '*really*' has to be converted to '*fine*'. The string distance here is 6 as it took only 6 steps for the conversion. That is why MSD (GTN, CTN) = 6.

Now, ER = (6/37) × 100 = 16.22%

A = 100 − ER = 100 − 16.22 = 83.78%

We built a Java Desktop application using NetBeans IDE to calculate the MSD, Error rate and the Accuracy using the same algorithm explained above. Before applying this, we did do a sanity check of the human and Google translation to ensure that synonyms were not counted as errors, e.g., If the human chose '*films*' and Google chose '*movies*' we 'cleaned' this data so the same word was used by the human as Google had.

2.3   Calculating Translation Understandability

Understandability of the translation is defined as the extent to which the translated text makes sense. An inaccurate translation may still be understandable, e.g.

'*I rely like pizza*' is understandable as '*I really like pizza.*'

We propose a formula to calculate understandability (U) as:

$$U = (NMIU/NMIC) \times 100\% \tag{3}$$

Where, NMIU = Total items of meaningful information understood.

NMIC = Total items of meaningful information present in the original text.

Here a piece of meaningful information is a phrase or sentence that has a meaning outside of other parts of the text. For example, in a Nepalese letter,

N: मेरो नामे दविस भुजेल हो मा क्लास ६ मा पद्रथु तर्मा कर्ता मा अद शोउ.

CTN: My name is Diwas Bhujel. I am in class 6. Which one are you in?

NMIC = 3 (full name, class and a question).

GTN: My name is Bhujel ho in class 6 how much is it to show?

This text has only two pieces of meaningful information (NMUI = 2):

- First information (Name): Even though only the surname is retained by Google, for the child it is understandable and only Bhujel will be taken as the name.
- Second information (Class): The sentence is not complete but the phrase '*in class 6*' helps the reader to understand that the writer is in class 6.
- The third piece of information is no longer meaningful. The question asked makes no sense.

The understandability for this piece of Google translated text will be:

$$U = (2/3) \times 100\% = 66.67\%$$

We recruited 92 English children and 36 Nepalese children to look at the translated texts (GTNs and GTEs) so we could measure understandability. These children used a digital app on which they first read a letter that introduced a child from the other country; they were then asked to write this again as if they were introducing that person to a third person. In this way the aim was to see what the child was able to understand from the translation. The children were allowed to do as many letters as they wanted to in 10 min – any letter looked at by several children was assessed for each child and then an average understandability score was used for analysis. The children's 're-phrased letters' were compared with the original (pre-translated texts) in order to determine the understandability scores.

3 Results

Table 1. Accuracy and Understandability of translation of Nepalese letters

Letter Code	|CTN|	|GTN|	Max (|CTN|, |GTN|)	MSD	ER	A	U
N1	186	140	186	79	42.47	57.53	65
N2	129	98	129	68	52.71	47.29	50
N3	93	108	108	57	52.78	47.22	50
N4	155	146	155	71	45.81	54.19	80
N5	117	86	117	73	62.39	37.61	46.7
N6	97	103	103	63	61.17	38.83	46.7
N7	116	120	120	60	50.00	50.00	75
N8	164	150	164	109	66.46	33.54	35.7
N9	220	192	220	74	33.64	66.36	73.8
N10	128	75	128	78	60.94	39.06	40
N11	169	171	171	93	54.39	45.61	42.5
N12	174	178	178	105	58.99	41.01	50
N13	140	130	140	64	45.71	54.29	50
N14	108	98	108	41	37.96	62.04	89.3
N15	490	258	490	347	70.82	29.18	25

The accuracy of translation for Nepalese letters varied from 29.18% to 66.36%. (M = 46.92, SD = 10.62). Understandability ranged from 25 to 89.3 (M = 54.65, SD = 18.01) and was higher than accuracy for most of the letters but the difference was not significant (t(14) = −0.78, p = 0.445). The two are correlated with p = 0.885.

The accuracy of translation for English letters varied from 39.46% to 68.64%. (M = 5s5.24, SD = 7.03). Understandability ranged from 72.23 to 100 (M = 90.08, SD = 10.32) and was significantly higher than accuracy (t(21) = −13.08, p < 0.05). The two are not correlated with p = −0.002.

4 Discussion

4.1 Does Accuracy Predict Understandability?

For Nepalese letters, it did appear that accuracy and understandability were correlated but this was not the same for English letters translated into Nepalese. Even with low accuracy, the text can still sometimes be understandable as seen with the letters N4 from Table 1, and E8 from Table 2.

4.2 Loss of Information and Understandability

During the translation it was observed that there was a loss of some phrases or sentences. This had a direct effect on understandability because the reader of the translated

Table 2. Accuracy and Understandability of translation of English letters

Letter Code	|CTE|	|GTE|	Max (|CTE|, |GTE|)	MSD	ER	A	U
E1	114	91	114	40	35.09	64.91	75
E2	176	198	198	76	38.38	61.62	80.95
E3	218	223	223	77	34.53	65.47	96.88
E4	250	226	250	113	45.20	54.80	100
E5	332	240	332	201	60.54	39.46	85
E6	137	109	137	60	43.80	56.20	100
E7	286	242	286	130	45.45	54.55	93.75
E8	96	70	96	49	51.04	48.96	100
E9	232	217	232	95	40.95	59.05	80.95
E10	118	103	118	37	31.36	68.64	93.75
E11	317	270	317	181	57.10	42.90	86.11
E12	376	342	376	168	44.68	55.32	90
E13	498	525	525	266	50.67	49.33	97.78
E14	109	90	109	54	49.54	50.46	100
E15	222	192	222	97	43.69	56.31	100
E16	256	199	256	110	42.97	57.03	100
E17	389	321	389	191	49.10	50.90	72.73
E18	412	411	412	174	42.23	57.77	77.08
E19	141	121	141	62	43.97	56.03	73.33
E20	151	115	151	74	49.01	50.99	78.57
E21	247	227	247	94	38.06	61.94	100
E22	206	185	206	99	48.06	51.94	100

text is not able to see the text that is lost. Out of 15 Nepalese letters, only 6 letters retained all the information after translation and 3 retained half, or less, of the information. For the 22 English letters, only 15 letters retained all the information, 6 retained one less and only 1 retained two less information. It would have been possible to calculate understandability as a ratio of the possibilities available after translation – this would result in higher understandability scores but would not represent the understandability in terms of what was initially intended – this is some work we are looking at further.

4.3   Understandability is Individual

The understandability really depended on the individual rather than the letter itself. For example: one letter had 8 pieces of meaningful information and after translation it retained 7 of them. When given to 5 different children, one appeared to understand all of them, 3 understood 6 of them, one understood just 4. There were exceptional cases where all the children understood same number of information, however, this only occurred in 1 GTN and 3 GTEs.

4.4   Creative Children

In some cases, when the children didn't understand a piece of text, they added some extra information either by guessing or by being creative. If they guessed something right, we wouldn't know that because it will show as if they understood it but when they came up with something completely new, it is interesting to see their creativity and imagination. Looking at the 214 individual responses by English children to GTNs, 88 of them had new things expressed which varied from 1 to 4 new things for a text. From a total of 75 responses from Nepalese children to GTEs, only 6 added something creative. For example:

- Nepalese text: मेरो नाम उर्मिला हो। मेरो घर कलारीमा छ। मा क्लास ७ मा पढ्छु। मेरो सकुलको नाम श्री शारदा माध्यमकि सकुल, रावाबेसी, वडा नम्बर-२, खोटांग हो।
- CTN: My name is Urmila. My home is in **Kalari.** I study in class 7. My Schools name is Shree Sharada High School, Rawabesi, **Ward number-2,** Khotang.
- GTN: My name is Urmila. I live in Kharpa. My house is in **blackberry** I read in class 7. My school name is Sri Sharada Secondary School, Raveshesi Village, **Vada No. -2**, Khattang.
- Child's response: Her house is in **Blackburn**. She is in **year 2**.

The use here of Blackburn instead of blackberry and year 2 instead of Vada No. -2 shows that the child tried their best to make sense of the text given to them and wrote what they thought might be the information.

5   Conclusion

We have shown that the accuracy of Google Translate in this study varied a lot and was relatively low. Looking at the mistakes made we do know that accuracy tended to depend on the text itself rather than the translation software used. Children's text is generally error prone, as see in [8], and the context of this work with many proper nouns will have been a challenge for Google Translate. Generally, understandability was higher than the accuracy. The context allowed children to make some reasonable guesses like, for example, guessing year 2 for Vada No. -2.

Our choice to measure accuracy at a character level had an effect as it probably gave higher error rates than a word level score might have done. Given that we measured understandability at a phrase level, it would be interesting to compare accuracy measures at both phrase and word levels – this would also lead us to consider making other baselines for understandability as suggested in the discussion. These are possibilities for future work.

Our decision to use children's re-interpretation of text in order to assess understandability was shown to be effective but was variable in so far as different children understood different things. We are working further on the concept of understandability and refining our metrics.

Acknowledgements. We thank all the children for the participation, the Teachers for the assistance and support and the Head Teacher for allowing us to do the study in the School. This work was partially funded with a grant from UKRI AHRC.

References

1. Abdel Azim ElShiekh, A.: Google translate service: transfer of meaning, distortion or simply a new creation? An investigation into the translation process & problems at Google. English Lang. Lit. Stud. (2012). https://doi.org/10.5539/ells.v2n1p56
2. Bahdanau, D., et al.: Neural machine translation by jointly learning to align and translate. In: 3rd International Conference on Learning Representations, ICLR 2015 - Conference Track Proceedings (2015)
3. Douglas, S.P., Craig, C.S.: Collaborative and iterative translation: An alternative approach to back translation. J. Int. Mark. **15**, 30–43 (2007)
4. Evans, L.: Language, translation and the problem of international accounting communication. Acc. Audit. Acc. J.
5. Groves, M., Mundt, K.: Friend or foe? Google translate in language for academic purposes. Engl. Specif. Purp. **37**(2015), 112–121 (2015). https://doi.org/10.1016/j.esp.2014.09.001
6. Hutchins, W.J.: Machine Translation over fifty years. Hist. Épistémol. Lang. **23**(1), 7–31 (2001). https://doi.org/10.3406/hel.2001.2815
7. Jabak, O.: Assessment of Arabic-English translation produced by Google Translate. Int. J. Linguist. Lit. Transl. (2019). https://doi.org/10.32996/ijllt.2019.2.4.24.
8. Lamichhane, D.R., Read, J.C.: Investigating children's passwords using a game-based survey. In: IDC 2017 - Proceedings of the 2017 ACM Conference on Interaction Design and Children, pp. 617–622 (2017). https://doi.org/10.1145/3078072.3084333
9. Levenshtein, V.: Binary codes capable of correcting deletions, insertions, and reversals. In: Soviet Physics Doklady (1966)
10. Nadhianti, M.: An analysis of accuracy level of google translate in English-bahasa Indonesia and bahasa Indonesia-English translations. Sastra Inggris-Quill (2016)
11. van Rensburg, A., et al.: Applying Google translate in a higher education environment: translation products assessed. Southern Afr. Linguist. Appl. Lang. Stud. **30**(4), 511–524 (2012). https://doi.org/10.2989/16073614.2012.750824
12. Soukoreff, R.W., MacKenzie, I.S.: Measuring errors in text entry tasks: an application of the levenshtein string distance statistic. In: Conference on Human Factors in Computing Systems - Proceedings (2001)

Gamification Design on Popular Science Education for Children with Hemopathy Based on Serious Game Theory

Xiaoyue Li, Ren Long$^{(\boxtimes)}$, and Hongzhi Pan

Huazhong University of Science and Technology,
Wuhan, Hubei, China
longren@hust.edu.cn

Abstract. The causes of children with hemopathy are complex and the conditions are varied. It is difficult for children and their families to recognize the diseases. Meanwhile, due to the weak self-control ability, children will have negative emotions such as fear, loneliness, pain during hospitalization. Gamification is considered to be an effective way to promote changes in mood, attitude and behavior. Therefore, in order to solve disease cognition problems in children and reduce their negative emotions, the gamification design method of serious game theory will be applied to the popular science education of children with hemopathy to design a gamification education software.

A combination of methods, including questionnaire and interview method, literature search method and story telling will be adopted in this design to have an in-depth understanding of gamification design, children with hemopathy, children's game design, popular science education and other aspects, and to determine the software framework, game mechanics and educational content. The software is mainly composed of 5 layers including task, game, Q&A, science education and situation recording. Among which the game layer contains four different types of game modules which involve the knowledge of hemopathy, treatment process and living habits, etc. This design will gamify popular science cognitive education through motivation, reward, achievement and other elements, so as to achieve children's systematic knowledge of hemopathy, reduce their negative emotions, and improve treatment adherence. The effectiveness of the software needs to be further tested.

Keywords: Children with hemopathy · Gamification design · Serious game · User experience

1 Introduction

As a common malignant tumor in children, children with hemopathy have a serious impact on children's physical and mental health [1]. School-age children are the main group of patients with children with hemopathy, and the diseases of children with hemopathy are diverse. Symptoms vary by age and condition. Therefore, it is difficult for

C. Stephanidis et al. (Eds.): HCII 2021, CCIS 1419, pp. 216–225, 2021.
https://doi.org/10.1007/978-3-030-78635-9_30

the children and their families to recognize the disease, and the hospitalization caused by the disease will also lead to negative emotions of children, such as fear, loneliness and pain. It is found that there are mainly three problems in the treatment process: the psychological condition of children, parents' anxiety and the sense of rejection from the outside world. Currently, there are few popular science software or games for children with hemopathy, and there are many problems existing in the education of hemopathy, such as the old model, boring knowledge, poor results, etc. Therefore, it is of great significance to contribute to the design field of children with hemopathy. Aiming at the problems of children with hemopathy as well as reducing their negative emotions, the goal is to design a popular science software of hemopathy knowledge, which is interesting and easy to popularize. Gamification is a core design concept. It is hoped that games can be integrated into popular science education, which can not only make children, parents and others who are interested in hemopathy correctly understand and learn the knowledge related to hemopathy, but also effectively divert children's attention to relieve their emotions.

2 Principle Description

2.1 Method

In this study, under the guidance of serious game theory, the scientific nature of hemopathy education is combined with the fun and entertainment of games, the knowledge of children with hemopathy, treatment methods and processes as well as good living habits are integrated into a challenging and interactive game so as to conduct the gamification design of popular science software of hemopathy knowledge. The innovative education mode of gamification is adopted as an important tool for popularizing knowledge and relieving emotions.

2.2 The Exposition and Application of Gamification

Today, gamification design has become pervasive in every aspect of our lives as a means to enhance and motivate user experience. It can turn a boring task into an enjoyable one that the user actively participates in and completes. Most software on the market today uses the concept of gamification to increase user preference and engagement.

In the context of gamification design, many authors have summarized game elements that repeatedly occur in gamification design. In the book "*For the Win*", *Werbach* and *Hunter* defined that "in the game system, gamtification is a tool that adopts the game elements to improve the user experience and user engagement" [2], In addition, they built a three-level DMC pyramid structure (Fig. 1), which distributed 30 game elements on three levels, from top to bottom: dynamics, mechanics, and components, as shown in the figure. In the later stage of gamification design, DMC pyramid structure should be combined for analysis and understanding, and selected elements should be used according to the design objectives and target users.

Fig. 1. DMC pyramid structure

2.3 Serious Game Theory

As an emerging hotspot in the field of digital game learning, the concept of serious game was first proposed by *Abt* [3] in 1970. In addition to enhancing the enjoyable gaming experience, Serious Game is also seen as an innovative means to solve social problems and enhance social and cultural inclusion. It adopts the expression form and mechanism of the game to introduce the knowledge and skills of medicine, education, scientific research, politics and other fields as the elements of the game, which has a wide range of application scenarios. This effectively promotes the popularization of knowledge and skills, and also enhances user experience. The applications of serious games mainly fall into three categories: popularization of knowledge, learning of skills, and change of attitude and behavior [4]. The popularization of knowledge is usually applied in the field of education, with clear learning objectives and content, such as language, medical knowledge and other educational games.

2.4 Analysis of Characteristics of User Group

School-age children are the user group targeted in this study. In the process of designing children's products, it is necessary to accurately analyze all aspects of children's characteristics so as to make a design that meets the needs of user groups.

- Physical characteristics of children:
  The physical function of school-age children is not fully developed, and the development varies from person to person. Meanwhile, the development of various functions of the body is affected by both internal and external factors, which are periodical consecutive [5]. The development of the nervous system of the school-age children of this stage is not yet perfect, and the specific performance is: they are more sensitive to the stimulation of the outside world, with a weak ability to receptivity and adaptive ability. In addition, school-age children's hearing is more acute and more sensitive to various sounds in the outside world. However, because the growth rate is too fast, coupled with the immature body, it is easy to bring fatigue.

- Psychological characteristics of children:
School-age children are quick to receive and respond to information from the outside world. They will fully use their vision, hearing, touch and smell to help them perceive information from the outside world. At this time, the cognitive structure of children has been restructured and improved, therefore, their psychological development speed is very fast, with a certain self-cognition ability, the ability to distinguish between right and wrong, and can quickly judge their own interests and hobbies, consciousness tendency, etc. The psychological characteristics of children at this stage are mainly shown as follows: strong observation ability to the outside world, exploration and curiosity, rich imagination, strong desire to win and lose, feeling information by physical touch, enjoying expression and imitation. But they are impatient, and it is difficult for them to maintain interest in things for a long time.
- Behavior Characteristics of Children:
School-age children love to play and explore. They love new and challenging things. In daily life, when faced with new things, they like to learn by practising. At the same time, children at this stage have a rich social life, and peers play an important role in their lives. School-age children show significant improvements in their ability to focus and control themselves as they age, but they still have deficits in allocating their attention. They have short attention spans and are characterized by instability and inconsistency.

Analysis of the User Group of Chiildren With Hemopathy. As school-age children, the physiological, psychological and behavioral characteristics of patients with hemopathy mostly conform to the above description. However, the disease leads to poor physical function and development of the children. In addition, in the face of a closed ward environment and long-term painful treatment, children's psychological status is more fragile and sensitive, prone to produce closed, sadness, fear and other negative emotions. At the same time, the enclosed environment limits the range of movement of children. Children can carry out a relatively single activity, their practical needs, expression needs, social behavior needs can not be met. The unclear cognition of medical products and medical means will also lead to distrust and rejection of children.

Persona. First of all, after contacting the local hemopathy care ward, the basic situation of the children group with hemopathy was learned, and then the target users gained insight through questionnaire interview and video observation. Then, an in-depth excavation of users' behaviors revealed that the problems of children with hemopathy were mainly caused by uncooperative treatment and poor physical and psychological quality, which were mainly affected by unclear cognition, painful treatment process, excessive behavior restrictions, unstable physical state as well as depressed mood. Through the analysis of user clustering, *Alan Cooper* characters method is used to build the "An 8-year-old patient with hemopathy who has lived in a hemopathy ward for a long time has a sense of exclusion and fear of treatment. He wants to understand the knowledge of hemopathy and treatments that can be used to cooperate with the treatment, as well as to alleviate the pain associated with the treatment" image, classical user role model as shown in Fig. 2.

User Map. The classic user role model is used as the experimental object. The design goal is to make the children correctly recognize the disease and relieve the negative

User Profile	User Behavior	User Goals and Difficulties
	Background introduction	**User goals**
	Lily is a child with hemopathy, because of her younger age, she has less awareness of blood diseases.Daily treatment (chemotherapy, blood draw, puncture, etc.) made her feel pain and resistance, The closed environment of the unfamiliar ward also made Lily feel restless during the hospitalization.	1.Correct knowledge of hemopathy. 2.Eliminate fear of treatment and cooperate with treatment. 3.Adapt to hospital life. 4.The design can be interesting and challenging to achieve the purpose of transferring pain.
N a m e : Lily		
G e n d e r : Female	**Behavior**	**Difficulties**
A g e : 8	There will be psychological resistance when in contact with doctors and nurses, which is manifested in the fear of not cooperating with treatment and seeing doctors and nurses.In the ward life, she looks forward to entertainment time most, like drawing and kneading plasticine.	1.Children's activity space in the hospital is small, concentrated in the ward. 2.The enclosed environment makes the child lose most of the social activities, and it is easy to feel lonely. 3.The child is young, has limited cognitive ability, and has poor coordination.
Education Background: 3rd grade of elementary school		
Identity : children with hemopathy		
Character: introverted, irritable		

Fig. 2. Persona

emotions such as fear and pain. To better convey user journey information, story drawing is used to simulate user's behavior process to construct a user journey map designed by the gamification of Children with hemopathy science education. It is mainly composed of six parts: user demand, behavioral touch point, idea motivation, stage process, pain point discovery and opportunity point (Fig. 3). The behavioral process of hemopathy children can be divided into four stages: finding needs, finding goals, user experience, feedback and motivation, and social sharing. Through the behavior exploration of target users, users' needs, behaviors and emotions, as well as driving factors and goals can be found. Then, the pain points of target users are further explored based on their behavior in the journey chart, and feasible opportunity points are analyzed.

User needs	1.Divert attention 2.Interesting and interactive 3.Scientific knowledge efficiently 4.Simple operation 5.Expand children's social activities 6.Has a reward mechanism.7.No need for help from outside (doctors, parents).			
Behavior	The child in the ward picks up the tablet during the break	Search for interesting and attention-grabbing apps on iPad	The child starts to use the app	The child ends the use of the app
Idea motivation	Use the iPad to collect knowledge about related diseases or play games to relax	Find an attractive app that interests you	Start using the app, learn and play knowledge, relax the mood, and recognize diseases	Achieve today's learning goals and relieve emotions
Stage	Find the need	Find the target	Experience app	Feedback and rewards
Pain point	Children lack the learning path of hemopathy knowledge;	The traditional form of popular science is boring; less attractive	The effect of traditional science popularization learning is mediocre; and lack of social behavior	The traditional form of popular science is difficult to maintain continuous learning behavior
Opportunities	The necessity of popular science design for children's hematology knowledge	We can incorporate gamification design into the design	Learning through games to increase interest in learning	Set rewards and points to satisfy children's sense of accomplishment

Fig. 3. User journey map

3   Method Description (Design Criteria)

3.1   Gamification Design of Science Education for Children with Hemopathy

Erickson argued that "games are the most natural way for children to heal" [6], so gamified design is one of the most applicable tools of popular science education at present. The gamification design of popular science education for children with hemopathy should follow three psychological characteristics of children: psychological characteristics of fear, psychological characteristics of color and psychological characteristics of fun [7].

The Psychological Characteristics of Fear. Combined with the two conditions of fear in children: based on their fear of the unknown and the fear of the pain they have suffered, there is no doubt that the causes of pain in children are the lack of knowledge about hemopathy, the fear of great pain caused by medical means, and the avoidance and rejection of medical equipment. At the same time, the closed treatment space and limited social activities all lead to the children's psychological characteristics of autism and fear. The design should be based on the psychological characteristics of children's fear, to help children correctly understand the disease, medical equipment and medical treatment, while alleviating negative emotions.

The Psychological Characteristics of Color. Children are extremely sensitive to color recognition. Colors also have a significant effect on children's emotions. A large number of studies have shown that blue, green, yellow, orange and other bright lively colors made children happier and more relaxed, increased their interest in things, but also significantly enhanced their imagination, creativity and attention. However, low-lightness colors, such as black, gray and white, stimulated nerve cells in children's brains, increasing their frustration, making them anxious and dull, and distracting. Children with hemopathy who have been exposed to white and blue wards for a long time have a low mood and anxiety. In the design, rich bright colors should be used to enhance the interest of children and attract their attention.

The Psychological Characteristics of Fun. School-age children have strong curiosity, so fun design can keep children highly interested. Studies have shown that fun toys could attract 70% of children's attention and produce a lot of fun. Meanwhile, it could also promote the interaction between medical staff and parents and children, establishing a good relationship of trust and reducing the difficulty of nursing [8]. Interesting design refers to the design elements in a lively, interesting and gamified form, so as to bring children a pleasant and relaxed emotional experience. In the design, attention should be paid to the expression of design elements to create a relaxed and pleasant experience environment for children.

3.2 Design Strategies Based on Serious Game Theory

There are three main stages in the process of children using software:

The Pre-start Stage. As a result of the immature psychological and physiological development of children, their reactions to things are superficial and direct. Children mainly focus on software color, style and other aspects. Bright and lively colors, vivid and interesting patterns, and lively and pleasant sounds can all satisfy the curiosity of children, stimulate their interest, and promote their experience of the product.

The Operation Stage. Due to long-term exposure to a closed ward, hemopathy children lack exercise, weak physical skills, lack of attention, and will reject boring content or difficult operations. Therefore, the easy operation of the software and the content of the rich, interesting and interactive is particularly important. At the same time, the form and hierarchy of the software also affect the experience of children to some extent. In the design, the teaching form of knowledge and the story and hierarchy of the software should also be considered.

The Post-reflection Stage. Considering the children's desire to win and lose and the need to be recognized, appropriate reward mechanisms should be adopted after the end of software learning, along with psychological guidance and emotional care, so as to meet the emotional needs of children and enhance their sense of experience and participation.

Combined with the design points of the above three stages, four product requirements are summarized: visual demand, auditory demand, form demand and interaction demand.

Visual Demand. In the design, the visual elements that need to pay attention to include color, graphics, text, texture and so on. As for colour, it is necessary to use a lively and bright color, but also cannot be too bright-colored. It is necessary to include a soft main tone to achieve the unity of color. In terms of graphics, a cute and easy design style should be used to meet the children's requirements for fun. In the text, using a lively font, formal font should be avoided. At the same time, the number of words should be controlled in order to avoid children with agitated anxiety.

Auditory Demand. Most children like relaxed, cheerful and rhythmic sounds. Therefore, whether it is background music or sound effects, the melody should be cheerful and relaxed to help children maintain a happy mood in the process of using the software. At the same time, children have delicate eardrums, and music and sound effects can be fun and rhythmic without being too loud.

Form Demand. Based on Serious Game Theory, design should also focus on content structure and hierarchy. The degree of difficulty of knowledge learning and the progressive relationship of the content should be in line with children's characteristics of curiosity and poor patience. Incorporating knowledge about hemopathy into different fun games and challenging ways of getting through challenges can increase children's interest and improve their learning efficiency.

Interaction Demand. Interactions are very important to gamification design. Ergonomics and user behavior should be studied before interaction forms are set up. Children are not interested in complex operations and abstract forms of interaction and they many get depressed. Therefore, in the design process of the product, the interactive button should be intuitive and eye-catching, the interactive form should be simple but rich, and the operation form should meet the cognitive range of children. In addition, the interactive form of play also helps to improve the learning efficiency of children.

4 Case Studies

4.1 Design Orientation

Based on the above research results, a prototype software for gamification of children with hemopathy education has been designed and named "Little E Paradise". The four purposes of software are as follows:

- Guide users to correctly understand hemopathy;
- Transfer users' negative emotions of anxiety and pain;
- Alleviate the loneliness of users in the closed environment and increase the social behavior of users;
- Improve users' compliance with treatment.

4.2 Program Design

Function Framework. The software mainly has four functions: popular science knowledge, entertainment games, reward mechanism and situation record.

There are five layers: task layer, game layer, answer layer, knowledge popularization layer and situation recording layer (Fig. 4). The game layer contains four game modules with different types of games. Based on the cognitive needs and entertainment needs of users, games of different modules are used to learn the knowledge of homeopathy, the treatment process of hemopathy and how to develop good living habits (Fig. 5).

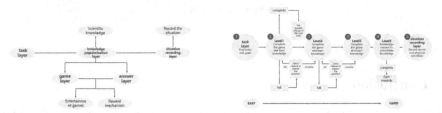

Fig. 4. Four functions and five layers   **Fig. 5.** User flow

Software Mode. The task layer runs through the process of software learning. By issuing tasks every day, users' enthusiasm can be improved and knowledge learning can be effectively completed. In the four game modules of the game layer, users can complete the game levels in turn by sliding, clicking and other interactive forms. Users can learn about hemopathy step by step by defeating viruses and collecting medical items. Meanwhile, the user's interest and patience can be enhanced by the rich game form and the fun game challenge. During the operation of the software, the system will reward users with points and props according to their game conditions, so as to satisfy users' sense of achievement and enhance their motivation for learning. If the game fails, the system will develop complications of hemopathy that correspond to the game content (nausea, hair loss, etc.), which will be used as a warning. In addition, users will be given a chance (answer layer) to answer questions about the basics of hemopathy, treatments and so on so that they can continue playing the game if they are correct, or the game will fail if they are wrong. The system ends the game with a pep talk that prevents the user from feeling frustrated. In the game layer, users can also interact with peers (chat, play together, etc.) to enhance users' social contact.

The knowledge popularization layer is combined with the game layer and the answer layer, which combines teaching with fun. It teaches knowledge to users through interesting games and challenging answer mechanisms, breaking the traditional boring knowledge learning method.

The situation recording layer usually appears when the user finishes the software operation. The user can record the experience of this time or the mood and physical condition of the day, which is convenient for the medical staff to view and manage in the background.

Interface Effects and Interactive Operations. The interface of the software includes the main page, character card, backpack, map, etc. Its interaction mode is also shown below (Fig. 6).

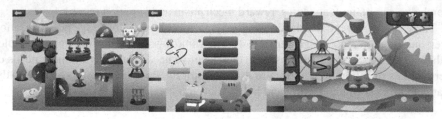

Fig. 6. The interface

5 Conclusion

Through literature analysis and research, this design puts forward the idea of applying serious game theory and gamification to popular science education. After theoretical analysis, investigation of actual situation, construction of user roles as well as simulation of user journey, a feasible and scientific gamification software called Little E Paradise for children with hemopathy education is designed.In addition to being a tool to popularize the knowledge of children with hemopathy, Little E Paradise can effectively alleviate the negative emotions of children with hemopathy so as to achieve the purpose of improving treatment compliance.

Due to the limitation of time, there are still some defects and limitations existing in the design, and the effect of the software needs to be further tested. The design is still under continuous improvement and iteration. In the future, several tests and experiments will be carried out to verify the feasibility of the design. With the development of digital technology and the further maturity of VR and AR technology, the popular science form of children with hemopathy knowledge will be diversified, and there is still a great space for development in the form of expression and interaction. The author hopes that the research and design of this paper can provide inspiration for the popularization of knowledge of children with hemopathy in the future.

References

1. Jemal, A., Siegel, R., Ward, E., et al.: Cancer statistics. CA Cancer J. Clin. **56**(2), 106–130 (2006)
2. Deterding, S., Sicart, M., Nacke, L., O'Hara, K., Dixon, D.: Gamification: using game-design elements in non-gaming contexts. In: CHI 2011 Extended Abstracts on Human Factors in Computing Systems, pp. 2425–2428 (2011)
3. Abt, C.C.: Serious games: the art and science of games that simulate life. Simul. Gaming **1**(4), 435–437 (1970)
4. Stewart, J.: The potential of digital games for empowerment and social inclusion of groups at risk of social and economic exclusion: evidence and opportunity for policy. Joint Res. Cent. (1), 3–9 (2013)
5. Liu, Y., Zhang, X.: Research on emotional design of electronic products for school-age children based on user experience. Xi'an Polytechnic University (2018)
6. Erikson, E.H.: Studies in the Interpretation of Play. Genet Psychol Monogr, p. 561 (1940)
7. Zheng, J., Wang, X., Wu, D.: Research on medical product design based on children's psychological characteristics. https://doi.org/10.19461/j.cnki.1004-8626.2020.08.015
8. Qin, Q., Yin, H.: Research on the extensibility design of children furniture. Taiyuan University of Technology (2012). https://doi.org/10.19554/j.cnki.1001-3563.2013.18.005

Research on the Design of Body Fat Meter for Children Based on Human-Computer Interaction Behavior

Wei Li and Junnan Ye(✉)

East China University of Science and Technology, Shanghai 200237, People's Republic of China

Abstract. The health of young children is one of the most important social concerns at present, and the phenomenon of childhood obesity is gradually becoming a topic of concern in many countries. The influencing factors that lead to childhood obesity are formed according to age, gender, and scale of eating habits. Methods: This paper promotes the early development of children's health by capturing their behavioral habits. Children's movement habits, color sensitivity, and pattern liking are scaled. The purpose of this paper is to investigate and design a physical fitness testing device specifically designed for children. The device was used to measure body fat percentage (BEP) in children. The results show that the monitoring of body fat percentage and trace elements in children is used to monitor changes in children's body health index in real time, to obtain interaction and products designed specifically for children, and to advocate and advise on children's body signs through mobile.

Keywords: Human-computer interaction · Child health · Obesity · Body fat percentage · Prevention and control

1 Introduction

1.1 Social Background

Childhood and adolescence are the most critical periods for children's development, and as technology advances and people's living standards improve, more attention is being paid to the nutritional health of children. Currently, the problem of excessive obesity in children is also becoming increasingly evident. Body mass index (BMI): BMI = weight (kg)/[height (m)]^2. Therefore, it is proposed to improve the problem of overweight and obesity in children by designing to assist in the detection of physical health in children.

Parents' perceptions of their own weight were also significantly related to children's BMIp (body mass index percentile). The perception that a child is overweight is associated with an increase in child weight regardless of the child's actual weight, which is similar to the finding that perceptions of one's own overweight lead to weight gain in children [1]. The current national prevalence of overweight in children and adolescents aged 6–17 years is 9.6% and obesity is 6.4%; the prevalence of overweight in adults aged 18 years and older is 30.1% and obesity is 11.9%.

© Springer Nature Switzerland AG 2021
C. Stephanidis et al. (Eds.): HCII 2021, CCIS 1419, pp. 226–232, 2021.
https://doi.org/10.1007/978-3-030-78635-9_31

1.2 Industry Background

Both child and parental concerns about being overweight were associated with higher child body fat and higher BMIp, similar to previous findings [2]. Since parental concern is the only significant interaction for children of obese or overweight parents, these findings are particularly salient because these children have the highest risk for overweight and obesity later in life. For parents who are concerned about their child's weight, better outcomes have been found when parents avoid criticizing their child's weight or avoid encouraging their child to lose weight while encouraging healthy eating and exercise [3]. The language used by parents is also important, with adolescents preferring "unhealthy weight" or "weight problems" to "heavy," "big," or "large" [4]. The methods and phrases used by parents are particularly important because they overestimate their children's overweight and obesity [5].

1.3 Research Significance and Value

A body fat meter is not an instrument to diagnose a specific disease, but an instrument to quickly determine body composition and evaluate the physical condition of the subject. Body composition determination and evaluation is a comprehensive discipline that studies the human body [6]. Body fat meters are commonly used in medical institutions and fitness facilities, but the market for children's body fat meters is relatively small. Children have different needs for body fat meters, and those used indoors at home are more focused on the home environment and easy storage. The traditional body fat meter used by the public in hospitals and fitness institutions is not suitable for children's human-computer interaction behavior. Through industrial design, the children's body fat meter is different from the traditional composition analyzer in the existing market, which is more suitable for children's use and home scenario, more in line with children's characteristics, and in line with the children's home environment and family members' use needs.

2 Body Fat Meter for Children

2.1 The Principle of Body Fat Meter Detection

In recent years, experts and scholars from many countries have used many methods and developed different devices for human composition analysis, all of which have their own advantages and disadvantages. The determination of human composition by bioresistance resistance method has the advantages of being fast, simple, accurate, non-invasive and risk-free, and has now become the globally recognized method of choice [7].

2.2 Bioelectrical Impedance Principle

Bioelectrical impedance analysis (BIA) is a technique to determine body water by electrical methods. When a weak alternating current signal is introduced into the body, the current flows with body fluid that has low resistance and good conductivity. The amount

Measurement Method	Test time	Dependent Variables	Advantages	Disadvantages
Underwater weighing method	About 30 minutes	Body Density	Traditional "gold" measurement standard with excellent accuracy for Db	The tester cannot move during the test, the subject needs to be completely immersed in water, and the RV needs to be measured accurately
Air Replacement Method	About 5-8 minutes	Body Density	Fast testing and easy process	Further reliability studies are needed to test
Human parameters method		Circumference and length of human body segments	Measurement is relatively simple	The results are not very accurate and there are few quantitative studies
Bioresistance method		Human electrical impedance value	Fast and simple testing process, BIS is able to perform analysis of different parts of the body and measure more variables	Need for human hydration status

Fig. 1. Comparison of measurement methods

of moisture determines the tolerance of the pathway through which the current passes, and this can be expressed by a measured value called impedance. However, the value of impedance and resistance differ in the human body by only about 2–3 Ω. Since such a difference in resistance can be neglected, the value of resistance can be used as an approximate substitute for impedance in the resistive resistance method for living organisms [8].

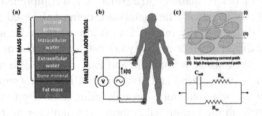

Fig. 2. Bioelectrical impedance schematic

3 Human-Computer Interaction Behavior

3.1 Human-Computer Interaction

So far, human-computer interaction technology has gone through three main eras: the early stage of manual operations, the last night control language and interactive command language stage, and the graphical user interface (GUI) stage [9]. Ergonomics is a multidisciplinary interdisciplinary discipline, and the core problem of research is the coordination between human, machine and environment in different operations. It is of great research value and significance.

3.2 Human-Computer Interaction for Children

By analyzing the size, mode of operation, and characteristics of the applicable population of existing products, the size and mode of operation of the product that is most suitable for the user's operational use are studied. The future paradigm of human-computer interaction technology tends to be specific to the user's task and should not be limited to one or several generic models [10]. There is also some research in educational software for children in China, such as a pen- and voice-based multi-channel storytelling system for children produced by the Institute of Software Research, Chinese Academy of Sciences [11].

Human-computer interaction can help children to better interact with the product and help them grow. With the progress of technology, interaction methods like voice recognition and gesture recognition are recognized by a large number of users because they are more in line with people's habits [12].

Touch gesture interaction. Currently one of the most important interaction methods for children's products, touch gestures can be well accepted by children, the difficulty of operation is low, using simple gestures to complete the operation.

Image interaction, children are younger, less sensitive to words, the mind is not yet mature, children will have many psychological reactions to patterns, which makes it possible to use more bionic images and more bright colors in the design of children's products.

4   Construction of a Design Process for children's Body Fat Meter Based on Human-Computer Interaction Behavior

Fig. 3. Overall design flow chart

4.1   Analysis of children's Interaction Behavior

Children have great curiosity about the products when interacting with them, and the design needs to reduce uncontrollable factors, and the products should not have harm or other side effects on children. Children are in the growth and development stage, children's height, hand size, foot length, weight are smaller than adults. In the traditional human-computer interaction tools, grasping, stepping, touching and other tools are set according to the average size of adults, there are certain difficulties in the use of children users. In the interaction, children's ability to observe things is weak, so the interaction process can't be designed too complex, the operation as simple as possible, and there are obvious guiding prompts. Medical products also need to be used under the care of parents, and should be designed with child locks and other similar means to prevent children from accidentally touching them.

4.2 Analysis of children's Health Needs

Children's health needs to be considered in many ways. Children's physical signs change significantly from infancy to toddler to adolescence, and children's health needs to be designed with different health programs for different age groups. To address the problem of childhood obesity, a simultaneous approach is needed in many aspects, including diet, sleep, outdoor activities, parental encouragement and intervention, and interest development. Healthy diet, children's health needs need rich and nutritious food, with good fruit and vegetable and protein intake, and a reasonable diet to provide children's body with the required energy.

4.3 Analysis of Children's Psychological Expectations

It is difficult for children to pay attention to something for a long time, but children are strongly attracted to animations, sounds, and other means. Timely and significant feedback should be given to children in the process of human-computer interaction, which can make children realize that the operation just happened has changed significantly because of their own participation. Children's imagination is rich and can be reasonably used to improve children's concentration and interest in the product, and the transfer between different states of physics should be designed to be relatively simple. After completing an operation, appropriate encouragement can help children become more interested and motivated by the product and the software, and related research shows that children like to share with each other and complete tasks together, so it can be designed better for multi-user interactions.

5 Design Practice

5.1 Ultrasonic Height Meter Design

Ultrasonic height meter design: the existing market body fat meter is basically a physical measurement of height devices, and larger, and the indoor environment is more abrupt, and can't record the change in height for a long time, which is not conducive to the use of children, based on the body fat meter, the addition of ultrasonic height meter, and the measured data can be stored to the cloud synchronization, record the growth of children's changes.

Fig. 4. Body fat meter design for children

5.2 Gripping Electrode Design

According to the market analysis, the traditional body fat meter on the market are designed to put the hand electrode on top of the column, and the wire is exposed, such design is not reasonable, and it takes up a lot of space indoors, and is not suitable for children to use, this design will be the overall column cancellation, the hand electrode is designed as a flat shape, when not in use can be disassembled, convenient storage, and through the modeling semantics of the elephant, the elephant's trunk is abstracted, when using children will not produce a sense of rejection.

Fig. 5. Scenarios for the use of body fat meters for children.

6 Conclusion and Expectations

Children's home body fat meter adopts bioelectrical impedance principle, which is measured in the body through current conduction, so it does not cause any harm, can be reused, low cost, and is widely used in medical field and fitness field, but lacks practical input in children's field. The design of this children's home body fat meter fully takes into account the use of indoor scenes in the home, and makes a breakthrough in appearance by eliminating the existing traditional column and adopting the bionic mentality of an elephant, which makes the overall shape look very harmonious. And the overall data can also be uploaded to the cloud, big data analysis and calculation, to give professional advice to help children improve their health, based on the body fat meter, the addition of ultrasonic height measurement instrument, and the measured data can be stored to the cloud synchronization, record the growth of children's changes, in the sense of view can give a lovely, warm visual feeling, and can be designed in sets, the type of animals Can be unfolded design, through different bionic design, installation is also very convenient and simple, allowing users to use more comfortable.

References

1. Robinson, E., Sutin, A.R.: Parental perception of weight status and weight gain across childhood. Pediatrics 137(5), e20153957 (2016)
2. Kral, T.V., Moore, R.H., Compher, C.W.: Maternalconcern about child weight in a study of weight-discordant siblings. Public Health Nursing 32(2), 132–142 (2015)
3. Gillison, F.B., Lorenc, A.B., Sleddens, E.F., Williams, S.L., Atkinson, L.: Can it be harmful for parents to talk to their child about their weight? A meta- analysis. Preventive Med. **93**, 135–146 (2016)

4. Puhl, R.M., Himmelstein, M.S.: A word to the wise: adolescent reactions to parental communication about weight. Child. Obes. **14**, 291–301 (2018)
5. He, J., Fan, X.: How accurate is using parent-reported height and weight for screening children and adolescents for overweight and obesity? Meta-analyses at both population and individual levels. Childhood Obesity **14**(5), 302–315 (2018)
6. Dong, S., Wang, H.: Human-Computer Interaction. Beijing University Press (2004)
7. Han, T., Sun, Y., Yao, Z.: Design of human body composition analyzer – an implementation of bioelectrical impedance principle. Beijing Biomed. Eng. **26**(6), 629–633 (2007)
8. Pu, J., Wang, G., Dong, S.: Multi-channel user interface study. Comput. Appl. (2001)
9. Peng, F., Wang, D.: Multi-pen interaction-based storytelling system for children. Comput. Eng. Des. **30**(13) (2009)
10. Ren, S.: Bioelectrical impedance measurement technology. China Med. Device Inf. **10**(01), 21–25 (2004)
11. Gudivaka, R., Schoeller, D.A., Kushner, R.F.: Single and multi frequency models for bioelectrical impedance analysis of body water compartments. Japplphysiol **87**, 1087–1096 (1999)
12. Zhao, Y., Chen, S., Jing, S., Jing, T.: Design and research of ergonomic keyboard. J. Shandong Univ. Technol. **31**(5), 433–440 (2001)

"X-8": An Experimental Interactive Toy to Support Turn-Taking Games in Children with Autism Spectrum Disorders

Beste Özcan$^{(\boxtimes)}$ (iD), Valerio Sperati(iD), Flora Giocondo(iD),
and Gianluca Baldassarre(iD)

Institute of Cognitive Sciences and Technologies National Research Council
of Italy ISTC-CNR, Rome, Italy
{beste.ozcan,valerio.sperati,flora.giocondo,
gianluca.baldassarre}@istc.cnr.it

Abstract. *Turn-taking* is a type of interaction where two individuals alternate a behaviour (e.g. during a conversation). Such competence – which is a fundamental key in the social behaviour – is often compromised in children with Autism Spectrum Disorders (ASDs). Neurodevelopmental therapists report how it is extremely difficult to teach this skill to young ASDs, yet it would be very important. In the current proposal we present an early prototype of interactive toy called *X-8*: it is a soft, wearable, six-legged octopus able to distinguish between two people, and produce different luminous patterns according to the user who is touching it. The toy can then potentially support therapists in set up sensory-motor games based on *turn-taking rules*. A first proof of concept is described and possible activities are proposed.

Keywords: Autism spectrum disorders · Turn-taking · Interactive technology · Transitional wearable companion · Therapy

1 Introduction

Autism Spectrum Disorder (ASD) is a neurodevelopmental condition characterised by important life-long impairments in the social, communicative and affective areas [1]. Early rehabilitative interventions – possibly within the first years of life – have proved to be effective in ameliorating the severity of the condition. Probably due to the plasticity on the nervous system [5], behavioural treatments are in fact more effective at a young age, in stimulating and strenghtening the basic social competences which are critical for the cognitive development (e.g. imitation, eye-contact, joint attention [7]).

In this context, interactive technologies seem to be a promising tool to support the therapeutic activity [2]. In fact, it was observed that most of children diagnosed with autism (from now on ASDs), show a clear attraction toward

C. Stephanidis et al. (Eds.): HCII 2021, CCIS 1419, pp. 233–239, 2021.
https://doi.org/10.1007/978-3-030-78635-9_32

technological devices. This intrinsic interest can then be exploited to maintain an high child's engagement during the therapeutic activities.

In this work-in-progress we present a simple – yet interesting – experimental, interactive toy called *X-8*. The prototype is designed to support *turn-taking* games, namely playful activities where two people (the child and the therapist in our case) must take turns. *Turn-taking* is a general social competence, often impaired in ASDs, which is pivotal for all communications activities featuring a reciprocal back-and-forth exchange [4]; this skill relies in facts on a complex social-cooperative coupling, precise in time, and based on several signals (visual, auditory, verbal and nonverbal) [8].

Surely the proposed device does not want to compete with much more sophisticated tools (as humanoid robots); yet we argue it can be still interesting for therapists, because of its simplicity, ease of use, and versatility as a potential supporting tool.

2 Related Works

Innovative technologies (e.g. interactive environments, robotic platforms, virtual reality) seem to be effective to support the therapeutic activity in ASD. [2]. About the *turn-taking*, robots have been used in some promising, exploring studies [6,13]. Unexpectedly, very few works were found, which exploit simpler – yet interesting enough – technological devices other than robots, to train the *turn-taking* competence in ASDs.

In [9] the authors developed an interactive system called *COLOLO* composed of two wirelessly connected spherical toys; the spheres (one held by the therapist and one by the child) are designed to emit luminous and vibrational feedback if the *turn-taking* game roles are complied. A similar approach, based on interactive lighting blocks which interact when positioned in each other's vicinity, was used in [3].

In the current work-in-progress we focused on a single device; in particular, we wanted to explore the technical possibility for the proposed toy, to detect autonomously the identity of the two players, namely the child and the therapist, so to respond differently according to the role in the game. We then present a simple proof of concept, showing the potential of the device in supporting *turn-taking* activities.

3 Design Concept of "X-8" First Prototype

3.1 Design Considerations

The design of *X-8* is based on the concept of *Transitional Wearable Companion* (TWC) [10]. A TWC is an interactive "smart" toy with the following features: (i) it is potentially able to arouse emotional attachment and reassuring feelings, thanks to its soft material and the *wearability* characteristic; (ii) it can be perceived as a playmate, thanks to the pleasant animal shape; (iii) it can stimulate simple social games (based on imitation and joint attention), exploiting the

Fig. 1. On left, the turn-taking concept: *X-8* can emit different lights and sounds according to the user who touches its tentacles. On right, the wearability concept: the tentacles, thanks to small weights, adapt to shoulders and gently hug the child, so that *X-8* can be easily worn around the neck.

attractiveness of coloured lights and sounds, supported by the inner electronics (see Fig. 1). The concept of TWC – as a potential supporting tool in therapy – is currently in a promising experimentation phase on young children diagnosed with ASD [11].

X-8 was designed as a six-legged octopus (which makes it a very special octopus!). Textile materials (external cotton envelope, internal soft padding) are hypoallergenic and fireproof. Within each leg there is a small pocket filled with linen seeds: these pouches make legs a little bit heavier, so that *X-8* can easily adapt its shape if placed on human body, and can consequently be comfortably carried on the child's shoulders. About this point, it was interestingly observed how weighted vests can exert a calming effect on some ASD children [12]. Pockets with linen seeds have another additional, appealing feature: they could be taken out, heated in microwave, and placed back, so that *X-8* becomes pleasantly warm, so enhancing the potential reassuring effects of the toy.

Concerning the interactive behaviour, each tentacle is able to respond to human touch emitting coloured lights (and brief amusing sounds in the next version of the prototype), namely sensory stimuli which are very rewarding for young children. The toy is able to autonomously detect the user's identity: in the context of an hypotetical therapy session including two actors, *X-8* can "understand" if its tentacles are touched by the child or the therapist. This feature makes it possible to set up several games based on *turn-taking* rules.

3.2 Technical Specifications

In this first prototype, *X-8* electronics is based on a *Arduino Uno* board that (once engineered and miniaturised) will be hidden in the octopus body. Luminous patterns are emitted through embedded addressable leds, nicely diffused by the soft padding. The device can detect the human touch through capacitive sensors and conductive patches, stiched on the six tentacles. In order to discriminate between the users touches, each tentacle presents also a magnetic sensor: if the therapist wears a ring embedding a little magnet, his/her touch will activate both the capacitive and magnetic sensors (see Fig. 2). This simple system lets X-8 to autonomously "understand" who is touching its tentacles. The solution obviously works only for two users, but we think it is not an important limitation, as many *turn-taking* activities are based on two people only. A first proof-of-concept, showing the feasibility of the solution, can be observed at this link https://bit.ly/31lfUv3.

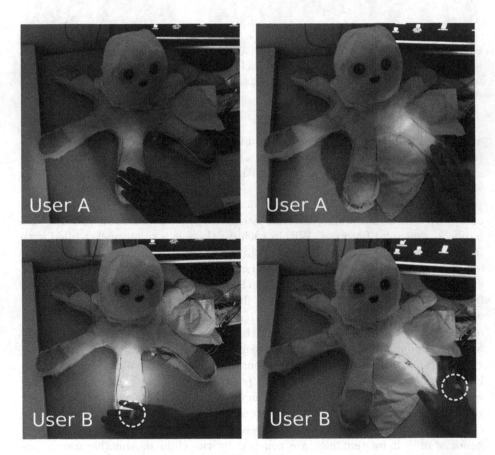

Fig. 2. In this functional test, the toy responds with magenta color to user *A* and with green to user *B*. The discernment is possible thanks to the small, discreet magnetic ring worn by user *B* (highlighted in yellow) which is detected by the sensors. The shown prototype, as a work-in-progress, is still partially disassembled: all electronics will be hidden by an external envelope. (Color figure online)

3.3 Proposals on Possible Games

Once the device is able to detect the identity of the users, several games based on *turn-taking* rules can be conceived, i.e. they can be easily implemented in the device software. As an example, if we figure a typical therapeutic session, with child and therapist sitting next to each other, with *X-8* placed in the middle (*floortime* therapy), the following proposals, featuring an increasing complexity, can be imagined:

– **Proposal 1**: different colors are associated to each user, e.g. magenta to the child and green to the therapist (as in Fig. 2). The child can touch the toy and make it glow in magenta, but he/her has to wait for therapist's touch to observe the toy glowing in green (hopefully, a *desired* outcome which the child wants to observe too). This is obviously the most simple activity, and it is already possible with the current prototype.
– **Proposal 2**: the toy glows briefly in magenta, indicating that it is the child's turn to touch the toy. If he/she touches any of the tentacles, *X-8* emits a generalised rewarding pattern, featuring several colours on all legs (as a rainbow); then the toy turns dark and, after few seconds, glows briefly in green, indicating that now it is the therapist's turn. If the child touches the toy in the place of the therapist, *X-8* recognises the violation of the rule, and does not produce any reward pattern. This activity is more complicated, and features a fixed sequence of turns: first the child, then the therapist, then all over again.
– **Proposal 3**: a random tentacle glows intermettently in green or magenta, indicating which user has to touch the active tentacle. If the rule is respected (i.e. the correct user touches the correct leg) *X-8* emits a generalised luminous rewarding pattern; then the game starts again with another random tentacle and a random colour (green or magenta). This activity is more complex than previous one, as it requires more attentional resources and features a non-fixed sequence of turns.

The above mentioned games are only proposals, made possible by improving the *X-8* software. It is easily feasible then further improve the system with the addition of a tablet, connected to the toy via Bluetooth, where the therapist can select – through an App – which game is more adapt to the child.

4 Conclusion and Future Work

We presented the first version of a toy prototype, which can potentially support *turn-taking* activities in young children diagnosed with ASD. In the next phase we are going to complete the device, through the following steps: (I) the improvement of the inner electronics – also with the addition of auditory feedback – to make the toy usable in a real therapeutic session; (II) the design of several, different games, through the development of a specific software; (III) the development of a control App, to let the therapist to select the current game, and save the behavioural data for research purpose.

Once the toy is competed, we plan to test the effectiveness of *X-8* in a pilot experimental session involving a therapist and a child diagnosed with ASD. This phase will be carried out in collaboration with neurodevelopmental researchers. Our main goal is to provide the therapist with an effective, versatile, easy-to-use tool, which can be helpful in training and reinforcing the *turn-taking* competences in this type of children.

Acknowledgments. This work has received funding from the European Union's Horizon 2020 Research and Innovation program under grant agreements No. 94587 (project *PlusMe: Transitional Wearable Companions for the therapy of children with Autism Spectrum Disorders*) and No. 952095 (project *IM-TWIN: from Intrinsic Motivations to Transitional Wearable INtelligent companions for autism spectrum disorder*).

References

1. American Psychiatric Association: Diagnostic and Statistical Manual of Mental Disorders: DSM-5. Washington DC, 5th edn. (2013). https://doi.org/10.1176/appi.books.9780890425596
2. Boucenna, S., et al.: Interactive technologies for autistic children: a review. Cogn. Comput. **6**(4), 722–740 (2014). https://doi.org/10.1007/s12559-014-9276-x
3. Brok, J.C.J., Barakova, E.I.: Engaging autistic children in imitation and turn-taking games with multiagent system of interactive lighting blocks. In: Yang, H.S., Malaka, R., Hoshino, J., Han, J.H. (eds.) ICEC 2010. LNCS, vol. 6243, pp. 115–126. Springer, Heidelberg (2010). https://doi.org/10.1007/978-3-642-15399-0_11
4. Holler, J., Kendrick, K.H., Casillas, M., Levinson, S.C.: Editorial: turn-taking in human communicative interaction. Front. Psychol. **6**(DEC), 1–4 (2015). https://doi.org/10.3389/fpsyg.2015.01919
5. Izadi-Najafabadi, S., Rinat, S., Zwicker, J.G.: Rehabilitation-induced brain changes detected through magnetic resonance imaging in children with neurodevelopmental disorders: a systematic review. Int. J. Dev. Neurosci. **73**(November 2018), 66–82 (2019). https://doi.org/10.1016/j.ijdevneu.2018.12.001
6. Kozima, H., Nakagawa, C.: Social robots for children: practice in communication-care. In: International Workshop on Advanced Motion Control, AMC 2006, pp. 768–773 (2006). https://doi.org/10.1109/AMC.2006.1631756
7. Neimy, H., Pelaez, M., Carrow, J., Monlux, K., Tarbox, J.: Infants at risk of autism and developmental disorders: establishing early social skills. Behav. Dev. Bull. **22**(1), 6–22 (2017). https://doi.org/10.1037/bdb0000046
8. Noel, J.P., De Niear, M.A., Lazzara, N.S., Wallace, M.T.: Uncoupling between multisensory temporal function and nonverbal turn-taking in autism spectrum disorder. IEEE Trans. Cogn. Dev. Syst. **10**(4), 973–982 (2018). https://doi.org/10.1109/TCDS.2017.2778141
9. Nunez, E., Matsuda, S., Hirokawa, M., Yamamoto, J., Suzuki, K.: Effect of sensory feedback on turn-taking using paired devices for children with ASD. Multimodal Technol. Interact. **2**(4), 1–18 (2018). https://doi.org/10.3390/mti2040061

10. Özcan, B., Caligiore, D., Sperati, V., Moretta, T., Baldassarre, G.: Transitional wearable companions: a novel concept of soft interactive social robots to improve social skills in children with autism spectrum disorder. Int. J. Soc. Robot. **8**(4), 471–481 (2016). https://doi.org/10.1007/s12369-016-0373-8
11. Sperati, V., et al.: Acceptability of the transitional wearable companion "+me" in children with autism spectrum disorder: a comparative pilot study. Front. Psychol. **11**(May), 1–9 (2020). https://doi.org/10.3389/fpsyg.2020.00951
12. Stephenson, J., Carter, M.: The use of weighted vests with children with autism spectrum disorders and other disabilities. J. Autism Dev. Disord. **39**(1), 105–114 (2009). https://doi.org/10.1007/s10803-008-0605-3
13. Wainer, J., Robins, B., Amirabdollahian, F., Dautenhahn, K.: Using the humanoid robot KASPAR to autonomously play triadic games and facilitate collaborative play among children with autism. IEEE Trans. Auton. Ment. Dev. **6**(3), 183–199 (2014). https://doi.org/10.1109/TAMD.2014.2303116

Children's Reality Understanding of Magic Show in the Video

Jiaqi Wu, Zhuo Zhang, Yi Zhou, and Na Xu[✉]

Central China Normal University, Wuhan 430070, Hubei, People's Republic of China
xuna511@icloud.com

Abstract. The purpose of the present study was to explore children's understanding of whether a magic show that they saw in a video depicted reality. Moreover, the research aimed to explore the difference between 5-year-old children and adults in judging the reality of the magic show. The results showed that the children's understanding of the reality of the magic show was similar to that of adults, but there was a significant difference in the justifications given by the children and the adults for their levels of belief. The children mainly used redundant justifications, while the adults provided factual justifications. More research could further explore the neuro mechanism underlying children's understanding of reality. This is of great value to deal with the issue of safety when children interact with the media.

Keywords: Understanding of reality · Magic show · Justification · Video

1 Introduction

In 2013, the news media reported the Lianyungang incident in which children burned their playmates in imitation of the animation of the cartoon characters Pleasant Goat and Big Wolf [1]. In a similar incident, a boy swallowed magnets, imitating what he saw during a magic show [2]. These incidents showed that children's blind imitation of fantastical events in a video may endanger their safety and even threaten their lives. These events directed researchers to pay closer attention to children's understanding of the reality of events in videos.

In today's world, children are exposed to a huge variety of material, both recorded and live, on a wide range of electronic devices. According to the statistics from Common Sense Media in 2020, 2-to-4-year-old children in the United States mainly used screen media to watch TV and videos, which accounted for about three-quarters (73%) of all their screen time [3]. In 2019, a questionnaire survey of 720 parents of children aged 2 to 6 in China also indicated that 74% of children used electronic media for watching videos and animated shows [4]. These surveys showed that at this time, the main use of electronic media in China and the United States was to watch videos.

There are many real and fantastical events in the videos that children view. Their ability to understand the reality status of events has been discussed frequently in recent years. In the study by Flavell, 54% of 3-year-old participants said that real objects would

C. Stephanidis et al. (Eds.): HCII 2021, CCIS 1419, pp. 240–246, 2021.
https://doi.org/10.1007/978-3-030-78635-9_33

not fall out of the upside-down TV [5]. Wright found that children aged 5 and 7 tended to think that the events happened in a TV video was not real [6]. Other research explored the differences of reality understanding between 4-to-6-year-old children and adults. It used fantastical and real events in animated videos and found that 4-year-old children's ability to distinguish fantastical and real events was lower than that of 6-year-old children and adults, while there was no significant difference between adults and children aged 5 and 6 [7]. These studies consistently showed that children aged 5 to 6 could accurately distinguish between fantastical and real events.

Different from TV programs and animations, a magic show is a unique kind of performance, which can present a variety of effects which violate physical principles. Rosengren and Hickling's research in 1994 showed that 4-year-old children thought the live magic show they saw was real, while 5-year-old children did not [8]. Subboksty and his colleagues used a live magic show for experiments, and found that 4-year-old children knew the difference between ordinary and magical events. Only 6-year-old and older children denied that magic could happen in real life. But after watching the magic show, children aged 4 and 6 accepted the explanation of the show as being magic, while 9-year-olds and adults did not [9]. Prior studies on children's understanding of the reality of live performances of magic reflected the influences of age and viewing experience, but they lacked research on children's understanding of the reality of a magic show on video, as well as in-depth discussion of the participants' justifications.

The present study compared 5-year-old children's understanding of the reality of a magic show in a video with that of adults in order to explore the influence of age and viewing experience. The hypotheses were: there were significant differences between 5-year-old children and adults in judging the reality of a magic show in a video; compared to the adults, children's viewing experience significantly affected the understanding of reality in a video magic show; there were significant differences between children and adults in their justifications for judging reality status.

2 Methods

2.1 Participants

Thirty Chinese-speaking children were randomly recruited from a kindergarten in Wuhan, China (15 girls, $M_{age} = 67.27 \pm 2.77$ months). Thirty Chinese-speaking adults were also randomly recruited from Central China Normal University, which was affiliated with the kindergarten (14 males, $M_{age} = 286.93 \pm 14.39$ months).

2.2 Tools and Materials

Based on the classification of experimental materials in Phelps and Woolley's research [10], we designed four types of magic show which violated different physical rules, including violating gravity (GR), violating perceptual constancy (PR), violating inertia (IR), and violating object constancy (CR). In the study, each type of magic show had two videos. Each of these violated the same physical rule and contained two different forms of magic. Therefore, there were eight videos of a magic show that children watched in the present study. An undergraduate from the magic club in the University was invited to film the eight videos of magic shows. All magic videos were performed by the same magician in the same setting. In this study, we also took pictures of all the performance props and paired them with the video one by one. Eight magic props pictures (Fig. 1) and video clips were randomly arranged in the PowerPoint file.

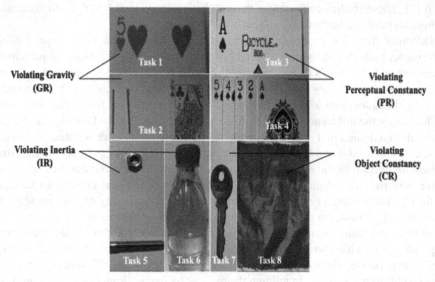

Fig. 1. Magic props pictures

2.3 Procedure

The whole experiment lasted about 20 min. The experiment was divided into two parts: interview and magic video task. In the interview part, the experimenter confirmed that children and adults understood the videos they had viewed. The participants were asked, "Do you know what a magic show is?" If the participants didn't understand and could not answer, the experimenter explained it with examples. After making sure that the participants understood the meaning of "magic show," they were asked two empirical questions, "Have you ever seen a magic show?" and "Did you go to a magic show?" Then participants were asked whether they had experienced viewing a magic show in a video or in real life.

Then the experimenters opened the PowerPoint file of the magic show video. They asked the participants to listen and answer carefully during the whole process. In order to ensure that the participants could focus on the changes of props when watching the magic show, the experimenters needed to present the props pictures used in the video to the participants before playing each video. Then the participants were asked to report what objects they saw, and to answer whether they had seen those objects changed from previous magic shows, so as to remind the children to pay attention to changes in the objects.

After playing the videos with the magic show, the experimenters asked the participants what changes to the scene had occurred. If the participants couldn't answer, the experimenters played the video again. The participants were then asked, "Do you think the changes you saw in the video could take place in real life, or just in a magic show?" (0 = only in a magic show; 1 = could happen in real life) The second question was the degree of certainty of their answers (0 = somewhat sure; 1 = very sure). In order to ensure that the children could clearly give the degree of their certainty, the experimenter showed them a bar chart representing "somewhat sure" and "very sure". The third question was, "Why do you think the event could/could not happen in magic or real life?" They were given enough time to think and answer.

2.4 Coding of Justifications

Based on the coding method of children's justifications in Shtulman and Carey's study [11], two graduates evaluated all participants' oral reports. Coding could be divided into three types. First, factual justifications referenced facts about the world that would preclude an event's occurrence (e.g., "*a water cup floating in the air* was impossible because of gravity"). Second, hypothetical justifications gave a concrete and operable hypothesis in place of the actual event under consideration (e.g., "*a carpet could fly in the sky* if it was in cartoons"). Third, redundant justifications gave no specific information beyond what was already in the video or what children had responded to the judgment questions. In addition, if the justification mentioned words like magic and magic show, the justification should belong to redundant justifications [11].

3   Results

Independent sample t-test results indicated that there was no significant difference between children and adults in judging the reality of the magic show ($t = -0.51$, $p > .05$). However, there was the main effect of video type on the judgment of children and adults ($F (3,232) = 7.297$, $p < .001$, $\eta_p^2 = 0.09$). Second, through independent sample t-tests, it was indicated that, surprisingly, children's viewing experience (including watching live shows that they might have seen at an earlier time) and adults' viewing experience (including watching live shows) did not significantly affect their judgment of reality. All adults had viewing experience. The adults' experience of viewing live shows did not affect their judgment on the reality status of the events ($t = -.211$, $p > .05$). Among children, the results indicated no significant difference for their reality status judgments, whether they had viewing experience or not ($t = -.365$, $p > .05$). Similarly, the children's live viewing experience did not affect their judgments ($t = -.332$, $p > .05$). Finally, through multivariate analysis of variance (MANOVA), there were significant differences between children and adults in their justifications of reality understanding for 8 magic show videos ($p < .001$). The detailed results are shown in Table 1.

Table 1. Means and standard deviations of reality status judgments by age groups

| | Magic show watching experience | | | | | | | | Live magic show watching experience | | | | | | | |
| | Without watching experience | | | | With watching experience | | | | Without watching experience | | | | With watching experience | | | |
	GR	PR	IR	CR	GR	PR	IR	CR	GR	PR	IR	CR	GR	PR	IR	CR
Children	0.18 ± 0.60	0.27 ± 0.65	0.73 ± 0.90	0.36 ± 0.81	0.16 ± 0.50	0.26 ± 0.45	0.63 ± 0.83	0.21 ± 0.42	0.17 ± 0.58	0.22 ± 0.52	0.78 ± 0.90	0.26 ± 0.62	0.14 ± 0.38	0.43 ± 0.53	0.29 ± 0.49	0.29 ± 0.49
Adults					0.07 ± 0.25	0.23 ± 0.57	0.57 ± 0.77	0.27 ± 0.64	0.13 ± 0.34	0.13 ± 0.34	0.75 ± 0.86	0.19 ± 0.54	0.00 ± 0.00	0.36 ± 0.74	0.36 ± 0.63	0.36 ± 0.74

4 Discussion

The study indicated that children and adults were more likely to believe that magic only happened in a video, rather than in real life. The children's viewing experience did not significantly affect their judgment of the authenticity of what they saw in the video. However, children's justifications of their understanding of reality were significantly different from those of the adults.

First, 5-year-old children's and adults' reality judgments about the magic show in the video were similar. This result was consistent with prior research that had demonstrated that children have the ability to accurately distinguish between fantastical and real events at the age of 5–6 [7, 12]. Based on previous research about children's judgments of the reality of live magic performances, this result supplemented information about their judgments of reality in the events portrayed in the magic show video. The similarity of the results from children and adults might be due to the fact that the magic events they viewed violate physical principles such as inertia, gravity, object constancy and perceptual constancy. These events rarely appear in real life. Therefore, 5-year-old children might be surprised when they were faced with fantastical events, and thought that these events would not happen in real life [4].

Second, the study found that the children's viewing experience as prior experience did not significantly affect their understanding of reality. The results were inconsistent with the previous studies which had proved that children distinguished fantasy from reality through prior direct or indirect experience [13, 14]. For example, in Marterli's study, children aged 8 to 10 might misjudge a fantastical image as a real image due to their contact with video games [13]. Woolley and his colleagues' research in 2004 indicated that children aged 3 to 5 tended to believe in fantasy because of their contact with the Candy Witch fantasy characters [14]. In prior researches, participants directly interacted with the virtual characters and games while this study's participants watched magic show in the video. The different way to interact with fantasy may lead to different results. Moreover, children in the present study were 5-year-olds, and their cultural background was different from the background of the children in the prior study. Future research can confirm whether the viewing experience has an impact on the understanding of the reality of a magic show in a video.

Although there was no significant difference between children and adults in the reality judgments, this study found that there was significant difference between children and adults in their justifications. There may be two reasons for this result: one is that the ability to explain judgments increases with age. Second, children and adults have different way of thinking. Previous study has shown that with the increase of age, children's hypothetical and redundant justification will gradually decrease, while factual justification will gradually increase. At the age of 6, children display a factual justification pattern as adults [15]. Shtulman proposed that children made judgments directly according to their intuition after understanding the event, while adults usually reflected on the rationality of their intuition, and children's reflection often appeared after the judgment [16]. In general, we can infer that cognition differences between children and adults lead to significant differences in their justifications.

This research only indicated that the ability of 5-year-old children to recognize and understand reality was similar to that of adults, but it did not explore the influence of age and individual experience on children's understanding of reality. Future research is warranted to explore children's neuro mechanism of their reality understanding from these aspects: different cultural backgrounds, age differences and individual experience.

Acknowledgments. The study reported in this article was supported by the Fundamental Research Funds for Central Universities, China (Project No. CCNU20QN039).

References

1. Beijing times. http://media.people.com.cn/n/2013/1219/c40606-23881783.html. Accessed 15 Nov 2020. (in Chinese)
2. Chongqing Evening News. https://www.chinanews.com/sh/2014/02-14/5835983.shtml. Accessed 15 Nov 2020. (in Chinese)
3. Rideout, V., Robb, M.B.: The Common Sense census: Media use by kids age zero to eight, San Francisco, CA: Common Sense Media (2020)
4. Chen, X.Y., Wang, Y.F., Zhao, J.Y., Meng, Q.: The development characteristics and mechanism of children's distinguishing fantasy from reality. Progress Psychol. Sci. **027**(007), 1232–1237 (2019)
5. Flavell, J.H., Flavell E.R., Green, F.L., Korfmacher, J.E.: Do young children think of television images as pictures or real objects? J. Broadcasting Electron. Media **34**(4), 399–419 (1990)
6. Wright, J.C., Huston, A.C., Reitz, A.L., Piemyat, S.: Young children's perceptions of television reality: determinants and developmental differences. Dev. Psychol. **30**(2), 229–239 (1994)
7. Li, H., Boguszewski, K., Lillard, A.S.: Can that really happen? Children's knowledge about the reality status of fantastical events in television. J. Exp. Child Psychol. **139**, 99–114 (2015)
8. Rosengren, K.S., Hickling, A.K.: Seeing is believing: Children's explanations of commonplace, magical, and extraordinary transformations. Child Dev. **65**(6), 1605–1626 (1994)
9. Subbotsky, E.: Magical thinking in judgments of causation: can anomalous phenomena affect ontological causal beliefs in children and adults? Br. J. Dev. Psychol. **22**(1), 123–152 (2004)
10. Phelps, K.E., Woolley, J.D.: The form and function of young children's magical beliefs. Dev. Psychol. **30**(3), 385 (1994)
11. Shtulman, A., Carey, S.: Improbable or impossible? How children reason about the possibility of extraordinary events. Child Dev. **78**(3), 1015–1103 (2007)
12. Li, M.Y., Wang, Q.: Investigation and research on the use of multimedia at home by children aged 3–6 – a case from Beijing. J. Educ. **10**(06), 95–102 (2014). (in Chinese)
13. Martarelli, C.S., Gurtner, L.M., Mast, F.W.: School-age children show a bias toward fantasy classifications after playing a platform game. Psychol. Pop. Media Cult. **4**(4), 351–359 (2015)
14. Woolley, J.D., Boerger, E.A., Markman, A.B.: A visit from the candy witch: factors influencing young children's belief in a novel fantastical being. Dev. Sci. **7**(4), 456–468 (2010)
15. Li, H.: The influence of television on children's executive function: the perspective of authenticity judgment. Central China Normal University, pp. 55–56 (2014)
16. Shtulman, A.: The development of possibility judgment within and across domains. Cogn. Dev. **24**(3), 293–309 (2009)

Designing for Older People

mHealthINX – A Virtual Reality-Based Occupational Stress Management Solution for Older Employees

Elisabeth Broneder[1]([✉]), Fabian Wagner[1], Christoph Weiß[1], Julia Fritz[2], Miroslav Sili[1], and Matthieu Arendse[3]

[1] Center for Digital Safety & Security and Center for Health & Bioresources, AIT Austrian Institute of Technology GmbH, Vienna, Austria
elisabeth.broneder@ait.ac.at
[2] terzStiftung, Berlingen, Switzerland
[3] tanteLouise, Bergen op Zoom, The Netherlands

Abstract. Stress-related diseases such as depression, anxiety and cardiovascular diseases are one of the main causes for sick leaves in older employees, aged 55+, in Europe. Mental disorders and work-related depression cost up to € 620 billion annually. mHealthINX seeks to alleviate these problems by providing a user-friendly solution that supports older employees in promoting and strengthening their mental health. It consists of (a) a hand-held stress-measurement device, (b) a mobile app that provides personalized interventions and enables the user to assess and elaborate the personal stress level via questionnaires and self-reported assessments and, (c) Virtual Reality (VR) glasses that offer immersive interventions where the user can blank out the stressful work-environment. VR is a promising technology that can offer innovative and immersive mental health interventions within a relaxing virtual environment. Users can choose their own relaxing surrounding to walk around and learn to cope with stressful situations via interventions like mindful relaxations and relaxing games. This provides an innovative way to support the user in coping with occupational stress. The provided interventions can be performed both during the work time and within a more private setting at home.

Keywords: Virtual reality · Promoting mental health · Occupational stress management · User experience · UX

1 Introduction

Being exposed to a chronically stressful working environment increases the chances of developing health problems. This is especially true for older workers where occupational stress is a key factor for developing mental disorders [1]. The risk for developing disorders like depression leads to a higher number of sick leaves compared to younger employees [2]. Moreover, a poor psychological working environment can lead to employees wanting to retire earlier [3]. Studies have shown that virtual exercises can reduce objective stress,

© Springer Nature Switzerland AG 2021
C. Stephanidis et al. (Eds.): HCII 2021, CCIS 1419, pp. 249–256, 2021.
https://doi.org/10.1007/978-3-030-78635-9_34

anxiety and depression in people with stress-related disorders [4]. Virtual Reality (VR) is a powerful tool for mental health applications. The high level of immersion that VR offers can help employees to escape stressful environments and learn how to cope with stressful situations. Some few existing VR solutions deal with stress reduction and mental health disorders, but none of them target the population of older employees. Soyka et al. [5] and Thoondee et al. [6] conducted studies in which they used 3D generated relaxing environments to tackle chronic stress. Anderson et al. [7] showed the usefulness of 360° videos and stills in VR for stress reduction. The age of the participants in all three cited studies was between 20–45 years. Other research regarding stress reduction and mental health improvement using VR can be found in [8–10]. Those solutions, however, are designed to assist patients already suffering from mental disorders and not for preventing them – especially in working environments.

The mHealthINX system is an innovative stress management tool that supports older employees in promoting and strengthening their mental health by helping them to relax and analyze as well as deal with stressful situations. The VR-based stress management component of the system provides an easy to use yet powerful tool allowing users to escape stressful situations by diving into a relaxing virtual world. The virtual environment offers employees different interventions like mindfulness interventions, relaxation and deflection exercises. Figure 1 illustrates the VR application in action.

Fig. 1. The VR stress management component. Left: user testing the interventions. Right: menu with the different interventions the user can pick from.

2   The mHealthINX System

The mHealthINX system consists of three different components: (a) A hand-held device records an ECG signal and a photoplethysmography signal, which allows to approximate the user's stress level. (b) A mobile app enables users to assess and elaborate the personal stress level via self-reported assessments and questionnaires. Based on the measured and reported stress level, the mobile app suggests personalized interventions that are determined by an intelligent logic in the backend. (c) In addition to the interventions in the mobile app, an innovative VR stress-management component – described in more detail in the following – offers immersive interventions where the user can blank out stressful work-environments.

For the VR application the VR glasses "Oculus Quest 2" (OQ2)[1] have been chosen based on the system requirements and market availability. In the first months of the project the Oculus Go[2] was used, but due to its announced end of life the consortium switched to the OQ2. This situation highlights the enormous progress and the fast pace in the VR sector. As development environment the game engine Unity3D[3] is used. At the current stage of the project, we implemented the first VR interventions: relaxing environments like photospheres and a 360° video, two relaxing games, and a mindful walk. This setup is currently tested at the end-user partners terzStiftung in Switzerland and TanteLouise in the Netherlands. Examples of the currently implemented interventions are depicted in Fig. 2.

Fig. 2. The different types of interventions. The left image shows an relaxing environment. In the middle image one of the relaxing games is demonstrated. The mindful walk, in which a bird guides the user through a forest, can be seen on the right side.

2.1 Relaxing Environments

As mentioned before, the VR component provides relaxing environments that users can dive into whenever they have the feeling that their stress level rises. In the category of relaxing environments, photospheres and 360° videos are implemented. Photospheres are extended panoramic photos that allow the user to look up and down in addition to the full 360° on the horizontal axis. They create the illusion of being at the shown place by surrounding the user. Nowadays, they can be easily recorded with modern smart phones. 360° videos are videos where a view in every direction is recorded simultaneously using an omnidirectional camera or a collection of cameras. In this project the Insta360 One R is used, which uses two 180° cameras pointing in the opposite direction. Currently five photospheres, displaying different landscapes and a 360° video, displaying a walk through the woods are provided. The photospheres and videos are easily extendable since they are provided by the backend.

---

[1] https://www.oculus.com/quest-2/.

[2] https://en.wikipedia.org/wiki/Oculus_Go.

[3] https://unity.com/.

2.2 Relaxing Games

In a literature study conducted at the beginning of the project, relaxing games were identified as suitable mental health interventions that can be enhanced if implemented in a VR version. Currently, two games are implemented. The first is a game, where users have to pick mature fruits before they fall to the ground, where they get eaten by animals. The challenge is to pick and throw them into a basket in time and reach certain points. The second game – a concentration game – focuses on a scenario where users are requested to build a tower by stacking stones. This tower has to stay steady for a few seconds. Since user movements, hand gestures, controllers' movement and the VR glasses are tracked, users can freely move around and grasp these virtual items. This provides a fully immersed feeling during the relaxing games.

2.3 Mindfulness-Based Interventions

Mindfulness interventions are an important therapeutic approach, and therefore a critical part of good physical and mental health [11]. Thus, the VR application also considers this category of intervention. The current prototype offers a mindful walk through a virtual landscape. Users can walk through a relaxing environment – consisting of meadows, wood and a waterfall - while learning something about procrastination. Towards the final prototype, this type of intervention will be enhanced by adding more interactive elements and defined mindfulness content.

3 Design and Development Methodology

mHealthINX utilizes a user-centered design approach. At the beginning of the project, end-user requirements were collected both in Switzerland and the Netherlands by the end-user partners terzStiftung and TanteLouise. The requirements workshop included questions about what participants do if they feel tense during the workday, what helps them to relax after work, which landscapes and sounds are relaxing for them, and in what way they can imagine using a relaxation tool or system.

During development, end-users are frequently providing feedback via user workshops, taking place at both end-user organizations. The first user workshop took place in September 2020, where the first prototype was tested, containing photospheres, a 360° video, and a game where the user can build a tower by stacking stones. The results of the first end-user workshop are described in Sect. 4. In the second workshop, which takes place in March 2021, an updated version of the prototype is tested that includes an updated version of the 360° video, an additional game, and a mindful intervention. In the final workshop, taking place in July 2021, end-users will again evaluate a new version of the prototype, including additional mindfulness interventions and games. The feedback will again be incorporated in the developments towards the final prototype, tested in field trials starting in December 2021.

3.1 UI and Interaction Design

Since the target group of mHealthINX are older employees and therefore mostly unfamiliar with VR, the user interface was designed to be simple and easy-to-understand. Figure 1 shows the main menu that is placed within the virtual environment. In the menu bar the four different intervention categories can be selected. When selecting a category, all the interventions from this category are displayed as thumbnails that are easy to understand. Since the UI is designed particularly for VR, the menu bar is placed within the 3D environment as a 3D object. In the first prototype, the menu is controlled by pointing on the UI elements via the laser pointer of the Oculus GO controller and selecting them via a button. In the second prototype, this interaction is also kept for the Oculus Quest 2. The menu bar concept is the same during the interventions. When displaying the menu bar, the 3D environment is considered so that it does not overlap with objects within the intervention scene. During a photosphere intervention, users can easily switch to other landscapes in order to find the one that relaxes them the most.

3.2 Interaction During the Games

Since the games constitute a more interactive intervention type, especially in VR, a special focus is placed on user interaction during the games. During the aforementioned stone game, the tower has to stay upright for a few seconds to win the game. Since the Oculus Go controller is only tracked in 3 Degrees of Freedom (DOF), the stones were moved via a laser pointer controlled by the controller movements and a button on the controller. This felt not intuitive since the hand-movement of the user was not tracked in the translation axes. For the second prototype the OQ2 is used which offers new possibilities of interacting with game elements. Both the glasses and the controller are tracked in 6 DOFs. Stones can be picked up by reaching out to them via moving the controller towards them and making a grabbing gesture by simultaneously holding the side, front and upper button of the controller. This way a more natural way of interaction can be reached compared to the interaction provided by the Oculus Go controller. In the fruit game the same way of interaction is used – but the user can additionally throw the fruits into a basket by performing a throwing movement.

4 Results

At the beginning of the project, a requirements analysis has been conducted in the form of a survey with potential future users. A total of 105 people took part in the survey in Switzerland and 229 people in the Netherlands. In Switzerland 77 of the users were women and 28 men. In the Netherlands 201 were women and 26 men. In addition to questions about stress management and user behavior, the survey also asked about attitudes toward VR glasses. When asked which landscape relaxed the participants the most, most participants from Switzerland chose mountains, forests and rivers, while those from the Netherlands tended to choose the beach, the sea and forests. The second question was about the sounds. We asked the participants which sounds they find relaxing. Here, a difference between the two countries can be seen. Whereas in Switzerland the chirping of birds, rain, and leaves in the wind was found to be particularly relaxing, the Dutch participants found the sounds of the forest and the sound of water more pleasant. In the end, they were asked where they would use a VR system for relaxation. Users from both countries claimed that they would prefer to use it at home, and half of the participants could imagine using such a VR solution.

The first user workshops took place in both countries in September 2020. They took place in both countries at the same time and were organized according to the same procedure. In Switzerland 5 persons and in the Netherlands 24 users participated in the workshop. A total of 5 men aged 55 to 72 participated in Switzerland, and 21 women and 3 men aged 50 to 65 participated in the Netherlands. All participants are currently in permanent employment. The workshop was divided into two parts not to overload the participants with an abundance of information. For this reason, it was decided to let the participants work creatively in the first part. In the second part, they had the opportunity to test the already completed prototypes. The same people participated in both parts of the workshop.

Fig. 3. Expressions from the first end-user workshop

4.1   Test Sequence During the Workshops

The World Café method was used for the first workshop. World Café is a creative and collaborative approach for brainstorming in groups. In an atmosphere that is as pleasant as possible, similar to a coffee house, small subgroups exchange ideas at high tables and network their knowledge. To further stimulate or deepen the discourse, participants change tables and groups several times during the World Café. The results are documented in the form of visualizations or texts on "paper tablecloths" at the bar tables. Using prepared guiding questions, the participants exchange ideas at eye level across specialist and organizational levels. To help participants better understand what mHealthINX is about and how the system can be used, three scenarios were presented. Each scenario described the application of the respective subarea.

After a brief exchange among the participants about their experiences with stress, stress symptoms, and stress causes, the mHealthINX system was presented to them, and the functionalities of the different parts (mobile app, Smart PWA, and VR glasses) were explained. Subsequently, the following questions were asked for each part of the system:

- What should the system be able/not be able to do?
- In which situation should it offer support?
- Where could there be difficulties with the application?

Due to the COVID-19 pandemic and the security concepts of the respective end-user partners, the method was slightly adapted. The participants did not move from table to table as usual in the method, but the respective group posters were passed on by the workshop leader. Instead of standing, the users sat at tables. This way, the necessary safety distance could be maintained, and personal contacts were kept as low as possible. Figure 3 gives an impression of this procedure.

4.2 Results

When asked what they would like the VR glasses to be capable of, participants mentioned a few special requests, such as having personal images, environments, or music integrated. When asked what the system should not provide, users provided more specific answers. It should not be addictive or overburden the user, thereby triggering a stress situation again. In general, they feel that the Photospheres are apt, but they see the potential for improvement in the background music. Some find the stone stapling game inside the VR glasses stressful at the beginning since they had to get used to the new hardware. In summary, they find the idea of using VR glasses to reduce their stress level pleasant.

5 Summary and Outlook

This work highlights the goals, the VR stress management component and first user involvement results of the EU project mHealthINX. It underlines the potential of VR interventions for promoting mental health using examples of three types of interventions that aim at reducing occupational stress. Although similar VR applications for stress management exist, they have not been specially designed and tested within the age group 50+. As outlined in Sect. 4, end-users see the potential of using VR glasses to reduce stress but have some trouble in adapting to the new hardware they are not yet experienced with. They gave valuable feedback that has been incorporated in the second prototype, which is currently tested in Switzerland and the Netherlands. In our future developments we will evaluate and incorporate the feedback from the second workshop and implement additional interventions – especially mindfulness interventions – that have a proven effect in stress management. A further prototype will be tested in the third workshop and the user feedback will be again incorporated into a final prototype and tested in long-lasting field trials in Switzerland and the Netherlands.

Acknowledgment. The project mHealthINX is co-funded by the AAL Joint Programme (AAL-2019–6-78-CP) and the following National Authorities and R&D programs in Austria, Switzerland, and the Netherlands: FFG, Schweizer Eidgenossenschaft, ZonMw.

References

1. Lunau, T., Wahrendorf, M., Dragano, N., Siegrist, J.: Work stress and depressive symptoms in older employees: impact of national labour and social policies. BMC Public Health **13**, 1086 (2013). https://doi.org/10.1186/1471-2458-13-1086
2. Götz, S., Hoven, H., Müller, A., Dragano, N., Wahrendorf, M.: Age differences in the association between stressful work and sickness absence among full-time employed workers: evidence from the German socio-economic panel. Int. Arch. Occup. Environ. Health **91**(4), 479–496 (2018). https://doi.org/10.1007/s00420-018-1298-3
3. Wahrendorf, M., Dragano, N., Siegrist, J.: Social position, work stress, and retirement intentions: a study with older employees from 11 European countries. Eur. Sociol. Rev. **29**, 792–802 (2012). https://doi.org/10.1093/esr/jcs058
4. Baños, R., Botella, V., Quero, S., Garcia-Palacios, A., Alcañiz Raya, M., Botella, C.: A virtual reality system for the treatment of stress-related disorders: a preliminary analysis of efficacy compared to a standard cognitive behavioral program. Int. J. Hum. Comput. Stud. **69**, 602–613 (2011). https://doi.org/10.1016/j.ijhcs.2011.06.002
5. Soyka, F., Leyrer, M., Smallwood, J., Ferguson, C., Riecke, B., Mohler, B.: Enhancing stress management techniques using virtual reality. In: Proceedings of the ACM Symposium on Applied Perception, pp. 85–88 (2016). https://doi.org/10.1145/2931002.2931017
6. Thoondee, K.D., Oikonomou, A.: Using virtual reality to reduce stress at work. In: Computing Conference, London, UK, pp. 492–499 (2017). https://doi.org/10.1109/SAI.2017.8252142
7. Anderson, A., Mayer, M., Fellows, A., Cowan, D., Hegel, M., Buckey, J.: Relaxation with immersive natural scenes presented using virtual reality. Aerospace Med. Hum. Performance **88**, 520–526 (2017). https://doi.org/10.3357/AMHP.4747.2017
8. Shah, L., Torres, S., Kannusamy, P., Chng, C., He, H., Klainin-Yobas, P.: Efficacy of the virtual reality-based stress management program on stress-related variables in people with mood disorders: the feasibility study. Arch. Psychiatric Nurs. **29** (2014). https://doi.org/10.1016/j.apnu.2014.09.003
9. Veling, W., Lestestuiver, B., Jongma, M., Hoenders, R., Driel, C.: Virtual reality relaxation for patients with a psychiatric disorder: crossover randomized controlled trial. J. Med. Internet Res. **23** (2021). https://doi.org/10.2196/17233
10. Ioannou, A., Papastavrou, E., Avraamides, M., Charalambous, A.: Virtual reality and symptoms management of anxiety, depression, fatigue, and pain: a systematic review. SAGE Open Nurs. **6** (2020). https://doi.org/10.1177/2377960820936163
11. Khoury, B., Sharma, M., Rush, S.E., Fournier, C.: Mindfulness-based stress reduction for healthy individuals: a meta-analysis. J. Psychosom. Res. **78**(6), 519–528 (2015). https://doi.org/10.1016/j.jpsychores.2015.03.009

Designing Towards an Application to Find a Nurse

Hélène Fournier[1,2,3]([envelope]) [ID], Keiko Katsuragawa[1,2,3,4] [ID], Karanpreet Singh[5],
Nabil Bin Hannan[4], and Irina Kondratova[1,2,3] [ID]

[1] Human-Computer Interaction, Digital Technologies Research Centre,
National Research Council Canada, Moncton, NB, Canada
{helene.fournier,keiko.katsuragawa,irina.kondratova}@nrc-cnrc.gc.ca
[2] Human-Computer Interaction, Digital Technologies Research Centre,
National Research Council Canada, Waterloo, ON, Canada
[3] Human-Computer Interaction, Digital Technologies Research Centre,
National Research Council Canada, Fredericton, NB, Canada
[4] Computer Science, University of Waterloo, Waterloo, ON, Canada
nbinhannan@uwaterloo.ca
[5] Computer Science, University of New Brunswick, Fredericton, NB, Canada
k.singh10@unb.ca

Abstract. In this fast-paced technological era, the demand and the
usage of applications which make our life easier have increased dramatically. This need has grown especially for the aging population who
require help more than ever. Older adults (65+) need an effective way
to communicate with a healthcare professional in case they require any
advice about their health or schedule an in-person checkup. The current COVID-19 pandemic has accelerated the push for remote check-ins
and virtual care especially for older adults who are medically or socially
vulnerable. Remote health services are being promoted as a means of
preserving the patient-health care provider relationship at times when
in-person visits are not practical or feasible, especially during COVID-19
and in the future. This paper describes an application to support vulnerable older adults in their home, with more responsive home health care
services which can potentially reduce the number of unnecessary trips
to the hospital for non-emergency situations. The process of designing
the application will be described, including workflow, storyboards, and
key steps in the validation process. The paper will also discuss future
research directions.

Keywords: Home health care services · Virtual care · Aging in place ·
HCI · Human factors · Vulnerable populations

1 Introduction

This paper presents research and development efforts to address the gaps in
home health care services that are essential in supporting older adults to live

© Her Majesty the Queen in Right of Canada 2021
C. Stephanidis et al. (Eds.): HCII 2021, CCIS 1419, pp. 257–264, 2021.
https://doi.org/10.1007/978-3-030-78635-9_35

independently at home for longer and to successfully age in place, with a glimpse into future research directions. A key factor in successfully aging in place is the ability to manage the health and well-being of an aging population [4]. Digital technologies play a major role in providing alternative health and wellness options, including mHealth, tele-health and virtual care options as part of comprehensive health care services [4,14,18,23]. The COVID-19 pandemic has accelerated the push for virtual care and tele-health options for public and individual health [14]. However, the current pandemic has also created a paradox for older adults, with safety measures such as staying at home and physical distancing having both protective and harmful effects [21]. Social distancing may work to exacerbate the existing digital divide by contributing to increased social isolation, loneliness, and depression among vulnerable older adults [21]. Our research has revealed that older adults have experienced fear, anxiety, and stress during the pandemic [13]. Factors such as fear, stress and anxiety can contribute to increases in blood pressure, trigger panic attacks and chest pain [20], and the thought of having to go to hospital emergency services can contribute to increases in stress levels as well. Stress responses may also be exacerbated by the on-going pandemic situation especially for older adults who are experiencing prolonged periods of social isolation and fear. The next section will present findings from the literature related to health and wellness applications aimed at supporting older adults to live safely and independently at home for longer, and to age in place.

2   Digital Technologies for Health, Well-Being, and Aging in Place

Research in the field of gerontechnology has highlighted important challenges for an aging population given a rapidly evolving technology landscape, with older adults (65+) described as being at risk of 'digitally marginalization' due to lower tech savviness, social isolation, and a lack of social support from peers [16,25]. Instead of contributing to the digital divide, communication technologies (e.g., ICT, internet, email, video, and text messages) have been shown to encourage social connectedness by providing meaningful social interaction and a sense of independence for older adults; thus reducing feelings of loneliness and social isolation experienced by many older adults [2,10]. Positive attitudes toward technology use among older adults were linked to better self-rated health, fewer chronic illnesses, higher subjective well-being, and fewer depressive symptoms [6]. The literature also underscores the importance of other mediating factors in the integration of new technologies into an individual's daily life including: a willingness and acceptance by the end-users, support (individual, family and community level), comfort in using technology and self-confidence in trying new technologies and devices in their daily lives [26].

As the population steadily ages, so does the need for alternative health and wellness options, including home health care, tele-health and virtual care options as part of comprehensive health care services [4,14,23]. Home-based health care is not meant to replace the mainframe system of hospitals, clinics, and physicians but rather to empower older adults to become agents in their own personal health and wellness, which is key in successfully aging in place [7,11,15,19]. The literature in the area of HCI and human factors related to digital health and assistive technologies underscores the urgency in addressing the needs of a rapidly aging population in order to support older adults in living independently at home for longer [23].

Older adults encompass an incredibly diverse group of users [12] therefore, increasing digital engagement of older populations in health care will require a more detailed understanding of their individual history of digital engagement, preferences for devices, including their own personal devices (i.e., BYOD), as well as supporting daily routines in order to provide new value [8]. Older adults face barriers that include lack of familiarity and access to tools and services, discomfort in requesting assistance, issues of trust, and concerns around privacy [11].

Continued availability and promotion of tele-health services might play a prominent role in increasing access to services during the public health emergency and beyond [14], however, our research has underscored important gaps in social and technology support for older adults which need to be addressed in more depth [13]. The application presented in this paper is aimed at providing help in accessing more timely and responsive home health care and potentially reducing unnecessary trips to the hospital.

3 Home Health Care Context

Each year, Canadians make over 14 million visits to hospital Emergency Department (ER) and more than 1.4 million visits to the ER are potentially avoidable [5]. The province of New Brunswick (Canada) has recently seen a spike in ER visits which combined with a shortage of human resources, has put extra strain on medical and nursing staff [24]. Canada's older population is expected to number 10.4 million by 2037 [3], with the Atlantic Provinces having the highest concentration of older adults (Nova Scotia has the highest proportion of older adults, at 16.6%, New Brunswick at 16.5%, and Prince Edward Island at 16.3%) [9]. Tele-health and home health care applications are poised to play an important role in enabling people to live more independent lives [19] with potential long-term benefits for improving appropriate ER utilization, as well as help to reduce the immense costs associated with chronic health conditions among older adults [14,15,19].

The New Brunswick (Canada) Extra-Mural Program is made up of over 900 professionals who provide home health care services across the province, with 28,989 patients having received home health care services in 2019–2020 [22]. The Web Application described in the next section aims to support older adults in their home by providing key communication technologies for improving the responsiveness of home health care services, while at the same time, helping to reduce anxiety among vulnerable older adults with chronic medical conditions (e.g., high blood pressure, heart disease, lung disease, etc.), and potentially avoiding unnecessary trips to the ER.

4   Collaborative Interface Design

A collaborative interface design approach was used to develop the 'Find a Nurse' Web Application, including, user interface (UI) and user experience (UX) considerations, building user case scenarios and a workflow for the sequence of processes involved for end-users (i.e., older adult and nurse), as well as validation of the steps involved. These design and development processes will be described next.

4.1   UI/UX Prototyping

Figma [1], a design/prototyping tool was used for designing the user-interfaces. The tool provided a web-based vector graphics editor and a prototyping tool which was used during the design phase to build user-interface designs and walk-throughs for the 'Find a Nurse' Web Application.

4.2   Building Use Case Scenarios and Workflow

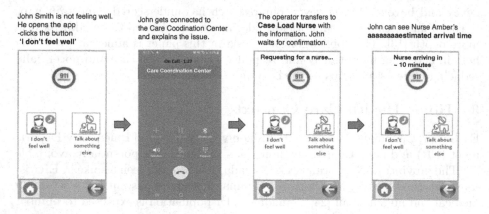

Fig. 1. Older adult's interface walk-through

Older Adult's Interface Walk-Through. Mock-up designs were created where an older adult could log in to a smartphone application and would see three main buttons to communicate. The first button is for a 911 emergency call when the older adult is unable to go to the hospital or treat themselves at home. The second button is the most important one in our scenario for the older adult who does not feel well. In this scenario, the older adult activates a call for assistance to a Care Coordination Centre which connects to a Case Load Nurse. The Case Load Nurse assesses the urgency of the call and either provides assistance by phone (i.e., tele-health) or can dispatch a nurse to the client's home as required. The older adult can see the status of the estimated arrival time on the screen of their smartphone which can reduce unnecessary stress. Figure 1 shows the walk-through storyboard for an older adult who is not feeling well and needs a nurse to visit them at home.

Nurse's Interface Walk-Through. In this scenario, Fig. 2 shows the nurse's interface walk-through where the available nurse receives a text from the Case Load Nurse, that is, the nurse who manages the appointment requests. The available nurse accepts the appointment request depending on her availability. The nurse's status changes to 'Busy' as soon as they press the 'GO' button and they are presented with a GPS navigation screen to guide them towards the destination. After completing the visit, their status changes back to 'Available'.

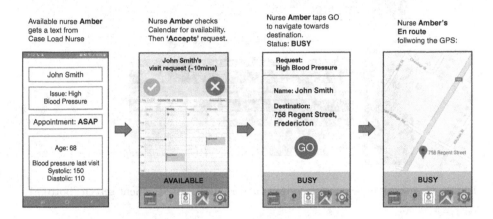

Fig. 2. Nurse's interface walk-through

Case Load Nurse's Interface Walk-Through. The Case Load Nurse receives the transferred call from the Care Coordination Centre. The Case Load Nurse has access to the contact information, appointment history, upcoming appointment information of clients who are registered with the Extra-Mural Program as shown in Fig. 3 top. The Case Load Nurse books an appointment by looking at the requests management screen, Fig. 3 bottom where the status of the nurse is colour-coded to enhance the decision making process for booking the appointment.

Subject Matter Interview and Validation Process. After designing the user interface screens, a subject matter expert, a nurse with the Extra-Mural Program, validated the designs. A semi-structured virtual interview was conducted as part of the validation process. The questions asked during the interview were related to the background information about the Extra-Mural Program, day to day activities performed by the nurses, devices they use, and what information the nurses have access to while on the road. The validation of key concepts, terminology and workflow was followed by a series of refinements of the initial interface designs. Stakeholder engagement on potential uses of the Find a Nurse Web Application are still underway in order to address current gaps in responsiveness and efficiencies of home health care services as experienced by older adults.

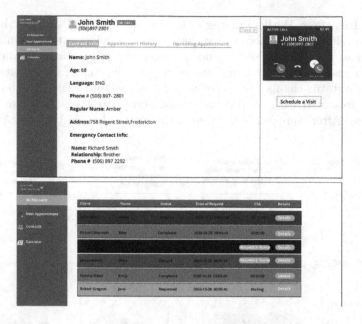

Fig. 3. Case load nurse's interface (top) and requests management screen (bottom)

5   Conclusion

The current COVID-19 pandemic has accelerated the push for remote check-ins and virtual care especially for older adults who are medically or socially vulnerable. Remote health services are being promoted as a means of preserving the patient-health care provider relationship at times when in-person visits are not practical or feasible, especially during COVID-19 and in the future. The literature in the area of HCI and human factors related to digital health and assistive technologies underscores the urgency in addressing the needs of a rapidly aging population in order to support older adults in living independently at home for longer. Our research has revealed that older adults have experienced fear, anxiety, and stress during the pandemic which in some cases can lead to unplanned visits to the ER. The Find a Nurse Web Application described in this paper is aimed at improving the responsiveness of home health care services by empowering older adult with additional communication functionalities to get immediate medical assistance and support at home, as a part of their circle of care. Technology support will be key in building innovative long-term health care services in the future, for keeping older adults living safe and independent at home for longer, and for mitigating the widening health care demand and supply gap. Future studies should include older adult users as co-designers in order to encourage ownership and empowerment in the management of their personal health and well-being, and possibly influence technology adoption for aging in place as well. Future advances in research and development in these areas are anticipated under the National Research Council Canada, Aging in Place Program [17].

References

1. Figma. https://www.figma.com/
2. Baecker, R., Sellen, K., Crosskey, S., Boscart, V., Neves, B.B.: Technology to reduce social isolation and loneliness. In: ASSETS14 - Proceedings of the 16th International ACM SIGACCESS Conference on Computers and Accessibility, pp. 27–34 (2014). https://doi.org/10.1145/2661334.2661375
3. Canadian Institute for Health Information: infographic: Canada's seniors population outlook: uncharted territory. https://www.cihi.ca/en/infographic-canadas-seniors-population-outlook-uncharted-territory
4. Cavoukian, A., Fisher, A., Killen, S., Hoffman, D.A.: Remote home health care technologies: how to ensure privacy? Build it. Privacy Des. Identity Inf. Soc. **3**(2), 363–378 (2010). https://doi.org/10.1007/s12394-010-0054-y
5. CBC/Radio Canada: 1 in 5 emergency department visits in Canada could be treated elsewhere—CBC news, November 2014. https://www.cbc.ca/news/health/1-in-5-emergency-department-visits-could-be-treated-elsewhere-institute-reports-1.2826366
6. Chopik, W.J.: The benefits of social technology use among older adults are mediated by reduced loneliness. Cyberpsychol. Behav. Soc. Netw. **19**(9), 551–556 (2016). https://doi.org/10.1089/cyber.2016.0151, https://www.liebertpub.com/doi/10.1089/cyber.2016.0151
7. Dishman, E.: Inventing wellness systems for aging in place. Computer **37**(5), 34–41 (2004). https://doi.org/10.1109/MC.2004.1297237
8. Gilbert, M.E.: Digitally engaging older populations in healthcare requires new practices to be effective. Gartner (January), 1–21 (2020)
9. Elections Canada: Research Note - Canadian Seniors: A Demographic Profile, November 2012. https://www.elections.ca/content.aspx?section=res&dir=rec/part/sen&document=index&lang=e
10. Findlay, R.A.: Interventions to reduce social isolation amongst older people: where is the evidence? Ageing Soc. **23**(5), 647–658 (2003). https://doi.org/10.1017/S0144686X03001296
11. Fischer, S.H., David, D., Crotty, B.H., Dierks, M., Safran, C.: Acceptance and use of health information technology by community-dwelling elders. Int. J. Med. Informatics **83**(9), 624–635 (2014). https://doi.org/10.1016/j.ijmedinf.2014.06.005
12. Gregor, P., Newell, A.F., Zajicek, M.: Designing for dynamic diversity, p. 151 (2002). https://doi.org/10.1145/638276.638277
13. Kondratova, I., Fournier, H., Katsuragawa, K.: Review of usability testing methods for aging in place technologies. In: HCI International 2021 (2021)
14. Koonin, L.M., et al.: Trends in the use of telehealth during the emergence of the COVID-19 pandemic – United States, January-March 2020. MMWR. Morbidity Mortality Weekly Report **69**(43), 1595–1599 (2020). https://doi.org/10.15585/mmwr.mm6943a3
15. Mitzner, T.L., et al.: Older adults talk technology: technology usage and attitudes. Comput. Hum. Behav. **26**(6), 1710–1721 (2010). https://doi.org/10.1016/j.chb.2010.06.020

16. Munteanu, C., et al.: Designing for Older Adults: Overcoming Barriers to a Supportive, Safe, and Healthy Retirement. The Disruptive Impact of Fin-Tech on Retirement Systems, pp. 104–126 (2019). https://doi.org/10.1093/oso/9780198845553.003.0007

17. National Research Council: Aging in place proposed program plan, October 2020. https://nrc.canada.ca/en/research-development/research-collaboration/programs/aging-place-proposed-program-plan

18. Pan, A., Zhao, F.: User acceptance factors for mHealth. In: Kurosu, M. (ed.) HCI 2018. LNCS, vol. 10902, pp. 173–184. Springer, Cham (2018). https://doi.org/10.1007/978-3-319-91244-8_14

19. Panagopoulos, C., Menychtas, A., Tsanakas, P., Maglogiannis, I.: Increasing usability of homecare applications for older adults: a case study. Designs 3(2), 23 (2019). https://doi.org/10.3390/designs3020023

20. Sheps, S.G.: Anxiety: A cause of high blood pressure?. https://www.mayoclinic.org/diseases-conditions/high-blood-pressure/expert-answers/anxiety/faq-20058549

21. Smith, M.L., Steinman, L.E., Casey, E.A.: Combatting social isolation among older adults in a time of physical distancing: the COVID-19 social connectivity paradox 8(July), 1–9 (2020). https://doi.org/10.3389/fpubh.2020.00403

22. The New Brunswick Extra-Mural Program: How we're doing (2021). https://extramuralnb.ca/en/how-we-are-doing/

23. Vasilyeva, E., Pechenizkiy, M., Puuronen, S.: Towards the framework of adaptive user interfaces for eHealth. In: Proceedings - IEEE Symposium on Computer-Based Medical Systems, pp. 139–144 (2005). https://doi.org/10.1109/cbms.2005.101

24. Vitalité Health Network: Vitalité health network asks moncton residents to reduce use of the emergency department, March 2021. https://www.vitalitenb.ca/en/news/vitalite-health-network-asks-moncton-residents-reduce-use-emergency-department

25. Xie, B.: Older adults, computers, and the internet: future directions. Gerontechnology 2(4) (2003). https://doi.org/10.4017/gt.2003.02.04.002.00

26. Zamir, S., Hennessy, C.H., Taylor, A.H., Jones, R.B.: Video-calls to reduce loneliness and social isolation within care environments for older people: an implementation study using collaborative action research. BMC Geriatrics 18(1) (2018). https://doi.org/10.1186/s12877-018-0746-y, https://bmcgeriatr.biomedcentral.com/track/pdf/10.1186/s12877-018-0746-y.pdf

What Functions on the Medicare Plan Finder Do Older Medicare Beneficiaries Use?

Mohammad Shahidul Kader$^{(\boxtimes)}$, Wi-Suk Kwon, Salisa Westrick, Kassandra Ross, Yi Zhao, and Xiao Huang

Auburn University, Auburn, AL 36849, USA
mzk0089@auburn.edu

Abstract. The Medicare Plan Finder (MPF), a decision support tool on Medicare.gov, provides functions to help older users simplify their plan selection, but many users may be unaware of MPF functions, cannot locate them, or do not have desire to use them voluntarily. Existing literature offers little knowledge on older adults' utilization of MPF functionality and human-computer interaction on MPF. Therefore, this study seeks to find 1) the relative usage of each MPF function toward plan decision and 2) assistance needed to improve MPF function usage. An observational study of 29 participants aged 65+ years was conducted during the Medicare open enrollment period of 2019. Each participant was paired with a counselor in a plan selection task using MPF, where they initially navigated MPF by themselves (i.e., self-moment) and then were allowed to ask their counselor for assistance. Data were collected through participants' task screen videos and participant-counselor speech audios. Five MPF functional themes, plan details, sort plans, filter plans, compare plans, and star ratings, were identified as key functions impacting Medicare plan decision-making processes. Participants' voluntary use of MPF functions was very rare, if any, during the self-moment. However, with the counselor guidance, the use of the key five functions became noticeably increased. These findings indicate meaningful contributions of the intervention of counselors (i.e., human agents) towards older users' MPF function usage and suggest a need for an intelligent agent system that can supplement human agents through real-time, on-screen, conversation-based assistance for older users.

Keywords: Medicare plan finder · Function · Older adults · Healthcare decision tools

1 Introduction

With the advancement of communication technology, e-healthcare decision tools are increasingly available. However, the elderly population finds it challenging to learn these web-based tools due to cognitive aging [1]. Medicare is a health insurance to the U.S. population aged 65 and above and younger population groups with certain conditions [2, 3]. In 2018, about 60 million U.S. citizens received Medicare health insurance, among whom 52 million were aged 65 and older [4]. Medicare Plan Finder

© Springer Nature Switzerland AG 2021
C. Stephanidis et al. (Eds.): HCII 2021, CCIS 1419, pp. 265–272, 2021.
https://doi.org/10.1007/978-3-030-78635-9_36

(MPF) is an e-healthcare decision support tool available on the official Medicare website, Medicare.gov, which allows users to research and compare a wide range of Medicare insurance plans by availing various functions (e.g., sort plans, filter plans, and compare plans) to help informed plan selection decisions [5].

During the annual Medicare open enrollment period, beneficiaries should review Medicare insurance plan choices and decide on a plan that best fits their health needs [4]. However, older Medicare beneficiaries find MPF quite challenging to use due to the wide variability of plan alternatives and plan attributes and users' literacy gaps (e.g., low computer literacy, low health literacy) [2, 3, 6]. Concerns exist that many older users are unaware of MPF functions, cannot locate them, or are not likely to voluntarily use them. However, existing Medicare literature has provided little knowledge on older users' utilization of MPF functionality, a gap addressed in this study. Further, in 2019, the Centers for Medicare & Medicaid Services (CMS) redesigned the MPF interface with goals to provide more user-friendly and flexible navigation [7]. It is necessary to understand users' experience with the new MPF interface for further improvement of the usability of this tool.

As per a recent study, only 7% of Medicare plan switches are done solely through MPF, while 71% of the switches are done with human agents [8], such as counselors from the State Health Insurance Assistance Program (SHIP) [9]. Given this high reliance on human assistance and the shortage of counselors relative to the large population of older users who need assistance, a critical need exists for improving the role of human agents in helping Medicare beneficiaries' autonomous MPF use as well as the development of an intelligent system that can supplement human assistance, such as artificially intelligent (AI) conversational agent.

To address the aforementioned needs, this study seeks to answer two research questions: 1) *What are older users' relative rate of usage of the various decision-support functions available on MPF while they make a Medicare plan decision*, and 2) *How counselors' assistance impacts older users' MPF function usage*? An observation study was conducted to answer these research questions.

2   Relevant Literature

2.1   Functions on MPF

MPF avails decision support functions to help users simplify decision processes and lead to an optimal plan selection [7]. The current MPF, which was redesigned in 2019, is structured with multiple pages, among which three key types of pages are used for plan selection decision-making, including 1) search results pages, 2) plan details pages, and 3) compare plan pages. These pages are designed to offer critical functions to streamline users' Medicare plan selection process by enabling them to search Medicare plans of which prescription drug coverage meets their drug needs, customize plan search results to their needs by sorting or filtering them, evaluate detailed attributes of each Medicare plan, and compare up to three plans at a time side-by-side on key attributes [8] (see Fig. 1). The current study explores the relative usage of these MPF functions by older users during their Medicare plan selection decision-making process.

Fig. 1. An example search-results page and MPF functions (marked with arrows) on it

2.2 Counseling Interventions

Trained counselors, such as ones who work for SHIP, pharmacists, or faculty and students from pharmacy schools trained on Medicare, work with an individual beneficiary either in person or via telephone. In most of these counseling sessions, it is the counselor, rather than the beneficiary, who collects and enters the beneficiary's medication and other information in MPF and navigates MPF to search, identify, and compare plans with proper cost and coverage options on behalf of the beneficiary [9–11]. Because it is the counselor who conducts the computer task on MPF, beneficiaries tend to be passive in their learning of MPF functions during counseling sessions, which can perpetuate their need to return for counselor assistance rather than autonomously perform the MPF task in future years. Several research topics of Medicare counseling have been investigated in the past literature, including the effectiveness of Medicare outreach programs, counseling psychology perspectives, and utilization of certified human agents [2, 12, 13]; however, no studies have been done to examine the impact of counselor intervention on beneficiaries' learning (use) of MPF functions. Given the pivotal role of MPF in Medicare plan selection and the expanding access of computing devices among older people, it is critical to investigate the potential role of counselors in not only assisting in older beneficiaries' plan selection for the year but also improving their self-efficacy of using MPF functions, which may, in turn, allows them to complete the task themselves in subsequent years without a counselor intervention.

3 Method

3.1 Study Design

The current study used a grounded theory approach to identify older beneficiaries' use of MPF functions and counselors' role in improving it via an observational study of 29 participants (65+ years of age, 14 women and 15 men) during the open enrollment period of 2019. Participants, recruited through flyers circulated in local senior centers in a southeastern U.S. city, arrived at the research facility and completed an informed consent process. Then, they completed a questionnaire asking about their personal information, medication list, and preferred pharmacies. Afterward, each participant was paired with a trained Medicare counselor. Counselors helped their participants enter their MPF login, if available, or their prescription drug and pharmacy information, if no prior-established login information is available, on MPF. Then, participants took over the computer from their counselor and performed the Medicare plan selection task on MPF. Participants were instructed to take a moment to explore MPF by themselves at the beginning of the MPF task until they had questions. During this self-moment, participants were asked to *think aloud* (i.e., saying whatever thoughts that came to their mind as they did). Further, participants were encouraged to ask counselors for guidance when they did not know the meaning of the information that they saw on the MPF screen or what to do next on the MPF. Once participants asked an initial *task-relevant* question (i.e., questions relevant to information or navigation on MPF; requests just to clarify the initial instructions or merely social questions were considered task-irrelevant), the counselors were allowed to provide unsolicited verbal guidance as they saw it fit until the participants reached a final plan selection. Throughout the session, participants had control over the computer even during the time that the counselor intervened in plan selection. Participants' MPF task screens were video-captured, while the participant-counselor speeches were audio-recorded.

3.2 Data Coding and Coding Guide

Task-screen video data and participant-counselor speech transcript data were coded using a qualitative data analysis program, *Atlas.ti*. Coding scheme development follows the grounded theory steps including 1) open coding, breaking the data into discrete parts with labels, 2) axial coding, categorizing, and connecting the discrete codes, 3) selective coding, refining themes. As a result, five key MPF functional themes, including *plan details*, *sort plans*, *filter plans*, *compare plans*, and *star ratings* emerged to constitute the coding scheme (see Table 1). Based on this coding scheme, participants' speech transcripts and computer mouse actions on task screen videos were scrutinized for instances where they spoke on each of the five functional themes or acted (clicked) on a functional button/link corresponding to each theme. Further, counselors' speech transcripts were also evaluated for instances where they gave verbal guidance related to each of the functional themes. Two coders performed the coding independently, which resulted in the inter-coder agreements of 93.9%, 93.9%, and 83.7% for the user action, user speech, and counselor speech coding, respectively. The two coders negotiated on all disagreed-upon codes to determine their final code.

4   Findings

4.1   Older Beneficiaries' Voluntary MPF Function Usage

As presented in Table 1, participants' self-moment computer action analysis revealed that only zero to six participants among the 29 participants autonomously used each of the five MPF functions, which suggests that older beneficiaries are rarely able to utilize the MPF functions without assistance. Six participants used the *compare plans* function,

Table 1. User usage and counselor intervention frequencies by MPF functions

Function Theme	Description	Frequency				
		No. of users before intervention		Counselor intervention	No. of users after intervention	
		Speech	Action		Speech	Action
Plan details	Users can check out detailed attribute information of an individual plan	3	3	24	13	28
Sort plans	Users can sort the plans appearing on the search results page by a) the lowest yearly drug deductible, b) lowest drug + premium cost, c) lowest monthly premium, or d) lowest health plan deductible (only applicable to Medicare Advantage plans) within the results	15	1	27	10	28
Filter plans	Users can refine the search results by filtering to show only ones that a) meet a specific star rating criterion (e.g., "0 stars & up"), b) are offered by a certain insurance carrier, c) are accepted across the U.S. or d) cover certain healthcare benefits (e.g., vision, hearing; only applicable to Medicare Advantage plans)	2	1	24	13	28
Compare plans	Users can select up to three plans at a time from the search results for side-by-side comparisons	2	6	14	6	15
Star rating	Users can check other customers' ratings on various attribute qualities and overall quality of a plan	2	0	27	10	28

which was the most utilized function during the self-moment. However, considering that only one participant employed the *sort plans* or *filter plans* function of MPF to refine the search results during the self-moment, the mere use of the *compare plans* function does not necessarily reflect decision optimization as the plans selected to be compared were not likely to be those that best matched the participants' need criteria. This observation is indirectly supported by the result that 15 participants spoke about sorting plans during their self-moment, which suggests that they might have felt overwhelmed by the long list of plans in the search results and realized the need to refine the plan search results, yet only one participant was able to act on it by using the *sort-plans* function on MPF until counselors intervened.

4.2 Counselor Intervention for Older Beneficiaries' MPF Function Use

The triangulation of data across participants' and counselors' speech transcripts and participants' task-screen videos before and after counselors' interventions (see Table 1) strongly suggests a potential impact of counselor intervention in improving participants' MPF function usage while selecting a plan on MPF. Contrary to participants' rare voluntary use of MPF functions before counselor interventions, all but one participant used four of the five functions, including *plan details, sort plans, filter plans*, and *star ratings*, and more than a half of the participants utilized the remaining function, *compare plans*, after counselors had started to intervene (see Table 1). These usage patterns are well-aligned with the patterns in the number of participants to whom the counselors spoke about the functions, which show a lower frequency for the compare-plan function ($f = 14$) as compared to the other four functions ($24 < f_s < 27$) (see Table 1).

5 Discussions and Implications

Applying an observational approach, the findings of this study provide at least four contributions to the literature. First, this study provides an overview of the decision-support functions of the recently redesigned MPF, which future research may delve into as to their roles in Medicare decision-making of various groups of users. Second, the findings suggest that older users rarely use MPF functions on their own; and if any, they are more inclined to use *compare plans* and *plan details*. But, MPF functions that can help users refine the plan search results to match their own needs, such as *sort plans* and *filter plans*, are hardly used voluntarily. This finding suggests a need for emphasis on these functions on the MPF interface to improve older users' efficacy of using these MPF functions as well as their optimal Medicare plan decision outcome. Third, the counselor intervention on MPF functions and the contrast in older users' function usage before and after counselor intervention observed in this study clearly suggest the meaningful contribution of counselors towards participants' MPF function usage for streamlined decision-making. This finding indicates that the role of a counseling session may be expanded beyond providing the given year's plan selection advice to educating MPF functions to eligible beneficiaries. The effectiveness of a counseling session may be enhanced by such improved user-interface assistance need mapping and targeted counseling. Future research is desired on the short- and long-term effects of this expanded role of counselors in improving beneficiaries' autonomous use of MPF for Medicare information gathering and decision-making. Finally, this study enriched the methodological approach by capturing user-counselor interaction through a study integrating observations of computer-task behaviors and user-counselor conversations. Studies considering observations from user-counselor interactions have been very rare in Medicare research. The integrative knowledge from both the user and counselor ends helps generate recommendations to sophisticate counseling strategies.

Beyond the immediate contributions to Medicare literature, the interface design recommendations from this study are applicable to decision support systems for a wide range of complex e-healthcare decisions as well as other consumer decision contexts, particularly targeting older decision-makers or other underserved population groups negatively impacted by a lack of domain knowledge or interface experience. Further, insights generated from this study on counselor roles can be transferred to the design of intelligent agent systems that may provide interventions supplementing human intervention where human resources are lacking or expensive.

Acknowledgment. "This project was supported by the Alabama Agricultural Experiment Station, the Hatch program of the National Institute of Food and Agriculture, U.S. Department of Agriculture, and the Auburn University Intramural Grant Program."

References

1. Li, Y., Baldassi, M., Johnson, E.J., Weber, E.U.: Complementary cognitive capabilities, economic decision making, and aging. Psychol. Aging **28**(3), 595–613 (2013)
2. Abaluck, J., Gruber, J.: Choce inconsistencies among the elderly: evidence from plan choice in the medicare part D program: reply. Am. Econ. Rev. **106**(12), 39623987 (2016)
3. Barnes, A.J., Hanoch, Y., Rice, T.: Can plan recommendations improve the coverage decisions of vulnerable populations in health insurance marketplaces? PloS One **11**(3), e0151095 (2016)
4. CMS initiative (2019). https://www.cms.gov/newsroom/press-releases/medicare-plan-finder-gets-upgrade-first-time-decade. Accessed 21 Feb 2021
5. Hoadley, J., Cubanski, J., Neuman, T.: Medicare part D in 2016 and trends over time. KFF, 16 September 2016. https://www.kff.org/medicare/report/medicare-part-d-in-2016-and-trends-over-time/. Accessed 21 Feb 2021
6. Zhao, Y., Diggs, K., Chen, Z.X., Hohmann, N., Kwon, W.S., Westrick, S.C.: Qualitative exploration of factors influencing the plan selection process by medicare beneficiaries. J. Managed Care Specialty Pharm. **27**(3), 339–353 (2021)
7. McGarry, B.E., Maestas, N., Grabowski, D.C.: Assessing the redesigned Medicare plan finder tool: room for improvement. Health Affairs, 8 November 2019. https://www.healthaffairs.org/do/, https://doi.org/10.1377/hblog20191106.803045/full/. Accessed 21 Feb 2021
8. Healthcare team (2019). https://www.medialogic.com/blog/healthcare-marketing/new-medicare-plan-finder-review-from-a-medicare-user/. Accessed 21 Feb 2021
9. Hohmann, L.A., Hastings, T.J., McFarland, S.J., Hollingsworth, J.C., Westrick, S.C.: Implementation of a medicare plan selection assistance program through a community partnership. Am. J. Pharm. Educ. **82**(9), 6452–6452 (2018). https://doi.org/10.5688/ajpe6452
10. Leonard, C.E., Cohenour, F.V., DeLoach, L.A., Galdo, J.A.: Impact of an open enrollment service on costs for medicare part D beneficiaries. J. Am. Pharm. Assoc. **57**(3), S225–S228 (2017). https://doi.org/10.1016/j.japh.2017.03.005

11. Massey, C., Aungst, T.D., Evans, P., Bartlett, D., Silva, M.A.: Cost savings impact of a pharmacist-initiated teleservice program for medicare part D reviews. J. Am. Pharm. Assoc. **58**(1), 56–60 (2018)
12. Griol, D., Callejas, Z.: Mobile conversational agents for context-aware care applications. Cognit. Comput. **8**(2), 336–356 (2016)
13. Hollingsworth, J.C., Teeter, B.S., Westrick, S.C.: Evaluation of student outcomes after participating in a medicare outreach program. J. High. Educ. Outreach Engage. **19**(2), 139–154 (2015)

A Study to Explore Behavioral Dynamics and Expectations of the Elderly People from Last Mile Delivery Services

Sundar Krishnamurthy(✉) and Sumeetha Suppiah

KPIT Technologies Ltd., Bangalore, India
{sundar.krishnamurthy,sumeetha.s}@kpit.com

Abstract. With the sudden advent of the pandemic and the unimaginable difficulties and loss of life that's followed, one of the key populaces in focus has been in the elderly who are particularly vulnerable to the pandemic. Its estimated that over 8.6% [1] of the population in India are elderly and out of that 14.4% [2] live alone or away from immediate family members. Even before the pandemic descended and led to strict lockdowns severely limiting the mobility, elderly people have had a difficult situation especially considering how they procure essentials like groceries, food and medications. On the other hand, imposition of lockdown across the country has led to an exponential growth of last mile delivery services offering doorstep access to essentials like food, medicines and groceries etc. Last mile delivery services are projected to grow 300% [3] adding hundreds of thousand users. Most of these platforms offer well-crafted experiences across multiple technology platforms including web and smartphone. However, the expectations and the experiences of the elderly people who wish to procure essentials is significantly fragmented by their affinity and literacy of technology platforms as well as their persistent behaviors which are resistant to embrace the technological avenues. In this study, we attempted to study the behavioral dynamics and expectational elements of the elderly population in India and how last mile delivery service impact could impact their ability to procure essentials. This study involves conducting an online survey with the elderly, taking assist from their family members in some instances. Post the survey, personal interviews and inferential analysis are conducted to draw meaningful insights. The study delineates observations of the elderly with an intent to understand how the last mile delivery platform could lend themselves to better fit their mind models.

Keywords: Elderly · Last mile delivery · Human computer interaction · Pandemic situation · Essentials · Behavioral modalities · User experience

1 Introduction

Over the last few decades, the population percent of elderly has been consistently growing in India with the trend projected to continue to an estimated 20% of the population by 2050 [4]. Improvements in healthcare coupled with better nutrition etc., have led to

© Springer Nature Switzerland AG 2021
C. Stephanidis et al. (Eds.): HCII 2021, CCIS 1419, pp. 273–281, 2021.
https://doi.org/10.1007/978-3-030-78635-9_37

increased longevity of people. Traditionally, families in India follow the practice where elderly persons cohabit with their children or with younger relatives, a concept known as joint family. This provided elderly people stability and access to essentials and care. However, in recent years, the percentage of elderly people living alone has increased. A report published in January 2021 [5] estimated about 5.7% of the country's elderly people are living alone without the support of family. While there are many factors that contribute to this, primary reasons include children migrating away from the city where the elderly person resides, children moving away after marriage and in some cases, elderly persons having had no children etc.

In many instances, elderly people are active and are able to go out and buy essentials on a regular basis. Most of the elderly people consider groceries, medicines and food as essential. However, many of them also eschew modern technology assisted delivery platforms for a more traditional shopping experience in local grocery shops and pharmacies. In many cases, they have been shopping at the same shop for decades and so, have a very good relationship with shopkeepers. Another trend among elderly people is that they are accustomed to cash transactions as less inclined to use cards or net banking. However, the advent of Coronavirus pandemic in early 2020 led to a major disruption to the shopping patterns of elderly people. At the time when there was close to 500 Covid 19 cases in India, as a precautionary measure, the Govt of India ordered a countrywide lockdown [6] which lasted till May 3, followed by phased relaxation. During this time all shops were either closed or in case of essential services, restricted to limited operational hours. This, by itself caused a lot of hardships to elderly persons, coupled with the fact that they were determined to have higher vulnerability to the virus.

Last mile delivery services which provide doorstep access to essentials and ecommerce products have seen significant growth in recent years in India. However, during the pandemic, last mile delivery platforms saw unprecedented demand when they were allowed to operate with the intention that delivering to the doorstep would reduce the necessity for people to venture out. Many of the last mile players prioritized delivering essentials and staggered out deliveries to customers to cope with the demand and moved to a cashless, prepaid transactional model to reduce human contact [7]. This proved to be a boon during lockdown as it facilitated access to essentials with focus on safety while also becoming convenient mode of purchase after an initial couple of months. For elderly people, however, this amounts to a paradigm shift in the behavioral dynamics of their shopping activities and presents multiple challenges from technological, behavioral and economic standpoint. This study attempts to understand some of the expectations of the elderly to be able to use last mile delivery services, the challenges they might face and also the human interface considerations which can go a long way in enabling them to use last mile delivery as a means for procuring essentials.

2 Method

The study involved about 50 participants from Tier 1 and Tier 2 cities in India. In order to understand the behavioral aspects related to senior citizens, the study was conducted with participants in the age group 60, and above which was further classified into 3 categories. The study involved a survey of participants to acquire quantitative metrics pertaining to the procurement of essentials, smartphone literacy and last mile delivery as well as a qualitative understanding of behavioral elements pertaining to the shopping habits and the impact of the pandemic. Based on the personas derived from this study a further contextual observation was conducted with participants where they were asked to perform sets of curated tasks with the popular last mile delivery platforms. This further helped solidify the understanding of the expectations of elderly people and how the last mile delivery platforms performed against the mental model of the participants. Furthermore, this study was performed gender blind as the initial focus was on understanding the overall behavior of the elderly.

3   Results

3.1   Demographic Analysis of the Participants

For the study, of the 43 participants, about 79% were in the age group of 60 to 70 years while 7% were in the 70 to 80 years group. Only 14% of participants were above 80 years of age (Fig. 1). Furthermore, around 63% of the respondents were from tier 1 cities with the rest from tier 2 cities.

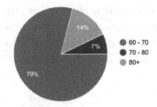

Fig. 1. Age wise age range participants of this activity

3.2   Living Situation of Participants

Based on the participants in the survey, about 60% of participants were living with immediate family, while 30% were living with extended family and about 9% lived alone. (Fig. 2).

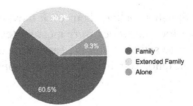

Fig. 2. Living situation

3.3 Health and Active Status

Majority of participants indicated that they are healthy and active (~65%) while only 7% of the respondents were completely dependent on family for managing the day-to-day activities (Fig. 3).

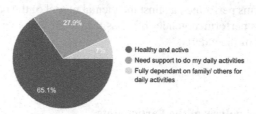

Fig. 3. Lifestyle and active status (%)

3.4 Shopping for Essentials

Majority of the respondents (68%) indicated groceries and medicine as essentials while 17% indicated food was also part of essentials. About 44% of the respondents indicated that they preferred to go out and purchase essentials in the pre-pandemic times while about 18% indicated a preference to shop online (Fig. 4).

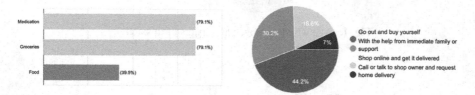

Fig. 4. Shopping for essentials

3.5 Online Shopping Behaviors

Among the participants who shop online about 60% have been shopping online for 1 to 5 years. Groceries and food deliveries were most preferred for online purchases. Over 80% of participants were satisfied with the ease of shopping online. Most of the participants (80%) used smartphones in lieu of desktop computers for online shopping (Fig. 5).

Fig. 5. Online shopping behaviors

3.6 Smartphone Literacy

Smartphone ease of use among the elderly persons who shop online was split 50:50 with half of them indicating easy to use while the other half were neutral. Android was the most prevalent smartphone (63%) primarily due to cost effectiveness and availability of lower priced models. From the perspective of knowledge and know-how of smartphone usage,

– 60% said they are able to install apps without help
– Only 20% said they could setup smartphone by themselves
– 50% said they use smartphones regularly for daily activities
– 80% said they use smartphones for calls, messaging, WhatsApp and more
– 70% said they use smartphones regularly for shopping online as well.

3.7 Impact of Pandemic

With the advent of Covid 19 pandemic and the lockdowns that ensued, there has been an impact in behaviors pertaining to shopping for essentials. 83% of participants indicated that the pandemic affected the way they shopped for essentials. About 35% of the participants have used online shopping completely while 32% have used it sometimes. However, 32% of participants still didn't use online shopping and resorted to other means of procuring essentials including relying on family. When asked if they would prefer to shop post pandemic, 36% of participants indicated yes, 39% indicated that they would shop online sometimes and 25% indicated that they would prefer to shop in stores (Fig. 6, Fig. 7 and Fig. 8).

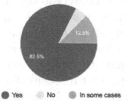
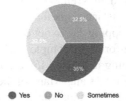
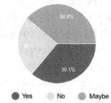

Fig. 6. Procuring essentials in Pandemic,   **Fig. 7.** Purchasing online since Lockdown,   **Fig. 8.** Plan on continuing online shopping post Pandemic

4 Observations and Analysis

Based on the study about the behavioral elements of elderly persons, there are 2 primary types that emerge. One, a traditionalist and the other a modernist. The traditionalist's key behaviors are more in favor of in person shopping and general non inclination towards technology platforms. The modernists, however, display a combination of behaviors of traditionalists but with an interest to embrace technology platforms including for shopping. With respect to general shopping behavior, both groups have a similar tendency including shopping in discrete intervals (e.g., once or twice a month for groceries and medications) and show preference for planning the purchases beforehand including items to purchase.

For the former group, in the case of grocery shopping, there is a strong preference to shop at a single shop in most cases and deviate only under circumstances like if the shop is closed or some critical items are not in stock. In fact, most of the participants (~58%) indicated that they had developed a personal rapport with the shopkeepers which enabled them to get the shopkeeper to deliver goods home by shopping over telephone calls. Cash is the preferred mode of payment since it's in-person interaction. Similarly, for medications, most participants (~60%) visit a preferred pharmacy with an indicated (~94%) satisfaction as it makes the purchasing easier. However, food shopping seems to be adhoc with majority of the respondents rarely going out for shopping food. Even in the cases, its mostly from restaurants that are nearby (~70%).

The latter group has a more fragmented behavior when ordering online particularly food which ranged from regular (~40%) to rare (~40%). Since many of the last mile shopping platforms don't show where the product is stored and shipped from, there is some anxiety associated with quality and efficiency of the same despite many of the platforms providing real time updates. In some cases, they also depend on their younger family members to interact with the platform. Cash on delivery was a preferred mode of payment since many are unsure of credit cards and online payments, particularly from a security standpoint even though they used credit cards for in person shopping. However, with the pandemic leading to the stoppage of cash on delivery, many are forced to provide credit card or net banking details (in some cases with help from family members).

4.1 Physical, Cognitive and Technological Barriers

For many of the participants, including those who use online shopping, there are certain barriers that prevent them from fully embracing the last mile delivery as options for shopping essentials. In some instances, participants in the former group feel that they don't have access to online shopping due to not owning smartphones or computers. Furthermore, they feel that the platforms are complex to learn, and they might end up making mistakes as opposed to shopping in person. Infact, the perceived complexity of online shopping was the top reason for the same. Many of the participants have been habituated to the more tactile feel of shopping in person whereas the digital divide and the more ephemeral nature of shopping by looking at pictures was not as convincing. The latter group, while using smartphones mostly for online shopping still in many cases needed help from family members, especially for payments. Furthermore, internet disruptions, unhelpful error messages, issues with visibility of content, complex user interfaces were barriers. Very few online platforms provide options to set regional languages as opposed to English. Knowledge of online payments and concerns about security also persists [8]. Usage of the apps on smartphones also presents physical difficulties including content readability due to reduced vision, typing experience and more. Providing alternatives like phone call based ordering could also be explored to augment the smartphone only experience.

4.2 Familiarity and Confidence

The study also unearthed another key area where shopping behaviors are influenced. There is a high level of confidence and familiarity that has been developed with the one-to-one relationship between the elderly persons and shopkeepers as indicated in Sect. 4 introduction. Online shopping platforms don't present the same level of confidence, particularly for groceries and food, where the users can choose the items to purchase but not where it will be shipped. In the case of food deliveries, the platforms clearly indicate the restaurant where the food is made which increases the confidence. If the last mile platforms allow users to choose the store and then place an order for the items, it would improve the affinity of the users. In some cases, it might be difficult for the last mile platforms as well since many of these grocers and pharmacies are small and might not be connected to the platform.

4.3 Interaction Complexity

Most of the respondents in the study indicated complexity, both perceived and experienced as a primary reason for difficulties in shopping online. Many of these platforms are primarily smartphone apps that require elderly persons to have basic smartphone literacy. Furthermore, the apps are not designed for comfortable viewing for elderly people who have age related vision deterioration. In many cases, the affordances in the interface are not easy to manipulate by elderly persons. In the contextual observation, the participants were asked to perform a set of tasks including finding a restaurant and placing the order and also searching and adding basic grocery items and making the payment.

In the task which required finding a restaurant in the list and selecting an item from the menu, most participants were able to perform while they had trouble with the concept of 'cart' and the payment steps. But in the task which required them to search for an item and then find a restaurant to shop from, most of the participants found difficulty in typing, and identifying search results. The results were similar to the task which required adding grocery items for shopping. Adding items from the list was possible while the concept of 'shopping basket' and payment methods seemed to confuse the participants. Also, navigating the app screens and using the software keyboard were indicated as primary physical interaction challenges among the participants (Fig. 9).

To improve the usability for the elderly people, the last mile platforms should reduce the number of interactions. Storing predefined lists of groceries, medications will be useful. Large images of products help offset the content readability issues. Leveraging accessibility features in the smartphone platforms helps. Furthermore, reducing dependency on typing by introducing voice-based search or scanning written lists will help in not only improving the usability but also bridge the divide between online and in-person shopping experience. Better representations of concepts like 'cart' or 'basket 'and simplified online shopping will be critical to improve the user experience.

Fig. 9. Physical & cognitive challenges of using the app

4.4 Economics

As noted from the analysis, there is a higher preference for elderly persons to make payments in cash as opposed to other forms. While cash on delivery is advantageous, the nature of pandemic has resulted in this mode of payment currently deemed as unusable. But there continues to be an inherent lack of trust in providing credit card details to online apps. However, in the post pandemic situation if the cash on delivery option becomes available again, it might lead more elderly people to embrace last mile delivery option. Another standpoint that was observed from the survey is that delivery charges are an unnecessary expenditure which is not present for in-person shopping. Furthermore, the understanding that the shopkeeper who has a relationship would provide better deals for the purchases as opposed to online shopping also prevents many of the elderly persons, especially those who are not well to do or on pensions/savings, to eschew online shopping in favor of in person shopping. Online discounts can help mitigate this particular perspective though.

4.5 Reliability

The study also indicated that most of the participants have expectations that the shopping experience be reliable. For the traditionalist group of participants, in person shopping offers a high degree of reliability since they can purchase the products on the spot and familiarity with the shopkeeper helps with the same as well. While last mile platforms do provide details on delivery date and time, only food delivery services provide a real time update and more accurate timeline for when the product will be delivered. Another aspect that impacts the reliability is that for online platforms, products are shipped from a central warehouse which could lead to delays due to traffic etc. Tie-ups with local shops, and providing the ability to shop from there could help with the reliability of online shopping which will also meet one of the key expectations from this group.

4.6 Post Pandemic Shopping Expectations

Irrespective of how the elderly persons used to shop earlier, the Covid pandemic had significantly disrupted these expectations. In many cases, senior persons are not allowed by the family to go out due to the fear of acquiring coronavirus. This behavior could continue in the post pandemic situation for the next year or so until most of the population is vaccinated and becomes immune to the virus and its variants [9].

This leads to modified expectations and behaviors that the elderly persons will need to embrace. First, the barriers that currently exist must be mitigated to allow elderly people to use the services comfortably. Also, adding more features to help senior people interact with greater ease and providing an interaction model that better mimics their mind model is also important. Last mile delivery services could benefit from this if they can demonstrate that it can be a greatly viable alternative to traditional shopping behaviors.

5 Conclusion

While last mile services are growing exponentially, they are more or less targeted to a younger user base. Even though most of elderly people have not embraced online delivery platforms, the impact of the pandemic will surely necessitate more elderly people, especially those who have been shopping out in person to evaluate leveraging the last mile delivery platforms. While the study so far has indicated some of the primary expectations and behavioral calibrations required for technology platforms to be usable to this segment of users, a further study focusing on gender-based behaviors, impact of tutoring elderly people to use these services and more could help unearth even more valuable data.

References

1. https://science.thewire.in/health/to-be-a-senior-citizen-during-indias-covid-19-epidemic/
2. https://social.un.org/ageing-working-group/documents/seventh/AgewellFoundationSubmiss ion.pdf
3. https://jungleworks.com/last-mile-delivery-evolving-market/
4. Share of population over age of 60 in India projected to increase to 20% in 2050: UN. https:// economictimes.indiatimes.com/news/politics-and-nation/share-of-population-over-age-of-60-in-india-projected-to-increase-to-20-in-2050-un/articleshow/68919318.cms
5. Longitudinal Ageing Study in India (Wave 1). https://www.iipsindia.ac.in/sites/default/files/ LASI_India_Report_2020_compressed.pdf
6. https://en.wikipedia.org/wiki/COVID-19_lockdown_in_India
7. https://locus.sh/resources/bulletin/how-india-dealing-with-essential-deliveries-at-times-of-lockdown/
8. https://www.thehindubusinessline.com/opinion/columns/from-the-viewsroom/outcasts-in-a-digital-world/article9709231.ece
9. https://www2.deloitte.com/content/dam/Deloitte/global/Documents/About-Deloitte/COVID-19/gx-last-mile-customer-delivery-after-covid-19.pdf

Service Design for Elderly People with Dementia and the Role of Technology Mediation

Qiang Li[✉], Jingjing Wang, Tian Luo, and Dayong Ma

Shenyang Aerospace University, Shenyang, China
qiangli@sau.edu.cn

Abstract. The world is entering an aging society in which the problem about the aged becomes a public concern especially the difficulties those elderly people with dementia are facing. The purpose of this study is to provide insight into the needs of elderly people with dementia through the user centered service design methods, and to explore the role of technology mediation, such as how VR (virtual reality), serious games and other digital technologies meet the needs of different levels of elderly people with dementia. Some previous studies only focused on the basic needs in home and it can be met by ICT (Information and Communication Technology) products such as Smart Home System or Living Lab environment. However, the overall system to meet the needs of all aspects of elderly people with dementia, considering different stakeholders and integrated with new digital technologies needs to be designed. In order to investigate the real needs of elderly people with dementia, the user centered research methods such as personas, stakeholder analysis and user travel map are used and four types of user needs and their corresponding user behavior, content and solutions are defined. And the Dementia Care app which can meet the needs of dementia people in all aspects is designed. Finally, the role of technology mediation is discussed. In the future work, the design will be developed and applied to the elderly people with mild dementia to improve their ability to live independently and the role of new digital technologies will be verified.

Keywords: Dementia · Service design · Virtual reality · Serious game

1 Introduction

Populations are aging the entire world and it is one of the major challenges that the world is facing in the coming decades. Due to the outcome of two fundamental forces—falling fertility and rising longevity, China is one of the world's most extreme examples of these demographic challenges [1]. And the prevalence of elderly people with dementia who are 65 and older in China is growing quickly. So Chinese society are facing many of the challenges related to family care-giving for elders with dementia. However, informal care at home can be extremely expensive and in some cases it is not possible at all. Considering the difficulties of informal care, the use of new technological products can substantially support the elderly people with dementia to live independently. There are

© Springer Nature Switzerland AG 2021
C. Stephanidis et al. (Eds.): HCII 2021, CCIS 1419, pp. 282–288, 2021.
https://doi.org/10.1007/978-3-030-78635-9_38

a few studies which expect to use technologies to improve the wellbeing of elderly people with dementia such as Smart Home System or Living Lab environment [2, 3]. And even the new VR (Virtual Reality) technology and serious games can be used to improve the cognition ability of elderly people with dementia [4–6]. And robot therapy for prevention of dementia at home has also been tried and verified [7–9]. However, there is a lack of holistic and systematic research on the needs of elderly people with dementia and the role of technology mediation according to different needs need to be verified. The purpose of this study is to use service design methods to analyze the user needs and experience, and an app is designed to meet user needs and support the independent living ability of elderly people with dementia. And the roles of technology mediation such as VR (Virtual Reality), Serious Game, and Wearable intelligent products to help elderly people with dementia and improve their wellbeing are discussed.

Dementia is defined as a chronic disease which cause permanent and gradual cognitive decline [10]. And the Alzheimer's disease is the most common type of Dementia. It is more likely to occur in elderly people and as the number of elderly people grows the percent of people with Alzheimer disease increases clearly. A study allowed categorizing the dementia progress into 7 stages. [see Table 1].

Table 1. The level of Dementia

Diagnosis	Stage	Signs and symptoms
No Dementia	1: No Cognitive Decline	No memory loss, and is mentally healthy
No Dementia	2: Very Mild Cognitive Decline	Normal forgetfulness associated with aging. Symptoms are not evident to loved ones or the physician
No Dementia	3: Mild Cognitive Decline	Increased forgetfulness, slight difficulty concentrating, and decreased work performance. Average duration: 7 years
Early-stage	4: Moderate Cognitive Decline	Decreased memory of recent events, and difficulties traveling alone to new locations. Average duration: 2 years
Mid-Stage	5: Moderately Severe Cognitive Decline	Have major memory deficiencies and need some assistance to complete their daily activities (dressing, bathing, preparing meals). Average duration: 1.5 years
Mid-Stage	6: Severe Cognitive Decline	Require extensive assistance to carry out daily activities. They start to forget names of close family members and have little memory of recent events. Average duration: 2.5 years
Late-Stage	7: Very Severe Cognitive Decline	Have essentially no ability to speak or communicate. They require assistance with most activities (e.g., using the toilet, eating). Average duration: 2.5 years

2   A Practical Case of Service Design with Dementia Care as an Example

This study uses the process and a method of service design to investigate the elderly people with dementia, and uses the smart phone app (Dementia Care) as the core system to meet the needs of patients with dementia. The design process comprehensively considers most stakeholders through systematic analysis, and combines virtual reality, serious games and wearable hardware technology, aiming to improve the life experience of patients with dementia as a whole.

2.1   Design Methods and Process

Service design is a holistic way for a business to gain a comprehensive, empathic understanding of customer needs [11]. The most typical characteristic of service design is that it thinks of the various stake-holders involved in creating, providing and consuming a service. In the service system design of Dementia Care, the digital technologies such as virtual reality and serious game are integrated in the system.

2.2   User Analysis

Designing a service system requires participation and opinion from all stakeholders such as internal stakeholders from the different organizational functions, external stakeholders such as user groups and supply teams. The first step of our service design project for dementia people is to find the important stakeholders in the service system and identify the characteristics of these stakeholders through different user-centered research methods such as observation, shadowing, personas and service safari etc. In this study the stakeholders are classified as three groups: service receiver (core), service provider (direct) and service supporting system (indirect). According to the analysis results, three parts of the important stakeholders (Policeman, Family Members, Caregivers, Hospital, and Dementia Center) will be applied and integrated into the Dementia Care APP. The stakeholders' structure is shown in Table 2.

Table 2. The stakeholder analysis

Stakeholder level	Stakeholders	Services provided
Core	End users (Elderly People with Dementia)	Personal information Users of services
Direct	Family members of user	Providing family care and emotion
	Caregivers of user	Providing family care
	Regional Police	Providing outdoor help
Indirect	Hospital	Providing emergency treatment and hospital care
	Dementia Center	Providing professional Alzheimer's disease advice and therapy

User Personas. User personas or User Role Models are used to classify users' behaviors, patterns, goals, skills, attitudes, hopes, needs and environment for the service, product or anything else which is relevant for the design challenge. In this study we used personas to access the deep level of needs and experiences of people with dementia. We designed 4 personas based on the results of the stakeholder analysis. The center user (elderly people with stage 5 of dementia) is Mr. Wang (the elderly people with dementia), who lived by himself. And Lily is his daughter who has her own 3 family members of herself. Lady Zhang is a home care-giver for the elderly people with dementia. Through user role modeling, the needs of different user roles are identified, as shown in Fig. 1.

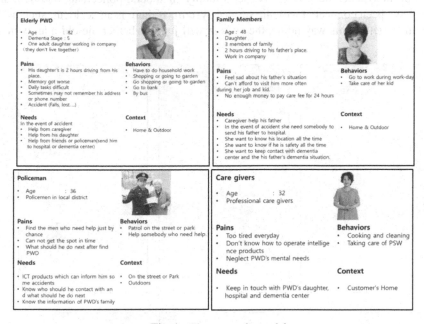

Fig. 1. The user role model

Customer Journey Map. Customer journey map is a service tool to describe the experiences, subjective responses, and feelings that customers or users use when they are using products or services. And the customer journey map can help us more in-depth understanding of users, auxiliary classification of users. In this study the tool of customer journey map for elderly people with dementia is used based on user personas.

Analysis results based on both customer journey map and User Role Models show that different level of needs from explicit, observable, tacit to latent are found. And even mild forms of dementia are associated with a diminished quality of life, unsafe feelings, poor self-esteem, anxiety and social isolation. And the elderly people with dementia need not only the help of daily activities but also to preventing and slow the progression of dementia even can effectively alleviate the patients' anxious and depressive emotions so as to raise the curative effect. And the care-givers and other stakeholders should focus on not only the supervision, worries and anxiety, but also a growing sense of frustration.

In order to meet the various needs of elderly people with dementia, the service system has different function modules and integrates various digital technologies to enhance the cognitive ability of elderly people with dementia.

2.3 APP Design

The design of Dementia Care APP takes elderly people with dementia as the center and integrates VR content, serious game and intelligent digital technology to enhance their cognitive abilities. The Dementia Care app contains six functional modules (see Fig. 2) and important stakeholders such as user's family members, policeman, and dementia center have been connected with the service system. If there is an accident, such as the old man forgetting his way home, the system will judge whether the old man is in the

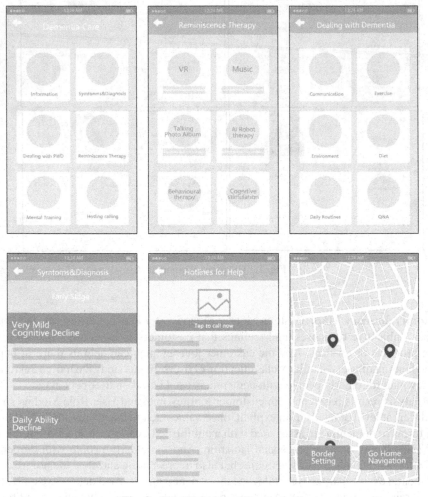

Fig. 2. The UI design of Dementia Care

activity setting range. If it is out of the range, it will automatically send an alarm to his family or the preset police.

3 Discussion on the Role of Technology Mediation

In this study a few kinds of digital technologies are used to help elderly people with dementia. One is to use GPS functions in the APP to monitor or capture the path of the patients and know their locations. By doing so, the system can inform about risky situation to direct stakeholders on behalf of the user. Other digital technical mediation such as music, old photos, serious games or VR can be used to slow the progression of dementia by stimulating and improving dementia people's cognitive ability. In the same time traditional methods such as exercise, diet, mental activities and socializing also be integrated and applied in this service. The relation between different technological methods and how can they met the needs of people with dementia is presented in (Table 3).

Table 3. The user needs and technological solutions

Types	Needs level	Behaviors	Detail contents	Solutions
Explicit	Physical needs	Daily activities	Dressing, medication, eating, drinking, washing, toileting	Diet, exercise ICT products
Observable	Cognitive needs	Mental activities	Hobbies, entertainments	Serious games, mental activities
Tacit	Affective needs	Socialization	Families, Friends	VR, socialization
Latent	Experience needs	Comprehensive	Feeling of satisfaction Self-confidence	Comprehensive

4 Conclusion

Based on the analysis of the elderly people with dementia, different level of needs from explicit, observable, tacit to latent are identified. And the smart service system Dementia Care is designed integrated with different digital technologies to support the life of the elderly people with dementia. The future research will focus on the usability testing of the service system. The effectiveness of digital technologies such as virtual reality and serious game still need to be studied and verified. There is a very broad space for research on the use of new digital technology to improve the cognitive ability of elderly people with dementia.

Acknowledgement. The work was supported by both Liaoning Province Education Department (JYT2020098) and Key R & D project of Science and Technology Department of Liaoning Province.

References

1. National Research Council, Committee on Population. Beyond six billion: Forecasting the world's population. National Academies Press (2000)ss
2. Boumpa, E., Gkogkidis, A., Charalampou, I., et al.: An acoustic-based smart home system for people suffering from dementia. Technologies **7**(1), 29 (2019)
3. Pino, M., Benveniste, S., Picard, R., et al.: User-driven innovation for dementia care in France: The LUSAGE living lab case study. Interdisc. Stud. J. **3**(4), 251 (2014)
4. Hodge, J., Balaam, M., Hastings, S., et al.: Exploring the design of tailored virtual reality experiences for people with dementia. In: Proceedings of the. CHI Conference on Human Factors in Computing Systems **2018**, 1–13 (2018)
5. McCallum, S., Boletsis, C.: Dementia games: a literature review of dementia-related serious games. In: Ma, M., Oliveira, M.F., Petersen, S., Hauge, J.B. (eds.) SGDA 2013. LNCS, vol. 8101, pp. 15–27. Springer, Heidelberg (2013). https://doi.org/10.1007/978-3-642-40790-1_2
6. Moyle, W., Jones, C., Dwan, T., et al.: Effectiveness of a virtual reality forest on people with dementia: a mixed methods pilot study. Gerontologist **58**(3), 478–487 (2018)
7. Wada, K., Shibata, T., Musha, T., et al.: Robot therapy for elders affected by dementia. IEEE Eng. Med. Biol. Mag. **27**(4), 53–60 (2008)
8. Tamura, T., Yonemitsu, S., Itoh, A., et al.: Is an entertainment robot useful in the care of elderly people with severe dementia? J. Gerontol. A Biol. Sci. Med. Sci. **59**(1), M83–M85 (2004)
9. Wada, K., Shibata, T., Asada, T., et al.: Robot therapy for prevention of dementia at home. J. Robot. Mech. **19**(6), 691 (2007)
10. Williams, J.W., Plassman, B.L., Burke, J., et al.: Preventing Alzheimer's disease and cognitive decline. Evid. Rep. Technol. Assess. **193**, 1–727 (2010)
11. Lockwood, T.: Design thinking: Integrating innovation, customer experience, and brand value. Simon and Schuster (2010)

Study on How Fatigue Affects Gait of Older Adult Rolling Walker Users

Jo Yee Sharmaine Lim[1]($\boxtimes$) and Tetsuya Hirotomi[2]

[1] Graduate School of Natural Science and Technology, Shimane University, Matsue, Shimane 690-8504, Japan
n21m109@matsu.shimane-u.ac.jp
[2] Institute of Science and Engineering, Academic Assembly, Shimane University, Matsue, Shimane 690-8504, Japan
hirotomi@cis.shimane-u.ac.jp

Abstract. Older adults with limited mobility are prescribed rolling walkers to prevent falls, but incorrect usage may cause accidents. The purpose of this study is to investigate the effects of fatigue on gait, including rolling walker usage, of older adult rolling walker users. In our approach, the usage is modelled by distance from rolling walker and gait velocity. The normal gait area is determined by the 5th and 95th percentile of these data. The deviance rate for every 10 s is calculated by the ratio of data exceeding the normal gait area. Three older adult rolling walker users participated our data collection. They walked from the entrance of their room in a nursing home to the canteen (outbound) and back (inbound). Outbound route data was used to determine area of normal gait while inbound route data for analysis. Through video analysis, 16 abnormal walking behaviors were noted and then compared to deviance rate that exceeded threshold value of 0.2. Five behaviors related to fatigue and another 11 abnormal behaviors were successfully detected by the deviance rate. It also detected eight slight changes in gait. These changes were difficult to detect through observation. Detecting and alerting these changes may be useful for caregivers to supervise older adults who may be at risk of falling.

Keywords: Older adults · Rolling walker · Fatigue · Gait

1 Introduction

Older adults with limited mobility are often prescribed rolling walkers to help prevent falls [1, 9]. Compared to healthy older adults, those older adults are more easily fatigued and gait patterns may differ compared to healthy older adults.

However, little information is known about the effects of fatigue on older adult rolling walker users. Therefore, the main objective of this paper is to investigate how fatigue affects gait of older adult rolling walker users. In this paper, a method for detecting fatigue from gait pattern is presented. It should be noted that the term "gait" in this paper also includes the usage of a rolling walker while walking.

© Springer Nature Switzerland AG 2021
C. Stephanidis et al. (Eds.): HCII 2021, CCIS 1419, pp. 289–297, 2021.
https://doi.org/10.1007/978-3-030-78635-9_39

2 Related Work

Injuries caused by falls lead to a considerable and long-term loss in quality of life resulting in high healthcare costs because of substantial increases in problems with self-care and usual activities compared to healthy older adults [3]. Nagano et al. [6] reported that fatigue induced by six minutes of fast walking led to an increased older adult's tripping risk due to reduced minimum foot clearance. Besides that, a few studies on healthy older adults who do not require ambulatory devices reported that fatigue increases gait velocity, step length, and the risk of tripping [2,4,6]. However, to the authors knowledge, no study examined the effects of fatigue on gait of older adult rolling walker users.

3 Identifying Deviance from Normal Gait

We proposed a method to detect fatigue by "deviance rate". This method calculates and identifies the deviance of gait from an older adult rolling walker users' (hereafter referred to as the participant) normal gait pattern using the following data collected: distance of participant from rolling walker and gait velocity. The data are collected at 0.1 s intervals using a rotary encoder and distance sensor attached to a rolling walker (see Fig. 1) [5].

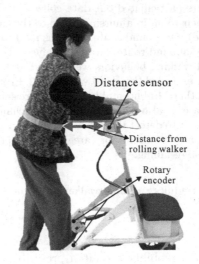

Fig. 1. Frequency graph showing participant's area of normal gait

Participant's distance from rolling walker is plotted against gait velocity in a frequency graph and is considered a visualization of the participant's gait pattern during ambulation. Subsequently, the 5th and 95th percentile of both participant's distance from rolling walker and gait velocity are calculated and marked on the graph (see Fig. 2). Gait data that fall within the marked area is deemed normal gait. After obtaining participant's normal gait pattern, the number of data exceeding the normal gait area was counted and divided by the total subset size to obtain the ratio of data exceeding the normal gait area as shown in Eq. 1. The ratio is called "deviance rate".

$$\text{Deviance rate} = \frac{\text{Number of data exceeding normal gait area}}{\text{Total number of data}} \tag{1}$$

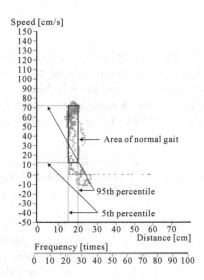

Fig. 2. Frequency graph showing participant's area of normal gait

4 Experiment

4.1 Participants

Data was collected from three female nursing home participants who used rolling walkers to navigate the inside the home in daily life. Details of participants are tabulated in Table 1.

Each participant's gait abilities were assessed with a Timed "Up & Go" (TUG) test [7]. According to Shumway-Cook et al. [8], older adults whose TUG scores ≥ 13.5 s are considered as fallers. Participant 01 and 03 took more than the cut-off time and Participant 02 could not fully complete the TUG, stopping midway.

Table 1. Participant demography

Participant	Age	TUG [s]	History of fall (location)	Distance travelled, one-way [m]
01	76	22.8	No	23.0
02	77	N/A	No	16.2
03	87	77.5	Yes (Toilet)	16.5

4.2 Procedure

Data Collection. Participants were asked to walk starting from the hallway outside participants lodging in the nursing home to the canteen located at the end of the hallway (outbound route) and back (inbound route). The entire walking process was recorded on video. A caregiver supported our data collection to monitor the participant's conditions and prevent accidents.

Data Analysis. Video data was manually annotated to extract timeline of notable events, such as changes in body movement, stopping before reaching goal, and visible changes in participant's distance from rolling walker and gait velocity.

Outbound route data was used to generate participants' gait pattern and obtain area of normal gait, although data indicating participant's distance from rolling walker of more than 80 cm were excluded from graphs as the distance sensor used has a range of up to 80 cm. Inbound route data was then analyzed. The deviance rate is calculated similar to how a moving average is calculated. A fixed subset size of 10 s (equivalent to 100 units of data) was used. Within the subset, the deviance rate was calculated. Then, the calculation was repeated after "moving" the subset by one data unit (i.e. subset of data 1 to 100 is "moved" one data unit to include data 2 to 101).

The deviance rate was then plotted on a line graph. For this study, 0.2 was taken as the exploratory threshold of deviance rate and peaks more than or equal to the threshold value was marked.

Each marked peak was classified into the following three types. A peak with a label beginning with the number representing the participant ID had the corresponding event extracted from video analysis. Labels having "_f" postfix indicated events that were observed to be related to fatigue. The peaks with the labels starting with letters A, B, and C showed that no event was extracted by video analysis during that period.

4.3 Results

Participant 01 completed both outbound and inbound route without needing to rest in between while participants 02 and 03 required a short break after outbound route and were allowed to sit and rest before starting inbound route.

Figure 3, 4, and 5 show the frequency of gait data with normal gait area while walking the outbound route, the deviance from the normal gait area while walking the inbound route, and the deviance rate graph with peak labels, respectively.

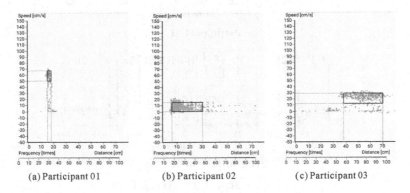

(a) Participant 01   (b) Participant 02   (c) Participant 03

Fig. 3. Frequency graph and area of normal gait (outbound route)

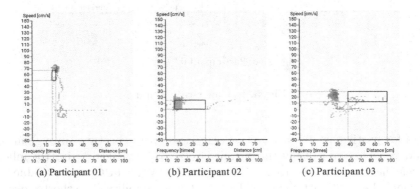

(a) Participant 01   (b) Participant 02   (c) Participant 03

Fig. 4. Frequency graph showing deviance from normal gait (inbound route)

Participant 01 did not require a rest after completing outbound gait but stood still for a while (label 1a in Fig. 5(a)) before conducting a "J" shaped turn (1b) and resuming gait of inbound route. Participant 01's frequency graphs for outbound and inbound route (Fig. 3(a), Fig. 4(a)) show that participant 01 had increased gait velocity and distance from rolling walker during inbound route which is consistent with their elevated deviance rate (label A1 in Fig. 5) even though video recording showed no visible changes in gait. The increase in gait velocity and distance from rolling walker was difficult to detect through video analysis. At 1c, participant 01 slowed down as she was approaching the chair, and as she neared the chair, she maneuvered the rolling walker to support herself while getting into the chair.

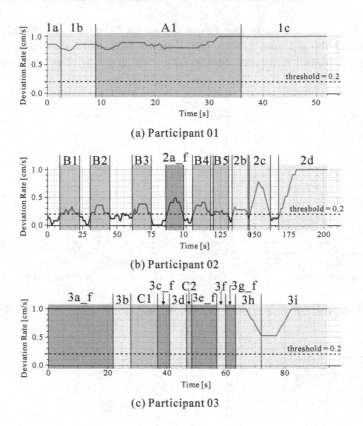

(a) Participant 01

(b) Participant 02

(c) Participant 03

Fig. 5. Deviance rate graph

As for participant 02, her gait velocity was fairly constant throughout out-bound and inbound gait but the distance from rolling walker during the inbound gait was nearer compared to outbound gait. From the TUG scores (Table 1), it was concluded that participant 02 had the lowest mobility. The shorter distance from rolling walker during inbound route may be due to participant 02 feeling tired and requiring more support from rolling walker to continue walking. The shorter distance between participant 02 and the rolling walker may have con-tributed to the peaks B1 through B5 in the deviance graph in Fig. 5(b) although not visible on video recording. However, events labelled 2a_f, 2b, 2c, and 2d were changes in gait that were visible on video recording and event at 2a_f was deemed fatigue related because participant 02 stopped walking midway through inbound route, prompting accompanying caregiver to encourage participant to continue walking. At 2b, participant 02 slowed down as they were nearing the chair and came to a complete stop directly in front of the chair at 2c, causing a steep spike in deviance rate. Caregiver had to intervene and assist participant in correctly maneuvering the rolling walker and sitting down (2d).

Participant 03 changed the way they held and used a rolling walker during the inbound gait, causing participant 03's shortened distance from rolling walker (Fig. 4(c)). This also caused participant 03 to obtain a high deviance rate during inbound gait. Throughout inbound gait, participant 03 kept their head lowered and looked directly at the floor while walking, indicated by labels 3a_f, 3c_f, 3e_f, and 3g_f (Fig. 5(c)). The subsequent events following this (labels 3b, 3d, 3f, and 3h) indicate when accompanying caregiver intervened by reminding and encouraging participant to look forward while walking. At 3h, participant looked up after being reminded by caregiver and slowed down as they were approaching the chair. Finally at 3i, the participant maneuvered the rolling walker to support themselves while getting into the chair.

5   Discussion

Overall, a total of five fatigue related events (events with "_f" postfix) were detected using video recordings. All the five fatigue related events were successfully detected by deviance rate method. The precision at which this method was able to detect fatigue has achieved the objective of this study.

This method was also able to detect certain changes in gait that may be related to fatigue but not visible through video recordings (events with labels beginning with uppercase alphabets). From the video data obtained, excluding fatigue related events, 3 events where changes in gait occurred were detected for participant 01 and 02. For participant 03, five events were visibly detected. However, deviance rate method detected an additional 1, 5, and 2 events where changes in gait occurred for participants 01, 02, and 03 respectively. These events are tagged with labels beginning in uppercase letters in Fig. 5. Among the events that were detected only through deviance rate method (events A1, B1–B5, and C1–C2), events B1 through B5 for participant 02, events C1 and C2 for participant 03 should have been assisted by a caregiver. For participant 02, spike in deviance rate at B1 through B5 was due to participant moving closer to the rolling walker for more support during ambulation and by alerting a caregiver, participant 02 can be given further assistance, reducing the risk of falling due to applying too much force on one end of the rolling walker. As for participant 03, alerting a caregiver can allow the caregiver to keep an eye on the participant so that she can walk with proper posture and correctly use a rolling walker.

However, in this study, the outbound route was set from 16 to 23 m because of the participant's gait abilities. This short distance may result in higher deviance rate of participant 01 and 03. Future studies are required to determine the proper walking distance for calculating the normal gait area.

6   Implications for Practice

The deviance rate method could be useful in a nursing home or other care facility settings whereby staff are alerted when an older adult rolling walker users exhibit abnormalities. Nursing home and care facility staff are able to check in on the user and maybe prevent a fall or accident from happening. For outdoor gait of the users, it can advise users to either rest or slow down to prevent tripping or falling.

7   Conclusion

The proposed deviance rate method is a straightforward way to detect fatigue especially in situations where users cannot be constantly supervised or strapped to certain equipment to monitor fatigue. By setting the threshold of participants' deviance rate at 0.2 and analysing indoor gait of real rolling walker users, we were able to detect visible and non-visible changes in participants' gait. Even small changes within a participants' area of normal gait could be detected.

Due to the COVID-19 pandemic, visitation and recruiting of institutionalized older adults was discouraged, therefore data from a prior study without fatiguing protocols were used. Future studies with appropriately designed experiments are required to further assess the accuracy of the deviation rate method as well as set an appropriate threshold for it. With this study, the need to identify if a consistent pattern or patterns is present in fatigued gait of older adult rolling walker users and if so, what are those patterns or characteristics.

Acknowledgement. A part of this study was supported by JSPS KAKENHI with grant number JP20K12765.

References

1. Ajimi, A., Tokuda, K., Mizuno, T.: Going-out status of elderly users of rollators and traffic issues to address. IATSS Rev. **35**(2), 131–138 (2010). http://ci.nii.ac.jp/naid/40017299287/
2. Granacher, U., Wolf, I., Wehrle, A., Bridenbaugh, S., Kressig, R.W.: Effects of muscle fatigue on gait characteristics under single and dual-task conditions in young and older adults. J. NeuroEng. Rehabil. **7**(1) (2010). https://doi.org/10.1186/1743-0003-7-56
3. Hartholt, K.A., et al.: Societal consequences of falls in the older population: injuries, healthcare costs, and long-term reduced quality of life. J. Trauma - Injury, Infection Critical Care **71**(3) (2011). https://doi.org/10.1097/TA.0b013e3181f6f5e5
4. Helbostad, J.L., Leirfall, S., Moe-Nilssen, R., Sletvold, O.: Physical fatigue affects gait characteristics in older persons. J. Gerontol. - Ser. A Biol. Sci. Med. Sci. **62**(9) (2007). https://doi.org/10.1093/gerona/62.9.1010
5. Hirotomi, T., Hosomi, Y.: Gait analysis on the use of four-castered walker and elderly-simulation suit. In: Proceedings of the 2008 International Conference on Bioinformatics and Computational Biology, BIOCOMP 2008 (2008)
6. Nagano, H., James, L., Sparrow, W.A., Begg, R.K.: Effects of walking-induced fatigue on gait function and tripping risks in older adults. J. NeuroEng. Rehabil. **11**(1) (2014). https://doi.org/10.1186/1743-0003-11-155
7. Podsiadlo, D., Richardson, S.: The timed "up & go": a test of basic functional mobility for frail elderly persons. J. Am. Geriatr. Soc. **39**, 142–148 (1991)

8. Shumway-Cook, A., Brauer, S., Woollacott, M.: Predicting the probability for falls in community-dwelling older adults using the timed up and go test. Phys. Therapy **80**(9) (2000). https://doi.org/10.1093/ptj/80.9.896
9. Stevens, J.A., Thomas, K., Teh, L., Greenspan, A.I.: Unintentional fall injuries associated with walkers and canes in older adults treated in U.S. emergency departments. J. Am. Geriatr. Soc. **57**(8) (2009). https://doi.org/10.1111/j.1532-5415.2009.02365.x

CogRehab: A Personalized Digital Approach to Cognitive Rehabilitation

António Mota[1], Paula Amorim[2,3(✉)], Ana Gabriel-Marques[3], Helder Serra[1], Marta Koc-Januchta[4], Helder Zagalo[1], and Beatriz Sousa Santos[1]

[1] DETI/IEETA, University of Aveiro, Aveiro, Portugal
[2] University of Beira Interior, Covilhã, Portugal
[3] Rovisco Pais Medical and Rehabilitation Center, Tocha, Portugal
[4] Media and Information Technology (MIT), University of Linköping, Norrköping, Sweden

Abstract. While there are already several digital platforms to support cognitive rehabilitation allowing therapists to create sessions, they often overlook the importance of taking into consideration patients' personal values and interests (personalization) to promote their engagement in rehabilitation. This paper proposes a personalized digital approach for cognitive rehabilitation. It presents a web-based prototype developed in collaboration with domain experts of a national Rehabilitation Center using a user-centered approach. This prototype allows therapist to create personalized exercises with content relevant to patients' life, interests or personality, assign them to patients, and monitor their performance. It was evaluated regarding usability and assessed by two domain experts who suggested improvements to the prototype and put forward ideas for extending the approach.

Keywords: Cognitive rehabilitation · Personalization · Web-based prototype

1 Introduction

Cognitive impairment "is the decline of intellectual functions such as thinking, remembering, reasoning and planning. It is common among older people but the effects range from mild forms of forgetfulness to severe and debilitating dementia." [1]. It has always been present throughout human history and people who suffer from this condition can have extreme difficulties in everyday tasks, like driving a car or sustaining a conversation, and might even need assistance for the rest of their lives. Unable to mentally keep up with the cognitive demands of daily life, people with cognitive impairment are prone to fatigue, depressive mood, irritability and exhaustion [2]. The list of possible causes is extensive, ranging from traumatic brain injury (TBI), stroke, or even genetic disorders [3]. A 2019 report by the Center for Disease Control and Prevention points out TBI as one of the major causes of death and disability in the United States [4]. From 2006 to 2014, the number of TBI-related emergency department visits, hospitalizations, and deaths increased by 53% [4]. Another primary factor is aging, which is worrisome if one considers the rapid inversion of the population pyramid, a problem that is increasing in our society. It is predicted that by 2050 the number of people aged over 65 will be

© Springer Nature Switzerland AG 2021
C. Stephanidis et al. (Eds.): HCII 2021, CCIS 1419, pp. 298–308, 2021.
https://doi.org/10.1007/978-3-030-78635-9_40

a sixth of the global population. As years go by, age-associated neurological diseases are more likely to occur. For example, the risk of suffering a stroke is doubled above 55 [5]. As consequence of these factors, there will be a boost on health-care costs to fulfill the needs of this transformed society. As such, it becomes more and more important for health-care systems to develop cost-effective rehabilitation. Considering the previous data, it is also important to recognize that cognitive disability is particularly expensive, especially because those with this kind of disability resort to hospital stays three times more often than other patients [4]. On the other hand, computerized therapeutic exercises can be useful to simplify the procedure, overall reducing costs while increasing patients' engagement and adherence to therapy. It can also be adapted to be used in tele-rehabilitation scenarios [6].

This paper presents a digital approach to cognitive rehabilitation supporting the preparation of personalized exercises taking into consideration patients' individuality. It is organized as follows: Sect. 2 is concerned with cognitive rehabilitation and how it can be supported by technology; Sect. 3 describes the proposed approach and a prototype; Sect. 4 presents the results of evaluation; and Sect. 5 draws conclusions and presents ideas for future work.

2 Cognitive Rehabilitation Supported by Technology

This section provides a very brief overview of cognitive rehabilitation concepts relevant for this work, as well as how technology may support it. One of them is engagement, which is essential for active learning to occur [7]. It is known that greater commitment reflects in an enhancement of content understanding and skill development [8]. From a clinical point of view, "the 'engaged patient' is perhaps identified as being the desirable patient, one who is easy for providers to work with." [6, p. 664]. In addition, the level of engagement has also been associated with the decrease of depression levels [6]. According to Blumenfeld et al. the four predominant factors for motivation and cognitive engagement are [9]:

Value – intrinsic value, involving personal interest; instrumental value, related to the perception of how tasks are linked with activities of daily living and attainment value, referring to personal importance on accomplishing the task;

Competence - the feeling of competence and ability to succeed has great influence on how much determination and persistence is given in the execution of a task;

Relatedness - expressions of "interest of well-being" by instructors and colleagues promote feeling of belonging;

Autonomy - the possibility of choosing and planning activities stimulates disposition to face challenges.

From these factors, the most interesting and possible to attain in the rehabilitation process is value [9]. By developing meaningful personalized exercises, based on patients' interests and daily life, and by promoting innovative ways of interaction, it is expected to achieve a higher motivation and a successful engagement in the tasks. Regarding competence, it is also important to give supportive feedback, recognition and encouragement throughout the patient rehabilitation journey. By doing this, one aims to maximize the efficacy and patients recovery.

Over the years, with the advancement of technology, the cognitive rehabilitation process has been increasingly computerized and tele-rehabilitation, consisting on the delivery of rehabilitation from remote locations through communication technologies, is becoming more and more accessible and interesting [10].

This work focus on computer-based cognitive rehabilitation (CCR), consisting essentially in the use of software usually involving the execution of cognitive game-like tasks [11, 12]. This type of software is not only developed for traditional computers but for various electronic devices including tablets and mobile phones. It is also important to stress that CCR is not about using technology to support cognitive disabled people, like electronic memory aid devices or personal virtual assistants (which are compensation techniques), but rather an active rehabilitation process which uses the same hardware. This therapy has been increasingly adopted due to the advantages it adds over traditional cognitive rehabilitation treatments [12]. In a medical context, CCR adds "(…) intensity, specificity and salience of treatment" [12, p.19]. By increasing these, it is also expected to increase the "experience-dependence" neuroplasticity. A good example is the paper and pencil tasks replacement. These are simple exercises that require reading some instructions and writing the solution according to the task. These tasks can be multiple-choice questions, sequencing some pictures, connecting diagrams, etc. The major reason paper and pencil exercises are one of the most used tools for the rehabilitation is because they existed before computers, didn't require specific instructions to use and have an extensive number of templates available. Still, analyzing, selecting and developing exercises that are adequate to a patient require time and effort which are already limited due to countless tasks neuropsychologist already manage.

Often, new digital platforms emerge aimed at migrating those traditional paper and pencil exercises that are so important in stimulus therapy or process training. These platforms have great potential of increasing the intensity, allow task prescription and may be able to change the engagement that patients have in the rehabilitation. Examples of such platforms are NeuroUP, COGWEB, Rehametrics, Cognifit and Guttmann Neuro Personal Trainer (GNPT). By researching the publicly available assets of these platforms (websites, demo videos, images, etc.), it was understood that generally they provide a vast number of digital exercises that can be executed in multiple platforms (laptops, tablets, smart TVs, etc.), some of them can also be printed and executed as traditional paper and pencil exercises. Other platforms also provide virtual reality immersion exercises, as Rehametrics (https://rehametrics.com/) that advertises itself as "(…) the only virtual reality rehabilitation platform that enables the treatment of physical and cognitive functions from the same solution". Regarding the exercises scope, the majority are focused on ADLs (Activities of Daily Living) aiming to retrain one or multiple areas of cognition such as Executive Function, Language and Memory, among others. Another relevant features of these platforms are performance monitoring, difficulty adaptability and neuropsychological assessments. While most are not available for demonstration without subscription, there is a paper describing the features of GNPT and their technical implementation, as well as the principles behind them [13].

Based on the clinical experience of the domain experts, literature analysis, as well as on the features and limitations of available digital platforms, such as using always the same set of exercises and not allowing including personal materials, a need for a different approach to computer supported cognitive rehabilitation based on customized exercises was identified. Also, it would be useful to make it generalizable to tele-rehabilitation scenarios, deemed increasingly feasible. These motivated our work.

3 Personalized Cognitive Rehabilitation Prototype

As mentioned, while there are several CCR platforms, they are configurable not customizable. However, it is paramount to make therapies more personal so that they motivate patients to have a total commitment to their recovery. In this context, personalization of an exercise may consist on using images with the patient's family members or objects related to their professional activity, while the configuration refers to the number of images, for example.

To develop the proposed personalized approach, it was employed a user-centered design (UCD) [14], starting by defining two personas (the therapist and the patient), as well as several persona-based scenarios. While personas are user models with the main characteristics of the target users relevant for the situation, including their needs and motivations, persona-based scenarios are "concise narrative descriptions of one or more personas using a product to achieve specific goals" [15, p.112]. Personas and scenarios help better understand the target users and their context of use and ease eliciting requirements. The following three scenarios were identified representing the main therapist activities that should be supported:

– Preparation of rehabilitation sessions (multiple sets of personalized exercises);
– Analysis of patient's performance;
– Management operations.

Another scenario was created to support the execution of exercises by the patient. After some meetings on site with the health professionals, a set of possible exercises were identified that could be migrated from the traditional paper and pencil exercises. With a clearer picture of the background and the target users, as well as the scenarios describing how the platform will be used by them, it was easier to perform a deeper analysis on what were its essential requirements.

Regarding functional requirements, after analyzing the user needs and the context of usage of the application, it was understood that the required application would need to run in multiple devices (tablets, laptops, etc.) in order to allow therapy to be delivered anywhere. Two dashboards should be developed, one for the health professional and other for the patients. The first needs sections for user management, cognitive exercises configuration and review, patient performance visualization and a final section for overall notification of treatments. The latter would instead be the place for execution of the exercises so it needs to be more minimalist but focused on details that might help patients to use the application easily.

Based on this analysis of the users' goals and motivations, the following main functional requirements were identified (visually summarized in Fig. 1):

Add, delete and modify patients - therapist need to be able to register and manage patients in the platform in order to assign them exercises.

Create, delete and modify exercises - the exercises should be intuitive to create and in the most dynamic and personalized possible way. This means that they should support text, images and other type of media in its creation.

Clone exercises - since there are many patients who may benefit from the same exercise template, but modifying the content in order to personalize it to other patients.

Create, delete, modify sessions - it should be possible to create a collection of exercises and assign it to patients, creating sessions.

Execute exercises - When assigned a session, patients need to execute exercises.

Exercise execution metadata extraction - all the patient interaction with the system should be recorded during the exercises (mouse clicks, key typing, times, etc.).

Automatic correction - whenever possible, exercises execution should be automatically assessed.

Review sessions - when a session is completed, therapists should access patient's performance.

Data visualization - the platform should be capable of analyzing patient's performance over time and build automatic graphs on their improvement.

Run the platform in tablets and laptops - the platform should be able to run in tablets and laptops in order to allow the sessions to be executed outside the clinic.

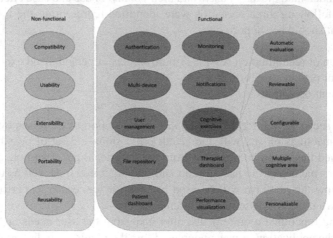

Fig. 1. Identified requirements for CogRehab based on the users needs, motivations and usage context

Since this application would be running in a diverse set of devices, either clinical owned devices or patient's personal devices, the application is required to be portable and compatible with other software that might be present in the system. Usability is a requirement that is important not only for the design method that was chosen for the development (user-centered design) but also for the care to be taken when working with patients with these disabilities. In order to allow further development beyond the scope of this work, extensibility and reusability are important non-functional requirements.

Finally all privacy and security issues are fundamental requirements in any application involving personal data and should be fully addressed as future work.

The decision of developing a prototype as a web application relies on the fact that the technology stack of web applications enables clients to run it without installing anything besides a regular browser. It also provides other advantages to clients such as seamless upgrades or availability from any machine with internet connection.

A first prototype was developed to demonstrate the concept and test the usability and acceptability of the proposed solution and identify aspects to improve. The prototype consists of a web application developed with ReactJS as frontend, Django as backend and PostegreSQL as the application database. Additionally, Django includes a lightweight and standalone web server that hosts the frontend and also exposes a REST API to the database. Any needs for storage are fulfilled by the web server. Figure 2 shows a high-level diagram of the prototype architecture.

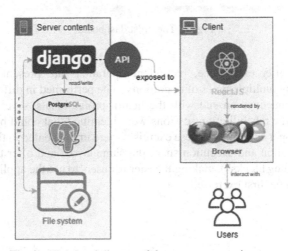

Fig. 2. High-level diagrm of the prototype arquitecture.

The result of all implementations is a web platform that acts as a user interface for all the functionality described. The entry point is the login page, essential to guarantee authentication of users and redirect patients and health professional to the appropriate dashboards. The therapist dashboard (Fig. 3) is an area where therapists can manage all the patients and exercises of the application, and additionally analyze the rehabilitation progress, allowing patients and exercises management, as well as obtaining overall information, as defined in the requirements.

To make it easier to navigate, a dashboard with a fixed top and side navigation bar was implemented. The top navigation bar is dedicated to content specific for that user such as: notifications, user settings and profile management. The side bar is a more general navigation drawer split into two categories: management and exercise creation. In the management section, therapists can browse through patients and exercises and do management operations. The creation section is dedicated to exercises creation as it provides a set of templates that the therapist can use to create exercises that fit their needs. Figure 3 shows the homepage of the therapist's dashboard showing the overall information section.

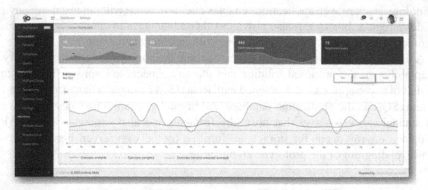

Fig. 3. Therapist dashboard.

To improve user experience, redundant operations are present throughout the platform allowing multiple types of operations to be performed in different ways.

After some meetings on site with the health professionals, several exercises frequently used in the rehabilitation sessions were identified that could be migrated from the traditional paper and pencil. These exercises were implemented in the platform such as their configuration and execution share the same layout and offer the same type of resources ("building blocks"), making it easier for users to use the application once they get familiar with the first exercise.

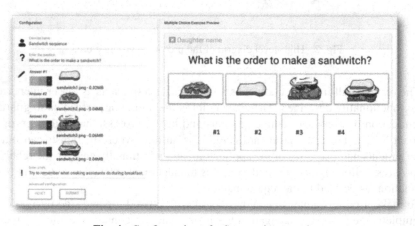

Fig. 4. Configuration of a Sequencing exercise.

To achieve personalization, all exercise types offer the therapist the possibility of adding multiple types of resources according to the template (e.g. images, text or videos) (Fig. 4). The exercises that the therapist can create are provided by the application as a "template" where all content may be added by the therapist in the multiple formats available. A preview of the exercise is also provided during its creation, updated in real time so the therapist can see how it will look to the patient. Four types of exercises are available: Multiple-choice, Reaction time, Sequencing, and Fill the gap (Figs. 4, 5 and 6).

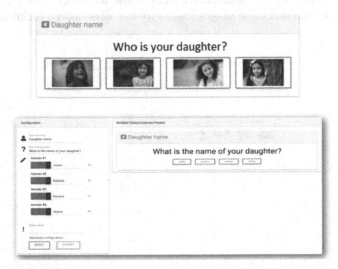

Fig. 5. Personalized multiple-choice exercise with a photo of a family member (top) and using text resources (bottom).

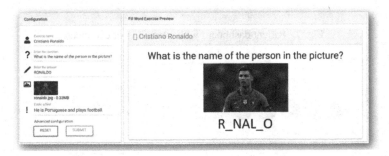

Fig. 6. "Fill the gap" exercise configuration

The patient dashboard allows only exercise execution. The main component is a sequential timeline of the exercises assigned for the patient to execute sequentially (Fig. 7). At the beginning of a session and after finishing the exercises, patients are asked regarding their mood and the difficulty of the session through dialog boxes (Fig. 8).

4   Prototype Evaluation

The prototype was analyzed by means of heuristic evaluation by two usability evaluators having experience in using usability evaluation methods. They used the heuristics set and severity scale proposed by Nielsen [16]. The evaluators identified seven unimportant potential usability issues ("Cosmetic problem only: need not be fixed unless extra time is available on project"), and two minor usability issues ("Minor usability problem: fixing this should be given low priority"), mainly related with the "visibility of system status" heuristic [17]. As result of the evaluation notes together with the post-evaluation discussion performed at the end of the process, it was possible to collect an overview feedback of the whole system and some suggestions to fix the identified problems proposed by the evaluators.

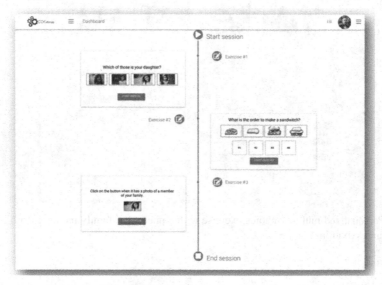

Fig. 7. Patient dashboard with a timeline of exercices.

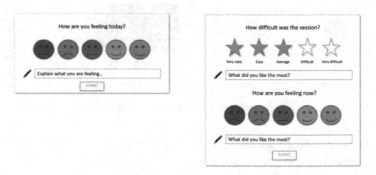

Fig. 8. Questions to obtain patients' feedback.

Regarding the application navigation the evaluators felt that is was easy and intuitive. The left navigation panel is very helpful since it provides an easy way of logically switching between patient related operations and exercise operations. It was also mentioned that the approach of shifting between therapist and patient without being necessary to go back the login page is very adequate and saves a lot of effort.

Regarding the patient dashboard, the general opinion is that it is very minimalist which makes the user focus on the main timeline displayed in the center of the page instinctively.

As a consequence of the heuristic evaluation, the prototype was improved and then evaluated by two domain experts who assessed the features implemented and pointed out that all the requirements were met with exception of a type of exercise – Fill the gap – which was different from what they expected. The experts also pointed out some usability issues and suggested increasing the size of the exercises preview, and allowing re-organizing the exercises on the therapists' view, as well as including simple instructions on how to perform exercises, and automatically open the next exercise, after completion of the previous one, on the patients' view. Besides these suggestions, therapists experts also proposed a number of new features that could be implemented in the platform which show the need for a new iteration of requirements definition and development. These features are presented as future work in the next section.

Although planned, it was not possible to perform tests with patients due to the SARS-CoV2 ongoing pandemic.

5 Concluding Remarks and Future Work

Personalization is considered relevant to foster cognitive rehabilitation as it may increase patients' motivation and engagement, thus potentially improving adherence to therapy routines and possibly their effectiveness. However, existing digital platforms are configurable, not personalized. This paper proposes a personalized digital approach for cognitive rehabilitation, and presents a prototype developed in collaboration with domain experts using a user-centered approach. It was evaluated concerning usability and assessed by two domain experts who put forward the following ideas for extending the approach, that are possible avenues for future work:

– implement a dynamic difficulty task assignment based on the results of baseline performance during the exercises to improve rehabilitation effectiveness;
– enable therapists to create templates for new types of exercises, thus extending the range of possibilities;
– improve feedback regarding the execution of exercises as it may increase patients' motivation and engagement;
– ensure security features to protect personal patients' information;
– add a chat supporting communication between patients and therapists, allowing patients, for instance, to report difficulties or give their opinion on their progress. This feature would be even more relevant in tele-rehabilitation scenarios.

Another important future work is to perform further evaluation, namely involving more domain experts as well as patients, first in clinical environment, and later in tele-rehabilitation scenarios.

Acknowledgements. The authors are grateful to the evaluators who assessed the prototype regarding usability and suggested improvements. This research was partially funded by National Funds through the FCT - Foundation for Science and Technology, in the context of the project UIDB/00127/2020.

References

1. Robertson, D., Savva, G., Kenny, R.: Frailty and cognitive impairment-a review of the evidence and causal mechanisms. Ageing Res. Rev. **12**(4), 840–851 (2013)
2. Fasotti, L.: Rehabilitation of slowed information processing. In: Wilson, B., Winegardner, J., van Heugten, C., Ownsworth, T. (eds.) Neuropsychological Rehabilitation, pp. 161–171. Routledge (2017)
3. Crowe, L., Brown, A., Greenham, M.: Other neurological conditions affecting children. In: Wilson, B., Winegardner, J., van Heugten, C.M., Ownsworth, T. (eds.) Neuropsychological Rehabilitation - The International Handbook, pp. 113–123. Routledge (2017)
4. Peterson, A., Daugherty, L., Breiding, M.: Surveillance report of traumatic brain injury related emergency department visits, hospitalizations, and deaths – United States, 2014. Centers for Disease Control and Prevention, U.S. Department of Health and Human Services. https://sta cks.cdc.gov/view/cdc/78062. Accessed 22 Feb 2021
5. Abbott, R., Rodriguez, B., Burchfiel, C., Curb, J.: Physical activity in older middle-aged men and reduced risk of stroke: the Honolulu Heart Program. Am. J. Epidemiol. **139**(9), 881–893 (1994)
6. Bright, F., Kayes, N., Worrall, L., McPherson, L.: A conceptual review of engagement in healthcare and rehabilitation. Disabil. Rehabil. **37**(8), 643–654 (2015)
7. Chi, M., Wylie, R.: The ICAP framework: linking cognitive engagement to active learning outcomes. Educ. Psychol. **49**(4), 219–243 (2014)
8. Carini, R., Kuh, G., Klein, S.: Student engagement and student learning: testing the linkages. Res. High. Educ. **47**(1), 1–32 (2006)
9. Blumenfeld, P., Rogat, T., Krajcik, J.: Motivation and cognitive engagement in learning environments. Cambridge University Press, The Cambridge Handbook of the Learning Sciences (2006)
10. Cotelli, M., et al.: Cognitive telerehabilitation in mild cognitive impairment, Alzheimer's disease and frontotemporal dementia: a systematic review. J. Telemed. Telecare **25**(2), 67–79 (2017)
11. Van Heugten, C.: Novel forms of cognitive rehabilitation. In: Wilson, B., Winegardner, J., van Heugten, C., Ownsworth, T. (eds.) Neuropsychological Rehabilitation, pp. 425–433. Routledge (2017)
12. Politis, A., Norman, R.: Computer-based cognitive rehabilitation for individuals with traumatic brain injury: a systematic review. Perspect. ASHA Sp. Inter. Groups **1**(2), 18–46 (2016)
13. Solana, J., et al.: Improving brain injury cognitive rehabilitation by personalized telerehabilitation services: Guttmann neuropersonal trainer. IEEE J. Biomed. Health Inform. **19**(1), 124–131 (2015)
14. Bass, L.J., Gornostaev, J., Unger, C. (eds.): EWHCI 1993. LNCS, vol. 753. Springer, Heidelberg (1993). https://doi.org/10.1007/3-540-57433-6
15. Cooper, A., Reimann, R., Cronin, D., Noessel, C.: About Face: The Essentials of Interaction Design, 4th edn. Wiley, Hoboken (2014)
16. Nielsen, J.: Usability Engineering. Morgan Kaufmann (1993)
17. Severity Ratings for Usability Problems. https://www.nngroup.com/articles/how-to-rate-the-severity-of-usability-problems/. Accessed 22 Feb 2021

Medicare Plan Decisions: What Strategy Do Older Adults Use for e-Healthcare Decision-Making and What Intelligent Assistance Do They Need?

Kassandra Ross[(⊠)], Wi-Suk Kwon, Salisa Westrick, Mohammad Shahidul Kader, Yi Zhao, and Xiao Huang

Auburn University, Auburn, AL, USA
mkr0028@auburn.edu

Abstract. Medicare Plan Finder (MPF), an e-healthcare tool on Medicare.gov, is designed to support beneficiaries in selecting a Medicare plan. The large number of plans and complexity of plan attributes make decisions arduous for older adults, whose decisions can suffer from cognitive aging. No studies have explored the optimization of older adults' decision strategies while making a plan decision. We applied decision strategies (LEX = plan selection based on a prime attribute; SAT = selecting an initial plan that satisfies minimum attribute cutoffs; MCD = comparing two plans at a time until a winner is selected; EBA = successively eliminating plans that do not meet attribute criteria; and WAD = comparing multiple plans for attribute trade-offs) from consumer theories to observational data from 29 participants (65+ years) selecting a plan using MPF with counselor assistance. Transcripts were analyzed to identify (1) participant strategies and (2) counselor intervened strategies. Before counselors' first intervention, 7 participants used no strategy, while 19 used only one strategy, mainly SAT. Most often, counselors promoted LEX ($f = 29$), followed by MCD > SAT > EBA > WAD (fs = 26, 23, 19, & 12). With counselors' intervention, participants came to use two ($f = 17$; most frequently, SAT then LEX [$f = 7$]) or more strategies. From 88 counselor interventions, participants adopted a strategy about 58%. Our findings highlight how older adults' e-healthcare decision strategies are impacted by on-task interventions and inform the development of real-time artificial intelligence (AI) decision assistants for Medicare plan decisions.

Keywords: e-Healthcare decision · Decision strategies · Older adults

1 Introduction

In an effort to enhance declining Medicare enrollment, in 2003, the Medicare Modernization Act was designed to extend beneficiary options across Medicare [1], which resulted in a sudden increase of Medicare plan options. In 2021, almost 1,000 Medicare Prescription Drug plans are being offered to beneficiaries across the U.S. [2]. A plethora

© Springer Nature Switzerland AG 2021
C. Stephanidis et al. (Eds.): HCII 2021, CCIS 1419, pp. 309–317, 2021.
https://doi.org/10.1007/978-3-030-78635-9_41

of literature cites the negative consequences of large choice sets on optimal decision-making of plan choices [e.g., 1, 3]. Previous studies have found that older adults suffer from the effects of cognitive aging [4], impairing the processes of complex decision-making [5, 6], a necessity in a Medicare Part D plan selection. In addition to a large choice set size of plan alternatives, older adults choosing a Medicare plan must also consider several plan attributes that may fit their needs (e.g., monthly premium, deductible amount, medication coverage) which vary between alternatives. Previous studies have found that many older adults often opt for simple choices whilst having to juggle complex information, potentially compromising an optimal choice for themselves [7].

Because plans often change attributes annually [8], and users' medication needs may also change, beneficiaries should evaluate the selection each year during Medicare open enrollment. To assist the decision process, the Medicare.gov website offers the Medicare Plan Finder (MPF), a decision support tool designed to help beneficiaries in simplifying a plan selection. As the only avenue for Medicare beneficiaries to gain knowledge and compare plans to make an informed plan selection, unfortunately, the MPF fails to curb decision complexities for older adults (65+ years old), who constitute the majority of Medicare beneficiaries. Given that many older adults suffer deficiencies in internet competency and health literacy [9], the MPF serves as a precarious venue for plan decision-making. Further, studies have shown that Medicare users' general knowledge regarding Medicare plans is lacking [10]. At times, older beneficiaries may seek the assistance of Medicare counselors or trained specialists who help aid in a plan selection [11]; however, counselors' assistance has been mostly limited to providing advice on plan information itself, rather than training older users in using the MPF for longer-term efficacy in their Medicare plan decision-making.

In this observational study, we investigated older Medicare beneficiaries' use of decision strategies while selecting a Medicare plan on the MPF with the assistance of a counselor. Further, we examined the decision strategies promoted by counselors and how the counselor intervention impacted older users' decision strategies employed on the MPF. In this pursuit, our goal was to address the optimization of decision strategies to inform not only Medicare beneficiaries' optimal plan decision needs, but also future innovations in real-time intelligent decision assistants for the MPF.

2 Literature and Research Questions

2.1 Decision Strategies on the MPF

A decision maker's selection of a strategy is based on a combination of (1) their cognitive ability, (2) the amount of decision alternatives available (i.e., number of plans to select from), and (3) the decision end goal (i.e., desired plan attributes) [12]. Decision strategy literature has discussed five decision strategies frequently employed by consumers that vary in level of required cognitive elaboration and decision outcome compensation (i.e., non-compensatory [without trade-offs] or compensatory [with trade-offs]). The five strategies include, from least to most complex, Lexicographic (LEX), Satisficing (SAT), Elimination-By-Aspects (EBA), Majority of Confirming Dimensions (MCD), and Weighted Adding (WAD), as detailed in Table 1. Naturally, while making complex consumptive choices like a Medicare plan selection, a decision-maker must utilize and switch between multiple strategies to accommodate an influx of information and streamline the decision-making process to make an optimal choice [13].

In 2019, Medicare revamped its MPF interface with the intention that users may readily be able to infer alternative (i.e., plan) and attribute information [14]. The MPF interface, accessed on a computer desktop or mobile device, includes various functions supporting the use of each of the five decision strategies during a plan selection process (see Table 1). For example, a 'Sort Plans' function makes allows users to sort numerous plans appearing on the search results page by deductible, drug, and premium amounts, which assists users in employing a LEX strategy (e.g., choosing the best [cheapest] plan on one of these cost attributes). A 'Filter' function allows users to refine search results by eliminating plans that do not meet a certain criterion (e.g., plans rated with less than 3 stars), thereby supporting the EBA strategy. An 'Add to Compare' function on the MPF enables users to select up to three plans for side-by-side comparisons on key attributes, thus facilitating the employment of MCD and WAD strategies.

2.2 Older Adults' Decision-Making

Many scholars agree that human decision-making is a widely complex and variable process where humans often utilize heuristics or mental shortcuts that ease the cognitive burden surrounding decision complexities and expedite a decision process [18]. The concept of bounded rationality, or limited rational mind in human decision-making due to limited cognitive capabilities and/or decision constraints, suggests that people often seek an *acceptable* solution by potentially foregoing an *optimal* decision [15]. Previous decision-making studies on older adults in a health-related context have revealed the effects of cognitive aging on the use of heuristics. For example, older adults were seen to less likely select optimal health-related options when given a larger decision choice set size than a smaller one [6]. Further, they were seen to rely more on the number of positive attributes provided by each option in a decision set instead of carefully ruminating on attribute options [6]. Furthermore, decision-makers combine and/or switch through multiple strategies during a cognitive task [19]. Strategy switches tend to lead to higher decision accuracies but require mental costs, which may explain the age-related differences in strategy switching, where older adults tend to switch less often than younger adults [5].

In the context of Medicare plan decisions on the MPF, an average of 25 to 35 stand-alone Medicare Prescription Drug plans are available to each Medicare beneficiary, a large choice set for older adults to process. Because Medicare insurance companies adjust plan options, coverage provisions, and costs from year to year [8], it is critical for users to review their plan choices and make informed decisions annually. Due to the complex nature of Medicare decision environments, some decision strategies and their combinations are more optimal than others for a plan decision. For instance, if users only employ the WAD strategy from the decision onset to compare 25–35 plans across multiple attributes, or only employ the SAT strategy to evaluate attribute details of one plan at a time, they are likely to abandon the decision process quickly due to mental fatigue. On the other hand, an optimal plan choice may be the result of using decision strategy switches or combinations [5]. For example, if a user refines search results by filtering plans from their initial choice set that do not meet their needs (i.e., the EBA

Table 1. Decision strategies applied to users and counselors in a selection task.

Decision strategy	Description and example application on MPF
Lexicographic (LEX)	Selecting the best alternative on a single attribute [13]; e.g., a MPF user employs the 'Sort Plans' by premium function on MPF to sort search results by lowest to highest monthly premium to find the plan that that has the cheapest (i.e., lowest) premium
Satisficing (SAT)	Selecting an alternative that meets a predetermined minimum cutoff for any key attributes considered, by reviewing one alternative at a time [15]; e.g., a MPF user investigates plan information one after another using a 'Plan Details' function on the search results page to find any plan that meets their minimum criteria (i.e., "acceptable" range) on key attributes, such as monthly premium, annual estimated cost, or star rating
Elimination-By-Aspects (EBA)	Successively eliminating plans that fail to meet a predetermined standard/cutoff value on one or more attributes until reaching a final choice [16]; e.g., a MPF user utilizes the 'Filter' by star rating function to eliminate plans rated with less than 3 stars
Majority of Confirming Dimensions (MCD)	Repeatedly comparing two alternatives at a time on key attributes through trade-offs until a winning alternative is finalized [17]; e.g., a MPF user repeatedly compares two plans at a time side-by-side to pick a winner by using the 'Add to Compare' function
Weighted Adding (WAD)	Comparing multiple alternatives (e.g., 3+) on multiple attributes simultaneously for value trade-offs in order to select an alternative with the highest total value [12]; e.g., a MPF user utilizes the 'Add to Compare' function to compare multiple plans (e.g., 3) from search results on key attributes to select a final plan

strategy), and then compare the remaining plans 2–3 at a time (i.e., the MCD strategy), they are able to review all relevant attributes across plans in a way that optimizes their time and cognitive faculties. However, many older adult users are unaware of or cannot locate appropriate MPF functions, which may lead to their under-utilization of diverse decision strategies convenient for Medicare plan decision optimization. Hence, applying the five common consumer decision strategies described in Table 1, this study seeks to answer the question *(RQ1), Which decision strategies are enacted by older users of the MPF during a Medicare plan selection task?*

2.3 Counselor Interventions

Medicare counselors help beneficiaries collect and streamline their health and financial information with the goal to find a plan that best suits beneficiary needs [20]. A previous study found that participants who used counseling assistance were almost twice as likely to switch to a new Medicare plan than those who did not receive assistance [21]. Although the assistance of Medicare counselors appears useful for users' making plan choices [21, 22], previous research has seldom examined the impacts of their facilitation on users' decision strategy utilization on the MPF. This study addresses this gap by answering *(RQ2), How do Medicare counselor interventions impact decision strategies employed by users?*

3   Method

An observational study was conducted during the 2019 Medicare open enrollment period with 29 older Medicare beneficiaries (65+ years old, 15 male and 14 female) recruited through flyers circulated in senior-serving agencies surrounding a southeastern university in the U.S. Participants were paired with a trained Medicare counselor to complete a plan selection task using the MPF on the Medicare.gov website. After counselors entered participants' prescription drug and pharmacy information in the MPF to pull up plan search results applicable to participants' information, the participants took over the computer and conducted the remaining plan selection task. Utilizing a think-aloud approach, participants were encouraged to speak their thoughts during the MPF task. Participants first took a moment to navigate the MPF and evaluate the plans on their own, and then were allowed to ask counselors for information or navigational guidance if needed. Upon being asked the first meaningful question (i.e., relevant to Medicare plan selection) from the participant, counselors were finally allowed to intervene by providing verbal guidance on MPF functions conducive to participants' optimal decision strategies. Text transcriptions of audio recorded participant-counselor conversations throughout task duration were coded using Atlas.ti, a qualitative data analysis program, to identify (1) the decision strategies used by participants and (2) the decision strategies intervened by counselors. Two coders independently performed the coding, with inter-coder agreement as 84.2% for user strategies and 89.7% for counselor-intervened strategies; any coder disagreements were resolved through negotiation.

4   Findings

4.1   Older MPF Users' Decision Strategies Prior to Counselor Intervention

Our data showed that prior to counselor intervention, seven participants were not using any decision strategy at all, meaning they were sitting idly or acted confused, while 19 participants were using a single strategy (see Table 2). The SAT strategy was used most frequently first ($f = 12$), meaning that participants were typically scrolling the initial search results page and examining one plan after another as they appeared; participants were attempting to choose any plan that met a minimum or acceptable criteria cutoff for attributes considered, with the goal to merely satisfy the task. The second most frequently used strategy was WAD ($f = 4$), where participants compared multiple plans across multiple plans at once mentally or by using the Add to Compare function. As previously discussed, both SAT and WAD decision strategies are the least optimal for efficient decision-making from a large choice set, yet both were revealed overwhelmingly at participants' task onset. The MCD strategy was used twice, followed by EBA which was used once, and no participant used LEX first.

Table 2. Decision strategies used by participants and intervened by counselors.

Decision strategy	No. of participants who used the strategy before counselor intervention	Counselor intervention			No. of participants who used the strategy at least once throughout decision-making process
		No. of times counselors promoted the strategy	No. of times counselors intervened to promote switching to the strategy from another strategy	No. of times the intervened strategy was adopted by participants	
No strategy	7				
LEX	0	29	26	13	11
SAT	12	23	17	9	18
EBA	1	19	15	7	12
MCD	2	26	21	15	20
WAD	4	12	9	7	12
SAT + EBA	2				
WAD + EBA	1				
Total	29	109	88	51	29

4.2 Impact of Counseling Decision Interventions

The analysis revealed that counselors promoted a decision strategy a total of 109 times throughout all decision tasks, 88 of which constituted interventions to facilitate participants to switch to a different strategy (see Table 2). LEX was the strategy most frequently promoted by counselors, followed by MCD, SAT, EBA, and WAD. When promoting the LEX strategy, counselors prompted participants for their single most important attribute to sort the initial plan search results by a simple cognitive strategy to streamline the decision process. Given WAD being the most cognitively exhausting strategy, it was least promoted through counselor interventions, as it would not be useful until the user's choice set was narrowed down to a relatively small number of plans. Of the 88 counselor attempts to switch participants' strategies, 51 (58%) successfully led to a strategy switch that counselors promoted (see Table 2). During the counselor-promoted switches, MCD and LEX were the most frequently adopted strategies, followed by SAT and EBA/WAD.

Counselor interventions also resulted in participants' increased utilization of multiple decision strategies throughout their task. Before counselor intervention, the average number of strategies used by participants was 0.86 strategies, with only three participants using a combination of two strategies, and no participants using more than two strategies (see Table 2). However, with counselors' intervention, the total number of unique decision strategies used by participants increased to an average of 2.52 strategies, with the majority of participants employing two strategies ($f = 15$), followed by three strategies ($f = 7$), four strategies ($f = 5$), and one strategy ($f = 2$). MCD was the most widely adopted strategy ($f = 20$) (see Table 2). Further, when participants used two or more strategies, they overwhelmingly had a tendency to use SAT first ($f = 16$) and MCD last ($f = 15$) (see Table 2).

5 Implications

This study demonstrates how older adults implement decision strategies during an e-healthcare decision task, specifically in the selection of a Medicare Prescription Drug plan, and how older users' decision strategies are impacted by human agents' real-time strategy interventions. Our findings reveal that many older users may not employ the most optimized decision strategy combinations for a Medicare plan selection if left without assistance. Our data reveal that older users often followed counselors' advice by implementing intervened decision strategies. Theoretically, our study is the first of its kind to apply decision strategies grounded in seminal decision theories to a Medicare context. This provision contributes not only to the extension of decision strategy research, but to the specific requisites of Medicare related decisions, which researchers have called for a simplification of presented plan information [22]. Further, contributions to the discourse of decision-making for older adults are provided. As the current body of literature reports studies centered around broad decision situations and older adults, our study extends this discussion to an important and complex healthcare situation. Not only does this provide insights on decisions where multiple attributes and alternatives are being considered, but it also addresses critical and high-risk healthcare needs. Importantly, our study demonstrates key findings that can be implemented in optimizing not only live counseling sessions, but the development of conversational artificial intelligence (AI) agent technologies to supplement human counselors, calling to a critical need [22]. Given the scarcity of trained counselors to the number of older adults that routinely make Medicare and other e-healthcare related choices [21], our study highlights the necessity of designing AI agents for healthcare decisions, addressing a gap in human-computer interaction literature that largely overlooks such contexts and aging populations, which may grossly benefit.

Acknowledgement. This project was supported by the Alabama Agricultural Experiment Station, the Hatch program of the National Institute of Food and Agriculture, U.S. Department of Agriculture, and the Auburn University Intramural Grant Program.

References

1. McWilliams, J.M., Afendulis, C.C., McGuire, T.G., Landon, B.E.: Complex medicare advantage choices may overwhelm seniors—especially those with impaired decision making. Health Aff. **30**(9), 1786–1794 (2011)
2. An overview of the Medicare Part D prescription drug benefit. https://www.kff.org/medicare/fact-sheet/an-overview-of-the-medicare-part-d-prescription-drug-benefit/. Accessed 23 Feb 2021
3. Hanoch, Y., Wood, S., Barnes, A., Liu, P.J., Rice, T.: Choosing the right Medicare prescription drug plan: the effect of age, strategy selection, and choice set size. Health Psychol. **30**(6), 719 (2011)
4. Sudore, R.L., et al.: Limited literacy and mortality in the elderly: the health, aging, and body composition study. J. Gener. Internal Med. **21**, 806–812 (2005)
5. Ardiale, E., Lemaire, P.: Within-item strategy switching: an age comparative study in adults. Psychol. Aging **27**(4), 1138–1151 (2012)
6. Besedeš, T., Deck, C., Sarangi, S., Shor, M.: Age effects and heuristics in decision making. Rev. Econ. Stat. **94**(2), 580–595 (2012)
7. Mata, R., von Helversen, B., Rieskamp, J.: Learning to choose: cognitive aging and strategy selection learning in decision making. Psychol. Aging **25**(2), 299–309 (2010)
8. Marzilli Ericson, K.M.: Consumer inertia and firm pricing in the medicare Part D prescription drug insurance exchange. Am. Econ. J. Econ. Pol. **6**(1), 38–64 (2014)
9. Abaluck, J., Gruber, J.: Choice inconsistencies among the elderly: evidence from plan choice in the medicare part D program. Am. Econ. Rev. **106**(12), 3962–3987 (2016)
10. Huffman, K.F., Upchurch, G.: The health of older Americans: a primer on Medicare and a local perspective. J. Am. Geriatr. Soc. **66**(1), 25–32 (2018)
11. Zhao, Y., Diggs, K., Chen, Z.X., Hohmann, N., Kwon, W.S., Westrick, S.C.: Qualitative exploration of factors influencing the plan selection process by medicare beneficiaries. J. Manag. Care Spec. Pharm. **27**(3), 339–353 (2021)
12. Payne, J.W., Bettman, J.R., Johnson, E.J.: The Adaptive Decision Maker. Cambridge University Press, New York (1993)
13. Bettman, J.R., Luce, M.F., Payne, J.W.: Constructive consumer choice processes. J. Consum. Res. **25**(3), 188–217 (1998)
14. Klein, M., Kranovich, M.: Changes to 2020 medicare plan finder. https://www.milliman.com/en/insight/changes-to-2020-medicare-plan-finder. Accessed 23 Mar 2021
15. Simon, H.A.: A behavioral model of rational choice. Quart. J. Econ. **69**, 99–118 (1955)
16. Tversky, A.: Elimination by aspects: a theory of choice. Psychol. Rev. **79**, 281–299 (1969)
17. Russo, J.E., Dosher, B.A.: Strategies for multiattribute binary choice. J. Exp. Psychol.: Learn. Mem. Cogn. **9**, 676–696 (1983)
18. Kahneman, D., Slovic, S.P., Slovic, P., Tversky, A. (eds.): Judgment Under Uncertainty: Heuristics and Biases. Cambridge University Press, Cambridge (1982)
19. Walsh, M.M., Anderson, J.R.: The strategic nature of changing your mind. Cogn. Psychol. **58**(3), 416–440 (2009)
20. Hohmann, L.A., Hastings, T.J., McFarland, S.J., Hollingsworth, J.C., Westrick, S.C.: Implementation of a medicare plan selection assistance program through a community partnership. Am. J. Pharm. Educ. **82**(9), 6452 (2018)

21. Han, J., Urmie, J.: Medicare part D beneficiaries' plan switching decisions and information processing. Med. Care Res. Rev. **75**(6), 721–745 (2018)
22. Zhou, C., Zhang, Y.: The vast majority of medicare part D beneficiaries still don't choose the cheapest plans that meet their medication needs. Health Aff. **31**(10), 2259–2265 (2012)

Design of Elderly Care Service in Rural Community with Mutual Assistance Mode—A Case Study of B Rural Community in A Town, Beijing

Yinan Zhang(✉), Wenjing Li, and Limin Wang

Beijing City University, Beijing, China

Abstract. Guided by the concept of mutual assistance mode, this paper designs a systematic service design scheme to resolve practical elderly care problems in rural communities, such as the sense of loneliness, low self-worth and monotonous lifestyles among the elderly. On the premise of keeping the basic lifestyle of the elderly in rural communities, multiple elderly care resources are integrated. Through mutual assistance and spontaneously participating community activities among the elderly, the inner vitality of the elderly in rural communities can be inspired; and then, the elderly can be taken cared and comforted within the mode of mutual assistance. Therefore, in such elderly care service system, the elderly will be transformed from being served to participants and contributors. It is hoped that the elderly will realize their self-worth as well as enhance their happiness.

Keywords: Rural communities · Mutual assistance · Service design · Spiritual needs

1 Background

By 2019, China's elderly over 65 years old has reached 175.99 million, in which rural elderly accounts for about 70% in the country's total elderly population. This indicates that China's rural areas are facing severe aging and elderly care problems. Through the analysis of the elderly care modes, it is found that the rural elderly care problem is complex and peculiar. Problems like complex age group, monotonous life styles, scattered systems, displacement of policies in rural elderly care service, all together aggravate the difficulty of rural elderly care.

At present, the most serious consequence of the laid-back elderly care service and a lack of family care is the suicide phenomenon among elderly in rural areas. According to the research data of Liu Yanwu[1], the number of suicides among the elderly in rural areas in the 1980s accounted for 24% of the total suicides number, while this proportion has increased to 79.19% from 2000 to 2010. The high suicide rate of the rural elderly

---

[1] Yanwu Liu. Suicide and Crisis Intervention in Rural Older Persons (1980–2009) [J]. Southern population. 2013, 28(2):57–64,56.

© Springer Nature Switzerland AG 2021
C. Stephanidis et al. (Eds.): HCII 2021, CCIS 1419, pp. 318–326, 2021.
https://doi.org/10.1007/978-3-030-78635-9_42

indicates that there is no suitable elderly care service provided to senior people. To solve the problem of rural elderly care, people should attach importance to the basic material needs as well as spiritual needs of the rural elderly, which means to fundamentally enhance the well-being of the rural elderly.

2 Current Situation of Elderly Care Service in Rural Areas of China

The construction of rural community elderly care mode should not only follow the national policy, but also take senior people's willingness and needs into accounts. In China, there are mainly four modes for the elderly care.

2.1 Home-Based Care Service Mode

In this mode, offspring or other family members shoulder the responsibility to take care of the elderly, including supplying materials and spiritual comfort. Currently, this mode is commonly found in rural areas.

2.2 Social Security-Based Care Mode

The social security-based mode mainly raise money from individual, collective and government way to ensure the life security of the elderly. But this mode is confined to requirements, senior people who are qualified to enjoy this mode does not have the legal dependent, lost their the labor ability and do not have stable income. Plus, unless the elderly come of a certain age, they cannot receive the pension.

2.3 Community Nursing Service Mode

The community becomes the carrier of senior people's living place, life style and leisure activities. It also provides the elderly with nursing resources for living, medical treatment and other services. In the process of social transformation in China, the function of the community is diversifying, and the community nursing service mode has gradually become an important supplement to the home-based care service mode.

2.4 Mutual Assistant Mode

In 2017, the Chinese government put forward the concept of rural mutual assistant elderly care service for the first time, which goes: giving full play to the role of the elderly organizations, to villagers' mutual assistant service organizations and to social service institutions; encouraging those high-mobility elderly to provide voluntary services to low-mobility elderly, and exploring to construct a voluntary-mutual assistant cycle mechanism. The core of mutual assistant mode lies in mutual aid service rather than placing infrastructure. Based on the reality, taking the population situation, elderly care resources, public facilities into accounts, the current rural mutual assistant care mode shall look for an appropriate mutual assistant elderly care service mode.

These four elderly care modes have their own pros and cons (the elderly care analysis in rural communities). By analyzing those four modes thoroughly, it is feasible to recommend a method that promotes mutual assistance elderly care mode and raises the awareness of rural elderly. Under the great pressure of the aging population in rural areas of China, handling the problem of caring the rural elderly will generate a positive and long-term impact on the stability of the whole society and the construction of the countryside (Table 1).

Table 1. The elderly care analysis in rural communities

Modes	Features	Advantage	Disadvantage
Home-based care service mode	Support by family members Material and spiritual comfort	Enjoy family warmth	Unable to meet the needs of the elderly when the family structure changes
Social security-based care mode	Provide minimum pension Multi-faceted support by the collective and the state	Sharing Home-based care burden	Difficulties in fund-raising, and the payment is not timely
Community nursing service mode	Community provides a variety of resources for the elderly	Multi-level/multi-faceted services	Many rural communities do not have the complete service facilities
Mutual assistant mode	Mutual aid service Based on the reality	Awaken the vitality of the elderly	Failure to achieve service goals when service awareness is backward

3   Current Situation of B Rural Community in a Town of Beijing

3.1   B Community Situation and Elderly Care Mode Analysis

In total, there are three phases for B community in A Town, Beijing. There are more than 2100 residents, of which 268 are over 65 years old, accounting for about 13% of the total population of the community. Through the preliminary investigation and the visiting to the elderly over 65, it is found that the current elderly care mode is the traditional home-based nursing care mode, and the community nursing care mode is the supplementary.

B community elderly care services mainly cover life care, health care, recreation and basic education activities. According to the survey, the elderly cannot select those service freely. In other words, needs from the elderly cannot be met timely. In addition, the content of community nursing care service can only meet the shallow demand of the elderly; while the in-depth demand, that is psychological and spiritual needs, are calling for continuing improvements.

3.2 Investigations and Interviews

With a preliminary understanding of the basic family situation of the elderly in community B, 180 elderly people were interviewed and invited to fill out questionnaires. Then 30of those elderly people who are over 65 were selected to conduct in-depth interviews so as to better understand the elderly living habits, daily activities, living conditions and so on. Based on the generated data and in-depth interviews, features among the elderly in the community B are summarized as follows:

- A sense of low self-worth
  The elderly in different situations may gradually lose their personal and social value with the increase of age. Some elderly farmers can only take care of their grandchildren at home after the land has been expropriated; some low-educated elderly people have difficulties in learning electronic products and then may be left behind in the intelligent age.
- The growing loneliness among the elderly
  Due to the special geographical location of community B, which locates on the edge of urban areas. Some young people move to urban areas for their career plans. The number of empty-nesters, those who live alone and those who have been left behind is increasing. Without the company from family members, people in this special elderly group may lose their spiritual sustenance. Then the elderly feel even more lonely and are often in bad moods.
- Dull life with monotonous activities
  The life of 80% elderly people in community is relatively fixed. Their daily activities are mostly around the family. In the conversation with them, it is found that activities organized by the community are monotonous and they hardly have multiple choices. Hence, the participation rate is low and they gradually lost interest in community activities.

Based on the above analysis, Summarize the key points of the design of the B community mutual assistance elderly care service system:

- Material needs
  The government provides policy support, financial support, and public facilities; the society provides medical security, voluntary services, and life care services; the community integrates multiple elderly care resources to provide elderly care services for the elderly in the community.
- spiritual needs
  With the support of the government, society, and family, the community provides emotional sustenance and spiritual filling for the elderly in the community through mutual assistance activities.

On the basis of making full use of local government, community resources and social resources. It is hoped to combine current resources with healthy and active elderly people in the community so as to form a mutual assistant nursing care system with warmth (Fig. 1).

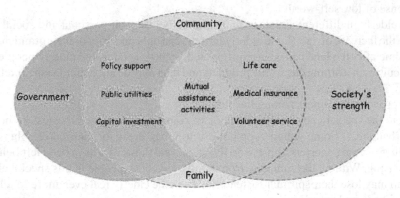

Fig. 1. Key designing points in mutual assistant care service in Community B

4 Design of Mutual Assistant Elderly Care System for Rural Community B in Town A, Beijing

4.1 User Research

From the user portrait I and II, we can see that the elderly are inclined to have the negative emotion of loneliness, the low self-esteem that they can do nothing, and the psychological burden caused by health problems. At the same time, it is expected to increase more community elderly activities, provide community psychological counseling, to enhance the self-worth of the elderly through mutual help etc. (Figs. 2 and 3).

Fig. 2. User portrait1   **Fig. 3.** User portrait II

4.2 User Journey Analysis

After understanding the user's sore point, the mutual contact point between the "help" receiver and the "helped" giver can be found so as to lay a foundation for the mutual assistance elderly care service system:

- Life Care: The elderly who can move flexibly can help those low-mobility to do chores.
- Community activities: Encouraging the elderly to join activities so as to increase interactions and communications, therefore, it is expected to improve vitality and self-esteem among the elderly.
- Education activities: The elderly with strong learning abilities can help those with weaker learning abilities to master electronic products etc. (Figs. 4 and 5).

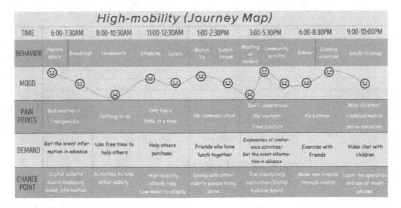

Fig. 4. User schedule

4.3 Blueprint for Mutual Assistant Care

In this design, the elderly population of rural communities will be divided according to their abilities. They are divided into different mutual assistant groups according to their

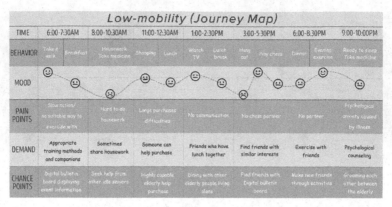

Fig. 5. User schedule2

different abilities. Community committees, social work organizations, volunteers and other elderly care resources will support the community mutual assistant groups (Figs. 6 and 7).

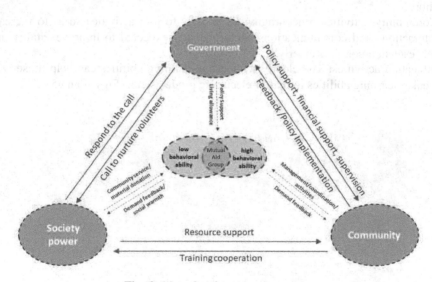

Fig. 6. Mutual assistant service system

In the serving process, the staff will guide the junior elderly with high-mobility to take the initiative to help and accompany the senior with low-mobility. Secondly, according to different interests and strengths of them, the staff will help the elderly to organize activities to plan cultural and recreational activities. In addition, through publicity, it is hoped to encourage more elderly people to participate in community activities (Fig. 8).

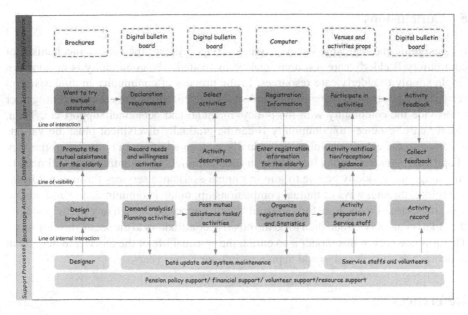

Fig. 7. Service blueprint

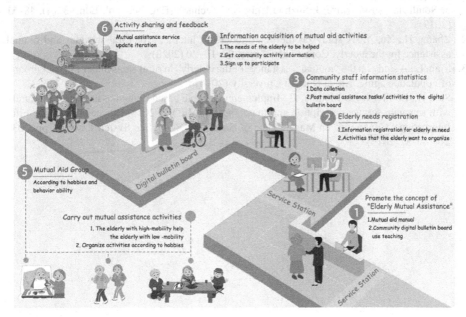

Fig. 8. Service flows

5 Conclusions

By designing the mutual assistant nursing service system, the supply mechanism of community B elderly care resources can be innovated. The community is no longer a single supply of elderly care resources. In the process of community mutual assistant service; the government, community and social organizations can cooperate altogether to provide the community with the policy, financial and personnel support etc. Then, elderly care resources to community B can be gradually diversified; plus, the various needs from the elderly can also be gradually met. In addition, in response to the lack of spiritual activities among the elderly in rural communities, communities still need to encourage more elderly people to join in mutual assistance services through publicity. Therefore, through ways of mutual companionship, mutual communication and mutual care; the elderly can be transformed from "being supported" to actively participating in the elderly care service and then to be the positive contributors to the social development. The ultimate goal of this model is to enrich the spiritual life of the elderly, to help them to achieve self-worth and to add happiness in their senior years.

References

1. Zhang, Y., Wang, Y.: A study on the model of mutual assistance and pension in rural areas of South Jiangsu Province. J. Suzhou Univ. Sci. Technol. (Eng. Technol. Edn.) **32**(4), 48–51 (2019)
2. Zhang, H., Xu, Y.: A study on the new model of "internet" for rural wisdom and mutual assistance for the elderly. Comments Observ. **02**, 19–20 (2020)
3. Man, L.: A study on the "mutual assistance for the elderly" in rural areas under the background of population aging. Xihua Normal University (2016)
4. Sun, H., De Florio, V., Blondia, C.: Implementing a role based mutual assistance community with semantic service description and matching. In: MEDES 2013: Proceedings of the Fifth International Conference on Management of Emergent Digital Eco Systems, no. 10, pp. 203–210. ACM (2013)

Design Case Studies

Product Meaning-Making in High-Tech Companies: A Case Study of DJI Drones

Lin Cheng[⊠]

Institute for Design Innovation, Loughborough University London, London, UK
L.Cheng-20@student.lboro.ac.uk

Abstract. The aim of this paper is to investigate how the product meaning is actually constructed in high-tech companies. The research method is based on the Circuit of Culture model, a closed loop of five main cultural processes as defined by Du Gay et al. [1], to analyse DJI drones from five perspectives. The findings of this case show that high-tech firms rely on innovation of technologies for producing the meanings. The conclusion of this paper is that technological innovation, in terms of high-tech enterprises, is the main method to acquire and consolidate users, especially in new technology field, then, through consumers' social practices to produce symbolic mean-ings, which further develop the meanings of products. This case study em-phasises the technological in-novation plays an important role for product meaning-making in high-tech enterprises and analyses how technology af-fects the formation of product culture and meaning.

Keywords: Technological innovation · Product meaning · Product culture

1 Introduction

Consumers are increasingly valuing the cultural meaning of products. "Meaning-making," define by Du Gay et al., is a creative-oriented approach to generate symbolic mean- ing towards products, services, and brands [1]. However, many still use "meaning-mak- ing" as a buzzy word, it is unclear that how the principles of meaning-making can con- tribute to shaping products' cultural value. High-tech companies refer to those enter- prises gain profit and growth through new and rapidly developing technology. The pa- per analyses DJI drones to research how high-tech companies complete their product meaning-making by the Circuit of Culture. The Circuit of Culture is a closed loop con- sisting of five main cultural processes, namely Representation, Identity, Production, Consumption and Regulation, and defined by Du Gay et al. [1] as shown in Fig. 1. Although each of the five elements will be analysed separately in this paper, in fact, they are correlate, so that they have to be understood as a whole.

C. Stephanidis et al. (Eds.): HCII 2021, CCIS 1419, pp. 329–336, 2021.
https://doi.org/10.1007/978-3-030-78635-9_43

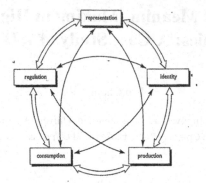

Fig. 1. The Circuit of culture (Du Gay et al., 1997).

2 Analysis

It is essential to define whether the DJI drone is cultural or not, otherwise, the analysis may not be meaningful. Because when a product is cultural, it could be meaningful. Du Gay et al. state that a product can be identified as cultural in five aspects: 1) Whether it is constructed as a meaningful entity that can be discussed, thought about and imagined; 2) Whether it is associated with the social practices of particular culture and lifestyles; 3) Whether it connects with a certain group of people and places; 4) Whether it is given a social identity; 5) Whether it is represented to media of communicate or visual languages [1].

A simple judgement is based on the above five conditions. Firstly, when people discuss topic of the drone, DJI is a brand that cannot avoid, as well as immediately conjure up images of users controlling drones and the concept of a 'flying camera'. Secondly, due to the growth of independent media, the market for consumer-grade drones has been expended and many self-media people use their drones to film and share their lives. Thirdly, many technological enthusiasts, photographers, self-media people and hobbyists are big fans of DJI's drones which are found frequently in cities, rural areas, tourist attractions and schools. Finally, DJI drone is an international brand as product technical advantages and a large number of videos and images taken with DJI drones are being shared on the Internet. So DJI drones are indeed cultural and meaningful.

2.1 Representation

Du Gay et al. point out that the term culture has two meanings- "culture as 'whole way of life' and culture as 'the production and circulation of meaning'" [1]. Therefore, in Representation, there are two points will be discussed: meanings and lifestyles. As for how people give meanings to DJI's drones will be analysed in detail in the next section Identity. As regards the meanings of product, advertising is one of the main methods to construct contemporary identities [2]. Similarly, Slater founds that advertising makes consumers create demand for commodities to solve some personal problem [3]. So, the following will be an analysis of what DJI's drones are trying to represent through its advertisements. Advertisements of DJI drones can be classified three types.

Product Introduction Type. This type of advertisement focuses on the functions of product. Expressing the cutting edge technology and technological innovation of DJI's drones, which is the basis of DJI's products culture. Figure 2 is a screenshot from the DJI - This Is Mavic Air 2, the link is https://www.youtube.com/watch?v=IwoyGb-NWDs& t=21s.

Fig. 2. This Is Mavic Air 2 (DJI, 2020).

Showpiece Type. These advertisements show videos shot with DJI drones and are focused on the performance of the product. DJI drone user's passion for the outdoors, life, nature and challenges is expressed. Figure 3 is a screenshot from the DJI World – The Story of Aisholpan, the link is https://www.youtube.com/watch?v=CFk8XWKDtkA.

Fig. 3. The story of Aisholpan (DJI, 2017).

Storytelling Type. This type of video is created by filmmakers shooting the drone and focuses on the consumer's evaluation of the product, meanwhile express the sincere and quirky minds of DJI drone users and share a 'different world'. Figure 4 is a screenshot from the DJI Profiles - Time is Fluid film, the link is https://www.youtube.com/watch?v=pQvGrLKSMfU.

Fig. 4. Time is fluid (DJI, 2017).

On the other hand, although drones have not 'bred' a new way of life, they have enhanced and changed parts of people's lifestyles. This view is supported by Du Gay et al. who writes that contemporary, postmodern culture is dominated by images. The basis of these visual cultures is those countless images and videos, recorded by lens, which are typeset, cropped and retouched into newspapers, posters, photographs, newspapers, films, television and videos [1]. Drones have enriched the language of the lens description, with a large number of aerial and overhead shots appearing in various visual expressions. Photographers, self-media people and even amateur photographers, for example, are willing to add drones to their travel kit because the view from a drone is not what human can do with their eyes. Simply put, the conventional photography equipment makes it difficult to record overhead moving views and drones can extend their lenses, which not only shows drones use value, but demonstrates DJI's concept of seeing the world from a different perspective.

2.2 Identity

Viktor Frankl states that people can discover meaning through doing a deed, experiencing a value, and experiencing suffering [4]. So what do consumers do with their drones? The applications of DJI's drones could be broadly classified into three types of consumer, professional and corporate and agricultural. These three types correspond to three client groups respectively.

The consumer level drones (Fig. 5) targets at amateur photographers who use drones to enrich their spare time, for example, to record travel photos and videos or simply as a toy, for them the DJI drone works in the entertainment, leisure and fashion.

In terms of the professional level (Fig. 6), the user group is more complex than the other two types. There are some enthusiasts who choose the professional level drones not for work but pursuing product performances; Others who has an immediate need for work, such as film making. For this segment of customer, drones are essential equipment to express their thoughts better.

For corporate and agricultural level (Fig. 7), this category is likely to be purchased by large companies that use drones for, such as, resource surveying, leak detection. So for them, drones are supplementary tools to improve efficiency and reduce risk to employees.

Fig. 5. Phantom 4 Pro V2.0 (DJI, 2018).

Fig. 6. Inspire 2 (DJI, 2016).

Fig. 7. Matrice 300 RTK (DJI, 2020).

2.3 Production

Production is not only the manufacturing process but involves' 'all forms of conscious intervention in the organisation, execution, distribution and circulation of goods and services' [5]. Thus, this section focuses on the cultural perspective of drone production. Furthermore, because of the subtle association between Production and Consumption, the influence of Consumption on the Production of DJI drones will be discussed.

Production in Culture. Each new technology can generate and replicate existing cultures and 'breed' its own culture [1]. Through the research and development of flight control technology, gimbal technology, obstacle avoidance algorithm, vision algorithm and map transmission technology, DJI has integrated low power consumption, intelligent flight control, stable gimbal technology and comprehensive image solution, excellent intelligent obstacle avoidance system into a drone. All of the above mentioned DJI's independent technologies are in the leading international position, which is the product culture of DJI's technology innovation mentioned in the Representation section.

While DJI is constructing its own brand culture, it is extending its product catalogue, including gimbal cameras (Fig. 8), gimbals (Fig. 9) and stabilisers (Fig. 10), so that the entire DJI photography product chain had been completing. In the same vein, Oswald in her book notes 'indicates that the double-axis structure of brand discourse contributes to the brand's long-term value and growth' [6].

Fig. 8. Gimbal camera zenmuse X7 (DJI, 2017).

Fig. 9. OM 4 (DJI, 2020).

Fig. 10. RS 2 (DJI, 2020).

Production and Consumption. The Production and Consumption of a product must be associated if it is to be fully understood and have social significance [1]. In terms of the DJI drone's market and consumer base, personally, it is aimed at photography enthusiasts, professional photographers or self-media people. In terms of enterprises and companies, it targets on various resource companies (e.g. oil and gas, power and land surveying) and government administration services (e.g. fire and rescue). For them, the most important things for drones are the products of quality, stability and low failure rates. As regards internationally, it has broken the stereotype of Chinese companies attracting consumers with cheap prices and instead conquered the market with high quality products. The most typical example of this is probably the continued suppression to DJI by the US government that continues to increase taxes on DJI products, making their price far more expensive than the American brand 3D Robotics. However, 3D Robotics is still unable to gain a larger market share and more customers in the USA, which is due to the maturity and leadership of DJI's drone technology.

2.4 Consumption

Both the poor and the rich, as consumers, tend to consume products that have a 'status' value rather than just a 'use value' [1]. In addition, Oswald further explains the 'identity' value that brands satisfy consumers' emotional needs for relationships, identity and self-identity, thus making consumers' brand-seeking behaviour known as symbolic consumption [6]. Then symbolic consumer behaviours of DJI drones were summarised and found that is in accord with Oswald's three symbolic purpose of products: 1) Customers create meaning with products. 2) Products are considered by others as significant status or identity symbols. 3) Clients' self-symbolism is extended [6].

2.5 Regulation

In human history, there were no flying objects like drones that were relatively low cost and could be operated by the general public, so new policies were introduced to deal with civilian drones in different countries and regions. In China, if you would like to fly the drone in some cities with air bases, you need to apply to the government in advance.

In the USA, the FFA (Federal Aviation Administration) states that there are currently (2007) no altitude restrictions, but specific authority is required to fly within national airspace [7]. The EU introduced a new policy related to drones in 2018 to ensure civil aviation safety and environmental protection [8].

While governments have introduced policies to regulate drones, questions have also been raised about the privacy and ethical problems of drones which invades private space. So, what is public space? What is private space? What are the differences between them? There are differences between public and private space in both material and symbolic aspects, material in terms of the relative difference in space (e.g. office and home) and symbolic in terms of the different things (e.g. collective and rational things versus personal and sensual things). This is because manoeuvrable high mobility of drones coupled with high performance cameras make it easy to invade from public to private space, for example, long-range surveillance and tracking.

3 Conclusion

Each part of Circuit of Culture has different responses to DJI drones, broadly speaking, it finds that the DJI drone 'bred' its own culture and is endowed meanings. These meanings are composed of two parts: use value and 'identity' value. First of all, the pivotal technology generates the use value of the product. Then, its identities and representation are reflected in society through public activities and practices, which grants the commodity could be given symbolic meanings. So the use value of a product is generated when it is used, in contrast with the 'identity' value which takes a process. Furthermore, in terms of high-tech enterprises, technological innovation is the main method to acquire and consolidate users, especially in new technology field, then, through consumers' social practices to produce symbolic meanings, which further develop the meanings of products.

References

1. Du Gay, P., et al.: Doing Cultural Studies : the Story of the Sony Walkman (1997)
2. Mathur, N. (ed.): Consumer Culture. Modernity and Identity, London, Sage (2014)
3. Slater, D.: Consumer Culture and Modernity. Polity (1999)
4. Frankl, V.: Man's Search for Meaning (1985)
5. Julier, G.: The Culture of Design. Sage (2013)
6. Oswald, L.: Doing Semiotics: A Research Guide for Marketers at the Edge of Culture. Doing Semiotics. Oxford Scholarship Online (2020). https://doi.org/10.1093/oso/9780198822028.003.0001
7. Dolan, A.M., Thompson, R.M.: Integration of drones into domestic airspace: Selected legal issues. Domestic Drones: Elements and Considerations for the U.S., pp. 1–41 (2014)
8. Bassi, E.: European drones regulation: Today's legal challenges. In: 2019 International Conference on Unmanned Aircraft Systems, ICUAS 2019, pp. 443–450 (2019). https://doi.org/10.1109/ICUAS.2019.8798173.

Developing a Parametric System for Pointe Shoe Customization

Marilena Christodoulou[1]([✉]) [iD], Isidro Navarro Delgado[1]([✉]) [iD],
and Pau de Solà-Morales[2]([✉]) [iD]

[1] Polytechnic University of Catalonia, Barcelona, Spain
{marilena.christodoulou,isidro.navarro}@upc.edu
[2] Universitat Autonoma de Barcelona, Barcelona, Spain
pau.solamorales@eina.cat

Abstract. The objective of this study is to define the parameters that need to be considered while designing a pointe shoe and using a graphical algorithm editor, to prove that a parametric system could be developed for designing and making pointe shoes that will be adaptable to all feet.

In the old days, the shoemakers would design and make the shoes for each person individually. Later on, with the mass production this became impossible. However, the new technologies nowadays, allow us to have a production of non-normalized repetitive components directly from the digital data. This realization leads to the idea of a project that is the functional customization of the Pointe Shoes in order to help the user, reach the highest level of performance.

A Pointe Shoe is worn by ballet dancers while performing the dancing technique called "en pointe". However, pointe work causes pain, blisters, calluses, and disfigurement of the feet. Dancers, pointe shoe fitters, and podiatrists agree that finding shoes which fit correctly and adjust throughout your career could help to avoid feet injuries. The different parts of the shoe require different performance, depending on the different parts of the foot. Each dancer has particular feet, with variations of toe length and shape, arch flexibility, and mechanical strength. Instead of having the dancer's feet adjusted on the point shoes, the idea is to have the shoes, uniquely "adapt" according to the morphology of the feet. The foot is not just a passive weight-bearer, it must assume positions and execute movements beyond its normal limits. Therefore, the parameters to take in account are classified in anatomical, mechanical, assembly and material.

From the study, it is deduced that the above parameters may be the key to define a proposal for a solution to the design of Pointe shoe.

Keywords: Parametric design · Algorithm · Mass customization

1 Introduction

1.1 Related Work

Until now, in mass production systems, the consumer/user remained anonymous, as well as their personalized needs. The aim of companies was to sell as much standardized

C. Stephanidis et al. (Eds.): HCII 2021, CCIS 1419, pp. 337–342, 2021.
https://doi.org/10.1007/978-3-030-78635-9_44

products as possible, in this case shoes, without getting to know the user, their needs, or demands (Boër and Dulio 2007). One of the advantages of parametric design and digital fabrication is that the manufacturer can have a direct link with the anatomical and aesthetic demands of the user, opening up new possibilities for product customization. Mass customization is about producing goods with a high degree of personalization with near industrial efficiencies. Many footwear companies are moving towards the future by experimenting and trying to get closer to satisfying consumer needs using contemporary technology and adjusting to new design techniques.

For example, New Balance have collaborated with Nervous System in order to develop 3D-printing midsoles for running shoes. The innovation of this design stands behind the introduction of underfoot pressure data from runners as the parameter for the design of the midsole. In this way, the designers are able to generate variations of the cushioning density, allowing them to customize the way that a runner performs.

These midsoles, instead of a uniform foam, form a structure that can be adapted to the performance data of different runners. The basic data used, is the pressure data from a foot strike by the user, that is recorded by a grid of sensors under the foot, demonstrating the force as the foot hits the ground and pushes off over time. Nervous System, instead of dealing with structural optimization, decided to create a platform that allowed them to experiment with variables that would respond to the data in several ways. Dealing with the midsole as a foam structure was one of the approaches that they followed. Their idea was to develop a foam structure that would perform as a natural foam structure. Moreover, their idea was to create an anisotropic, macroscopic foam structure that would be controlled according to the running data, with its geometry to be adapted to different forces (Gibson et al. 2015).

In addition, since 2015, Adidas has been working on their 'Futurecraft' project, introducing the future in sports footwear, with the ambition that customers, in a few years, will be able to enter an Adidas store, run on a treadmill, and leave the store with an instantly 3D-printed shoe. Futurecraft is an open-source collaboration and craftsmanship that consists of a series of 3D-printed prototypes of a running shoe midsole that tries to imitate a runner's footprint. Scanning a runner's foot, getting his footprint and pressure points, would allow every athlete to have his midsoles personalized in order to help him reach their peak performance. A customized midsole requires a cushioning with a variation of properties that can be adapted to the needs of every athlete and to his anatomical characteristics. Using a mixture of UV curable resin and polyurethane, they were able to print a midsole with a variation of lattice structures in the heel and forefoot in such a way that it responds to the different cushioning needs.

1.2 Innovation

Following a centuries' tradition, point shoe making process it's an artisanal craftsmanship. With the exception of Gaynor Minden that in the last years started introducing machines in a specific part of the manufacturing process, pointe shoe making industries work with specialized, trained and hard to replace, artisans. The need for modernizing also stands for the material that is being used. The traditional pointe shoes' section, answers to cardboard, paste, burlap, little nails, and even newspaper (Barringer and

Schlesinger 2004). On the other hand, customized point shoes it is not an option for the majority of dancers.

The integration of digital technologies in the designing process, as well as the digital fabrication in the manufacturing process, implies the introduction of new materials. The objective of this investigation is to try and implement digital design and manufacturing to the pointe shoe making process, opening in this way the door for redefining the design, ergonomics and comfort of the shoe. The use of 3D scanning technology and parametric it's an important part of the investigation, as it will allow to personalize the design of the shoe for every individual according to his/her anatomical characteristics or even, personal taste.

2 Methodology

The first part of our investigation it is concentrated on the geometrical aspect of the problem. Using 3D scanning technology and the theoretical background related to foot and dancing anatomy, we defined the geometrical variables that need to be taken in account while designing a pointe shoe and its specific parts (see Fig. 1).

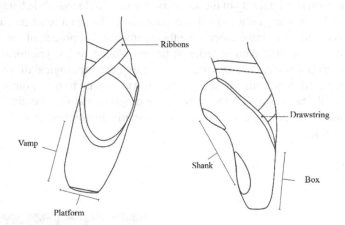

Fig. 1. Anatomy of the traditional pointe shoe.

A 3D scanner can give us an exact 3D model of any object, that's why scanning different types of feet was very helpful in order to have a more complete topological analysis. This analysis helped us to define better the variables for developing the parametric system. The 3D models of the scanning were also used for the development of the parametric system. For the 3D scanning we used a Structure Sensor connected to a computer along with the software SKANECT (see Fig. 2).

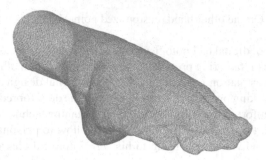

Fig. 2. 3D scanned right foot in pointe position.

Five women's feet were scanned. Three of them were dancers and two of them have never danced in their lives. Scans were done with a naked foot, pointed as much as possible. In order for the scan to be done, the structure sensor had to be rotated 360 degrees around the foot to accomplishing the best result possible. It has to be noted that a pointed foot, depending on the physical characteristics of each person, modifies some of the basic dimensions of the shape of the foot. For example, the width length of the foot, depending on the flexibility of the metatarsals can be reduced while being on pointe positions. For that reason, a scan was also done with the feet in a relax position.

The defined variables, only concerning the geometrical approach of the study were translated into measurable data in order to be introduced to the graphical algorithm editor. These variables were fundamental for building the topological diagram of each foot (see Fig. 3). After defining these variables, it was crucial to map points of the foot so that they could be considered for drawing the diagram and thus be able to take the measurements. These points, corresponded to a specific anatomical part of the foot.

These variables are:

- Foot Length
- Arch of the foot

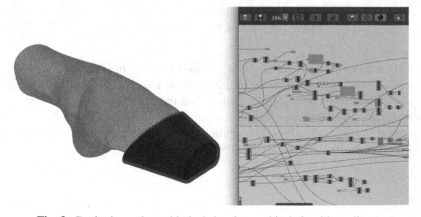

Fig. 3. Designing a shoe with the help of a graphical algorithm editor.

- Heel width
- Foot width
- Toe type
- Toe Length

The designing of a shoe using a graphical algorithm editor was made in parts because each part of the shoe has different requirements as per performance and needs to support a different part of the foot. Pointe shoe making process is an artisanal craftsmanship working with the same materials for at least two centuries. In this project, it was very crucial to study and understand the performance of the traditional materials with the purpose of understanding their properties and be able to propose new materials. One of the advantages of the digital era is that you can link human data to the design and manufacturing. 3D printing as an addictive manufacturing process, allows us to transform digitally developed 3D models into physical objects (see Fig. 4).

Fig. 4. 3D printed prototype using PLA filament

For that reason, most of the parts of the shoe, 3D printing was proposed as a fabricating process. The different requirements of the different parts of the shoe need different material properties. For some parts (for example the box) we used PLA filament because the box it's the part of the shoe that need to be strong for supporting the whole body. In other parts of the shoe (for example the inside cushioning) we used TPU filament that is a much more flexible material.

3   Conclusions

The scanning provided us with a 3D mesh that we were able to import in a 3D software and work with a proper 3D model in order to get the right dimensions. After that, were able to develop a parametric system, depending on the geometry of each foot. The samples we got from the scanning, though, only gave us information for a very few foot typologies. Future work could be done scanning more feet, maybe up to 100, from different ages and maybe even from male dancers. The prototyping was focused mainly on additive manufacturing and only on two types of materials. Future investigation, should be focused on trying a bigger variation of materials and maybe introduce other ways of digital fabrication. Overall, even though the parameter of the applied forces were taken in account while designing the shoe, they were not calculated. A study should be done on how the system could be further developed adding the applied forces while the shoe is being used also as a parameter.

References

Au, S.: Ballet and Modern Dance, 3rd edn. Thames & Hudson Ltd., London (2012)

Barringer, J., Schlesinger, S.: The Pointe Book, 3rd edn. Princeton Book Company, Pennington (2004)

Barringer, J., Schlesinger, S.: The PointeBook: Shoes, Training and Technique. Princeton Book Company, Pennington (1991)

Boër, C.R., Dulio, S.: Mass Customization and Footwear: Myth, Salvation or Reality? A Comprehensive Analysis of the Adoption of the Mass Customization Paradigm in Footwear, from the Perspective of the EUROShoE (Extended User Oriented Shoe Enterprise) Research Project. Springer, London Limited (2007)

Chatfield, S.J.: Kinesiology and Medicine for Dance, January 1993

Clifton, G.: The Coefficient of Friction of the Pointe Shoe and Implications for Current Manufacturing Processes, Senior Seminar in Dance, Fall (2009)

Gibson, I., Rosen, D., Stucker, B.: Additive Manufacturing Technologies, 2nd edn. Springer, New York (2015). https://doi.org/10.1007/978-1-4939-2113-3

Haas, G.J.: Dance Anatomy: Your Illustrated Guide to Improving Flexibility, Muscular Strength and Tone. Human Kinetics (2010)

Johnson, S.: Emergence: The Connected Lives of Ants, Brains, Cities and Software. Penguin Books (2002)

Klenerman, L., Bernard, W.: The Human Foot: A Companion to Clinical Studies. Springer, London (2006)

da Costa, L., Hentschel, P., Sacco, I.C.N.: Biomechanical Approach to Ballet Movements: A Preliminary Study, January 2009

Simmel, L.: Dance Medicine in Practice: Anatomy, Injury Prevention, Training. Routledge, Taylor & Francis Group (2014)

Spahiu, T., Galantucci, L.M., Piperi, E.: 3D Low Cost Scanning Systems for Extracting Foot Dimensions, November 2015

Spahiu, T., Piperi, E., Grimmelsmann, N., Ehrmann, A.: On the possible use of 3D printing for clothing and shoe manufacture. In: Conference Paper, November 2016

Sun, L.S.: Accessing Axis (3D Printed Fashion), November 2014

Tang, Y.M., Hui, K.-C.: Human foot modeling towards footwear design. Computer-Aided Design, December 2011

D'Arcy, W.T.: On Growth and Form. Dover Publications, Inc., New York (2010)

Design of Intelligent Household Mushroom Cultivation Equipment

Cheng Huang and Wei Yu[✉]

College of Art Design and Media, East China University of Science and Technology,
Shanghai, China
weiyu@ecust.edu.cn

Abstract. The COVID-19 epidemic disrupted the normal order of global social operation, and also caused a great impact on people's outlook on life, nature, ecology and health, which triggered people's collective reflection, regression and even reconstruction of their thinking mode, cognitive mode and behavior mode. The resulting concepts of life first, harmony between man and nature, health have given new thoughts to design activities. This research will be based on the above background, guided by the concept of green ecological design and healthy living, the optimization design of indoor living space as the goal, ecological interaction as the innovation point, and relying on the expression form of indoor micro-landscape product design, and finally help people to have friendly interaction with nature, environment and products, and achieve harmonious coexistence of life community. Because edible fungi are rich in edible, nutritious and ornamental value, this paper takes domestic edible fungi planting equipment as the starting point of micro-landscape product design, studies and analyzes the planting conditions and methods of edible fungi, the needs and behaviors of users, the use environment, functions, structure, use mode, ergonomics and ecological interaction mode of planting equipment, and then designs a domestic edible fungi planting equipment. Taking this as a bridge, we can realize the collision between micro-landscape and people's thinking and emotion, and Imitate the unity of man and nature of the ancients, and conform to the current form of the times.

Keywords: Intelligent planting · Edible fungi · Micro-landscape · Ecological interaction

1 Introduction

1.1 Research Background

The ultimate benchmark of all civilizations, the final balance of human right and wrong, depends on the promise of survival that the mountains and rivers can give. The global climate anomaly, the fire in Amazon rain forest, the break of Antarctic glacier, the deadly heat wave, Ebola raging in Africa, nature is warning us in his way, but we didn't pay attention to it, until this worldwide COVID-19 epidemic is closely related to each of us.

From a painful experience. In the post-epidemic era, we began to rethink.

© Springer Nature Switzerland AG 2021
C. Stephanidis et al. (Eds.): HCII 2021, CCIS 1419, pp. 343–350, 2021.
https://doi.org/10.1007/978-3-030-78635-9_45

The ecological view of the unity of man and nature and the health view of the supremacy of life have become the theme of the times. As a higher intelligent creature selected by nature, human beings should know clearly that we belong to a part of nature, and society also belongs to an extension of nature, and we are nature. We have the obligation to take part in the evolution of nature carefully, to fear nature and life, and to realize the friendly symbiosis between people and people, people and nature.

Living at home during the epidemic period has given people more time to examine happiness at home, and the needs of smart lifestyle and aesthetics of life at home have become prominent. The home industry has ushered in a critical period of digital transformation revolution.

In the era of great health, people's health awareness is soaring, and the health care industry is gaining momentum. In the future, people will be more willing to pay for health, especially put forward higher requirements for food safety, and pay more attention to healthy diet, reasonable collocation, adequate nutrition and freshness.

1.2 Research Contents

This study will focus on the ecological system composed of people and environment, medium environment, micro environment, utensils and things, take the green ecological design and healthy living concept as the guide, take the optimization design of indoor living space as the goal, take ecological interaction as the innovation point, and rely on the expression form of indoor micro-landscape product design, and finally help people, nature, environment and products to carry out friendly interaction in indoor micro-landscape environment, so as to achieve harmonious symbiosis of the living community.

Edible fungi, as a good health product, has edible value, nutritional value and aesthetic value. Moreover, edible fungi have higher requirements on planting conditions, and it is difficult for ordinary families to plant them. Based on the above characteristics, this study will take the domestic edible fungi planting equipment as the breakthrough point, and discuss the expression form of indoor micro-landscape related product design. Using edible fungi to decorate the courtyard balcony, beautify the living environment, and harvest certain labor achievements will gradually become a new fashion for people to enjoy healthy life, optimize the home environment and experience farming civilization.

2 Design Strategy Research

A new micro-ecological innovative design idea of "diet+ecology+ micro-landscape+smart home" can be constructed by integrating healthy living with four elements: diet structure, green ecological design, micro-landscape design based on edible fungi, and smart home design. It provides necessary basis for subsequent design practice.

2.1 Healthy Living and Diet Structure

In the era of great health, the concept of human wealth has been reshuffled, and health demands have become the first. The 21st century is destined to be a century in which health and life receive unprecedented attention. Health is closely related to daily habits, diet, work and rest, exercise and psychology. Among them, the concept of nutrition and diet is particularly prominent.

There are many kinds of edible fungi. Since ancient times, they have been called the holy products of health care because of their high edible value and nutritional and medicinal value. Studies have found that edible fungi have good pharmacological effects in anti-tumor, cardiovascular system protection, anti-oxidation and gastrointestinal protection [1]. Because of its particularity in color, shape and growth habit, edible fungi also have high aesthetic value [2].

Common edible fungi include mushrooms, fungus, straw mushrooms, etc., while the more valuable edible fungi include tricholoma matsutake, ganoderma lucidum, hericium erinaceus, truffle, etc. Understanding the growth characteristics and nutritional structure of different strains and embedding the results of family cultivation into daily diet will provide a new model of healthy life and diet structure.

2.2 Green Ecological Design

The concept of "ecosystem" was first put forward by British biologist Tansley, who believed that the ecosystem is mainly composed of two parts, namely, the biological complex on the earth and the complex of various natural factors in the ecological environment, and that the biological interaction with the environment in which it is located can keep the ecosystem in balance [3]. The interrelation between ecology and science, literature, politics, economics and sociology has formed ecological laws, which have been applied to solving problems such as human survival, social development and global strategy.

With the development of science and technology, the relationship between human beings and nature has changed rapidly, and the development of science and technology and material has led to the dilemma of human society moving towards the struggle between man and nature in ecology and alienation and destruction in culture. Therefore, the concept of green ecological design based on ecological system and ecological philosophy gradually stepped onto the historical stage.

Green ecological design conforms to ecological principles and ecological philosophy, gives full play to the initiative of design activities in sustainable development, and turns the design core into the purpose of how to guide human beings to save themselves.

2.3 Indoor Micro-landscape Design Based on Edible Fungi

Micro-landscape originates from potted art, which is usually based on small decorative containers and designed by aesthetic principles. Indoor micro-landscape design introduces the design concept of ecological space into indoor environment design, and integrates the aesthetics of life in a square inch, which has both green environmental protection and ornamental value [4]. Understanding the concept connotation of micro-landscape design from the ecological perspective is the logical starting point for the construction of environmental design theory at the ecological level.

Understanding the growth characteristics of different edible fungi strains, combining them into a miniature ecological space with interest and appreciation, forming a small ecological system, can add vitality and vitality to the indoor space composed of urban reinforced concrete.

2.4 Smart Home Design

Smart home design refers to a design mode that applies intelligent systems to the living space of home and provides more humanized services under the background of big data. As a classic case of environmental design, smart home has the dual attributes of natural science and human social science, which can accurately reflect the immediate needs of consumers for their environment, and provide scientific and accurate home space optimization solutions and all-round information exchange services [5]. Smart home is the inevitable trend of the development of home living space.

3 Design Practice of Edible Fungi Planting Equipment

3.1 Analysis of Planting Methods and Conditions of Edible Fungi

In order to grasp the functional points needed by the planting equipment, we should first understand the planting process and methods of edible fungi, and then understand the necessary conditions and elements in the planting process of edible fungi, and get them to a certain numerical range.

Analysis of Planting Methods. Preparation of nourishment: soybean straw and corn straw can be used as cultivation materials for edible fungi, and rice bran and corn meal can be used as auxiliary materials. The preparation of nourishment goes through four steps of germinating, sterilizing, mixing and bagging [6]. Sowing work: before sowing, the nutrients and planting devices should be sterilized to prevent the growth of mutant strains. It is more appropriate to sow at about 25 °C. Cultivation: put the inoculated nutrient package on the planting rack for cultivation, which requires multiple inspections, strengthening ventilation and cooling, and paying attention to the change of nutrient temperature. In this process, no light is required before the mycelia extend into nutrients, and the mycelia are irradiated with astigmatism after they are full, so as to stimulate their fruiting. Management of fruiting: after fruiting, pay attention to increasing ventilation and humidification to provide weak scattered light. When mushroom buds appear, open the nutrition bag and remove the old bacteria blocks on it, so that the mushrooms grow more orderly. Harvesting: picking mushrooms in time after maturity, gently unscrewing them from the planting bag, so as to pick, hold and release them lightly and minimize the mechanical damage to mushrooms. After the first batch of mushrooms are harvested, the residual stipes, broken mushrooms and dead mushrooms should be cleaned, and the planting bags should be soaked in water for 48 h to prepare for the second batch of mushrooms to grow.

Analysis of Planting Conditions. The growth of edible fungi requires higher environmental conditions such as temperature and humidity, moisture content of culture medium, light and ventilation. Therefore, strict control of environmental parameters in the process of planting edible fungi is an important basis to ensure the quality and yield of edible fungi. The environmental requirements parameters in the normal production process of edible fungi are as follows. Temperature: after inoculation, the temperature should be controlled at 20–30 °C, and after mushroom buds appear, the culture temperature should be maintained at 25–27 °C [7]. Water content: The most suitable water content of culture medium is 60%. Air humidity: The air humidity is generally controlled at 80%-85% during mushroom bud formation, and it needs to be controlled at 85%-90% during fruiting body growth. Light intensity: no light is required after inoculation, and astigmatism is required after hyphae are full. Light needs 1–10 × 1 at the early stage of mushroom bud occurrence, 50–100 lx at the middle and late stage of mushroom bud occurrence, and weak light is required for fruiting body growth.CO2 concentration: Edible fungi perform the same respiration as mammals during their growth, so it is necessary to strengthen the ventilation effect of edible fungi cultivation site [8].

3.2 Function and Structure Analysis of Edible Fungi Planting Equipment

According to the environmental factors required for edible fungi planting, the equipment system needs to be composed of a plurality of detection terminals and a control host, and the detection terminals and the test host are connected by radio equipment, as shown in Fig. 1.

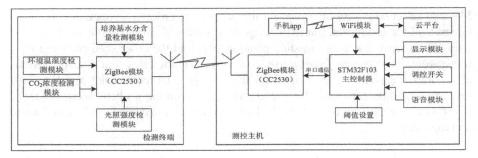

Fig. 1. Control host connection equipment

The detection terminal consists of indoor temperature detection equipment, nutrient moisture detection equipment, indoor air humidity detection equipment, illumination intensity detection equipment and CO2 concentration detection equipment. The control host consists of a main controller, a display device, a switch, a voice device and a network connection device.

After summarizing the data, each detection device sends the environmental parameters to the control host through the radio equipment, and then the control host analyzes the environmental parameters. If the environmental change is detected, the LED lamp tube, cooling fan, hot fan, humidification module and ventilation module linked with it are controlled to make automatic intelligent adjustment, or the user can make remote adjustment through the client.

YL-69 type detection sensor is used for moisture detection equipment of nutrients, and a digital hygrometer based on DHT22 sensor is used for indoor temperature and humidity detection equipment. The whole equipment adopts digital scheme for collection, transmission and display, which has high precision and stability, and provides digital interface for network access [9]. The MG811 CO2 sensor is used for CO2 concentration detection, which can output the detected CO2 concentration in the air to the control host in the mode of 0-2V voltage signal. TSL2561 photoelectric sensor is used as the intensity detection equipment of ambient light. The regulating switch can control the power on and off of the equipment. The voice equipment adopts SYN6288 equipment, and SYN6288 is connected with the main controller through serial port.

3.3 Man-Machine Scheme Analysis

After market analysis and user investigation, the target users of this product are mostly 25–60 years old, and the average height of men in this age group is about 170 cm. The height of this equipment should not be higher than the height of human body, and the top height should be located around the waist. Considering that the height of most indoor houses, in order to make the equipment use the existing vertical space to stack up. Therefore, the height, length and width of the equipment are finally determined to be 130 cm, 73 cm and 35 cm.

3.4 Material and Color Analysis

Material selection is very important for the product. In order to increase the ornamental value of the equipment, transparent injection shell with strong hardness is used for the outermost arc frame and module planting box, and the other shell parts are non-transparent injection shell. In order to echo the green ecological design concept, degradable composite particleboard is used for the base part. Different color matching will give products different visual effects and styles. Based on the aesthetic needs of indoor micro-landscape, the equipment finally draws up the color matching of black and white and log color.

3.5 Ecological Interaction Analysis

Technical Support. The team led by Helene Steiner invented a technology that can read the sensor signals of plants and send them to communicate with them. Edible fungi planting equipment is equipped with this technology, and we can communicate with plants from a new perspective. It can better explore the physical characteristics of plants, make clear the adaptability of the current environment and optimize it accordingly, and deeply explore the inner world of plants and feel the magical charm of natural science. Creatively set up a new multi-dimensional interaction model between man and nature, and use it as a bridge to realize the collision between micro-landscape and man in thinking and emotion.

Factor Analysis. Edible fungi are rich in trace elements, proteins and various bioactive substances, and different bioactive substances correspond to different medicinal and health care values. A healthy diet structure requires the matching of different strains. Therefore, the equipment needs to rely on the client, combine the nutritional structure needed by the human body and the health value of edible fungi, and provide a systematic cultivation selection scheme. The whole planting process should follow the principle of green ecology and maximize the utilization of resources on the premise of ensuring the maximum fruiting rate. It is necessary to embody the design principles of indoor micro-landscape, analyze the living conditions of different strains, place strains with similar living conditions in the same planting module, and gather the aesthetics of life in a square inch to form an ecological system and realize the optimization of indoor ecological space. As an integral part of the smart home system, this device is also applicable to the technology, principle and purpose of smart home, and forms an "ecology" together with other smart devices.

3.6 Design Effect

The following is the overall effect and multi-angle view of household edible fungus planting equipment (see Fig. 2 and Fig. 3).

Fig. 2. Renderings

Fig. 3. Multi-angle view

4 Conclusion

In the post-epidemic era, this study takes people's rethinking of life, nature, ecology and health as the background, and takes healthy living and diet structure, green ecological design, indoor micro-landscape design of edible fungi and smart home concept as the key elements. Innovatively, this paper puts forward a new ecological interaction mode of micro-landscape in the era of great health, which takes edible fungi planting equipment as an interactive bridge, breaks the traditional thinking limitation of interaction between people and utensils, and helps people to have friendly multi-dimensional interaction with nature, environment and products in indoor micro-landscape environment, so as to achieve harmonious coexistence of life community.

References

1. Ma, T.: Research progress on pharmacological effects of common edible fungi. Chin. Fruits Vegetables (02), 45–49 (2019)
2. Chu, X., Gong, P., Liang, Z., Chen, M., Cui, X.: Application of potted edible fungi in balcony vegetables. Chin. Edible Fungi **36**(05), 79+82 (2017)
3. He, W., Liu, J.: Diversified harmony and intersymbiosis: construction and development of ecological philosophy. Shandong Foreign Lang. Teach. **41**(01), 12–24 (2020)
4. Yu, T.: Analysis of the aesthetic construction of micro-landscape. Beauty Times (I), (08), 86–88 (2019)
5. Chen, X.: The new trend of home interior development under the background of big data-smart home. J. Hebei Eng. Univ. (Soc. Sci. Ed.) **36**(02), 29–31 (2019)
6. Grimm, D., Wösten, H.A.B.: Mushroom cultivation in the circular economy. Appl. Microbiol. Biotechnol. **102**(18), 7795–7803 (2018). https://doi.org/10.1007/s00253-018-9226-8
7. Guo, P., Yang, L.: Study on high-yield cultivation techniques of pollution-free edible fungi. Chem. Des. Newsl. **45**(04), 260 (2019)
8. Zhang, W.: Study on the cultivation techniques and popularization of edible fungi. Hubei Agric. Mech. (02), 16 (2019)
9. Yang, H.: Design of Mushroom Greenhouse Management System Based on ZigBee Technology. Qufu Normal University (2017)

Service Design of Stray Cat Feeding Based on the Theory of Sustainable Development

Xinrong Li[✉] and Jiawei Dai[✉]

University of Leeds, Leeds, UK
{ml19x19,ml192jd}@leeds.ac.uk

Abstract. With the rapid advancement of information technology, the increasing pressure of life and the accelerated pace of life, more and more people become addicted to keeping cats. Then the pet industry can be seen everywhere, such as pet feeding, pet health, pet beauty, pet sharing platform. At the same time, more and more people are willing to join in the rescue of stray cats. In this context, there are various problems in feeding stray cats, such as inconvenience to buy food, unhealthy cats, fear of feeders, and the growing ecological pressure on society caused by the rapid reproduction of stray cats. Given the above problems, the innovative design of cat feeding is carried out. The main innovative contents include the following:

(1) Automatic cat food feeder: allowing users to buy cat food anytime, anywhere. The hardware information framework of the feeder is designed, and the innovative design of products is carried out.
(2) Cat canteen app: Constructing the framework of purchasing-caring rescue-sucking cat platform, realize the reward of purchasing cat food, and donate to the community cats for sterilization after reaching a certain value, forming a cat-human-social integrated service system. A product-service system suitable for cat public welfare project is proposed, which enables the resources of cat rescue to be allocated reasonably to mobilize the enthusiasm of users to rescue stray cats and solve social problems.
(3) Community and caring organizations use pet feeders to track and analyze the cat's footprints. After cultivating enough trust, they carry out TNR activities on cats to solve the problem of overbreeding more humanely.

The design can become a goal and direction of cat rescuing and provide ideas and solutions for integrating pet public welfare project design.

Keywords: Sustainable design · Stray cat rescue · Feeder design · Service design · HCI

1 Introduction

As Albert and Bulcroft 1 supported that pets are becoming more and more important in contemporary families. It is showed that the cost of feeding cats and dogs, such as

C. Stephanidis et al. (Eds.): HCII 2021, CCIS 1419, pp. 351–357, 2021.
https://doi.org/10.1007/978-3-030-78635-9_46

licenses, grooming, and veterinarians, exceeds US$5 billion, while the cost of raising babies is only US$3 billion. With the development of the economy and society, pets play an important role in the emotional connection of the family. For example, some parents believe that pets are very important to the growth of their children, so they are willing to raise a pet to accompany their children 1. At the same time, pets will also become emotional substitutes to a certain extent 1. For those who have special experiences or who have experienced major changes in their lives, pets can give them the courage and support to live 1. The above reasons all explain that pets take up an increasing proportion of people's lives in modern times, and pets have become a social issue that cannot be ignored. However, in this context, many problems such as fast-paced life and high pressure in life have also caused people to abandon pets. And in many cities, pet cats can easily become stray cats or wild populations, causing great pressure on the ecology 2. To begin with, wild cats not only cause predation of other wild animals, but stray cats and wild cats carry pathogenic bacteria, which poses a threat to residents 2. Besides, stray cats have a high reproductive capacity. In areas with high cat density, they often receive complaints from the public about cat behaviours, such as courtship barking and feces. Therefore, some actions must be taken to control the number of stray cats, which can maintain social stability and ecological security.

At this stage, Trap-Neuter-Return (TNR) is an effective means to control the number of stray cats. The TNR program is one of the most effective and humanitarian methods because the purpose of this program is to reduce the number of stray cats on the premise of not harming individual cats 3. This article will take the TNR plan as the leading solution to solve the problem of overproduction of stray cats because most residents will support the plan regardless of whether they like cats or not 3.

In society, many organizations are set up to rescue stray cat sustainably. The aim of rescuing stray cat should not be limited to cut down the number of stray cats. It is necessary for people to keep safe and healthy from stray cats. For instance, an organization in the United Kingdom is dedicated to collecting money to feed and rescue stray cats, besides, they also try to find the new owner of them. However, Existing institutional rescues of stray cats are traditional. Using online and offline events to raise money, the website publishes information about stray cats. The site has a single touchpoint for users, making it difficult for users to participate in the whole activity. On the hardware side, most of the existing devices deliver recyclable water bottles to replace cat or dog food, and most of these machines are placed in parks. The project is in line with the concept of sustainable development, but the operation cost of the project is high, which is mainly reflected in two aspects. On the one hand, the requirements for water bottles are higher, and water bottles need to be of a specific shape and brand. On the other hand, there are labour costs associated with recycling and reusing water bottles. For the national conditions of China, investment and maintenance costs are relatively high.

This paper will explore how to use the existing resources to build a sustainable development of the rescue system for stray cats, which can not only meet the needs of users but also solve serious social problems. Furthermore, in the process of designing, the article will explore how to use the concept of HCI to improve the user experience of hardware. As Peter W and John M said, HCI is a useful tool for the designer to apply technology, because HCI has the function to analyse the thinking, value, experience of people 4.

In this project, many stakeholders are included to support the operation of the system. The target group is city residents who like cats and stray cats.

2 Methodology

The methodology included a literature review, the questionnaire and one-to-one interview. The literature review is conducted to understand the concept of sustainable design and human-computer interactive design. The result of the literature review can help designers. The questionnaire was conducted which gain the attitude of people toward the stray cat, and it is helpful for the designer to realize the potential of this project. A one-to-one interview with target users who has the experience of feeding stray cats.

2.1 Questionnaire

The questionnaire was conducted on the Internet, and N = 50 participants attended this research. Figure 1 shows that Cloud-Cat-Keeping people are mainly between 19 and 34 years old. People are willing to see pictures of cats on the Internet and use cats as account photos. At the same time, people are willing to spend money on cats.

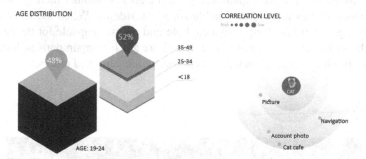

Fig. 1. The result of questionnaire

2.2 One-to-One Interview

At this stage of the interview, people with experience in feeding stray cats are invited to participate in the process. In this step, some points of opportunity are identified, and then we involve the end-user in the whole process to collaborate with the designer. HCI pay more attention to the aspect of interface design to create a more useful system, but the modelling of users can give better support to the collaboration between human and computer 5. Furthermore, the methods of HCI are focused on the usability of hardware and software at first instead of transporting the content of the interface to the users who used the system for the first time. Therefore, from the perspective of ended user to think about the questions, they can give the project more useful and interesting ideas than designers. The interviewer took part in the whole process of creating ideas. Some problems, which they met in their experience of feeding cat, were talking about. In the beginning, they shared some experience of feeding cat. Sometimes, it is hard for them to buy some food for the cat when they met a stray cat occasionally. Then, at night, it is very easy to get hurt because of the weakness of light. Besides, one of the interviews said that she enjoyed watching cat eat food. She thought it is interesting and she also took some photos to postpone on the internet.

The result is target users lack a special and convenient place for them to buy cat food where offers good light. It is an opportunity to offer a platform for users to find and see stray cats. Then, there will have a community for them to share photos and their stories.

3   Final Solution

3.1   Automatic Cat Food Feeder

The product aims to increase the practicability and make the product serve the public welfare agency, so the production cost needs to be reduced. Besides, the feasibility and operability of the project need to be increased, the cat feeder is combined with the community public seat which can be seen in Fig. 2. Because the two products have the same attributes. Public seats belong to the infrastructure which is a necessary element in the local community. The combination reduces the area of another facility and reduces the cost, which makes it more acceptable for the residents. When the habit of cat is considered, leg support is changed to a cat hole and a space capsule for the cat to drill. Figure 3 shows the architecture of the feeder. There are four main parts of hardware to support this product: feeding, picturing, lighting, purchasing and others.

 RENDERING

Fig. 2. The final rendering of hardware

Figure 4 present the touchpoint of the feeder, the sensor mode is combined with the manual mode. When the cat approaches the feeder or passes through the sensor, and then the sensor will send out instructions to feed the pet cat. When the user completes the step of purchasing, the cat food can be dropped out by turning the red cross knob at the top which can be seen in Fig. 5, and the interaction between user and hardware can increase the user experience of the feeder.

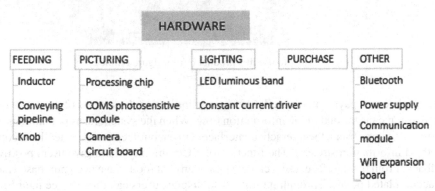

Fig. 3. The architecture of hardware

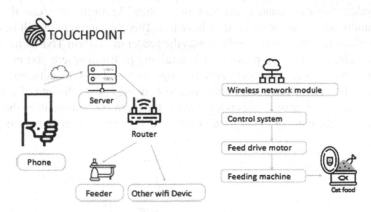

Fig. 4. The touchpoint of hardware

3.2 Cat Canteen App

The user scans the QR code on the hardware which is shown in Fig. 2 to enter the mobile phone, and the mobile phone information architecture is presented in Fig. 6. The mobile phone transmits the instructions to the server, and the server transmits the instructions to the router, and the router controls the feeder to feed the cat. The mobile terminal is divided into three information streams. The homepage is the cat feeding interface, and the user can choose the number of servings and weight of cat food. When the user selects

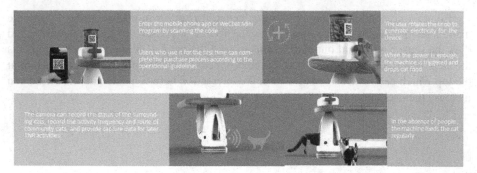

Fig. 5. How to use this product (Color figure online)

and completes the payment, they will enter a page indicating the success of the purchase, which also means the end of the information flow. When the system turns potential users into mobile phone users, the interactive interface will encourage users to enter the second and third information streams. The function of "Community" is to give users positive feedback. From the interface, users can see how many cat foods have been purchased and the accumulated points. Through intuitive data display, users can directly see their love behaviour, so users increase their dependence on the product and a sense of trust. This is beneficial to the long-term development of the project. When the user's love points reach a certain value, they can donate to the community they like, or the stray cats they like or the community where the stray cats they have fed. This part of the fund will be donated to the Love Rescue Organization, which uses the feeder to perform TNR behaviour and sterilize the cat. And the app provides a fundraising platform where you can provide information about injured stray cats. After the operator confirms the authenticity of the information, the system can accept donations to help the cat. At the end of the year or month, the app will give users an annual report, the main content includes the number of rescued cats, the number of cat food purchased. This setting can give users positive

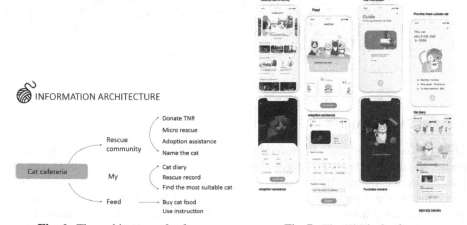

Fig. 6. The architecture of software   **Fig. 7.** The Hi-Fi of software

feedback, which is more conducive to the cat's later rescue activities. The establishment of the app platform also has another meaning. It is to establish a platform that society and the public can trust. Through this platform, all kinds of love rescue assistance can be gathered together, which is more conducive to rescue stray cats. Figure 7 shows the Hi-Fi of the cat canteen app, in this picture, the interface style is shown.

4 Conclusion

The public welfare platform of "Cat Feeding-Information Sharing-Rescue" has been built. This platform integrates many stakeholders into a whole, and with the promotion of the project, the target users will gradually expand. As a result, the situation of stray cats will be greatly improved. In the future, this system will be involved more touchpoints and stakeholders to make it more sustainable. Besides, according to the usability test and the feedback from the user, the interaction of the feeder and cat canteen app will be improved depending on the HCI concept.

References

1. Uetake, K., Yamada, S., Yano, M., Tanaka, T.: A survey of attitudes of local citizens of a residential area toward urban stray cats in Japan. J. Appl. Anim. Welfare Sci. **17**(2), 172–177 (2014). https://doi.org/10.1080/10888705.2013.798558
2. Albert, A., Bulcroft, K.: Pets, families, and the life course. J. Marriage Fam. **50**(2), 543–552 (1988)
3. Crawford, H.M., Calver, M.C., Fleming, P.A.: A case of letting the cat out of the bag—why trap-neuter-return is not an ethical solution for stray cat (Felis catus) management. Animals **9**(4), 171 (2019). https://doi.org/10.3390/ani9040171
4. Wright, P., McCarthy, J.: Empathy and experience in HCI. In: Proceedings of Conference on Human Factors in Computing Systems, pp. 637–646 (2008)
5. Rich, C., Sidner, C.L., Lesh, N.: COLLAGEN: applying collaborative discourse theory to human-computer interaction. AI Mag. **22**(4), 15–25 (2001)

User Preference and Suitability-Aware Eyeglasses Recommender System

Shimpei Maruoka[1]([⊠]), Emmanuel Ayedoun[2], Hiroshi Takenouchi[3], and Masataka Tokumaru[2]

[1] Graduate School of Kansai University, 3-3-35 Yamate-cho, Suita-shi, Osaka 564-8680, Japan
k709082@kansai-u.ac.jp
[2] Kansai University, 3-3-35 Yamate-cho, Suita-shi, Osaka 564-8680, Japan
{emay,toku}@kansai-u.ac.jp
[3] Fukuoka Institute of Technology, 3-30-1 Wajiro-higashi, Higashi-ku, Fukuoka 811-0295, Japan
h-takenouchi@fit.ac.jp

Abstract. This paper proposes a system that uses Interactive Evolutionary Computation (IEC) to recommend eyeglasses based on user aesthetic preference and suitability. The system presents the user with various eyeglasses, and the user evaluates the design based on aesthetic preference. Then, the system uses an Interactive Genetic Algorithm (IGA) to optimize the design based on the user and suitability evaluation. An experiment was conducted to determine the effectiveness of the proposed system toward optimizing eyeglass design. In the experiment, subjects were presented with two versions of the proposed system, which differed in the selection process adopted for the IGA. After system interaction, the subjects answered a questionnaire to determine any differences between the two versions. As new designs were generated, the system was could optimize the eyeglass design, to improve preference and suitability evaluations. We also found a difference in the optimization performance and user satisfaction of the two proposed methods.

Keywords: Recommender system · Interactive evolutionary computation · Eyeglass design

1 Introduction

Interactive evolutionary computation (IEC) refers to optimization technologies that use human subjective evaluation to improve system outputs. IEC is particularly effective for problems involving human sensitivity, where a quantitative solution is difficult to determine. Systems using IEC include retrieval systems for clothes, images [1], and design generation support systems for interior layout and clothes [2,3].

Most of the IEC systems proposed so far optimize a solution reflecting only users' preferences. However, for clothing and accessories, apart from the users

© Springer Nature Switzerland AG 2021
C. Stephanidis et al. (Eds.): HCII 2021, CCIS 1419, pp. 358–365, 2021.
https://doi.org/10.1007/978-3-030-78635-9_47

subjective preference, optimization using third persons' opinions on the extent to which the item would suit a given user has also been proposed. Users don't determine the system out with such optimization methods, it is driven by other's impressions. Although it would be interesting to combine preference and suitability for optimization, conventional IEC systems are not suitable for this purpose because of their single evaluation criterion-based optimization approach.

To tackle such an issue, a design support system that considers preference and suitability have been proposed [4]. In this study, rules for eyeglasses suitability were handcrafted by the system designer and defined in the system in advance. However, such handcrafted suitability rules cannot be generic or robust enough to encompass all the subtle factors that come into play when evaluating the item suitability for a given user.

In this paper, we propose an eyeglass recommender system that uses eyeglasses suitability data collected from real people, to generate eyeglasses designs that are not only the following users' preferences but also suit them. Our approach involves carefully accumulating evaluation data of eyeglasses suitability from real people, which we then incorporate in a conventional IEC. Evaluation results are presented and implications are discussed.

2   Proposed System

2.1   Overview of the Proposed Eyeglasses Recommender System

In this paper, we propose a system for recommending eyeglasses designs based on user's preference and suitability, using suitability evaluation information collected from real people. Figure 1 shows an overview of the proposed system. This system is equipped with a database that stores the suitability evaluation information obtained from numerous evaluators that have previously used the system. By incorporating this evaluation information into the IEC, the proposed system optimizes the eyeglass design by considering the design preferences and suitability. To achieve this optimization, the system is equipped with two interfaces: one for suitability evaluation and the other for design optimization.

When using the suitability evaluation interface, the system displays images of a user wearing eyeglasses, and the evaluator rates by deciding whether the face and eyeglasses in the presented image are well or not. This process is repeated until a predetermined number of eyeglasses are evaluated. In this way, the system can accumulate information on the suitability of eyeglasses for various faces.

The eyeglasses design optimization interface randomly generates an initial set of eyeglasses designs, which are evaluated by users based on their personal design preferences. Then, the system generates the next generation of designs based on the user's evaluation and evaluators' suitability data stored in the database. By repeating these operations for several generations, the system can generate eyeglasses designs that reflect the user's preference and suitability.

2.2   Suitability Evaluation

Three types of information are stored in the suitability evaluation database, namely, face information, eyeglass information, and face eyeglass of the

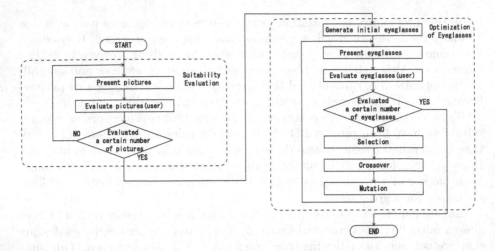

Fig. 1. Operation flow of the proposed system

suitability evaluation data. The face information is stored in the database in the form of various imaginary face photographs, eyeglasses information containing feature values for various eyeglasses designs, and suitability evaluation information stores the percentage of users who evaluated a given combination of face and eyeglasses as GOOD (i.e. suitable). This is called the percentage of GOOD p_{good} and it is calculated using Eq. 1, where N is the number of previous users that evaluated the suitability of the image, and N_{good} is the number of users who evaluated it as GOOD.

$$p_{good} = \frac{N_{good}}{N} \tag{1}$$

Note that the design optimization interface compares the face information stored in the database to select the face that most resembles the user's face. This is achieved using features such as the size, arrangement, and color of each face feature.

2.3 Optimization of the Eyeglasses Design

In this paper, we propose two types of Interactive Genetic Algorithm (IGA) as design optimization methods for eyeglasses recommendations that combine user's preference evaluation value and percentage of suitability (i.e. p_{good}).

(A) Non-linear conversion method

In the non-linear conversion method, p_{good} is used to calculate the suitability evaluation value E_{match}, which is a real number on a five-point scale, using Eq. 2. The function in Eq. 2 is designed so that a design is considered sufficiently suitable if its p_{good} is higher than a certain value.

$$E_{match} = -3.9322p_{good}^2 + 7.9322p_{good} + 1 \tag{2}$$

Then, the evaluation value E is calculated from E_{match} and the evaluation value of the user's preference, E_{user}, using Eq. 3. This evaluation value E is the fitness value upon which the selection and crossover processes are performed. Here, α is the suitability reflection rate, which is a real number in the range $[0,1]$. The system can determine the ratio of the user's preference and the suitability to be incorporated in the design optimization, by varying the value of α.

$$E = (1 - \alpha)E_{user} + \alpha E_{match} \tag{3}$$

(B) Individual roulette method

The preference evaluation value E_{user} and the percentage p_{good} are used as fitness indexes in the individual roulette method. In the selection process, roulette based on E_{user} and roulette based on p_{good} is implemented. Following that, each roulette is used to select an individual to be the parent. At this time, half the number of individuals per generation is selected from each roulette. After selecting the parent individuals, the individuals selected from both roulettes are crossed to produce two child individuals. The design features that consider the user's preferences and suitability are reflected in the next generation of eyeglass design through these operations.

2.4   Eyeglasses Chromosomes Representation

In the proposed system, chromosomes are used to represent eyeglass designs in terms of frame shape and color. As shown in Fig. 2, the frame shape is represented by 3bits, and the frame color is represented by 12bits: 4bits for hue (H), 4bits for saturation (S), and 4bits for brightness (V). Therefore, the total length of genetic information per chromosome is 15bits, which means that a total of 32,768 designs can be expressed following this representation.

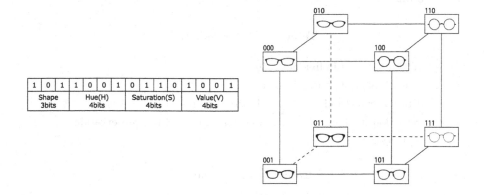

Fig. 2. Chromosomes of eyeglasses

3   Experiment

3.1   Experiment Summary

This experiment aimed to evaluate the performance of two proposed optimization methods and to investigate users' degree of satisfaction with the proposed system. After implementing a suitability evaluation database for each subject, the subjects used the proposed system via the design optimization interface, which was implemented as an iOS application. Here, both the system embedding the Non-linear conversion method (App A) and the system with the individual roulette method (App B) are used. The experiment was completed after participants answered a questionnaire on both apps.

Table 1 shows the parameters of the GA in the experiment. Based on elite preservation, in App A, the elite is preserved based on the evaluation value E, which considers preference and likeness, whereas App B preserved the elite based on the preference evaluation value E_{user} and the percentage p_{good}, respectively. The subjects were eight males and females in their 20s, and the suitability evaluators were seven males and females in their 20s as well. The questionnaire items are shown in Table 2. All questions were designed using a 5-point likert-style scale.

3.2   Suitability Evaluation Database

In the experiment, pseudo-data on the percentage of GOOD evaluations based on evaluators' reponses were created. Here, 32 eyeglasses design differing only in terms of color were presented to the evaluators along with subjects' face pictures. The evaluators were instructed to select 5 suitable and unsuitable eyeglasses. Then, the difference between the number of suitable and unsuitable eyeglasses for each design was calculated. Finally, the five colors with the highest difference were considered suitable, while the five colors with the lowest difference were considered unsuitable.

Table 1. GA parameters

The number of individuals	10
The number of generations	15
Crossover method	Multi-point crossover
Selection method	Roulette wheel + Elite preservation
Mutation rate	5%

Table 2. Questionnaire

Q1	Did eyeglasses design evolved according to your preference?
Q2	Were you satisfied with the final presented eyeglasses?
Q3	Did you feel any difference in the eyeglasses presented by A and B?

Based on suitable and unsuitable colors, the color suitability score $Score_{color}$ for an eyeglass design was calculated using Eq. 4. Here, $Distance_b$ is the smallest Euclidean distance in L*a*b* color space between a given design's color and suitable colors. Similarly, $Distance_w$ is the smallest Euclidean distance in L*a*b* color space between the color of the design and unsuitable colors.

$$Score_{color} = \frac{Distance_w}{Distance_b + Distance_w} \times 50 \qquad (4)$$

To determine the suitability of the shape, we use the suitability information for combinations of face and frame shapes provided by the eyeglasses brand JINS [5]. Here, the degree of similarity between the eight frame shapes is expressed at three levels for each of the four face shapes. These three levels of similarity are expressed as $Match_{shape}$, and the similarity score $Score_{shape}$ of a frame shape for a certain eyeglass design is calculated using Eq. 5.

$$Score_{shape} = 20 \times Match_{shape} - 10 \qquad (5)$$

From $Score_{color}$ and $Score_{shape}$, the percentage of GOOD for a certain eyeglasses design p_{good}, is calculated using Eq. 6.

$$p_{good} = \frac{Score_{shape} + Score_{color}}{100} \qquad (6)$$

3.3   Experimental Results

Figures 3 and 4 show the results of the experiments for App A (Non-linear conversion method) and App B (Individual roulette method). Figure 5 shows the results of the questionnaire survey.

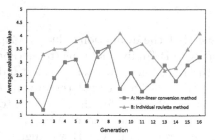

(a) Transition of evaluation value

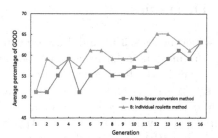

(b) Transition of percentage of GOOD

Fig. 3. Transition of the evaluation value of subject No. 8

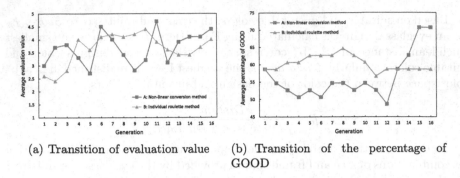

(a) Transition of evaluation value (b) Transition of the percentage of GOOD

Fig. 4. Transition of evaluation value of subject No. 5

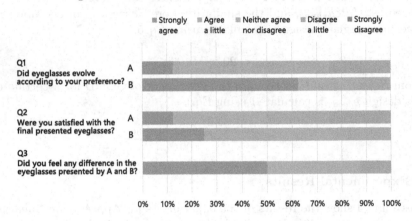

Fig. 5. Results of questionnaire answers

4 Discussion

As shown in Figs. 3(a) and 4(a), we can see that the evaluation values for App A (Non-linear transformation method) and App B (Individual roulette method) are higher in the final generation than in the initial generation. This result indicates that App A and App B can optimize their designs so that the preference evaluation values were high. Similar results were obtained for all subjects. Interestingly, the evaluation results of App B were higher than that of App A.

Figures 3(b) and 4(b) show that p_{good} for App A and App B was higher in the final generation than in the initial generation. Here, there was no change in values between initial and final generations for App A across all subjects. However, for App B, p_{good} was higher for the final generation than for the initial generation for five subjects including subjects' No. 5 and 8. Also, p_{good} in App B was higher in App A for all subjects except subject No. 5.

Thus, we can deduce that App B outperformed App A in terms of optimization performance. This is because the characteristics of preferred and suitable designs were easily passed on to the next generation using the individual roulette method. We assume that the optimization performance was affected due to App A emphasis on the overall evaluation value, whereas App B ensures that each evaluated highly individual is passed on to the next generation.

Figure 5 shows that for App A, half of the subjects positively answered Q1. However, all the subjects gave positive answers for App B. The same trend was observed in the answers to Q2. From the answers to Q3, all the subjects considered there was a difference between the design presented by App A and App B. Hence, we can conclude that the subjects considered a difference between App A and App B, and App B can present eyeglasses designs that provided the subjects with a higher degree of satisfaction.

5   Conclusion

In this paper, we proposed an eyeglasses recommender system that combines user's preferences with suitability data for design optimization. We also reported the results of an experimental evaluation that was conducted to investigate its effectiveness. From the experimental results, we found that individual roulette method-driven systems not only outperformed the other systems in terms of optimization performance, but it also triggered a higher satisfaction level among the subjects. However, it is worth mentioning that only pseudo-similarity data were used in this present study. Hence, future studies will focus on further evaluating the effectiveness of the proposed system using similar data collected from real users.

References

1. Urai, T., Tokuamaru, M.: User Kansei clothing image retrieval system. J. Adv. Comput. Intell. Intell. Inf. **18**(6), 1044–1052 (2014)
2. Unemi, T.: SBArt4 for an automatic evolutionary art. In: 2012 IEEE Congress on Evolutionary Computation in 2012 IEEE World Congress on Computational Intelligence (WCCI 2012), Brisbane, pp. 2014–202 (2012)
3. Sugahara, M., Miki, M., Hiroyasu, T.: Design of Japanese Kimono using interactive genetic algorithm. In: 2008 IEEE International Conference on Systems, Man and Cybernetics (SMC 2008), Singapore, pp. 185–190 (2008)
4. Sakaguchi, T., Onisawa, T.: Support system for glasses design matching user's face. In: 27th Fuzzy System Symposium (FSS 2021), TD1-1, Fukui, pp. 597–602 (2011)
5. Megane no erabikata (in Japanese). https://www.jins.com/jp/guide/eyewear/select_glasses.html. Accessed 16 Mar 2021

Detection of Hand Strength Distribution with E-Textile-Based Tactile Glove for Peach Harvesting

Daisuke Miyada[1] and Lei Jing[1,2(✉)]

[1] The Graduate School of Computer Science, The University of Aizu,
Aizu-wakamatsu, Japan
[2] Research Center for Advanced Information Science and Technology (CAIST),
The University of Aizu, Aizu-wakamatsu, Japan
leijing@u-aizu.ac.jp

Abstract. In recent years, the aging of agricultural workers has become more serious due to the declining birthrate and aging population. Thus, fewer people are teaching young people harvesting techniques, such as how to pick a peach from the tree. So far, such training practice is proofed to be costly since its unit price is high (e.g. each one costs about two to five USD in Japan) and the peach is prone to be damaged for incorrect pick approach. Moreover, for the correct pick approach, it requires to distribute the force over the hand to avoid damaging the delicate peach. But for the traditional training method, a learner needs to repeat the trial-and-error process to get the correct hand feeling since the hand force is invisible. In this paper, to visualize the hand force, we propose a E-textile tactile glove. The glove is sewed with soft piezo-resistive sensors which can detect 26 points of force all over the hand. And a 2D GUI is designed for hand force visualization. According to the qualitative experiments, the tactile glove can detect and visualize the hand strength distribution in real time.

Keywords: E-textile · Glove · Pressure sensor

1 Introduction

Fruit tree production is thriving in Fukushima Prefecture. In particular, peaches are the second largest producer in Japan, accounting for 25% of the total yield. On the other hand, the number of farmers in Fukushima prefecture who grow fruit trees is decreasing year by year. According to data from the Ministry of Agriculture, Forestry and Fisheries, it has decreased by about 40% in the last 20 years. According to a survey by Japan's Agricultural Products Promotion Organization, peach yields in Fukushima Prefecture have decreased by 19.6% over the past decade. One of the causes is the difficulty of learning harvesting techniques. Since peaches are generally delicate fruits, harvesters often mistakenly injure them during harvesting. In addition, it takes time to learn, and the

C. Stephanidis et al. (Eds.): HCII 2021, CCIS 1419, pp. 366–372, 2021.
https://doi.org/10.1007/978-3-030-78635-9_48

practice cost is high considering the risk of peaches used for practice during that time. Therefore, we developed gloves that can visualize the pressure and thought that we could practice quantitatively by collecting pressure data at the time of harvest.

To this end, this research is to develop the E-textile-based tactile glove to detect and visualize the hand strength distribution wile peach harvesting.

2   Related Researches

Our lab had a fingertip pressure glove as part of hand posture detection in a previous research [1]. It used Touch Detection to measure pressure on each knuckle. However, the detection accuracy was coarse. In addition, it had an electrode plate in his gloves, which made it a little difficult to operate. Byung Woo Lee and Hangsik shin proposed a pressure sensor using a sheet with a piezo-resistive effect called Velostat [2]. This is a composition in which a square Velostat is sandwiched between insulation covers of the same shape. It used up to 3×3 sensors to detect sitting in a chair. However, the number of sensors was small and there was little information to estimate. References [3] increased the number of these sensors and applied them to gloves. This enabled 26 pressure detection, but only 2 on each finger. [4] greatly increased the number of sensors to 32 × 32, and also succeeded in subdividing. Although the accuracy of hand state estimation has improved due to the increase in the amount of pressure detection information, the production of gloves is complicated. Therefore, reference [5] proposed a method using an embroidery machine as a pressure sensor that can be made more easily. Here, the conductive cloth was targeted, and Velostat was not used.

The feature of our research is that by sewing a pressure sensor directly on a commercially available glove with a sewing machine, it is possible to make a glove with the convenience of making a glove and the accuracy not inferior to the above.

3   Glove System

3.1   System Outline

Figure 1 shows an overall system diagram. The pressure sensors were arranged vertically and horizontally to correspond to the matrix. The detection control of each row and column is performed by a multiplexer, and the Raspberry Pi 3model B controls the multiplexer and displays the measured data. The series of circuits including the sensor is equivalent to the non-inverting amplifier circuit, and the output voltage Vout currently is as follows:

$$V_{out} = (1 + \frac{R}{R_{Velostat}}) \cdot V_{in} \tag{1}$$

Vin indicates the + input voltage of the amplifier, R indicates the resistance connected to the amplifier side, and R Velostat indicates the resistance of Velostat. Therefore, from the equation, the resistance of Velostat is as follows:

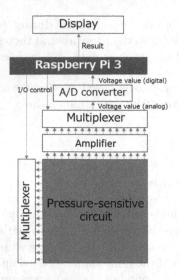

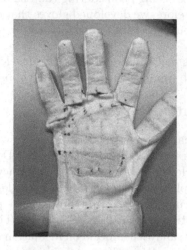

Fig. 1. System structure

Fig. 2. External view of E-textile-based glove

$$R_{Velostat} = (\frac{V_{in}}{V_{out} - V_{in}}) \cdot R \qquad (2)$$

The pressure estimate is calculated from the equation and the equation. This allows for quantification.

3.2 Glove Design

Attach a 1 × 2 sensor to the thumb, a 1 × 3 matrix sensor to the other fingers, and a 4 × 3 matrix sensor to the palm. The sensor was one for each joint of the finger, and the palm was referred to the reference [7] arrangement. In this arrangement, the central part is left open, and three places (fingertip ball, thumb ball, and hypothenar ball) are set as detection points around it. The appearance of the gloves is shown in Fig. 2.

3.3 Producing Process

Figure 3 shows a procedure for making gloves.

1. Draw a rough wiring diagram with a cloth pen.
2. Open a commercially available glove from the little finger side to the index finger and divide it into two with the back of the hand and the palm. However, it is difficult to sew the thumb, so sew directly by hand without opening only the thumb.
3. Create sensors for each finger and palm and sew them on the palm divided by two with a sewing machine.

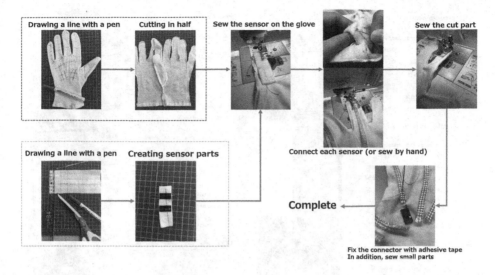

Fig. 3. The process of making a glove

4. Sew the conductive ribbon, which is an output connector, on the fabric on the back of the hand with a sewing machine.
5. Connect the connections of each part directly by hand sewing.
6. Finally, sew the part divided by 2 again.

4 Evaluation

4.1 Experiment

Experimental Outline. The experiment is divided into three parts. First, it is a test of the sensor alone. The purpose is to calculate the regression equation for the resistance and pressure of the sensor, which was already mentioned in Sect. 3.3. Next is a test with a Textile sensor. The purpose is detection using a plurality of sensors. In the experiment, an object is placed on the textile sensor on a table to measure the accuracy of object detection. The last test is to attach a sensor to the glove and hold or grab an object. In this experiment, Python 3.6.6 is used, and the output result is displayed on jupyter-notebook.

Experiment Contents

– Experiment 1
  The purpose of this experiment is to compare the detection when an object is placed on the created textile pressure sensor with the actual bottom surface. The size of the textile in Experiment 1 is 5 rows and 6 columns, which is the same size as the gloves used in Experiment 2, and the distance between each point is 15 mm. This experiment was performed on a desk, with 3 rectangular shapes, 2 circular shapes, and a "9" shape, for a total of 6 patterns.

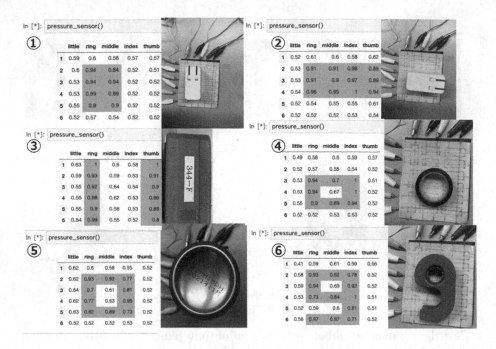

Fig. 4. Result of experiment 1

– Experiment 2

The purpose of this experiment is to detect the movement of an object and compare the actual state while wearing the created gloves. This time we used a smartphone, a ball, and a mug.

4.2   Result

– Experiment1

Figure 4 shows the results of Experiment 1. ① and ② are placed on the vertical and horizontal sides of the rectangular parallelepiped. You can clearly distinguish that the vertical and horizontal sizes are different. Also, ③ is a whiteboard cleaner, which has a dent in the center. Then, from the experimental results, the shape with a hole in the center is detected and it is found to be correct. ④ is a vinyl tape with a diameter of mm, and ⑤ is an aluminum can with a diameter of mm on the bottom. In both cases, the central part is empty, which matches the detection result. ⑥ is the side surface of the cellophane tape. This is modeled after "9" and is very characteristic. The detection result also shows a feature that looks like "9", which shows that it is correct.

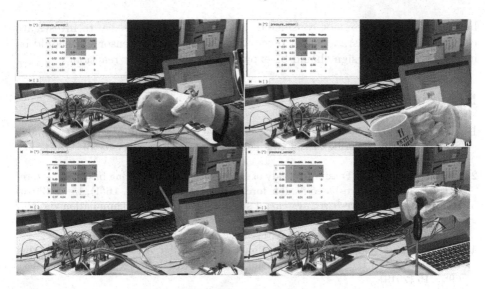

Fig. 5. Result of experiment 2

- Experiment2

  Figure 5 shows the result of experiment 2. When I actually put on gloves, each reaction was seen. The reaction when grabbing a peach with three fingers is small. This indicates that the force applied to the peach is small. Also, when I grabbed the mug, it was heavier than the peach, so the reaction of my fingertips was strong. On the other hand, I tried two ways to hold the driver. The first is to hold it with your entire hand. This was especially strong when the fingertips were bent and brought into close contact, and the reaction was strongly shown. The other is to hold it like tightening a screw with your fingertips. When tightening a screw, force is applied to the fingertips, and since it is held only by the fingertips, the force is particularly applied to the fingertips compared to other ways of holding. As a result, both showed the same reaction as expected. Therefore, it was shown that the pressure can be detected with this glove and the strength of the force can be visualized.

5   Conclusion

5.1   Achievement

In this research, we designed a digital glove that uses velostat to detect and visualize pressure. In addition, it was efficient to use a sewing machine for creation, and the sensor accuracy of the gloves was also good.

5.2   Future Work

The first issue for the future is to make a quantitative estimate of pressure. In this study, the strength of pressure was visualized rather than the change in voltage, but reflexive logic was not considered. Therefore, it is necessary to investigate the pressure and resistance more precisely. In addition, the sensor size should be increased and the design should be expanded to show a finer reaction.

References

1. Suzuki, Y.: E-textile-based motion capture glove for VR input. Master of Computer Science and Engineering in the Graduate School of the University of Aizu (2020, Unpublished)
2. Lee, B.W., Shin, H.: Feasibility study of sitting posture monitoring based on piezore-sistive conductive film-based flexible force sensor. IEEE Sens. J. **16**(1), 15–16 (2016)
3. Liu, H., et al.: A glove-based system for studying hand-object manipulation via joint pose and force sensing. In: 2017 IEEE/RSJ International Conference on Intelligent Robots and Systems (IROS), pp. 6617–6624, September 2017
4. Sundaram, S., Kellnhofer, P., Li, Y., Zhu, J.-Y., Torralba, A., Matusik, W.: Learning the signatures of the human grasp using a salable tactile glove. Nature **569**(7758), 698–716 (2019)
5. Aigner, R., Pointner, A., Oreindl, T., Parzer, P., Haller, M.: Embroidered resisteive pressure sensors: A novel approach for textile interfaces. In: CHI 2020 Paper, no. 178, pp. 1–13 (2020)

Printed Absorbent: Inner Fluid Design with 3D Printed Object

Kohei Ogawa[1]([✉]), Tatsuya Minagawa[1], Hiroki Hasada[1], and Yoichi Ochiai[1,2]

[1] University of Tsukuba, Tsukuba, Ibaraki, Japan
wizard@slis.tsukuba.ac.jp
[2] Pixie Dust Technologies, Inc., Chiyoda, Tokyo, Japan

Abstract. *Printed Absorbent* is a novel concept and approach to interactive material utilizing fluidic channels. In this study, we created 3D-printed objects with fluidic mechanisms that can absorb fluids to allow for various new applications. First, we demonstrated that capillary action, based on the theoretical formula, could be produced with 3D-printed objects under various conditions using fluids with different physical properties and different sizes of flow paths. Second, we verified this phenomenon using real and simulated experiments for seven defined flow channels. Finally, we described our proposed interaction methods, the limitations in the design of fluidic structures, and their potential applications.

Keywords: Metamaterials · Digital fabrication · Capillary action · 3D printing · Inner color · Liquid

1 Introduction and Related Work

Using 3D printing technology, it is possible to design objects wherein different regions have different material properties. Recently, researchers started exploring methods to control material properties by using microstructures. In particular, metamaterial absorbers have been used with light and acoustics. A light absorber is applied to prevent diffuse reflection, heat radiation, and to efficiently generate solar energy [3]. Other studies have succeeded in producing a breathable, acoustic metamaterial structure that allows for 94% sound insulation [2].

Research on methods to add functionality by structural design to 3D-printed objects has been widely explored [1,4,5], and we aimed to further these efforts by embedding programmable absorbability into 3D-printed objects. Through our research, we intend to contribute to the field of human-computer interaction (HCI) by expanding the scope and design opportunities of interactive programmable materials research by introducing a mechanism for fluid absorption. The design of inner structures that can retain liquids in 3D-printed objects has not been extensively studied. To achieve this, it is necessary to design a structure that considers factors such as surface tension and dripping. In addition, in

© Springer Nature Switzerland AG 2021
C. Stephanidis et al. (Eds.): HCII 2021, CCIS 1419, pp. 373–381, 2021.
https://doi.org/10.1007/978-3-030-78635-9_49

K. Ogawa et al.

order to add liquid absorbency to 3D printed objects, it is necessary to verify the structure that forms a water column that causes capillary action in the structure.

In this study, we first investigated the properties of a 3D-printed capillary tube using basic experiments. We investigated and simulated the capillary action of seven 3D-printed capillary tubes with different flow paths that we defined. In this paper, we present our results with a discussion and description of the limitations of the flow channel design patterns in which capillary action occurred. Finally, we demonstrate the effectiveness of each design and provide examples of its application in daily life and as a coloring technique for 3D-printed objects.

2 Capillary Action by 3D Printed Object

2.1 Principles of Capillary Action

In this paper, we propose a concept for a material that absorbs liquids without the need for external energy by designing a structure in which capillary action occurs. Capillary action [8] is the ability of a liquid to flow in narrow spaces without the assistance of, or even in opposition to, external forces such as gravity. Specifically, if the diameter of the capillary is small enough, the combination of adhesion and surface tension between the liquid and the wall of the tube will propel the liquid.

Capillary action can be expressed by the following equation.

$$h = \frac{2T \cos(\theta)}{\rho g r} \tag{1}$$

where T is the surface tension, θ is the contact angle, ρ is the density of the liquid, g is the gravitational acceleration, and r is the inner radius of the pipe.

To provide liquid absorption properties to a 3D-printed object, three parameters need to be considered: surface tension, density of the liquid, and radius of the tube. Surface tension is controlled by the material of the 3D-printed object, and the density and temperature of the liquid. For example, if the liquid is water and the material is glass, the surface tension is 0.0728 N/m at 20 °C. Therefore, one way we can adjust the surface tension is to adjust the resin of the 3D printer. Surface tension can also be controlled by changing the density of liquids. However, we recommend using water because of the ease to obtain liquids and the fact that the liquids are kept and colored within the structure. Temperature also affects surface tension; it decreases as temperature increases. This is because heat agitates the molecules causing the distance between the molecules to increase, which decreases surface tension. However, our experiments were conducted in an average environment on Earth, so it was assumed that there would be no extreme temperature change.

Finally, the radius of the tube was calculated on a computer during the 3D-modeling process. It is also the easiest way to ensure the desired height of the liquid is achieved by capillary action. By adjusting these parameters capillary action can be controlled.

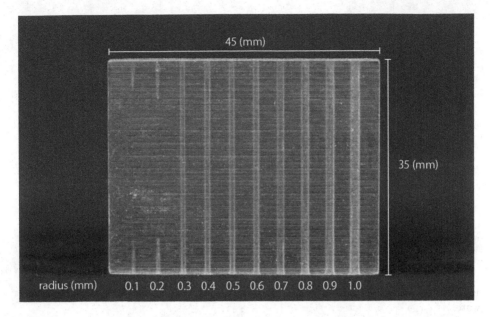

Fig. 1. The experimental shape had eight tubes with radii between 0.3 and 1.0 mm, at 0.1 mm intervals.

2.2   Property Test

We examined changes in capillary action by varying the parameters discussed in the previous section and bringing them into contact with a liquid. The 3D-printed model used for the validation was a cylindrical tube with holes of different radii, as shown in Fig. 1. This shape is a rectangular parallelepiped, with the following dimensions: a height of 35 mm, width of 45 mm, and depth of 5 mm, with capillary tubes placed at 4 mm intervals. The radius, r, of the capillary tube varies in size from 0.1 mm to 1.0 mm at intervals of 0.1 mm. The holes of the tubes with radii of $r = 0.1$ mm and 0.2 mm were blocked because the characteristics of the 3D printer used did not allow the removal of the support material. This is discussed further in Sect. 5. Therefore, eight pipes in the shape were used in the experiment.

In this study, capillary tubes with different diameters and liquids with different densities were used to compare the rising height in the capillary tubes. The liquids used were water, vinegar, soy sauce, salt, sugar, and alcohol. Table 1 shows the densities of the liquids. Table 2 shows the results of the experiment.

Table 1. Six liquids with different densities used in this study.

Liquid	Water	Vinegar	Sugar s.	Salt s.	Soy sauce	Ethanol
Density (g/cm^3)	1.0	0.7892	1.0	1.08	1.15	1.2

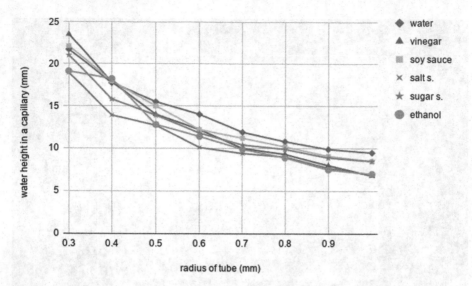

Fig. 2. Liquids of different densities (sugar s. is 20% sugar water, salt s. is 20% salt water)

As per the theoretical equation, the results show that the smaller the radius, r, the larger the rising height, h, of the liquid in the capillary tube. This was also the case when the density of the liquid was low. However, even though a change in rising height was observed, there was no significant difference based the density of the liquid.

We confirmed that capillary action can be generated with 3D-printed objects. In addition, the diameter of the tubes can be easily and accurately adjusted during the 3D-modeling process. In the next section, we show the results indicating the behavior of the liquids in seven different channel geometries.

3 Experimental Result

To verify whether capillary action would occur on contact with liquid, the following seven 3D channel geometries were dipped in liquid.

- Tube Size Changes (case1)
- Surface (case2)
- Groove (case3)
- Bending (case4)
- Branch (case5)
- Combined Structure of Pipe and Surface (case6)
- Siphon Principle (case7)

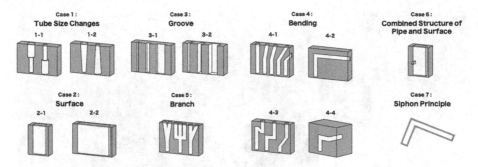

Fig. 3. Classification of channel geometries used in this study: (case 1-1) Discrete variation. (case 1-2) Continuous variation. (case 2-1) Narrow. (case 2-2) Wide. (case 3-1) Shallow groove. (case 3-2) Deep groove. (case 4-1) General bending structure. (case4-2) Right angle with a long horizontal leg. (case 4-3) General bending structure. (case 4-4) Right angle with a long horizontal leg. (case 5) Branched structure. (case 6) Combined pipe and surface structure. (case 7) Siphon principle.

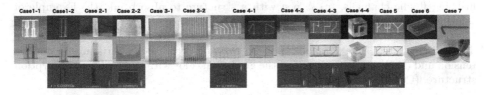

Fig. 4. Results for each channel geometry: (case 1-1) Discrete variation. (case 1-2) Continuous variation. (case 2-1) Narrow. (case 2-2) Wide. (case 3-1) Shallow groove. (case 3-2) Deep groove. (case 4-1) General bending structure. (case 4-2) Right angle with a long horizontal leg. (case 4-3) General bending structure. (case 4-4) Right angle with a long horizontal leg. (case 5) Branched structure. (case 6) Combined pipe and surface structure. (case 7) Siphon principle.

Figure 2 shows the results of a simulation based on a volume-of-fluid solver of OpenFOAM[1] and the results of experiments conducted with a 3D-printed model. The experimental results showed that capillary action occurred in all shapes (Fig. 4).

4 Application

In this section, we present six examples to demonstrate the potential of *Printed Absorbent* approach based on the results of Sect. 3.

---

[1] https://www.openfoam.com/.

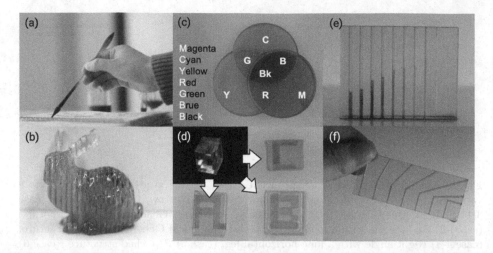

Fig. 5. *Printed Absorbent* is a novel concept and approach to an interactive material utilizing fluidic channels: (a) A pen with a structure to absorb ink, (b) Example of coloring a 3D object with a 3D shape, (c) The appearance of subtractive color mixing, (d) 3D ambigram created by designing an internal structure. It is possible to recognize different characters from various angles, (e) A liquid kept inside a structure by surface tension and (f) Example of absorbing the gradation color with the proposed absorption structure. (Color figure online)

4.1   Glass Dip Pen

The results of case 3 in Fig. 4 show that 3D-printed objects with a grooved structure on their surface can produce capillary action when in contact with a liquid. The glass pen, shown in Fig. 5(a) is an example of the application of capillary action using a grooved structure. The tip of the pen has a groove through which the liquid rises, enabling the pen to write letters using the liquid held in place by capillary action and surface tension. By collaborating this principle with a 3D printer, we have created a glass dip pen made with a 3D printer [6,7]. It can be designed and 3D printed on a computer using 3D CAD software, thus greatly reducing the cost of manpower, technology and time in manufacturing.

4.2   Internal Painting

The results of Sect. 3 show that capillary action occurs when a structure with small cylindrical holes comes in contact with a liquid.

3D-printed objects can be colored by moistening them with colored water. It is also possible to absorb the liquid into the object only by making contact with colored water, which can be removed easily through contact with a cloth or other material with stronger absorption abilities. It can be used to fill an arbitrary character in an object with colored fluid, as shown in Fig. 5(b). In addition, we can easily create objects that present information like ambigrams using small-scale 3D shapes that can be filled through contact with a liquid (Fig. 5(d)).

4.3   Mixing of Colors and Multiple Color

Using a 3D printer, it is possible to print transparent 3D objects. By creating a multilayered transparent structure with channels, it is possible to represent many colors using only the three primary colors. In addition, as shown in Figure (e) and (f), it is possible to apply different colors to each structure with a single contact. The procedure is as follows: First, an arbitrary image is printed on an OHP sheet using a water-based inkjet printer. The sheet can then be moistened with a small amount of water and then contacted with a 3D-printed object. Which can then be colored in multiple colors. The object can also be lifted up, but due to surface tension, the colored water will not leak out.

5   Limitations and Discussion

To use the proposed method, it is necessary to select a 3D printer with high printing modification abilities and that support transparent materials. Table 2 shows the performance of different 3D printers. For example, the fused deposition modeling (FDM) method does not have a high printing resolution, so it is not possible to print flow paths narrow enough for capillary action.

Table 2. Performance comparison of three 3D printers with different printing types.

	replicator+[a]	Form2[b]	Objet 260 Connex3[c]
Printing method	FDM	SLA	Polyjet
Material	PLA	Clear resin	Vero Clear
Layer thickness	100 μm	25 μm	16 μm

[a]https://www.makerbot.com/3d-printers/replicator/
[b]https://formlabs.com/ja/
[c]https://www.stratasys.com/3d-printers/objet260-connex3

The method layers filaments by melting them with heat, which makes it difficult to print models finer than the size of the filament itself. On the other hand, stereolithography apparatus (SLA) has a high printing accuracy and should be suitable; however, the Form 2 used for the validation could not print with a high printing accuracy because of the room temperature and inadequate maintenance. The Objet 260 Connex 3 (Stratasys Inc.) is used in this study to achieve our purpose; it is a polyjet 3D-printing system. The UV-curable liquid resin was injected from the nozzle of the head, and the object was modeled by laminating while curing with UV light. In addition, the injected resin is composed of extremely fine particles; therefore, a smooth model surface could be achieved.

The 3D printer used in this study had a maximum printing accuracy of less than 200 μm, making it possible to print very small structures.

However, we faced a problem with the support agent that filled the flow path at the end of printing. Ultrasonic cleaners are available to dissolve support material; however, because of the fine structures that we printed, removing the support material was difficult. Therefore, we confirmed the removal of all the supporting agent by inserting a metal needle into the flow channel. Consequently, the support material was removed by hand and, depending on the structure of the flow channel, some structures could not be completely cleared. It is possible to print simple, vertical tubes without filling the tube with support material; however, more complex internal structures can be blocked. This problem could be circumvented by using another 3D printer. However, there was no other 3D printer available that had the same accuracy as the Objet 260 Connex 3 and did not also allow support material to enter the flow channel. However, once the problem of clogged support material was solved, the applications were made possible.

6   Conclusion

We propose a design, referred to as *"Printed Absorbent"*, in which objects printed by a 3D printer absorb liquids. In this study, we decided to embed capillary structures into a 3D model to add absorbency of liquids. Therefore, we conducted experiments to validate the phenomenon in objects created using 3D printing technology based on the defining equation of capillary action. Subsequently, we presented design patterns that define the generality of this approach. In the evaluation, experiments were carried out in a real environment and in a simulation to demonstrate the effectiveness of each of the seven design patterns. Capillary action occurred for all seven categories tested. Finally, we present three types of applications, describing the applicability of *Printed Absorbent* as a design method for 3D-printed models that absorb liquids.

References

1. Ballagas, R., Ghosh, S., Landay, J.: The design space of 3D printable interactivity. Proc. ACM Interact. Mob. Wearable Ubiquit. Technol. **2**(2) (2018). https://doi.org/10.1145/3214264
2. Ghaffarivardavagh, R., Nikolajczyk, J., Anderson, S., Zhang, X.: Ultra-open acoustic metamaterial silencer based on fano-like interference. Phys. Rev. B **99**, 024302 (2019). https://doi.org/10.1103/PhysRevB.99.024302. https://link.aps.org/doi/10.1103/PhysRevB.99.024302
3. Hajian, H., Ghobadi, A., Butun, B., Ozbay, E.: Active metamaterial nearly perfect light absorbers: a review [invited]. J. Opt. Soc. Am. B **36**, F131 (2019). https://doi.org/10.1364/JOSAB.36.00F131
4. Ion, A., Kovacs, R., Schneider, O.S., Lopes, P., Baudisch, P.: Metamaterial textures. In: Proceedings of the 2018 CHI Conference on Human Factors in Computing Systems, CHI 2018, p. 1–12. Association for Computing Machinery, New York (2018). https://doi.org/10.1145/3173574.3173910

5. Iwafune, M., Ohshima, T., Ochiai, Y.: Coded skeleton: shape changing user interface with mechanical metamaterial. In: SIGGRAPH Asia 2018 Technical Briefs, SA 2018. Association for Computing Machinery, New York (2018). https://doi.org/10.1145/3283254.3283255
6. Ogawa, K., Tanaka, K., Minagawa, T., Ochiai, Y.: Design method of digitally fabricated spring glass pen. In: ACM SIGGRAPH 2018 Posters, SIGGRAPH 2018, pp. 6:1–6:2. ACM, New York (2018). https://doi.org/10.1145/3230744.3230809. https://doi.acm.org/10.1145/3230744.3230809
7. Tanaka, K., Ogawa, K., Minagawa, T., Ochiai, Y.: Design method of digitally fabricated spring glass pen. In: ACM SIGGRAPH 2018 Studio, SIGGRAPH 2018, pp. 3:1–3:2. ACM, New York (2018). https://doi.org/10.1145/3214822.3214825. http://doi.acm.org/10.1145/3214822.3214825
8. Young, T.: An essay on the cohesion of fluids. https://doi.org/10.1098/rstl.1805.0005

Design of Conceptual Compatibility Between Door Weight of Direct Visual Perception and Door Operating Force

Heng-Hui Shih[1], Shih-Bin Wang[2(⊠)], and Chih-Fu Wu[3]

[1] Fujian University of Technology/Design Innovation Research Center of Humanities and Social Sciences Research Base of Colleges and Universities in Fujian Province, Fujian, China
[2] Department of Innovative Product Design, Lee-Ming Institute of Technology, New Taipei City, Taiwan
wsb@mail.lit.edu.tw
[3] Department of Industrial Design, Tatung University, Taipei, Taiwan

Abstract. This research develops an actual door operation force measurement system and divides the door operation force into 5 levels as the basis for the door operating force score. First, we used the developed index to design doors with light, medium, and heavy visual weight scores. Then their actual door operating force scores were evaluated and regression analysis was performed. From the obtained regression equation, the door visual weight score can be used to predict the door operating force score, and the corresponding actual door operating force can be further found. The results show that a door whose actual door operating force consistent with its direct visual perception of door weight (DVPDW) can be designed, a door design that conceptual compatibility between DVPDW and door operating force can be completed.

Keywords: Direct visual perception of door weight · Door operating force · Conceptual compatibility

1 Introduction

Required operating force is a crucial factor for successful operation of man-made artifacts. To evaluate existing industrial artifacts and environments for the improve-ment of product design development processes, Preiser and Smith (2010) proposed seven UD principles based on the concept of availability. One of the most important principles stipulates that the design of man-made artifacts should enable operators to operate the artifact effectively and comfortably with minimal effort. Also, Norman (2011) had thoroughly reviewed and evaluated the capabilities and limitations of doors and frames. Despite of the diversities of doors, he manifested that door types are mainly selected based on the strength requirements and aesthetic factors. Although physical load is a vital aspect to operating doors and it is extremely influential in our everyday lives, only a few scholars have analyzed the operation of doors based on door operating force (DOF).

Generally, door weight is one of most direct and important factors influencing required DOF. Door operators generate an instinctual evaluation of door weight based

© Springer Nature Switzerland AG 2021
C. Stephanidis et al. (Eds.): HCII 2021, CCIS 1419, pp. 382–390, 2021.
https://doi.org/10.1007/978-3-030-78635-9_50

on their perceived door appearance/attributes and environment factors. Previous studies conducted experiments for DVPDW and developed a door visual weight reference designing index that can predict the door visual weight score (Shih et al. 2016). However, this index is only the door weight image of direct visual perception in the psychological cognition. In actual door operation, the actual operating force of the door is directly sensed through the touch of the hand. How to design a door whose DVPDW is consistent with the operating force that meets human requirements is a topic worthy of further study.

2   Methodology

2.1   DOF Measurement System

Hinged doors generally require operators to push to enter and pull to exit a room. Garg et al. (2014) comprehensively investigated and determined maximum acceptable pushing and pulling forces. Wang and Wu (2015) investigated the pulling and pushing loads of hinged doors and found that operators largely considered pulling to be more energy intensive. They developed a method to test the actual operating force of hinged doors. The researchers designed a lightweight aluminum four-arc pulley to open the test door using a metal rope actuated by a motor. The advantage of this measurement method is that the required operating DOF can be measured simultaneously. This system can be used when the door is pulled by a motor and the handle bar on the door is replaced by a pulling force meter. These conditions are inapplicable for measuring the DOF physically exerted by operators. Therefore, this system was re-designed into a door measuring system suitable for human operation.

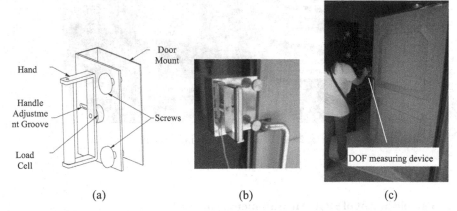

Fig. 1. The DOF measuring device (a) Schematic representation, (b) Actual installation, (c) Operating situation

The door handle is a key component for human operation. Thus, a DOF device was designed in the form of a push bar, as shown in Fig. 1(a). This device comprises a force sensor (tension/compression load cell) and a door handle joined with a pair of screws. Through this device, pushing and pulling forces received during door operation can be detected by the load cell. The device mount comprises of a groove that is wide enough to fit over the door panel of a door. The entire device can then be secured to the door panel using screws. The DOF measuring device used in this experiment is illustrated in Fig. 1(b). An example of the operation of the DOF device is illustrated in Fig. 1(c).

A signal processing system of the operating force for the hinged door was developed here to deal with the transmission of force signal, which consisted of four parts: (1) force sensor (Load Cell, LCM300, measuring scale ± 112 N), (2) Signal Amplifier (WGA-100B), (3) Data Recorder (GRAPHTEC GL220), (4) Computer (along with the self-developed data acquisition software and the analysis software of MS Excel), as shown in Fig. 2.

The signal transmissions were described as follows. Once the door was pushed, the pushing force was then detected by the Load Cell, and the generated force signals were transmitted to the signal amplifier through the signal line. The analogue signals were sent to the Data Recorder and then transferred into digital signals, which were then sent to the computer. Also, the self-developed data acquisition software was used to read and record the data, and finally the MS Excel software was applied for data processing to obtain the time-varying force diagram.

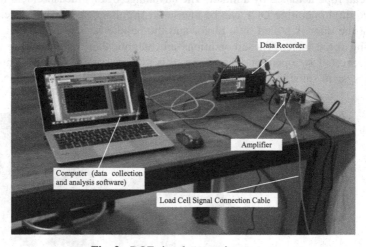

Fig. 2. DOF signal processing system

2.2 Establishment of DOF Measurement Standards

To establishing DOF standards, we consider how people's different levels of sensitivity to DOF may affect their expectation for operating forces. Generally, people are able to distinguish a difference of 5 N (0.5 Kgw) or more, but less able to distinguish a force difference between 1 N and 3 N (0.1 Kgw and 0.3 Kgw), leading to biased force evaluations. To accurately evaluate the force required to operate hinged doors, an appropriate

DOF range and DOF categories should be established. Usually, hinged doors equip with door closer (DC) to close or hold doors automatically. In the present study, test doors were separately fitted with a light door closer (LDC) and a heavy door closer (HDC). The aforementioned DOF measuring system was adopted to measure the DOF of the test doors and the results were used as the maximum and minimum evaluation range. The experiment entails operators physically pushing on the DOF measuring device attached to the test door, as illustrated in Fig. 1(c).

Using the aforementioned configuration, the DOF measuring signals of numerous operations were collected. The measurement results of three operations are illustrated in Fig. 3. Signals with a steeper gradient denote that the door was opened faster, and thus they present a larger force peak. Referencing the definition of required DOF proposed by Wang and Wu (2015), the signal with the gentlest slope and smallest peak value was adopted as the required DOF value. Thus, the required DOF for the operation of the test door equipped with the LDC was 23.2 N. This value was selected as the minimum evaluation range for the operating force of the DVPDW measurement. The force signal is presented in negative values because pushing force was measured.

Similarly, the measurement results for three operations were selected for the test door equipped with the HDC, as shown in Fig. 4. For comparison purposes, the signal with the gentlest slope and smallest peak value was adopted as the required DOF value for the test door equipped with the HDC. Thus, the required DOF for the operation of the test door equipped with the HDC was 47.2 N. This value was selected as the maximum evaluation range for the operating force of the DVPDW measurement.

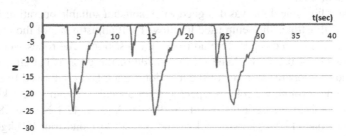

Fig. 3. Operating force measurements for the test door equipped with the LDC

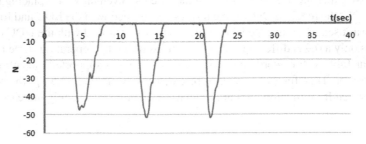

Fig. 4. Operating force measurements for the test door equipped with the HDC

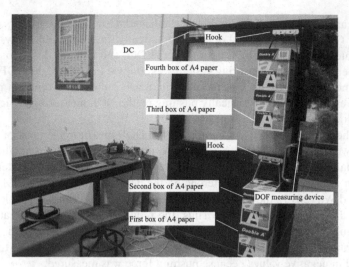

Fig. 5. Adjusting the required DOF of the test door

Based on the aforementioned observations, the operating window for measuring the pushing force of the DVPDW measurement was between 23.2 N and 47.2 N. Using this window, operating force can characterized into five levels to accurately evaluate operators' operating force. As the operating window is exactly 24.0 N, levels increased in increments of 6 N.

A weight-adjustable door was designed to establish a suitable operating force standard. Figure 5 illustrates the setup used to allow DOF adjustments of the test door. To increase DOF, hooks and ropes were added to the test door. The ropes were then tied around boxes of A4 paper and hung on the inside of the door as hanging weights to adjust the required operating force of the test door. Each box comprised five packages of paper weighing roughly 2.5 kg per package for a total of roughly 12.5 kg per box. The required DOF of the door increased to 29.6 N, 35.7 N, 42.1 N, and 48.2 N with the addition of one (12.5 kg), two (25 kg), three (42.5 kg), and four (50 kg) boxes of A4 paper. Based on these results, the addition of each box of paper added roughly 6 N to the required DOF. Hence, the boxes were ideal for representing the force levels of the DVPDW experiment. In order to eliminate the inconvenience of replacing the LDC with the HDC, the required DOF of the test door equipped with the LDC and four boxes (48.1 N) was used to replace the DOF of the test door equipped with the HDC (47.2 N), which was only a 0.9 N difference. The definitions of the five operating force levels are recorded in Table 1. It is worth noting that the door hinges supported the entire weight of the test door. Therefore, despite each box of paper weighing 12.5 kg, the operating force generated from rotation resistance and door-opening inertia only increased by 6 N per box.

Table 1. Operating force levels in the DVPDW experiment

Operating conditions	Force level	DOF size
No DC		9.8 N
LDC	Level 1	23.2 N
LDC door with one box of A4 paper	Level 2	29.6 N
LDC door with two boxes of A4 paper	Level 3	35.7 N
LDC door with three boxes of A4 paper	Level 4	42.2 N
LDC door with four boxes of A4 paper	Level 5	48.1 N
HDC DOF		47.2 N

3 DVPDW Experiment

3.1 Test Door Design and Creation

The DVPDW reference indicator function proposed in (Shih et al. 2016) is expressed in Eq. (1). This function can be used to predict the DVPDW score for any factor–level combination.

$$Y = \beta_0 + \sum_{j=1}^{n} X_j(\beta_i) \tag{1}$$

where n denotes the number of factors (n = 5); β_0 is the constant term (overall average preference, $\beta_0 = 4.072$); and $X_j(\beta_i)$ refers to the utility coefficient for the ith level in the jth factor (Myung 2003), as shown in Table 2.

Table 2. Results of conjoint analysis (Shih et al. 2016)

Factor	Part-worth utility coefficients (Constant Term 4.072)					
(%)*	Level 1	Level 2	Level 3	Level 4	Level 5	Level 6
X1(grain) (5.904%)	Straight (−0.036)	Cathedral (0.036)				
X2 (color) (45.623%)	Yellow (−1.141)	Orange (−0.288)	Red (0.139)	Purple (0.536)	Blue (0.752)	Green (0.002)
X3 (density) (9.251%)	Loose (−0.052)	Medium (0.021)	Dense (0.031)			
X4 (depth) (14.247%)	None (−0.114)	Shallow (−0.116)	Deep (0.230)			
X5 (handle) (24.975%)	Knob (−0.013)	Lever (−0.087)	T bar (0.100)			

*%: Relative importance

Test doors with three DVPDW weights (light, moderate, and heavy) were designed using the reference indicator function and used to conduct physical tests. The designs of the three test doors for the DVPDW experiment are listed in Table 3. Their DVPDW scores (Y) were given by Eq. (1).

Table 3. The three test door designs for the DVPDW experiment

DVPDW	A (Grain)	B (Color)	C (Density)	D (Depth)	E (Handle)	Conjoint Analysis DVPDW Score
(a) Heavy	Straight	Blue	Medium	Deep	T-bar	5.139
(b) Moderate	Straight	Red	Medium	Shallow	T-bar	4.180
(c) Light	Straight	Yellow	Medium	Non	T-bar	2.902

3.2 Questionnaire Design and Data Collection

Thirty-two students were recruited for this experiment. None of the respondents had previously operated the original door. The respondents comprised 15 men and 17 women aged 19 to 25. A pre-experiment questionnaire was first administered to collect the respondents' basic demographics, including age, height, weight, and health (major surgery, visual impairment). The experiment procedures were also explained to them.

The respondents were instructed to complete a questionnaire concerning the perceived level of effort required to operate the doors based on their DVPDW. The level of effort is measured on a 7-point Likert scale, where 1, 2, 3, 4, 5, 6, and 7 represent "no effort," "slight effort," "little effort," "moderate effort," "relatively large effort," "large effort," "extremely large effort," respectively.

Then, the respondents were instructed to physical push the test doors and evaluate the DOF level. They were required to naturally approach the door, use their hands to push the door, and determine whether their physical evaluations were consistent with their perceived evaluations. A research assistant was stationed behind the door during the experiment to add or remove boxes to adjust door weight until respondents' physical evaluations were consistent with their perceived evaluations. Respondents' perceived DOF levels were then recorded. Once all 32 respondents completed a test door, the door panel was replaced with the next one. The experiment was complete once all three test doors were evaluated to obtain DOF scores (Z).

4   Analysis and Discussions

4.1   DVPDW Reference Indicator Function to Estimate DOF

The conjoint analysis DVPDW scores (Y) in Table 3 and the DOF scores (Z) in DVPDW experiment were collated into Table 4. If the two scores are correlated, regression relationships can be established to formulate estimations.

The results of a correlation analysis indicated that the conjoint analysis DVPDW scores were significantly correlated with the DOF scores ($r = 0.999$; $p = .014 < 0.05$).

Table 4. Conjoint analysis DVPDW scores and DOF scores comparison

DVPDW type	Conjoint analysis DVPDW score (Y)	Test door DOF Score (Z)
(a) Heavy	5.139	3.2188
(b) Moderate	4.180	2.3438
(c) Light	2.902	1.3438

Thus, the regression model achieves favorable goodness of fit ($F = 523.58$, $p = .028 < 0.05$) and the explanatory power of the independent variables on the dependent variables achieved $R^2 = 0.998$, suggesting that the conjoint analysis DVPDW scores (Y) can be used to estimate the actual DOF scores (Z). The original regression equation can be expressed as follows:

$$Z = 0.835Y - 1.100 \tag{2}$$

In the DVPDW experiment, DOF was categorized into five levels, as illustrated in Table 1. The results of the correlation analysis indicated that the DOF levels achieve a significant correlation with DOF ($r = 1$, $p = .000 < 0.01$) and the explanatory power of the DOF scores (Z) on DOF ($\hat{Z}$) achieve $R^2 = 0.9998$. Therefore, a regression model exists ($F = 15370$, $p = .000 < 0.01$). The original regression equation can be expressed as follows:

$$\hat{Z} = 6.24\,Z + 17.04 \tag{3}$$

Using the two regression equations above, Eq. (2) was incorporated into Eq. (3) to create the following equation:

$$\hat{Z} = 5.2104\,Y + 10.176 \tag{4}$$

Using Eq. (4), the conjoint analysis DVPDW scores (Y) can be directly used to estimate actual DOF ($\hat{Z}$). Results indicated that the estimated DOF for the light, moderate, and heavy test doors were 37.0 N, 32.0 N, and 25.3 N, respectively.

5 Conclusion

The experiment results confirmed that the application of the DVPDW design reference indicator and DVPDW measurement method developed in the present study could effectively estimate DOF. When designing doors, designers can consider DVPDW principles to aid operators in generating an accurate expected DOF that is consistent with the actual DOF of the door, thereby actuating intuitive operator-door interaction, improving operators' door operations, and reinforcing operation safety.

References

Garg, A., Waters, T., Kapellusch, J., Karwowski, W.: Psychophysical basis for maximum pushing and pulling forces: a review and recommendations. Int. J. Ind. Ergon. **44**, 281–291 (2014)

Myung, R.: Conjoint analysis as a new methodology for Korean typography guideline in web environment. Int. J. Ind. Ergon. **32**(5), 341–348 (2003)

Norman, T.L.: Integrated Security Systems Design: Concepts, Specifications, and Implementation. Elsevier Butterworth-Heinemann, Amsterdam (2011)

Preiser, W., Smith, K.H.: Universal Design Handbook, 2nd edn. McGraw Hill Professional, New York (2010)

Shih, H.H., Wu, C.F., Wang, S.B.: Development of a reference designing index of door weight based on direct visual direct perception for door operation. In: 2016 International Conference on Applied System Innovation (ICASI), pp. 1–4. IEEE, May 2016

Wang, S.B., Wu, C.F.: Design of the force measuring system for the hinged door: analysis of the required operating torque. Int. J. Ind. Ergon. **49**, 1–10 (2015)

Seat Design Based on Subconscious Behavior

Ruoyue Tang[1], Luwei Chen[2(✉)], and Geqi Lin[3]

[1] Zhejiang Gongshang University Hangzhou College of Commerce, Hangzhou, Zhejiang, China
[2] China Jiliang University College of Modern Science and Technology, Hangzhou, Zhejiang, China
[3] Hangzhou Gallerie Couture Furnishing Co., Ltd., Hangzhou, Zhejiang, China

Abstract. Homogeneity emerges in the seat design. While, the innovation merely on exterior shape cannot satisfy the increasing multidimension need of users. Through the analysis of the contribution of subconscious behavior to design, this paper constructs a design process based on subconscious behavior and conducts the related design practice with this design process. Based on the observation and analysis of the subconscious behavior in the process of sitting, this paper builds the initial seat design model with the subconscious behavior, and approvals the completed design project with the integration of the consideration of dimensions, materials, processes. Then the design project is verified by the physical model test. This project targets to design a seat which breaks the homogeneity of the market as well as meets the subconscious needs of users.

Keywords: Subconscious behavior · Seat · Design

1 Subconscious Behavior and Design

According to Freud's "iceberg theory" related to subconscious behavior, which compares human consciousness to iceberg, claims the conscious part accounts only for 5%, while the subconscious part accounts for the rest 95% [1]. It's inevitable that some behavior and motivation is caused by the subconsciousness. These are objective behaviors under various mental situation, such as emotional hint, and potential need [2]. Psychological research claims that the subconscious awareness has a deep and imperceptible effect on the user's overall perception of the product [3]. By the study of subconscious behavior research, the previously hidden need can be revealed. Incorporating the design thinking of user's subconscious behavior into the design process embodies the "user-oriented" design principle, which remarkably enhances the user's experience, and promotes product diversification.

There is a joint relationship between repetitive behavior, inertial behavior and subconscious behavior. The repetitive behavior leads to the occurrence of the inertial behavior, while the inertial behavior is the basement of the subconscious behavior . Subcon-

C. Stephanidis et al. (Eds.): HCII 2021, CCIS 1419, pp. 391–398, 2021.
https://doi.org/10.1007/978-3-030-78635-9_51

scious behaviors dominate people's life. The private subconscious behaviors, which related to the individual experience expression exists. While the generalized subconscious behavior is a more popular existence in groups [4]. Designers need to pay attention to this general subconscious behavior, observe and sort out these universal and repetitive inertial behaviors in order to apply them in related design.

2 Seat Design Method and Process Based on Subconscious Behavior

Norman proposed in design psychology theory that humans are reflected in three dimensions including of instinct, behavior, and introspection. The design of seat should also meet these three kinds of emotional need. The first impression resulted of the material, color, and proportion, as well as the comfortableness when siting on are the important factors which determine whether the need from the instinct dimension is meet or not. The related potential need can be explored thought the observation and organization of the subconscious behavior in the action of sitting. It influences the user self-interpretation among the contact process with the targeted product that whether users feel subtle care on this product and whether the cost performance fits the expectation, which furtherly determines if the user introspection dimension need is satisfied or not [5]. Picture 1 is a structural illustration of the user need analysis of seat (Fig. 1).

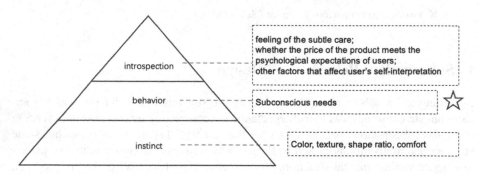

Fig. 1. User need analysis of seat.

Through the observation of the targeted user's subconscious behaviors involving in the motion and process of sitting, the subconscious behavior-based seat design seeks user's potential need in the behavior dimension, by which the design prototype is built for further modification. Based on this prototype, the need in both dimensions of instinct and introspection can be considered. Ergonomics verification, material and process selection, and product size adjustment are applied in the following design process. The last step is finishing the physical model to verify whether this design meets the corresponding user's subconscious behavior needs. The design process is shown in Fig. 2.

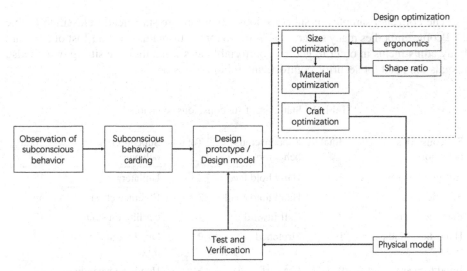

Fig. 2. Seat design process based on the subconscious behavior.

3   Design Practice

3.1   Design Prototyping

Based on the process above, the design practice begins with the collection and analysis of subconscious behavior. The behavior observation method was used to photograph the natural behavior during the usage of seats of the target groups of people, which in order to accumulate the usage samples for the further summary and analysis. Figures 3 and 4 show the photographs.

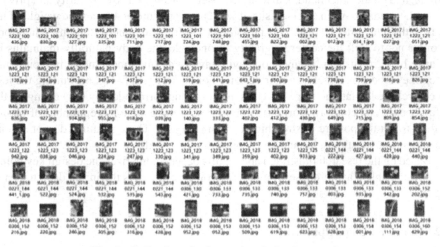

Fig. 3. Collection of subconscious behavior samples.

The collected samples of subconscious behaviors are statistically classified (Table 1). People embodies many subconscious behaviors in the natural state. Most of them are body adjustments in order to get the comfortableness when they are sitting, which also reveals the need for security, comfort, and relief of tension.

Table 1. Statistics of subconscious behaviors.

Subconscious behaviors	Total	Subconscious behaviors	Total	Subconscious behaviors	Total
Lift up and cross legs	32	Hand hold face	23	Unilateral tilt	18
Sit sideways	15	Hand hold head	20	Embrace chest	5
Play the phone	30	Calf inward	16	Curling on sofa	17
Hand-held clothes or bags	12	Stretched	24	One foot under the thigh	14
Bend forward	9	Leg rest	3	Hands between legs and pressed	12
Touch chin or mouth	21	Lie on back and slouching	19	Lean on furniture	19
Hands on knees	5	Leg crossed	20	Pick foot	2

Applying the monographic research method, through the long-term observation of a single individual (Fig. 5), this paper continues to analyze the deeper need behind the typical subconscious behavior shared by the users. For example, when the user rests, he often leans on the sofa and performs side blocking.

This behavior, on the one hand, finds a fulcrum for the head, which relieves neck fatigue, and on the other hand, it also allows users to gain a sense of security and privacy due to the shading. When a person sits, it will cause pressure of 4 times the weight of his body to the intervertebral disc. This pressure is 1.4 times amount of standing. Therefore, in order not to shift the center of gravity to one side, the body naturally maintains its balance by tilting its legs. Many people will have some small movements in their hands when they sit down, which is a manifestation of anxiety relief (Fig. 6). Putting the legs up can relieve leg fatigue (Fig. 7). The sense of being surrounded by the curling on the sofa is peace and comfort. During the observation, there are a large number of people willing to get the posture of stretching or lying (Fig. 8). These postures do not require the support of waist muscles and can achieve a relaxing effect.

Based on the research illustrated above, this paper summarizes the design key points showed in Table 2 and proposes the design prototype which is the initial design idea in Fig. 8.

3.2 Further Design Optimizations

Product Size Establishment. After the further data consulting, appropriate range of the size of each part of the seat is get under the ergonomic consideration [6, 7]. Considering

Fig. 4. Individual observation.

Fig. 5. Small movements.

Fig. 6. Cross leg.

Fig. 7. Stretch.

Table 2. Design key points.

Subconscious behavior	Potential need	Design key point
Leaning on the sofa, side block	Relieve neck fatigue Shading, sense of security	Design a shading, surrounding, leaning function
Curled up on the sofa	Feeling of being surrounded	
Cross leg	Relieve fatigue of legs and waist	Reasonable sitting width and depth
Stretching, and lying	Relieve waist fatigue	
Put the leg up	Relieve leg fatigue	Design a ottoman for legs
Small hand movements	Relieve anxiety	Design a hand-playing device

the design points, the seat width and seat depth should be larger within a reasonable range. By repeatedly adjusting each size within the available range to achieve the appropriate shape ratio, the final product size is determined.

Selection of Material and Crafts. To control to entire cost of this seat, the main material of the seat is 18 mm birch plywood. Then, the CNC cutting is selected to process the plate. Choosing this process can not only save materials during processing, but also

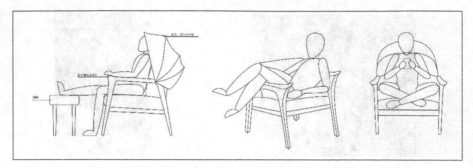

Fig. 8. Initial design.

greatly save transportation costs due to the ease of transportation. 304 stainless steel is selected for the connection material. The cover is made of translucent white frosted PP (polypropylene) plastic board.

3.3 Physical Model Test

In the preset usage scenario, the user can unfold and fold the plastic board to obtain shading, relying on and privacy (Fig. 9). Users can relax their waist and back by putting the feet on the ottoman, cross-legged, and reclining (Fig. 10). What's more, users can play with small objects on the armrests from time to time to relieve potential anxiety emotions (Fig. 11).

Fig. 9. The preset usage scenarios (one).

The real person is invited to test the physical model, through the observation and recording of the user experience (Fig. 12), it can be seen that the tester has restored the preset usage scenario without specific thinking, which verifies the rationality of this seat design the its related design process based on the subconscious behavior analysis.

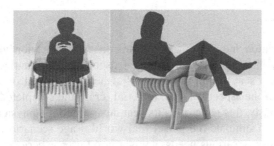

Fig. 10. The preset usage scenarios (two).

Fig. 11. The preset usage scenarios (three).

Fig. 12. Physical model test.

4   Conclusion

Throng the observation and analysis of the subconscious behavior lying in the process of "sitting", this paper explores the potential user need, summarizes the design key points, establishes a seat design prototype. Furthermore, based on the consideration and optimization of the aspects of size, material, craft, the completed design project is finished. Continuously, this paper puts its seat design into the physical model and real user test, in order to simulate the preset real-world usage scenarios. The final design of seat meets the user's various needs, gains a good user experience with a relatively low production cost. The design method that conducting the design base on the user subconscious behavior to explore the potential user need gets reasonable significance of the achievement of good user experience and design optimization.

References

1. Ishii, H.: Tangible Media Group. Tangible Bits: Towards Seamless Interface between People,Bits and Atoms. NTT Publishing Co. Ltd., Tokyo (2000)
2. Sun, X., Li, S., Jin, W.: Application research on interaction design based on unconscious user design. Packaging Eng. **32**(20), 69–72 (2011)
3. Liu, B., Xin, X., Liu, Y.: Subconscious interaction design methods based on theory of neuropsychology. Packaging Eng. **37**(10), 70–74 (2016)
4. Li, Z.: Application analysis of subconscious behavior in interaction design. Art Educ. **12**, 173–174 (2019)
5. Jin, R., Xie, H.: Research on user subconscious motivation strategy oriented to interaction design. Design. **10**, 181–183 (2012)
6. Yang, Y., Li, G.: The application of human body size percentile in chair furniture design. Furniture. **4**, 55–58 (2013)
7. State Technical Supervision Bureau: GB10000–88. Chinese adult body size. China Institute of Standardization and Information Classification and Coding (1989)

Optimal Design of Rescue Motor Boat Based on Ergonomics

Yibing Wu[✉], Zhengyu Wang, Meiyu Zhou, Jinyao Zhang, Yajing Xu, Lu Zhong, Hanwen Du, and Li Wang

School of Art Design and Media, East China University of Science and Technology, No. 130, Meilong Road, Xuhui District, Shanghai, People's Republic of China

Abstract. With the continuous advancement of technology and materials and the continuous changes in demand, the design of vehicles has gradually changed from machine-oriented to human-oriented, and the goal of the design is to bring the driver a safer and more comfortable experience. At present, some Chinese motorboats for specific purposes mostly rely on imports, such as marine emergency motorboats. The emergence of this phenomenon has caused a mismatch between the size of the motorboat and the size of the Chinese driver. So it may lead to reduced driving comfort, muscle fatigue, reduced rescue efficiency, and safety issues, thereby affecting the completion of offshore rescue work.

Now, the manufacture of domestic motor boats is short of the standard size of Chinese human body, so it is urgent to design a motorboat suitable for China's offshore rescue. Based on this, our research first collected relevant Chinese and foreign literature, and summarized the reference data of similar motorboats which have been put into production, combined with ergonomics and material structure analysis, and proposed the design of composite motorboats suitable for China's offshore rescue. Secondly, a good motorboats design provides a comfortable experience while maintaining superior performance. We designed experiments, collected data on Chinese human bodies, and designed the size and structure of motorboat according to the data. Finally, after analysis and comparison of several related resin, fiber and core materials suitable for this composite motorboat, finally selected unsaturated polyester resins, glass fiber and PVC foam core materials respectively. We also performed pressure calculations to verify the safety of the material design, and completed the design of a emergency motorboats suitable for offshore rescue in China.It provides a reference direction for the better combination of ergonomics and motorboats design, and makes a beneficial attempt under the close combination of design theory research and material selection.

Keywords: Ergonomics · Structural design · Glass fiber · Rescue motorboat · Product design

1 Introduction

China has a coastline of 18,000 km, and with the continuous development of the economy of coastal cities, there are many shallow waters around the sea, such as the South China

© Springer Nature Switzerland AG 2021
C. Stephanidis et al. (Eds.): HCII 2021, CCIS 1419, pp. 399–405, 2021.
https://doi.org/10.1007/978-3-030-78635-9_52

Sea [1, 2]. Because drivers rarely have the opportunity to adjust their position during driving tasks, professional driving can lead to neuromuscular fatigue and discomfort [3]. A comfortable driving posture can ensure that the lumbar curve and lower back muscles are in a normal state, covering the front and rear view, and improving the driving safety. However, some of China' s motorboats for specific purposes, such as marine emergency motor-boats (later all replaced by EMBs), are mostly rely on imports, which caused a mismatch between the size of the motorboat and the size of the Chinese driver, so it may affect the driver's driving posture, lead to their workload and muscle fatigue damage. Improper sizing and material selection may threaten the driver's safe operation, taking into account reliability and safety factors [4], Chinese existing national standards are old and poorly targeted for design, not fully covering the target user and may be more targeted at furniture-type sizes rather than special-purpose tools like EMBs.National studies has increasingly focused on changing anthropometric data, such Norway and some countries in Europe and the United States. The old anthropometric data cannot meet the needs of today's design needs [5]. We should respond to the country's changing anthropometric data and select the appropriate materials to design a more secure EMB that is suitable for China's offshore first aid.

2 Analysis and Design of Size of Motorboats

2.1 Hot Selling Motorboat Data

Based on the study of the world's motorboat manufacturers, the following selected Yamaha motorboat models that are popular in the motorboat market, and collected their size information (see Fig. 1):

Model	Length(mm)	Width (mm)	Height (mm)	Net Weight(kg)
FZS	3370	1230	1160	361
FX SVHO	3560	1230	1230	378
VX 700S	3220	1170	1160	240

Fig. 1. Size information about Yamaha motorboats hot sale models

2.2 Experimental Design of Chinese Body Size Standards

At present, the parameters provided in GB 10000–1988 "Chinese adult human body size" are usually used as the design basis, which conforms to the principle of ergonomics on the theoretical level, but from 1988 to 2021, the size of the Chinese people's bodies varied from generation to generation, This can directly lead to the design of products based on past standards that are not compatible with current body size conditions, so in this design, eight police officers from the Huangpu District of Shanghai were invited to measure their body size to make this design of EMB more suitable for coastal rescue in China.

Analysis of related literature revealed that most of the designs selected the data of height, weight, thigh length, calf length, waist circumference, hip circumference, shoulder width, sitting height, seated hip width, seated eye height, seated elbow height, and seated shoulder height in terms of measurement data [6–11]. By analyzing and combining the data needed in the reference motorboat design, the following 9 data were selected and measured in this EMB design: height, weight, upper arm, forearm, thigh, calf, sitting shoulder height, sitting knee height and sitting hip width. The data are summarized in Fig. 2.

Subjects Tested	Age	Height (mm)	Weight (kg)	Upper Arm (mm)	Forearm (mm)	Thigh (mm)	Lower Leg (mm)	Sitting Shoulder high(mm)	Sitting Knee Height(mm)	Sitting Hip Width(mm)
1	22	1753	72	332	255	505	377	626	565	403
2	24	1795	80	345	283	510	412	653	575	415
3	24	1875	100	376	322	544	433	685	588	445
4	24	1707	70	338	258	466	348	675	523	415
5	22	1785	70	330	285	492	363	645	566	368
6	24	1745	80	330	280	515	418	640	550	370
7	22	1840	77	355	286	496	414	705	584	388
8	24	1823	72	345	285	472	385	688	565	395
Min	23.2	1779	75.3	342.1	281.1	495	388.3	658.3	561.2	297.1

Fig. 2. Measured data of 9 parts of eight subjects

2.3 Improved Design of Motorboat Size

Comparing the average data calculated from the measurement data of eight subjects and the size of motorboats currently on sale, the difference between the size of hot-selling motorboats and the relevant professional anthropometric data in China. Therefore, the next step is to improve the design of the EMB based on the measured body data: The length of the whole hull, longitudinal, upper and lower bulkhead is reduced in size, and the height of the steering wheel is increased to make it more suitable for Chinese EMB design. The specific dimensions and the model drawn with PRO / E software(see Figs. 3 and 4) are as follows:

Component	Length(mm)	Width(mm)	Height(mm)
Whole Hull	3300	1200	1100
Longitudinal Bone	3300	Top 80 Bottom 40	60
Lateral Bones	2500	Top 80 Bottom 40	60
Horizontal Baffle	1100	50	500
Connection Layer	3300	1200	70
Upper Bulkhead	3000	800	600
Lower Bulkhead	3000	1000	500
Steering Wheel	250	500	200

Fig. 3. EMB related dimensions

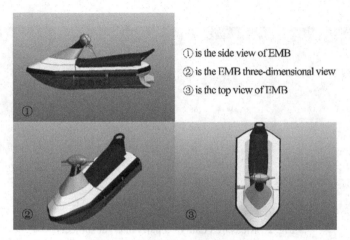

① is the side view of EMB
② is the EMB three-dimensional view
③ is the top view of EMB

Fig. 4. EMB drawn using PRO/E

3   Analysis and Design of Size of Motorboats

3.1   Design Features of Composite Motorboat Crew

Composites refer to materials with better performance than the original materials generated by combining two or more materials with different properties, generally consisting of resin as the matrix and fiber as the reinforcing material. Composites have the following advantages: excellent fatigue resistance; high vibration damping; large designability; easy processing, etc.

The structure design of the EMB hull is formed together in the course of material formed by the composite process of raw materials of various components. These materials will form composite materials and structures with different properties according to different composite effects; The strength of composite materials exceeds the yield limit of steel materials normally used as hulls when the right materials and technology are selected, but the modulus of elasticity is low compared to metal materials. Therefore, for some high performance boat manufacturing and design, the use of engineered composite motorboat hulls is the best choice among them.

3.2 Material Analysis and Selection

Selection of Resins. So far, the most frequently used resin for design in boats is unsaturated polyester resin.Considering that domestic boat materials are chosen more from an economic point of view, we selected three resins from unsaturated polyester resin, epoxy resin and phenolic resin for comparison. Finally, 189 # unsaturated polyester resin was selected as an excellent FRP resin for hull production, with appropriate viscosity, good mechanical properties, and water resistance. In this motorboat design, choose dragon Pearl 189 # unsaturated polyester resin.

Selection of Fibers. The choice of fiber is generally made between glass fiber and carbon fiber. In the current research level of ship materials, almost all of the fibers chosen are Alkali-free glass fibers. Glass fiber is by far the most commonly used fiber in composite boat design, which has strong mechanical properties, electrical insulation and heat resistance. The disadvantage is that it is not suitable for use in acidic environments. Carbon fiber has high strength and modulus, but the disadvantage is that the axial shear modulus is relatively low, poor impact resistance, and more difficult to process.

After comparing the two fibers, due to the maturation of the glass fiber, the price advantage, and the high corrosion resistance of motorboats, alkali-free glass fiber was selected, with the specification of EWR 60(600g/m^2 per unit weight), whereas the density of glass fiber selected in this case is generally 2.5 to 2.7 mg/cm^3.

Selection of Core Material. The composite core material required for EMB is usually made of rigid foam, which can meet the following shipbuilding requirements: high strength; good craftsmanship; no deformation or curling due to reaction with resin in the sandwich state; more affordable, etc. This time, among the four core materials, PVC, PS, PU, and SAN, We learned through analysis and comparison that the PVC foam with better performance can produce a core material with high stiffness under extreme environment. In this motorboat design the core material was selected from the solid H-80 PVC of DIAB of Sweden, which has a density of 80 kg/m^3, thickness of 19.5 mm, tensile strength of 2.6 Mpa, compression strength 1.5 MPa, shear strain of 40% and shear strength 1.6 MPA.

3.3 Determination of the Structural Form of Motor Boats

According to the motorboat reference requirements and the reference model of the motor boat, the following can be obtained:

In this EMB design, the bottom of the hull is layered with fiberglass as well as resin, and in each layer there will be a corresponding directional angle; the structural difference between the wall and bottom materials lies in the sandwich structure, meaning that a foam core needs to be laid in the middle of the layup. The mechanical properties of the core are not high, but the core can withstand the shear strength of the whole structure.

3.4 Design Security Validation

After the design of the size structure of EMB and the selection of related materials, in order to verify the safety of EMB design, several structural parts of motorboat were selected to calculate the pressure.

(1) Calculation of pressure P(KP) for the motorboat bulkhead:

$$\text{Watertight bulkhead} \quad P = 10\,h \tag{1}$$

In formula (1): h means the vertical distance(m) at which the pressure point is transplanted to the bulkhead vantage point, which in this design is 0.5 m, so P = $10 \times 0.5 = 5$ kPa.

(2) Water Tank Bulkhead: P = (9.81 + 0.5a) h.

$$
\begin{aligned}
P &= 10 \quad (h + 2/3hp)\\
P &= 10 \quad (h + 1.0)
\end{aligned}
\tag{2}
$$

In formula (2): Hp-is the relative vertical distance (m) from the ceiling of the tank to the top of the pipe. In this design is 0.2 m, h-is the vertical distance (m) from the point of calculation of pressure to the top of the tank, in this design, the midpoint of the bearing area is 0.25 m, so the values calculated by the above three formulas are 4.265 kPa, 3.28 kPa and 12 kPa respectively, hence the maximum value is 12 kPa.

(3)

$$\text{Collision bulkhead} : P = 12.5\,h \tag{3}$$

In formula (3): h-the vertical distance (m) from the relative point of the pressure in the bulkhead to the relative highest point of the bulkhead, p = $12.5 \times 0.5 = 6.25$ kPa.

Through the verification, the size and material design of the EMB can meet the basic safety requirements of the marine motorboat.

4 Conclusion

Focusing on the design of EMB that is suitable for the standard size of the Chinese human body. Based on the reference data of the hot selling motorboat, combined with ergonomics and material structure analysis, the body data of 8 police officers in Huangpu District, Shanghai were collected, with their data as a reference to improving the design of Chinese EMB. Several materials needed for composite motor boats were analyzed and compared, finally choosing Dragon pearl card 189 # unsaturated polyester resin, alkali-free fiber square cloth for the fiber and solid H-80 PVC for the core material. And after the design, in order to ensure the safety of the design, the pressure calculation of the relevant parts was carried out according to the size and material selection, completing this practice of combining ergonomics and material science. And it provides a direction for the combination of ergonomics and Chinese special-purpose vehicles, a theoretical basis and foundation for research in related fields, and a design basis for the dimensional design of fire trucks or ambulances, etc.

In addition, there are some limitations in this study, first of all, the number of samples chosen is relatively small,only eight police officers in Shanghai were selected as samples. Due to the vast territory of China, there may also be some variations in body size standards across the region. In future research, it is planned to expand the sample size, summarize and generalize the more extensive data base on human size in China.

References

1. Wang, X., Yan, F., Su, F.: Changes in coastline and coastal reclamation in the three most developed areas of China, 1980–2018. Ocean Coast. Manage. **204**(1), 105542 (2021)
2. Zhou, X., et al.: Integrating island spatial information and integer optimization for locating maritime search and rescue bases: a case study in the South China Sea. ISPRS Int. J. Geo-Inf. **8**(2), 88 (2019)
3. Lecocq, M., et al.: Neuromuscular fatigue profiles depends on seat feature during long duration driving on a static simulator. Appl. Ergon. **87**, 103–118 (2020)
4. Sagot, J.C., Gouin, V., Gomes, S.: Ergonomics in product design: safety factor. Saf. Sci. **41**(2–3), 137–154 (2003)
5. Rokne, B.A.: Anthropometry of Norwegian light industry and office workers. Appl. Ergon. **2001**(32), 239–246 (2001)
6. Arunachalam, M., Singh, A.K., Karmakar, S.: Determination of the key anthropometric and range of motion measurements for the ergonomic design of motorcycle. Measurement **159**, 107751 (2020). https://doi.org/10.1016/j.measurement.2020.107751
7. Chen, Y.-L.: Predicting external ischial tuberosity width for both sexes to determine their bicycle-seat sizes. Int. J. Indus. Ergon. **64**, 118–121 (2018)
8. Jung, E.S., et al.: Coach design for the Korean high-speed train: a systematic approach to passenger seat design and layout. Appl. Ergon. **29**(6), 507 (1998)
9. Ghaderi, E., Maleki, A., Dianat, I.: Design of combine harvester seat based on anthropometric data of Iranian operators. Int. J. Indus. Ergon. **44**(6), 810–816 (2014)
10. Deros, B.M., et al.: Incorporating Malaysian's population anthropometry data in the design of an ergonomic driver's seat. Procedia-Soc. Behav. Sci. **195**, 2753–2760 (2015)
11. Mehta, C.R., et al.: Review of anthropometric considerations for tractor seat design. Int. J. Indus. Ergon. **38**(5–6), 546–554 (2008)

Service Design for a Hand-Painted Map of the North Bund in Shanghai

Junnan Ye[✉], Jingyang Wang, Menglan Wang, Xu Liu, and Siyao Zhu

East China University of Science and Technology, Shanghai 200237, People's Republic of China

Abstract. As a significant part of promoting economic growth and attracting tourists' attention, souvenirs have always been attached importance by cultural and creative industries. This dogmatic design thinking can lead to the souvenirs being insipid or too serious, which does not make it a relaxing or enjoyable experience for visitors. In addition, the current souvenir design tends to focus only on the sales process, without considering that the product may form multiple touch-points with tourists during the whole journey. In view of the existing shortcomings, the Emotional Design concept and Service System construction method are innovatively applied to tourist souvenir design. The hand-drawn maps of tourists participating in the whole process were taken as the research object, and the North Bund Sightsight Area of Shanghai Hongkou District, which has rich historical resources and future development advantages, was taken as the research scope. In the design practice, first of all, the Kano Model is used to analyze the subjective questionnaire and summarize the tendency in the emotional needs of potential users. Then, the service design tool is used to comb the stakeholders and draw the customer journey map and service blueprint.

Keywords: Souvenirs · Emotional design · Service design

1 Introduction

Whether the destination is a rural area or a developed city, one of the most important values of tourism development is to allow tourists to experience a unique regional culture. Tourist souvenirs as a commodity with artistic and practical at the same time, this means that the charm of culture become a commercial value consumed here, this not only helps to build closer to the communication platform of life, promote regional culture spread to the world, is also to dig more effectively bring enduring power of regional culture [1].

For the North Bund of Hongkou District, Shanghai, which reflects the history of cultural collision between the East and the West, there are abundant resources available for the development of regional tourism souvenirs. However, there are no products that can be regarded as the name card of the region. Therefore, this paper is devoted to exploring how to improve the design intervention in tourism services, to interact with consumers from an emotional perspective, to build a sound tourism service system based on tourist souvenirs, in order to effectively convey the regional culture, enrich the satisfaction of tourists' cultural experience and emotional experience, enhance the sense of happiness of local residents, and help upgrade the tourism industry of the North Bund.

© Springer Nature Switzerland AG 2021
C. Stephanidis et al. (Eds.): HCII 2021, CCIS 1419, pp. 406–413, 2021.
https://doi.org/10.1007/978-3-030-78635-9_53

2 Introduction

2.1 Design Resources of the North Bund

The north Bund in HongKou district has unique design resources, such as riverside landscape, bearing culture of historical architecture, modern city landmarks and so on, they jointly form a recognizable high landscape in the region, these resources in hand-drawn map making and it is worthy of deep mining in the construction of travel service system design elements. The water body in the city is a rare natural resource. At present, the total open area of the North Bund Riverside is 310,000 square meters, and the total green area of the riverside is 137,000 square meters. The total length of all kinds of footpaths is 6.3 km, and all along the river are connected by winding green land.

Huangpu River brings Hongkou District not only a large area of water-friendly space and park green space, but also water sightseeing and commerce and shipping resources. Among them, the Gongminglu Ferry in the North Bund area, after surpassing the vicissitude of a century of history, has been reopened to the public after renovation in 2009, and has become the representative of sightseeing and shipping on both sides of the Huangpu River [2].

The North Bund is rich in Shanghai culture resources. It can be said that Hongkou is the epitome of Shanghai culture under the blending of modern Chinese culture and western culture. The cultural exchange between the east and the west has created a large number of Shikumen buildings in the North Bund. This study focuses on the old buildings planned to be maintained and developed by the government of Hongkou District, and historical landmarks such as Tilanqiao Prison, Shanghai Postal Museum and Suning Polaro-Carlton Hotel with architectural features of Shikumen style are selected as the focus of the map drawing. Historic sites, such as the Jewish memorial, are also highlighted in hand-drawn form. This allows visitors to understand Shanghai's recent history in a context that is close to the historical reality, rather than being bogged down in boring written descriptions.

The modern urban landscape of Hongkou District concentrates on the riverside area of the North Bund. The North Bund area is the top priority in the development of Hongkou District. Located at the confluent of Huangpu River and Suzhou River, the waterfront along Suzhou River and Huangpu River is 3.53 km long, forming the "Golden Triangle" together with Lujiazui. According to the planning of the municipal government, this study selected 37 buildings to mark points on the map.

2.2 Research Status of Tourism Souvenirs in the North Bund

In terms of service upgrading to enhance tourism experience, Hongkou District Government has upgraded the regional guide system in 2020 [3]. Scholars of landscape planning have also made many attempts on the topic of how to repair old buildings as old as old ones in urban reconstruction and renovation [4]. I believe that the improvement of hardware facilities can attract more tourists, but after that, the improvement of soft power in more detail is the more critical work. In 2018, Hongkou District has officially promulgated policies on revitalizing tourism. Encouraged by relevant policies, the literary and art circles have sorted out the regional culture of the North Bund. The source of culture is mainly divided into red culture, Shanghai culture, urban culture, shipping culture and so on [5]. Although similar studies have been carried out extensively, they are limited to theoretical aspects. From the perspective of practice, the design of tourist souvenirs is the most relevant to cultural communication. Therefore, this study tries to make up for this gap by using the concept of emotional design.

2.3   Research Status of Tourism Souvenirs in the North Bund

Based on the emotional design concept, this study used service design tools and Kano model to sort out the design requirements and determine the function Settings of hand-drawn maps. Emotional design refers to the designer's targeted design based on the emotional level of human brain, so as to make the product conform to the attitude or experience required by the target consumer group, generate an emotional driving force, and apply it to the product, so as to increase the value of the product.

Most existing research focus on industrial product design [6], game design [7], software development and other fields [8], and the design of tourist souvenirs related to cultural mining is also one of the representative fields [9]. The essence of tourism commemorative book is not a simple commodity, but a carrier to transmit culture. In view of this, the designer must integrate this design concept into the emotion of people's instinctive level, behavior level and reflection level in the emotional design.

In 1991, Bill Hollins put forward the concept of "service Design" in the field of Design in his book Total Design [10]. The service design tools used in this study include tourist user journey map and service system map. User journey map is a full-stage process analysis tool used to observe and capture the user's behavior path at different stages [11]. And the final reasonable service system can be summarized as a service system diagram.

The Kano model was proposed by Professor Noriaki Kano in 1984 [12]. Through qualitative and quantitative description of user needs, the model classifies and sorts user needs, and analyzes the impact of user needs on user satisfaction, so as to find specific product demand elements.

3   Product Service Design System Construction

The design strategy of tourism souvenir and service system proposed in this study is divided into two parts, which respectively involve the investigation of three elements of user demand, product function and use environment, as well as the study of the relationship between the three elements.

The study of environment, namely, mastering regional history, culture and modern development, and obtaining information through literature collection and field visit, is the basis of designing tourist souvenirs. In addition to regional historical documents, this study also focuses on policy documents. The determination of consumer groups and the research of product functions are carried out through the Kano model to seek the optimal combination of functions according to consumer needs. The subjects of this study are mainly foreign tourists, supplemented by local residents. Although the knowledge base is different, they all need to have a deeper understanding of the characteristic culture of the region they live in. Finally, it is determined that the essential demands of the hand-drawn map of the North Bund are wayfinding and collection, the expected demands are walking guide and high standard aesthetic appreciation, and the charm demands are stamp punching. The research on the relationship between the three elements is realized through the service design tool. This research is represented by combing the service touch points and the user journey map. By sorting out the relationship between the three elements, a more complete service system can be obtained (Fig. 1).

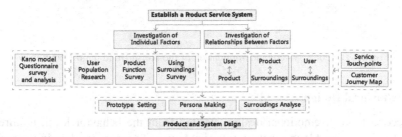

Fig. 1. Tourism souvenir and service system design strategy.

4   Tourism Souvenir Service Design Strategy

In his book Emotional Design, Professor Norman elaborated the three levels involved in emotionalization. Instinct level, involving the product's external morphological characteristics, including color, style, touch and other intuitive first feelings.

Behavioral level refers to the functionality, usability and user experience of tourist souvenirs. On the reflective level, emotional communication is established between users and products, which sometimes needs to be realized through interaction design. In this study, the emotional needs of tourists in the reflective level are met mainly through the construction of tourism service system.

4.1   Visceral Design

The first level of emotional design is the level of instinct. The first level of emotional design is the instinctive level, which appears before consciousness and thinking and emphasizes the immediate emotional effect. The charm of hand-painted painting is precisely that it provides warm and intimate first impression for the audience, which is very important in the design of tourist souvenirs with the deep purpose of cultural communication. The instinctive layer of emotional design requires products to provide lively aesthetic feeling, soft and friendly visual and tactile experience. In this study, this goal was first achieved through the medium of hand painting. In addition, the reinterpretation of city landmarks by hand-drawn maps conveys a kind of poetic life, which is also derived from regional characteristics, and is a secular way to study history and culture [13]. Hand-drawn maps also use a fresh and lively color scheme on the color system. Four main colors and two auxiliary colors were determined based on the area features of the North Bund urban water system, green landscape and Shanghai architecture (Fig. 2).

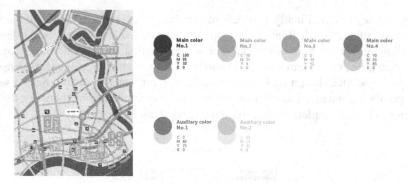

Fig. 2. The color system and application of the North Bund hand-drawn map.

4.2 Behavioral Design

The second level of emotional design, starting from the behavior level, requires the product to be reasonable in function and easy to use. As a core product in the series of tourist souvenirs, designers have high requirements for its functions.

In order to reduce the learning cost for tourists to read hand-drawn maps, this study uses the Kano model to screen these functions, in order to classify user needs and find out one or several important functions that tourists and residents need most. According to the relationship between the type of user demand and user satisfaction, the Kano model divides user demand into five categories: Must-be Quality, One-dimensional Quality, Attractive Quality, Indifferent Quality and Reverse Quality [14].

The following figure shows the nonlinear relationship between user demand and user satisfaction in the Kano model (Fig. 3).

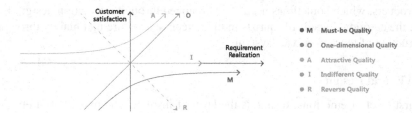

Fig. 3. Kano model.

In this study, users were invited to answer questions on urban forums and campus websites, and the respondents were screened through simple questions before formal questionnaires. The study did not limit respondents to non-residents, as the cultural excavation project, which centers on hand-drawn maps, can also be helpful for people who want to learn more about their city. Influenced by the epidemic, most of the questionnaires were sent online.

In order to more intuitively represent the functional preferences of potential consumers for hand-drawn maps and clarify the design direction, this study used the functional evaluation obtained from the questionnaire results according to the classification of Kano model, and concluded a four-quadrant graph with the Better Worse coefficient [15]. The formula is shown following.

$$Better(SI) = (A + O)/(A + O + M + I))$$ (1)

$$Worse(DSI) = (-1)(O + M)/(A + O + M + I)$$ (2)

The absolute value of the Worse coefficient is adopted in Fig. 4.

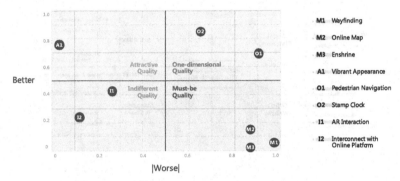

Fig. 4. Better-worse coefficient analysis quartile map.

Finally, a total of 124 questionnaires were collected by electronic and paper methods, and 102 valid questionnaires were obtained after eliminating obvious illogical data.

According to the Kano model and the analysis of the Better Worse coefficient, the Must-be Quality of the hand-drawn map of the North Bund are wayfinding, collection and online map. The One-dimensional Quality is the walking distance and walking time between the scenic spot. The appearance of the map is also valued, visitors expect a map with fresh and bright colors. The Attractive Quality for a map with a stamp may have something to do with the fact that most tourists plan to keep paper maps as souvenirs at the end of their trips. However, whether the hand-drawn map is connected to the official website of the tourism industry and other online platforms, and whether the AR punch card function is added is not recognized by most people. It can be seen from the data that there is Indifferent Quality, which may be related to the tourists' concern about the additional traffic costs incurred during AR interaction. In further interviews, interviewees said that AR interaction is still worth trying as long as it forms a topic. At the same time, the high quality of information will be an important factor in attracting them to visit online platforms. Therefore, the study decided to use both as alternative features for later iterations.

4.3 Reflective Design

Reflection level of emotional design is an important part of enhancing user satisfaction and loyalty. Obviously, the functions and services provided by tourist souvenirs must fit the action pattern of travelers during the whole journey, so that they can resonate well with consumers. At the same time, for local residents, a tourist souvenir design with an accurate grasp of the local cultural background can also have a profound impact. It can stimulate their interest in understanding the living environment and enhance their sense of cultural identity. At the reflective level, this study mainly ponders how to construct a service system around the hand-drawn map of the North Bund, so as to provide tourists with a more comprehensive tour guide, and tries to integrate cultural excavation into the life of local residents in a dynamic attitude with the combination of urban planning. The functional modules and service system of the hand-drawn map are sorted as Fig. 5.

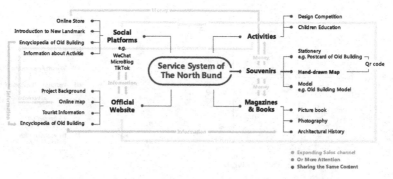

Fig. 5. Service system around the hand-drawn map.

5   Discussion

The design strategy proposed in this paper is based on the principle of emotional design, and the overall goal is to combine the in-depth exploration of regional culture with the design of high-quality tourism souvenirs. Optimize the overall design idea from the perspective of service design, construct the tourism service system, and make it possible for the attractive commemorative products to become a part of the city's public utilities. Due to the support from the government, the exposure rate of the project can be easily obtained in the early stage, and the balance of income and expenditure can be achieved in the later stage when the maintenance costs are included. It can be said that the income pressure of similar projects is relatively small, so the commercial operation part is not discussed in depth in this paper. However, the design strategies presented in this article have also taken into account how to make more money later on, with details such as more spin-off lines around the core product.

References

1. Weijia, L.U., Renke, F.H.E., Xiao, S., Dihu, T.: Creative products design based on the culture of Yuelu Academyn. Packaging Eng. **36**(24), 105–109+114 (2015)
2. Lin Feng, F.: Construction of the Global Shipping Resources Disposition Center by the Shanghai International Shipping Center. J. Soc. Sci. **6**, 28–36+187–188 (2010)

3. Li Haihong, F.: Discussion of greenway planning strategies of high-density district——taking Hongkou district of Shanghai as an example. Landsc. Architect. **04**, 72–77 (2019)
4. Du, C., Wang, F., Yuanyuan, S.: Features preservation and renewal in No. 63 neighborhood, Hongkou district, Shanghai. Planners **36**(15), 43-48 (2020)
5. Wang Meng, F., Jiang Huafu, S.: Fully explore the connotation of Hongkou cultural resources. Journal **01**, 59–61 (2018)
6. Zhang Jing, F., Yin Jiayi, S.: Research on emotional of coffee machine based on the KANO model method. Design **34**(05), 76–78 (2021)
7. Huang Siyuan, F., Zhang Li, S.: Interaction design of music mobile games from the perspective of emotional experience. Design **34**(05), 72–75 (2021)
8. Zhang Pei, F., Li Yi, S.: Application of emotional design in software interface design. Electron. Technol. Softw. Eng. **24**, 70 (2014)
9. Yang Qichun, F.: Tourism souvenir design based on emotional design. Packaging Eng. **42**(02), 279–281 (2021)
10. Zhang Qing, F., Lou Ming, S., Zhang Linghao, T.: Innovation Strategies of Local Life Information APP Products from the Perspective of Service Design. Packaging Eng. **39**(14), 153–157 (2018)
11. Wu Chunmao, F., Li Pei, S.: User experience map and construction of touchpoint information analysis. Model Packaging Eng. **39**(24), 172–176 (2018)
12. Kano Noriaki, F., Seraku Nobuhiko, S., Takahashi Fumio, T., et al.: Attractive quality and must-be quality. J. Jpn. Soc. Qual. Control **14**(2), 1–18 (1984)
13. Su Xiaojing, F., Liushilun, S.: Research on critical issues of Jiangnan cultural. Zhuangshi **03**, 37–39 (2017)
14. Yu Senlin, F., Chen Xiyue, S.: Innovative design of outdoor speaker based on fuzzy-Kano model. Packaging Eng. **41**(24), 202–208 (2020)
15. Xiong Yunjia, F., He Renke, S.: Design of Business Intelligence System Interface Based on Carnot and Four Quadrant Model. Packaging Eng. **41**(10), 242–247 (2020)

Research on Longquan Celadon Cultural and Creative Products Based on Kansei Engineering

Lu Zhong[✉], Zhengyu Wang, Meiyu Zhou, Hanwen Du, Li Wang, Yibing Wu,
Jinyao Zhang, and Yajing Xu

School of Art Design and Media, East China University of Science and Technology, No. 130,
Meilong Road, Xuhui District, Shanghai, People's Republic of China

Abstract. With the development of the tourism industry, the cultural and creative products of tourism have shifted to diversified products, and its development plays a vital role in the prosperity of regional economy, the promotion of local cultural characteristics, and the building of local tourism brands. The traditional firing technique of Chinese Longquan celadon is the first and only ceramic product to be included in the world-class intangible cultural heritage list whose products are also prominent in Longquan tourism cultural and creative products. This study takes the design of Longquan celadon cultural and creative products as an example to explore the shape design of celadon products. Firstly, we use the questionnaire method to integrate the Kansei words and establish the product sample library and Kansei word library of Longquan celadon. Then, we combine the user needs and design elements, and use Likert scale to quantify users' perceptual cognition. Thirdly, we achieve dimensionality reduction of the Kansei words by factor analysis. Finally, we obtain the strategies of the cultural and creative products design of Longquan celadon. This study bridges the differences in cultural perceptions of multiple stakeholders, provides a new method for cultural innovation design aided by Kansei engineering, and provides a reference basis for the future design of Longquan celadon cultural and creative products.

Keywords: Chinese porcelain culture · Longquan celadon · Kansei engineering · Cultural and creative product design

1 Introduction

In recent years, as people's needs have shifted from material to spiritual culture, more and more attention has been paid to the study of users' emotional needs in the design field, and perceptual design has become an effective and logical design method in the process of product development [1]. Kansei engineering, proposed by Nagamachi in the 1970s, is an engineering that attempts to transform users' perceptions of products into a basis for designers to design and manufacture products [2], and is a user-oriented and human-centered technology [3, 4]. It combines sensibility and rationality, and its main goal is to design and develop new products [5] that are easier to accept based on the

© Springer Nature Switzerland AG 2021
C. Stephanidis et al. (Eds.): HCII 2021, CCIS 1419, pp. 414–420, 2021.
https://doi.org/10.1007/978-3-030-78635-9_54

users' emotion, so as to provide people with a higher quality and more comfortable life [6].

With the rapid development of global knowledge economy and experience economy, people have attached more importance to spiritual and cultural consumption, and the rapid development of tourism has promoted the prosperity of cultural and creative industries. Each country and region has its own unique culture, and the cultural derivatives lead to the unique perceptual images. The traditional firing technique of Chinese Longquan celadon originated in the Northern Song Dynasty (960–1127 AD) and has a history of about 1,000 years. It reached its heyday in the Southern Song Dynasty (1127–1279 AD) and Yuan Dynasty (1279–1368 AD), and declined in the Ming dynasty (1368–1644 AD) [7]. It is the first and only ceramic product to be included in the world-class intangible cultural heritage list [8]. Longquan celadon works have a unique aesthetic connotation, being attractive mainly by virtue of the glaze color and the strong sense of glassy light. Longquan celadon cultural and creative products played a positive role in the inheritance of intangible cultural heritage, but they still face higher and more specific requirements in terms of innovative design, cultural heritage and adaptation to user needs. Recently, a large number of modern imitation Longquan celadon vases and the related cultural and creative products have been produced by different kilns in China, but the inheritance of empirical skills lacks logical theoretical guidance [8]. Coupled with the multi-layered attributes of traditional Chinese culture [9] and the cognitive differences among people with different knowledge backgrounds [10], the existing celadon cultural and creative products are not enough to fully reflect the cultural value of Longquan celadon. The focus of cultural creative products is to grasp the perceptual image of users by improving the relevance of design elements and cultural connotations, so as to increase the users' identification with traditional culture [10]. Therefore, this study aims to use Kansei engineering theory to assist design, analyze the shape characteristic elements of Longquan celadon, build the cultural image knowledge base of Longquan celadon vases, and conclude the strategies of the design of its cultural and creative products. The results of the experiment will help to bridge the differences in cultural knowledge perceptions among heritage experts, designers and users in the design of cultural and creative products, and promote the development of cultural and creative industries.

2 Experimental Materials and Procedure

2.1 Kansei Words

First, through the collection of Kansei words in many reports, magazines and papers related to Longquan celadon vases, 132 Kansei words are selected and the word library of Longquan celadon vases is established. Then, the words with similar meanings, ambiguous semantics and little relevance are eliminated by the means of questionnaire method and panel method, and the study finally gets 7 Kansei words that can represent the characteristics of Longquan celadon. Finally, 7 pairs of Kansei words are obtained by taking the opposite meaning, which are in order as follows: vulgar-elegant, complicated-simple, rough-exquisite, dull-dynamic, modern-ancient, light-steady, tough-soft. Therefore, the multidimensional semantic dimension reduction is realized.

2.2 Experimental Samples

First, samples of Longquan celadon vase are widely collected through product catalogs, the official website of Longquan celadon, museum websites, related reports and shopping websites. The sample collection is based on the principle of morphological similarity and suitability for the study to ensure the comprehensiveness and correctness of the results. Then, a total of 252 samples are obtained, and the sample library of Longquan celadon products was established. Next, the study classifies the samples by the group discussion method and KJ analysis method. After removing similar samples and abnormal samples, 51 sample pictures are retained.

In order to eliminate the interference of other visual factors to the greatest extent, obtain targeted visual data of the research objects, and improve the accuracy of the experiment, the study divides the Longquan celadon vase body into 3 regions: the mouth, the body, and the bottom, based on the morphological composition elements, using the methods of feature quantification, scattering, and brainstorming (see Fig. 1).

1-Vase Mouth

2-Vase Body

3-Vase Bottom

Fig. 1. Vase area division.

After multivariate scale analysis and cluster analysis, 4 types of geometrically shaped Longquan celadon vases, namely, straight-mouth vases, girdle-mouth vases, dish-mouth vases, and Cong-shaped vases, are selected as experimental samples for the study. Then we select 28 representative images from the same perspective in 4 types of vases from the above 51 samples. At the same time, the consistency such as contrast, background, grayscale and size of sample images is ensured to eliminate the influence of factors such as color, texture and brightness on the experimental results. Finally, we use Photoshop software to depict the basic outline shapes of the vase mouth, body and bottom of various samples (see Fig. 2).

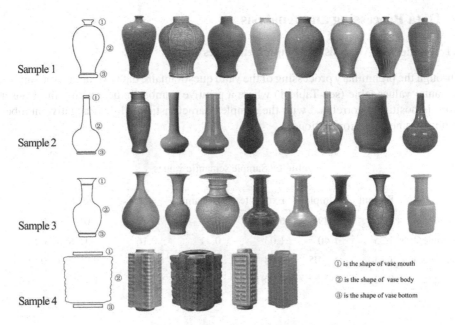

Fig. 2. Experimental samples and basic outline shapes.

2.3 Perceptual Image Questionnaire

The research uses the Likert seven-level scale, combined with the product samples and Kansei words of the above-mentioned Longquan celadon vases, to establish a questionnaire on the perceptual needs of Longquan celadon. The score "0" is the dividing line, and the negative numbers indicate the degree of agreement with the left adjectives. The greater the absolute value, the higher the degree of agreement, and the stronger the subjects feel about the imagery on the side; the same goes for the positive number. Subjects score the degree to which the sample fits the Kansei words according to their own feelings to quantify the perceptual cognition. For example, in the evaluation of "modern-ancient", "−3" means very modern, "−2" means relatively modern, "−1" means somewhat modern, "0" means no obvious tendency, "1" means somewhat ancient, "2" means relatively ancient, and "3" means very ancient.

2.4 Experiment Subjects and Procedure

The study chooses 69 subjects, including 32 males and 37 females, with an average age of 24.1 years. All the subjects have normal or corrected vision, no color blindness or other eye diseases.

All the subjects are asked to fill in the same questions in the same order via mobile phones or computers. We distribute 69 questionnaires totally, collect 63 valid questionnaires, and record scores from −3 to 3 for each sample. After collecting data, the research conducts a numerical analysis of sample semantic by Excel and a factor analysis by SPSS.

3   Data Processing and Analysis

3.1   Numerical Analysis of Sample Semantics

Through the preliminary processing of the valid questionnaire data, we obtain the sample semantic values table (see Table 1) where a positive number indicates that the Kansei word is positively correlated with the sample characteristics, while a negative number indicates a negative correlation.

Table 1. Sample semantic values.

	Elegant	Simple	Exquisite	Dynamic	Ancient	Steady	Soft
Sample 1	1.14	0.79	0.54	0.37	1.22	1.06	0.78
Sample 2	1.25	1.40	1.03	0.41	0.16	−1.78	0.56
Sample 3	1.33	−0.05	0.98	0.40	1.22	0.97	0.51
Sample 4	0.02	−1.22	−0.81	−1.02	1.27	1.7	−1.57

It can be concluded from the table that the most significant Kansei words in sample 1 are elegant and ancient in order, and sample 1 also gives people a stable, simple, exquisite, dynamic and soft feeling. The most significant Kansei words in sample 2 are light, simple, elegant and exquisite in order, which also gives people a feeling of softness, dynamism and simplicity. In sample 3, the most significant Kansei words are elegant, simple, exquisite and steady, and it gives people a sense of movement and softness as well. The most significant Kansei words in sample 4 are stable, tough and simple, but it gives people the impression of being dull and rough instead.

3.2   Factor Analysis

By screening data with initial eigenvalues which are greater than 1 in the total variance explanation table (see Table 2), the study obtains 2 factors explaining 97.745% of the total

Table 2. Total variance explained.

Component	Initial eigenvalues			Extraction sums of squared loadings		
	Total	% of variance	Cumulative %	Total	% of variance	Cumulative %
1	5.496	78.517	78.517	5.496	78.517	78.517
2	1.346	19.228	97.745	1.346	19.228	97.745
3	.158	2.255	100.000			
4	5.576E−16	7.966E−15	100.000			
5	1.130E−16	1.615E−15	100.000			
6	−5.225E−17	−7.464E−16	100.000			
7	−1.113E−15	−1.590E−14	100.000			

data variance, which indicates that the factors can summarize most of the information of the 7 pairs of Kansei words and the experimental data can reflect the objective facts more effectively.

Based on the analysis of the component matrix (see Table 3), the following Kansei words contribute more to factor 1: ancient and stable, and the following Kansei words contribute more to factor 2: exquisite, simple, elegant, dynamic and soft. The result of factor analysis shows that when Longquan celadon vases are considered ancient, they are usually considered stable; when Longquan celadon vases are considered to have a sense of delicacy, they usually give people a feeling of simplicity, elegance, dynamism and softness.

Table 3. Component matrix[a].

	Component	
	1	2
Elegant	.940	.323
Simple	.947	−.140
Exquisite	.960	.191
Dynamic	.949	.314
Ancient	−.659	.751
Steady	−.774	.630
Soft	.927	.356

Finally, according to the contribution rate, the study screens out 2 Kansei words, ancient and exquisite, as the final guiding words. Then the study collates the corresponding Longquan celadon cultural and creative product design strategies by analyzing the common morphological characteristics of the samples with high semantic values (see Fig. 3).

Kansei words	Design strategies
Ancient	Reduce the ratio of product height to cross-sectional width; Use full, large curves or use a combination of curves and straight lines with a pronounced rise in the surface; The overall product is narrow at the top and wide at the bottom, with the center of gravity concentrated in the lower part of the product.
Exquisite	Superimpose several simple geometries, and the product form is slender; Add details, and add a slender cylindrical shape to the product structure; Reduce line corner turns, and there is no visible bumps on the surface of the product; The cross-section of the product is mainly concentric circles, and the width of the cross-section of different parts is richly varied.

Fig. 3. Cultural and creative product design strategies.

4 Conclusion

This research makes full use of the procedures and methods of Kansei engineering to study the shape characteristics of Longquan celadon vases, and constructs a mapping relationship between the design elements of Longquan celadon vases and perceptual images, providing a new idea and method for cultural innovation design aided by Kansei engineering. The results of the research can bridge the differences in cultural perceptions of multiple stakeholders, guide the cultural and creative product design of developers, and enhance users' overall aesthetic experience and cognition of Longquan celadon, so that Longquan celadon's cultural and creative tourism products will be more in line with users' perceptual needs in the future.

However, this research also has certain limitations, such as the singleness of the subjects and the small number of subjects which contribute to the lack of representation in the study. Therefore, future studies can address the issue by expanding the sample size for more detailed discussion.

References

1. Guo, F., et al.: A proposal of the event-related potential method to effectively identify Kansei words for assessing product design features in Kansei engineering research. Int. J. Indus. Ergon. **76**, 102940 (2020)
2. Göken, M., Alppay, E.C.: A case study on Turkish tea glasses and Kansei engineering. In: Fukuda, S. (ed.) AHFE 2019. AISC, vol. 952, pp. 319–328. Springer, Cham (2020). https://doi.org/10.1007/978-3-030-20441-9_34
3. Nagamachi, M.: Kansei engineering: a new ergonomic consumer-oriented technology for product development. Int. J. Indus. Ergon. **15**(1), 3–11 (1995)
4. Coronado, E., Venture, G., Yamanobe, N.: Applying Kansei/affective engineering methodologies in the design of social and service robots: a systematic review. Int. J. Soc. Robot., 1–11 (2020)
5. Nagamachi, M., (ed.) Kansei/Affective Engineering. CRC Press, Boca Raton (2016)
6. Hashizume, A., Kurosu, M.: "Kansei Engineering" as an indigenous research field originated in Japan. In: Kurosu, M. (ed.) HCI 2016. LNCS, vol. 9731, pp. 46–52. Springer, Cham (2016). https://doi.org/10.1007/978-3-319-39510-4_5
7. Zhu, T.Q., et al.: Study on the material and manufacturing technology of different types of Longquan ware imitations from Dapu Kiln of Guangdong Province in the Ming Dynasty of China (ad 1368–1644). Archaeometry **60**(1), 42–53 (2018)
8. Zhang, B., et al.: PIXE study on recovery of making-technology of Chinese Longquan celadon made in the Southern Song Dynasty (1127–1279 CE). Ceramics Int. **45**(3), 3081–3087 (2019)
9. Leong, B.D., Clark, H.: Culture-based knowledge towards new design thinking and practice—a dialogue. Des. Issues **19**(3), 48–58 (2003)
10. Zhu, S.S., Dong, Y.N.: Evaluation of Liangzhu cultural artifacts based on perceptual image. Appl. Mech. Mater. 2187 (2013). https://doi.org/10.4028/www.scientific.net/AMM.268-270.1986

Dimensions of User Experience

Usability Study on the User Interface Design of Tablet Note-Taking Applications

Yi-Hung Hsu$^{(\boxtimes)}$ and Chien-Hsiung Chen

Department of Design, National Taiwan University of Science and Technology, No.43, Keelung Road, Sec. 4, Da'an Dist., Taipei City 10607, Taiwan
cchen@mail.ntust.edu.tw

Abstract. The purpose of this study is to explore the interface usability of commonly used functions with the existing note-taking applications (Apps), and propose design improvements and suggestions. The participants used Apple iPad and Apple pencil to operate the note-taking Apps for five tasks. The results were examined by the repeated measures one-way ANOVA. The results indicated that three of the five note-taking tasks showed significant differences. The findings generated from post-experiment interview and observation showed that: (1) When adding a note page, it would be better to place the new symbol on the left or middle of the page to allow users to click. (2) When inputting notes, it would be better to use "T" as the icon for text input. In addition to the toolbar, the entire display area could be operated with Apple pencil to input data. (3) The erase method used the eraser icon and detected the area and range of the Apple pencil swing to determine whether to erase a large area or make a detailed correction. In the way of finding notes, in addition to date, name, type, text input should also be provided to find note records, which is convenient for users to search.

Keywords: Take note · Interface usability · Tablet · Handwriting recognition · System usability scale (SUS) · Usability evaluation

1 Introduction

The tablet sales are growing worldwide and changing the landscape of personal computing. This is true of mature markets as well as emerging ones [1]. The behavior of using digital pen and tablet to take notes is widely used in many fields. For example, taking notes on a tablet can reduce cognitive pressure and is an important tool for learning foreign languages [2]. Multiple means of content representations and possible ways of expressions provided students with options in learning. The disadvantages are that the tablet requires extensive training [3]. In similar products of the eBook usability study, it was found that the participants were not satisfied with the navigation effects [4]. Therefore, it is important to investigate the usability of related products. Usability testing is an essential skill for usability practitioners, i.e., professionals whose primary goal is to provide guidance of product developers for the purpose of improving the ease-of-use of their products [5]. Usability analysis is an important step in software development in

© Springer Nature Switzerland AG 2021
C. Stephanidis et al. (Eds.): HCII 2021, CCIS 1419, pp. 423–430, 2021.
https://doi.org/10.1007/978-3-030-78635-9_55

order to improve certain aspects of the system. However, it is often a challenge espe-cially when it comes to evaluating applications running on mobile devices because of the restrictions posed by the device and the lack of supporting tools and software available to collect the necessary usability data [6]. The purpose of this study is to explore the usabil-ity of commonly used functions of the existing note-taking Apps and propose design improvement suggestions. The results can be provided for researchers and developers as future references.

2   The Three Samples of Tablet Note-Taking Applications

A total of three tablet note-taking application (App) samples were adopted in the exper-iment. The first sample is the Notability that is a tablet note-taking application. After clicking the App, four areas will be generated, which are the upper toolbar, the lower toolbar, the left note area menu, and the right note content area. In the upper toolbar, there are three tools, namely edit, share and add. In the editing function, a user can stack or delete notes in each note area. Adding tools can add note topics and note group topics. Note group topics are the branch of the note subject. The toolbar below provides func-tions such as setting, online consultation, storage and trash can. In the setting function, a user can adjust the font, style, font size and the classification color of the theme line. The handwriting function area provides fine-tuning of detailed parameters. Notability APP also provides practical options, such as privacy protection setting password function and synchronization backup to the cloud. The magnifying glass of the upper right side pro-vides text input to find notes. The imported part can be combined with personal Google Cloud Drive and Dropbox, and can directly access cloud space files. When using, a user needs to set the note theme and the next-level note group theme first, open a new note work area, set whether to import the photo area or other spaces, email pictures when using it, and open the default file name of the note. The opening time can be changed if necessary. In the new work area, the upper left is the output function, which can directly output the prepared notes to the cloud space or return to the note group theme. The upper areas are respectively text input, drawing tool stroke thickness and color, clear tool, cut and paste tool, recording tool and individual page display functions.

The second sample is the FeeNote. After clicking the icon to enter, a user can see the main tools listed below. There are five items, i.e., "Latest", "Folder", "+", "Calendar", and "Me". The latest is the current page and folder. After clicking, the content of the note can be classified into "All", "My Life", "My Work", "Others", and "To-Do" according to the preset method, and manage different contents in different colors. Click the calendar function, a user can find the notes you edited in the past according to the date. In the "Me" item, a user can set a password to lock the notes and upload the notes to the cloud drive. After entering the main screen of the App, the main tools are placed in the upper and lower sections. The bottom is the delete and reply button and the writing area. The top is the text, upload, pen tool, Apple pencil, importing pictures, recording, sound and other functions. The App presets grid lines. If a user uses text input, s/he can arrange the input text. If a user uses a pen tool, s/he can draw in the note area to help text notes explained.

The third sample is the GoodNotes that has a simple design. Click to go to the main screen, there are two icons in the upper corner, the lower are "file", "search", "share", "collection" and other items, the middle part is the main note area, click the middle "+" to add notes. Notes can be sorted and searched by date, name, and type. After clicking the note editing area, two toolbars will appear above the notes. The upper toolbar is for editing basic functions, such as sharing, searching, and replying. The second toolbar is the note editing tool, including pens. Type tools, erasers, simple drawing tools, taking pictures and using existing pictures. Different from other notebook apps, this App has a presentation pen function but no recording function. When a user clicks on the second row of toolbars and selects the icon, the detailed items of the icon will be displayed on the right side for the user to select. The gear pattern in the upper right corner is "Settings", which can be set for more detailed functions, such as backup. The three note-taking Apps are on the rankings in the Apple store and all adopt paid versions. The three tablet note-taking App interfaces are shown in Table 1.

Table 1. The three tablet note-taking App samples for the experiment

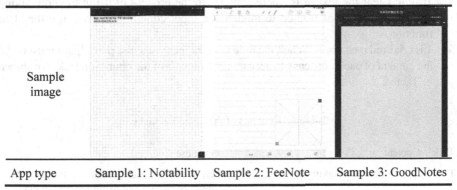

Sample image			
App type	Sample 1: Notability	Sample 2: FeeNote	Sample 3: GoodNotes

3 Methods

The experiment was conducted mainly in quantitative manner, supplemented by qualitative method. The quantitative part included the analysis of task performance and the questionnaire of System Usability Scale (SUS). The qualitative part includes post-experiment interview and observation.

3.1 Participants, Experimental Tools, and Environment

A total of 36 participants (M = 20.22, SD = 1.48) were invited to take part in the experiment by using a convenience sampling method. They were all between 18 and 23 years old. The experimental period is from October 17th to November 3th, 2020. The task operation was conducted by using an Apple pencil. The experimental environment is free of interference and with well illumination in a university classroom. The experimental data were collected by Google forms.

3.2 Experimental Tasks

About the task design, in order to understand whether a user can operate the functions of the interface when using the note-taking App, the task design is based on the main functions of each note-taking Apps. In the end, five tasks were planned in the experiment. The aim of the task design and its operation method are explained as follows:

(1) Task 1: Open a new note-taking area. Open the note-taking area is a function that must be used when using the note-taking App.
(2) Task 2: Import a picture from the photo database. Note-type Apps often use pictures or import online pictures to assist or add to the content of the note.
(3) Task 3: Enter a piece of note content. The text input is the note-type function that the App must use. With Apple Pencil, participants can use the drawing function for text input. In this function, many note-taking Apps can adjust the parameters according to the user's needs, so that the user has a better experience.
(4) Task 4: Clear the text of the note content. In the process of using the note-taking App, if a participant wanted to modify the input content, s/he will use the clear function.
(5) Task 5: Find past notes. When the note content increases, the participant must make the content of each note easy to access. The contents of the operation tasks are shown in Table 2.

Table 2. Contents of the operation tasks.

Task	Content	Purpose
1	Open a new note-taking area	Open the note-taking area is a function that must be used when using the note-taking App
2	Import a picture from the photo database	Note-type Apps often use pictures or import online pictures to assist or add to the content of the note
3	Enter a piece of note content	The text input is the note-type function that the App must use. With Apple Pencil, participants can use the drawing function for text input
4	Clear the text of the note content	In the process of using the note-taking App, when a participant wanted to modify the input content, he/she will use the clear function
5	Find past notes	When the note content increases, the participant must make the content of each note easy to access

3.3 Statistical Tool and Questionnaire

When the participants operated the tasks, the researcher recorded each of their task completion time. After the operation was completed, the participants were asked to fill in the questionnaire of System Usability Scale (SUS). The SUS is divided into ten Questions, five positive questions and five negative questions, and are designed with a five-point Likert scale. The participants' task completion time, the records of the SUS were analyzed by the repeated measures one-way ANOVA. When the participants operated the tasks, the researcher would observe the participant's response pertinent to each task, and conduct post experiment interview with some participants. The content of the interview is about the task satisfaction of the experiment procedure and the advantages and disadvantages of each user interface design. The participants were also encouraged to provide suggestions regarding functional improvement.

3.4 Procedure

The experimental design adopts a repeated measures one-way ANOVA design. A convenience sampling method was adopted. The experimental equipment is an Apple tablet, and the Apple pencil is used to offer clicking and note-taking operations. Before the experiment, the content of each task was clearly described to the participant. The researcher records the task completion time, and participants must fill in the questionnaire of System Usability Scale (SUS) after all the tasks were completed. The experiment adopts a counter-balancing design to avoid order effects and sequence effects. The order of the user interface is based on the number 1 assigned for Notability, the number 2 assigned for FeeNote APP, and the number 3 assigned for the GoodNotes. The experimental procedure was in the order of 123, 132, 213, 231, 312, 321, and the data results were recorded and analyzed by using the repeated measures one-way ANOVA.

4 Results and Discussions

4.1 The Results of Task Completion Time

There existed significant differences in the first, the third, and the fourth task. That is, the repeated measures one-way ANOVA result of task 1 revealed significant difference amount the three Apps ($F = 7.57$, $P = 0.00^* < 0.05$). Among them, participants' task performance of the FeeNote ($M = 10.48$, $SD = 5.90$) and GoodNotes ($M = 13.14$, $SD = 8.88$) was better than the Notability ($M = 18.47$, $SD = 11.71$). The repeated measures one-way ANOVA result of task 3 showed significant difference amount the three Apps ($F = 18.36$, $P = 0.00^* < 0.05$). The participants task performance of the GoodNotes ($M = 22.06$, $SD = 11.01$) and Notability ($M = 21.55$, $SD = 9.64$) was better than the FeeNote ($M = 52.58$, $SD = 40.07$). In addition, the repeated measures one-way ANOVA result of task 4 illustrated significant difference amount the three Apps ($F = 5.12$, $P = 0.00^* < 0.05$). More specifically, participants' task performance of the GoodNotes ($M = 6.63$, $SD = 3.90$) was better than Notability ($M = 10.52$, $SD = 4.89$), and the Notability ($M = 10.52$, $SD = 4.89$) was better than the FeeNote ($M = 20.70$, $SD = 28.96$). The results generated from the repeated measures one-way ANOVA of all the five tasks are shown in Table 3.

Table 3. The repeated measures one-way ANOVA results of all five tasks (in second)

	Notability M(SD)	FeeNote M(SD)	GoodNotes M(SD)	F	P	Post Hoc (LSD)
Task 1	18.47 (11.71)	10.48 (5.90)	13.14 (8.88)	7.57	0.00*	FeeNote = GoodNotes < Notability
Task 2	14.16 (6.23)	11.25 (4.85)	11.11 (6.40)	2.70	0.07	
Task 3	21.55 (9.64)	52.58 (40.07)	22.06 (11.01)	18.36	0.00*	GoodNotes = Notability < FeeNote
Task 4	10.52 (4.89)	20.70 (28.96)	6.63 (3.90)	5.12	0.00*	GoodNotes < Notability < FeeNote
Task 5	10.26 (9.90)	9.12 (6.27)	11.29 (17.10)	0.32	0.72	

* Significantly different at $\alpha = 0.05$ level (*$P < 0.05$)

4.2 SUS Result

SUS is a fast and low-cost scale with a total of ten questions using the five-point Likert scale. There are five positive questions and five negative questions, and the score ranges from 0 to 100 [7]. The SUS items have been developed according to the three usability criteria defined by the ISO 9241-11: (1) The ability of users to complete tasks using the system, and the quality of the output of those tasks (i.e., effectiveness), (2) the level of resource consumed in performing tasks (i.e., efficiency), and (3) the users' subjective reactions using the system (i.e., satisfaction) [8]. The results generated from the repeated measures one-way ANOVA are shown in Table 4. It was found that there were not significant differences among the three drawing APPs ($F = 0.82$, $P = 0.37 > 0.05$). However, the average values of FeeNote is lower than the average score of 68. This means that there is still room for improvement.

Table 4. The repeated measures one-way ANOVA results of SUS

	Notability M(SD)	FeeNote M(SD)	GoodNotes M(SD)	F	P
SUS	67.67 (14.97)	57.75 (21.70)	71.00 (16.36)	0.82	0.37

4.3 Discussions

Based on the above quantitative data together with the researcher's observation and interview data, the research results were generated as follows: (1) When opening a new note area task, a user would focus on his/her attention on the left or bottom of the screen, placing the new symbol at the bottom, using a circular icon with a light blue design.

GoodNote uses the top left side to place the new symbols. Notability uses the shape of a piece of paper and a pen as the icon, and then uses the symbols of the new note category. This design has visibility and predictability. However, poor visual designs will cause confusion to users and should be redesigned [9]. (2) In Notability App, a user could use Apple Pencil to directly click on the "T" text icon and input data onto the note area by drawing. This design is the same as that of GoodNote. Users can quickly understand and use it, but FeeNote's handwriting area is designed at the bottom right of the note area. Although this design can organize the text written by the user in a limited block, users without user experience need more time to find the text input area. The method is not designed according to the user's mental models [10]. (3) In the area of clearing and correcting notes, both the function icons of GoodNote and Notability use the eraser symbol. At the top of the toolbar, Good Note will determine whether the Apple pencil is completely deleted according to the range of the user swiping the Apple pencil, so it can be cleared quickly. To all unnecessary content, Notability can choose the size of the clear brush, and it also affects the efficiency of clearing. FeeNote puts the clear icon under the note area, and uses the clear symbol of the keyboard as the clear icon, but this design is not compatible with users' schemata and should be redesigned [11].

5 Conclusion

From the above-mentioned discussions, the significant part of the experimental results indicated that when adding a note page, place the new symbol on the left or middle of the page to allow users to click When inputting notes, use "T" as the icon for text input. In addition to the toolbar, the entire display area can be operated on Apple pencil to input data. The erase method uses the eraser icon and detects the area and ranges. The Apple pencil can swing to determine whether to erase a large area or make a detailed correction. In the way of finding notes, in addition to date, name, and type, the text input should also be provided to help find note records, which is convenient for users to search.

Regarding the recommendations of future research, more participants can be invited for the experiment to help compare whether there are differences in the design of various functions because of various user experience. It is hoped that the research results can be good design references for future design applications.

Acknowledgements. Financial support of this research study by the Ministry of Science and Technology under the grant MOST 108-2410-H-011-008-MY3 is gratefully acknowledged.

References

1. Terrenghi, L., Garcia-Barrio, L., Oshlyansky, L.: Tablets use in emerging markets: an exploration. In: Proceedings of the 15th International Conference on Human-Computer Interaction with Mobile Devices and Services, pp. 594–599. MobileHCI, Germany (2013)
2. Roy, D., Brine, J., Murasawa, F.: Usability of English note-taking applications in a foreign language learning context. Comput. Assist. Lang. Learn. **29**(1), 61–87 (2016)
3. Valstad, H.: Introducing the iPad in a Norwegian High School: How do Students and Teachers React to This Technology. Institutt for datateknikk og informasjonsvitenskap, Norway (2011)

4. Richardson, J.V., Mahmood, K.: eBook readers: user satisfaction and usability issues. Library Hi Tech (2012)
5. Lewis, J.R.: Usability Testing. Handbook of Human Factors and Ergonomics. Wiley, New York (2006)
6. Balagtas-Fernandez, F., Hussmann, H.: A methodology and framework to simplify usability analysis of mobile applications. In: 2009 IEEE/ACM International Conference on Automated Software Engineering, pp. 520–524. IEEE, New Zealand (2009)
7. Brooke, J.: SUS: a "quick and dirty" usability. Usability evaluation in industry, p. 189 (1996)
8. Borsci, S., Federici, S., Lauriola, M.: On the dimensionality of the system usability scale: a test of alternative measurement models. Cogn. Process. **10**(3), 193–197 (2009)
9. Norman, D.A.: The Psychology of Everyday Things, Basic books (1988)
10. Norman, D.A.: Some observations on mental models. Mental Models **7**(112), 7–14 (1983)
11. Davies, M.: Concept mapping, mind mapping and argument mapping: what are the differences and do they matter? High. Educ. **62**(3), 279–301 (2011)

Implementation of Action Maps and Interaction Prototypes as a Strategy to Improve Information Architecture and Interface Design in an Academic Management Platform

Sara B. Ibarra-Vargas[✉] and César Augusto Arias Peñaranda

Institución Universitaria Pascual Bravo, Medellín, Colombia
{s.ibarrava,cesar.arias}@pascualbravo.edu.co

Abstract. Organizations have found a great ally in information technologies to achieve success in their management processes. For universities, for example, information systems and platforms are essential to support the academic and administrative management of their institutional mission. These platforms, whether proprietary or licensed, serve institutions not only as a data repository but also as a scenario for managing and systematizing processes and procedures. The Pascual Bravo University Institution in Medellín, Colombia, has articulated its academic management processes through the University Academic Information and Control System or SICAU (in its Spanish acronym) platform, a proprietary development that perhaps has not achieved a coherent integration between information architecture and interface design. That is, the information experience specified in the backend (data architecture) is not integrated or reflected in the experience of the different users in the frontend (interface design). The objective of this case study is to propose the design of the interface level interaction (graphic elements and feedback) for the SICAU platform in the teaching module at the Pascual Bravo University Institution. It is concluded that the analysis on action maps allows to identify gaps on the information architecture. The interaction analysis model proposed in this research facilitated the design of interactions with the purpose of improving the user experience (UX) and attributes in the platform's backend.

Keywords: Action maps · Interaction prototypes · Interface design · User experience

1 Introduction

The use of ICTs oriented to the development of management platforms for teaching administrative activities is a clear trend in the context of higher education. Educational institutions have adopted and adapted actions that allow them to set up virtual spaces with ICT resources - Information and Communication Technologies - to improve their administrative, training, content dissemination and management tasks for their stakeholder groups. These implemented information systems serve as a model to be repositories of

© Springer Nature Switzerland AG 2021
C. Stephanidis et al. (Eds.): HCII 2021, CCIS 1419, pp. 431–439, 2021.
https://doi.org/10.1007/978-3-030-78635-9_56

institutional traceability, communication platform or educational management model where students, teachers, administrative staff and employees interact. The implementation of these virtual extensions brings with it the centralization of the administrative activity in a virtual platform that aims at facilitating the processes around the information that the teacher manipulates around their figure and academic performance, courses in charge, groups of students and other processes resulting from his work; this makes the number and type of interactions that occur between such management platforms, teachers and other groups of users involved to be increasingly varied.

Information systems must propose different interaction scenarios for the user according to the amount of data to be managed and other users who must manipulate the information. It is frequent that the operation tasks are proposed from the organization level and the interaction flow from the software possibilities, consequently, the user-machine interaction process falls short because of its focus on the information architecture. In the design of the platform, the development team focuses its efforts on the backend -code structure seeking the optimization of server resources related to the accumulation and manipulation of data to deliver meaningful information to each interested area within the academic institution. But, the light definition on the frontend -interface design, feedback to action or cutback of paths in the execution of an activity during the use of the platform, causes that executing a simple action becomes a complex act among several operational possibilities [1, 2]. The development of screens as human interaction elements brought with it an increase in interface design, usability and user experience options [3]. However, the focus on frontend interaction design continues to aim its attention at the problem of time on task completion, losing reflection on the paradigm shifts that can be achieved in the way information is managed from user-screen-object relationships [2, 4].

The possibilities of intervention from interaction are based on two axes: one, in the basic principles of design, the ways elements are configured and their formal aspect at the levels of interface and affordance; and two, ergonomics, in terms of information and communication devices and the ways in which stimuli are processed through the senses [5]. On these two axes, the definition and analysis of the process of use, sequence, frequency and intensity, in the different moments of interaction is articulated [6]. Consequently, these moments are projected in the light of the design context and the interaction evaluation: cognitive ability, physical ability, sensory ability and functional ability [7]. A tool that has proved useful for the representation of the relationships between the information devices functions and the interactions that take place during their use are action maps [6, 8]. This graphical tool reconstructs the sequences that are used as a mapping where the different functions are discovered as inputs that the user can tour when interacting on the screen. Thus, action maps simplify the identification and evidence of coincidences (repetitions) during periods of use.

2   Methodology

The development of this experimental project was guided by agile methodologies due to the affinity for working with software development groups from the information architecture, and the CDIO methodology due to its affinity with the work paths proposed in the creative disciplines for interface design. The research on the interactions in the academic management platform SICAU was carried out in the teaching module, in the version of the first quarter of 2020. This platform is used by about 300 teachers who are part of the Pascual Bravo University Institution. The methodological implementation was carried out in three stages: (i) description of interaction levels on the interface, (ii) creation of action maps, and (iii) prototype execution.

Description of the Interaction Levels on the Interface. The teaching module interface comprises 15 action blocks, grouped into 7 categories: information, teaching assistance (without action options), research, approved plans, work plan, academic control and reservations. Figure 1 shows the SICAU platform interface in the teaching module. From the main page interface of the teaching module, it is possible to distinguish 4 hierarchical levels: 1. Section headers as those titles that frame a group of options; 2. Main icon in background, the figure is presented in white outlines within a colored circumference; 3. Main icon in figure; 4. Text to directly recognize the activity suggested by the icon. Each of the action blocks recognized in the main interface of the teaching module were characterized according to these 4 hierarchical levels to identify common configuration/action elements.

The choice of actions on which the detailed analysis of the interactions would be carried out was based on a recognition of the frequency of use per semester by the teachers. This exercise made it possible to identify the actions with the highest interaction during such period and on which it would be relevant to begin the process of updating and enhancing user experience. After this acknowledgement, the categories "grade recording" and "work plan" were chosen to carry out detailed analysis of the reciprocal action, and to project the interface design so as to improving user experience and communication with the system. For each of the two selected categories, detailed analyses were performed on action possibilities, hierarchies and interface formal attributes for both actions. The analyses on interaction levels were based on universal design principles [9], design fundamentals [10] and Gestalt principles [7, 11].

Creation of Action Maps. The cognitive path was executed using action maps. These maps were created based on the routes [12, 13]that the teacher users must carry out to complete the activities selected in the categories "grade recording" and "work plan". For each of the categories, an action map was developed to graphically project the action possibilities on the SICAU platform interface. After this mapping, the iteration and reprocessing cycles are identified for both cases and the events are systematized in order to match them up with the results of the information architecture analysis and thus become an input for improvements in the prototype execution. Table 1 shows the systematization of the events for the category "work plan" with the activity "new work plan".

Prototype Execution. The proposed improvements in each of the interfaces and information blocks are taken to the interaction flow prototype development. Second level prototypes are created from the analysis and systematization of the information obtained in the previous moments. Such prototypes detail UX aspects in milestone moments of use, defined from the action maps. Mock-ups are developed in a tool such as Balsamiq for the creation of wireframes of the proposed platform solution. Balsamiq is a software

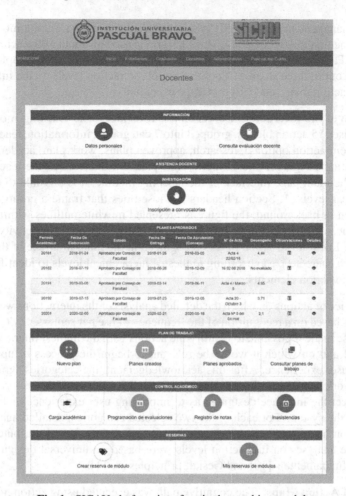

Fig. 1. SICAU platform interface in the teaching module.

implemented for rapid interface prototyping. For each of the selected categories, rapid prototypes were made in order to determine whether the patterns or actions developed within the SICAU platform were appropriate according to the action map proposed in the previous phase. Figure 2 presents the initial proposal for the "work plan" category interface with the "new work plan" activity. The proposed interface in the base prototype reduces use regularity and integrates the information that matches with other modules within the platform and that are related to the teaching function.

3   Results

The following is a description of the results of each of the moments carried out during the research:

Table 1. Event systematization - Activity New work plan.

Information blocks	Decision making	Actions to be performed	Reprocess
Home page for activity	1. Submit plan for approval 2. Confirmation of action	1. Send 2. Cancel	1. Error due to sending a work plan without being filled out
Personal information	N/A	1. Continue to fill out	N/A
Direct teaching activities	1. Observations on the assignment	1. Enter number of students 2. Enter number of hours 3. Continue to fill out	1. Enter number of students 2. Enter number of hours
Support to teaching activities	1. Verification of associated activities	1. Enter number of hours 2. Continue to fill out	1. Enter number of hours 2. Decimal adjust to record exact times on role
Research activities	1. Verification of associated activities	1. Project selection 2. List products 3. Enter number of hours 4. Continue to fill out	1. Enter number of hours. 2. Decimal adjust to record exact times on role
Extension activities	1. Verification of associated activities	1. Enter number of hours 2. Continue to fill out	1. Enter number of hours. 2. Decimal adjust to record exact times on role
Working hours	N/A	1. Enter activities on the grid 2. Enter remarks 3. Continue to fill out	1. No correspondence with decimal values filled in the previous blocks vs. whole value assignment on the grid
Intersemester schedule	N/A	1. Enter activities on the grid 2. Enter remarks 3. Continue to fill out	N/A

(continued)

Table 1. (*continued*)

Information blocks	Decision making	Actions to be performed	Reprocess
Evidence	1. Warning about evidence assignment 2. Review assignments 3. Submit for approval	1. Select associated evidence 2. Assign link 3. Save	N/A

Source: Own creation.

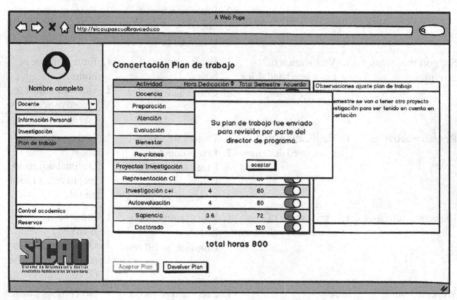

Fig. 2. Initial proposal prototype for the "work plan" category interface with the "new workplan" activity.

Description of Interface Interaction Levels. There is disagreement between the possibilities of action within the interface and actual actions to carry out the activity thoroughly. This is evident through buttons that remain active to complete an operation without any data to process. The use of color or hierarchy in the other blocks seems to happen randomly. Moreover, there were no direct associations with the further action in the use of 60% of the icons. This issue leads to a greater tendency for human error and reprocessing that negatively impacts other user roles or information blocks in the platform.

Creation of Action Maps. The action map that corresponds to the category "new work plan" consists of a greater number of levels or blocks of information to execute the activity due to the specifications that must be defined on it, however, some of them could be automated. This map presents a simple work structure from the actions, since no more than three movements are required to execute several of them. Nevertheless, reprocesses are registered in 6 of the 9 information blocks (66.6%), which shows that the information architecture has some gaps on the integration of information in its databases. The action map that corresponds to the activity "grade recording" generates a couple of iteration cycles that could confuse the teacher user in the use sequence and increase the related tasks development time.

Prototype Execution. A couple of usability tests were run on the base prototype. These tests were related to the perception of information blocks, hierarchies and use sequences. The results of these tests were input for the development of high-fidelity prototypes. The layout of the interactive interface was carried out on Adobe XD software since it allowed the integration of feedback elements in the use sequence use that this research aimed at. Figure 3 shows the interface and integration on the information architecture of the implemented high-fidelity prototype.

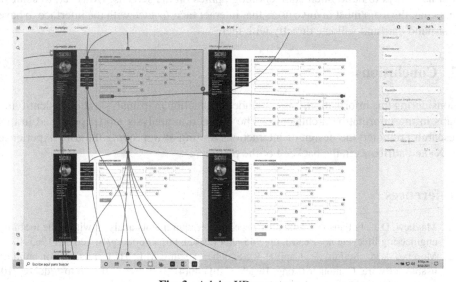

Fig. 3. Adobe XD prototype

4 Discussion

Improvements in the design of the SICAU platform interface articulated the knowledge of creative disciplines such as industrial and graphic design with Gestalt theory and systems engineering in block programming. The creation of action maps allows the identification of gaps in the information architecture and promotes interdisciplinary work between designers and software engineers. As a result, the user experience and the team's perception of the system were improved. This working path, when facing the project, allows for an interdisciplinary and transdisciplinary work, since each of the people involved in the process contributes from their area of knowledge to the creation of the product that is being developed, but is constantly feeding from other fields of study that contribute to both individual and collective knowledge. This approach facilitates work not only from a disciplinary point of view, but it also gives importance to the generation and confrontation of knowledge by the participants, which is applicable to any project that will be conducted and that involves the construction, design or redesign of a particular system.

The implementation of action maps as a representation of the routs users can take when interacting with the on-screen interface. The potential represented using action maps in interface design lies in the possibility of demonstrating the complexity of the relationships during the process of use and promoting, through functional and operational matches, the interactions between the practical, aesthetic and symbolic dimensions of the interface. Thus, the action map based on user interaction nodes in various activities opens up new possibilities for the software development and interface design team to find new ways to build interaction choreographies on the screens. However, to achieve this goal, the team must involve users that interact face-to-face with the interface to have first-hand data and validate directly with them.

5 Conclusions

Considering this information, it is concluded that action map analysis allows identifying gaps in the information architecture. The interaction analysis model proposed in this research promoted the design of interactions aiming at improving the user experience (UX) and attributes in the backend of the platform.

References

1. Mayhew, D.J., Follansbee, T.J.: User experience requirements analysis within the usability engineering lifecycle no. Beaird, pp. 945–954 (2012). https://doi.org/10.1201/b11963-48
2. Moreno, A.M., Seffah, A., Capilla, R., Sánchez-Segura, M.I.: HCI practices for building usable software. Computer (Long. Beach. Calif) 46(4), 100–102 (2013). https://doi.org/10.1109/mc.2013.133
3. Lilliam, D., Cancio, P., Mercedes, I., Bergues, M.: Usabilidad de los sitios Web, los métodos y las técnicas para la evaluación Usability of Web sites, methods and evaluation techniques. Rev. Cuba. Inf. en Ciencias la Salud 24(2), 176–194 (2013). http://scielo.sld.cu
4. Hart, M.A.: Designing interactions by bill moggridge. J. Prod. Innov. Manag. (2008). https://doi.org/10.1111/j.1540-5885.2008.00294_1.x
5. Kim, G.J.: Human factors as HCI theories. Human-Computer Interact. Fundam. Pract. pp. 205–208 (2015). http://jlc.jst.go.jp/DN/JST.JSTAGE/rika/28.205?from=Google
6. Herreño, E., Ibarra Vargas, S.B.: Modelo da análise de dispositivos digitais para simplificar a interação humana. In: Anais do 4° Congresso Sulamericano de Design de Interação, pp. 190–197 (2012)
7. Lim, Y., Stolterman, E., Jung, H., Donaldson, J.: Interaction gestalt and the design of aesthetic interactions. In: Proceedings of 2007 Conference on Designing pleasurable products and interfaces - DPPI 2007, p. 239 (2007). https://doi.org/10.1145/1314161.1314183

8. Fileno, E.F.: Design de interação e a percepção das tecnologias Interaction design and perception of technologies (2009)
9. Labrada, S.M.: Principios del proceso de Diseño de Interfaz de Usuario, vol. 1, pp. 143–155 (2020)
10. Wucius, W.: Principios del diseño en color, pp. 1–110 (1992)
11. Gómez Reynoso, J.M., Echavarría Álvarez, E.G., Reynoso, G., Álvarez, E., Manuel Gómez Reynoso, J.: Midiendo el Impacto de las Teorías Gestalt en el Diseño de Interfaces Gráficas de Usuario (2011). http://aisel.aisnet.org/amcis2011_submissions%0A. http://aisel.aisnet.org/amcis2011_submissions/59
12. Norman, D.A.: The Design of Future Things, vol. 18, no. 4. Basic Books (2007)
13. Norman, D.A.: Walk-through: a usability experiment. InformationWeek **773**, 66 (2000). http://search.ebscohost.com/login.aspx?direct=true&db=aph&AN=2796171&site=ehost-live

Understanding Trust in Social Media: Twitter

Catherine Ives-Keeler[✉], Oliver Buckley, and Jason Lines

School of Computing Sciences, University of East Anglia, Norwich NR4 7TJ, UK
{c.ives-keeler,o.buckley,j.lines}@uea.ac.uk

Abstract. In this paper we investigate how users can be perceived on Twitter by looking at a selection of tweets, and how the type of personality traits and language can effect trust. We present participants with a selection of tweets and gather their initial opinions of the Twitter users presented by using a Likert scale (https://www.simplypsychology. org/likert-scale.html) and free text box for participants to share their opinions, hosted on Microsoft forms. This paper presents preliminary results based on the data gathered from a questionnaire created by the researcher, highlighting factors that impact how participants perceived the Twitter users. It was found that participants valued content, profile pictures and the display name more than likes and retweets. They did not like the more aggressive or opinionated users and had more of a neutral or positive reaction to the more light-hearted users.

Keywords: Trust · Misinformation · Twitter

1 Introduction

With the increased popularity of social media platforms, such as Twitter, comes an increase in social media bots and the spread of misinformation [1]. Twitter is an open platform which has made the creation and automation of bots easy for users to set up and post tweets on their behalf. Misinformation is a growing problem on social media, especially during the pandemic era, as discussed by H. Rosenberg et al. [2], so it is important to understand factors that impact what users trust on social media, when and why they share information.

Understanding trust in social media is vital, including assessing factors which make users want to tweet, retweet or like certain pieces of information or news, and what are users more sceptical about. If we can pin-point different characteristics or personality traits, this could help determine factors that lead to how information spreads around social media. In this paper we want to investigate the spread of information and factors that make users more or less likeable and how a select set of tweets from a user can be perceived. We hope the outcome of this experiment will give us an insight as to the type of language and personality traits that participants find most trustworthy and engaging when using social media. The outcome of this experiment could lead to further work including how fake news spreads on social media, and how misinformation can spread due to a large number of users retweeting incorrect information.

© Springer Nature Switzerland AG 2021
C. Stephanidis et al. (Eds.): HCII 2021, CCIS 1419, pp. 440–447, 2021.
https://doi.org/10.1007/978-3-030-78635-9_57

2   Background and Relevant Literature

The motivation behind this study is to understand trust within social media, with a focus on why a Twitter user may be perceived as more or less trustworthy. One particular area of interest is how the language used can alter our perceptions of a user, and whether it can make a tweet more appealing to like or retweet. With the growth of social media in recent years, studies have emerged looking at personality and perception on social media, as discussed by Qiu L. et al. [3]. In this paper they looked at measuring the big 5 personality traits by collecting tweets from users over a 1 month period to observe if personalities can manifest in micro-blogging, the chosen social media platform for this study was Twitter. It was found that Out of the 5 traits only agreeableness and neuroticism could be judged accurately, they judged these traits by associating posts with specific linguistic markers, and observers rated the participants' personality of the basis of their tweets.

Another study that focused on predicting the big 5 personality traits from social media posts was discussed by Azucar, D et al. [4] in which their research aimed to develop automated methods to extract and analyse these digital footprints to predict personality traits. In this study they conducted a series of meta-analyses to determine the predictive power of digital footprints collected from social media over big 5 personality traits, finding that the accuracy of predictions is consistent across big 5 traits, and that accuracy improves when analyses include demographics and multiple types of digital footprints. Both of the papers discussed motivated our research and help to highlight the importance of personality on social media and how it can be measured.

Research conducted by D. Sterrett et al. [5] discuss what news to trust on social media and how social media platforms are becoming increasingly popular news sources. It was found that two cues could impact opinions of news on social media: the trustworthiness of the person who shares a story and the credibility of the news outlet reporting the story. This research was part of the motivation behind our study, highlighting how news can spread around social media and what factors can effect its trustworthiness. One of the interesting areas focused in this study is if people are more likely to trust an article on social media if it is shared by a public figure they trust than by one they do not trust.

These studies highlight the importance of understanding personality types on social media, by researching and understanding areas around predicting personality on social media [6] and who to trust we were motivated to create this study. Our hypothesis for this study is that users who come across as having strong personalities or strong views will generate stronger opinions and be more actively disliked than those who share more typical, 'mundane' posts.

3   Method

3.1   Procedure

For this study it was decided that a quick and effective way of collecting insightful results in a relatively short period of time was a questionnaire, this is the best platform to gather the information we wanted to analyse. We decided to use Microsoft forms as a link to a form can be easily created and shared, results gathered on this platform can easily be exported to an excel file for analysis and it had the functionality to have a Likert scale and optional free text responses.

A questionnaire was designed and created by the researcher to gather opinions about how Twitter users are perceived by a number of random participants. To execute this, a range of fake users and tweets were created based on research on how users interact on Twitter and generating believable tweets, which were then created to look like a genuine screen shot from Twitter by using tweetgen[1]. Research conducted behind the creation of these tweets was based on observing language and interactions between a range of users, from public figures to users who have few followers that post regularly, and verified users. We created a range of fake users with different views, characteristics and personalities, a mix of profile pictures or no profile pictures, randomly generated names and a variation of likes and retweets to make the accounts as genuine as possible. A bot account and a troll account were created to observe how participants perceived these users and if they are more sceptical of them, or even acknowledge that they might be a troll or bot.

The participants were shown 5 random tweets by each fake user then filled out a Likert scale, answering questions based on if they trusted the user or would retweet any of the tweets from that user, questions used can be seen in Fig. 1. At the end of the questionnaire a free text option was provided for participants to discuss any thoughts they had while reading the Tweets and if there were any factors that impacted their responses. This free text option is designed to provide more information as to how the selected Twitter users were perceived and any specific features that may make them stand out. After gathering this information from the responses, we have gathered a wide range of information that can be analysed using various text processing techniques such as removing punctuation and stop words in order to finalise the term frequency.

3.2   Participants

The participants in this experiment were recruited by using a Snowball sampling procedure [7] and posting about the questionnaire on social media. A total of 75 participants filled out the questionnaire, including 44 responses to the first free text option and 55 responses to the second free text option. This experiment was not aimed at a particular demographic, we aimed for a mixture of Twitter and non-Twitter users to ensure we could gain a range of responses. A brief description of the experiment was given to the users before they were shown any tweets, giving them a basis of what to expect from the questionnaire ensuring they understood what they were consenting to. We requested the participants email address in case they wished to withdraw their responses from the experiment at any time. No other personal or demographic information was gathered to ensure participant anonymity. Participants were not informed that the users

---

[1] https://www.tweetgen.com/create/tweet.html.

presented in this experiment were fake until the end of the questionnaire during the debrief, this deception was intended so that the participants started the experiment believing they were real users and provide genuine responses to the content. This experiment received the universities ethical approval, following the appropriate guidelines and ensuring no personal data was gathered from the participants unless absolutely necessary.

4   Preliminary Results

4.1   Quantitative Results

As part of the data collection, participants filled out a Likert scale answering 8 different questions after they had read through 5 tweets from each different user, 10 users in total. Some of the questions for this section include asking participants if they would retweet this user, if they trust the information discussed and if they think the users are a social media bot or troll, the participant then selects their responses between 'Strongly disagree' to 'Strongly agree' as shown in Fig. 1. All 75 participants responded to each of these questions.

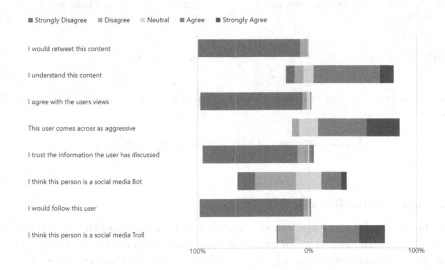

Fig. 1. Result from likert scale

From the results it was found that participants generally had the same responses to not liking, trusting or wanting to retweet tweets of the Twitter accounts that expressed very strong views. For example the results shown in Fig. 1 is from a user who expressed very strong controversial political views, showing that there was a majority response to each questions implying that most participants viewed them in the same way. The Twitter users that shared more personal information had more of a neutral responses compared to users who were sharing information or expressing political views. The Twitter user that was created to resemble a bot was overall mostly viewed as a bot by the participants (65.3%), though not everyone agreed. There was more of a positive or neutral responses to the cat account (an account made to look like it is the cat tweeting rather than a human) and the users that appeared to be younger. Though there was nothing to specify the exact ages of any of these Twitter users, participants assumed that if they looked younger in their profile pictures then it was actually them and a few participants made comments comparing how they viewed the 'younger' users compared to the 'older' users.

Overall most users had a mixed results, but generally there was a majority response for each user if the participants found them to be trustworthy or not and if they would share any of their tweets. The cat account, example in Fig. 2a was most trustworthy (28% agree - strongly agree), the account that came across as very right wing, Sully in Fig. 2b came across as the least trustworthy (94.5% disagree - strongly disagree).

(a) Tweet from 'human pretending to be their cat' account

(b) Tweet from 'old right wing male' account

Fig. 2. Examples of tweets used in the experiment

4.2 Qualitative Results

For the analysis of results gathered from the free text option of the questionnaire, we looked at term frequency for each response and looked for any common factors that participants mentioned which could have impacted their response. Out of the 75 participants that filled out the questionnaire, 44 responded to the free text option giving them the opportunity to discuss any further information they could share about the users that impacted their responses to the questions. The second free text option was to gain information from participants about if there were any factors such as profile picture or number of likes that affected their responses. The results of the term frequency analysis can be seen in Tables 1a for the first responses and 1b for the factors.

While analysing the text responses from participants it was noted that these tweets generated some fairly aggressive responses, with some participants providing feedback such as "Most users were thick as shit" and "these people suck, twitter is just filled with the insane babblings of children and idiots". A lot of the negative responses provided by the participants were due to the overly opinionated and political accounts, however they felt more positively towards the more light-hearted and 'fun' accounts. There were several participants that stated they do not regularly use Twitter and do not see the purpose in it. Results also showed a mixture of participants considering likes and retweets while others did not acknowledge they were there, a lot of people appeared to focus on the content of the tweets rather than the users profile. It was also mentioned regularly that grammar and spelling effected how a lot of participants felt about the users, with several participants mentioning that they did not like users that used strong language or had frequent spelling mistakes. Most participants preferred a 'genuine' looking profile image rather than one that looked like a stock image photo or no profile photo. Profile photos are the only way participants might assume the age of the user, some participants expressed that they disliked how the 'older' users came across compared to the 'younger' users however the age of the users is never mentioned, participants based this purely on information provided like profile picture or making assumptions based on the content of the tweets. One participant stated they are more likely to trust users who shared the same views as them, implying they would share information regardless of where it comes from if it is something they already believe. Word clouds were created from the free text results after removing stop words as a visual representation of the key elements participants mentioned, as shown in Fig. 3a and 3b. Figure 3b shows the key factors that impacted their responses were likes, profile pictures, content and discussion around potential bot accounts.

 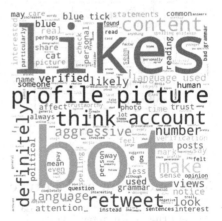

(a) Further thoughts on users   (b) Factors that impact responses

Fig. 3. Wordclouds created using responses from the questionnaire

Table 1. Term frequency for how many times a word was used in the free text responses

Thoughts	
Word	**Word count**
tweet	23
users	16
twitter	12
people	11
information	11
account	10
bot	8
user	7
political	7
follow	7
views	6
felt	6
content	6
none	5
social	5
media	5
across	5
agree	5
news	5
interesting	4
posting	4
politics	4
aggressive	4
things	4
come	4
opinions	4
5g	4
cat	4
though	4
different	4

Factors	
Word	**Word count**
like	34
user	27
tweet	23
bot	22
profile	16
picture	15
would	14
language	14
didnt	14
think	13
content	12
account	11
used	11
blue	10
also	10
definitely	9
aggressive	9
twitter	9
retweets	8
really	8
grammar	7
number	7
look	7
likely	7
views	6
spelling	6
verified	6
dont	6
people	5
posts	5

(a) Thoughts   (b) Factors

5   Conclusion and Future Work

Overall the preliminary results of our study show us that there are specific factors that impact how a user is portrayed based on what and how they share posts on social media. Our research identified that a user's profile picture and the actual content of their tweets are the two most significant factors in determining whether a user will share a post on social media. The language, spelling and grammar will play a role in the user's decision making process. This information is key when understanding what makes a user more attractive, engaging and why other social media users would interact with them.

Based on the preliminary results from this experiment, we have gained an insight into some of the key factors that play a role in how a Twitter user might be perceived based on a small sample of what they might discuss on Twitter. After a more in-depth analysis is carried out on these results, it could lead to further experiments around deception; if participants have a certain expectation before viewing users tweets does this alter their perception of the person, leading into a discussion on the halo effect [8] in social media. An experiment like this could include creating a similar questionnaire to the one generated for this experiment, but populated only with bots, can we deceive participants into thinking bots are actual users and vice versa? This has the potential to lead into more work covering how bots are perceived on social media and if people can find a bot trustworthy. Future experiments similar to this also open up new paths to further text and sentiment analysis, looking at how language used can alter the sentiment of a social media post.

References

1. Wang, P., Angarita, R., Renna, I.: Is this the era of misinformation yet: combining social bots and fake news to deceive the masses. In: Companion Proceedings of the The Web Conference 2018. International World Wide Web Conferences Steering Committee, Republic and Canton of Geneva, CHE, pp. 1557–1561 (2018)
2. Rosenberg, H., Syed, S., Rezaie, S.: The Twitter pandemic: the critical role of Twitter in the dissemination of medical information and misinformation during the COVID-19 pandemic. CJEM **22**(4), 418–421 (2020). https://doi.org/10.1017/cem.2020.361
3. Qiu, L., Lin, Q., Ramsay, J., Yang, F.: You are what you tweet: personality expression and perception on Twitter. J. Res. Pers. **46**(6), 710–718 (2012)
4. Azucar, D., Marengo, D., Settanni, M.: Predicting the Big 5 personality traits from digital footprints on social media: a meta-analysis. Pers. Individ. Differ. **124**, 150–159 (2018)
5. Sterrett, D., Malato, D., Benz, J., Kantor, L., Tompson, T., Rosenstiel, T., Sonderman, J., Loker, K.: Who shared it?: deciding what news to trust on social media. Digit. Journal. **7**(6), 783–801 (2019)
6. Golbeck, J., Robles, C., Turner, K.: Predicting personality with social media. In: CHI 2011 Extended Abstracts on Human Factors in Computing Systems (2011)
7. Goodman, L.A.: Snowball sampling. Ann. Math. Stat. **32**(1), 148–170 (1961)
8. Nisbett, R.E., Wilson, T.D.: The halo effect: evidence for unconscious alteration of judgments. J. Pers. Soc. Psychol. **35**(4), 250–256 (1977)

Utilitarian or Relational? Exploring Indicators of User Orientation Towards Intelligent Agents

Hankyung Kim[1(✉)], Hoyeon Nam[1], Uichin Lee[2], and Youn-kyung Lim[1]

[1] Department of Industrial Design, KAIST, Daejeon, Republic of Korea
{hkkim31,hoyeonnam,younlim}@kaist.ac.kr
[2] Department of Computer Science, KAIST, Daejeon, Republic of Korea
uclee@kaist.ac.kr

Abstract. When interacting with an agent, some users with utilitarian orientation tend to treat an agent as an instrumental tool, while others with relational orientation find the design of humanlike features more pleasing. Along with technological advances in user modeling and prediction algorithms, intelligent agents nowadays can personalize their interaction by identifying such orientation of users towards them. While prior work has revealed several behavioral signs resulting from such difference in orientation, little attention is directed to more fundamental cues that precede the occurrence of actual interaction. In light of this issue, this study explores intrinsic properties of users related to their utilitarian or relational orientation towards intelligent agents. Qualitative analysis of responses revealed three user propensities contributing to individual differences in orientation: tolerance to unpredictability, sensitivity to privacy, and sensitivity to an agent's autonomy. We discuss future directions for leveraging our findings to design personalized interaction in intelligent agents.

Keywords: Intelligent agents · Personalization · Orientation · Interaction design

1 Introduction

Intelligent agents promise personalization, or "a process of changing a system to increase their personal relevance" [3]. The trend in personalization has accelerated along with technological advances in user modeling and prediction algorithm. Channels for personalization have also been diversified as intelligent agents are appearing in forms of various products and services, ranging from smart thermostats to movie recommender systems. Accordingly, how to design more sophisticated personalization in intelligent agents has become a key research interest.

Among many important user characteristics to be considered in such personalization is orientation, or a mental schema [1], of users towards intelligent agents. Although the Computers are Social Actors (CASA) paradigm points to the need for social interaction between users and agents [13], there exist individual differences in the level of preference for such sociality. It has been suggested that when interacting with an agent, some users with utilitarian orientation tend to treat an agent as an instrumental tool, while others

© Springer Nature Switzerland AG 2021
C. Stephanidis et al. (Eds.): HCII 2021, CCIS 1419, pp. 448–455, 2021.
https://doi.org/10.1007/978-3-030-78635-9_58

with relational orientation find the design of agent sociality more pleasing. Even given with the same visible form factor of an agent, these individual differences exist [5].

Previous research has shown a potential of personalizing interaction strategies of agents based on such user orientation. For example, prior studies suggested that different recovery [8] and politeness [9] strategies of robots were appropriate for users with different orientation. More recently, Liao et al. [11] showed interaction with intelligent agents should be designed differently considering user orientation. For a user with high social-agent orientation, an agent should improve conversation and present a personality. For a user with low social-agent orientation, an agent should convey features from conventional information-search tools, avoid humanized features, and improve its transparency and affordance. These findings all point to opportunities for user-orientation-based personalization of an agent's behavior styles and service contents.

For this to occur, an agent should first be able to infer the user's orientation. A collection of studies has identified several user behaviors as possible predictors of orientation, such as greeting [7], pronouns [14, 15], as well as socializing questions, politeness, or agent-grounding questions [11] of users. While these factors add valuable insights to the design of personalized interaction, they are resultant behavioral "phenomena" evoked by user orientation and therefore can only be captured throughout interaction. To support personalization irrespective of the actual occurrence of interaction, it is necessary to know more fundamental properties of users that are potentially associated with different orientation toward agents. For example, Lee et al. [10] showed a user's tendency for parasocial interaction can be used to infer his or her attitude towards hedonic and utilitarian robots. More relevant to our research is Kim and Lim's work [6] which illustrates the differences in user perception on adaptive services that produce varied orientation of users.

Advancing this line of work, this research explores inherent properties of users that can be used as cues for their orientation towards agents. Our questionnaire-based study reveals three types of user propensity that can be used to infer orientation: tolerance for unpredictability, sensitivity to privacy, and sensitivity to an agent's autonomy. We conclude by discussing how designers of intelligent agents can utilize these findings to design personalized service and interaction style.

2 Study Method

We designed a scenario-based online questionnaire to explore user characteristics associated with either utilitarian or relational orientation of theirs towards intelligent agents as in Fig. 1. Our aim was to investigate what inherent tendencies of users shape their high-level orientation in general, irrespective of particular contextual subtleties. This means that we needed to minimize any influence that would create context-dependent differences when experiencing two distinct types of agents. Therefore, instead of observing people in separate cases, we decided to let all participants read the same predefined scenarios. Also, the aim of this study was not to categorize participants according to the pre-defined user characteristics, but rather to deductively discover those characteristics and how they are associated with user orientation. We therefore designed our study to be exploratory and collected qualitative data, letting participants freely articulate their visceral preference on each scenario. Instead of interview, therefore, we asked the same open-ended questions to all participants, as we wanted to minimize intervention or biases introduced by an interviewer which might affect participants' perception, but also to give them enough freedom to answer the rationales behind their preference for scenarios [12, 16]. We recruited participants who experienced using at least one AI-infused product or system (e.g. intelligent personal assistant, AI speakers) to ensure they had a basic understanding of intelligent agents. Participants were recruited via social media and our university's networks.

We designed these agents and scenarios as in Fig. 1, based on Kim and Lim's [6] findings on two initial mental models of users toward intelligent agents which parallel utilitarian and relational orientations respectively, namely Getting-Things-Done (GTD) Agent and Companion Agent mental models. Their findings identified two key factors that determine services to be provided by the GTD Agent and the Companion Agent. The two factors are: (1) the main value that each agent pursues (i.e., efficiency-centered support by the GTD Agent vs. personally nuanced support by the Companion Agent); and (2) the scope and the processing logic of data used (i.e., factual-level interpretation of only essential data by the GTD Agent vs. semantic interpretation of diverse data by the Companion Agent).

In the questionnaire, participants were first provided with a short introduction, an informed consent, and questions for basic demographic information. After this, participants were presented with two agents simultaneously in the form of two different scenarios (Fig. 1) that included common everyday situations that an agent could provide its support, expecting participants could intuitively grasp the characteristics of each and the differences between both. After scrutinizing the scenarios of both agents, participants rated their preference for the agents and explain the reasons. They rated preference for each agent using a slider scale from "0: not preferred at all" to "100: most preferred" and described in detail the reasons for each score (B-Q1 and B-Q2 in Fig. 1, presented in random order). Then, they were asked to rate relative preference between two agent types using a 7-point scale with "strongly prefer the GTD Agent" and "strongly prefer the Companion Agent" on each side, also describing in detail the reasons for the score (B-Q3 in Fig. 1). This item was to ask participants to rate their orientation, i.e. those who preferred the GTD Agent were deemed to hold utilitarian orientation, and vice versa.

For the analysis, among a total of 309 participants, we aimed to focus on participants who had more firmly set orientation, in expectation of gaining clearer predictors. We chose to only analyze participants who preferred (i.e., chose "2" or "6" in Q3) or strongly preferred (i.e., chose "1" or "7" in Q3) either the GTD Agent (N = 130) or the Companion Agent (N = 69). This resulted in keeping 199 participants in total (Female = 100) with an average age of 27.4 (SD = 8.63, MIN = 20, MAX = 60).

The data were analyzed by five researchers. The lead author initially scrutinized all 199 participants' open-ended answers and wrote memos. After this, four other researchers also participated in the discussion and conducted thematic analysis [4] to derive key themes. We then developed initial codes, focusing on the underlying reasons for preference and hence factors contributing to the shaping of orientation, rather than user needs and behaviors in consequence of differences in orientation. We iteratively conducted coding until we reached a consensus on emergent themes.

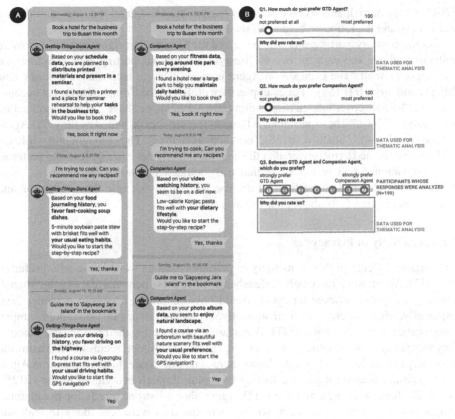

Fig. 1. (A) Service scenarios for GTD Agent (left) and Companion Agent (right); (B) Items in the questionnaire and data used for analysis.

3 Findings

From the analysis, we found three key factors that can be used as indicators of individual differences in user orientation to agents. The detailed findings are as follows.

3.1 Tolerance for Unpredictability

We found that participants differed in to what extent they were tolerant for unexpected service contents. Participants who preferred the GTD Agent considered an intelligent agent as an extremely advanced computer after all, expecting it to do better what computers could usually do: "What I want from an agent is not to understand me and empathize with me, but to save my time and effort by searching on behalf of me for the information I really need (P90)." As a result, these participants expected logicalness, speed, accuracy, and efficiency as the primary values pursued by an agent, being reluctant to get unpredicted and novel services that did not match their mental model of agents. Preferring "suggestions that are not exceptional (P116)," some participants even mentioned that overly creative suggestions were perceived as suspicious "advertisement (P3,

P26)." These participants wanted services reasonable enough so that they could infer and understand the rationale behind all the time.

On the contrary, participants who preferred the Companion Agent appreciated more collective advice and care for overall lifestyle, thereby supporting self-reflection and self-improvement: "The Companion Agent is more likely to help me get to know new things about myself (P153)." For example, they preferred the Companion Agent because it would "help discover hidden disposition (P167, P171)" or "have a positive impact on daily habits (P160)." These participants thought the services provided by the GTD Agent as "passive (P134)," "shallow (P188)," or "tactless (P151)." They thought that while the GTD Agent seemed to merely predict the next most likely behavior by learning patterns, the Companion Agent was the one that truly understands users. Accordingly, these participants welcomed suggestions of unexpected nature that help them reflect on and discover interesting facts about their life as a whole.

3.2 Sensitivity to Privacy

Participants differed in their sensitivity to privacy issues as well. Those who preferred the GTD Agent were extremely defensive against their personal data being shared. These participants believed an agent should have minimum access to personal data. Especially, what mattered was their subjective feeling of privacy invasion. For example, some participants perceived the GTD Agent as more protecting their privacy even though they were aware that the same data were used: "[The GTD Agent] seems like it is using the necessary data only (…) although I know there is no difference. [The Companion Agent is] unpleasing because it gives a feeling of seeing through everything in me (P125). "Overall, those who preferred the GTD Agent showed strong needs for maintaining proper distance between an agent so that personal data were less likely to leak and the agent could not grasp everything about them, criticizing the Companion Agent as "creepy (P15, P101)" and "stalker-like (P53)."

On the other hand, participants who preferred the Companion Agent believed an agent utilizing personal data to tailor services as beneficial and even "interesting (P157)." Service contents based on a wide scope of personal data were more appreciated as well: "I would think 'wow, can it even do that?' when the agent takes many factors into account instead of only using information related to a certain task (P199)." Furthermore, these participants even believed that disclosure of personal information was a catalyst for the relationship between an agent and them. An agent with a comprehensive understanding of users was perceived as friendly, far from being creepy. Participants appreciated the Companion Agent knowing more deeply about them and paying attention to trivial preferences and interests of theirs. Positive words such as "a best friend (P143, P147)" or "a family member (P135, P198)" were frequently used when participants were describing the Companion Agent.

3.3 Sensitivity to an Agent's Autonomy

Participants' orientation was also associated with the level of willingness to allow an agent to have autonomy. Participants who preferred the GTD Agent were vigilant in that an agent might think and judge on behalf of them, eventually taking away "free will (P27)" of humans: "I do not want to delegate my right of decision-making to a computer. After mobile phones were invented, few people possess the ability to memorize phone numbers. Just like that, I am afraid my ability to judge and decide by myself will degenerate if the Companion Agent takes over. (P36)" For these participants, the main body of the decision should always be themselves. Also, it was important for them to have the feeling of control in the overall relationship. They insisted an agent should not "cross the line (P53, P85, P96)" and stay as a tool.

Participants who preferred Companion Agent, conversely, were willing to delegate their decision-making process to an agent: "Utilizing data to generate suggestions is a job that I cannot do, so I think I can get something [from the Companion Agent] that I could not come up with (P180)." These participants hardly cared about whether or not they are having the feeling of control, and they even considered an agent which decides and behaves on their own to be convenient and smart. Also, these participants were relatively less concerned with an agent having overall autonomy. Instead, they even emphasized the expected role of an agent as, literally, an "equal (P193)" companion and not a "master-servant (P135)" relationship.

4 Discussion

Unpredictability, privacy, and autonomy have been central topics of discussion regarding the design of intelligent agents, but to our knowledge, this is to the first study explicitly identifying these factors are associated with user orientation to agents. Our findings open up opportunities for more human-centered personalization with users' orientation to intelligent agents taken into consideration. Coming back to the motivation of this study, we suggest that designers apply our findings to designing an agent's personalization services based on user orientation. For users with utilitarian orientation, an agent should (1) exploit essential data only, (2) generate results within the boundary of users' expectation, and (3) ensure users feel in control by, for example, ensuring them to make the final decision. For users with relational orientation, an agent should (1) strengthen the feeling of intimacy by communicating that it is utilizing diverse data, (2) think on behalf of users to unfold the possibilities rather than narrowing down, and (3) proactively take care of users and shepherd them to become better selves. Figure 2 shows an example with these suggestions applied.

With this in mind, in future, it remains to be explored how individual differences in propensity can be detected. One way is to find out relevant user traits that an agent can simply identify. For example, studies investigated an individual's phone-use behavioral features and traits associated with propensity to trust [2] or cooperation [17], demonstrating ways to unobtrusively infer users' qualitative characteristics. In a similar vein, we encourage future researchers to investigate observable behavioral signals that can imply an individual's tendency to embrace unpredictability, protect privacy, and value autonomy. Another way is to let users self-report their propensity. For instance, without seeming to pry, intelligent agents can ask purposeful questions during an onboarding stage to inquire desired levels of access to personal data or autonomy of an agent. Also, designers can let users directly customize such levels. While providing specific design guidelines for this goes beyond the purpose of this paper, we underscore the necessity of tactically designed probing interaction to unveil a user's propensity to unpredictability, privacy, and agent autonomy.

▼ For a user with **utilitarian** orientation

I'm tying to cook. Can you recommend me any recipes?

Your **food journaling history** shows that you favor **fast-cooking soup dishes.**

The following recipes in the Soup category are likely to fit well with your usual eating habits:

5-min soybeen paste stew

11-min onion soup

8-min spicy Tantanmen

▼ For a user with **relational** orientation

I'm tying to cook. Can you recommend me any recipes?

Your **usage history of entertainment-related apps** shows that you are interested in diet now.

I know many nice diet recipes! How about low-calorie Konjac pasta for today's dinner?

Fig. 2. Example of personalized recommendations for users with different orientations.

Meanwhile, we note that we probed properties of users that affect their general orientation towards intelligent agents as a whole. Users' orientation might be associated with other situational factors, such as the type of information provided. Also, a user's orientation might evolve over time [6, 11]. We hope our work motivates longer-period exploration in a less controlled study environment as future research.

5   Conclusion

In this paper, we investigated possible indicators of users' orientation towards intelligent agents. Our scenario-based questionnaire study shows individual differences in users' tolerance for unpredictability, sensitivity to privacy, and sensitivity to an agent's autonomy are associated with such orientation. We suggest considering them into the design of personalized service and interaction style, supported by further investigation of methods for eliciting them. We hope our study will be a step toward a deeper exploration of human-centered personalization in intelligent agents.

Acknowledgement. This work was mainly supported by Institute of Information & Communications Technology Planning & Evaluation (IITP) grant funded by the Korea government (MSIT) (No.2016-0-00564, Development of Intelligent Interaction Technology Based on Context Awareness and Human Intention Understanding) and partially supported by the National Research Foundation of Korea (NRF) grant funded by the Korea government (MSIT) (No. NRF-2021R1A2C2004263).

References

1. Abelson, R.P.: Psychological status of the script concept. Am. Psychol. **36**(7), 715 (1981)

2. Bati, G.F., Singh, V.K.: "Trust Us" mobile phone use patterns can predict individual trust propensity. In: Proceedings of the 2018 CHI Conference on Human Factors in Computing Systems, pp. 1–14. ACM (2018)

3. Blom, J.: Personalization: a taxonomy. In: CHI'00 Extended Abstracts on Human Factors in Computing Systems, pp. 313–314. ACM (2000)

4. Boyatzis, R.E.: Transforming Qualitative Information: Thematic Analysis and Code Development. Sage (1998)

5. Friedman, B., Kahn Jr., P.H., Hagman, J.: Hardware companions? What online AIBO discussion forums reveal about the human-robotic relationship. In: Proceedings of the SIGCHI Conference on Human Factors in Computing Systems, pp. 273–280. ACM (2003)

6. Kim, D.J., Lim, Y.K.: Co-performing agent: design for building user-agent partnership in learning and adaptive services. In: Proceedings of the 2019 CHI Conference on Human Factors in Computing Systems, pp. 1–14. ACM (2019)

7. Lee, M.K., Kiesler, S., Forlizzi, J.: Receptionist or information kiosk: how do people talk with a robot? In: Proceedings of the 2010 ACM Conference on Computer Supported Cooperative Work, pp. 31–40. ACM (2010)

8. Lee, M.K., Kiesler, S., Forlizzi, J., Srinivasa, S., Rybski, P.: Gracefully mitigating breakdowns in robotic services. In: 2010 5th ACM/IEEE International Conference on Human-Robot Interaction, pp. 203–210. ACM (2010)

9. Lee, Y., Bae, J.E., Kwak, S.S., Kim, M.S.: The effect of politeness strategy on human-robot collaborative interaction on malfunction of robot vacuum cleaner. In: RSS Workshop on HRI (2011)

10. Lee, N., Shin, H., Sundar, S.S.: Utilitarian vs. hedonic robots: role of parasocial tendency and anthropomorphism in shaping user attitudes. In: Proceedings of the 6th International Conference on Human-robot Interaction, pp. 183–184. ACM (2011)

11. Liao, Q.V., Davis, M., Geyer, W., Muller, M., Shami, N. S.: What can you do? Studying social-agent orientation and agent proactive interactions with an agent for employees. In: Proceedings of the 2016 ACM Conference on Designing Interactive Systems, pp. 264–275. ACM (2016)

12. Müller, H., Sedley, A., Ferrall-Nunge, E.: Survey research in HCI. In: Ways of Knowing in HCI, pp. 229–266 (2014)

13. Nass, C., Steuer, J., Tauber, E.R.: Computers are social actors. In: Proceedings of the SIGCHI Conference on Human Factors in Computing Systems, pp. 72–78 (1994)

14. Ogan, A., Finkelstein, S., Mayfield, E., D'Adamo, C., Matsuda, N., Cassell, J.: "Oh dear stacy!" social interaction, elaboration, and learning with teachable agents. In: Proceedings of the SIGCHI Conference on Human Factors in Computing Systems, pp. 39–48. ACM (2012)

15. Purington, A., Taft, J.G., Sannon, S., Bazarova, N. N., Taylor, S.H.: "Alexa is my new BFF" social roles, user satisfaction, and personification of the amazon echo. In: Proceedings of the 2017 CHI Conference Extended Abstracts on Human Factors in Computing Systems, pp. 2853–2859. ACM (2017)

16. Singer, E., Couper, M.P.: Some methodological uses of responses to open questions and other verbatim comments in quantitative surveys. Methods Data Analyses J. Quant. Methods Surv. Methodol. 11(2), 115–134 (2017)

17. Singh, V.K., Agarwal, R.R.: Cooperative phoneotypes: exploring phone-based behavioral markers of cooperation. In: Proceedings of the 2016 ACM International Joint Conference on Pervasive and Ubiquitous Computing, pp. 646–657. ACM (2016)

The Dimension of Mobile Phone Fluency: A Focus Group Interview

Xinze Liu[1,2], Yan Ge[1,2], Cheng Wang[3], Qian Zhang[1,2], and Weina Qu[1,2(✉)]

[1] CAS Key Laboratory of Behavioral Science, Institute of Psychology, Beijing, China
quwn@psych.ac.cn
[2] Department of Psychology, University of Chinese Academy of Sciences, Beijing, China
[3] School of Psychological and Cognitive Sciences, Peking University, Beijing, China

Abstract. The user experience of mobile phone products has been widely concerned, while the fluency of mobile phone will also affect the user experience. However, the factors that affect the fluency of mobile phone have not been fully discussed. Present study used semi-structured focus group interviews with 25 participants to explore the definition of smartphone fluency and the influencing factors of smartphone fluency. The interview results showed that among the 13 factors which affect mobile phone purchase, fluency is the most important factor. Fluency refers to the degree of ease with which an individual is able to perform some tasks. It usually means a high level of experience or practice. By coding and analyzing the user's evaluation, this study summarized six factors that affect smartphone fluency experience, including connection (visual sense when frames or tasks switch), response delay (the time interval between a user completing an operation and the smart phone providing a recognizable response), nonoperational system failure (the misoperation during mobile phone operation which are not related to lack of knowledge), visual experience (sharpness, distinguishability, color matching), operation error rate (error rate when users operate a mobile phone), simplicity (the minimum number of operation steps required to complete a task). This study defines the fluency of mobile phones and identifies the dimensions of smart phone fluency, which can provide research basis for improving fluency experience, and provide new research ideas for future direction of user experience improvement.

Keywords: Smart phone fluency · Focus group interview · User experience

1 Introduction

Mobile phone products have become an indispensable communication tool in daily life. According to the statistics of the Ministry of Industry and Information Technology of the People's Republic of China (2021), as of December 2020, there are 1594.07 million mobile phone users in China, with 1–2 mobile phones per capita. Therefore, more and more enterprises, researchers and engineers pay attention to the user experience of mobile phone.

On the one hand, researchers from the performance (Gaudette et al. 2016; Ma et al. 2013), appearance (Si and Liu 2015), application (Ahmad et al. 2014), interface design

© Springer Nature Switzerland AG 2021
C. Stephanidis et al. (Eds.): HCII 2021, CCIS 1419, pp. 456–463, 2021.
https://doi.org/10.1007/978-3-030-78635-9_59

(Rasche 2013), security (Mylonas et al. 2011), physical properties (Sutika et al. 2018) and other aspects to evaluate the usability of mobile phones and improve the product satisfaction of mobile phones. On the other hand, the researchers put forward some integrated models to evaluate mobile phone products. Ren et al. (2017) summarized four evaluation dimensions of smart phone experience: performance experience, sensory experience, usability experience, and emotional experience. Kim et al. (2018) proposed a mobile phone product satisfaction model in different situations and emotional states by using item identification. Li (2015) proposed a 6-dimensional mobile user experience evaluation system. However, the current mobile user experience evaluation system is not well compatible with the concept of smart phone fluency, which needs further discussion.

Smart phone fluency is a common subjective feeling when consumers purchase and evaluate mobile phones. The use of the word "smart phone fluency" may appear in a variety of situations, such as the smoothness of task switching, the task response speed and the startup or shutdown of applications. However, few studies have investigated this area to determine the definition of smart phone fluency and explore its structure. Therefore, this study aimed to develop the components of smart phone fluency. Present study adopted focus group interviews to investigate the problems users encounter regarding smart phone fluency and to qualitatively identify operational definitions of fluency.

2 Method

2.1 Participants

All the participants had experience with more than two smartphone operation systems, especially more than half a year's experience using the IOS system of iPhone. Three groups (graduate students, office workers and telecommunication engineers) were chosen as they may have different experience and attitude to smartphone fluency. Each group was interviewed respectively because they have similar background and may have similar opinion and more discussion. There are totally 25 participants joined the interview, aged from 20 to 40 (Mean = 27.28, SD = 4.36), including 11 males and 14 females.

2.2 Procedure

Three focus group interviews were conducted in which the participants were students, office workers, and engineers. A total of 7–10 interviewees participated in each interview. One moderator was in charge of each interview, and one assistant was responsible for recording information during the interview. Each interview lasted approximately 2 h, and the entire procedure was recorded by a camera. Before the interview, the participants were informed that the process would be videotaped for scientific research and that the contents of the video recording as well as their personal information would remain strictly confidential. All participants signed the informed consent form.

To ensure consistency across groups in the questions asked, we used a semi-structured questioning approach to allow some flexibility in the topics raised and level of participation within the groups. First, the moderator asked about smart phone usage, such as the brand and system currently in use, the reason for choosing them, which smart phone gives a better overall experience, and why. Second, the moderator investigated the factors related to smart phone fluency, such as how the participants understood smart phone fluency, their previous experiences in which fluency was negatively influenced, and other factors that may affect smart phone fluency. Third, specific scenarios affecting smart phone fluency were investigated. In this part, the moderator asked questions from the perspective of different modules and different operations. Different modules included networking applications, shopping applications, video applications, and audio applications. Different operations included turning the smart phone on and off, system upgrades, unlocking and locking the screen, and switching between applications. After the interview, all participants received 100 yuan as a reward.

3   Results

3.1   Impact Factors of Smartphone Purchases

The impact factors of smartphone purchases were surveyed by one question "When purchasing and selecting smartphones, which aspects of smartphone performance should be paid more attention to?" According to the record of each participant' comments, their answers were coded and classified into 13 types by the authors. The frequency of each type of impact factors mentioned by the participants was counted. The results were showed in Table 1 for three groups. Fluency, hardware parameters, battery power, appearance design, and screen size were the top five impact factors of smartphone purchases. Different groups had slightly different views, but fluency was the aspect of smartphone performance that most concerned all three groups, as it was the most frequently identified issue.

3.2   The Dimensions of Smartphone Fluency

According to the comments of participants in the interview, the authors discussed the structure of smartphone fluency based on three questions: 1) how to understand smartphone fluency; 2) factors affecting smartphone fluency experience under different modules and operations; 3) other issues of fluency experience. We summarized 6 aspects related to smartphone fluency. The first aspect is connection, which is defined as a visual sense of connection when switching frames or tasks (whether there were pauses or interruptions) (i.e., the rate of switching between applications). The second aspect is response delay, which is defined as the time interval from completing an operation to the device providing a recognizable response (i.e., the response time to a command). The third aspect is nonoperational system failure, which is defined as the mobile breakdowns caused by hardware configuration, software and the compatibility of the two rather than faulty operations (i.e., a device does not work when the user is typing). The fourth aspect is visual experience, which is defined as the sharpness, distinguishability and color matching of the screen and image quality. (i.e., the display of dynamic effects). The fifth aspect is the operation error rate, which is defined as the error rate when individuals operate a mobile phone and the lapses are not caused by the users' lack of mobile-related knowledge (i.e., using 3D Touch by mistake). The sixth aspect is simplicity, which is defined as the number of operations needed to complete a task (i.e., meeting the user's needs with the fewest steps). Then, one experimenter coded the comments of each participant. Table 2 showed the statistic results of each aspect that has been mentioned by participants.

Table 1. 13 impact factors of smart phone purchase.

	Graduate students (N = 7)	Office workers (N = 8)	Engineers (N = 10)	Total (N = 35)
Fluency	3	2	3	8
Hardware parameters	0	2	2	4
Battery power	1	0	3	4
Appearance design	2	1	1	4
Screen size	3	1	0	4
Screen resolution	1	1	1	3
Safety	0	2	1	3
Hand feeling	1	1	0	2
Camera function	2	0	0	2
Others' opinion	1	0	0	1
Price performance ratio	1	0	0	1
Durability	1	0	0	1
Habituation	0	0	1	1
Total	16	11	12	39

4 Discussion

In a sum, the main contribution of our research was we founded the important role of fluency in the experience of smartphone using and defined the dimensions of smartphone fluency.

4.1 Dimensions of Smart Phone Fluency

Through the focus group interviews, six main components of smart phone fluency were identified: nonoperational system failure, simplicity, connection, response delay, visual experience and operation error rate. In different modules and operations, these problems were mentioned frequently and were then extracted as elements of the structure of smart phone fluency. Next, each component of smart phone fluency will be discussed in connection with related studies.

Table 2. The structure of smart phone fluency.

Component	Number of times mentioned	Examples
Nonoperational system failure	63	Does not work when typing
Simplicity	33	Minimum number of operation steps required when completing a task
Connection	30	Rate of switching between applications; stability of the system; whether the system becomes stuck when opening an application
Response delay	25	Response time to a command; response time of turning the phone on and off
Visual experience	12	Display of dynamic effects; quality of screen or image
Operation error rate	7	Touch by mistake

Nonoperational System Failure. If mobile breakdowns result from hardware configuration, software and compatibility, users will be seriously inconvenienced. Some users complain that they frequently encounter certain minor problems, for example, that the keyboard cannot open and there is no input after typing. In the user experience evaluation model (Ren et al. 2017), a similar concept is system stability, which was one of the subelements of the performance experience. It was determined by whether the system frequently shut down, restarted, or flash quit automatically. To improve smart phone fluency, decreasing the possibility of nonoperation error rate caused by the hardware should be emphasized in the hardware configuration.

Simplicity. Simplicity refers to the minimum number of operating steps needed to complete a task. It means that common tasks should be simple to accomplish (Constantine 1994). Simplicity is also crucial to generating better smart phone fluency and user experience. From the users' perspective, they want to use the lowest number of steps to achieve their goals. The more custom and optional items are required, the more users become confused. However, when the interaction process is designed simply and clearly, users can complete tasks easily and quickly (Ji et al. 2006).

Simplicity is an important dimension of user experience. Park et al. defined the constituents of user experience as three elements: usability, affect and user value. Simplicity was a subelement of usability as well as affect because it referred to the way a product worked and how it looked, respectively (Park and Lee 2011). In a user experience evaluation model (Ren et al. 2017), the author mentioned that the minimum steps to complete a certain task should be evaluated to improve the usability experience. Additionally, in the heuristic evaluation checklist, simplicity and minimalist design were mentioned, which emphasized that questions and language used in mobile interfaces should be clear and concise, and the time to achieve a goal should be minimized according to Fitt's Law (Yáñez Gómez et al. 2014).

Connection. Connection, as another component of smart phone fluency, refers to the visual sense when frames or tasks switch. If there are pauses or interruptions when switching between applications, or if a device often becomes stuck in other operations, users tend to feel frustrated. Although users may tolerate slowness, they will hardly tolerate interruptions or pauses because they become confused about the system status. It is better to keep users informed about what the smart phone is doing (Nielsen 1994).

Response Delay. Response delay refers to the time interval between a user completing an operation and the smart phone providing a recognizable response. In our study, response delay was described as the mobile phone sometimes getting stuck and reacting slowly in the operation process. If the response delay is too long, it is perceived as a negative user experience in terms of smart phone fluency.

Response time has been widely studied in usability and human factor studies by many researchers because it is a key factor in the productivity of human-computer interactions (Zhao et al. 2017). Yáñez et al. (2014) developed a new checklist for heuristic evaluation of mobile interfaces in which response time was a subelement of visibility of system status. In the checklist, response time was investigated by checking whether the response times were appropriate for the users' cognitive processing and appropriate for the task, whether there were observable delays and whether users were kept informed of the system status. Therefore, response time did play a role in the usability test of mobile interfaces. Time delay during human-computer interactions would increase negative user emotions, task error rate, work stress and perceptual sensitivity (Hoxmeier and DiCesare 2000; Luck et al. 2006; Owen-Hill et al. 2014; Szameitat et al. 2009; Yang and Dorneich 2015). Therefore, response delay, as an aspect of smart phone fluency, has an important impact on user experience.

Visual Experience. Visual experience, which is closely related to screen and image quality, refers to sharpness, distinguishability, color matching, etc. It is also related to smart phone fluency because whether the interface is smooth and whether animation is in accordance with human visual perception can affect the user experience to a certain degree. In the user experience evaluation model, appearance, screen size, interface style and color matching were four of the subelements of sensory experience, and the aesthetic value of interactive systems could affect users' satisfaction and perception of usability (Koutsabasis and Istikopoulou 2013; Lindgaard and Gitte 2007; Sauer and Sonderegger 2009). The visual appearance of the phone could also have a positive effect on performance by reducing the time required to complete tasks and improve reading comprehension (Cuddihy and Spyridakis 2012; Sonderegger and Sauer 2010). It was noted that the smart phone should be designed to be attractive, with a well-designed visual layout (Yáñez Gómez et al. 2014). Additionally, the interface should be concise and elegant, and the colors of the interface should be harmonious. In the future, the better understanding of human's visual cognition could also contribute to the design of human-computer interface (Wu et al. 2014).

Operation Error Rate. The operation error rate means the error rate when users operate a mobile phone, and the lapses are not caused by a lack of mobile-related knowledge. For instance, users sometimes touch 3D Touch by error, which has a negative influence on fluency experience. Because it is hard for users to prevent their own operation errors, it is advisable for the smart phone developer and designer to eliminate error-prone conditions. Additionally, before users commit to an action, it is optimal to present them with a confirmation option, which was one of 10 usability heuristics for user interface design (Nielsen 1994). In the user experience evaluation model (Ren et al. 2017), fault tolerance was one of the subelements of usability experience, and the author mentioned that it is beneficial to provide guidance and feedback in time to help the users avoid and correct errors.

4.2 Limitations and Future Directions

This study used focus group interviews to explore the important impact of fluency on mobile phone using experience and the dimensions of mobile phone fluency, but there are still some limitations in this study. The focus group sample was very small, with only 25 people; thus, the results can hardly represent the opinions of a large sample. Future studies need to verify the wide applicability of the results in a larger population. In addition, this study identified the dimensions of mobile phone fluency, but did not give quantitative design suggestions. Future research can further explore the fluency design parameters of user satisfaction through laboratory experiments.

References

Ahmad, N., Boota, M.W., Masoom, A.H.: Smart phone application evaluation with usability testing approach. J. Softw. Eng. Appl. **7**, 1045–1054 (2014). https://doi.org/10.4236/jsea.2014.712092

Constantine, L.: Collaborative usability inspections for software. In: Proceedings of the Software Development'94 (1994)

Cuddihy, E., Spyridakis, J.H.: The effect of visual design and placement of intra-article navigation schemes on reading comprehension and website user perceptions. Comput. Hum. Behav. **28**(4), 1399–1409 (2012). https://doi.org/10.1016/j.chb.2012.03.002

Gaudette, B., Wu, C.-J., Vrudhula, S., IEEE: Improving smartphone user experience by balancing performance and energy with probabilistic QoS guarantee. In: Proceedings of the 2016 IEEE International Symposium on High-Performance Computer Architecture, pp. 52–63 (2016)

Hoxmeier, J.A., DiCesare, C.: System response time and user satisfaction: an experimental study of browser-based applications. In: AMCIS 2000 Proceedings, p. 347 (2000)

Ji, Y.G., Park, J.H., Yun, M.H.: A usability checklist for the usability evaluation of mobile phone user interface. Int. J. Hum.-Comput. Interact. **20**(3), 207–231 (2006). https://doi.org/10.1207/s15327590ijhc2003_3

Kim, K.-J., et al.: Evaluation of smartphone user experience: identification of key evaluation items and their relationships. Int. J. Mob. Commun. **16**(2), 167–189 (2018)

Koutsabasis, P., Istikopoulou, T.G.: Perceived website aesthetics by users and designers: implications for evaluation practice. Int. J. Technol. Hum. Interact. **9**(1), 116–121 (2013)

Li., J.W.: Evaluation System Research and Implementation of the Smart Phone User Experience. Beijing University of Posts and Telecommunications, Beijing (2015). (Chinese)

Lindgaard, G.: Aesthetics, visual appeal, usability and user satisfaction: what do the user's eyes tell the user's brain? Aust. J. Emerg. Technol. Soc. **5**(1), 1–14 (2007)

Luck, J.P., Mcdermott, P.L., Allender, L., Russell, D.C.: An investigation of real world control of robotic assets under communication latency. In: Paper presented at the ACM SIGCHI/SIGART Conference on Human-robot Interaction (2006)

Ma, Z., Qiao, Y., Lee, B., Fallon, E.: Experimental evaluation of mobile phone sensors. In: ISSC 2013: 24th IET Irish Signals and Systems Conference, 20–21 June 2013. https://doi.org/10.1049/ic.2013.0047

Mylonas, A., Dritsas, S., Tsoumas, B., Gritzalis, D., IEEE: Smartphone Security Evaluation: The Malware Attack Case (2011)

Nielsen, J.: Heuristic evaluation. usability inspection. Methods **13**(3), 377–386 (1994)

Owen-Hill, A., Suárez-Ruiz, F., Ferre, M., Aracil, R.: Effect of video quality and buffering delay on telemanipulation performance (2014)

Park, B.W., Lee, K.C.: A pilot study to analyze the effects of user experience and device characteristics on the customer satisfaction of smartphone users. In: Kim, T., Adeli, H., Robles, R.J., Balitanas, M. (eds.) Ubiquitous Computing and Multimedia Applications. UCMA 2011. Communications in Computer and Information Science, vol 151, pp. 421. Springer, Berlin, Heidelberg (2011). https://doi.org/10.1007/978-3-642-20998-7_50

Rasche, P.: Haptic-loading interface design for better smartphone user experience (2013)

Ren, H.B., Zhou, J., Feng, W.Q.: Evaluation of the smart phone user experience based on MTS. Packaging Engineering (Chinese) (2017)

Sauer, J., Sonderegger, A.: The influence of prototype fidelity and aesthetics of design in usability tests: effects on user behaviour, subjective evaluation and emotion. Appl. Ergon. **40**(4), 670–677 (2009). https://doi.org/10.1016/j.apergo.2008.06.006

Si., Y.Q., Liu., L.: Study on the influencing factors of the intelligent mobile phone user experience. Software (Chinese) **36**(3), 111–115 (2015)

Sonderegger, A., Sauer, J.: The influence of design aesthetics in usability testing: Effects on user performance and perceived usability. Appl. Ergon. **41**(3), 403–410 (2010). https://doi.org/10.1016/j.apergo.2009.09.002

Sutika, T., Funilkul, S., Triyason, T., Supattatham, M., Assoc Comp, M.: Quality of Smartphone User Experience Analysis: Focusing on Smartphone Screen Brightness Level for the Elderly (2018)

Szameitat, A.J., Rummel, J., Szameltat, D.P., Sterr, A.: Behavioral and emotional consequences of brief delays in human-computer interaction. Int. J. Hum Comput Stud. **67**(7), 561–570 (2009). https://doi.org/10.1016/j.ijhcs.2009.02.004

Wu, C.C., Wick, F.A., Pomplun, M.: Guidance of visual attention by semantic information in real-world scenes. Front. Psychol. **5** (2014). https://doi.org/10.3389/fpsyg.2014.00054

Yáñez Gómez, R., Cascado Caballero, D., Sevillano, J.-L.: Heuristic evaluation on mobile interfaces: a new checklist. Sci. World J. (2014)

Yang, E., Dorneich, M.C.: The effect of time delay on emotion, arousal, and satisfaction in human-robot interaction. In: Paper Presented at the Human Factors & Ergonomics Society Meeting (2015)

Zhao, W.G., Ge, Y., Qu, W.N., Zhang, K., Sun, X.H.: The duration perception of loading applications in smartphone: effects of different loading types. Appl. Ergon. **65**, 223–232 (2017). https://doi.org/10.1016/j.apergo.2017.06.015

A Study of Motivation, Preferences, and Pain Points Regarding Participation in Career Related Mentorship

Arpit Mathur$^{(\boxtimes)}$ and Carrie Bruce$^{(\boxtimes)}$

Georgia Institute of Technology, Atlanta, GA 30332, USA
{arpit.mathur,carrie.bruce}@gatech.edu

Abstract. Seeking mentorship and advice is a key activity in a graduate student's career development, specifically when transitioning from academia, and looking for job opportunities. While multiple sources of career related information are available to graduate students, there are multiple benefits in getting this information through a mentor. This paper presents a user research study to understand the motivations, preferences and pain points of various participants of career related mentor-mentee relationships. Semi-structured Interviews were conducted with 24 participants, comprising (i) graduate students, (ii) industry professionals, (iii) professional career advisors, and (iv) recruiters. Further data was collected from 76 participants through surveys. The data revealed insights and patterns pertaining to mentorship related scheduling, initiation, information needs, incentives and strategies. The analysis of this data resulted in a set of design recommendations for digital mentorship platforms to enhance the nature of these interactions, and in turn provide a better experience to both the mentor and the mentee.

Keywords: Human-computer interaction · Career development Human resources · Mentor-Mentee relationships · User research

1 Introduction

Human-computer interaction students who are seeking an internship or other employment must be skilled in building their resumes and portfolios, searching for pertinent positions, navigating application processes, and negotiating position details. While various sources for these types of career-related information are available to graduate students, there are potential benefits to practicing and refining these skills with a mentor or advisor. Mentors and advisors can be employment specialists, such as campus career services staff who assist students in developing job seeking skills or university recruiters who connect with students to identify potential hires. Other possible mentors and advisors include faculty, peers, and HCI-related professionals who perhaps have less specialized experience in job seeking skills or placement, but likely have other useful knowledge or advice for the student. Despite the availability of mentors or advisors, it is not

© Springer Nature Switzerland AG 2021
C. Stephanidis et al. (Eds.): HCII 2021, CCIS 1419, pp. 464–471, 2021.
https://doi.org/10.1007/978-3-030-78635-9_60

always easy for HCI students to identify the appropriate person to contact for specific information needs or advice. Additionally, students can have difficulty getting responses from people they do not have a formal mentoring or advising relationship with, resulting in delays, insufficient information, and unsatisfactory experiences.

The objective of this study was to learn about the preferences and incentives of HCI graduate students and industry professionals to participate in mentorship or advisement relationships. We believe that incorporating these characteristics into a digital solution would significantly improve the job hunt experience of graduate students. We conducted semi-structured interviews, surveys, and a competitive analysis, and this paper highlights the results of our research work. We end this paper by highlighting design recommendations that can improve the user experience of online mentoring platforms.

2 Related Work

Many studies have been conducted on understanding the role of technology to support individuals during their job hunt. [1] compares the query results specific to an individual's job hunt with general search query trends. The study identifies specific attributes of these queries, arguing that optimization of search engines around these attributes can improve user experience. Other literature also explores the role of mentoring in career development. [2] presents a mentoring roadmap and network model on the basis of an extensive literature review. The advent of the internet has enabled online mentorship to play a huge role in career development, due to its potential to nurture more effective communication between mentors and protgs. [3] studies the nature of online mentoring, by studying career advice given through online Q/A forums. Their research work built a taxonomy of three different types of career requests (best practices, career threats, and time-sensitive requests). [4] identifies various stages of a typical online mentorship process, and also suggests multiple strategies to optimize value at each stage. Multiple studies have also been conducted to understand the nature of mentorship in the context of academia. [5] investigated the motivations, nature, and outcomes of mentorship programs for undergraduate students, and reported the positive impact of this relationship on future graduate roles. [6] presents a program for female undergraduate computer science students, advocating the value of mentoring for career development.

3 Study Objectives

The objective of this study was to understand preferences and motivations for students and mentors in existing mentoring relationships. We believe that incorporating these preferences into mentoring platforms will help increase participation and make digital mentorship more effective. We studied the following preferences: (i) incentives/motivations for participation (ii) medium of communication (iii) preferences for choosing mentor/mentee. We also wanted to learn to what degree existing solutions incorporated these preferences.

4   Methodology

We conducted semi-structured interviews with individuals experienced in career related mentorship, to get some qualitative findings about their experiences. We then conducted a survey to generalise these findings to a broader audience. We also conducted a competitive analysis in parallel to benchmark the array of existing offerings in mentoring platforms.

4.1   Semi-structured Interviews

Participants. We recruited 24 participants (M = 10, F = 14) with experience in engaging in job related mentorship and advisement activities. 7 participants (S1 - S7) were graduate students enrolled in (MS) Master of Science programs across the United States of America. 7 participants (M1–M7) were industry professions in various technical roles (such as User Experience Researchers, Software Developers, User Experience Designers, Product Management, Data Analysis etc.). 5 participants (A1–A5) were Professional University Career Advisors at the Georgia Institute of Technology. The final 5 participants (R1–R5) worked in recruiting, with varying job titles (such as Recruiting Manager, Campus Recruiter, Recruiting Analyst etc.). Recruitment for the study was voluntary, and no compensation was provided for participation.

Procedure. A semi-structured interview was conducted with each participant to understand their preferences, perceptions and motivations pertaining to their experiences with mentoring and advisement relationships. The duration of the interview typically varied between 45 min to an hour. The interviews were conducted remotely, telephonically or through video calling platforms, depending on the participant's preference. Prior to the interview, the participants were required to sign a consent form, educating them about their rights as a participant, as well as permitting the researchers to use the collected data for academic purposes.

Each participant was interviewed with a different script, focusing on a different set of research questions. For S1–S7, the questions were focused around the information needs of graduate students, and their preferences for direct interaction with an expert to get that information. For M1–M7, the questions revolved around motivations and incentives to participate in mentorship activities. For A1–A5, the questions focused on the major issues that students face in their experience. Finally, for R1–R5, the questions focused on the information dissemination practices followed by recruiters, and how they evaluate candidates on the basis of their approach.

Data Collection and Analysis. The data were collected by noting down the answers in a notebook while conducting remote interviews. We also recorded the call in order to revisit the findings. Prior consent was taken from each participant before recording the call (Fig. 1).

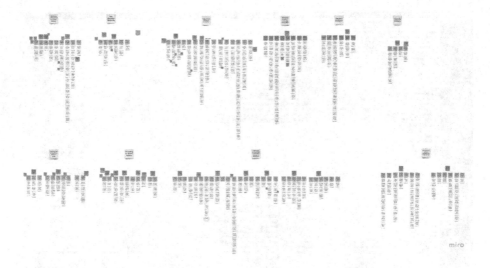

Fig. 1. User quotes analysed through a bottom-up affinity diagram

The collected data was analysed through a bottom up affinity diagramming technique. Participant quotes were written down on sticky notes, and similar notes were grouped together to produce themes. This mapping was done on four levels, with the themes becoming narrower down the map. The themes reflect the various pain points, motivations, characteristics, and opportunity areas relevant to the study.

4.2 Survey Design

An online survey was created to generalize the qualitative findings from the interviews. The survey was filled anonymously by 76 participants. 55 participants identified themselves as graduate students who have experiences with mentors and 21 participants identified themselves as industry professionals with mentoring experience. Students were questioned about their information needs as they navigate their job hunt, while industry professionals were questioned about their motivations to engage in mentoring relationships. Both sets of participants were questioned about preferred medium of communication as well.

4.3 Comparative Study

We identified 13 mentoring platforms that graduate students typically use to get career related mentorship. These platforms were identified through the interviews. A competitive benchmarking was conducted identifying 6 feature domains (Messaging, Profile View, Profile Discovery, Group sessions, Personalised Mentorship, Mentor verification). Features of different platforms that cater to these domains were documented (Fig. 2).

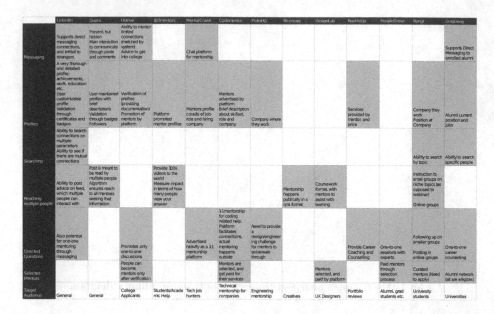

Fig. 2. A competitive matrix to evaluate various existing tools and their functionality

5   Results

5.1   Motivations

Finding Commonalities. Commonalities between a mentor and a mentee are a big facilitator of these relationships at both ends. Mentors try to look for common characteristics with potential mentees. "Seeing someone in the same shoes I was in a few years ago really drives me to take time out to give advice to students." report M2. "I usually only respond to people that belong to the same Alma mater as me" reported M3. "As a woman, I resonate with the problems women have to face in the workplace. So I really look out for women that reach out to me for help." reported M1.   Mentees, find it easier to approach industry professionals that have characteristics in common. "I typically look for Indians in the people page of a company website, because I find it easier to approach them." reported S1.

The survey illustrated that Empathy was the biggest personal motivation for mentoring (Fig. 3 (a)). 17 mentors reported that Alma matter was one of the biggest characteristics that stood out as they consider responding to potential mentees.

Visibility. Mentors are also motivated by the visibility of their actions in their network. Being identified as a mentor or advisor by their network proves to be an incentive for them to take time out for these activities. This can also be in the form of achievements of their mentees. "If I'm taking out time to help out

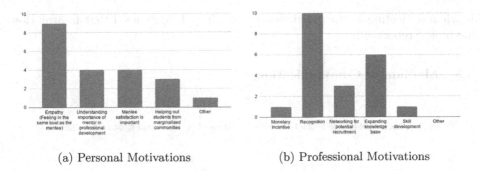

(a) Personal Motivations   (b) Professional Motivations

Fig. 3. Motivations for mentors to engage in mentoring relationships

a student, I would like it if my network finds out that I contributed to their achievements." reported M5.

The survey illustrated that the biggest professional motivation for mentors was recognition (Fig. 3 (b)).

5.2   Information Needs

Reliability. Students reported that the advantage of a direct interaction with a mentor was the desire for human intellect, which led to increased trust. Students found information about a company's work culture and a job description more reliable if they directly interacted with a mentor figure from that company. "I prefer reaching out to people over reading a blog post because I trust that the people will be more honest about a company's work culture" reported S2. "Static resources can be outdated, but I can trust that an alum is telling me the most up to date information" reported S5.

The survey illustrates that they preferred reaching out to industry professionals to learn about work culture (45 responses) and job description (40 responses), information that is readily available online.

Personalised Feedback. Direct interaction with a mentor also lets students receive personalised feedback on job application material such as resume, portfolio, etc. "Seniors and Alumni can review my portfolio before I apply to a specific company" reported S3.

Static Resources. Static resources were better for standard/objective pieces of information. The students also said that static resources help them avoid awkward conversations. "I prefer finding out details about a role's compensation online, than asking another person how much they earn" reported S5. "I wish there was a way I could just click a button and get a referral, and avoid the awkward conversation" reported S1. Static sources are also more reliable for time sensitive information, as people may be unresponsive or busy. "I don't like it when a meeting is scheduled to a point where I don't need that information anymore" reported S2.

5.3 Medium of Communication

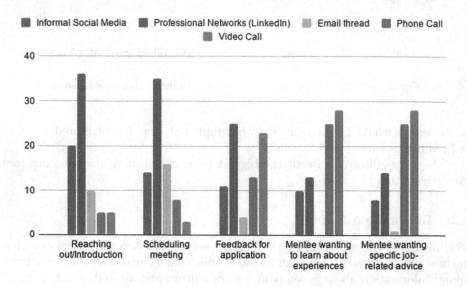

Fig. 4. Preferred medium for mentoring activities

The interviews revealed that the participant's preference for medium of communication depended on the mentoring stage, as well as the mentoring activity. The survey data further illustrates this point. Participants prefer textual communication for initial connection and scheduling, but they prefer video conferencing for feedback sessions, career counseling etc. (Fig. 4)

6 Design Recommendations

The study highlights a few areas of opportunity to redesign existing solutions and platforms that assist in the development and maintenance of mentoring relationships between students and industry professionals.

Scheduling. A majority of existing solutions afford connection of individuals through a textual format, while the mentoring activities happen outside the platform through other mediums such as a telephonic or video call. Textual mediums were reported as being inefficient for scheduling purposes. Mentoring platforms need to design better mechanisms to schedule meetings.

Profile Design. Most existing platforms incorporate the concept of a profile page through which potential mentors and mentees can get more information ahead of connecting. While these pages highlight the achievements of said individuals, a big motivation to engage in mentoring relationships that has been identified has learning about similar struggles the participants might have gone through. The platform can encourage participation in these relationships by highlighting commonalities for a given profile with the given user.

Gamification. Gamification can be incorporated into these platforms in the form of labels to identify participants involved with good mentorship behaviour. This can be a way for mentees to offer gratitude to mentors, and the visibility of these labels in their professional networks can incentivise mentors. Mentors were also concerned with evaluating their own mentorship performance, which can be measured through these labels.

7 Conclusion

The study illustrates some common motivations, preferences and pain points pertaining to career related mentorship for graduate students. (i) Finding commonalities between a mentor and a mentee was a strong motivation to engage in these relationships. (ii) Mentors are motivated by the visibility of their mentoring activities in their professional network. (iii) Direct Interactions with mentors is in general important, but not appropriate for topics such as compensation, job descriptions etc. (iv) Mentees require static resources such as blogs, FAQs etc. where they can get information difficult to procure from mentors. We also illustrate some recommendations illustrating how these insights can improve the design and development of existing mentoring tools.

References

1. Behrooz M., Zahedi, M.S., Campos, R., Farhoodi, M.: Online job search: study of users' search behavior using search engine query logs. In: The 41st International ACM SIGIR Conference on Research and Development in Information Retrieval (SIGIR 2018), pp. 1185–1188. Association for Computing Machinery, New York (2018). https://doi.org/10.1145/3209978.3210125
2. Montgomery, B.L.: Mapping a mentoring roadmap and developing a supportive network for strategic career advancement. SAGE Open (2017). https://doi.org/10.1177/2158244017710288
3. Tomprou, M., Dabbish, L., Kraut, R., Liu, F.: Career mentoring in online communities: seeking and receiving advice from an online community (2019). https://doi.org/10.1145/3290605.3300883
4. Kang, M., Yoo, Y.R., Park, Y.: Analyzing online mentoring process and facilitation strategies. Procedia - Soc. Behav. Sci. **46**, 5158–5162 (2012). ISSN 1877-0428, https://doi.org/10.1016/j.sbspro.2012.06.400
5. Cohoon, M.G., et al.: Mentoring computer science undergraduates. WIT Press (2004)
6. Doerschuk, P.: A research and mentoring program for undergraduate women in computer science. S2H - 7 (2004). https://doi.org/10.1109/FIE.2004.1408747

User Experience of Agent-Mediated Interactions with Multiple Conversational Agents

Hoyeon Nam[✉], Hankyung Kim, and Youn-kyung Lim

Department of Industrial Design, KAIST, Daejeon, Republic of Korea
{hoyeonnam,hkkim31,younlim}@kaist.ac.kr

Abstract. In the human-computer interaction (HCI) practice, there have been increasing interests in systems consisting of multiple conversational agents (CAs). However, existing studies pointed out that the interactions with multiple CAs require a high level of users' mental efforts. To cope with this issue, we introduce a mediator agent (MA): a single CA which mediates interactions between a user and multiple CAs. Although there are existing studies that imply the potential of a CA as a mediator in a multi-party context, understanding of user expectations on MA is still lacking. In this work, we conducted an improvisational acting-based Wizard of Oz study to explore user experience (UX) of MA-mediated interactions with multiple CAs. Twelve participants experienced interactions mediated by a virtual MA and interviewed about their expectations on a MA. Qualitative analysis of interview data revealed user expectations on a MA, including user-preferred types of agent-mediation such as confirmation-based mediation and transparency-oriented mediation.

Keywords: Conversational agents · Mediator agent · User experience

1 Introduction

One of the noticeable phenomena in human-computer interaction (HCI) practice is the proliferation of conversational agents (CAs) [8]. Due to the difficulty of developing open-domain CAs [4], HCI practitioners have focused on designing systems consisting of multiple closed-domain CAs. For instance, LG introduced HomeChat [7], a multi-CA system composed of various device-based CAs (Fig. 1).

On the HCI research side, researchers have actively reported studies on interactions with multiple CAs. They have focused on technical aspects of interactions like conversation failure recovery and turn-management [2, 3]. Those studies pointed out that interactions with multiple CAs required a high level of user mental load. As a solution to the interactional issue of multi-CA systems, we propose a mediator agent (MA): a single CA which mediates interactions between a user and multiple CAs. Although existing studies imply the potential of a CA as a mediator in a multi-party context [10], understanding of user expectations on MA is still lacking.

In this work, we conducted an improvisational acting-based [9] Wizard of Oz study to explore user experience (UX) of MA-mediated interactions with multiple CAs. Qualitative analysis revealed user expectations on a MA.

© Springer Nature Switzerland AG 2021
C. Stephanidis et al. (Eds.): HCII 2021, CCIS 1419, pp. 472–476, 2021.
https://doi.org/10.1007/978-3-030-78635-9_61

Fig. 1. LG HomeChat [7].

2 Method

To explore the UX of agent-mediated interactions, we utilized the Wizard of Oz method to simulate the experience with a virtual MA and CAs. Studies on interactions with CAs generally use the hi-fidelity Wizard of Oz method based on precisely-defined protocols [3, 11]. However, we conducted improvisational acting-based Wizard of Oz to explore possible UX [5] rather than capture feasible scenarios constrained by current technological limitations. In our study, four wizards followed simple instructions to perform improvisational acting as a virtual MA and three closed domain CAs.

2.1 Study Setup

Since text-based interaction is one of the most representative types of interaction in a multi-CA context, we conducted Wizard of Oz based on a text messaging platform. We used a domestic text-messaging app [6] for setup. We created two chat rooms: chat room A for a user-MA interaction and chat room B for MA-CA interactions (Fig. 2).

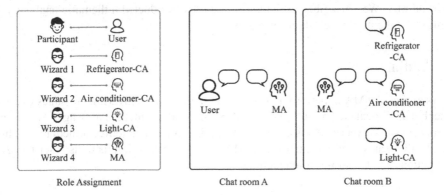

Fig. 2. Study setup.

2.2 Instructions for Wizard-Actors

We recruited four designers who had experience in CA design. After a brief explanation of the study process, we assigned roles to the designers and provided simple instructions. The instructions for wizard-actors consisted of the following.

- A refrigerator-CA makes conversations on refrigerator-related topics like food, cooking, diet, shopping, and user's health.
- An air conditioner (AC)-CA makes conversations on AC-related topics like air-conditioning, temperature, humidity, and cleaning.
- A light-CA makes conversations on light-related topics like sleep and emotion.
- A MA performs various types of user-friendly mediation: from delivering one's messages to the other one to intelligent mediation.
- A MA accepts a user' request when a user expresses expectations on mediation

2.3 Instructions for User-Actors

We recruited 12 participants who had experience in interaction with commercial CAs. After a brief explanation of the study process, we assigned a user-role to participants and provided instructions. The instructions for user-actors consisted of the following.

- A user is always aware of the existence of three CAs in chat room B
- A user makes conversations with a MA when s/he wants to interact with CAs.
- A user freely requests a specific type of mediation that s/he expects a MA to perform.

2.4 Study Process

We invited a participant and the MA-wizard to chat room A and four wizards to chat room B at the appointed time. They set their profile names as their assigned role and started a chat session. Fifteen minutes after the chat began, we stopped the chat session and met the user online. We interviewed users mainly on their expectations and experience with a virtual MA. We transcribed all interview data and conducted a thematic analysis [1] to draw out the user expectations on a MA.

3 Findings

Users expected a MA to perform not simple mediation like delivering messages to each other but intelligent mediation based on understanding the content of messages. However, there were some experiential issues when MA performed the intelligent mediation. This section illustrates user expectations on MA in two types of interactions: user-to-CAs interactions and CAs-to-user interactions.

3.1 User Expectations on Agent-Mediation in User-to-CAs Interactions

Assigning a Task to a Suitable CA. In our study, users provided various kinds of virtual tasks to CAs through a MA: *"Hey MA, tell refrigerator-CA to buy some eggs online (P6)."* However, users usually did not explicitly mention which CA the task was for in their messages: *"Ask about the weather on weekends (P2)."* Users expected MA to assign the task to the appropriate CA on behalf of users.

Shaping User's Request into CA-Available Tasks. Moreover, users tried to provide complex tasks which required the collaboration of multiple CAs: *"I invited my friends to my house. Please prepare a house party (P4)."* Rather than questioning how to deal with the complicated request, the MA-wizard shaped the request into feasible tasks: *"I tell fridge-CA to buy some finger foods and light-CA to set mood lights (MA-wizard)."* This intelligent type of mediation allowed users to ask for tasks in a natural manner.

Confirmation-Based Mediation. Sometimes users felt a lack of control from those intelligence-driven mediations. In the interview session, users listed up the types of tasks that should not be assigned or shaped by a MA: works related to privacy, finance, and security: *"I was surprised when the MA said that it allowed fridge-CA to buy something. I had never asked for that at all. I hoped MA would be proactive, but there were certain types of tasks that MA should not handle without my permission (P11)."* According to the significance of tasks, MA should regulate its agency and gently ask for the user's confirmation.

3.2 User Expectations on Agent-Mediation in CAs-to-User Interactions

Summarization of Reports from CAs. Regardless of whether users asked for information, users received information from CAs periodically: *"According to refrigerator-CA, apples are on sale now! (MA-wizard)."* When the MA kept reporting various information in a short period, users were stressed out and asked MA to deliver only important news: *"I asked MA to filter out insignificant information and give a summary with essentials. I think it is quite similar to how assistants report to their boss (P3)".*

Transparency-Oriented Mediation. Generally, users appreciated MA's summarization. However, they felt curious about how MA processed the information. Furthermore, users showed their wants to access chat room B. To cope with the curiosity issue, users adopted various strategies: *"I was curious about what's going on behind the MA. So, I asked a MA to provide both a summary and all of the information gathered (P8)".*

4 Conclusion

By conducting an improvisational acting-based Wizard of Oz study, we revealed user expectations on agent-mediation: users expected a MA to manage users' requests and process CAs' information. Also, we found the user-preferred types of agent-mediation: confirmation-based mediation and transparency-oriented mediation. We hope that our knowledge will guide HCI practitioners to design a MA meeting user expectations.

Acknowledgments. This work was mainly supported by Institute of Information & Communications Technology Planning & Evaluation (IITP) grant funded by the Korea government (MSIT) (No.2016-0-00564, Development of Intelligent Interaction Technology Based on Context Awareness and Human Intention Understanding), and partially supported by the National Research Foundation of Korea (NRF) grant funded by the Korea government (MSIT) (No. NRF-2021R1A2C2004263).

References

1. Braun, V., Clarke, V.: Using thematic analysis in psychology. Qual. Res. Psychol. **3**(2), 77–101 (2006)
2. Candello, H., Pinhanez, C.: Recovering from dialogue failures using multiple agents in wealth management advice. In: Moore, R.J., Szymanski, M.H., Arar, R., Ren, G.-J. (eds.) Studies in Conversational UX Design. HIS, pp. 139–157. Springer, Cham (2018). https://doi.org/10.1007/978-3-319-95579-7_7
3. Chaves, A.P., Gerosa, M.A.: Single or multiple conversational agents? An interactional coherence comparison. In: Proceedings of the 2018 CHI Conference on Human Factors in Computing Systems, pp. 1–13. ACM (2018)
4. Griol, D., Molina, J.M.: Building multi-domain conversational systems from single domain resources. Neurocomputing **271**, 59–69 (2018)
5. Jung, J., Nam, H., Lim, Y.K., Lee, K.P.: Beauty and the beast: an IoT design method based on improvisational acting. In: Proceedings of the 2017 ACM Conference Companion Publication on Designing Interactive Systems, pp. 61–66. ACM (2017)
6. KaKaoTalk. https://www.kakaocorp.com/service/KakaoTalk?lang=en. Accessed 20 Feb 2021
7. LG Homechat. http://www.lghomechat.com. Accessed 20 Feb 2021
8. Luger, E., Sellen, A.: "Like having a really bad PA" the gulf between user expectation and experience of conversational agents. In: Proceedings of the 2016 CHI Conference on Human Factors in Computing Systems, pp. 5286–5297. ACM (2016)
9. Medler, B., Magerko, B.: The implications of improvisational acting and role-playing on design methodologies. In: Proceedings of the 2010 CHI Conference on Human Factors in Computing Systems, pp. 483–492. ACM (2010)
10. Toxtli, C., Monroy-Hernández, A., Cranshaw, J.: Understanding chatbot-mediated task management. In: Proceedings of the 2018 CHI Conference on Human Factors in Computing Systems, pp. 1–6. ACM (2018)
11. Vtyurina, A., Fourney, A.: Exploring the role of conversational cues in guided task support with virtual assistants. In: Proceedings of the 2018 CHI Conference on Human Factors in Computing Systems, pp. 1–7. ACM (2018)

Continuance Intention to Use Cloud Services in Educational Institutions

Dijana Peras[✉] and Renata Mekovec

Faculty of Organization and Informatics, Department of Information Systems Development,
University of Zagreb, Varaždin, Croatia
{dijana.peras,renata.mekovec}@foi.hr

Abstract. Continued use of technology depends on numerous factors that arise from different dimensions, such as the characteristics of the organization, environment, tools, and users. Trends in cloud service (CS) related research are focused on technology capabilities, cost reductions, and profit increases in small and medium-sized enterprises (SMEs). Although the use of technology depends on the intention of the users, their perception in this particular research area is neglected. Most of the papers from this research domain explore the initial acceptance of CS, although the initial acceptance of technology does not guarantee its continued use. The objectives of the proposed research are: 1) to identify the factors related to the continuance intention to use CS in education institutions (EI), and 2) to develop a conceptual model for the continuance intention to use CS in EI. The main research question of the proposed paper is: "Which factors are related to the continuance intention to use CS in EI"? To identify the factors, an overview of the state of the art will be presented, including: a) a review of the CS used in educational institutions, and b) an analysis of existing models and factors related to the continued use of technology. Furthermore, since the biggest concerns of the CS users are data loss/leakage and data privacy, the review of the impact of privacy perception on the continuance intention to use CS will be made. The identification of factors is the first step towards determining the direction of further development of CS for EI and towards strategic planning and organization of teaching models that include the use of CS. Further efforts will be directed on the development of an instrument for measuring the continuance intention to use CS in EI.

Keywords: Cloud services · Educational institutions · Continued use of technology

1 Introduction

Cloud services (CS) are considered to be one of the most promising technologies used in education [1]. Unlike solutions for business users, which are mainly based on hybrid cloud and local data storage, education is dominated by software as a service (SaaS) implemented as a public cloud, where users have the ability to access the tools and content from various devices but do not manage cloud infrastructure or tool capabilities [2]. In face-to-face teaching, CS serve as a substitute for other media (board and book) and

C. Stephanidis et al. (Eds.): HCII 2021, CCIS 1419, pp. 477–484, 2021.
https://doi.org/10.1007/978-3-030-78635-9_62

expansion of their capabilities (interactive presentations and videos). In hybrid teaching, they are used for sharing materials and virtual collaboration. In online teaching, they support the entire process (from initial planning of learning outcomes and selection of materials to evaluation and final reflection) [3]. The reasons for using CS in EI are numerous. They provide easier communication and collaboration, flexibility, dissemination of knowledge, and save time and costs [4]. CS are available through a web browser, so the data is stored on remote servers. Users can simultaneously open documents, edit them, comment and review changes, take notes, and communicate from anywhere in the world. According to their functionality, cloud tools can be divided into cloud communication tools (e.g. Zoom, GoToMeeting, BigBlueButton), cloud management tools (e.g. Asana, Trello, Zoho Projects), cloud storage tools (e.g. Dropbox, Box), and cloud productivity tools (Microsoft 365 and G Suite). The most commonly used SaaS tools in EI around the world are Google G Suite for Education (including Drive, Meet, Hangouts, etc.), and Microsoft Office 365 (including Sway, OneDrive, Yammer, Teams, etc.) [5].

Despite the many opportunities they provide, many CS providers have difficulty retaining users [6–8]. Namely, CS carry certain risks. Users are particularly concerned for data considered sensitive and generally prefer local storage over cloud storage [7]. According to a survey conducted in May 2020, users of CS are most concerned about the loss and leakage of information (69% of respondents) and data privacy (66% of respondents) [9]. Disclosure of personal data entails consequences, such as a change in the perception of privacy and the termination of the use of technology [10]. Due to the state of emergency in the world caused by the COVID-19 pandemic, many EI have recently adopted CS. However, it remains unknown whether and to what extent CS will be used under normal conditions. Educational institutions (EI) in the context of this paper refer to secondary schools and higher education institutions that conduct education through university and professional studies and include universities (faculties and art academies within it), polytechnics, and colleges. Continuance intention refers to factors that contribute to the successful usage of technology for a long time.

The lack of empirical research dealing with the key factors influencing the continued use of CS in EI was stated by several authors [11–14]. To ensure the preconditions for the development and continuous application of CS despite the stated risks, it is necessary to identify the factors of their continued use [15]. Understanding the preferences of users and their underlying values is necessary to be able to respond to these needs and to enable CS providers to design services that are better suited to their beneficiaries.

2   Research Methodology

The proposed research will utilize a combined methodological framework. The research will consist of a theoretical and an empirical part.

2.1   Theoretical Framework

The first part of the research consists of a review, analysis, and synthesis of relevant and available literature from the problem area. The following research question has been defined: "What factors are related to the continuance intention to use cloud services in educational institutions?" An initial review of the literature on the Web of Science, Scopus, Science Direct, and IEEE Xplore Digital Library platforms was made. The following search string was defined: ("cloud services" OR "cloud computing" OR "cloud usage" OR "cloud storage" OR "SaaS") AND ("continuance intention" OR "continued use" OR "intention to use"). The selection of papers consisted of two parts: 1) the title and abstract were screened and the papers were classified as included or excluded, and 2) included papers were read and the factors that were used in research of CS continuance intention were extracted.

Most reviewed studies have integrated more than one theory, and the models were complex. Many studies used the Expectation-Confirmation Model of IS Continuance (ECM-IS) as a basis [16], and integrated other constructs relevant for the context of the research [7, 13, 17–23]. Theories such Technology Acceptance Model (TAM) [18, 19, 22, 23], Diffusion of Innovation Theory (DOI) [23, 24], IS success model [17, 21, 23, 25], Technology-organization-environment (TOE) framework [13, 21, 24–26] have also been used to predict continuance intention. However, most of these theories pay more attention to the factors that influence users in the phase of the initial adoption than to the factors that influence the continued use of technology [16], and may be inappropriate to predict continuance intention [27].

Constructs like satisfaction [17, 20, 23, 28], perceived usefulness [7, 17–22], confirmation [17, 20, 23], perceived ease of use [17, 18, 21, 22, 25], and attitude [19, 22] remained consistent over time in predicting technology continuance intention [29]. According to the results of a recently made systematic overview of the variables in continuance intention to use an information system (IS) [29], attitude and satisfaction are the best predictors of continuance intention. However, those variables do not fully capture user continuance behavior regarding CS in EI. New constructs begin to appear, such as utilitarian value [23, 28, 30], accessibility [25, 31], and collaboration [32, 33]. Their importance needs to be further examined to enrich the theoretical model. Furthermore, privacy perception stands out as an important factor in the CS initial acceptance [34, 35], but its impact on the continuance intention in this particular context has not yet been explored. The need for the construct of privacy perception is derived from research conducted in different contexts in which privacy vulnerabilities negatively affected the continued use of technology and customer retention. The protection of personal data has an important role in EI. CS used by EI have different features, privacy policies, and terms of use than those used by individuals to ensure that their business policies comply with data protection regulations.

Hypotheses Development. A dissatisfying experience with service can decrease user's attitudes towards CS. Furthermore, when users feel CS are satisfactory, they intend to continue using them. Previous research has provided abundant evidence to support this relationship. Here, we believe that feeling satisfied would enhance users' attitude and continuance intention to use CS. Therefore, it is proposed:

H1: Satisfaction will positively affect continuance intention to use CS in EI.
H2: Satisfaction will positively affect attitude related to CS in EI.

Attitude refers to the degree to which a user perceives a positive or negative feeling related to CS. The positive link between attitude and continuance intention has received strong empirical support in previous studies. We, thus, believe that the attitude of the users about CS would be a good predictor of continuance intention. Therefore, it is proposed that:

H3: Attitude will positively affect continuance intention to use CS in EI.

Utilitarian value refers to the cognitive evaluation of CS in terms of purpose fulfillment and problem-solving. It represents users' goal-oriented reasons for starting a task. Prior research has demonstrated the significant impact of utilitarian value on satisfaction across a wide range of contexts. Furthermore, users choose to continue using the service if they perceive that they offer great value. Therefore, we assume that utilitarian value will positively affect both users' satisfaction and continuance intention to use CS.

H4: Utilitarian value will positively affect continuance intention to use CS in EI.
H5: Utilitarian value will positively affect satisfaction with CS in EI.

Accessibility refers to the extent to which the CS are made available to users. When services are not restricted to a particular area, they tend to be more used. Users are more satisfied because they can access CS regardless of their location at any given time, and the continuance intention to use CS is higher. Therefore, it is proposed:

H6: Accessibility will positively affect satisfaction with CS in EI.
H7: Accessibility will positively affect continuance intention to use CS in EI.

The success of EI depends in large part on effective collaboration among users. The application of new technology is crucial to satisfy the needs of users and to support their collaboration. Based on these arguments, we propose:

H8: Collaboration will positively affect satisfaction with CS in EI.
H9: Collaboration will positively affect continuance intention to use CS in EI.

In this paper, privacy perception is defined as personal space that is exclusively under the control of the individual, who decides when, how, and to what extent his personal data can be collected, used, and transferred to a third party. The results of previous research indicate that increased control and perceived sense of ownership over personal data decreases the negative attitudes towards CS. The perception of a low level of privacy may affect users' attitudes towards using CS. Thus, the following hypothesis is formulated:

H10: Perceived privacy will have a positive influence on attitude towards CS in EI.

Users who share more personal information with CS providers are more likely to have richer experiences (e.g. single sign-on, automatic synchronization, etc.). Previous studies pointed out that users tend to protect their personal data to prevent data leakage. Furthermore, negative privacy perception has a major negative effect on utilitarian value. Thus, we propose the following:

H11: Perceived privacy will positively affect the utilitarian value of CS in EI.

When users are afraid that disclosure of their personal data will harm them, their perceived value of service decreases, which prevents their intention to continually use the service. In correspondence with the literature, we assume that perceived privacy will positively affect both satisfaction and continuance intention to use CS in EI. Thus, the following hypotheses are proposed:

H12: Perceived privacy will positively affect satisfaction with CS in EI.
H13: Perceived privacy will positively affect continuance intention to use CS in EI.

The identification of constructs is followed by the design of the conceptual model presented in Fig. 1.

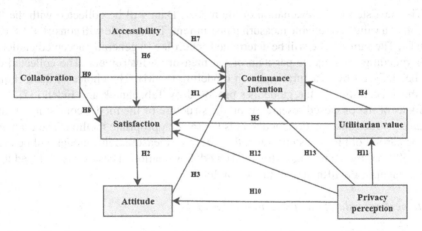

Fig. 1. The conceptual model of continuance intention to use CS in EI

The listed steps have led to the achievement of the first and second goal of the research:

1) *to identify relevant factors related to the continuance intention to use CS in EI.*
2) *to develop a conceptual model of continuance intention to use CS in EI.*

2.2 Empirical Research

As part of the research, a new measuring instrument will be developed. The development of a measuring instrument will follow the guidelines proposed by DeVellis [36]:

1) determining the object of measurement, 2) generating a set of items, 3) determining the method of measurement, 4) evaluation of items by experts, 5) selection of a sample, 6) determination of the construct validity, 7) determination of the reliability of the measuring instrument, and 8) optimization of the length of the measuring scale.

After determining the constructs of the model, the items will be created following the results obtained from the literature review. The initial set of items will be at least twice as large as the desired final scale. Items will be measured using a semantic ordinal scale. The importance of each particle in the context of the research will be assessed by experts. The value of the content validity ratio (CVR) will be calculated. Experts will also assess the clarity and conciseness of the items. A sample for the pilot research will consist of available CS users from EI. The construct validity will be measured by factor analysis. The reliability of a measuring instrument based on its internal consistency will be measured by McDonald's omega coefficient. The last step is the optimization of the length of a measuring instrument. These steps will lead to the achievement of the third and fourth goal of the research:

3) *to develop an instrument for measuring variables related to the continuance intention to use CS in EI; and*
4) *to examine the validity and reliability of the developed measuring instrument.*

The next step is the evaluation of the model. Data will be collected with the final version of a valid and reliable measuring instrument. The sample will consist of CS users from EI. The sample size will be determined according to generally accepted guidelines recommending 10 subjects per item of the measuring instrument. The collected data will be analyzed by structural equation modeling (SEM). The choice of the technique was made according to the guidelines proposed by Tabachnick and Fidell [37]. Since the focus of the proposed research is on the structure of the model consisting of latent variables, structural equation modeling is the most appropriate method. The evaluation will be carried out in two steps. First, the external (measurement) model will be evaluated, followed by the internal (structural) model evaluation. These steps will lead to the achievement of the fifth goal of the research:

5) *to perform validation of the proposed model.*

3   Conclusion

A relatively small number of papers investigating the continuance intention to use CS was detected by literature review, even though it is a technology that is at the peak of its life cycle. The proposed research will contribute to the mentioned area by developing an instrument for measuring variables related to the continuance intention to use CS in EI. Scientific contribution in the field of social sciences is the cognition of the possibilities and application of developed artifacts in the context of EI. A significant contribution is reflected in the inclusion of new constructs that are beginning to appear in research related to CS: utilitarian value, accessibility, collaboration, and privacy perception. Understanding the factors of continuance intention to use CS will help service providers to determine the direction of the development of educational applications and plan CS promotion programs, which in turn should increase ease of use and efficiency for users.

References

1. González-Martínez, J.A., Bote-Lorenzo, M.L., Gómez-Sánchez, E., Cano-Parra, R.: Cloud computing and education: a state-of-the-art survey. Comput. Educ. **80**, 132–151 (2015)
2. Asadi, Z., Abdekhoda, M., Nadrian, H.: Understanding and predicting teachers' intention to use cloud computing in smart education. ITSE **17**(1), 14–27 (2019)
3. Ćosić, K.: Hrvatske škole preselile se u oblake, Portofon (2020). (in Croatian). https://www.portofon.com/savjeti/hrvatske-skole-preselile-se-u-oblake. Accessed 11 July 2020
4. Orehovački, T., Babić, S., Etinger, D.: Identifying relevance of security, privacy, trust, and adoption dimensions concerning cloud computing applications employed in educational settings. In: Nicholson, D. (ed.) AHFE 2017. AISC, vol. 593, pp. 308–320. Springer, Cham (2018). https://doi.org/10.1007/978-3-319-60585-2_29
5. Akande, A.O., Van Belle, J.-P.: The use of software as a service by students in higher education institutions: a systematic literature review. In: Proceedings of the 18th Annual International Conference on Electronic Commerce: e-Commerce in Smart connected World, pp. 1–6 (2016)
6. Burda, D., Teuteberg, F.: Exploring consumer preferences in cloud archiving – a student's perspective. Behav. Inf. Technol. **35**(2), 89–105 (2016)
7. Goode, S.: Keeping the user in the cloud: a cognitive social capital antecedent to use continuance and trust-commitment in personal cloud storage services. Behav. Inf. Technol., 26 (2018)
8. Trenz, M., Huntgeburth, J., Veit, D.: How to succeed with cloud services? Bus. Inf. Syst. Eng. **61**(2), 181–194 (2019)
9. Top cloud security concerns 2020. Statista. https://www.statista.com/statistics/1172265/biggest-cloud-security-concerns-in-2020/. Accessed 03 Nov 2020
10. Fox, G.: Understanding and enhancing consumer privacy perceptions in the cloud. In: Lynn, T., Mooney, J.G., van der Werff, L., Fox, G. (eds.) Data Privacy and Trust in Cloud Computing. PSDBET, pp. 59–78. Springer, Cham (2021). https://doi.org/10.1007/978-3-030-54660-1_4
11. Ibrahim, M.S., Salleh, N., Misra, S.: Empirical studies of cloud computing in education: a systematic literature review. In: Gervasi, O., Murgante, B., Misra, S., Gavrilova, M.L., Rocha, A.M.A.C., Torre, C., Taniar, D., Apduhan, Bernady O. (eds.) ICCSA 2015. LNCS, vol. 9158, pp. 725–737. Springer, Cham (2015). https://doi.org/10.1007/978-3-319-21410-8_55
12. Arpaci, I., Kilicer, K., Bardakci, S.: Effects of security and privacy concerns on educational use of cloud services. Comput. Hum. Behav. **45**, 93–98 (2015)
13. Qasem, Y.A.M., Abdullah, R., Jusoh, Y.Y., Atan, R., Asadi, S.: Cloud computing adoption in higher education institutions: a systematic review. IEEE Access **7**, 63722–63744 (2019)
14. Ali, M.B.: Multiple perspective of cloud computing adoption determinants in higher education a systematic review. Int. J. Cloud Appl. Comput. **9**(3), 89–109 (2019)
15. Halilović, S.: The influence of service quality on satisfaction and information system continuance intention. Market-Tržište **27**(1), 18 (2015)
16. Bhattacherjee, A.: Understanding information systems continuance: an expectation-confirmation model. MIS Q. **25**(3), 351 (2001)
17. Cheng, Y.-M.: Drivers of physicians' satisfaction and continuance intention toward the cloud-based hospital information system. Kybernetes (2020)
18. Tripathi, S.: Understanding the determinants affecting the continuance intention to use cloud computing. J. Int. Technol. Inf. Manage. **26**(3), 30 (2017)

19. Wu, B., Chen, X.: Continuance intention to use MOOCs: Integrating the technology acceptance model (TAM) and task technology fit (TTF) model. Comput. Hum. Behav. **67**, 221–232 (2017)
20. Bøe, T., Gulbrandsen, B., Sørebø, Ø.: How to stimulate the continued use of ICT in higher education: integrating information systems continuance theory and agency theory. Comput. Hum. Behav. **50**, 375–384 (2015)
21. Yang, H.-L.: User continuance intention to use cloud storage service. Comput. Hum. Behav., 14 (2015)
22. Wang, C.-S., Jeng, Y.-L., Huang, Y.-M.: What influences teachers to continue using cloud services? The role of facilitating conditions and social influence. Electron. Libr. **35**(3), 520–533 (2017)
23. Dağhan, G., Akkoyunlu, B.: Modeling the continuance usage intention of online learning environments. Comput. Hum. Behav. **60**, 198–211 (2016)
24. Martins, R., Oliveira, T., Manoj, T., Tomás, S.: Firms' continuance intention on SaaS use – an empirical study. Inf. Technol. People (2019). Accessed 22 Mar 2021
25. Eze, S.C., Chinedu-Eze, V.C.A., Okike, C.K., Bello, A.O.: Factors influencing the use of e-learning facilities by students in a private Higher Education Institution (HEI) in a developing economy. Humanit. Soc. Sci. Commun. **7**(1), 133 (2020)
26. Walther, S., Sarker, S., Urbach, N., Sedera, D., Eymann, T., Otto, B.: Exploring organizational level continuance of cloud-based enterprise systems, p. 19 (2015)
27. Veeramootoo, N., Nunkoo, R., Dwivedi, Y.K.: What determines success of an e-government service? Validation of an integrative model of e-filing continuance usage. Gov. Inf. Q. **35**(2), 161–174 (2018)
28. Guo, Z., Xiao, L., Van Toorn, C., Lai, Y., Seo, C.: Promoting online learners' continuance intention: an integrated flow framework. Inf. Manage. **53**(2), 279–295 (2016)
29. Franque, F.B., Oliveira, T., Tam, C., de Oliveira Santini, F.: A meta-analysis of the quantitative studies in continuance intention to use an information system. Internet Res. **31**, (2020)
30. Hong, J.-C., Lin, P.-H., Hsieh, P.-C.: The effect of consumer innovativeness on perceived value and continuance intention to use smartwatch. Comput. Hum. Behav. **67**, 264–272 (2017)
31. Arora, N., Malik, G., Chawla, D.: Factors affecting consumer adoption of mobile apps in NCR: a qualitative study. Glob. Bus. Rev. **21**(1), 176–196 (2020)
32. Qasem, Y.A.M., Abdullah, R., Yaha, Y., Atana, R.: Continuance use of cloud computing in higher education institutions: a conceptual model. Appl. Sci. **10**(19), 6628 (2020)
33. Arcila-Calderón, C., Calderín, M., Aguaded, I.: Adoption of ICTs by communication researchers for scientific diffusion and data analysis. EPI **24**(5), 526 (2015)
34. Arpaci, I.: Understanding and predicting students' intention to use mobile cloud storage services. Comput. Hum. Behav. **58**, 150–157 (2016)
35. Alotaibi, M.B.: Exploring users' attitudes and intentions toward the adoption of cloud computing in Saudi Arabia: an empirical investigation. J. Comput. Sci. **10**(11), 2315–2329 (2014)
36. DeVellis, R.F.: Scale Development: Theory and Applications, vol. 26. Sage Publications, Thousand Oaks (2016)
37. Tabachnick, B.G., Fidell, L.S., Ullman, J.B.: Using Multivariate Statistics, vol. 5. Pearson, Boston (2007)

Recommended by Google Home

The Effects of Gender Stereotypes and Conformity When Interacting with Voice Assistants

Florian Schneider(✉)

Julius-Maximilians University Wuerzburg, 97070 Würzburg, Germany
florian.schneider@uni-wuerzburg.de

Abstract. Voice-enabled personal assistants like Google Home have been adopted by the masses (Hoy 2018). As speech is the main channel for communication between humans (Flanagan 1972) and is an innate human behavior (Pinker 1994), interacting with a voice interface is intuitive and easy (Cohen et al. 2004). Studies conducted under the Computers Are Social Actors (CASA) paradigm indicate that speech-output and interactivity are two main factors to elicit social reactions in users (Nass et al. 1993). Users have been shown to adopt human principles like conformity and gender stereotypes when interacting with computers (Nass and Moon 2000).

As voice assistants are able to send social cues, we assumed that subjects would show social reactions towards a Google Home smart speaker. Focussing on the social norm of conformity, we measured if participants show more conformal behavior towards the voice assistant depending on their own gender and the gender of the assistants' voice.

A laboratory experiment with 62 participants was conducted. Participants interacted with a Google Home speaker that either used a male or a female voice to present them with different social dilemma situations. In addition, the voice assistant always argued for participants to choose the less likely (as determined in a pretest) of two possible choices presented.

Results show a significant interaction effect on conformity between voice assistant gender and participant gender. Female participants chose significantly more options recommended by a female voice assistant meaning female participants did show conformal behavior. Regarding gender stereotypes, the voice assistant was rated differently by participants depending on the gender of its voice. A female assistant was rated as significantly warmer while a male assistant was rated to be significantly more competent in line with previous findings on gender stereotypes in human-human communication (Spence and Helmreich 1979).

Keywords: Voice assistants · Media equation · Conformity · Gender stereotypes

1 Introduction

Conversational interfaces have already established themselves as one of the breakthrough technologies of the 21st century. With the launch of Siri, a conversational assistant

© Springer Nature Switzerland AG 2021
C. Stephanidis et al. (Eds.): HCII 2021, CCIS 1419, pp. 485–493, 2021.
https://doi.org/10.1007/978-3-030-78635-9_63

presented by *Apple Inc.* in 2011, voice-enabled technology has since been accessible to the masses. Initially, these services were only available on smartphones. However, since the *Amazon Echo* was released in 2014 followed by *Google Home* in 2016, there have been a variety of stand-alone devices, so-called smart speakers. These are equipped with intelligent personal assistants aimed at making everyday life easier (Hoy 2018). *Siri, Alexa, Google Assistant, Cortana,* and other intelligent assistants can currently perform basic functions that the user can trigger via voice command. They send messages, create shopping lists, retrieve information from the Internet or control other smart home devices - overall, they perform tasks on demand.

Spoken dialogue interfaces take advantage of human evolutionary behavior which is why interacting with them appears intuitive and easy (Cohen et al. 2004). Speech is the primary medium of human communication (Flanagan 1972; Nass and Gong 2000; Schafer 1995) and thus a means of interaction whose use one is usually unaware of. Voice assistants appear to have human characteristics like comprehending speech, generating voice and being inherently socially interactive (Purington et al. 2017) and thus send social cues to users that are usually exclusive to human-human communication. Based on the findings of research conducted under the Computers Are Social Actors (CASA) paradigm (Nass et al. 1994; Nass et al. 1993) these social cues trigger the same mindless application of innate social rules and heuristics as human-human interaction would. It has been shown that gender stereotypes (Nass et al. 1997) and conformity effects (Lee 2003) can both be found in human-computer interaction. However, no empirical research has been done regarding voice assistants specifically.

The present study sets out an empirical examination of the effects of gender stereotypes and conformity on the users' behavior towards a voice assistant, specifically a Google Home device.

2   Theoretical Framework

2.1   Speech in Human-Human Interaction

Speech is an essential aspect of human-human interaction (Flanagan 1972; Nass and Gong 2000; Schafer 1995) and, referring to socio-evolutionary research, an inevitable tool for survival (Nass and Gong 2000). In ancient times, it was a vital need of the homo sapiens to bond with other humans for hunting and for mating to make sure that the species will survive natural selection (Nass and Gong 2000). As speech was an easy to perceive and highly accurate cue of humanness, it became a central tool for interactions, such as building and maintaining social bonds, describing the environment and expressing internal processes. All of this led to the innate rule of decision to perceive everything that produces speech as a human being (Nass and Gong 2000).

Transferring it to technology results in the most humanlike interaction with technological devices so far. Technology evolves rapidly - from unidirectional communication of a user giving commands to the device and waiting for an answer to bidirectional communication between the technological agent and the human user. One of the greatest advantages of speech technology is the intuitive operation of the devices. Since spoken language skills are an innate behaviour (Pinker 1994) and do not have to be learned first, the handling of language-based systems is familiar and easy (Cohen et al. 2004). The technological progress and the resulting new conditions of technology use call for an in-depth analysis of the underlying psychological processes: If human users communicate with conversational agents will they adopt social norms originally known from human-human interaction?

2.2 Previous Research: Computers Are Social Actors

The theory of CASA maintains that social scripts are activated when interacting with a computer resulting in behavior that is well known from human-human interaction (Nass and Moon 2000). Several studies carried out in this domain were based on the same principle: a methodological approach known from interpersonal social research was taken and replicated in such a way that at one point the human being was substituted by a computer (Nass et al. 1994). Following this procedure, it was demonstrated that users classify computers into social categories such as gender and ethnicity, adopting predictions of stereotypic behavior and character traits (Nass et al. 1994; Nass et al. 1997; Nass and Moon 2000). Furthermore, people tend to attribute personality characteristics to computers (Nass et al. 1995) and adopt social norms such as politeness when interacting with computers (Nass et al. 1994) as well as smartphones (Carolus et al. 2019).

Speaking naturally with a computer is a truly ubiquitous method of user access (Cox et al. 2000). Giving the fact that a voice assistant is able to send social cues and thus appears to have human characteristics like comprehending speech, generating voice and being "inherently a socially interactive device, since it requires social interaction to function" (Purington et al. 2017), it is reasonable to assume that voice assistants are perceived as social actors and as a result treated as such.

2.3 Gender Stereotypes

Stereotypes are beliefs about certain characteristics, procedures and attributions of persons belonging to a certain group (Hilton and Hippel 1996). While stereotypes are not inherently negative, they often contain negative connotations when they describe members of out-groups (Fedor 2014; Hilton and Hippel 1996). Stereotypes are usually applied in most areas of everyday life and even occur when they convey a wrong picture of an in-group like the own gender (Costrich et al. 1975). For this study we only examine stereotypes regarding gender, so called gender stereotypes.

Gender stereotypes are defined as socially shared convictions regarding specific characteristics that are seen as typical for men or women (Ashmore and Tumia 1980; Eckes 2008). Previous research identified four basic concepts that are attributed to the different genders: women are affiliated with warmth and expressiveness while men are affiliated with competence and instrumentality (Deaux and LaFrance 1998; Eckes 2003; Sczesny et al. 2019). All four of these concepts proved to be stable over time (Bergen and Williams 1991; Spence and Buckner 2000) as well as consistent across different cultures (Williams and Best 1990).

Especially warmth and competence are identified by Fiske et al. (2007) as some of the most important dimensions for social cognition and have been a staple of gender stereotype research for years (Conway et al. 1996; Eagly 1987). Based on the Social Role Thoery by Eagly (1987) people tend to ascribe attributes to others based purely on their social role and the gender stereotypes that come with it while ignoring situational variables (Eagly 1987; Eagly et al. 2000).

The application of gender stereotypes has been shown in human-computer interaction (Nass et al. 1997), human-smartphone interaction (Carolus et al. 2018) as well as human-robot interaction (Mieczkowski et al. 2019) where even exterior of robots by itself resulted in different attributions of warmth and competence.

2.4   Conformity

An important factor in human-computer interaction research is conformity, especially regarding stereotypes (Lee 2003). Conformity research assumes that the existence of groups or even perceived groups puts social pressure on individuals and influences their decisions. In that case individuals are more likely to make decisions based on group values and norms and follow decisions made by other members of the group (Asch 1956; Hertz and Wiese 2016). Conformity can even influence decisions when the group opinion is regarded as false (Asch 1956).

Conformity is an important research object within the scope of gender stereotypes. Eagly (1983) notes that individuals are more likely to allow themselves to be convinced by men than by women. The same effects have been demonstrated in human-computer interaction by Lee (2003): when interacting with computers exhibiting male or female characteristics, subjects rated suggestions made by a male computer as more sensible when concerning a stereotypical masculine topic while the same was true for female computer and feminine topics (Lee 2003).

2.5   Hypotheses

The CASA literature indicates that users tend to perceive a computer as a social entity which leads to the application of social rules in interactions with computers. Gender stereotypes and the dimensions of warmth and competence have been examined before in human-computer interaction. A higher knowledge concerning the topics of love and relationships was ascribed to computers speaking with a female voice while higher knowledge of technology was ascribed to male computers (Nass et al. 1997). More recently, male avatars were rated to be more competent compared to female avatars who were rated to be warmer (Lee 2008). Additionally, these effects could also be shown with different colored smartphone cases. Smartphones with a pink case were rated to be warmer while smartphones with a blue case were rated to be more competent (Carolus et al. 2018). Similar results were also shown for robots (Mieczkowski et al. 2019). Based on these results we predict that a smart-assistants voice will act as a social cue during the interaction with the device thus triggering the same stereotypes:

H1a: A voice assistant using a male voice is rated to be more competent compared to a voice assistant using a female voice.
H1b: A voice assistant using a female voice is rated to be warmer compared to a voice assistant using a male voice.

As mentioned above, conformity can be tied to the own gender as well as the gender of interaction partners depending group membership. It has been shown in conformity research that individuals are more likely to be convinced by members of their own in-group (e.g. gender) (Eagly 1983). This was replicated in human-computer (Lee and Nass 2002) as well as human-smartphone interaction (Carolus et al. 2008). Based on these results we predict that similar effects will be observed during the interaction with a voice assistant:

H2a: A voice assistant using a male voice will lead to higher conformity from male participants compared to a voice assistant using a female voice.
H2b: A voice assistant using a female voice will lead to higher conformity from female participants compared to a voice assistant using a male voice.

3 Method

3.1 Participants

62 volunteers participated in our experimental study conducted at the University of Würzburg, including $n = 19$ (30.6%) male and $n = 43$ (69.4%) female subjects. Participants ranged in age from 19 to 38 years ($M = 22.37$ years, $SD = 3.19$ years). In terms of education, 87.1% reported to hold a higher education entrance qualification.

3.2 Procedure

To evaluate our research questions, we conducted a laboratory experiment with a between-subject factorial design (male voice-assistant/female voice-assistant). On arrival, subjects were randomly assigned to one of the conditions and were prompted to interact with a Google Home device which guided them through the entirety of the experiment using voice interaction.

After a short introduction that allowed participants to get used to interacting with the voice assistant, they were presented with five social dilemmas. The dilemmas are based on those used by Lee and Nass (2002) and have been translated into German. Each of the dilemmas has two possible solutions. We conducted a pretest to determine the solution that is less likely to be chosen for each dilemma. For each dilemma, the assistant gave a recommendation on how it would resolve that dilemma. This recommendation was always based on the less likely solution. Participants were then asked to rate these recommendations and whether they would make the same or another decision in order to measure conformity. Following the interaction with the voice assistant participants were then asked to fill in an online questionnaire to rate the assistant's warmth and competence using items derived from the Stereotype Content Model by Fiske et al. (2002). The scale consisted of two subscales (warmth and competence) with six items each (for warmth, e.g. 'warm', 'good-natured', 'friendly'; for competence, e.g. 'competent', 'capable', 'efficient'). All answers were given on a 5-point-likert-scale.

4 Results

Our first hypothesis stated that a male voice assistant is rated to be more competent. A one-way ANOVA between the experimental groups revealed that the voice assistants gender had a significant effect on competence ratings, $F(1, 56) = 5.91, p = .019$. A male voice assistant was rated to be significantly more competent ($M = 4.43, SD = 0.60$) than a female voice assistant ($M = 3.82, SD = 0.55$). Therefore, the hypothesis can be confirmed.

Hypothesis 1b focused on the dimension of warmth, where we expected a female voice assistant to be rated higher compared to a male voice assistant. As expected, there was a significant difference between the groups, $F(1, 56) = 5.35, p = .012$. Subjects perceived a female voice assistant to be significantly warmer ($M = 4.12, SD = 0.60$) compared to a male voice assistant ($M = 3.35, SD = 0.66$).

Our second hypothesis relates to the social norm of conformity. Contrary to expectations, male participants showed less conformity with a male voice assistant ($M = 4.00, SD = 0.81$) when compared to a female voice assistant ($M = 4.24, SD = 0.93$). However, this difference was not statistically significant, $t(17) = -0.62, p = .273$. Thus, hypothesis 2a was rejected.

Female participants on the other hand did show significantly more conformal behavior when interacting with a female voice assistant ($M = 4.38, SD = 0.77$) when compared to a male voice assistant ($M = 3.47, SD = 0.96$), $t(41) = -3.40, p < .001, d = 1.024$. Therefore, hypothesis 2b is confirmed.

5 Discussion

Gender stereotypes have been found to affect almost every area of our everyday life (Costrich et al. 1975) and can lead to conformal behavior based on gender (Eagly 1983). The goal of this study was to examine the effects of gender stereotypes and the resulting conformity during human-voice-assistant interaction based on previous CASA research. The results confirmed the significant effect of perceived gender on the assessment of voice assistants and on conformal behavior. Voice assistants using a male voice were rated to be significantly more competent and a voice assistant using a female voice was rated to be significantly warmer.

For conformity the results were mixed. Female participants did show more conformal behavior when interacting with a female voice assistant. The same effect could not be shown for male participants interacting with male voice assistants. It should however be noted that only 19 male subjects participated in this study so the sample size may have not been large enough to find any significant conformity effects for male voice assistants. In addition, due to the study being conducted in Germany, German voices were used for the Google Home voice assistants. While the female voice is the default voice of the device and quite sophisticated and technically sound it was harder to find an equally sophisticated male counterpart as the default male voice was still in active development when this study was conducted and did have some weaknesses regarding pronunciation and intonation compared to the female voice.

Still, the results can be seen as a verification that the social cues sent by a voice-based system causes the user to view the system as a social actor thus falling in line with previous research concerning conformity in human-human interaction and confirming that the perceived gender of a voice assistant directly affects the behavior of the user.

6 Conclusion

To summarize, transferring the CASA paradigm to voice assistants has been shown to be a heuristically fruitful approach for future analyses. They seem to elicit seemingly inappropriate social reactions in their users which are the result of psychological mechanisms deeply rooted in mankind.

The assumption of subjects perceiving a smart speaker as a social actor was confirmed by significant results regarding the application of gender stereotypes as well as conformal behavior. Female subjects were more likely to show conformity with voice assistants using a female voice. Additionally, a female assistant was rated as significantly warmer while a male assistant was rated to be significantly more competent which falls in line with previous findings on gender stereotypes. In conclusion, this study provides a further contribution to the extension of the CASA paradigm focusing on the technology of voice assistants. The indication that interacting with these assistants elicits social behavior opens new questions regarding the implications of gender stereotypes and how they are applied even when interacting with technology, especially in the highly relevant field of voice interaction.

References

Asch, S.E.: Studies of independence and conformity: I. A minority of one against a unanimous majority. Psychol. Monogr. Gen. Appl. **70**(9), 1–70 (1956). https://doi.org/10.1037/h0093718

Ashmore, R.D., Tumia, M.L.: Sex stereotypes and implicit personality theory. I. A personality description approach to the assessment of sex stereotypes. Sex Roles **6**(4), 501–518 (1980). https://doi.org/10.1007/BF00287882

Bergen, D.J., Williams, J.E.: Sex stereotypes in the united states revisited: 1972–1988. Sex Roles **24**(7–8), 413–423 (1991). https://doi.org/10.1007/BF00289331

Carolus, A., Schmidt, C., Muench, R., Schneider, F.: Impertinent mobiles. Effects of polite and impolite feedback on the evaluation of smartphones. Comput. Hum. Behav. **93**, 290–300 (2019). https://doi.org/10.1016/j.chb.2018.12.030

Carolus, A., Schmidt, C., Muench, R., Mayer, L., Schneider, F.: Pink stinks - at least for men. In: Kurosu, M. (ed.) HCI 2018. LNCS, vol. 10902, pp. 512–525. Springer, Cham (2018). https://doi.org/10.1007/978-3-319-91244-8_40

Cohen, M.H., Giangola, J.P., Balogh, J.: Voice User Interface Design. Addison-Wesley, Boston (2004)

Conway, M., Pizzamiglio, M.T., Mount, L.: Status, communality, and agency: implications for stereotypes of gender and other groups. J. Pers. Soc. Psychol. **71**(1), 25–38 (1996). https://doi.org/10.1037/0022-3514.71.1.25

Costrich, N., Feinstein, J., Kidder, L., Marecek, J., Pascale, L.: When stereotypes hurt: three studies of penalties for sex-role reversals. J. Exp. Soc. Psychol. **11**(6), 520–530 (1975). https://doi.org/10.1016/0022-1031(75)90003-7

Cox, R., Kamm, C., Rabiner, L., Schroeter, J., Wilpon, J.: Speech and language processing for next-millennium communications services. Proc. IEEE **88**(8), 1314–1337 (2000). https://doi.org/10.1109/5.880086

Deaux, K., LaFrance, M.: Gender. In: Gilbert, D.T., Fiske, S.T., Lindzey, G. (Hg.) The Handbook of Social Psychology, 4. Aufl., Bd. 1, pp. 788–827. Oxford University Press, Oxford (1998)

Eagly, A.H.: Gender and social influence: a social psychological analysis. Am. Psychol. **38**(9), 971–981 (1983). https://doi.org/10.1037/0003-066x.38.9.971

Eagly, A.H.: Sex Differences in Social Behavior: A Social-Role Interpretation. Lawrence Erlbaum Associates (1987)

Eagly, A.H., Wood, W., Diekman, A.: Social role theory of sex differences and similarities: a current appraisal. In: Eckes, T., Trautner, H.M. (Hg.) The Developmental Social Psychology of Gender, pp. 123–174. Erlbaum (2000)

Eckes, T.: Geschlechterstereotype: Frau und Mann in sozialpsychologischer Sicht, 2. Aufl. Frauen, Männer, Geschlechterverhältnisse: Bd. 5. Centaurus-Verl.-Ges (2003)

Eckes, T.: Geschlechterstereotype: Von Rollen, Identitäten und Vorurteilen. In: Becker, R., Kortendiek, B. (Hg.) Handbuch Frauen- und Geschlechterforschung, pp. 171–182. VS Verlag für Sozialwissenschaften (2008). https://doi.org/10.1007/978-3-531-91972-0_20

Fedor, C.-G.: Stereotypes and prejudice in the perception of the "other". Procedia Soc. Behav. Sci. **149**, 321–326 (2014). https://doi.org/10.1016/j.sbspro.2014.08.257

Flanagan, J.N.: Speech Analysis Synthesis and Perception, 2nd edn. Springer, Berlin (1972). https://doi.org/10.1007/978-3-662-01562-9

Fogg, B.J., Nass, C.: How users reciprocate to computers. In: CHI '97 Extended Abstracts on Human Factors in Computing Systems, pp. 331–332 (1997). https://doi.org/10.1145/1120212.1120419

Hertz, N., Wiese, E.: Influence of agent type and task ambiguity on conformity in social decision making. Proc. Hum. Factors Ergon. Soc. Annu. Meet. **60**(1), 313–317 (2016). https://doi.org/10.1177/1541931213601071

Hilton, J.L., von Hippel, W.: Stereotypes. Annu. Rev. Psychol. **47**, 237–271 (1996). https://doi.org/10.1146/annurev.psych.47.1.237

Hoy, M.B.: Alexa, Siri, Cortana, and more: an introduction to voice assistants. Med. Ref. Serv. Q. **37**(1), 81–88 (2018). https://doi.org/10.1080/02763869.2018.1404391

Lee, E.-J.: Effects of "gender" of the computer on informational social influence: the moderating role of task type. Int. J. Hum Comput Stud. **58**(4), 347–362 (2003). https://doi.org/10.1016/S1071-5819(03)00009-0

Lee, E.-J.: Gender stereotyping of computers: resource depletion or reduced attention? J. Commun. **58**(2), 301–320 (2008). https://doi.org/10.1111/j.1460-2466.2008.00386.x

Lee, E.-J., Nass, C.: Experimental tests of normative group influence and representation effects in computer-mediated communication. Hum. Commun. Res. **28**(3), 349–381 (2002). https://doi.org/10.1111/j.1468-2958.2002.tb00812.x

Mieczkowski, H., Liu, S.X., Hancock, J., Reeves, B.: Helping not hurting: applying the stereotype content model and BIAS map to social robotics. In: 2019 14th ACM/IEEE International Conference on Human-Robot Interaction (HRI), pp. 222–229. IEEE (2019). https://doi.org/10.1109/HRI.2019.8673307

Nass, C., Fogg, B., Moon, Y.: Can computers be teammates? Int. J. Hum. Comput. Stud. **45**(6), 669–678 (1996). https://doi.org/10.1006/ijhc.1996.0073

Nass, C., Gong, L.: Speech interfaces from an evolutionary perspective. Commun. ACM **43**(9), 36–43 (2000). https://doi.org/10.1145/348941.348976

Nass, C., Moon, Y.: Machines and mindlessness: social responses to computers. J. Soc. Issues **56**(1), 81–103 (2000). https://doi.org/10.1111/0022-4537.00153

Nass, C., Moon, Y., Carney, P.: Are people polite to computers? Responses to computer-based interviewing systems. J. Appl. Soc. Psychol. **29**(5), 1093–1109 (1999). https://doi.org/10.1111/j.1559-1816.1999.tb00142.x

Nass, C., Moon, Y., Fogg, B.J., Reeves, B., Dryer, C.: Can computer personalities be human personalities? In: Conference Companion on Human Factors in Computing Systems - CHI 95, pp. 228–229 (1995). https://doi.org/10.1145/223355.223538

Nass, C., Moon, Y., Green, N.: Are machines gender neutral? Gender-stereotypic responses to computers with voices. J. Appl. Soc. Psychol. **27**(10), 864–876 (1997). https://doi.org/10.1111/j.1559-1816.1997.tb00275.x

Nass, C., Steuer, J., Tauber, E.R.: Computers are social actors. In: Proceedings of the SIGCHI Conference on Human Factors in Computing Systems Celebrating Interdependence - CHI 94, pp. 72–78 (1994). https://doi.org/10.1145/191666.191703

Nass, C., Steuer, J., Tauber, E., Reeder, H.: Anthropomorphism, agency, and ethopoeia. In: INTER-ACT 93 and CHI 93 Conference Companion on Human Factors in Computing Systems - CHI 93, pp. 111–112 (1993). https://doi.org/10.1145/259964.260137

Pinker, S.: The Language Instinct: How the Mind Creates Language. W. Morrow and Co, New York (1994)

Purington, A., Taft, J.G., Sannon, S., Bazarova, N.N., Taylor, S.H.: Alexa is my new BFF. In: Proceedings of the 2017 CHI Conference Extended Abstracts on Human Factors in Computing Systems - CHI EA 17, pp. 2853–2859 (2017). https://doi.org/10.1145/3027063.3053246

Schafer, R.W.: Scientific bases of human-machine communication by voice. Proc. Natl. Acad. Sci. **92**(22), 9914–9920 (1995). https://doi.org/10.1073/pnas.92.22.9914

Sczesny, S., Nater, C., Eagly, A.H.: Agency and communion: their implications for gender stereotypes and gender identities (2019). https://doi.org/10.7892/boris.119396

Spence, J.T., Buckner, C.E.: Instrumental and expressive traits, trait stereotypes, and sexist attitudes: what do they signify? Psychol. Women Q. **24**(1), 44–53 (2000). https://doi.org/10.1111/j.1471-6402.2000.tb01021.x

Spence, J.T., Helmreich, R.L.: Masculinity & Femininity: Their Psychological Dimensions, Corrrelates, & Antecedents, 2. cloth print. Univ. of Texas Press (1979)

Williams, J.E., Best, D.L.: Measuring Sex Stereotypes: A Multination Study. Cross-Cultural Research and Methodology Series, Bd. 6. Sage (1990). http://www.loc.gov/catdir/enhancements/fy0655/90008295-d.html

Measuring and Evaluation of the Results of UI-Re-Engineering in the Nursing Field

Sergio Staab[✉], Johannes Luderschmidt, and Ludger Martin

RheinMain University of Applied Sciences, Wiesbaden, Germany
{sergio.staab,johannes.luderschmidt,ludger.martin}@hs-rm.de

Abstract. Since all systems and services are ultimately aimed at human users, it is essential to address the interaction between humans and machines. The acceptance of a system, i.e. the question whether a system is interpreted by a user as good or bad, is a complex construct of perception and evaluation processes. A disproportionately growing number of care recipients and the associated avalanche of data in all areas of modern care continuously increases the need for more efficient, higher-quality and at the same time more cost-saving options for care and its networking of relatives, doctors and nurses. As part of a project to digitize dementia residential communities, an information platform called "INFODOQ" was developed. The system serves as a transparent information, coordination and communication platform for various dementia residential communities to optimize the daily care and nursing routine. After completion, the system underwent several analytical and empirical evaluations in which nursing teams were involved. The subject of the work presented here is the presentation of the evaluation results, the subsequent reengineering process of nursing documentation and the presentation of a specially developed analysis tool. New insights into the interaction behavior of caregivers in digital nursing documentation and the optimal interface development are the results of this work.

Keywords: Reengineering · Health informatics · Interface development · UX

1 Introduction

Demographic change and the associated improvement in medical care and nutrition as well as changes in housing conditions have a lasting impact on the life expectancy of generations. In addition, reduced birth rates and the resulting ageing of society are leading to a decline in the population and a massive increase in people in need of care. This results in a large shortage of junior care staff. Forecasts by the German Federal Statistical Office [1] show that in the next 15 years more than 66,000 skilled workers will be lacking in outpatient nursing alone. The shortage of nursing staff will result in a loss of value added and overall losses of 35 billion euros by 2030 due to vacant positions. On average, the healthcare sector is growing more than one percent faster than the entire German economy per year and at the same time, it is one of the least digitized sectors. According to Haefker and Tielking [2], only 20% of clinics work with

© Springer Nature Switzerland AG 2021
C. Stephanidis et al. (Eds.): HCII 2021, CCIS 1419, pp. 494–501, 2021.
https://doi.org/10.1007/978-3-030-78635-9_64

electronic nursing documentation. Based on such figures, the question arises as to why information science is so little accepted in this sector in particular. On the one hand, the basis of this scientific work rests on the problem of the increasing number of people in need of longterm care. With this work we want to investigate this issue. We analyze the nursing software INFODOQ which is currently being actively used by two dementia residential communities. Furthermore, we establish metrics regarding acceptance and usability for the correct software development of nursing systems and reexamine them using the newly designed software. The following questions are fundamental for this work: Which requirements and problems arise during the interaction of nurses with digital nursing documentation? How can the user-friendliness of interfaces in nursing documentation be increased in the context of these points?

- Presentation of an information platform developed in collaboration with two dementia residential communities
- Investigation of requirements and problems by means of analytical and empirical evaluations
- Demonstration of improvements in interaction between nurses and software through our work
- Derivation of guidelines for the development of user interfaces in nursing documentation

In Sect. 2, this paper starts with an insight into opinions on acceptance criteria that generally exist for interactions with software in medical care settings. Section 3 describes the implemented nursing software INFODOQ. Section 4 contains the functionality of the analysis tool. Section 5 describes our usability analysis using the analysis tool. Section 6 contains the conclusion and guidelines for the development of software in the nursing sector.

2 Related Work

In the medical field, central administrative activities and services can be supported almost seamlessly by IT systems. According to Haefker and Tielking [2], the entry of information science into the narrower field of medical treatment and care is more difficult due to ethical, social and technical reasons. Many works in the field of software development are based on the heuristics for the design of interfaces formulated by Nielsen and Molich [3]. These include visibility of system status, correspondence between system and reality, user control and freedom, stability, flexibility and efficiency, an aesthetic and minimalist design as well as assistance in recognizing, evaluating and correcting mistakes. As part of the project UCARE (Gräfe and Rahner [4]) from 2017, a usability competence center was developed to support small and mediumsized software manufacturers in the care industry. Nielsen's ten heuristics are also taken up here and extended by the subjective perception of the viewer of a software.

In the work by Hielscher, Kirchen-Peters and Sowinski [5], the topic of the acceptance of nursing staff is addressed as follows: A decisive factor for the positive acceptance of the IT-supported documentation is the individual self-confidence in the direct handling of computers as well as the acceptance of the care process mapped in the documentation system. In addition, the social context of the group of colleagues and their acceptance of the technology represent a considerable factor, since nursing staff within work teams or shifts have a significant influence on the willingness to use the technology. It should be noted that technical settings should not be regarded as static variables. They can change during the introduction of IT systems and with increasing service life. The administration of the maintenance process is shifted "into the system" by digitizing the documents, away from management and specialists. This tends to reduce the scope for consideration and negotiation processes regarding the correctness or execution variants of the individual maintenance steps. Deviations are still possible, but automatically become justifiable and directly transparent for management. In this context, the obligation to provide reasons is to be regarded as very important.

Wechsler [6] describes possible contextual challenges within the development of a mobile health-related application on the basis of a mobile health project from 2015. She emphasizes that software designers have to adapt flexibly to the respective needs of nurses. In order to avoid discrepancies between the ideas of nurses and those of designers regarding the application, it should be ensured at the beginning of development that nurses understand that the design process requires their participation in order to achieve the best possible results. A possible way to do this would be to educate them about the value of design research activities in advance. The transfer of knowledge between nurses and designers should be designed efficiently. Both sides should commit themselves in advance to participate in the respective design process.

3   INFODOQ

INFODOQ [7] is a web-based information platform for use in outpatient residential care groups. The system was developed in response to the desire for a transparent information, coordination and communication platform for various dementia residential communities to optimize day-to-day care and nursing. A decisive factor for the digitalization of the documentation, which until now has only been available in analog form, is the enormous increase in performance. In addition to the reduction of redundant or incorrectly addressed information and communication channels and the simultaneous reduction of bureaucratic and administrative effort, the system ensures effective and efficient care and maintenance. Furthermore, the information platform offers a transparent way for the mobile use of information as well as for the coordination and scheduling of relatives, nurses and assistants.

4   Analysis Method

The analysis tool is based on four different analysis methods, which are described below. Interaction of the users. Atterer and Schmidt [8] describe a solution for detailed logging of user interactions with AJAX-based web applications. They generate protocol data via an intermediate proxy. This approach reaches far beyond the field of usability tests. The following user actions can be logged on HTML pages: Mouse movements (pixel coordinates, ID and HTML DOM tree positions of the elements over which the mouse pointer is moved), scrolling (pixel offset), clicks, ID and DOM tree position of the clicked element, selection of dropdown menu entries, keystrokes (displayed modification keys such as Shift/Alt/Ctrl), text selection in form fields and resizing of the browser window. In summary, various interaction events can be logged from the metadata of mouse interactions, scroll strokes, clicks, keystrokes and dwell time.

Performance Analysis. Tullis and Albert [9] describe in their book the calculation of performance indicators based on certain user behavior, scenarios or tasks. Regardless of the technology, users interact with a system in some way. These behaviors form the cornerstone of performance metrics. Performance metrics are among the most valuable tools for any usability professional. Tullis and Albert describe the following types of performance metrics as Performance Metrics: Task Success, Time on Task, Errors, Efficiency and Learning Ability.

Effort-based Analysis. In their work, Tamir, Komogortsev and Mueller [10] put forward the hypothesis that usability is a function of effort and time. The use of effort to measure usability assumes that the less effort it takes to achieve a certain goal, the more usable the software is. One approach to an analysis could be to set a set of goals and measure the effort and time a subject needs to achieve each goal. If developers estimate the effort and time required, it is possible to compare the observed effort with the estimated effort. If the observed effort is greater than the estimated effort, a problem arises that requires further investigation. One approach is to execute the task n times per user to determine the learning curve of the user himself. The fewer task executions are necessary until the effort curve per user E(u) stagnates, the faster the user seems to have adapted to the interface and the task structure. The calculation of the effort (E) determines the physical and temporal effort of a user per modification within a task execution. This includes the number of all mouse clicks (MCall), number of double clicks (MCD), number of mouse movements (MM) and number of scrolled pixels (SM). To analyze the usability, the average effort of all users has to be measured on an expert ideal line, i.e., the minimum effort E(e) that an expert would need to process the same modification. The area between the learning curve E(u) and the learning curve E(e) up to the point at which the slope of the effort E(u) is zero is to be regarded as the learning phase. The difference between curves E(u) and E(e) represents the comprehensibility of the interaction with regard to the task/the interface underlying the task. The greater the difference, the more difficult it seems to be to handle the software optimally. Figure 1 shows the average effort of user E(u) and expert E(e).

The line chart shows a series of data points connected by interpolated straight line segments. The horizontal axis counts up the task executions. The vertical axis describes the effort.

Psychological Reaction Analysis. Freeman and Ambady [11] present the real-time processing of their mouse tracking method for task evaluation in their work. Motor responses can be considered as the final result of a feed-forward pipeline of perception, cognition and action. Conclusions can be drawn about the temporal course of perceptual cognitive processing. This is done as follows: A trajectory is the measurement of a movement from a starting point in the context of a task to a target point over a distance. During each trajectory, three pieces of information are recorded: time (how many milliseconds have elapsed), the x-coordinate of the mouse (in pixels), and the y-coordinate

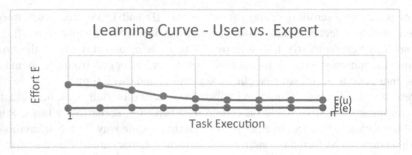

Fig. 1. Learning curve of user versus expert [9].

of the mouse (in pixels). The distance covered by each competitor is calculated as the "mean trajectory". This can be done by the number of competitors or by the number of attempts of a single competitor. Based on this basic data, analyses can now be carried out in many different ways, for example by measuring the spatial attraction.

5   Analysis

The previously described analysis procedures were developed in the analysis tool. In a 50-day usability analysis covering 3,135 documentation activities of 22 users, user behavior, performance, idiosyncrasies, competence, regularities, user irritations as well as the handling of different interfaces of one or more users were tracked, compared and analyzed. Figure 2 shows a partial overview of the data generated by the analysis tool.

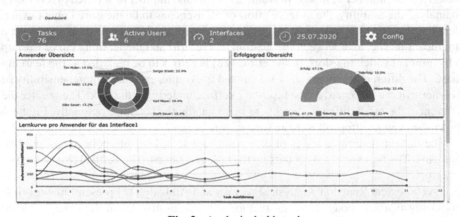

Fig. 2. Analysis dashboard

The analysis of the nursing documentation, shown in Fig. 3, revealed a high learning curve, various user irritations - including the wrong condition of buttons and images, and inconvenient use of the table, as well as slipping in columns and rows and high physical effort due to scrolling and clicking. Following empirical studies by Tractinsky [12] and

Kiurosu and Kashimuar [13], we then simplified the maintenance documentation in several steps. The new design of the nursing documentation is significantly slimmer, both in the header area by eliminating the static listing of resident images and in the footer area by removing the footer bar. Columns and rows have been masked by the hover effect, which improves clarity and should prevent slippage. The selection of all residents has been integrated into the table. The image of a resident changes by mouse interaction with the respective resident name in the listing or the table header. The space savings offer the user at first glance significantly more content of the documentation matrix.

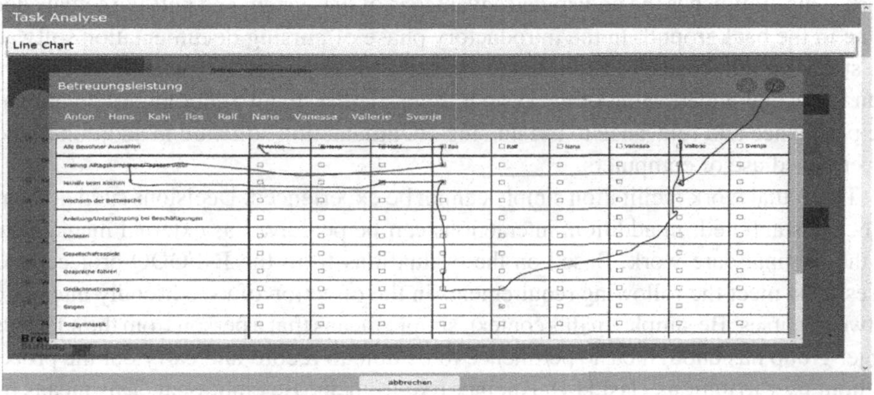

Fig. 3. Task- and mouse path analysis

If the mouse paths would show complex or even fluctuating trajectories between the respectively selected objects, there would be two possible conclusions: One user would not have understood the distribution of the objects, with several users a bad or misunderstood distribution of the objects on the respective interface could be concluded.

6   Conclusions

On the basis of the analysis tool described in the previous chapter, this chapter focuses on the digitization of transparent nursing documentation which is necessary but hardly articulated. The findings of the summative analytical methodology for evaluating the interaction of nurses with the INFODOQ system underpin various of the problems addressed. Even if the heuristics described by Nielsen [3] had previously been analytically identified by usability experts and integrated into the system, the requirements and problems of the nurses before and during the interaction are not only ensured by the design and function optimization. The subjective reference of each individual user turns out to be an important point. This includes perceptual characteristics such as hearing and sight as well as behavioral characteristics such as experience, motivation, individual preferences, abilities and knowledge. It should be noted that age generally represents a strong point of reference to the subjective limits described above. An interface from the point of view of a younger or older user does not seem to be pertinent for both. It can be assumed that users of a certain age on average no longer possess the same background knowledge in dealing with computer-aided systems as younger users. Their motivation to deal with new systems also decreases with increasing age. If individual self-confidence in the direct use of the computer is not strengthened, even small tasks such as registration seem to pose major obstacles. In the beginning, any design irritation is directly related to the acceptance of the entire system. Frequently, if a manager or a colleague is not immediately available for advice when problems arise, the hurdle seems insurmountable. After consultation with nurses, it turned out that the desired transparency of all interactions is rather perceived as the external management of the original care work. This diminishes the undisputed advantages of the system and puts the actual added value in the background. In the introductory phase of nursing documentation software, the stress for nurses due to additional work and time expenditure is significantly higher than the actual added value of the system. In particular, many older nurses do not have the pertinence and relevance to use nursing documentation software in addition to their experienced use of computers.

The actual work facilitation simply cannot be experienced. Decisions suddenly have to be substantiated; in addition, interactions can be perceived as external management of the original care work. Based on the evaluations from the INFODQ project, interfaces must meet the following requirements in the direction of user-friendly interaction between nurses: Be simple. In this context, simple means that a person from the addressed target group has enough basic pertinence to be able to record and carry out the process without user irritations Gast [14]. Another requirement: Be emotional. This means that a person from the addressed target group sees a fundamental usefulness with regard to the relevance of the subjective point of view. It should be noted that the knowledge contained in information is to be classified as relevant if it objectively serves to prepare a decision or to close a knowledge gap. If the system is simple and emotional, then a certain motivation arises which exceeds the threshold potential of the nerve cells of a user and thus allows the objective information to be processed. It should be noted that nursing documentation software must be designed to be brain-friendly by means of user experience and usability. This means objective knowledge must be prepared in the context of the internal reference of the target groups addressed and processes must be reduced to the essentials.

Objective knowledge must be enriched with emotional values in the context of the internal reference of the target groups addressed. It turns out that experienced computer users have a significantly higher competence. For them, user interfaces are much quicker to become functionally apparent and pertinent. Their perception process is much more pronounced through interaction with other systems. The structure of the system and the respective interfaces are more paramount. In addition, these users focus much more on usability and user experience, but also here the heuristics do not provide holistic user satisfaction. In everyday life, nurses must be able to access desired information much more quickly and easily. The heuristic of minimalism is a decisive approach that must be pursued in combination with user experience and usability measures. How can the user-friendliness of interfaces in nursing documentation be increased in the context of these points? User experience and usability measures can be understood as the simplification of objective knowledge by refining emotions that build fictional relevance. This means that objective knowledge must be designed in a way that is acceptable to the subject as a person (usability). During the process of information transfer, the user should be given an emotional part that builds up subjective relevance (experience). In order to support the development and commissioning of nursing documentation software, we extend the concept of dialogue design of usable systems by the principle of the ambience freedom of objects, i.e., the proportionality (benefit - user irritation) of each individual object. This means that the result of the use must be in the context of the granularity of the nursing documentation software in order to keep the previously described user irritation as low as possible. In this context, self-localization, clarity and simplicity are the characteristics of nursing documentation.

References

1. Sarodnick, F., Brau, H.: Methoden der Usability Evaluation – Wissenschaftliche Grundlagen und praktische Anwendung 3. Auflage. Hogrefe Verlag, Bern (2016)
2. Haefker, M., Tielking, L.: Altern, Gesundheit, Partizipation: Alternative Wohn- und Versorgungsformen im Zeichen des demografischen Wandels. Springer, Wiesbaden (2017). https://doi.org/10.1007/978-3-658-16801-8
3. Nielsen, J.: Usability Enginerring Kaufmann, San Francisco (1993). ISBN: 0-12-518406-9
4. Gräfe, B., Rahner, S., Root, E., Timmermanns, E.: Entwicklung eines Usability-Kompetenzzentrums zur Unterstützung von klein- und mittelständischen Softwareherstellern in der Pflegebranche (2017)
5. Hielscher, V., Kirchen-Peters, S., Sowinski, C.: Wissenschaftlicher Diskurs und Praxisentwicklungen in der stationären und ambulanten Langzeitpflege (2015)
6. Wechsler, J.: HCD mobile health project: post collaboration reflection of researcher and designer (2015). https://doi.org/10.1145/2846439.2846442
7. Bundesweites Journal für Wohn- Pflege- Gemeinschaften: Wissenschaft und Praxis zur Weiterentwicklung In Wohn-Pflege-Gemeinschaften 2018 (2018). https://www.kvjs.de/fileamin/dateien/soziales/fawo/wohn-pflege-journal_7-2018.pdf
8. Atterer, R., Schmidt, A.: Tracking the interaction of users with AJAX applications for usability testing (2007). ISBN: 978-1-59593-593-9. https://doi.org/10.1145/1240624.1240828
9. Tullis, T., Albert, W.: Measuring the user experience - collecting, analyzing, and presenting usability metrics (2013). ISBN 978-0-12-415781-1
10. Feldman, L., Mueller, C.J., Komogortsev, O.V., Tamir, D.: Usability testing with total-effort metrics (2009). https://doi.org/10.1109/ESEM.2009.5316022
11. Freeman, J.B., Ambady, N.: MouseTracker (2010). https://doi.org/10.3758/BRM.42.1.226
12. Tractinsky, N.: Aesthetics and apparent usability: empirically assessing cultural and methodological issues. ACM: 0-89791-802-9/97/03 (1997)
13. Kiurosu, M., Kashirnuma, K.: Apparent usability vs. inherent usability experimental analysis on the determinants of the apparent usability. ACM: 0-89791-755-3/95/0005 (1995)
14. Gast, O.: User Experience im E-Commerce. Springer, Wiesbaden (2018). https://doi.org/10.1007/978-3-658-22484-4

Information, Language, Culture and Media

Development of a Holistic Web-Based Interface Assistance System to Support the Intralingual Translation Process

Matthias Baumgart[✉], Claudia Hösel, Dominik Breck, Martin Schuster, Christian Roschke, and Marc Ritter

University of Applied Sciences Mittweida, 09648 Mittweida, Germany
{baumgart,hoesel,dbreck,mschust3,roschke,ritter}@hs-mittweida.de

Abstract. At the political and social level, easy-to-read texts are regarded as an important tool for creating barrier-free communication. In some countries, the right to comprehensible information is enshrined in law, which means that more and more standard-language texts have to be translated into easy-to-read texts. To support this intralingual translation process, previous approaches address the automation of specific sub-processes and thus focus on specific actors in the translation process. Interaction between those involved in the translation process is mostly decentralized and takes place using various applications. There is a lack of a holistic system that connects all actors involved in the process and allows interactions between the participants. This paper focuses on the implementation of a web-based assistance system and suitable interfaces that allow the representation of sub-processes of the intralingual translation process, taking into account the actors involved, and enable interactions between the participants. In order to store the data generated during the translation process in a structured and clear manner, various data management approaches could be used in this context and evaluated by means of functional tests. The results indicate that the interfaces between the actors have been optimized by the interaction components integrated in the system. Based on this, user-oriented further developments of web-based assistance systems can be carried out in the context of the intralingual translation process, whereby the system is to be used in real application contexts in the future in order to elicit the need for further assistance functions.

Keywords: Interface assistance system · Distributed systems · Easy-to-read

1 Introduction

Easy Language is a variant of standard language that is reduced at all linguistic levels and aims to enable people with learning difficulties to participate equally in information and communication. Easy Language is considered an important tool

© Springer Nature Switzerland AG 2021
C. Stephanidis et al. (Eds.): HCII 2021, CCIS 1419, pp. 505–511, 2021.
https://doi.org/10.1007/978-3-030-78635-9_65

on the political level for creating barrier-free communication, which has received support on the international level in recent years, e.g. in the Convention on the Rights of Persons with Disabilities [1].

The production of Easy-to-Read texts can be considered as an intralingual translation process, which essentially consists of four sub-processes - source text analysis, translation strategy creation, translation, text review [4]. The intralingual translation process is intellectually demanding and there are increasing efforts to provide computer support for this process. For the translation sub-process, various approaches have been presented in the past that address (semi-)automated text simplification. Approaches range from rule-based text simplification (e.g. Chandrasekar et al. 1996 [2], Siddharthan 2003 [8]), which focus on syntactic simplification of texts, to approaches that aim to simplify texts at the lexical level by integrating, for example, dictionaries. Swain et al. 2019 [12] propose an approach to text simplification involving additional lexical resources. Stodden & Kallmeyer 2020 [9] explore the relevance of different lexical and syntactic features in multi-lingual text simplification. More recent approaches attempt to align automated text simplification more closely with human behavior. For example, Sheang 2020 [7] presents an initial approach that incorporates context from surrounding sentences in text simplification, but explicitly notes that the quality of text simplification must be verified by a human. Suter et al. 2016 [11], who are developing a rule-based text simplification system for the German language, also stated for the qualitative evaluation of their system that difficult vocabulary would not be reduced as readably as a human would. Hansen-Schirra et al. 2020 [3] explicitly state for Easy Language that the quality of machine translation is often not yet comparable to a human translation and needs to be revised by humans. Approaches to text verification mostly address linguistic features on the text surface. Suárez-Figueroa et al. 2020 [10] use rule-based techniques, pattern recognition, and Natural language processing techniques to check compliance with easy-to-read guidelines for Spanish-language texts. Iglesias et al. 2020 [6] present, also for the Spanish language, a tool for readability checking of web pages that considers accessibility and usability aspects in addition to traditional linguistic features.

Existing approaches address the sub-processes of text simplification and text review as singular processes. The interactions between the actors involved in the translation process are largely ignored. This paper presents a holistic web-based assistance system that integrates the sub-processes of the intralingual translation process while taking into account the interactions between the stakeholders.

2   Methods

In order to implement a web-based assistance system with suitable interfaces that integrates the sub-processes of the intralingual translation process and allows interactions between the stakeholders involved in the process, a suitable system architecture is required. This was created on the basis of a systematic requirements elicitation and verified in functional tests.

2.1 Requirements

The basis for creating the software architecture was the elicitation and specification of requirements based on the international standard ISO/IEC 25000 "Systems and software engineering - Systems and software Quality Requirements and Evaluation" [5]. The elicited functional and non-functional requirements were systematically documented in requirements documents. Based on the requirements documents created, the properties and framework conditions of the software architecture were determined, analyzed and specified.

2.2 System Architecture

To achieve the intended objective, the system was developed in such a way that data can be distributed asynchronously and stored persistently. In addition, the provision of assistance functions for the creation of Easy-to-Read texts is essential. Based on these specifications, a software architecture was developed within various conceptual processes, which is shown in Fig. 1. Various functional complexes of the system are grouped into units and represented on multiple systems. The individual system components are addressed individually or in combination with different units within the substeps of the translation process. For the basic implementation of the distributed system, a web-based approach is chosen here, which is implemented using October CMS. The resulting modular architecture is divided into multiple sub-areas. These are divided into the transfer of data within the client-server system, the structuring and persistent storage of data, the distribution and virtualization of the individual system components, and the creation of various assistance systems to support the user. The data transfer within the system is realized by means of AJAX, the persistent data storage is done by MySQL. Docker is used for the distribution and virtualization of the individual components of the system. For the creation of the individual assistance functions of the application, Regular Expressions were used, among other things, to map the rules required for the creation of easy-to-read texts. The intralingual process of translating standard German texts into Easy Language begins with the analysis of the source text, which is carried out within the Application Unit. Translators and client can interact in this regard. The subcomponents "Import/Export Unit", "Datatransfer Unit", "Translation Unit" and "Assistance Unit" can be used to map the entire process.

As part of the process, (1) a source text is provided by the client using the Import/Export Unit. The uploaded and persistently stored file can then be read out and enriched by the client with various metadata within the Translation Unit and the test translation process can be started. The Storage Unit is used to store all system states. (2) Within the test translation process, it is possible for the translator to create a translation strategy tailored to the text. After a test translation has been created, it is stored in the system and forwarded to the client, who can iteratively evaluate the translation received. This can now result in several iterations of the test translation. (3) Once a test translation has

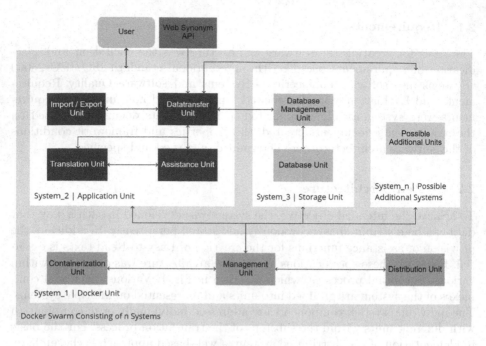

Fig. 1. Created software architecture

been produced and accepted by the client, the process of intralingual translation begins. Within this process step, various assistance functions are provided
to enable semi-automated translation. The Assistance Unit acts as the central
component in this process. (4) Once the final translation has been completed,
the review process follows. The translator forwards the translation to the target
group reader, who checks and evaluates it for comprehensibility. Based on the
assessment received in this way, the translator further adjusts the translation and
then forwards it to the client for further evaluation and, if necessary, approval.
Once the translation has been accepted by the client, the client can export and
download the final version of the text from the system using the Import/Export
Unit.

The system structure shown in Fig. 1 makes it possible to dynamically expand
the system by adding further subsystems and components. Thus, there is a
possibility of scaling and load distribution within the application.

2.3   Functional Tests

To check the functionality of the system architecture, test cases were derived from
the identified functional and non-functional requirements, checked for fulfillment
and documented accordingly. The test cases were structured according to a fixed
scheme: each test case consists of an assigned requirement, various dependencies
on other requirements, a description of the initial situation, a description of the
event to be performed, and a description of the expected result.

3   Results and Discussion

The functionality of the system architecture and the assistance functions was tested on the basis of functional tests. The test cases derived from the functional and non-functional requirements were successfully performed. Figure 2 represents an excerpt of the generated test document. The naming scheme for the ID of the test case is composed of the type of requirement (FR = Functional Requirements; QR = Quality Requirements), the abbreviation TC (Test Cases) followed by the number of the respective test case.

ID	EXPECTATIONS	STATUS
FRTC01	Asynchronus transmission of data	✅
FRTC02	Virtualization of the system	✅
FRTC03	Distribution of the system	✅
QRTC01	Reduction of the amount of data transferred	✅
QRTC02	Reduction of the time required to display the data	✅
QRTC03	Reduction of the necessary page impressions	✅
QRTC04	Transfer of data without blocking the system functions	✅
QRTC05	Components of the application are separable	✅
QRTC06	Components can be distributed across different systems	✅
QRTC07	Maintainability of the system through central administration of all components	✅
QRTC08	Maintainability of the system through central updating of services and components	✅
QRTC09	System resilience	✅
QRTC10	Distributed executability of the system	✅
QRTC11	Application scalability	✅
QRTC12	Isolation of the components from the OS of the host system	✅

Fig. 2. Excerpt of the generated test document

Based on the test documents, the choice of technologies used, AJAX for data transfer and Docker for the distribution of the system, is rated as reasonable and practicable. In this context, data volumes seem to be optimizable in terms of transfer volume when transferring via AJAX. Furthermore, selected parameters, such as word and sentence length, are checked rule-based and any rule violations are highlighted in the text. By connecting additional lexical resources, the frequency of the words used is also determined, displayed as hint text, and synonyms are suggested if necessary. The results of the functional tests also indicate that the interaction components integrated in the system are suitable for optimizing the interfaces between the stakeholders involved in the translation process. For specific activities within individual sub-processes, components were created and integrated that enable direct interactions between the actors involved. In the input, review, and correction of metadata, an activity within text analysis, the distributed system architecture and integrated interaction components enable direct feedback between translator and client. Likewise, when creating, reviewing, and correcting, the interaction components enable direct interactions between the actors involved in the process.

4   Conclusion

This paper focuses on the implementation of a web-based assistance system that integrates the sub-processes of the intralingual translation process and enables interactions between the stakeholders involved in the process. Based on comprehensive requirements documents, a system architecture was created and suitable assistance functions for the intralingual translation process were integrated. The functionality of the system architecture and the assistance functions was confirmed in functional tests.

In further studies, we will conduct evaluation experiments of the implemented parts of the system involving end users and optimize our system based on the results of the end user study. In the evaluation of the system with end users, it is also important to evaluate the implemented assistance functions with regard to their practical suitability. Since no dictionary optimized for Easy Language was used as a lexical resource, the relevance of the suggested synonyms in particular needs to be validated.

References

1. Convention on the rights of persons with disabilities. https://www.un.org/development/desa/disabilities/convention-on-the-rights-of-persons-with-disabilities/convention-on-the-rights-of-persons-with-disabilities-2.html. Accessed 16 March 2021
2. Chandrasekar, R., Doran, C., Srinivas, B.: Motivations and methods for text simplification. In: The 16th International Conference on Computational Linguistics (COLING), vol. 2, pp. 1041–1044 (1996)
3. Hansen-Schirra, S., Nitzke, J., Gutermuth, S., Maaß, C., Rink, I.: Technologies for translation of specialised texts into easy language. In: Easy Language Research: Text and User Perspectives, pp. 99–127. Frank & Timme (2020)
4. Hösel, C., Roschke, C., Thomanek, R., Rolletschke, T., Platte, B., Ritter, M.: Process automation in the translation of standard language texts into easy-to-read texts - a software requirements analysis. In: Stephanidis, C., Antona, M. (eds.) HCII 2020. Communications in Computer and Information Science, vol. 1226, pp. 50–57. Springer International Publishing, Cham (2020)
5. IEC International Electrotechnical Commission: ISO/IEC 25000 systems and software engineering - systems and software quality requirements and evaluation. https://www.iso.org/obp/ui/#iso:std:iso-iec:25000:ed-2:v1:en. Accessed 18 Mar 2021

6. Iglesias, A., Cobián, I., Campillo, A., Morato, J., Sánchez-Cuadrado, S.: Comp4Text checker: an automatic and visual evaluation tool to check the readability of spanish web pages. In: Miesenberger, K., Manduchi, R., Covarrubias Rodriguez, M., Peňáz, P. (eds.) ICCHP 2020. LNCS, vol. 12376, pp. 258–265. Springer, Cham (2020). https://doi.org/10.1007/978-3-030-58796-3_31

7. Sheang, K.C.: Context-aware automatic text simplification. In: Lloret, E., Saquete, E., Martínez-Barco, P., Sepúlveda-Torres, R. (eds.) CEUR Workshop Proceedings, vol. 2633, pp. 56–62. Bilbao, Spain (2020). urn:nbn:de:0074-2633-3

8. Siddharthan, A.: Preserving discourse structure when simplifying text. In: Proceedings of the European Natural Language Generation Workshop (ENLG), 11th Conference of the European Chapter of the Association for Computational Linguistics (EACL 2003), pp. 103–110 (2003)

9. Stodden, R., Kallmeyer, L.: A multi-lingual and cross-domain analysis of features for text simplification. In: Proceedings of the 1st Workshop on Tools and Resources to Empower People with REAding DIfficulties (READI), pp. 77–84. No. May, European Language Resources Association, Marseille, France (2020)

10. Suárez-Figueroa, M.C., Ruckhaus, E., López-Guerrero, J., Cano, I., Cervera, Á.: Towards the assessment of easy-to-read guidelines using artificial intelligence techniques. In: Miesenberger, K., Manduchi, R., Covarrubias Rodriguez, M., Peňáz, P. (eds.) ICCHP 2020. LNCS, vol. 12376, pp. 74–82. Springer, Cham (2020). https://doi.org/10.1007/978-3-030-58796-3_10

11. Suter, J., Ebling, S., Volk, M.: Rule-based automatic text simplification for German. In: 13th Conference on Natural Language Processing (KONVENS 2016), pp. 279–287. Bochum, Germany (2016). https://doi.org/10.5167/uzh-128601

12. Swain, D., Tambe, M., Ballal, P., Dolase, V., Agrawal, K., Rajmane, Y.: Lexical text simplification using wordnet. In: Singh, M., Gupta, P.K., Tyagi, V., Flusser, J., Ören, T., Kashyap, R. (eds.) ICACDS 2019. CCIS, vol. 1046, pp. 114–122. Springer, Singapore (2019). https://doi.org/10.1007/978-981-13-9942-8_11

Orientalism and Kung Fu Panda

Xu Chen[✉]

Nanjing University of Science and Technology, Nanjing 210000, China

Abstract. With the advent of globalization, more and more cultural elements of oriental countries have been discovered by Hollywood and become the basis and material for its film creation. However, ever since Hollywood first introduced the concepts of "Chineseness" and "otherness" in films, the western understanding of oriental cultural prejudice, namely Orientalism, has existed and gradually penetrated into the production of films, such as the film *Kung Fu Panda* with Chinese characteristics. Different people have different opinions about the Chinese culture reflected in the film. Based on the theory of Orientalism put forward by Said, this paper discusses the embodiment of Orientalism in Hollywood animated films and takes *Kung Fu Panda* as an example to analyze how to use oriental elements to convey western ideas and shape American heroes. Through the analysis, readers will have a deeper understanding of cross-cultural communication and Orientalism in Hollywood films. These films full of Chinese elements seem to express the essence of Chinese culture, but in fact it is just a commercial film full of eastern and foreign imagination, strongly permeating western ideas.

Keywords: Communication barriers · Cross-cultural communication · Orientalism

1 Introduction

With the advent of globalization, film as a medium has become an important way of cultural communication. More and more cultural elements of oriental countries have been discovered by Hollywood, which has become the selection basis and source of material for its theme creation, character image design, prop scene conception and so on. But orientalism, the western understanding of oriental cultural prejudice, has existed since Hollywood first introduced concepts of 'Chineseness' and otherness in its films, and this understanding has gradually penetrated into the production of films such as *Kung Fu Panda*, a film with Chinese characteristics. Some people think that the film is a good promotion of Chinese culture. Some people think that some of these cultures are different from traditional Chinese cultures.

Therefore, this paper will take Hollywood classic animated films as an example to discuss and analyze the embodiment of orientalism in the movies. First, this paper analyzes Said's orientalist theory on which it relies, followed by discussing how Hollywood animation films use oriental elements to convey western ideas and shape American heroes from the perspective of orientalism. Finally, through the analysis of literature research and case studies, this paper searched theories related to orientalism and Hollywood's

C. Stephanidis et al. (Eds.): HCII 2021, CCIS 1419, pp. 512–519, 2021.
https://doi.org/10.1007/978-3-030-78635-9_66

policy towards China and analyzed *Kung Fu Panda*. Through the above analysis, readers will have a deeper understanding of orientalism in Hollywood films. To conclude, these films full of Chinese elements seem to express the essence of Chinese culture, but in fact they are just commercial films full of oriental and exotic imagination, permeating western thoughts.

2 Literature Review and Theoretical Framework

As early as the end of the 18th century, "Orientalism" began to become an independent discipline. It originated from a series of British studies on eastern India, including language (Sanskrit), law, folk customs, literature and so on [1]. Orientalism, while being a discipline, is also a way of thinking for the western world to understand the eastern world and an embodiment of the west's attempt to dominate and rule the east [2]. Faced with the prejudice, misunderstanding and slander of the west against various cultural forms of the east, western scholars, represented by the Palestinian-American Edward Said, resisted and criticized the post-colonial behavior of the west.

Orientalism, published in 1978, became a classic work of post-colonial criticism. In the book, Said used "Orientalism" to summarize the post-colonial relationship between the western world and the eastern world. This concept refers to the theory and practice of the western representation of the east. For example, in American films, the narrative mode of latent orientalism and manifest orientalism is adopted, which is just a medium for the western representation of the east. Said's "orientalism" theory has strong ideological and political criticism, which is aimed at the western cultural hegemony and power politics. In the book *Orientalism*, Edward Said has made a clear definition of orientalism: 'Orientalism does not express an understanding of a world totally different from itself... In some cases, the desire or intention of the west to control, manipulate, or even annex' [2].

In the eyes of western countries in the 19th century, there was no real basis for the eastern world. Through some fiction, they viewed the east with an attitude of curiosity and even prejudice. For example, the word "Chineseness", which emerged in the 1970s and 1980s, is often understood being an ancient cultural paradigm that potentially constrains modern Chinese. In the west, although have some scholars have said the Chinese and westerners have common humanity, but China's image in the western popular culture, has always given China a strange, incredible "oriental" and stressed that China and the opposite characteristics of Chinese and western things, this is typical of orientalism. Moreover, western expressions of the east, including China, are often full of extreme expressions [3]. For example, from the 1850s, American traders, diplomats and missionaries emphasized the moral depravity of the Chinese, creating negative stereotypes of the Chinese in fiction, theatre and cartoons. They emphasize China's moral depravity, characterized by 'deceit, cunning, idolatry, tyranny, xenophobia, cruelty, infanticide and intellectual and sexual perversity' [4]. Or the rich, powerful, intelligent, mysterious, quiet and other positive characteristics mentioned in Marco Polo's travels. In the west, the history of China is far less important than the fiction about China, in which the China they see happens to reflect the archetype of China they imagine. In the same way, there are often two extreme forms of stereotype in their images of China.

The research objects of Edward Said are mainly academic work, travel notes and novels. However, "orientalism" not only exists in western literature, music, architecture and drama, but also widely exists in film and television work. The movie, accompanied by grand scenes and impressive sound effects, gives the audience unparalleled impact and the sense of reality. In the symbolic coding of the film, China is also defined as an exotic and opposite "other". "Oriental" emerges as an imaginary place that is contrary to the west in imagination, in space and time, and meaning and value. As a medium suitable for worldwide dissemination, film has been loaded with too many symbolic meanings and cultural assumptions at the beginning of its birth. The film originated at a time when western imperialism and colonialism were prevalent all over the world. Looking at western films, there are countless oriental elements such as kung fu, ethics, chivalry, traditional Chinese medicine, metaphysics, and violence aesthetics, which are like strange wonders, distant fairy tales and bizarre stories. This is a typical expression of "orientalism". This essay takes Hollywood movies, the representative of western films, as an example to analyze the classic performance of "orientalism".

At the very beginning of the birth of the film, the film basically undertook the mission of exploring the strange world, and the remote east naturally became the object of the photographer's attention. Through the study of early Hollywood films, orientalism in some films is not a reflection of the reality of the objective situation of the eastern countries, and often contains all kinds of prejudice and discrimination. In early Hollywood films, oriental was inextricably linked with "Yellow Peril." In the 1890s, the Yellow Peril appeared in Europe, and gradually became a tone of the west versus the east. This word is popular from the famous print "Peoples of Europe, guard your dearest goods." (see Fig. 1)

Fig. 1. Peoples of Europe, guard your dearest goods (Hermann 1895)

The picture could be interpreted as that the Europeans, led by one of the chief princes Saint Michael, will defeat the Buddha and dragon from the east to defend the European faith and homeland. It also reflected the recognition by European countries that east Asia had the potential to threaten the hegemony of Europe and the United States. The yellow peril caricatures the oriental, physically and psychologically, as weak, savage, coarse, violent, savage, immoral, pagan, and infantile [5]. For example, the fictional anti-hero "Dr. Fu Manchu" is impressive: he is thin and tall, bald, with two long, upside-down beards, and his never-smiling face is full of evil. But after the 1990s, the original orientalism was much weakened in terms of "hostility" or prejudice. The "global orientation" of the film market has led to changes in Hollywood in a series of aspects such as the materials, themes and shooting methods. Hollywood creates for the world, always looking for the best story no matter where it happens. The pyramids of Egypt, Solomon of India, Mulan of China... More and more oriental stories are being brought to the Hollywood screen. The eastern sentiment not only creates the cultural spectacle for the western audience, but also expands the market share of Chinese films and obtains the vast market resources for them. The 5,000-year-old Chinese culture and the spirit of Chinese culture, which includes martial arts, painting and calligraphy, Confucianism and Taoism, have all become the elements of Hollywood films.

China's film market is an irresistible target market for Hollywood studios due to its huge population base and increasing consumption power. "Oriental" is no longer synonymous with backwardness and poverty. In recent years, in particular, Hollywood studios have begun to project an image of the east that easterners love to see. In this context, Hollywood films are gradually trying to construct a new image of China, a new impression of the east, on the screen. Thus, "orientalism" from this new perspective was born. In addition to analyzing the Chinese film market, consumer market and audience, cultural influence is also an important aspect of the potential consideration of Hollywood films.

Hollywood takes the commercial value of Chinese elements very seriously, but paradoxically, uses them with great care. For example, the emergence of "China special feed" may also be closely related to such contradictory mentality. "China special feed" described here refers to the film version designed and released for the Chinese market by Hollywood producers and directors in the early stage of film creation and operation, which is different from the international version sold and distributed in other countries and regions except China [6]. In consideration of the global market, Hollywood edited the global version and "China special feed" into two versions, which are also a marketing method aimed at commercial considerations. Hollywood production of "China special feed" of the story will not be a real impact, will not change the original content, only the corresponding increase in one of Chinese elements, mainland increased focus on subject factors, at the same time, the mainland investors to cooperate with the film in the localization of deeper campaign, thereby enhance the audience's psychological recognition and acceptance, become the powerful tools for the movie marketing. The emergence of "China special feed" is also to cater for the taste of global movie fans, which is also a respect for the cultural environment and aesthetic differences in other countries and regions.

3 Analysis of Kung Fu Panda

Kung fu movies have long been a window for Hollywood and the western world to learn about China, from Hong Kong kung fu movies like Bruce Lee and Jackie Chan to the Oscar-winning *Crouching Tiger, Hidden Dragon*. In 1949, the Hong Kong film industry produced the first Wong Fei-hung film, and the incorporation of Chinese martial arts became outstanding [7]. In the impression of westerners, 'Chinese kung fu' is a relatively vague concept, referring to all Chinese or even all eastern martial arts that do not rely on modern firearms. All martial arts are simplified into one big label: Chinese kung fu. As a result, some incomprehensible information such as martial arts schools have been cut down, and the various forms of martial arts on screen are only repeated impressions of 'Chinese kung fu'. Among Hollywood kung fu films, *Kung Fu Panda* has received some attention from people who love kung fu culture. The co-director John Stevenson mentioned in an interview that many people are big fans of kung fu movies when they watch *Kung Fu Panda*. Doing kung fu well, doing martial arts well, is the film's biggest technical and artistic challenge. There are a lot of technicians involved in every aspect of the film, including professional teams and product designers, story artists and French animators doing martial arts, which actually ensures that certain martial arts moves are accurate and correct [8]. But despite their efforts to accurately use the cultural elements of Chinese kung fu, their concerns in trying to mimic kung fu to a very general statement. This film relies on western thoughts and behaviors and filters the general knowledge of kung fu, and still tells American stories.

The Americanization of Chinese elements in *Kung Fu Panda* is obvious to see. In 2007, in a massive online survey called '*Looking for 100 Chinese elements*' [9], the dragon dominated the top three in terms of "Chinese elements," while pandas, Chinese kung fu, Peking Opera, acupuncture and calligraphy also made the list. As a Chinese belief, the dragon represents nobility and auspiciousness. However, in western culture, the fire-breathing dragon is a synonym for ugliness and evil, and the dragon does not become the protagonist in Chinese animation. *Kung Fu Panda*'s dragon scroll is at the heart of the movie, and it has always been the biggest mystery factor in the film. At the end of the film, Po finally learns the true meaning of the wordless Dragon Scroll secret and reaches the highest level of wuxia. However, Po understands the wordless Dragon Scroll through a quintessentially American cultural idea: the belief that you can work miracles. By using Chinese elements to understand the nature of American culture, Hollywood still reflects American cultural thought.

From The aspect of character selection, The Furious Five – master Tigress, master Mantis, master Viper, master Crane and master Monkey – originated from Chinese Panthera Tigris Amoyensis, Red Crowned Crane, Tenodera Sinensis, Red-tailed Green Bamboo Snake and Golden Monkey respectively. (see Fig. 2) These animals are selected with Chinese characteristics. And the protagonist Po is a panda, panda is a unique symbol of China, they are gentle, cute appearance, easy to depict and exaggerated entertainment image. At the same time, the choice of pandas also avoids to some extent the restriction of the appearance characteristics of certain ethnic groups and avoids the unnecessary in-depth interpretation of the ethnic cultural background of the characters. The choice of "kung fu" and "panda" is an attempt to portray China in a straightforward way. This cultural penetration is actually more conducive to westerners' understanding of China than the real "China" [10]. Dreamworks chose the panda because it is more acceptable to western audiences. Since it is instantly recognizable, in the 26 years from 1957 to 1982, 23 pandas being presented as gifts given by China to 9 countries. Chinese kung fu, Chinese stories, and popular Chinese elements around the world, the presence of these

Chinese symbols in *Kung Fu Panda* is an important reason for the film's success. And the appellation Po also has Chinese characteristics, meaning the beloved baby, which is popular in traditional Chinese culture.

Fig. 2. The choice of characters – native animals of China

The film is permeated with American humor under the Oriental culture. Po's businessman background, fat physique and gluttony habits seem destined never to achieve a remarkable achievement. But he has a life beyond the ideal, desire to become the dragon warrior, to punish evil. As a result, the heavy body and the huge gap beyond reality turned into endless Hollywood style comedy elements, Po's secular weaknesses were endlessly exaggerated, and he often in the tense moments of tension funny, the strict relationship between teachers and students in the eastern way also in the collapse of laughter. Hollywood's approach is that since the mundane side of human nature is inevitable, it is necessary to treat it with tolerance as an endearing quality, or to turn it into a driving force and opportunity for success. Po's master takes his gluttony as the driving force for martial arts practice, and his heavy weight does play a big role against the enemy – ordinary individuals with weaknesses also have the possibility of achieving ideals.

In many Hollywood movies, the main character has a strong sense of personal heroism. Examples for this are Superman, Spider-man, Iron man… and the most exciting scene in the film is the final battle between the main character and the main villain. The end result, of course, is that the main character overcomes the main villain, saves the world, and the world returns to peace. This is the characteristic "heroism" of Hollywood films. In *Kung Fu Panda*, Po is an ordinary noodle shop manager's son, but because of the coincidence became the dragon warrior, from then on began his extraordinary martial arts warrior life, became the hero of worship. Although the furious five have great martial arts skills, the task of saving China falls to Po. Po began to practice kung fu assiduously, diligent in thinking, and finally got the secret of the dragon treasure code and understand the raccoon master "inner peace" of the supreme realm of martial arts, finally defeated Tai Lung, make the whole Chinese land to restore peace and vitality.

Some audiences were affected by the heroism advocated by the film. Since the Spring and Autumn Period in ancient China, the correct way of doing things handed down in China is to require people to be kind, upright, polite, wise and trustworthy. However, the American thought is quite different. The *United States Declaration of Independence* was issued after the American people fought hard against the British, which enabled them to promote the values of freedom and equality, to advocate people's fearless spirit of adventure, and to achieve happiness through unremitting efforts [11]. The difference in value evaluation makes the styles of eastern and western cultural works greatly different. The gentle and peaceful style of the east is far from the distinctive style of the west. Kung fu is a Chinese cultural heritage, in ancient times there are a variety of martial arts chivalry chivalrous justice, he helped the poor, only for the people to fight injustice but not famous. But in *Kung Fu Panda*, Po is worshipped by the people, which is not the style of Chinese martial arts, but the hero who is full of western "heroism", because he is so powerful that he is worshipped. Therefore, it runs counter to the martial arts spirit worshiped in China.

Every country has its own spiritual pillar. In the history of the United States, the American people gained their freedom and democracy through their own efforts, which formed the American spirit – the American dream. Because the development history of the United States is short and there has never been a feudal system, so this concept is more widespread and deeper than the eastern countries. Therefore, the American dream advocates freedom, democracy and equality, and only through unremitting efforts and struggles can people succeed. In the movie *Kung Fu Panda*, the idea of freedom and equality is reflected. For example, after the raccoon master took Po as his student, they were more like close friends in the process of training. In addition, Po from a young man who can't do any kung fu, through their own unremitting efforts to finally achieve success, to realize their dreams into a warrior. In the movie, there is always this spiritual theme, which advocates ordinary people to daydream, and its essence is to realize one's self-worth through unremitting efforts. In the *United States Declaration of Independence*, it is emphasized that all people are created equal and everyone has the right to pursue happiness. [11] This determined the subsequent attitude of the western people towards dreams. In the east, however, there is an emphasis on seeking truth from facts. A journey of a thousand miles starts with taking the first step instead of daydreaming. Different from the American dream, so different ideas make different attitudes and cultures.

4   Conclusion

Based on the analysis of the theory of orientalism and the oriental elements in Hollywood films, we find that orientalism frequently appears in the films of western countries. In the process of intercultural communication, cultural symbols with very different cultural images are endowed with specific cultural connotations, which are easier to be understood and recognized by people from other cultures. However, people should also realize that cross-cultural communication is unlikely to fully convey the "Chinese", Hollywood animation film in the deconstruction and reorganization of "orientalism", not completely is a representative of the orient itself and cultural traditions, is more of a station in the economic point of view, or is the output of the deeper cultural value perspective a need. On the surface, this is the communication and integration with different cultures in different countries and regions. The deep meaning is that Hollywood in the United States can gain its own value recognition through the image of others constructed in the movies.

References

1. Schwab, R.: The Oriental Renaissance: Europe's Discovery of India and the East, 1680–1880. Columbia University, New York (1984)
2. Said, E.W.: Orientalism. Sanlian Bookstore Press, Beijing (1999)
3. Zhou, N.: Between utopia and ideology: the two extremes of western Chinese views over the past 700 years. Acad. Issue (8), 11 (2005)
4. Richards, J.: China and the Chinese in Popular Film: From Fu Manchu to Charlie Chan. Bloomsbury Publishing, Bloomsbury (2016)
5. Wong, E.F.: On Visual Media Racism: Asians in the American Motion Pictures. Arno Press, New York (1978)
6. Lu, Y.B.: Research on Hollywood 'China Special Feed' in Cooperation Age. Soochow University, Soochow (2015)
7. Szeto, K.Y.: The Martial Arts Cinema of the Chinese Diaspora: Ang Lee, John Woo, and Jackie Chan in Hollywood. Southern Illinois University Press, United States (2011)
8. Edward, D.: EXCL: Kung Fu Panda Co-Director John Stevenson (2008)
9. Looking for Chinese 100 elements. Sohu Homepage. http://news.sohu.com/s2007/zgys/. Accessed 2007
10. Wang, G., Yeh, E.Y.Y.: Globalization and hybridization in cultural products: the cases of Mulan and Crouching Tiger, Hidden Dragon. Int. J. Cult. Stud. **8**(2), 175 (2005)
11. Thomas, J., Benjamin, F., John, A., Robert, R.L., Roger, S.: The United States Declaration of Independence. National Archives and Records Administration, United States (1776)

Can Users Distinguish Narrative Texts Written by an Artificial Intelligence Writing Tool from Purely Human Text?

Vivian Emily Gunser[1](✉), Steffen Gottschling[1] (iD), Birgit Brucker[1] (iD), Sandra Richter[2](✉), and Peter Gerjets[1](✉)

[1] Leibniz-Institut fuer Wissensmedien, Schleichstr. 6, 72076 Tuebingen, Germany
{v.gunser,p.gerjets}@iwm-tuebingen.de
[2] Deutsches Literaturarchiv Marbach, Schillerhoehe 8-10, 71672 Marbach am Neckar, Germany
sandra.richter@dla-marbach.de

Abstract. The present user study investigates narrative texts generated by an AI-tool (the Generative Pretrained Transformer 2 Model, GPT-2). In particular, we examined whether readers can distinguish texts written mainly by a GPT-2-based interactive interface for creative writing from texts written without this tool. Nine participants with a literature-specific professional background were provided with the first few lines of 18 unfamiliar poems and short stories written by classic authors (two texts per participant). They created two continuations for each of these texts, one without and one with the help of the AI-tool (only minor human edits allowed). In an evaluation phase, they were presented with all the continuations not written by themselves (16 triples of original continuation, human continuation, AI-based continuation) without knowing each continuation's category. Their task was to assign each continuation to the correct category. Results showed that participants misclassified 18% of the AI-based continuations (14% as written by other participants without AI-tool and 3% as being the original continuation). Additionally, participants misclassified 35% of the purely human continuations written by other participants (13% as being AI-based continuations and 22% as being the original). These findings indicate that even professionals are no longer able to perfectly distinguish between narrative texts mainly written by an AI-writing-tool and purely human text.

Keywords: GPT-2 · Literature · Artificial intelligence

1 Introduction

Artificial Intelligence (AI) in the form of self-learning algorithms is of increasing importance for our lives [1] and has already found its way into day to day applications such as internet searches or translations. Moreover, AI-tools are increasingly used in genuinely human activities such as art, music and literature. Here, the important question arises, what kind of role we envision for AI-tools in such creative areas. Traditional research in AI has tended to focus on imitating or stimulating human behavior, which

© Springer Nature Switzerland AG 2021
C. Stephanidis et al. (Eds.): HCII 2021, CCIS 1419, pp. 520–527, 2021.
https://doi.org/10.1007/978-3-030-78635-9_67

also applies to creative behavior, for instance in the area of literature [2]. However, AI engineering research traditionally has a strong interest in replacing human performance, which seems to be problematic in creative cultural domains. Therefore, we will build on a human-centered AI perspective in the following [3].

From a human-centered perspective, the best way of how human performance should be enhanced by means of AI is by using AI in terms of sets of tools that enable humans themselves to become more creative or productive. This might involve using AI-tools for "minor" tasks such as searching for better words or for tasks that humans cannot easily do on their own such as analyzing big amounts of data. By using AI-tools in this way, people might become more effective with the regard to their own work than without using technology. However, when it comes to critical aspects such as taking major decisions, making meaning or evaluating different interpretations, humans should take the responsibility on their own and not delegate it to AI-tools. One reason why AI-tools should not be seen as responsible agents is because they are not accountable, neither morally nor legally [4]. Therefore, to keep the level of performance high, AI-tools should not be treated as "teammates", but as tools that help humans to improve themselves [5].

Based on this background, we were particularly interested in this study how using existing AI-tools might enable human beings to be more productive in creative fields and in how creative AI-tools should be best designed to put users in charge of important decisions and leave them in control while simultaneously supporting creative processes, such as composing music or writing poems. More concretely, we investigated "writing continuations for poems" as one potential application scenario for using language-based AI-tools in the area of creative writing.

The specific application used in this study is an AI-tool (GPT-2) that uses an initial input of words for predicting which words might plausibly follow, thereby being able to continue written paragraphs. GPT-2 is a pre-trained transformer model which has been considered as one model for breakthrough for solving Natural Language Processing tasks [6]. In this study we investigated how GPT-2 might be used by humans in a creative writing scenario as a possible additional source for narrative ideas or linguistic images or expressions. The use of such a tool in a writing context raises several (research) questions: "What writing tasks can and should AI-tools do for us?", "Who holds the (psychological) copyright for text created in this way?", "Can the resulting text be considered a co-creation - a work co-created by humans and AI-tools?", "Can the aesthetic value of narrative texts be improved by the use of AI-tools?", and most importantly with regard to the present study, "Are AI-tools at all helpful in creating writings that are considered to be believable or authentic by human readers?"

It should be clear from the beginning that humans and AI-tools do not have the same backgrounds, reasons, and inspirations for writing narrative texts. For example, humans are influenced by their lived experiences, their emotional reactions, and their aesthetic preferences. All of these aspects are typically human and will not be shared with an AI-tool, which is just fulfilling a natural language task based on an algorithm that has been programmed by humans when continuing the writing of a narrative paragraph [7]. Despite these differences with regard to the mechanisms of text production, two questions still remain unclear: First, whether novice (or expert) recipients of narrative texts would be irritated or would actually even recognize it when these texts would have been heavily influenced by the input of a creative AI-tool. Second, whether novice (or expert) writers of narrative texts would consider creative AI-writing-tools as useful in the sense of taking texts that they have written with the help of such an AI-writing-tool as serious creative products.

With regard to the first question addressing text reception, Köbis and Mossin [8] have very recently shown that literature novices cannot differentiate AI-generated poetry from human-written poetry (by Maya Angelou). They conducted a so-called Turing-Test, that is used to investigate whether AI-generated behavior can be identified by humans when compared to human-generated behavior. This is a remarkable finding that raises the issue of whether novices in the future will still try to identify AI-generated texts when they have difficulties to do so. In contexts that are not related to human creativity such as sophisticated online bots that communicate human-like, it is already discussed that people may get used to writing bots and will not insist on humans writing anymore [9]. However, this might be very different for creative texts. Another issue raised by the study of Köbis and Mossin [8] is whether literature experts can distinguish creative texts heavily influenced by an AI-tool from texts purely written by humans. This issue is one focus of the current study.

Regarding the second question of text production, it has to be noted that research on co-creating narrative texts is very rare. However, there is some research in other art domains such as music composition [10]. Zacharakis and colleagues evaluated expert and novice music composers when engaging in human-computer co-creative processes. Participants were first asked to use a music tool to place chords at positions based on their personal preference. Secondly, they should harmonize a melody. Results showed that novices liked to use the tool more than experts but that their sophisticated use of the system was not on the same high level as the one of the expert composers. Nevertheless, outcomes of participants who interacted with the tool were more diverse, unexpected and complex than outcomes of a control group that did not use the tool at all to harmonize both melodies. The appreciation of the system as a tool for music composition depended on participants' expertise level with more expert participants being less impressed by using the tool. We might expect similar results for the co-creation of narrative texts with AI-tools. Therefore, a second focus of the current study is how experts with a professional background in literature might use an AI-tool for text generation in a creative writing scenario and whether they experience the texts written with the help of such an AI-writing-tool as authentic texts that can be taken seriously as creative products.

2 Materials and Methods

2.1 Participants

Participants were recruited from the Leibniz-Institut fuer Wissensmedien and the Deutsches Literaturarchiv Marbach and had a literature-related professional background. The sample consisted of eight female and one male participants whose age ranged from 22 to 55 years ($M = 34.67$, $SD = 13.27$) with either normal or corrected to normal vision.

2.2 Materials and Procedure

We conducted an exploratory study that was based on an AI-writing-tool based on GPT-2. All participants provided their informed consent at the beginning of the study, filled in a demographic questionnaire and participated in a text creation phase and in a text evaluation phase. During the creation phase, the first few lines of two poems were presented to the participants (18 unfamiliar poems; different poems for each participant). Participants were asked to first create their own attempt to continue some lines of the poems and then try to develop a second continuation of the same poem with the help of an AI-writing-tool. This resulted in three continuations for the beginning of each poem: The original continuation written by the poet (Franz Kafka, Friedrich Hölderlin, Robert Gernhardt or Paul Celan), an alternative continuation written by a human (participant), and a third alternative continuation written by the human with the help of the AI. In the AI-based continuation, human editing was severely limited to 25% of the words.

Subsequently, in the evaluation phase, participants were presented with all continuations not written by themselves (i.e., 16 triples of original continuation, human continuation, AI-based continuation) without knowing each continuation's category. Participants were asked to guess the correct category of each presented continuation and to comment on their decision. Eye-tracking data was recorded during this task to analyse the reception process for the different continuations using a SMI RED250 mobile eye-tracking device and Experiment Center 3.7 (SensoMotoric Instruments, Teltow).

The overall study took place in a group setting and lasted approximately 4 h (1 h for generating and 3 h for evaluating the text continuations).

2.3 Statistical Analyses

For the statistical analyses, the software IBM SPSS (version 25.0.0.0 – © IBM Corporation 2017) for Windows was used. The analyses were based on a significance level of 5%. Eye-tracking data was analysed using the statistical software R (version 4.0.3, R Core Team).

3 Results

3.1 Frequency Analysis of Participants' Evaluations

Participants evaluated 16 triples of poem continuations. They misclassified 18.18% of the AI-tool supported continuation (14.69% as written by other participants without AI-tool and 3.49% as being the original continuation, see Table 1). Additionally, they misclassified 34.97% of participants' continuation (12.59% as being AI-based continuations and 22.38% as being the original). For original continuations they misclassified 25.17% (7.69% as AI-based continuations and 17.48% as participants' continuation).

3.2 Qualitative Analyses of Comments on the Decision

Qualitative analyses revealed several types of comment categories. We identified "cosmetic" aspects (e.g., typos, spaces, case sensitivity, punctuation, line breaks, or former/variant spelling), structural aspects (e.g., rhyme scheme, number of verses, stanzas,

Table 1. Participants' classification frequencies (misclassifications in bold)

	Continuation type		
Participants' classification	AI-based	Participant	Original
Evaluated as AI-based continuation	81.82%	**12.59%**	**7.69%**
Evaluated as participants' continuation	**14.69%**	65.03%	**17.48%**
Evaluated as original continuation	**3.49%**	**22.38%**	74.83%

form, number of lines, direct speech, fit to the given beginning, or length), content aspects (e.g., story line, logic, fluency, or coherence), as well as "artistic style" aspects (e.g., phrasing, interjection, choice of words, use of language, syntax deviations, ellipsis, or humor and pointes of the story).

For the AI-based continuations that were classified correctly as AI-texts, 8.21% of the comments addressed cosmetic aspects (e.g., "small and big letters were often mixed up in the AI-based continuations" or "punctuation was wrong"), 40% addressed structural aspects (e.g., "different or missing rhyme schemes" or "metre and strophe schemes were not maintained"), 36.41% addressed content aspects (e.g., "topic and motives were too simple" or "missing consistency of the story"), and 15.38% addressed artistic style aspects (e.g., "AI seems to try to imitate", "language was too modern").

For participants' continuations that were classified correctly as participants' texts, 13.89% of the comments addressed cosmetic aspects (e.g., "more spelling errors"), 29.86% addressed structural aspects (e.g., "too short continuation" or "style, metre etc. maintained, therefore quite convincing"), 23.61% addressed content aspects (e.g., "coherent overall picture but not very coherent continuation of theme and motif"), and 29.16% artistic style aspects (e.g., "pointe is missing"). Moreover, 3.47% of the comments indicated processes of elimination (because, participants had already chosen which of the triple continuation were the original and which the KI-based text, this remaining continuation was identified as the participants' continuation).

3.3 Eye-Tracking Data

For the explorative analyses of eye-tracking data during the evaluation phase, areas of interest (AOIs) were defined around the original beginning of the poem and around each continuation within their respective conditions (see Fig. 1). Gaze points within a viewing angle of two degrees over a minimum period of 80 ms were defined as fixations. Due to technical issues and eye-tracking quality three participants had to be excluded from these analyses.

Two mixed effects linear regression models with overall dwell time on the poem beginning and its continuation as dependent variables, continuation type as predictor and random intercepts for participants and poems were calculated. There was no significant effect of continuation type on dwell time on the (original) beginning of the poem, $\chi 2(2) = 3.70, p = .157$, however, the analyses revealed that dwell time on the poem continuation differed significantly between continuation types, $\chi 2(2) = 10.47, p = .005$. Participants showed shorter dwell times (in ms) for the original continuations ($M = 21628, SD =$

Der Tag, an dem das verschwand

Am Tag, an dem das verschwand,
da war die uft vo Kagen.
Den Dichtern, ach, verschlug es gatt   Original Beginning
ihr Singen und ihr Sagen.

Sie wollten die Musik wie ein Lied klingen lassen,
das die Welt zum Zittern bringen würde.
Und die Musik, die sie singen wollten,
war das Lied aus dem Lied aus dem Lied der drei Bären.

Die Dichter wussten nicht, wie sie die Worte singen sollten.
Ihre Gesichter waren so verzer Continuation
Einige waren zu gut, um zu singen, andere zu großartig, um aufzutreten.

Tausend Jahre später schrieb der große Schriftsteller ein Lied in einer
Sprache,
die anders war als alle anderen,
und die Musik, die dazu gehörte.

Fig. 1. AOIs on an example poem during the evaluation phase.

16668) than for the AI-based continuations ($M = 31289$, $SD = 24960$), $b = -8842$, 95%-CI = $[-15890; -1822]$, or the participants' continuations ($M = 33306$, $SD = 27009$), $b = -11073$, 95%-CI = $[-18114; -40523]$. The dwell times on participants' continuations were similar to those on AI-based continuations, $b = 2231$, 95%-CI = $[-4816; 9269]$.

A mixed effects linear regression model with average fixation duration on the poem continuation as dependent variable, continuation type as predictor and random intercepts for participants and poems showed significant differences between continuation types, $\chi 2(2) = 24.50$, $p < .001$. Average fixation duration (in ms) was shorter for AI-based continuations ($M = 231.10$, $SD = 74.27$) than for the original continuations ($M = 296.14$, $SD = 172.70$), $b = 60.82$, 95%-CI = $[35.86; 85.78]$, or the participants' continuations ($M = 284.64$, $SD = 142.68$), $b = 44.96$, 95%-CI = $[20.93; 69.04]$.

4 Discussion

The results of this study show that the participants misclassified approximately 26.11% of all continuations (either original, participant, or AI-based), and with regard to AI-tool supported poems continuations solely participants still misclassified approximately 20%. This indicates that even experts with a professional background regarding literature experience some difficulties in differentiating between purely human written poetry and poetry written with a heavy influence of an AI-tool. This finding is particularly interesting as we made the decision task as easy as possible for participants: First, all participants experienced the process of creating alternative continuations on their own in an author role directly before they evaluated the continuations created by others. Therefore, they were experienced with regard to the type of continuations the AI-tool might suggest.

Second, participants knew in advance that, from the three continuations for each poem, there would be one continuation of each category (either original, participant, or AI-based; with the same beginning for all three). Thus, if they correctly classified two continuations, the third continuation was automatically classified correctly, too. Thirdly, participants were allowed to compare between all three continuations for each particular poem before they made their decisions.

Nevertheless, even under these simplifying conditions, over one fifth of the continuations were classified incorrectly. One can easily imagine that more realistic conditions (just reading a poem and classifying it as human or AI) would lead to much larger misclassification rates even in an expert sample as used in our study. Therefore, we might derive the following conclusions with regard to our main research interests: (1) Even literature experts experience difficulties in distinguishing creative texts heavily influenced by an AI-tool from texts purely written by humans. (2) When experts with a professional background in literature use an AI-tool for text generation in a creative writing scenario they experience at least some of the texts written with the help of such an AI-writing-tool as authentic texts that can be taken seriously as creative products.

The qualitative analysis of the comments on the continuations indicated four central aspects: the consideration of cosmetic, structural, content, and artistic style aspects. These identified aspects have to be considered in the context of future studies and particularly during designing study materials to avoid for example identifications of an AI-based text solely based on cosmetic issues to give the AI-tool a fair chance.

Regarding the exploratory analyses of online reading behavior via eye-tracking, the results suggest that the different poem continuations led to varying depth of text processing by the readers. The AI-based and participants' continuations were looked at for a longer amount of time than the original continuations, which suggests that the former two continuations took more time to categorize (potentially based on higher uncertainty). Additionally, the average fixation duration while reading the AI-based continuations was shorter than for the original and participants' continuations. Since average fixation duration is often considered to be positively linked to the general difficulty of the text [11], this could be an indication that the AI-based continuations are overall less complex and more predictable (regarding word sequences) than human-generated continuations (comprising original as well as participant continuations). Such a reduced complexity level, as potentially indicated by the shorter average fixation duration, might be one indicator that even well-programmed AI-tools are not able to replace humans when literary creativity is considered.

Furthermore, in this study, the AI failed to create textual structures that deviate from the regular grammatical or semantic order - as it is typical for modern poetry. Also, AI-tools tend to reproduce clichés when choosing words and expressions. Finally, AI-tools do neither recognize nor suggest elaborate literary genres; they produce expository texts of various kinds. Consequently, AI-engineering research that suggests replacing human performance might not work for creative literary work. Especially for literature professionals, however, the tool could serve as an additional inspiration that complements other sources authors profit from.

Limitations of this study might be the fact that we used GPT-2 and it would be interesting to investigate how results would change with the new GPT-3 pre-trained transformer model instead of the GPT-2 model. Furthermore, the number of participants in both the poem continuation phase as well as the poem evaluation phase consisted of a rather small sample. Therefore, further research with more participants is needed to replicate our results. Nevertheless, this study constitutes one of the first promising steps in the avenue of addressing human centered AI-tools - such as this promising and interesting GPT interface - in creative writing contexts, that should be continued in more complex creative writing scenarios (e.g., writing workshops, language classes in schools).

References

1. Makridakis, S.: The forthcoming Artificial Intelligence (AI) revolution: its impact on society and firms. Futures **90**, 46–60 (2017). https://doi.org/10.1016/j.futures.2017.03.006
2. Bernhart, T., Richter, S.: Frühe digitale Poesie. Informatik Spektrum **44**, 11–18 (2021). https://doi.org/10.1007/s00287-021-01329-z
3. Shneiderman, B.: Bridging the gap between ethics and practice: guidelines for reliable, safe, and trustworthy human-centered AI systems. ACM Trans. Interact. Intell. Syst. **10**(4), 1–31 (2020). https://doi.org/10.1145/3419764
4. Boden, M., et al.: Principles of robotics: regulating robots in the real world. Connect. Sci. **29**(2), 124–129 (2017). https://doi.org/10.1080/09540091.2016.1271400
5. Shneiderman, B.: Design lessons from AI's two grand goals: human emulation and useful applications. IEEE Trans. Technol. Soc. **1**(2), 73–82 (2020). https://doi.org/10.1109/TTS.2020.2992669
6. Strubell, E., Ganesh, A., McCallum, A.: Energy and policy considerations for deep learning in NLP. arXiv:1906.02243 (2019)
7. Mazzone, M., Elgammal, A.: Art, creativity, and the potential of artificial intelligence. Arts **8**(1), 26 (2019). https://doi.org/10.3390/arts8010026
8. Köbis, N., Mossink, L.D.: Artificial intelligence versus Maya Angelou: experimental evidence that people cannot differentiate AI-generated from human-written poetry. Comput. Hum. Behav. **114**, (2021). https://doi.org/10.1016/j.chb.2020.106553
9. Boneh, D., Grotto, A.J., McDaniel, P., Papernot, N.: How relevant is the turing test in the age of sophisbots? IEEE Secur. Priv. **17**(6), 64–71 (2019). https://doi.org/10.1109/MSEC.2019.2934193
10. Zacharakis, A., Kaliakatsos-Papakostas, M., Kalaitzidou, S., Cambouropoulos, E.: Evaluating human-computer co-creative processes in music: a case study on the CHAMELEON melodic harmonizer. Front. Psychol. **12**, 322 (2021). https://doi.org/10.3389/fpsyg.2021.603752
11. Rayner, K., Chace, K.H., Slattery, T.J., Ashby, J.: Eye movements as reflections of comprehension processes in reading. Sci. Stud. Read. **10**(3), 241–255 (2006). https://doi.org/10.1207/s1532799xssr1003_3

Participation in the Intelligibility Testing of Easy-to-Read Texts: Development of an Interface for People with Learning Difficulties

Claudia Hösel[✉], Susan Labude, Elisabeth Christoph, Christian Roschke,
Matthias Baumgart, and Marc Ritter

University of Applied Sciences Mittweida, 09648 Mittweida, Germany
{hoesel,slabude,echrist1,roschke,baumgart,ritter}@hs-mittweida.de

Abstract. Standard language texts pose significant challenges for some people because they do not understand the content due to the linguistic complexity. Transforming them into a simplified linguistic form can reduce these communicative hurdles. Easy-to-read texts enable people with learning disabilities to receive texts independently and thus form an important basis for equal participation in social life. In order to ensure a high level of comprehensibility of easy-to-read texts, simplifications are made not only to the language but also to the content. During manual translation, the simplifications made are checked by target group readers. In the case of (semi-)automated intelligibility checking, the check by target group readers is omitted. This paper focuses on the integration of the target audience of easy-to-read texts into the text review process. A web-based interface adapted to the reception needs is created and a rating system is integrated, through which people with learning disabilities can independently give feedback on the text comprehensibility. The interface will be evaluated in the form of a user study with brain-injured people. The results obtained indicate that both the web-based interface and the rating system are suitable for actively involving target group readers in the text review sub-process. The results of the study form the basis for the development of a system that takes into account the real text comprehension of the target group readers in addition to linguistic features when annotating texts in plain language.

Keywords: Easy-to-Read · Intelligibility testing · Interface

1 Introduction

Easy language is a form of barrier-free communication that aims to enable people with cognitive impairments to receive texts independently. For this purpose, simplifications are made on various linguistic levels and content reductions are made in order to reduce the complexity of the text and thus enable better text comprehension [6].

C. Stephanidis et al. (Eds.): HCII 2021, CCIS 1419, pp. 528–534, 2021.
https://doi.org/10.1007/978-3-030-78635-9_68

In the 1920s, research into concrete features that influence text comprehensibility formed the central object of investigation in readability research [8]. Based on the assumption that certain linguistic features on the text surface influence the difficulty of a text, the focus was on quantifiable parameters on the text surface. Various variables at the word and sentence level were identified and transformed into indices by means of which text difficulty could be objectively predicted. These traditional readability indices based on simple parameters, such as the Reading Ease Formula [4] or the SMOG Grading [9], are still used today for readability prediction. Correa et al. 2020 [3] use an online tool based on traditional readability formulas to assess text comprehensibility of health-related information. Other approaches combine traditional readability metrics with other linguistic features and use machine learning to automate text comprehensibility assessment. Keinki et al. 2019 [7] focus on computer-based readability testing of health-related texts and conclude that machine learning methods can usefully complement traditional readability formulas in predicting readability. Balyan et al. 2020 [1] use other linguistic features, such as syntactic complexity and lexical density, in addition to Flesch-Kincaid Grade Level for automated assessment of text comprehensibility. Naderi et al. 2019 [10] present a data-driven approach for predicting text comprehensibility of German-language texts that considers lexical and morphological features in addition to traditional readability features. Some of the features used to predict text comprehensibility are also reflected in the guidelines written for plain language (e.g. Inclusion Europe [6], Netzwerk Leichte Sprache e.V. [11]). For example, word length, which in traditional indices is used as a parameter in predicting text comprehensibility via the average number of syllables, is manifested in the use of short words in plain language. In addition to linguistic simplifications, various typographic features are also used to facilitate better text comprehension. Battisti et al. 2019 [2] propose a computational approach that considers text structure, typographic features, as well as image information in addition to linguistic features when assessing the complexity of easy-to-read-texts.

Although computational approaches to text comprehensibility assessment attempt to incorporate more complex Easy Language guidelines, the integration of target group readers in comprehensibility assessment seems to be an understudied field in the human-machine interface domain so far. Approaches that involve the target audience in the assessment of text comprehensibility, such as Vajjala & Lucic 2019 [12], are more likely to be found in the field of interlanguage translation. However, with the tendential exclusion of target group readers in comprehensibility assessment in the domain of Easy Language, an important input is lost. Because the Easy Language guidelines themselves are written in Easy Language, they do not provide concrete information, such as word or sentence length, which is why computer-assisted intelligibility testing in the Easy Language domain is fraught with uncertainty. The participation of target group readers in the comprehensibility testing of Easy Language texts could reduce these uncertainties. To enable target group readers to actively participate in comprehensibility checking, we create an interface adapted to their reception needs and integrate a user-optimized rating system that allows people with cognitive impairments to independently provide feedback on text comprehensibility.

2   Methods

In order to enable people with learning disabilities to participate independently in the process of comprehensibility testing, an interface is needed that meets the special reception needs of this user group. This paper focuses on the creation of an interface to meet the reception needs of people with cognitive impairments as well as the integration of a user-optimized rating system for evaluation by means of a user study involving brain-injured people. Figure 1 shows the basic methodological approach.

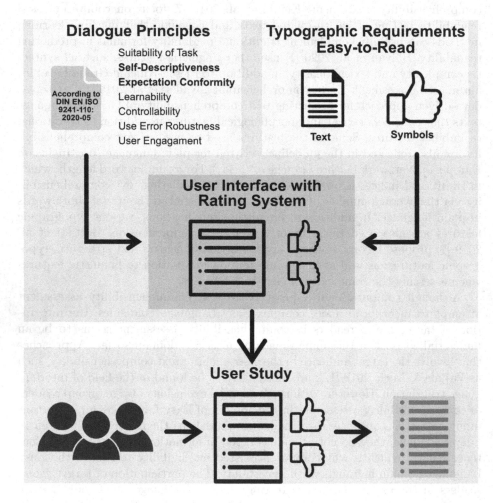

Fig. 1. Overview of the methodical approach

Table 1. Typographic recommendations for easy-to-read texts and implementation in the user interface.

Typographic Recommendations	Implementation
Usage of sans-serif font	Use of Open Sans font
Avoidence of italic font	Italic font explicitly not used
Avoidence of continuous capitals	Continuous capitals explicitly not used
Adequate font size (min. 14 pt.)	Font size of 20px
Adequate line spacing (min. 1:1.5)	Line spacing 1.5
Left-align text	Align text left

2.1   Creation of User Interface

The user interface was developed taking into account the principles and concepts of usability defined in DIN EN ISO 9241-110:2020-05 [5]. Against the background of the special reception needs of users, the self-descriptiveness of the interface and conformity to expectations were of central importance. When creating the interface, it was important to implement dialog steps and feedback for people with learning difficulties in a way that was understandable and consistent with their experiences.

In order to meet the reception needs of the users, the typographic recommendations defined by the association "Netzwerk Leichte Sprache e.V." were implemented [11]. Table 1 shows the typographic recommendations of Easy Language as well as the realization in the created interface. It can be seen that the interface fulfills all typographical requirements, whereby the text was left-aligned and continuous texts were implemented with a spacing of 1.5 lines. The font used is Open Sans, a sans-serif font optimized for web and mobile interfaces. The minimum font size in the interface is 20px. With the implementation of the typographic requirements of Easy Language, both the reception needs and the experiences of the target group were taken into account, which also fulfilled the conformity to expectations.

In order to actively involve people with learning difficulties in the process of checking the comprehensibility of Easy Language texts, a user-optimized evaluation system is necessary. Following the recommendations of the german association "Netzwerk Leichte Sprache e.V." [11] we developed a symbol-based easy-to-use rating system. For the evaluation of the intelligible the user has a thumbs-up symbol or a thumbs-down symbol at his disposal. By pressing a thumbs-up icon, the user can mark sections of text or headings as intelligible. Pressing a thumbs-down icon marks text sections or headings as unintelligible. The section-by-section assessment of text comprehensibility takes into account the structural peculiarities of Easy Language. This can also include a more difficult word, which is explained in the next line. Consequently, text comprehension can also only arise through the context of a paragraph, which would not be taken into account in a sentence-by-sentence evaluation. User ratings for text comprehension were stored in a database. The functionality of the symbol-based rating system could be confirmed in functional tests.

2.2 Evaluation of the Evaluation System

The evaluation function was evaluated in a user study of people who are dependent on Easy Language due to an acquired brain injury. Seven test persons between the ages of 31 and 34 participated in the user study, the majority of whom already had some experience in using computers. Participation was voluntary.

The test persons were informed about the procedure of the user study by their supervisor, who also gave them access to the interface. All test persons were shown the same text in Easy Language and asked to rate the comprehensibility of the text using the integrated function. During the experiment, a supervisor was always present to explain the task in case of comprehension problems. However, the testing and evaluation of text comprehensibility was done without assistance. After completion of the comprehensibility test, the test persons gave their supervisor feedback on the evaluation function. To enable comparability of the feedback, the supervisor was provided with an easily intelligible questionnaire, which the test persons worked through together with their supervisor. Since the test persons' memory and concentration are limited, the number of questions was limited to three and the granularity of the answers to the individual questions was kept low.

3   Results and Discussion

While the functional tests served to verify the functionality of the interface and the rating system, the user study evaluated whether the created web-based interface can be used independently by people with learning difficulties and whether the text comprehensibility can be rated independently via the integrated rating function.

The functional tests were successful, i.e. the functionality of the user interface and the rating system were confirmed. The user study showed that all test persons were able to independently assess the intelligibility of the displayed Easy Language text section by section using the integrated rating system. No test person requested assistance from their supervisor during the comprehensibility assessment. This indicates that the interface was adequate for the test persons' reception needs and that the symbolized rating system was intelligible and intuitive to use. This assumption is strengthened by the results of the test person survey. Nevertheless, it can be stated that the majority of the test persons already had initial experience with computers and were therefore fundamentally familiar with web-based interfaces. The extent to which these results can be transferred to people with learning difficulties without this prior knowledge requires further examination. Likewise, the target group requires further consideration. People who are dependent on Easy Language due to an acquired brain injury took part in the user study. The results of the user study indicate that the interface created and the rating system meet the reception needs of the test persons. However, it remains open whether the created interface and integrated rating system meet the reception needs of other Easy Language addressees. Easy Language is aimed at a heterogeneous group of addressees whose reception needs must be considered in a differentiated manner.

Overall, our results suggest that both the developed interface and the rating system are suitable for involving people with learning disabilities in the process of intelligibility assessment and for enabling them to independently and directly rate the intelligibility of Easy Language texts.

4 Conclusion

This paper addresses the participation of people with learning difficulties in the intelligibility testing of texts in Easy Language. To enable participation in intelligibility testing, we created a web-based interface adapted to the reception needs and integrated a symbol-based rating system that enables people with learning difficulties to independently rate the text intelligibility. The functionality of the interface and the rating system was confirmed in functional tests. In a user study with brain-injured people, we evaluated whether the interface and rating system can be understood by the target group and used independently in the context of a text comprehensibility test. The results indicate that the interface and rating system are understood by people with learning disabilities and used intuitively when assessing text comprehensibility. Accordingly, both the web-based interface and the symbol-based rating system appear to be suitable for engaging target group readers in the text rating sub-process. Due to the small number of test persons and their first previous experience with computers, it seems reasonable to extend the user study to a more heterogeneous and larger group of test persons in the future. It should also be examined to what extent the results can be transferred to the reception and user needs of other target groups of Easy Language. In the future, the results will form the basis for the development of a system which, when annotating texts in Easy Language, takes into account not only linguistic features but also the target group's actual understanding of the text.

References

1. Balyan, R., McCarthy, K.S., McNamara, D.S.: Applying natural language processing and hierarchical machine learning approaches to text difficulty classification. Int. J. Artif. Intell. Educ. **30**(3), 337–370 (2020). https://doi.org/10.1007/s40593-020-00201-7
2. Battisti, A., Ebling, S., Volk, M.: An empirical analysis of linguistic, typographic, and structural features in simplified German texts. In: Bernardi, R., Navigli, R., Semeraro, G. (eds.) Proceedings of the Sixth Italian Conference on Computational Linguistics, Bari, Italy, vol. 2481, p. 7 (2019). https://doi.org/10.5167/UZH-175963

3. Correa, D.J., et al.: Quantitative readability analysis of websites providing information on traumatic brain injury and epilepsy: a need for clear communication. Epilepsia **61**(3), 528–538 (2020). https://doi.org/10.1111/epi.16446
4. Flesch, R.: A new readability yardstick. J. Appl. Psychol. **32**(3), 221–233 (1948). https://doi.org/10.1037/h0057532
5. IEC International Electrotechnical Commission: DIN EN ISO 9241-110:2020 ergonomics of human-system interaction - part 110: Interaction principles. https://www.iso.org/obp/ui/#iso:std:iso:9241:-110:ed-2:v1:en. Accessed 23 Mar 2021
6. Inclusion Europe: Information for all. European standards for making information easy to read and understand. https://inclusion-europe.eu/wp-content/uploads/2015/03/2113-Information-for-all-16.pdf. Accessed 16 Mar 2021
7. Keinki, C., Zowalla, R., Pobiruchin, M., Huebner, J., Wiesner, M.: Computer-based readability testing of information booklets for German cancer patients. J. Cancer Educ. **34**(4), 696–704 (2018). https://doi.org/10.1007/s13187-018-1358-0
8. Klare, G.R.: Readability. In Pearson, P.D., Barr, R., Kamil, M., Mosenthal, P. (eds.) Handbook of reading research. Longman, New York (1984)
9. McLaughlin, H.G.: SMOG grading - a new readability formula. J. Read. **12**(8), 639–646 (1969)
10. Naderi, B., Mohtaj, S., Karan, K., Moller, S.: Automated text readability assessment for german language: a quality of experience approach. In: 2019 Eleventh International Conference on Quality of Multimedia Experience (QoMEX), pp. 1–3. IEEE, Berlin (2019). https://doi.org/10.1109/QoMEX.2019.8743194
11. Netzwerk Leichte Sprache: Die Regeln für Leichte Sprache (2013). https://www.leichte-sprache.org/wp-content/uploads/2017/11/Regeln_Leichte_Sprache.pdf. Accessed 20 Mar 2021
12. Vajjala, S., Lucic, I.: On understanding the relation between expert annotations of text readability and target reader comprehension. In: Proceedings of the Fourteenth Workshop on Innovative Use of NLP for Building Educational Applications, pp. 349–359. Association for Computational Linguistics, Florence (2019). https://doi.org/10.18653/v1/w19-4437

Hurdle Relay: A Participatory Design Method for Understanding the Information Gap Through Iterative Comparison

Keunwoo Kim[✉], Seoyeon Jang[✉], Hyeonju Park[✉], Kyung Je Jo[✉], Hankyung Kim[✉], and Youn-kyung Lim[✉]

KAIST, Daejeon, Republic of Korea
{alex1027,seoyeonj,hopedt2,kyungjejo,hkkim31,younlim}@kaist.ac.kr

Abstract. Some perceive poorer quality of information (i.e., information-poor) than others (i.e., information-rich) depending on diverse physical and social barriers. The unevenness of information experience is referred to as information gap. It is core to figure out the features that create such differences for researchers to understand the uneven experiences. The aim of our method is to help designers address the gap features: components of information gap such as clothes fabric or size in online-shopping. While few studies in HCI community attempted to identify the gap features, existing studies are often limited to exploration of gaps. We suggest Hurdle Relay, a method not only to identify the gap features but also to further understand how and why these gap features create different experiences. Hurdle Relay has two key concepts: role-switching of information-rich, and iterative comparison through a relay. We conducted a study on a movie captioning project for hearing-impaired as the case information gap is experienced. The study result showed that the researchers can use Hurdle Relay method to compare the features appearing/disappearing through a relay and understand the subjective gap features. We conclude by discussing the implications of our method for HCI designers.

Keywords: Information gap · Iteration · Participatory method

1 Introduction

We face various barriers in daily life as we interact with people or systems. The spectrum of barriers that people encounter spans widely from physical to language, social, and cultural barriers. Due to such barriers, some people gain relatively less amount and poorer quality of information than others (Fig. 1). In other words, people who struggle with the barrier become information-poor, and less struggling people become information-rich. For example, hard-of-hearing people are likely to experience difficulty in perceiving and understanding a movie

© Springer Nature Switzerland AG 2021
C. Stephanidis et al. (Eds.): HCII 2021, CCIS 1419, pp. 535–542, 2021.
https://doi.org/10.1007/978-3-030-78635-9_69

in comparison to those without disabilities. Likewise, people who wish to buy clothes online are likely to have a different level of information compared to those who view the product under their noses. In this paper, we refer to the features that create such information gaps (e.g. music or tones in movies, fabric, size, or color in shopping) as "gap features."

To successfully bridge information gaps from digital media and generate proper design solutions for people with poorer information, it is core to address which or where the gap occurs (i.e., gap features) in the early stage of the design process. Few studies attempted to identify the gap features using literature reviews and user studies [5,7]. However, existing studies are often limited to exploration of gap features. The subjective and contextual nature of the barrier requires designers to thoroughly understand how and why gap features are perceived differently. The goal of our method is to gain a deeper and holistic understanding of the gap features because, albeit the complexity, there has been little work on understanding the characteristics and meaning of the gap features specifically.

This paper suggests Hurdle Relay, an early-stage participatory design method to explore the information gap by allowing information-rich people to switch roles with information-poor in order to identify and address the gap features. Through a study on a barrier-free film project, Hurdle Relay succeeded in figuring out the gap features and creating diverse expressions to bridge those gap features. The findings offer a starting point for designers to bridge the information gap and showed the possibility of application of Hurdle Relay to different domains.

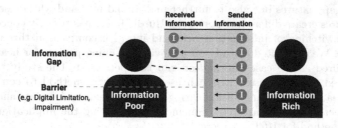

Fig. 1. Information gap: the experience difference between information-rich and information-poor

2   Related Works

A number of researchers conducted studies to understand the barriers in various domains including newcomers in open source software projects [7] and the visually impaired gamers in the online audiogame community [1]. It should be highlighted that, although domains differ, the information is inevitably generated based on the information-rich (i.e., existing users in open source software community and non-impaired gamers) experience. Because the information-rich is likely to continue being the information provider, figuring out why and how the information-rich creates the information gap would offer value in addressing it. While few studies implemented participatory design methods to utilize information-rich's ability to ideate solutions [5], little attempts have been made to invite information-rich to help understand the gap features composing the barriers. As the gap features occur from uneven experiences, perceiving the difference is key for addressing the information gap. One possible direction to maximize the information-rich's ability to identify the gap features is through empowering the participants to compare the experiences of both sides of the barrier by role-switching. The Role-Playing method has been used in varied ways [6] and Seland identified the benefits of the Role-Playing method in understanding user needs and quick idea creation in the early phases [4].

Furthermore, like Speed Dating method, rapid iteration of ideas is known to be helpful to explore the early stage concepts [2,3]. In case of information gap situations, different environmental and personal factors influence the function of barriers, resulting in making the gap features subjective and contextual. Rather than testing a single system that designers narrowed down, there required a method to experience and test multiple barriers as a relay to help build a holistic understanding of the gap features. Thus, we suggest an information gap-bridging method that 1) lets information-rich experience the barrier and compare the experiences, and 2) can iteratively explore the gap features based on a relay.

3 Method: Hurdle Relay

Hurdle Relay is an information gap-bridging method to explore the gap features through iterative comparison. Since understanding the whole information is impossible from an information-poor point of view, we must rely on information-rich people to identify the difference and find gap features. Thus, Hurdle Relay intentionally makes information-rich participants experience barriers of information. Through the comparison between situations with and without barriers, participants can find the gap features and struggle to bridge that gap. Each participant produces an artifact s/he considers proper to bridge the information gap based on a reflection in stepwise activities. These artifacts are handed over to the next participants to repeat the process and are analyzed as a whole by the researchers.

3.1 Process

Participants go through a process of activities as shown in Fig. 2. In phase 1, participants are asked to take their own approach to make the first artifact to close gaps in the information-rich point of view. Then, in phase 2, they are put into a situation where they experience the information gap from an information-poor point of view (e.g., watching a film without sound). Then, in phase 3, they experience the situation of phase 2 without the barrier (e.g., with sound) and compare the quality of information between the two situations, and make further ideas to improve the artifact of phase 2. Thus, the comparison is the driving force for participants to figure out gap features and to generate ideas to close the gap. Lastly, in phase 4, participants revise the artifact of phase 1 based on the reflections that are obtained through phase 2 and phase 3.

A participant's artifact from phase 4 is passed onto the next participant like a relay race. Through the relay, researchers can progressively reveal new gap features that are not identified from artifacts of previous participants. Figure 2 shows the process of how the artifact of each participant is passed onto the next participant. To lessen the burden, the participants are asked to mark ideas on how to make the artifacts using low-fi prototypes or tools. Following the ideas, researchers refine the artifacts to be more realistic to offer a more immersive experience to the next participant. As a result, the artifact from phase 4 of each participant is used as the source in phase 2 of the next participant. In other words, every participant experiences barriers based on the reflected result of the previous participant. The relay helps each gap feature to be repeatedly assessed by the next participants to be kept or filtered depending on its perceived value, leading to a continuous and collaborative effort to lessen the information gap.

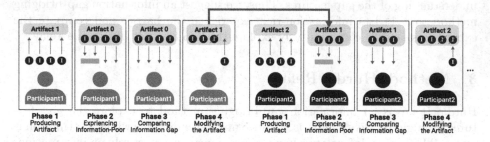

Fig. 2. Iterative relay process to figure out the feature patterns in artifacts

4   Case Study

4.1   Study Background

As a case study, we focused on the gap features that distinguish the experiences of hearing-impaired user groups in watching a film. Currently, most online video platforms offer mere subtitles for dialogue, and fewer organizations focus on reproducing existing films into barrier-free films—films that contain explanatory audio descriptions and captions to deliver narration, dialogue, and sound information to all audiences. While audio information takes a huge part in the film information, there is a low understanding of how to effectively modify films barrier-free due to an absence of structured gap features. Similar to other information gap situations, the barrier-free film requires information-rich (i.e. caption creators) to add materials to support hearing-impaired to understand existing films. To explore the effectiveness of Hurdle Relay, we conducted a study in the context of transforming existing films into barrier-free films for hearing-impaired audiences.

4.2 Study Process

The process of the case study contains a total of four phases and an interview as depicted in Fig. 3. Each participant was given a Google Slides link which contains captured scenes of 30 s-long film. In phase 1, we asked each participant to add the desired interactions (e.g. text, diagram, image. . .) to close information gaps that might have occurred due to hearing-impairment. We provided a subtitle in text for the participants to remove the burden of transcription. In phase 2, the participant watched a barrier-free film *in mute*. For the first participant, we showed him an existing barrier-free film as a starting point of barriers, and the rest participants watched the refined version of the artifacts prior participants have created. Each participant completed a questionnaire to summarise the film briefly, explain the characters, and express the mood they felt watching the film. Next, in phase 3, the participant watched the same video *with sound* and was asked to complete another questionnaire that consists of the same questions as in phase 2. By comparing the questionnaires from phase 2 and 3, the participant reflected on gap features and revised the expressions from phase 1 upon their reflections. In phase 1 and 4, we adopted Think-Aloud method to understand the participants' intention thoroughly. We conducted a post-interview to understand how s/he reflected from the other's artifacts and what gap features were considered to improve his or her own artifacts.

The case study was conducted via Zoom due to COVID-19. Hurdle Relay is not solely intended to be conducted online, and the materials used for making the artifacts could take either digital or analog form, as long as the artifact communicates with the researcher for its purpose to express the gap features. Researchers edited a video based on each artifact from phase 4 and passed the video to the next participant.

Google Slides was adopted to create artifacts of barrier-free films throughout the whole process. We chose Google Slides for mainly three reasons. Firstly, it allows a great degree of freedom for participants to express their ideas using text, diagrams, images, and so on. Secondly, Google Slides is a widely used tool, so supplementary instructions or guides were not needed. Lastly, the composition of the films could be easily transferred into the widescreen(16:9) of Google Slides.

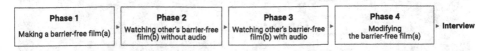

Fig. 3. The process of each participant in the study

Recruitment. The method was tested out with 5 college students aged from 19 to 26 who were recruited from on- and off-campus communities. To conduct a study with a mix of various people, we asked the participants about the experience with barriers, favorite genre of films, frequency of watching a film via pre-questionnaire. We aimed to cover several film genres for figuring out gap features from various moods and situations. At the same time, we assigned the film which each participant has not watched in order to make them fully experience the barriers during the case study.

5   Result

We obtained five raw artifacts of the movie scenes with visual and text elements that describe the audio information in the form of Google Slides. Researchers collaboratively transformed participants' artifacts in video format (i.e., barrier-free video) following the description in the artifacts and post-interview. We identified types of gap features that lead to information gaps and diverse ways of visual and textual expression to bridge these gaps.

5.1   Gap Features

The gap features were represented by what kind of sound the participants wanted to transfer in the artifact. As a result, the participants tried to deliver dialogue and tone of voice as key gap features. One of the participants wanted to express additional information of which character is talking in the group shot by different locations of the scripts. Another participant tried to describe the humorous situation in which one character subtly cuts off another one speaking by placing the interrupting dialogue crossing the interrupted dialogue (Fig. 4). The additional gap features like sound effects, background music, and atmosphere were also found in less frequency.

The visual expressions are the attempts to address the gap features focusing on how to deliver information sufficiently. For example, the participants conjugated scripts using different text locations, descriptions in brackets, or glyphs like exclamation marks, tildes, and dots. The participants also used screen filters to express the subtle meaning of sound.

Fig. 4. Artifact examples from phase 4. (Hit and Run Squad-Left, Keys to the Heart-Right)

5.2   Findings from Iterative Relay

The participants got reflections from watching the previous participant's artifact. Features that are considered valuable were reused, and features that hindered information in films disappeared in the next participant iteration. Through the post-interview and Think-Aloud during the study, the underlying reasons for the features disappearing and reappearing in iterations were clarified.

In our case study, we observed certain patterns of gap features through iterations. The dialogue and tone of voice continuously appeared after it was suggested, while background music, sound effect, and atmosphere repetitively disappeared and reappeared. The primary gap features (dialogue and tone of voice) and minor gap features (mood and sound effect for showing situational description) were figured. In Addition, the results inspired the designers to identify what is required to address each gap feature by analyzing participants' rationales for artifacts. In our study, transferring the tacit and subtle situational information was of the utmost importance to address dialogue and tone of voice.

Once certain patterns were found in the appearance of the features, researchers decided whether to stop the Hurdle Relay or to run more laps. It is worthy to remind that researchers have to compare the combined progress of the results rather than comparing with each adjacent participant iteration. For example, the different and common features of 1st and 2nd participants were compared with the features of the entire progress from 1st to 5th iterations. In our study case, the progress showed that visual effects such as vibration or moving texts disappeared and reappeared multiple times, while dialogue and tone of voice remained still through the iterations. We defined such a phenomenon as a pattern and decided that 5 participants were enough to offer valuable features for our study.

6   Discussion

6.1   Redefining Design Problems to Consider Subjective Gap Features

We found values of Hurdle Relay in re-defining the design problems. Testing our method in barrier-free film study succeeded in figuring out the priority among the gap features: 1) dialogue and tone of voice, 2) mood and sound effect, 3) situational description. The priority hints which gap features are the most subjective because while situational description bothered a few participants concentrating on the atmosphere, the other few felt strong needs about illustrating the situational information in detailed text. It is difficult to conclude which subjective gap features should be included to bridge the information gap at this point. However, as researchers identified the subjective and objective gap features, novel design problems to address the subjectiveness could be defined such as 'how to convey the situational description without bothering the most conventional viewers', or, to be more specific, 'how to utilize the objective gap features such as dialogue and tone of voice in order to express the situational information.'

6.2   Application to Different Domains

Hurdle Relay can be extended further to other domains where media functions as barriers and triggers the uneven information experience. Due to COVID-19, more online contents are replacing offline contents, functioning as barriers to users (i.e., online shopping of fashion and groceries, online conferencing and lectures). For example, in a service to help online shopping, information gaps are often created due to various types of physical features of the product (e.g. fabric, size, or color). Our method can be applied by creating online-friendly product descriptions with the sellers being intentionally restricted from physical information of products. The sellers would generate product descriptions for products to be sold online, based on reflections from experiencing previous participants' product descriptions with/without physically obtaining the product. As the iterations of sellers expand, the product descriptions would become more concrete, and the subjective gap features would be identified from the pattern of disappearing and reappearing, as a result to bridge the information gap of online shopping.

Acknowledgement. This work was supported by the National Research Foundation of Korea (NRF) grant funded by the Korea government (MSIT) (No. NRF-2021R1A2C2004263).

References

1. Andrade, R., Rogerson, M.J., Waycott, J., Baker, S., Vetere, F.: Playing blind: revealing the world of gamers with visual impairment. In: Proceedings of the 2019 CHI Conference on Human Factors in Computing Systems, pp. 1–14 (2019)
2. Davidoff, S., Lee, M.K., Dey, A.K., Zimmerman, J.: Rapidly exploring application design through speed dating. In: Krumm, J., Abowd, G.D., Seneviratne, A., Strang, T. (eds.) UbiComp 2007. LNCS, vol. 4717, pp. 429–446. Springer, Heidelberg (2007). https://doi.org/10.1007/978-3-540-74853-3_25
3. Dillahunt, T.R., Lam, J., Lu, A., Wheeler, E.: Designing future employment applications for underserved job seekers: a speed dating study. In: Proceedings of the 2018 Designing Interactive Systems Conference, pp. 33–44 (2018)
4. Seland, G.: System designer assessments of role play as a design method: a qualitative study. In: Proceedings of the 4th Nordic Conference on Human-Computer Interaction: Changing Roles, pp. 222–231 (2006)
5. Siek, K.A., LaMarche, J.S., Maitland, J.: Bridging the information gap: collaborative technology design with low-income at-risk families to engender healthy behaviors. In: Proceedings of the 21st Annual Conference of the Australian Computer-Human Interaction Special Interest Group: Design: Open 24/7, pp. 89–96 (2009)
6. Simsarian, K.T.: Take it to the next stage: the roles of role playing in the design process. In: CHI'03 Extended Abstracts on Human Factors in Computing Systems, pp. 1012–1013 (2003)
7. Steinmacher, I., Conte, T., Gerosa, M.A., Redmiles, D.: Social barriers faced by newcomers placing their first contribution in open source software projects. In: Proceedings of the 18th ACM Conference on Computer Supported Cooperative Work & Social Computing, pp. 1379–1392 (2015)

Research on Television Drama Derivative Creative Design from the Perspective of Service Design

Mengting Li and Hong Chen[✉]

School of Art Design and Media, East China University of Science and Technology, 130 Meilong Road, Xuhui District, Shanghai, China

Abstract. In recent years, the sustained development of television dramas culture industry has brought huge development space for television drama derivative products, and promoted the improvement of the link of television drama culture industry and the development of related IP derivative cultural and creative products. Television-derived cultural and creative products are one of the links in IP development of television dramas. At present, there are many types of home products, clothing products, decorative products and so on. However, in the face of huge development opportunities and the ever-developing trends of science and technology and consumption, it is necessary to systematically explore the design of television drama derivative cultural and creative products. This paper studies from the perspective of service design, and through the investigation and analysis of digital, physical, activity and space-derived cultural creation, studies the possibility of further development of cultural creation products derived from television dramas.

Keywords: Television dramas derivative · Derivative creative design · Service system

1 Background

TV dramas include TV dramas and online dramas. In recent years, the proportion of TV dramas has steadily increased, and the number of online dramas has been continuously increasing. From 2018 to 2020, the scale of investment in film and television dramas increased steadily. With the development of television drama industry, the television drama derivatives (TDDs) industry is rising and maintaining stable development. From 2015 to 2019, the investment scale of television derivatives industry increased steadily, which provided a good consumption environment of derivatives market with the continuous improvement of residents' income level. For example, in 2019, the broadcast volume of television dramas in *The Untamed* exceeded 6.49 billion, and it also achieved great success in derivative cultural creation design (DCCD), covering daily life, original soundtrack, mobile games with the same name, concerts and many other aspects. The crowdfunding amount of the original painting image memorial special code alone reached 3,731,177 yuan, and 9,729 people participated in the crowdfunding.

© Springer Nature Switzerland AG 2021
C. Stephanidis et al. (Eds.): HCII 2021, CCIS 1419, pp. 543–550, 2021.
https://doi.org/10.1007/978-3-030-78635-9_70

2 Overview of Television Drama Derivative Creation

2.1 Television Drama Derivatives Category

Cultural creative design derived from television drama is a creative product derived from the creativity of television content, which refers to the products closely related to television content based on the copyright of television works and relying on the content of television. Its main forms of expression are books, games, music, theme parks, stationery, toys, clothing, daily necessities, etc. Traditionally, television derivatives are divided into two categories: physical derivatives and digital derivatives. In recent years, derivatives have tried to combine with various fields and developed more creative forms. In this paper, television-derived cultural creation is summarized into four types: physical-derived cultural creation, digital-derived cultural creation, activity-derived cultural creation and spatial-derived cultural creation. The "periphery" of physical derivative creative design is usually well known to the consumers. The digital derivative creative products include games, music, movies, programs and digital design creative products. Activity-derived cultural creation and space-derived cultural creation are new forms in the pan-entertainment era. Activity-derived cultural creation includes meetings and concerts, while space-derived cultural creation includes theme parks, theme parks and theme pop-up shop.

2.2 Service Content of Television Drama Derivative Creative

The service content of TDD creation mainly includes derivative information acquisition, derivative creative consumption experience and experience feedback after watching drama series. The derivative services of consumer experience mainly include physical derivative creation, digital derivative creation, activity derivative creation and space derivative creation. In the timeline of consumers' experience, the former guides consumers to obtain the consumption information of follow-up services, and the four types of derivative cultural creations (DCC) overlap each other to form a service system. Derivative cultural creation service system provides multi-level consumption experience, enhances the emotional connection between consumers and dramas, and promotes the emotional value of TDD cultural creation (Fig. 1).

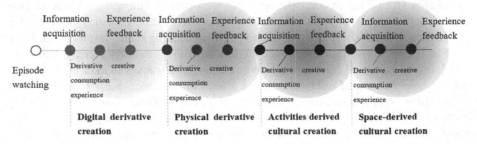

Fig. 1. Content map of television drama derivative cultural and creative services

3   The Development Status of Television Drama Derivative Creation

In this study, the top 10 episodes in 2019 and 2020 are taken as the research objects, including episodes on TV and online episodes, and statistics are made by using the bone-flower data in the database, Baidu search engine, social applications (microblogs) and public data of online shopping websites. It should be noted that the data of this study is as of December 20, 2020.

3.1   Physical Derivative Creation

110 types of derivative cultural and creative products on e-commerce platforms have been derived from research. Among them, mobile phone cases, cushions, canvas bags and thermos cups accounted for 52%. However, in terms of the number of buyers, the selected categories, such as Jianzhan cups (tea cup made by traditional Chinese technology), original painting set/setting set, blind box, etc., sold more. Mobile phone cases, pillows, canvas bags and thermos cups are low in cost, practical and can be purchased repeatedly. Dealers are mostly manufacturers of this kind of customized products. For them, these categories do not need complicated production technology or extra design, and can be customized by using official pictures.

In order to "rub the heat", the merchants produce quickly to gain profits, which leads to high degree of product homogeneity, lack of design creativity and cultural experience. And this part of the products lacks quality control, resulting in many products being shoddy. For consumers, although the selling price is low, the product quality is not satisfactory, and the combination of cultural and creative design and stories plot is lacking, which does not reflect the characteristics of drama series and cannot continue the attraction of film and television works to consumers (Table 1 and Fig. 2).

The product categories with small quantity but high sales volume in the survey are mostly concentrated in the official crowdfunding activities. In the survey, 20% of television dramas planned derivative crowdfunding activities, and 100% of them successfully reached the crowdfunding amount, of which 75% continued to sell products through the e-commerce platform after crowdfunding, shown in Table 2. The derivative creative categories of crowdfunding activities are mostly original stills, jewelry accessories and daily life categories. Although the price is slightly higher, the product has a sense of design, well-made, delicate and lovely or fresh and elegant, which fully fits the drama style and consumer portraits. Products can make consumers recall the relevant stories, arouse their cultural experience of the content of the drama series, and transform the audience into consumers to a greater extent. In addition, crowdfunding activities increase the playfulness of activities, enhance the interaction between consumers and officials, and stimulate fans' desire for consumption by means of "raising the flag" (giving extra gifts to all participants after reaching a certain crowdfunding amount).

Physical derivative cultural creation is still the main form chosen by the developer of cultural creation, but products with poor quality and lack of cultural connotation in design are not accepted by the market. The design and production of products lead to consumers having to wait for a long time to receive the products. In this process, consumers' attention to the drama series continues to decline.

Table 1. Investigation on the category of physical cultural and creative products in television

Products category	Quantity	Products category	Quantity
Mobile phone case	21	Notebook	3
Cushion	19	Brooch;1metal badge;1 acrylic badge	2
Canvas bag	9	Cotton doll	2
Mug/thermos	8	Post-it notespaper	2
Acrylic keychain	7	Accessory	1
Clothes	5	Scene splicing building blocks	1
Postcard	5	Jianzhan cup	1
Bracelets; earrings	5	Mobile phone support	1
Same products in episodes	4	Original painting feature set/setting set	1
Desk calendar	4	Bookmark	1
Umbrella	4	Blind box	1
Mouse mat	3		

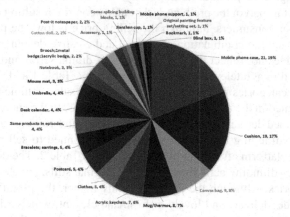

Fig. 2. Scale diagram of physical cultural and creative products of television dramas

In the era of experience economy, the emotional experience behind DCCD products has become the core of consumers' attention, and more consumers are willing to pay for the emotional value of DCCD products. Cultural and creative products with high quality, genuine copyright and creative design occupy a larger market share. The high success of crowdfunding shows that the promotion of interactive experience can stimulate huge consumption potential.

Table 2. Crowdfunding situation of television drama derivative creation

Episode name	Crowdfunding activities	Sum of money (¥)	Crowdfunding results, ratio
The Story Of MingLan	Peripheral Derivatives Millennium Intangible Treasure *Jianzhan Cap*	10504	Success, 105%
Go Go Squid!	Same derivatives	432399.5	Success, 864.8%
The Untamed	One song will never come to an end——*The Untamed Original Painting Image Memorial Special Code*	3731177	Success, 7462.35%
The Untamed	*The Untamed genuine authorized name scene series blind box-only envy forget envy not envy fairy*	940251	Success, 940.25%
Serenade of Peaceful Joy	Ancient Jewelry of Poetry Series	116589	Success, 233.18%

Data source: Modian.com

3.2 Digital Derivative Creation

In the era of pan-entertainment, because of its convenient access and changeable forms, the proportion of digital-derived cultural creations is gradually equal to that of physical-derived cultural creations. At present, digital derivative creations are mostly derivative programs, television drama shooting tidbits, mobile games and online games, video and audio (including theme songs, music videos and their products), etc. In the survey, all television dramas released their soundtrack albums on the music playing platform, among which 5% were music digital albums that needed to be paid for, and 45% needed music playing platform VIP to get them. Take *The Untamed* as an example. There are 18 songs in one album, which are sold in 20 yuan and have sold more than 1.5 million copies. Only the soundtrack digital album of television drama has brought huge income to the drama party.

New media technologies provides more and more forms for digital derivative cultural creation, such as VR video, interactive drama series, expression packs and so on. With the development of digital media market and technology, consumers are gradually getting used to the industrial mode of IP-centered transformation of film, sound, travel and diffuse forms. It is in this link that digital derivative cultural creation supplements the multi-sensory and strong sense of participation consumption experience that physical derivative cultural creation lacks.

3.3 Activities Derived Cultural Creation

Activity-derived cultural creation takes activity as the main form, which arouses the enthusiasm and interaction of participants to a greater extent. At the early stage of the drama series, the creative staff attended the fan meeting together. After the drama is played, the official concert is held, in which actors interact and sing theme songs, so as to enhance the adhesion of fans to television dramas. *The Untamed*, a television drama, held two concerts in Nanjing and Thailand, and *Love and Redemption* also successfully held a concert. *The Untamed*'s official microblog has also launched interactive and competitive online activities, including "Expression Pack Competition of *The Untamed*", "*The Untamed* 101", "Guo Feng Chen Qing Ling" and "*The Untamed* Graffiti Competition", which greatly satisfied the fans' desire to participate. The Untamed fans also participate in offline party activities held by micro stores, and meet the offline interaction needs of fans in the form of small theme markets.

Only 10% of the 20 television dramas researched and designed hold large-scale concerts. Although there are factors affected by the epidemic situation, it can still be seen that the official offline activities have not been taken seriously by the organizers. Most online topic activities focus on the content of drama series, and the audience lacks deep interactive participation. Under the leadership of fan economy, more dramas are increasing the audience's attention and interaction through activities-derived cultural creation, transforming ordinary audience into drama fans and cultivating more potential consumers.

3.4 Space-Derived Cultural Creation

Space-derived cultural creation mainly refers to theme parks and theme parks related to the content of television dramas. There is no derivative creation based on space carrier in the survey, but what we can see is that TV dramas such as *The Untamed*, *Sansheng Sanshi pillow* have all driven fans to go to the location to travel and punch in. According to C-trip ticket data, during the broadcast period in *The Longest Day In Chang'an*, the search volume of tickets to Xi 'an increased by 130% year-on-year, and the peak period increased by more than 200% year-on-year. In addition, according to the "2019 Xi 'an Tourism Raiders" released by Ma Honeycomb, the popularity of Xi 'an tourism has increased by 22% since the television was launched.

At present, there are few attempts on spatial derivative forms. An excellent television drama can bring tourists to its shooting place or the place in the drama content. The rise of tourism in television cities and taking photos in shooting scenic spots shows that the development potential of space-derived cultural creation of television dramas is huge.

3.5 Television Drama Derivative Creative Service

At present, there is no perfect service system in the field of cultural creation derived from television dramas. Most TDD creative designs simply choose the successful derivative creative types, which brings a single sense of experience and cannot meet the audience's comprehensive experience needs for derivative creative works. There is a lack of systematic consideration for television dramas applying various types of DCC, and the service contents of DCC are independent of each other. For example, the popularity of consumers attracted by digital DCC failed to guide consumers to obtain information of physical DCC. Various derivative cultural and creative contents should influence and complement each other, extend the audience's attention to dramas and form a complete chain of derivative cultural and creative consumption experience.

4 Television Drama Derivative Creative Development Strategy

4.1 Improve the Quality of Physical Derivative Cultural Creation

Under the experience economy, consumers' quality requirements for television dramas and derivative creations are improving, and consumers are not satisfied with simple printed materials without cultural experience. Product quality control should be guaranteed first in DCCD. In the aspect of design, pay attention to the elements that have emotional connection with consumers and reflect the cultural connotation of television dramas, and take them as the breakthrough point, which can better fit the audience's emotional memory of drama series and more accurately convey the cultural content of stories. In the process of selling DCC, adding activity elements, increasing interactivity and participation will achieve better sales results.

4.2 Increase the Form of Digital Derivative Creation

With the continuous development of media technology, it provides more possibilities for digital creation of television dramas. The increasing use of electronic devices has brought more potential consumers. New media technologies, such as VR video and interactive drama series, can bring consumers a more comprehensive and novel service experience. For example, the warm-up series launched by the variety *Crime Scene* is an interactive form, in which the audience participates in the series from the perspective of players and deduces different endings. Adding digital derivative creative forms will increase the dimension of consumption experience for consumers.

4.3 Try Space-Derived Cultural Creation

Space creative design can bring consumers a more immersive and all-round cultural experience, and the senses of sight, hearing and touch are satisfied. Compared with other categories, the design investment of space-based cultural creation is higher and the overall time line of the project is longer, but the benefits are huge. The television drama parties can unite with the local tourism industry to jointly create theme parks and theme tourism routes, so as to continue the influence of television drama on the audience and make better use of the long tail market.

4.4 Systematic Television Drama Derivative Cultural and Creative Services

At present, there is still a lack of systematic service system in the design of TDD works. There are many kinds of TDD works, which are incomplete and lack of correlation, and it is difficult for consumers to harvest TDD services with good experience. From the perspective of service design, systematic analysis shows that digital, physical, activity, and space are the four derivative types of cultural creation to provide a complete consumption experience. In the service process, the derivative service content provided first should guide consumers to obtain the information of the next service content. Digital-derived cultural creation can improve the audience's attention to the drama content, enhance the expectation value and increase the viscosity of drama pursuit. At the same time, it guides the audience to participate in online topic discussion, increases the interactivity of the drama series, and attracts more viewers to become potential consumers. In the discussion, we can obtain the information of cultural creation derived from physical objects and activities, increase the consumption experience, enhance consumers' like of drama series and prolong the long tail market of television dramas. Use the long tail market to guide consumers to experience theme parks and tourism industries derived from space, and further transform the commercial value of television dramas. Various types of DCC constitute a service system, which cooperates with each other, connecting the contact points between consumers and DCC into a complete experience path, and improving the loss of consumption power caused by the current independence of various types.

5   Conclusion

At present, China's television drama-derived creative design is developing, and there have been many attempts in television drama-derived creative design. Physical derivative cultural creation should pay more attention to quality and emotional connection between consumers and television dramas. Digital derivative cultural creation can be more integrated with media technology, and creatively convey the cultural connotation of television dramas. Activity-derived cultural creation appears in the appropriate marketing opportunities, enhancing the interaction between consumers and television dramas, and providing a more comprehensive cultural and creative service experience. Space creative design should combine tourism more, create theme tourism routes and theme parks, and meet the needs of consumers to experience the space environment of television dramas. Various types of DCC constitute a service system, paying attention to the emotional needs of consumers, providing a more coherent consumer cultural experience, integrating the content value of television dramas with the carrier of DCC, and creating higher value for the pan-entertainment industry.

References

1. Song, Y.: Analysis of the supply and policy of film and television cultural consumption-thinking about the market trend and industrial policy of film and television derivatives in 2018. J. Shanghai Univ. (Soc. Sci. Edition) **36**(06), 41–54 (2019)
2. Yao, X., Yan, Q., Liu,. J.: Research and practice of user experience design of Wenchuang products based on service blueprint. Packag. Eng. 1–10
3. Zuo, W.: User aggregation: marketing ideas of online dramas in the new media era-taking The Untamed as an example. Audiovisual **09**, 71–72 (2020)
4. Zou, Q., Da Me, G.: Research on the commercial value of Internet IP drama based on "fan economy". J. Shanghai Bus. Sch. **20**(06), 50–60 (2019)

Research on the Perceptual Experience Based on Text Mining—Taking Reclining Chair as an Example

Xianggang Lu$^{(\boxtimes)}$ and Meiyu Zhou

East China University of Science and Technology, Shanghai, China

Abstract. With the continuous improvement of product technical performance, more and more attention has been paid to the emotional needs of users. As a result, understanding the relationship between emotional impression and design elements is a vital procedure in product design, which is also an important part of Kansei Engineering. However, traditional questionnaire method has some shortcomings in this aspect, because it may cause misunderstanding of word meaning. Therefore, this paper uses a method called text mining technology, which is based on big data and can truly and effectively reflect the user's point of view. 3367 online reviews about reclining chairs were crawled from JingDong, one of the largest online shopping service platforms in China. Through word frequency statistics and text clustering, we can find the users' concerns, and study the relationship between design elements and emotional impression in a complete context. The results show that 'comfort' is the most frequently used emotional variable when using the recliner, which is related to various emotional variables. In addition, the reclining chair comments extracted from JingDong are divided into 15 clusters by python. The findings indicate that text mining technology and text clustering can effectively collect and analyze the users' emotional experience, and provide some guidance for the design of reclining chair.

Keywords: Kansei engineering · Text mining · Recliner · User reviews · Python

1 Introduction

With the progress of product development, production and other technologies, it is difficult to achieve product differentiation in terms of performance, price and functional characteristics. Maslow's hierarchy of needs theory points out an effective way for us to analyze the needs of product design, that is, to pay attention to people's emotional experience. In recent years, engineers have been making quantitative analysis of customers' emotional needs, which is called "Kansei Engineering" [1].

From the perspective of methodology, Kansei engineering has developed a variety of methods to collect emotional vocabulary to measure customers' emotions or impressions of products [2]. The common collection methods include literature review and interview, and then collect feedback through evaluation questionnaire. However, the amount of vocabulary collected from the literature is limited, and it may be divorced from the

© Springer Nature Switzerland AG 2021
C. Stephanidis et al. (Eds.): HCII 2021, CCIS 1419, pp. 551–561, 2021.
https://doi.org/10.1007/978-3-030-78635-9_71

vocabulary used in people's daily life. And the other method- interview, is limited by the number of participants. There are also shortcomings in the evaluation questionnaire. This kind of questionnaire usually adopts the evaluation scale defined by researchers or experts in advance, which may not be consistent with the conceptual structure of the respondents, thus affecting the evaluation process [3].

A good solution is to use web-based text mining technology. With the rapid development of e-commerce, people are increasingly shopping online and publishing their experiences of products. As an important way of consumer feedback, how to mine and analyze the comments has become a significant research direction of perceptual analysis of commodity evaluation [4]. Compared with traditional Kansei engineering methods, such as interview and questionnaire, text mining has more advantages. Because it identifies the users' own words, which ensures that the end user will not be semantic confused. In addition, with the help of big data, it can effectively and quickly collect more complete ideas from a large number of end users. More importantly, it is not limited by the perception, that means, we can not only evaluate on the basis of vision and experience but also other perceptions. Because the mined text is the emotional embodiment of the user's personal experience. At home and abroad, the research of mining emotional experience through online text is gradually emerging, involving many fields such as products, tourism and service. Xiong Wei et al. analyzed the word frequency and emotion of hotel customers' online reviews [5], Zhai Dongsheng et al. applied product review mining to competitive advantage analysis [6], Koltringer et al. extracted tourism destination brand image and cognition through automated web content mining [7], and Chen Zhixuan used text mining technology to extract perceptual image vocabulary of gas stove [8]. In recent years, the algorithm of processing network text is becoming more and more mature. Cheng zhengshuang proposed a sentiment analysis method based on support vector machine (SVM) to classify the positive, negative and neutral emotions in comments [9]. Liu et al. developed a recommender algorithm, which uses adverb based opinion feature extraction method to improve the accuracy in online comment analysis [10]. Wang et al. used support vector machine to study the selection of feature words in Chinese online reviews to improve sentiment classification [11].

Using the method of text mining to understand the user's emotional experience, most of the researches mainly focus on the classification of commendatory and derogatory emotions, subjective content recognition and economic value mining of online reviews. Most of the researches draw on the technologies and methods of information retrieval, natural language processing, machine learning, statistics and so on [12]. However, the relationship between perceptual intention and design elements is very important [3]. Therefore, this paper assumes that different design elements will lead to different affective variables, and attempts to collect and analyze user experience through text mining and cluster analysis, so as to understand users' implicit needs and natural feelings for products, and find out users' concerns and the relationship between design elements and emotional vocabulary. The target product of this case study is the recliner. The product reviews are obtained from Jing Dong, one of the largest online shopping service platforms in China. Python is used for data processing.

2 Research Method

The whole process of this study is to integrate text mining technology into Kansei engineering. First of all, a kind of suitable products that can produce emotional interaction with users is chosen. Secondly, a large number of user comments are collected from JingDong through text mining technology. The third step is to preprocess the data and convert the text document into a computer-readable data matrix. Then, based on the preprocessed file, word frequency analysis is carried out. Based on the data matrix, text clustering is carried out to classify the user's emotional experience. The similar emotional experience is classified into one category. With the increase of the number of common words in two comments, the probability of these comments being classified into the same cluster will also increase. Finally, representative clusters are selected according to the clustering results, and each cluster is analyzed to explain the relationship between perceptual intention and design elements.

2.1 Target Product and Data Sources

The main purpose of this study is to collect and analyze emotional words by mining online reviews, so as to understand users' feelings and how they feel when using products. To achieve this, the choice of product types is important, it has to require the ability to produce various types of emotional experiences. Reclining chair is a kind of chair closely related to ergonomics. The design of reclining chair needs to consider multiple dimensions of human body size. Its basic configuration is seat surface, back and footrest. Most of them have headrests and armrests. Some reclining chairs can adjust the angle of back and footrest electrically or manually. Some reclining chairs also have foldable, inflatable, roller, electric massage and other functions. Materials are also various, including polyester, metal, cloth, solid wood, rattan, leather, plastic, etc. With the improvement of people's living standards, the use of reclining chair has also increased. In many daily activities, such as watching TV and basking in the sun, reclining chair will be used, which is easier to reflect various emotions than office chair (according to material and size). Therefore, we chose the reclining chair as the product of this study.

The data source of network evaluation is one of the mainstream e-commerce websites, JingDong. It contains a large number of product categories, each category has a large number of products, and allows customers to publish their product experience and opinions, and evaluate the products they buy. All the information is stored in the database and can be collected.

First of all, in the search of "reclining chair" on JingDong, 350000 + products can be found, and 100 pages of results are displayed, with 60 products per page. According to the number of comments from high to low, 3015 reclining chairs have users' comments, among which 230000 + comments are for the first reclining chair. After crawling 3367 comments by Python, 123 duplicate comments were deleted during data preprocessing, leaving 3244 comments for analysis.

2.2 Data Preprocessing

The data preprocessing in this stage includes synonym replacement, word segmentation and stop word filtering. The first step is realized by Microsoft Office Word, and the second step is realized by python. In order to facilitate the word frequency analysis and clustering of the text, it is necessary to replace synonyms.

In order to turn short text into a language that can be understood by computer, the first step is word segmentation. Word segmentation is the process of extracting language units (such as words and phrases) from text. This study uses Jieba segmentation, and some errors were adjusted later.

The second step is to filter stop words. Stop words are very common words, which convey less information. It seems to have little value in text mining and analysis, but it will affect the efficiency and accuracy of text classification. Therefore, before comprehensive analysis, it is better to exclude stop words from the vocabulary set [13]. The commonly used stop words in Chinese include auxiliary words, prepositions, articles, conjunctions, and some meaningless words such as signs and adverbs of degree. In this paper, we use the downloaded Chinese stop word list and make manual adjustment according to word frequency statistics and text features.

2.3 Statistical Analysis

After filtering the stop words, each line of evaluation has become the text represented by separated characteristic words. By analyzing the word frequency of the filtered text file, we can see the frequency of each word, so as to understand which aspects consumers pay more attention to and the main emotional reaction of the product.

And then, we need to cluster the text and divide the comments into several categories in order to analyze the relationship between emotional words and the relationship between emotional words and design elements. The stop words have been removed before in the step of preprocessing. In order to prevent the impact on clustering, we delete the comments only about logistics, customer service and JingDong. Then we use VSM algorithm to construct the word bag space to turn the text into a digital language that can be understood by the computer. In this step, we need to build a vector for each evaluation, and the value of the vector is the number of times the words appear in all evaluations. Then, the number of words is converted into weight to determine the weight of each word in the classification. In clustering, the more the same words in the two comments, the more likely they are to be divided into a category. But we can't just consider the number of common words, so it's very important to give weight, which is based on IDF (Inverse Document Frequency). Finally, the Python SinglePass algorithm is used to cluster the comment text and output the number of comments and keywords of each category.

3 Results

3.1 Word Frequency Analysis of Reclining Chair Network Evaluation

On the basis of word segmentation and filtering stop words, we conducted a lexical frequency analysis to investigate the main emotional words and users' concerns. We deleted some emotional variables for the following reasons. First of all, lexical items such as "nice", "like" and "praise" are adjectives related to evaluation, which are deleted from the study because they are too many in the review. Second, words like "customer service" and "logistics" that have nothing to do with the product itself have been deleted. If these words are not removed according to the above criteria, the classification of comments through Python will be disturbed.

The first 60 high frequency words are extracted in Table 1. The total frequency of 60 valid parameters is equal to 10847. The most frequent word was "comfortable", followed by "quality" and "(folding, installation, cleaning, maintenance) convenience" (n = 1702; 1009; 615).The words "rest assured", "assembly" and "high-end" belong to low-frequency words (n = 39; 36; 35).

Table 1. The results of frequency analysis of reclining chair affective variables from online reviews.

Affective variable	Frequency	Affective variable	Frequency	Affective variable	Frequency
Comfortable	1702	Simple	159	Pillow	73
Quality	1009	Appropriate	154	Smell	72
Convenient	615	Portable	144	Carry	70
Strong	374	Design	120	Balcony	68
Occupied area	343	Cushions	120	Light	63
Good-looking	323	Office	119	Style	61
Workmanship	306	Cost performance	116	Soft	59
Size	302	Rest	112	Angle	50
Logistics	299	Texture	100	Brace	49
Service	291	Adjust	99	Ventilation	47
Install	283	Solid	93	Grade	47
Type	266	Fine	92	Perfect	45
Fold	244	Fabric	91	Voice	44
Noon break	216	Storage	89	Hospital	43
Appearance	213	Practical	85	Operation	41
Packing	204	Thick and solid	84	Material	39
Material quality	200	Ingredient	79	Firm	39
Colour	197	Peculiar smell	79	Rest assured	39
Customer service	180	Durable	78	Assemble	36
Decent	170	Substantial benefits	77	High-end	35

It can be seen from the word frequency table that the part of speech mainly includes nouns, adjectives and verbs, with 29, 21 and 10 respectively. Nouns are reflected in product attributes, use scenarios, services, etc. "quality", "occupied area", "workmanship", "type" and other words are relatively higher, indicating that consumers value the quality, volume and visual factors of reclining chairs. Nouns also include "material", "smell", "angle" and "pillow", which shows that these have a great impact on the user experience. Adjectives mainly show the user's visual feeling, use feeling, product material evaluation and other aspects. The most common ones are "comfortable", "convenient", "strong" and "good-looking", which indicates that the user mainly evaluates from the use experience, operation simplicity, stability and appearance. In addition, the users also pay attention to the size of the recliner, material texture and the amount of material used. Verbs include the interaction between the user and the recliner, such as "install", "fold", "adjust", etc., as well as the purpose of using the recliner, such as "break" and "rest", indicating that the difficulty of product installation will affect the product evaluation, and the adjustability and portability are also factors worthy of consideration. The extracted high-frequency words can be divided into four categories: product design elements, product use purpose, product usage and user experience evaluation.

3.2 Text Clustering

Python is used to perform data analysis to identify the evaluation group of reclining chair, and understand the relationship between design elements and emotional evaluation in the complete text. The results are shown in Table 2. Among the 3244 comments, 2789 were left after deleting those which were totally unrelated to product evaluation. Similar reviews were clustered and these comments were eventually divided into 15 representative categories.

Table 2. Cluster analysis results of emotional experience of reclining chair

Serial number	Number of comments (n)	The most commonly used keywords
1	298	Comfortable, quality, style
2	35	Sound, quality, strong, comfortable
3	72	Comfortable, size, satisfied, width, occupied area
4	104	Decoration, style, type, comfortable
5	156	Logistics, service, attitude, quality
6	137	Material quality, texture, good-looking, quality
7	47	Fold, convenient, occupied area, size
8	85	Installation, convenient, simple, workmanship

(*continued*)

Table 2. (*continued*)

Serial number	Number of comments (n)	The most commonly used keywords
9	102	Quality, workmanship, durable, strong, comfortable
10	21	Comfortable, satisfied, angle
11	63	Style, good-looking, high end, decent
12	84	Solid, weight bearing, quality, workmanship
13	37	Simple, operation, adjust, fold
14	127	Cheap, perfect, price, satisfaction
15	134	Comfortable, fabric, smooth, color, soft

Among all clusters, cluster 1 has the most comments (n = 298), and the most frequently mentioned keywords are "comfortable" and "quality". Cluster 2 and cluster 10 had the least comments, including words such as "voice" and "angle".

4   Discussion

The purpose of this study is to obtain the emotional parameters and related design elements of product experience from user reviews through word frequency analysis and text clustering analysis. The results show that there are different affective variables in the process of use.

On one hand, word frequency analysis shows that the most commonly used emotional word is "comfortable". In previous studies, the term "comfort" was considered as the core content of chair furniture design elements [14]. This indicates that the method of extracting affective parameters from user reviews in this study achieves the same results as traditional methods (such as interview and literature review).

On the other hand, the clustering results show that the comments belonging to each cluster contain a variety of emotional parameters. Cluster 1 is related to the comfortable and relaxed user experience when using the recliner, for example:

"It's great to send home by express!!After driving for a day, I packed the chair in ten minutes when I got home. When I lay down, I was going to the sky. It was so comfortable! Usually not much evaluation, this time I must praise!!I hope it's durable."

As the comments show, users emphasize comfort when expressing their emotional experience of the recliner, which represents a high degree of satisfaction. Clusters 2, 3, 10 and 15 contain information about the comfort experience and related design parameters. For example, cluster 2 involves the firmness of a recliner, for example:

"Good quality and cheap reclining chair, strong support, good fabric quality, reassuring load. It's very comfortable."

This indicates that the firmness of the reclining chair is related to the user's comfortable sensation, which may be because the firmness of the reclining chair will give people a "reassuring" feeling, thus bringing comfort. Therefore, we need to consider firmness as an important design element. In addition, some users will judge whether it is solid or not according to whether there is sound, which puts forward requirements for the fit between parts.

Clusters 9 and 12 are also related to firmness. Users describe the firmness of the chair by describing their weight, and judge its quality and durability by its firmness and workmanship. It is worth noting that durability is also a common word used by users. Examples of comments are as follows:

"My friend weighs more than 120 kg. It's good to sit. It's very strong. It should be durable."

"Adults and children can sit or lie down, the shaking range is very safe, the bearing capacity is very strong, we can see that the quality is very good, very satisfied with this shopping."

The results also show that group 3 represents the relationship between size and width and reclining chair comfort, as shown in the following comments:

"The chair is really good. This one is a little wider, very comfortable. Metal lock. It's light but strong. We can adjust the back angle when sitting on it. It's very convenient and comfortable."

"It's all right but a little narrower, it would be more comfortable if it were wider and thicker"

The height and length mentioned in comments are less, and they are not divided into clusters, which indicates that users pay more attention to width than these two dimensions.

Group 10 shows the relationship between the recliner's back angle and overall comfort, for example:

"The style is simple and generous. The back can be adjusted from many angles. It's very nice. It's very comfortable to lie on. The quality is also good. There's no smell. The bracket is all aluminum."

The results show that the adjustability of the back can bring higher satisfaction, which may be because the individual differences of each person's body, which leads to the need for a certain degree of "personalized customization". In addition, users will also want to be able to adjust the back when sitting in a recliner.

In addition, as shown in cluster 15, the material of the reclining chair is also related to the overall comfort, as follows:

"The chair is a little hard. It's not very comfortable to sit on."

"Because of the inflatable protection, the air cushion won't be stiff and elastic. The flocking surface is not cold and comfortable to lie on."

The above comments show that the tactile factors such as "soft and hard", "cold and hot" of the recliner will affect the comfort. The perception of "hard" and "cold" is regarded as a negative expression by the recliner users, while the "cool" used in the evaluation of the rattan chair is a positive expression.

Group 4 shows the relationship between the recliner and the user's environment, as shown in the following comments:

"My house has just been decorated, I felt that there were some shortcomings, so I bought a set of this. It's high-end and elegant and matches the layout of my house very well."

"The sofa is really good. It looks high-grade and decent. The quality is very good, neither too hard, nor too soft. It's very comfortable to sit on. It matches the decoration in the house very well. The color is beautiful. I'm satisfied with all aspects."

When buying recliner, users will also pay attention to the matching degree of recliner and decoration style, house pattern and room space. Therefore, it may be necessary to consider these factors when designing recliner.

Clusters 6 and 11 show the importance of visual parameters, for example:

"It's good-looking. It's comfortable to lie down. Easy to install. Very suitable for reading and watching TV while lying down. The fabric is perfect. It's worth recommending."

"The quality is very good, the material is good, strong and durable, the style is high-end and the customer service is considerate."

When users have a positive reaction to the recliner they buy, they will comment on visual aesthetics and comfort. And visual satisfaction will affect their evaluation of comfort to a certain extent. In the evaluation of product image, the words "good-looking" and "beautiful" can best represent the relationship with design parameters, because visual interaction is the first to occur before using it. The study also found that the affective variables of "good-looking" is related to color, style, texture and processing fineness. Consumers often use the words "high-end" and "decent" to express their visual impression of the reclining chair style.

Clusters 7, 8 and 13 are related to the operation of the recliner, as follows:

"Good quality!It's very convenient and comfortable to fold, but it needs some simple installation after delivery. Overall satisfaction."

"The chair is very comfortable. The key point is that it's easy to carry. You can rest anywhere you want. Moreover, the folded chair covers a small area, which is very good."

The comments in the above cluster show that users will interact with the recliner to install, fold, adjust and carry. They want these actions to be "convenient" and "simple". In addition, users often use the word "occupied area" to describe the effect of folding, which is a positive word.

5 Conclusion

The purpose of this study is to use text mining technology and algorithm technology to effectively and quickly collect affective variables from user comments, and analyze the relationship between affective variables and design elements, so as to avoid the shortcomings of traditional Kansei engineering methods to a certain extent.

The main findings of this study are as follows. First, the frequency of feature words is analyzed. When a customer uses a recliner, the most common emotional variable is "comfort". Therefore, it is very important to understand the design factors related to comfort when studying the design of reclining chair. Second, through text clustering, the comments are divided into 15 categories, and the words used by users are analyzed in specific and complete semantics to understand their relationship. It is worth noting that the size, visual form and touch of the chair affect its perceived comfort and overall impression.

The method used in this study is to mine emotional variables from user reviews, where big data can be used to collect the opinions of most users, and it is a complete idea rather than a single word. This study links the design elements of reclining chair with the emotional response of users, which may arouse the interest of reclining chair designers, because they hope to make more effective design. By letting designers and researchers think about the results of this paper, users can obtain higher satisfaction and experience.

References

1. Li, Q.: Phenomenology of design: a descriptive framework about experience, meaning creation and pursuit of practice. Design research, 2016: School of design and creativity, pp. 102–121. Tongji University (2019). (in Chinese)
2. Henson, B., Barnes, C., Livesey, R., Childs, T., Ewart, K.: Affective consumer requirements: a case study of moisturizer packaging. Concurr. Eng. **14**, 187–196 (2006)
3. Nuria, C., Carmen, L., Jose, M.B., Vicente, B.: Subjective assessment of university classroom environment. Build. Environ. 122 (2017)
4. Agarwal, B., Mittal, N., Bansal, P., et al.: Sentiment analysis using common-sense and context information. Comput. Intell. Neurosci. **2015**, 30 (2015)
5. Xiong, W., Guo, Y.: Text mining of hotel customer online reviews. J. Beijing Int. Stud. Univ. **35**(11), 38–47 (2013). (in Chinese)
6. Zhai, D., Xu, Y., Huang, L., Zhao, J.: Competitive product advantage analysis based on product review mining. Intell. Mag **32**(02), 45–51 + 66 (2013). (in Chinese)
7. Költringer, C., Dickingerm, A.: Analyzing destination branding and image from online sources: a web content mining approach. J. Bus. Res. **68**(9), 1836–1843 (2015)
8. Chen, Z.: Research on product perceptual image vocabulary based on online review mining. China Academy of Fine Arts (2019). (in Chinese)
9. Cheng, Z., Wang, L.: Sentiment analysis method of online reviews based on support vector machine. Electr. Technol. Softw. Eng. **16**, 3–4 (2019). (in Chinese)
10. Liu, H., He, J., Wang, T., Song, W., Du, X.: Combining user preferences and user opinions for accurate recommendation. Electron. Commer. Res. Appl. **12**, 14–23 (2013)
11. Wang, H., Yin, P., Yao, J., Liu, J.N.: Text feature selection for sentiment classification of Chinese online reviews. J. Exp. Theor. Artif. Intell. **25**, 425–439 (2013)

12. Zhang, Z., Ye, Q., Li, Y.: Review on sentiment analysis of Internet product reviews. J. Manage. Sci. **13**(06), 84–96 (2010). (in Chinese)
13. Ma, Z.: Research on Stop Word Processing and Feature Selection in Text Classification. Xidian University (2014). (in Chinese)
14. Shang, K., Luo, J., Wang, Z.: Seat comfort evaluation based on pupil detection. J. Forest. Eng. **4**(02), 152–157 (2019). (in Chinese)

Placing AI in the Creative Industries: The Case for Intelligent Music Production

Glenn McGarry(✉), Alan Chamberlain, Andy Crabtree, and Christopher Greenhalgh

Mixed Reality Laboratory, School of Computer Science, University of Nottingham, Nottingham, England, UK
{glenn.mcgarry,alan.chamberlain,andy.crabtree}@nottingham.ac.uk

Abstract. The digital transformation of the recording industry is one of the most well-known in recent times, with the Digital Audio Workstation (DAW) making new methods of music production available to amateurs and professionals in almost any setting beyond the traditional recording studio. However, the uptake of AI in this domain is seemingly impeded by DAW software architectures and a need for designers to better understand production practices and workflows. Our research addresses the latter of these challenges and in this extended abstract we present an overview of an ethnographic study that "gets inside" the work of the recording studio and exposes opportunities for the design of automated production tools. From a summary report of this work, we then aim to motivate or provoke novel conversations and future work in this problem space.

Keywords: Music production · Ethnography · Automation · Workflow

1 Background

In the modern music industry, the advent of the digital audio workstation (DAW) has radically redefined the concept of the 'studio' - triggering the decline of the 'traditional' recording studio sector [1, 2] - and introduced novel production methods, technologies, and workflows [3]. Professionals and amateurs alike can now equip any space - bedrooms, garages, or lofts - with a DAW and a new generation of affordable production software and hardware, to create a studio capable of producing high-quality recorded music that can be distributed through accessible digital marketplaces [4]. DAW technology has also developed to provide systems that can piece music together produced at different times and places – for example a band performance captured in a traditional recording studio might be layered with vocal performance captured in a home studio, before the finished song is mixed at a project studio. This makes for a more economical approach which has paved the way for small/medium recording studios to become predominant in this sector [5]; and affected professional practices, for example, the roles of producer and recording engineer are typically now rolled into one [6].

Despite prevalence of digital technologies, the recording industry is lagging in the prospective take-up and integration of state-of-the-art intelligent technologies to support creative processes and address the functional needs of modern music production practice

C. Stephanidis et al. (Eds.): HCII 2021, CCIS 1419, pp. 562–572, 2021.
https://doi.org/10.1007/978-3-030-78635-9_72

[7 cited in, 8]. In the following section, then, we explore works related to this problem space and position our research in contribution to addressing some of the prevalent issues.

2 Related Work

Recent developments in artificial intelligence in music (AIM) tend to focus on the mixing stage of production; blending and treating layers of multi-track audio into the final musical product. These include modelling the mixing process [9–13]; automating audio effects and mixing [14, 15]; instrument identification [16] for automated editing [17–19] and production workflows [20]; and process tracking for data provenance and project management [21–25]. The prospective take-up for these novel tools and concepts, however, is bound up in a particular set of design challenges. *Firstly*, there is a knowledge gap between the demonstratable possibilities for AIM, such as those above, and empirical understandings of real-world practices, in order to identify which tasks may be usefully automated [26], either through assistive features or full automation [8]. *Secondly*, most DAW platform architectures constrain the possibility of integrating AI outside of the third-party "plug-in" structure and so any significant redesign of the DAW to enable this should be underpinned by thorough analyses of real-world requirements [12].

2.1 Studies of Music Production in HCI

In AI design, HCI studies now play a crucial role in providing detailed understandings in different work domains [27], however recording studios are notoriously difficult to access as a study site, particularly in the professional realm [28]. Hence, existing studies typically involve interviews with production professionals [12, 13, 29] that render retrospective accounts that are detached from the setting and so are limited in the kinds of first-hand detail that can usefully explicate the work. A few ethnographic studies exist that conduct their inquiries from "within the flow of work" [30] and begin to piece together a picture of the contemporary music production landscape. These studies highlight: issues in the hand-over of song data between settings [31]; the appropriation of networked technologies to support remote music-making collaborations [32]; the ad hoc workarounds required to use incompatible production tools [33]; and the constraints of DAW design outside of the traditional production context [34, 35].

3 The Study

In contribution to the body of work discussed above, we conducted ethnographic studies of real-world professional music production practices and in this extended abstract, we report on one of those studies conducted in a 'traditional' recording studio.

In brief, the design ethnography [30] approach used involves immersing the researcher in the setting in order to understand, and describe the work as the participants do [36]. This requires attending to the "accountable features" [37] of the setting which include the social character of work (the interactions and accountability); work practices in context (the competencies, contingencies, and reasoning); and the ecology of the work (the spaces, tools, and resources).

The field data gathered in the studio includes field notes taken in real-time that sequence the actions and reasoning of the production activities; photographs of the setting and its organizing artefacts and resources; and video of the activities in real-time. The approximate run-time of video captured is: 12 h.

By way of analysis, vignettes extracted from the transcribed videos, field notes, and photographs were compiled into detailed field reports to describe and illustrate workflows; the methods and reasoning of the production activities; the collaborations and interactions; and the use and creation of production resources– all of which is reported more completely in the lead author's PhD thesis [38]. The full details of this complex and detailed work cannot be covered in the space allowed in this paper and so the following sections present a summary of the study scenario, an overview of the workflow, and some of the organizing features of the setting.

4   The Findings

The study observes a three-day recording session with a "Retro Rock" covers band. The session takes place in an archetypal 'traditional' recording studio, installed with sound proofed rooms and high specification digital and analogue multi track recording equipment operated from a control room (Fig. 1).

Fig. 1. The recording engineer's working position in the control room

The participants are the five band members (singer, guitarist 1, guitarist 2, bassist, and drummer) and the recording engineer who share the role of producer with the singer, and guitarist 1 to direct the recording activities and meet the artistic aim of producing a 'classic rock sound' that represents their live act. This presents the production process with the technical challenge of allowing musicians to perform together effectively while simultaneously separating and capturing sounds, which is a key feature of multi-track recording practice to optimize the control of sound layers in the mixing stage.

4.1 Day 1: Setup (2.5 h Observed)

In this section we explore the set up stage as shown in Fig. 2 and described below.

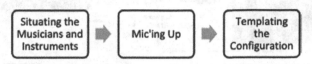

Fig. 2. The setup stage workflow

Situating the Musicians and Instruments

In order to separate sounds across the soundproofed zones of studio space, one live room is allocated as the band performance area; and the other as the vocal performance area. Upright acoustic screens are positioned around the guitar amplifiers to separate sounds further and lessen 'spill' – sounds that are unintentionally picked up by a microphone. In order to enable all of the members to coordinate their performances, the sound engineer sets up a communication loop, known as 'foldback', between the two live rooms and the control rooms consisting of talkback microphones and headphone feeds with a customizable mix of the instrument audio.

Mic'ing Up

Mic'ing up involves the choice and placement of microphones to capture a sound source, the methods and reasoning for which are contingent on several situational factors. In this scenario for example, microphones are used that are robust to loudness of the band instruments, which allows close positioning to reduce spill, while multiple microphones with different tonal qualities are used on the guitars that are then blended in order to shape the sound (Fig. 3).

Fig. 3. The recording engineer positions two microphones in front of a guitar amplifier

Two methods for organizing the dozens of audio channels used in mic'ing up are accounted for in the recording engineer's work. Firstly, mapping the microphone connections to the recording equipment determines the channel allocation and ordering of audio on the recording console; secondly, the engineer labels recording console channels and corresponding DAW tracks with information about the sound source and the microphone type used to record it (Fig. 4).

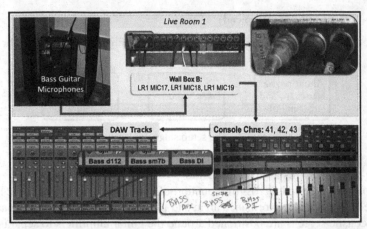

Fig. 4. An example of mapping and labelling the setup for recording bass guitar. The signal chain clockwise from top left: microphones > wall box > console channels > DAW audio tracks Labels refer to: an AKG D112 mic, a Shure SM7B mic, and the unamplified guitar signal converted through a Direct Input (DI) box

The resultant audio configuration then, is both spatially organized and textually annotated, physically on the recording console labels and digitally in the DAW, such that the navigation of controls in the flow of immediate work is supported and information that is prospectively useful for future stages of the process.

Templating the Configuration

In the finishing stages of setup, the mappings, and labelling applied in the DAW is saved as a template ready to be used in the recording stage, the reasoning for creating this resource is explored in the next section.

4.2 Day 2: Recording *(6 h Observed)*

In this section we explore the core workflow for the recording stage, which centres on capturing band performances in real-time as 'takes'. This requires high levels of coordinated action from all members involved, crucial to which is the foldback communication loop between the soundproof zones of the studio, the organization of audio in the control (Fig. 5) room, and the DAW template.

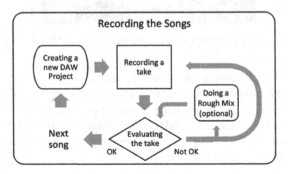

Fig. 5. The recording stage workflow

Creating a New DAW Project (song file)

The creation of each song is initiated through the DAW template, which is called upon frequently at the point decisions are made – sometimes planned, sometimes ad hoc - about which songs from the band's repertoire to record (Extract 1).

Extract 1. Creating a new DAW project

The band return to the studio after a break. The recording engineer (Paul) asks the guitarist (Richard) which song is to be recorded next.

Richard: It's Sharp Dressed Man

Paul: Sharp Dressed Man, right… [sits at the DAW; closes the previous recording; opens a new DAW song file from a template and names it 'Sharp dressed man'].

Paul: Tell you one thing, I'm glad I created all these templates yesterday. Don't half make this so much easier. 'specially like this cos it means … all the sessions (song files and audio data) are grouped together now as well so I've not got like … hundreds and hundreds of audio files all over the place [puts DAW in record mode]

Paul: [looks up to see if band are ready] (Into talkback mic) Are we all ready?
             (Inaudible reply from Live Room through talkback)

Paul: I'm rolling so whenever you're ready, Go for it.

Richard: Ready, 1 – 2 – 3 – 4… (The band perform Sharp Dressed Man by ZZ Top)

Crucially, the template supports the workflow for the recording stage and beyond ensuring consistent organization of multi-track audio in the production of each song, and that the correct mappings and labelling propagates throughout the process through to the eventual archiving of song data.

Recording and Evaluating Takes

The band make several attempts to perform each song, with each attempt called a 'take'. The DAW is left in record mode to capture takes in series, as if a tape machine were running, so that the flow of performances are uninterrupted. The aim of this approach is to record a take that is free from musical errors with the appropriate musicality and energy, which requires careful monitoring and evaluation in real-time (Extract 2).

Extract 2. Monitoring and Evaluating takes

The band are performing Sharp Dressed Man by ZZ Top, while the recording engineer (Paul) is monitoring from the control room. Dialogue is via talkback between the guitarist (Richard), the band, and Paul.

             //A mistake is made in the first guitar solo//

Richard: Sorry! Ready, straight in! (counts-in the band to restart the song)

Paul: (Into TB mic) Whoa! One second, just watch your speed (tempo) a bit, it was starting to race a little bit in that song [puts TB mic down]

Richard: (partly inaudible: gives directions to the drummer, counts-in) 1 – 2 – 3 – 4…

    //The band play another take of Sharp Dressed Man and three mistakes are made in guitar solo, the band discuss this then attempt two more takes of the guitar solo section//

Richard: (song ends) I think that one was alright, wasn't it?

Paul: Yeah, I think what I'll probably end up doing is take the last chunk of the solo that (was) good, but put it into the previous take … where there was a bum note, because the ending of the first take … was better. … But yeah, but I've got to basically fix that.

In lieu of taking notes about each take, the recording engineer's configuration captures the talkback microphones as part of the multi-track audio for each song, enabling the songs to be annotated with voice notes. In Extract 2 above, the members' collaborative conversations are captured directly from the flow of work, providing the recording engineer with a record of the production decisions made in situ that can be referred to in later processes: in this example, the decision to construct the song from different takes in the editing and mixing process following the recording session.

The Rough Mix

The rough mix provides a representation of the final product where further evaluation of the recorded songs are required. In this study scenario a rough mix is done for this reason, although it is done ad hoc in response to a critique of the sound from one of the band members. Nonetheless, the recording engineer is able to draw upon the contingencies of the setup that provide for the mixing stage, such as the labelling and organization of the multi-track audio, in order to accomplish the rough mix. In our study, this proved to be a useful collaborative resource as it satisfied the concerns of the band members about the quality of the production, however, in doing so it did impact the planned workflow and the recording time available in the studio.

4.3   Day 3: Overdubbing *(3.5 h Observed)*

Overdubbing involves layering instrumental and vocal performances over the songs created in the recording stage, in order to add new musical parts, or to double up or 'thicken' existing musical parts. This stage might be thought of as a 'workflow within a workflow' as it requires its own setup stage, to prepare for recording the overdubs (Fig. 6).

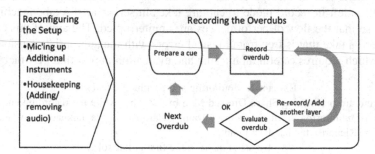

Fig. 6. The workflow in the overdubbing stage

Setting up requires adapting the recording configuration, firstly, to accommodate new instrumentation, and secondly, for 'housekeeping' to remove and reallocate redundant resources. This is particularly onerous task as reconfigurations cannot be applied globally to existing song data in the DAW meaning that each song must be manually recalled, reconfigured, and saved as a new version.

While similar in several ways to the recording stage, the critical difference in the overdubbing stage is that activities require interplay with pre-recorded song material and so the process begins with establishing musical cues to lead-in the musicians' performance at certain points in the song, for example where backing vocals are only sung on the chorus. So follows a process of establishing a cue point; recording the performance; collaboratively evaluating the performance; and, in some cases, experimenting with multiple layers of sound.

5 Discussion

As we have hopefully demonstrated from this study report, music production is a domain in which tensions exist between the art and the technologies of production, which in turn present several technical challenges. In order to address this, our study report focuses on workflows of recording studio production and features potential places for intervention with intelligent production tools that allow more control over the creative process.

For example, mapping and labelling audio is clearly an important aspect of music production work. It organizes audio spatially and annotates the configuration with key information that not only provides a retrospective account of the work done, but also prospectively provides the information to inform future activities (instrument types and recording methods). Automated labelling using instrument recognition has already been demonstrated as a result of this study [20], but could be taken further to relieve the repetition of duplicating labelling between the real and virtual production environments. It may be possible, for example, to retrofit analogue equipment with displays to transfer the digital labels to physical equipment, or alternatively transfer physical inscriptions to the digital domain via object character recognition technologies.

Conceptually, spill (or crosstalk) detection might also be a useful tool in the set-up process. DSP prototypes exist for cross-talk reduction in recorded material [39] and so applying this technology to real-time activities could be of significant utility. Using this application to 'cancel out' spill, however, could conceivably encourage bad recording practices and so might be better designed as an assistive technology to support the set-up process, for example finding the optimal positioning of instruments, microphones, and, crucially, performers.

The creation of voice annotations in the process also opens up hitherto unconceived possibility for the intervention of intelligent speech agents to automate the documentation of relevant production information, such as the evaluation of takes or editing decisions made in situ. Similarly, music structure analysis [18] might also be beneficial to the overdubbing process to identify transitional points in the music - verses, choruses etc. - that are likely to be cue points for adding new sound layers.

The study also highlights the requirement for a rough mix, which in our study scenario took the flow of work on a tangential course. This can, of course, significantly consume the limited time available in a recording studio and so the implementation of automated mixing tools, which exist conceptually [14, 15], has the potential to satisfy the requirement for a rough mix as a collaborative resource and smooth over the process.

Finally, we observe how templating the recording configuration provides a key processual resource for creating and managing song data, however, this approach falls short in the transition of those song data between stages of the process. This has been reported in our previous work [31] and contributed to the concept of the digital music object

(DMO) [20], which addresses a need for more flexible methods of generating, reusing, and reworking musical data in different production contexts.

6 Conclusion

In this extended abstract, we have shown that by using ethnographic methods that we can start to unpack and pinpoint where in the recording studio workflow AI-based technologies and automation might be used. In using this methodology and basing our understanding on this empirical 'data' we are able to offer insights into the actual issues and sites of intervention (in the workflow) where AI can be used. The aim of our paper is to present some of our ongoing work and to present our findings to the wider community. This set of studies informs an ongoing set of research challenges that span the concerns of many in the music industry – engineers, performers, producers and composers in starting to really understand where and what technologies might be used in such settings. We hope that this paper gives an initial insight into this world and that our findings are of interest to a range of researchers in different research communities.

Acknowledgements. This work was supported by the Engineering and Physical Sciences Research Council [grant number EP/L019981/1] project Fusing Semantic and Audio Technologies for Intelligent Music Production and Consumption, and [grant number EP/V00784X/1] UKRI Trustworthy Autonomous Systems Hub (as part of the Creative Industries theme).

References

1. Kirby, P.R.: The Evolution and Decline of the Traditional Recording Studio, p. 438. University of Liverpool (2015)
2. Leyshon, A.: The software slump?: digital music, the democratisation of technology, and the decline of the recording studio sector within the musical economy. Environ. Plan. A. **41**, 1309–1331 (2009). https://doi.org/10.1068/a40352
3. Byrne, D.: How Music Works. Canongate (2013)
4. Hoare, M., Benford, S., Jones, R., Milic-Frayling, N.: Coming in from the margins: amateur musicians in the online age. In: Proceedings of the 32nd Annual ACM Conference on Human Factors in Computing Systems - CHI '14, pp. 1295–1304. ACM Press, New York, New York, USA (2014). https://doi.org/10.1145/2556288.2557298
5. Théberge, P.: The end of the worldas we know it: the changing role of the studio in the internet age. In: Zagorski-Thomas, S. (ed.) The Art of Record Production: An Introductory Reader for a New Academic Field, pp. 77–90. Routledge (2012)
6. Watson, A.: Cultural production in and beyond the recording studio (2014)
7. Bromham, G.: How can academic practice inform mix-craft. In: Hepworth-Sawyer, R., Hodgson, J. (eds.) Mixing Music. Perspective on Music Production, pp. 245–56. Taylor & Francis, Oxon (2016)
8. Moffat, D., Sandler, M.B.: Approaches in intelligent music production. Arts **8**, 125 (2019). https://doi.org/10.3390/arts8040125
9. Hawkins, J. V: Automating Music Production with Music Information Retrieval (2013)
10. De Man, B., Leonard, B., King, R., Reiss, J.D.: An analysis and evaluation of audio features for multitrack music mixtures. In: 15th International Society for Music Information Retrieval Conference (ISMIR 2014), pp. 137–142 (2014)

11. De Man, B., Reiss, J.D.: A knowledge-engineered autonomous mixing system. In: Audio Engineering Society Convention, p. 135 (2013)
12. Pestana, P., Reiss, J.D.: Intelligent audio production strategies informed by best practices. In: AES 53rd International Conference on Semantic Audio, pp. 1–9 (2014)
13. Pestana, P.: Automatic Mixing Systems Using Adaptive Digital Audio Effects (2013)
14. Kolozali, S.: A framework for automatic ontology generation based on semantic audio analysis, pp. 1–10 (2014)
15. Wilmering, T., Fazekas, G., Sandler, M.B.: High-level semantic metadata for the control of multitrack adaptive digital audio effects. In: Proceedings of the 133rd AES Convention (2012)
16. Kitahara, T., Goto, M., Komatani, K., Ogata, T., Okuno, H.G.: Instrument identification in polyphonic music: feature weighting with mixed sounds, pitch-dependent timbre modeling, and use of musical context. In: Proceedings of the 6th International Society for Music Information Retrieval, pp. 558–563 (2005)
17. Fazekas, G., Sandler, M.: Structural decomposition of recorded vocal performances and it's application to intelligent audio editing, pp. 1–20 (2007)
18. Fazekas, G., Sandler, M.B.: Intelligent editing of studio recordings with the help of automatic music structure extraction. In: Proceedings of the 122nd Convention of the AES (2007)
19. Hargreaves, S., Klapuri, A., Sandler, M.: Structural segmentation of multitrack audio. IEEE Trans. Audio Speech Lang. Process. 20, 2637–2647 (2012). https://doi.org/10.1109/TASL.2012.2209419
20. Sandler, M., De Roure, D., Benford, S., Page, K.: Semantic Web Technology for New Experiences Throughout the Music Production-Consumption Chain, pp. 49–55 (2019). https://doi.org/10.1109/mmrp.2019.00017
21. Barkati, K., Bonardi, A., Vincent, A., Rousseaux, F.: GAMELAN: a knowledge management approach for digital audio production workflows. In: Proceedings of the Artificial Intelligence in Knowledge Management Work. ECAI 2012, pp. 3–8 (2012)
22. Barkati, K., Rousseaux, F.: Considering music production and culture management as an emerging digital ecosystem. In: Proceedings of the Fifth International Conference on Management of Emergent Digital EcoSystems, pp. 45–53 (2013). https://doi.org/10.1145/2536146.2536151
23. Barkati, K., Rousseaux, F.: How to understand digital studio outputs: the case of digital music production. Artificial Intelligence for Knowledge Management, pp. 151–169 (2013)
24. Fazekas, G., Sandler, M.B.: The Studio Ontology Framework. Information Retrieval Boston, pp. 471–476 (2011)
25. Wilmering, T., Fazekas, G., Sandler, M.B.: The audio effects ontology. In: Proceedings of the 14th international Society for Music Information Retrieval Conference (2013)
26. Reiss, J.D.: Intelligent systems for mixing multichannel audio. In: 17th DSP 2011 International Conference on Digital Signal Processing, Proceedings (2011). https://doi.org/10.1109/ICDSP.2011.6004988
27. Palanque, P.: Engineering Automations, pp. 1–2 (2018). https://doi.org/10.1145/3220134.3223044
28. Thompson, P., Lashua, B.: Getting it on record: issues and strategies for ethnographic practice in recording studios. J. Contemp. Ethnogr. 43, 746–769 (2014). https://doi.org/10.1177/0891241614530158
29. Ronan, D., Gunes, H., Reiss, J.D.: Analysis of the Subgrouping practices of professional mix engineers. In: 142nd Audio Engineering Society International Convention 2017, AES 2017 (2017)
30. Crabtree, A., Rouncefield, M., Tolmie, P.: Doing Design Ethnography. Springer London, London (2012). https://doi.org/10.1007/978-1-4471-2726-0

31. McGarry, G., Tolmie, P., Benford, S., Greenhalgh, C., Chamberlain, A.: They're all going out to something weird: workflow, legacy and metadata in the music production process. In: Proceedings of the 2017 ACM Conference on Computer Supported Cooperative Work and Social Computing - CSCW '17, pp. 995–1008. ACM Press, New York, New York, USA (2017). https://doi.org/10.1145/2998181.2998325

32. McGrath, S., Chamberlain, A., Benford, S.: Making music together. In: Proceedings of the Audio Mostly 2016 on - AM '16, pp. 186–193. ACM Press, New York, New York, USA (2016). https://doi.org/10.1145/2986416.2986432

33. Brooker, P., Sharrock, W.: Remixing music together : the use and abuse of virtual studio software as a hobby. In: Tolmie, P., Rouncefield, M. (eds.) Ethnomethodology at Play. Directions in Ethnomethodology and Conversation Analysis, pp. 135–155. Ashgate (2013)

34. McGrath, S., Hazzard, A., Chamberlain, A., Benford, S.: An ethnographic exploration of studio production practice. In: Proceedings of the 2nd AES Workshop on Intelligent Music Production, vol. 13, pp. 4–5 (2016)

35. McGrath, S.: Breaking the workflow: Design heuristics to support the development of usable digital audio production tools: framing usability heuristics for contemporary purposes. In: ACM's International Conference Proceedings Series, pp. 130–137 (2020). https://doi.org/10.1145/3411109.3411133

36. Garfinkel, H., Wieder, D.L.: Two incommensurable, asymmetrically alternate technologies of social analysis. In: Watson, G., Seiler, S.M. (eds.) Text in Context: Contributions to Ethnomethodology, pp. 175–206. Sage (1992)

37. Pollner, M., Emerson, R.M.: Ethnomethodology and Ethnography. In: Handbook of Ethnography. pp. 119–135 (2001)

38. McGarry, G.: Studies of the Social Character of Metadata in Modern Music Production (2020). http://eprints.nottingham.ac.uk/60392/

39. Seipel, F., Lerch, A.: Multi-track crosstalk reduction using spectral subtraction. J. Audio Eng. 145(4), EL329–333 (2018)

Elicitation of Requirements for an AI-Enhanced Comment Moderation Support System for Non-tech Media Companies

Marco Niemann[(✉)] [iD]

ERCIS, University of Muenster, Leonardo-Campus 3, 48149 Muenster, Germany
marco.niemann@ercis.uni-muenster.de

Abstract. Traditional (news) media companies are increasingly facing rising participation in their discussion sections and a simultaneous surge of abusive contributions. Legally required to prevent the dissemination of hate and threats, manual moderation is an increasingly daunting task for journalists and part-time community managers. Consequently, many comment sections are closed for economic reasons world-wide. While there is ongoing academic and practice research on machine learning (ML) systems to detect abusiveness or hate, the focus typically remains on this limited technical task. Integrations into systems for practical community management are still rare. Based on eleven semi-structured interviews with experts of four German newspapers of varying size (incl. an observation of their working patterns), complemented by insights from workshops on community management, we could identify five major functional requirements for creating such integrated systems. This range goes from the need for increased transparency and controllability to better support for team-based community management. In this paper, we outline each requirement's origin and implications for the development of integrated, artificial intelligence (AI)-enhanced comment moderation support system (CMSS).

Keywords: Abusive language · Hate speech · Comment moderation · Decision support system · Functional requirements

1 Introduction and Background

Journalism and journalists have a long-standing tradition of serving as gatekeepers. They filter the plethora of events and information occurring locally, nationally, and increasingly globally, deciding on the topics worthy of being reported upon [3]. However, the journalistic self-understanding goes beyond gatekeeping and extends to the facilitation of discourse and public debate [14,19,21]. Hence, participatory formats such as letters to the editor have a long-standing tradition [12,19], providing room for otherwise uncovered topics, criticism and feedback,

© Springer Nature Switzerland AG 2021
C. Stephanidis et al. (Eds.): HCII 2021, CCIS 1419, pp. 573–581, 2021.
https://doi.org/10.1007/978-3-030-78635-9_73

as well as appeals and calls to action [19]. As recent studies [12] confirm, even in 2020, such traditional participatory formats are still popular and contribute to both the image and economics of the publishing outlets.

However, letters to the editors did not fully fulfill their intended deliberative purpose, as requirements in terms of form, time to publication, and interactivity are still high. The internet and Web 2.0 flattened communication hierarchies and eliminated some of the hurdles pertinent to traditional formats such as letters to the editor [3,21]. Many newspapers added comment fora and debate sections to their websites to use this new participatory channel, hoping for active and insightful discussions between readers [6,17]. The high hopes linked to comment sections remained unfulfilled, as abusive and uncivil behavior soon became a massive problem as acknowledged by academics [5,18] and journalists [2,8]. As a result, beginning in the mid-2010s, a growing number of newspapers decided to shut down their comment sections, reaching a closure rate of up to 50% in Germany [16]. Despite the positive economic impact of participatory formats, comment moderation is highly resource-intensive—often to the point that financial and personal resources are deterred from the core news business: article writing [4,9,13]. This effect was found to have a more substantial effect on smaller outlets [13].

Throughout the past decade, an increasing number of academics and practitioners have set forth to experiment with ML and natural language processing (NLP) to use these upcoming technologies to tackle abusive comments [7,20]. While the research stream is reporting continuous improvements, there are still open challenges: Firstly, many publications focus on the technical refinement of used models [11,25]. While work in this direction is crucial, it is challenging to digest standalone for all interested parties lacking experts (typ. smaller outlets). Even approaches geared towards better interpretability are still more technical demonstrations than integrated solutions [22]. Secondly, a large part of the published works are carried out by major online media companies, working on solving problems faced by their internal teams [27]. Lastly, the integration of the research work into broadly applicable solutions is still ongoing. While several tools set forth to improve the commenting experience, many of them are tailored towards the creation of improved, more interactive, and insightful debates [15]. The moderation perspective, especially the AI-supported one, is mostly neglected ([24] being one of the few exceptions). This leads to the conclusion that news outlets in general and small ones in particular lack consideration in the ongoing research efforts.

To address this extant gap, this paper's research goal is the *elicitation of functional requirements of an AI-enhanced comment moderation support system for non-tech media companies.*

The remainder of this paper will unfold as follows: Sect. 2 presents the research method chosen for this paper. The identified requirements are presented and explained in Sect. 3 before the paper is concluded in Sect. 4.

2   Research Method

To obtain the requirements presented in this paper, semi-structured interviews were chosen as the primary source of information. These are among the most common and suitable methods to obtain functional requirements [1,10]. Furthermore, they provide valuable additional degrees of freedom to elicit potentially unexpected insights in the young domain of AI-enhanced CMSSs.

In total, eleven semi-structured interviews [23] were conducted with journalists and community managers of four newspapers. Among these were two local, one over-regional, and one national newspaper with circulations between ~10,000 and >300,000 newspapers daily. The interviews were centered on understanding their current working patterns (mode of operation and central tasks to be supported) and probing how they could imagine an AI-supported CMSS to support their daily work. Each interview was recorded (*with the interviewees' explicit consent*) and subsequently transcribed for further assessment.

As secondary sources of information, two further commonly used requirements elicitation methods [29] were applied: Participation in journalistic workshops[1] served to get a better domain understanding. The goal was to uncover potential pain points by observing discussions without explicitly nudging the people towards algorithmic solutions. Furthermore, three of the participating newspapers allowed us to observe their staff working on daily community management. Here additional gaps and pain points of the existing software solutions could be identified—sometimes, the interviewees even remembered additional issues they could not mention in the interview before.

The collected data was subsequently structured, analyzed, and interpreted to understand the sometimes plainly stated but often hidden requirements towards a modern AI-supported CMSS. Identified requirements were initially validated through discussions with researchers working in the same field, and some of the initially interviewed community managers.

3   Requirements for AI-Enhanced CMSS

Based on the previously outlined information sources, we could identify five major requirements towards AI-enhanced CMSS (for non-tech media companies). Each of them subsumes multiple minor requirements, which have the same overarching goal and were clustered accordingly. This paper's focus will be on functional aspects of a CMSS, as many non-functional requirements for platform software (e.g., performance, usability, ...) are domain-independent and already covered in other outlets. Each identified requirement will be described in more detail in the following subsections, enhanced by direct and indirect quotes. The interviews have been conducted in German, and the author translated quotes.

---

[1] Three workshops were visited before the COVID-19 pandemic. The first two had ~20 participants—mostly journalists and newspaper personnel—and centered around hate speech prosecution and management. The third had ~10 participants and centered on hate speech labeling and detection.

3.1   Team Moderation and Review Functionality

In nine out of eleven interviews, the massive team focus in practical community management is the most prominent insight. Currently, research on AI-supported community management mainly focuses on supporting individuals. However, there has been little indication so far that community management might require systems/CMSS to facilitate exchange and group work as well. Some interviewees stated that 70% of the comments get moderated individually, while for "the remaining 30%, I will ask my colleagues again". Other team leaders explicitly state that they "regularly encourage employees to share when there is a case that is not clear". As of now, many community managers have to copy comments to external tools (primarily *Slack*) to discuss them—typically lacking whatever meta-information their moderation system provides. What is missing is described as means to "Forwarding [comments to] different employees who can then take it over", as well as functionalities to enrich comments with internal information (e.g., about the user, or interpretations of the comment itself).

REQ$_1$: A CMSS should provide community managers with the ability to assign comments to other peers for review or assessment. This should be accompanied by a functionality to leave internal feedback for comments.

3.2   Interpretability and Transparency

More commonly reflected in extant literature was the demand for interpretability and transparency of AI and system decisions [26]. Six of our interviewees were concerned about having software "that [...] only tells me: delete the [comment/person]". From the interviews and observations, it could be derived that community managers are scanning and searching for specific keywords to make first decisions; as one interviewee put it: "We look of course for keywords that might be relevant". They would appreciate a solution that highlights words or passages that an algorithm deemed problematic to ensure a better and faster understanding of why a particular action should be taken with a comment. This increased transparency would also better accommodate the general moderation process, which the interviewees describe as "relatively fast scanning" with a targeted processing time per comment of sometimes 5 s and less. An alternative approach suggested is sorting of comments based on their criticality to ensure faster processing of out-of-control situations. Furthermore, interpretable cues and efforts towards transparency should be well thought-through, as one interviewee explicitly stated that poorly understandable flags and annotations get ignored.

REQ$_2$: A CMSS should always provide explanations for decisions or assessments created by the AI. This should be done through visual cues such as highlighting specific words or parts and providing additional information.

3.3   Control and Correction of Machine Decisions

Confronting community managers with ideas for the (semi-)automatic detection and deletion (or blocking) of comments typically led to reserved reactions. Many of our interviewees only interacted—if at all—with blacklists as automated solutions where they correctly observed that the context might get lost: "the danger: You have to see the whole context, how people write or use words of course." Even after receiving additional information and understanding that there are more sophisticated and context-aware means to classify comments, one typical answer to the question of whether they would trust the machine was: "Yes, [it] is hard." However, this does not indicate a rejection of machine support, as less intrusive measures were welcomed: "Where things are flagged as being of varying degrees of sensitivity. Something like that would be really good, I think". The majority of the interviewees agree more or less plainly that automation is desirable but not without human control. One participant summarized it as: "So security mechanisms, but otherwise, yes, I think that would be a good thing."

REQ$_3$: A CMSS should provide community managers with decisions in the form of suggestions that humans can override.

3.4 Decision Support Beyond AI

Throughout the interviews, one pattern kept reappearing: People explicitly asked for or outlined the desire for decision support mechanisms beyond an AI supporting them in comment assessment. Two of our interviewed newspapers are already using systems that provide them with information about the commenters: e.g., their registration time, number of comments, number of flags/interventions. They state that such information helps them interpret comments, make complex decisions, and justify them when comments themselves might be disputable. Another three interviewees of newspapers with nickname registrations listed the detection of duplicates as a pressing concern. The inability to permanently lock out people creates situations where comments have to be repeatedly assessed, taking away time from other tasks. Last but not least, an overview of moderation actions was described as a potential feature. Based on the impressions from some ticket-based systems, community managers see value in getting information on whether a comment—or even the overarching article and its thread—has already been dealt with. The described benefits include being able to track decisions even after users change comments and linked to REQ_1 to see whether colleagues already interacted with an ongoing discussion.

REQ$_4$: A CMSS should provide supportive information beyond AI decisions. This entails elements such as user statistics and an overview of moderation actions for comments and stories.

3.5 Openness of the System

The last aspect that kept reoccurring throughout the interviews can be summarized as the openness of the CMSS. Most of the newspapers we talked with operate multiple commenting opportunities (on-site, on Social Media, . . .) and/or are linked to other newspapers under one overarching corporation. Much of this has grown historically. Community managers often have to switch between systems which creates additional overhead, to the point of losing track of the accounts they have to check. Hence, four interviewees stated they would prefer to have one system to aggregate all the moderation work ("there are two systems now [...] would be cooler, of course, if it were just one system."). One outlet already uses a ticket system (*swat.io*) aggregating several sources, giving away a further requirement for this capability: CMSS cannot be content management systems at the same time but have to be independent.

Beyond this, three of the four outlets work with proprietary systems, and the two larger ones face issues regarding the extensibility and configuration of their systems. There were ongoing efforts to change to an open source system to gain additional degrees of freedom in one case. This does not only pertain to the overall CMSS but also the included AI aspect. While community managers are aware of existing proprietary solutions, they doubt their worth or that it even is a working AI system ("if it is real AI"). This indicates a so far uncovered gap: Academia can offer thoroughly evaluated AI models. There are available model registries [28]. However, no CMSS systems allow for configurable models. Thought further, even external model management and maintenance is up for consideration as most outlets lack internal knowledge to maintain an AI component.

REQ5: A CMSS should provide the ability to be extended and enhanced by its users (without paying any software vendor). The AI part should be externally manageable to ensure being up-to-date and avoid black box models.

4   Discussion and Conclusion

This study aims to provide requirements for CMSS that can provide AI support to non-tech media companies. Despite the plethora of extant AI models, there is still little knowledge on how to provide software artifacts that are of practical use to community managers in non-tech media companies.

Based on eleven interviews with community managers and journalists of four German newspapers, five central requirements have been identified and outlined in this paper. An overview of the requirements and associated cluster elements is depicted in Fig. 1.

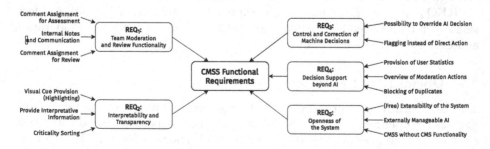

Fig. 1. CMSS Functional requirements and cluster overview

While there are systems fulfilling parts of these requirements, a CMSS adhering to all is unavailable to the best of our knowledge. Hence, our research agenda's next step is to develop a corresponding CMSS. With this software artifact, the requirements can be validated in a practice setting with our project partners (several German newspapers of various sizes). Based on their feedback, we expect to refine the identified requirements and complement them by additional ones emerging from the hands-on work with the artifact—which will again serve to refine the CMSS artifact. We hope to gain valuable insights into the acceptance of such systems in smaller newsrooms and which measures can be taken to increase the trust in both the system and the novel way of community management.

As a conceptual paper reporting about research in progress, some limitations remain: We are currently only considering the design of a CMSS, abstracting away all elements of such a system that would be commenter-facing. This is reflected in the exclusive consideration of the community manager's perspective. Communication and presentation to commenters and the generation of acceptance are issues to be addressed by future research.

Acknowledgments. The research leading to these results received funding from the federal state of North Rhine-Westphalia and the European Regional Development Fund (EFRE.NRW 2014–2020), Project: M⬤DERAT! (No. CM-2-2-036a).

Furthermore, I would like to thank Jens Brunk and Vera Steinhoff for their assistance in carrying out and transcribing the interviews used in this paper.

References

1. Agarwal, R., Tanniru, M.R.: Knowledge acquisition using structured interviewing: an empirical investigation. J. Manag. Inf. Syst. **7**(1), 123–140 (1990)
2. Bilton, R.: Why some publishers are killing their comment sections (2014). https://digiday.com/media/comments-sections/
3. Boberg, S., Schatto-Eckrodt, T., Frischlich, L., Quandt, T.: The moral gatekeeper? Moderation and deletion of user-generated content in a leading news forum. Media Commun. **6**(4), 58–69 (2018)
4. Braun, J., Gillespie, T.: Hosting the public discourse, hosting the public: when online news and social media converge. Journal. Pract. **5**(4), 383–398 (2011)
5. Coe, K., Kenski, K., Rains, S.A.: Online and uncivil? Patterns and determinants of incivility in newspaper website comments. J. Commun. **64**(4), 658–679 (2014)
6. Einwiller, S.A., Kim, S.: How online content providers moderate user-generated content to prevent harmful online communication: an analysis of policies and their implementation. Policy Internet **12**(2), 184–206 (2020)
7. Fortuna, P., Nunes, S.: A survey on automatic detection of hate speech in text. ACM Comput. Surv. **51**(4), 1–30 (2018)
8. Gardiner, B., Mansfield, M., Anderson, I., Holder, J., Louter, D., Ulmanu, M.: The dark side of Guardian comments (2016). https://www.theguardian.com/technology/2016/apr/12/the-dark-side-of-guardian-comments
9. Goodman, E.: Online comment moderation: emerging best practices - a guide to promoting robust and civil online conversation. Technical report, World Association of Newspapers (WAN-IFRA), Darmstadt, Germany (2013)

10. Hadar, I., Soffer, P., Kenzi, K.: The role of domain knowledge in requirements elicitation via interviews: an exploratory study. Requir. Eng. **19**(2), 143–159 (2014)
11. HASOC: Call for Participation (2019). https://hasocfire.github.io/hasoc/2020/call_for_participation.html
12. Hayek, L., Mayrl, M., Russmann, U.: The citizen as contributor-letters to the editor in the Austrian Tabloid Paper Kronen Zeitung (2008–2017). Journal. Stud. **21**(8), 1127–1145 (2020)
13. Hermida, A., Thurman, N.: A clash of cultures: the integration of user-generated content within professional journalistic frameworks at British newspaper websites. Journal. Pract. **2**(3), 343–356 (2008)
14. Juarez Miro, C.: The comment gap: affective publics and gatekeeping in the New York Times' comment sections. Journalism, 1–17 (2020)
15. Kim, J.: Moderating the uncontrollable. Intersect Stanford J. Sci. Technol. Soc. **10**(3), 1–9 (2017)
16. Köffer, S., Riehle, D.M., Höhenberger, S., Becker, J.: Discussing the value of automatic hate speech detection in online debates. In: Tagungsband Multikonferenz Wirtschaftsinformatik 2018. MKWI 2018, Lüneburg, Germany (2018)
17. Kolhatkar, V., Taboada, M.: Constructive language in news comments. In: Waseem, Z., Chung, W.H.K., Hovy, D., Tetreault, J. (eds.) Proceedings of the First Workshop on Abusive Language Online, pp. 11–17. ALW1, ACL, Vancouver (2017)
18. Muddiman, A., Stroud, N.J.: News values, cognitive biases, and partisan incivility in comment sections. J. Commun. **67**(4), 586–609 (2017)
19. Nielsen, R.K.: Participation through letters to the editor: circulation, considerations, and genres in the letters institution. Journalism **11**(1), 21–35 (2010)
20. Niemann, M., Welsing, J., Riehle, D.M., Brunk, J., Assenmacher, D., Becker, J.: Abusive comments in online media and how to fight them. In: van Duijn, M., Preuss, M., Spaiser, V., Takes, F., Verberne, S. (eds.) MISDOOM 2020. LNCS, vol. 12259, pp. 122–137. Springer, Cham (2020). https://doi.org/10.1007/978-3-030-61841-4_9
21. Papacharissi, Z.: Democracy online: civility, politeness, and the democratic potential of online political discussion groups. New Media Soc. **6**(2), 259–283 (2004)
22. Risch, J., Ruff, R., Krestel, R.: Offensive Language Detection Explained. In: Proceedings of the Second Workshop on Trolling, Aggression and Cyberbullying, LREC 2020, pp. 137–143, ELRA, Marseille (2020)
23. Robson, C., McCartan, K.: Real World Research: A Resource for Users of Social Research Methods in Applied Settings, 4th edn. Wiley, Hoboken (2016)
24. Schabus, D., Skowron, M.: Academic-industrial perspective on the development and deployment of a moderation system for a newspaper website. In: Proceedings of Eleventh International Conference on Language Resources and Evaluation, LREC 2018, pp. 1602–1605. ACL, Miyazaki (2019)
25. Vidgen, B., Yasseri, T.: Detecting weak and strong islamophobic hate speech on social media. J. Inf. Technol. Polit. **17**(1), 66–78 (2020)
26. Wich, M., Bauer, J., Groh, G.: Impact of politically biased data on hate speech classification. In: Proceedings of the Fourth Workshop on Online Abuse and Harms, pp. 54–64. ALW4, ACL, Stroudsburg (2020)
27. Wulczyn, E., Thain, N., Dixon, L.: Ex machina. In: Proceedings of the 26th International Conference on World Wide Web, WWW 2017, pp. 1391–1399. ACM Press, Perth (2017)

28. Zaharia, M., et al.: Accelerating the machine learning lifecycle with MLflow. Bull. IEEE. Comput. Soc. Tech. Comm. Data Eng. **41**(4), 39–45 (2018)
29. Zowghi, D., Coulin, C.: Requirements elicitation: a survey of techniques, approaches, and tools. In: Aurum, A., Wohlin, C. (eds.) Engineering and Managing Software Requirements, pp. 19–46. Springer, Heidelberg (2005). https://doi.org/10.1007/3-540-28244-0_2

Emotion Recognition via Sentiment and Critical Discourse Analysis in Catastrophic Contexts

Stefanie Niklander[✉]

Universidad Autónoma de Chile, Av Pedro de Valdivia 425, Santiago, Chile
stefanie.niklander@uautonoma.cl

Abstract. The study of emotions in a human computing interaction context has gained special attention during the last years. Different AI-based tools have emerged in order to smartly analyze content -and particularly emotions- in social networks with marketing, financial, and/or political purposes. However, effective emotion recognition is still a hard task due to the presence of ironies, sarcasm, hybrid languages, and argot in most people comments. Additionally, the presence of such components may be larger when the comment is related to a controversial concern such as the current coronavirus vaccine or political corruption scandals. In this paper, we explore the combination of AI-based and linguistic techniques, namely sentiment analysis and critical discourse analysis, in order to effectively study the emotions on social networks. We take as case study a set of important corruption episodes occurred in Chile, which has internationally been observed as its corruption index has systematically been increased from 2012. During this period, different respected institutions and companies have been involved in important corruptions cases. This concern in conjunction to other social aspects triggered the Chilean social outbreak at the end of 2019, which added to the COVID-19 pandemic have generated a very complex scenario for the whole country. This complicated situation has of course turned people more sensible and overreactive, making the social networks a proper test bed worth to carefully analyze. We illustrate interesting where the proposed technique combination allows us to properly identify people having negative, positive or neutral connotations related to a given topic.

Keywords: Emotion recognition · Emotions in HCI · Social sciences · Sentimental analysis · Critical discourse analysis · Artificial intelligence · Social networks

1 Introduction

Corruption scandals are increasingly frequent in the Chilean press. According to a study conducted by Transparency International, the corruption perception index remained the same as the previous survey. However, the worrying thing is that since 2012 there is a constant decline in the score. Moreover, the Chilean Center for Public Studies survey states that corruption is among the problems that the government of President Sebastián Piñera should devote greater effort to solve.

© Springer Nature Switzerland AG 2021
C. Stephanidis et al. (Eds.): HCII 2021, CCIS 1419, pp. 582–585, 2021.
https://doi.org/10.1007/978-3-030-78635-9_74

In Chile "corruption has not been an essential characteristic of the country's history" [1] nor has it been a great concern of the rulers or of society in general. However, corruption scandals began to come to light in the 1990s caused this issue to occupy space on the public and media agenda.

Due to this concern added to the Chilean social context where there is a social outbreak, it is necessary to study the news framing of the most visited online media in the country (Las Últimas Noticias). Based on the Critical Discourse and Sentiment Analysis, this research analyzes the media discourse on political corruption in Chile. The analysis will deliver the news frames of each of the news items. Further, this technique will provide us important information about who issued the message.

"A critical analysis has the fundamental objective of showing, through of discourse analysis, social and political problems" [2]. This procedure is possible since this technique allows decoding the ideology of the discursive producer from the value judgments issued in the informative note. This method studies written documents and is used in research studies when the purposes of are oriented towards formulating a general description based on inferences from the literature. The sentiment analysis determines the emotional tone behind each news frame.

In order to find out what is the media discourse that is transmitted to audiences on corruption, this article will analyze what is the journalistic treatment that the online newspaper "Las Últimas Noticias" gives to the subject. Specifically, the study will focus on the study of all the news related to corruption between October 2019 and July 2020.

It is useful to try to understand opinions, attitudes and emotions expressed in the news. We present interesting result, and we illustrate how certain discursive tools are used to understand and analyze the information disseminated by the mass media.

This paper is organized as follows: Sect. 2 presents the problem, results and discussion. Conclusions and some lines of future directions are given at the end.

2   Discussion and Results

There is a lot scientific literature on the concept of corruption from various epistemological approaches such as economics, political science, etc. However, some researchers maintain that it is a diffuse notion surrounded by a conceptual void. From a subjective perspective, a fact is corrupt when public opinion so decides.

The Critical Discourse Analysis of the corruption news frames in the analyzed period allows us to observe interesting findings. When we analyze the news of corruption in the newspaper "Las Últimas Noticias", 100% of them want to combat this scourge.

Fom de analysis, of the newspaper we observe that 37.5% of the news headlines are focused on ensuring that corruption does not go unpunished.

25% of them indicate that we must have zero tolerance for corruption and 16,6% of the news reports on politicians involved in corruption cases. 8.3% of them focus on reporting on methods to report corruption in Chile and another 8.3% affirm that this issue has become one of the most important for Chileans.

The remaining 4.1% report the constant struggle of both the public and private sectors to fight against this evil that attacks all societies.

In this way, after applying the analysis to the news of "Las Últimas Noticias", we affirm that the headlines published show a concern of the newspaper to combat this scourge. News related to different corruption cases was constantly published and the penalties received by the culprits were reported.

After applying the critical discourse, a sentiment analysis was carried out on the news headlines (via SentiStrength). Positive sentiment strength ranges from 1 (not positive) to 5 (extremely positive) and negative sentiment strength from −1 (not negative) to −5 (extremely negative). When we apply emotional computing we can observe that 70.8% of the covers of "Las Últimas Noticias" were rated as not negative (−1). 12.5% of the news items were classified as non-positive, 8.3% as negative (−2) and 4.1% as negative (−3) (Table 1).

Table 1. Sentiment ranges in the corruption news of "Las Últimas Noticias"

+5	0
+4	0
+3	0
+2	0
+1	12,5%
−1	70,8%
−2	8,3%
−3	4,1%
−4	0
−5	0

When we compare the results of the sentiment analysis with the Content one, we affirm that both analyzes complement each other. Although, these analyzes are unable to understand many of the expressions that are more dependent on certain contexts, the fact that they are capable of learning offers increasingly high margins of confidence in the results.

3   Conclusions

In this article we have studied the combination of sentimental and content analysis, with the purpose of enriching the analysis and obtaining more reliable, precise and accurate data. We have verified that the newspaper questions and criticizes corruption. In addition, with the sentiment analysis we were able to verify that the messages that were published on the subject were not as negative as we thought. To continue observing these phenomena we consider that it is needed to analyze more newspaper to enrich the research and obtain definitive results.

Acknowledgement. Stefanie Niklander is supported by Grant Universidad Autónoma de Chile/DIUA145.

References

1. Orellana, P.: Chile, un caso de corrupción oculta. Revista de sociología **21**, 257–272 (2007). https://doi.org/10.5354/0719-529X.2007.27528
2. Van Dijk, T.A.: La noticia como discurso. Comprensión, estructura y producción de la información. Paidós, Barcelona (1990)
3. Hodgson, Geoffrey y Jiang, Shuxia: La economía de la corrupción y la corrupción de la economía: una perspectiva institucionalista. Revista de Economía Institucional **10**, 55–80 (2008) (Colombia)

Exploring Korean Consumers' Responses Toward Over-The-Top Recommendation Services Focusing on YouTube Algorithm: A Text-Mining Approach

In-Hyoung Park⬭ and Jae-Eun Chung⁽⊠⁾⬭

SungKyunKwan University, Hoam Building, Seoul 51102, South Korea
jchung@skku.edu

Abstract. Since the COVID-19 outbreak, the over-the-top (OTT) platform, which is booming because of the increase in OTT service usage time owing to continuous lockdown, has induces the influx of new consumers and the increased consumption time of existing users through the recommendation service. Although the OTT service is drawing attention as the main video consumption channel, studies on the reaction to the recommendation service or the content from the consumers' perspective is remain insufficient. To determine the vivid response of consumers, we collected social media data related to the YouTube algorithm, which is a representative example of the OTT service, and compared the content consumed before and after the COVID-19 outbreak using text mining techniques. Contents extracted only after the pandemic were "Movie," "Fan-cam," "Musical," "Documentary," "Costume play," and "Diet." Moreover, before the pandemic, only one entertainment program appeared in the top 50, however, six entertainment programs were ranked in the top 50, after the COVID-19 onset. We identified terms representing consumers' cognitive, affective, and behavioral responses toward the YouTube algorithm and classified them into six categories. Furthermore, terms with similar meanings were identified, resulting in 28 categories. Network analysis was conducted to determine the relationship of the 28 categories previously identified. The centrality results indicate that consumers have both positive and negative responses to the YouTube algorithm. Through this study, we expect to understand consumers' reactions to the OTT platform's recommendation service, and to provide a guide for service providers to improve consumer satisfaction in the post-COVID-19 era.

Keywords: Post COVID-19 · OTT services · Recommendation services · Consumer behavior · Text-mining

1 Introduction

'Over-the-top' (OTT) services refer to online video streaming, wherein various media contents, such as dramas and movies, are offered via the Internet by third-party operators as well as existing telecommunications and broadcasting companies [1]. After the

COVID-19 outbreak in South Korea, the usage time of OTT users increased by 12.8% compared to that in February and January 2020, and the Korean domestic OTT service "Watcha!" also showed a 204% increase in usage compared to that in March and January 2020 [2]. Although OTT services have attracted the attention of researchers as one of the main video consumption channels, studies on consumer reactions to algorithm-based recommendation services are insufficient. Research on the recommendation service has mainly focused on technological, industrial, and marketing aspects and few studies have addressed it from the consumer's perspective. Therefore, this study examines the following research questions:

RQ 1: What is the difference in the content consumed through the YouTube algorithm before and after the outbreak of COVID-19 in South Korea?

RQ 2: Before and after the COVID-19 outbreak in South Korea, what are consumers' responses to the YouTube algorithms, and what are the relationships between the reactions?

2 Literature Review

2.1 OTT Service Platform

OTT Service. This is defined as a service that provides internet-based video and broadcasting content that can be consumed through various devices. The OTT service has the following characteristics. First, it can be used diverse range of devices. Owing to the popularization of smart devices and the development of the internet, OTT services can be used with more than one device [3]. This feature helps OTT service users to consume continuous content even if they change devices while viewing the content and allows them to consume different content through multiple devices simultaneously [3]. Second, OTT services are based on interactions between service providers and consumers [4]. As two-way communication over the internet became possible, consumers actively used the service through feedback and opinion presentation, beyond content selection and simple viewing, thus developing from one-way viewers to actual users [5]. The third characteristic is diverse content. In OTT services, the types of content have expanded, and simultaneously, the way consumers use OTT content has also changed. It has been used as a means of information acquisition and communication, apart from watching video content as in the past.

The importance of using the OTT platform is increasing as the time spent at home increases owing to the normalization of lockdowns. It has been confirmed that the spread of highly contagious or infectious diseases has a significant influence on changing consumers' media preferences [6].

YouTube. Youtube is one of the most successful OTT services. Owing to its open policy, anyone intending to upload video content can easily do. As a result, youtube is continuously building a variety of content that flows globally, such as 'how to' video (how to do make-up, cook, clean, etc.), or 'jik-cam' (a video that is filmed and edited by fans of a certain celebrity), which have not been covered in the traditional media [7].

2.2 Recommendation Service: YouTube Algorithm

Recommendation Service. The concept of personalization was introduced with the advancement of information and communication technology. The development of the Internet and artificial intelligence (AI) has transformed the media environment into a personalized user environment. Accordingly, it became possible to provide differentiated recommendation services based on individual consumer information, rather than providing the same services to all. This can satisfy the user's individual needs and, as a result, positively affect users' satisfaction and behavior.

Recommendation services that were used for the collection, classification, selection, and disclosure of information have been extended to the media field. OTT services, such as YouTube, also provide recommendation services based on different algorithms. Utilizing this service, YouTube has attempted to increase consumer viewing time because it generates revenue by inserting advertisements when consumers watch videos [7].

Existing research has mainly focused on identifying factors affecting these algorithms in the engineering field [8]. Although a few studies have examined users' motivations for the use of recommendation services based on surveys [3, 9] or focus-group interviews, further studies are required to uncover the reaction to the contents of the OTT platform and recommendation services based on actual users.

3 Methodology

Target OTT Service. We selected the YouTube algorithm as the target OTT service. YouTube has excellent accessibility as a free service and is the most consumed OTT service. Korean users' average viewing time is of 56 min a day [2].

Data Collection. To collect data that reflect consumers' vivid opinions on YouTube algorithms, social media posts on Facebook, blogs, Twitter, and online communities were crawled. Facebook was excluded from the collection due to the large amount of private information, as it is a closed network. Blogs, Twitter, and communities that tend to share their opinions on areas of interest and related issues with others were selected as data collection targets.

To collect social media data, "YouTube" and "Algorithm" were used as keywords. The collection period was from November 11, 2019 to December 10, 2019 (30 days) before the outbreak of COVID-19, and from August 31, 2020 to September 30, 2020 (30 days) after the outbreak. For data collection, 'Trend-Up 4.0' of Tapacross, a South Korean social media big data analysis company, was employed. As a result of data collection, 4,347 and 12, 644 data points were collected before the COVID-19 outbreak, respectively.

Data Cleaning. This is the process of extracting hidden meanings from text data. In previous studies related to social media posts, text-mining techniques have been applied to the analysis of consumer opinions on various products and services [11]. In this study, Term Frequency - Inverse Document Frequency (TF-IDF), frequency analysis, and network analysis techniques were used to analyze social media data. First, data irrelevant to the research topic were removed from the collected data, including advertising posts and article links. Documents such as 'Smart Store', 'Profits', and 'Photoshop', which were promotional documents related to the opening of YouTube channels, and those including 'Reporters' and 'News' were excluded as they were considered to be irrelevant to consumer reactions. Consequently, 3,516 data points before the COVID-19 outbreak and 9,924 post-COVID-19 data points were selected for analysis.

Second, among the selected data, data containing profanity, emoticons, abbreviations, and new words were modified or deleted. If such words are included, errors of misrecognized parts of speech may appear during morpheme analysis in the text mining process; therefore, a process of deleting or replacing words is required to improve the accuracy and validity of the results [10]. However, meaningful words that reflect the vivid opinions of consumers (e.g., 'Jik-cam' and 'hit the reality'), were not modified in order to reflect the consumer's reaction. This process was performed by the researchers manually using Microsoft Excel.

Third, to eliminate words that were irrelevant or meaningless to the research topic, a stopwordslist was used. Adverbs, conjunctions, and descriptive pronouns (e.g., 'this', 'that', 'and', and 'but') were designated as stopwords and removed. Morphological analysis was performed using R's KoNLP and tm packages on the corrected data. Additionally, words whose morphemes were not properly distinguished were processed using R's regular expression.

Process of Text-Mining. Morphological analysis was performed on the cleaned data. A morpheme analyzer was used based on SimplePos22 included in the KoNLP package, a Korean natural language analysis package of R. As a result of morpheme analysis, all words in the sentences were decomposed into morpheme units such as nouns, verbs, adjectives, and adverbs. For words that were difficult to analyze as morphemes because they were not registered in the Sejong dictionary, a morpheme dictionary was added using the MergeUserDic function. Thereafter, to grasp the subject of the content consumed through the YouTube algorithm, the nouns identified with the POS tag before and after the outbreak of COVID-19 were extracted and listed based on TF-IDF. In text mining, TF-IDF shows the importance of a word in a particular document from a group of documents [4]. Thereafter, frequency analysis was performed based on TF-IDF to determine the words that frequently appeared on social media before and after the COVID-19 outbreak. To analyze consumers' responses to the YouTube algorithm, the nouns and verbs that are the factors of the consumer's reaction are separated, and words with similar meanings are clustered to examine the contents efficiently. Adjectives are not included in cluster analysis because they are a major factor in determining consumer reactions [10]. In Research Question 2, we compared the cognitive, affective, and behavioral responses to the YouTube algorithm before and after the COVID-19 outbreak. However, because there were no significant differences in these responses between the two periods, we combined them for further analyses. In the next step, a frequency analysis for consumer responses was performed to extract words, which were then classified into six categories. First, they were classified into three categories: cognitive, affective, and behavior, and then further classified into two dimensions: positive and negative. In addition, to analyze the correlations between these reactions, network analysis was performed, followed by centrality analysis [10].

4 Results

4.1 Amount of Buzz About the YouTube Algorithm on SNS

Figure 1 shows that the amount of buzz about the YouTube algorithm on SNS has dramatically increased after the outbreak of COVID-19 in 2020.

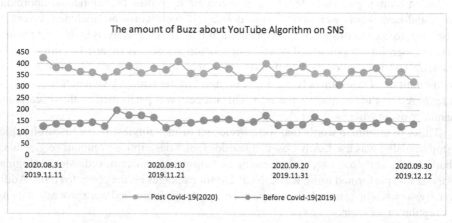

Fig. 1. Comparison of the amount of buzz about YouTube algorithm on SNS

4.2 Content Consumption Through the YouTube Algorithm

First, as shown in Table 1, we extracted and compared the content consumed through the YouTube algorithm before and after COVID-19 outbreak. Contents extracted differently from before and after the pandemic are "Movie," "Fan-cam," "Musical," "Documentary," "Costume play," and "Diet." These results imply that the increasing the number of consumers have indirect experiences through the movies, 'Jik-cam', musicals, documentaries, and costume play as recommended by the YouTube algorithms, because external activity restrictions and event cancelations hamper one from visiting movie theaters, visiting auditoriums, and travelling. Moreover, the fact that diet was extracted only during the post COVID-19 period is believed to be a phenomenon that occurs as the amount of activity decreases in proportion to the increase in the time spent at home. Moreover, before the pandemic, only one entertainment program appeared in the top 50; however, six entertainment programs were ranked in the top 50 after the COVID-19 onset. This reflects the consumption behavior of OTT service users to address the COVID-19 blues caused by the lockdown.

4.3 Cognitive, Affective, and Behavioral Response

Herein, we identified terms representing consumers' cognitive, affective, and behavioral responses toward the YouTube algorithm with frequencies of five and above and classified them into six categories (three types of responses (cognition, affection, and behavior)

Table 1. Content consumption through the YouTube algorithm

	Before COVID-19						Post COVID-19				
No.	word	TF-IDF	No.	word	TF-IDF	No.	word	TF-IDF	No.	word	TF-IDF
1	Pop	485.133	26	Promotional Video	23.724	1	Pop	1481.358	26	Highlight	62.886
2	Boy/Girl Band	190.587	27	Teacher	22.696	2	Boy/Girl Band	656.209	27	Radio	62.523
3	Pet	116.118	28	Drawing	21.505	3	Pet	354.575	28	I Pad	62.331
4	Animation	109.935	29	Knitting	20.703	4	Mukbang(food porn)	290.371	29	Munmyeongteuggeub(Youtube Channel)	60.486
5	Travel Back In Time	84.810	30	Oil Pastel Drawing	20.335	5	Movie	282.147	30	Legendary	56.592
6	Movie	77.610	31	Wedding Ceremony	18.398	6	Fancam	266.115	31	Twitch TV	55.086
7	Fancam	74.025	32	How to Knot	17.285	7	Soap Opera	248.538	32	Cross cutting	53.007
8	Climb The Chart	65.318	33	Learn Chinese	17.121	8	Game	231.397	33	V app	52.600
9	Singer	64.900	34	Twitch TV	16.672	9	Travel back in time	229.155	34	TicToc	45.321
10	Music Video	58.977	35	gong_sin(Youtube Channel)	16.129	10	Animation	215.068	35	Behind story	45.314
11	Mukbang(food porn)	55.470	36	Highlight	15.860	11	Singer	214.543	36	Challenge	39.755
12	Celebrity	54.305	37	Cross Cutting	15.366	12	Vlog	208.580	37	Gajjasanai(Youtube Channel)	39.288
13	Vlog	51.526	38	Vocaloid	15.053	13	Home Training	199.797	38	Beginagain(TV Show)	36.195
14	Classical Music	47.622	39	How to Clean	15.035	14	Climb The Chart'	185.558	39	Awards	35.005
15	Soap Opera	45.710	40	Cover	14.817	15	How to Cook	174.573	40	ASMR	34.057
16	Frozen	44.104	41	Legendary Video	14.014	16	Celebrity	164.519	41	Running Man(TV Show)	34.005
17	Trip	40.756	42	Dancing	13.440	17	Music Video	162.786	42	Negowang(Youtube Channel)	33.869
18	Headline News	39.010	43	Remix	13.440	18	Financial Technique	153.307	43	Infinite Challenge(TV Show)	33.670
19	How to Cook	36.591	44	Radio	12.957	19	Classical Music	144.937	44	Learn Japanese	32.016
20	Home Training	34.575	45	Time Traveling	12.544	20	ASMR	110.552	45	Collection	31.984
21	Game	32.906	46	Halloween	12.544	21	Musical	100.549	46	Fake News	30.493
22	Concert	32.566	47	ShinSeoYuGi(TV Show)	12.496	22	Trip	89.110	47	Documentary	28.925
23	Hymn	30.883	48	Review	12.288	23	Concert	76.513	48	CostumPlay	28.472
24	Financial Technique	26.184	49	Mimicry	12.288	24	Teacher	66.980	49	Organizer Decorating	28.450
25	ASMR	23.863	50	Learn Japanese	12.125	25	Diet(Loose weight)	63.254	50	How to Clean	28.153

* Yellow highlighted words are content extracted only after the COVID-19 onset.
* Green highlighted words are entertainment shows or channels.

× two of valence (positive and, negative)) Tables 2, 3 and 4. Furthermore, terms with similar meanings were identified, resulting in 28 categories (e.g., usefulness). One of the interesting behavioral responses is "reminding the past," implying recommending videos to remind users that they had enjoyed these videos in the past. "Digging" represents terms such as "playlist," "learn about" them, and "store" the videos, which suggests that users are "crazy about boy/girl band" depicted in the recommended videos.

Table 2. Cognitive response for the YouTube algorithm

Cognitive	Positive	Usefulness(31)	Convenience(20), Usefulness(11)
		Innovativeness(244)	A whole new world(156), smart(47), powerful(30), innovative(11)
		Customized(264)	Customized(142), similar(68)[a], variety(54)[b]
	Negative	Cannot understand(1312)	Cannot understand(1312)
		Not productive(15)	Not productive(15)

[a]Similar = similar to my taste, [b]Variety = various video clips related to own taste

4.4 Semantic Network Analysis

Figure 2 illustrates the results of the semantic network analysis based on the 28 categories previously identified in Tables 2, 3 and 4. Using UCINET, we calculated the degree,

Table 3. Affective response for the YouTube algorithm

Affective	Positive	Amazing(310)	Marvelous(179), amazing(120), thrilling(11)
		Enjoyable(210)	Enjoy(91), interesting(59), excited(46), happy(9), smiling(5)
		Good(65)	Good(65)
		Grateful(96)	Grateful(96)
		Healing(46)	Healing(46)
	Negative	Afraid(239)	Afraid(239)
		Irritated(144)	Irritated(66), messy(51), strange(27)
		Bored(73)	Bored(54), uninteresting(19)
		Ridiculous(69)	Ridiculous(42), unexpected(17), embarrassed(10)
		Dissatisfied(67)	Bad(35), not good(18), useless(8), biased(6)
		Regretful(23)	Hit with reality(23)

Table 4. Behavioral response for the YouTube algorithm

Behavioural	Positive	Intention for continued use (3608)	Follow(1918), keep using(1560), join the YouTube Premium service(59), look forward to(37), play on repeat(34)
		Choose (414)	Choose(293), search for(81), encounter(40)
		Reminding the past(383)	Remind(209), travel back in time(174)
		Digging(635)	Crazy about boy(girl) band(255), digging(163), making a playlist(134), Learn about(72), store(11)
		Share the taste(19)	Share the taste(19)
		Sleep with algorithm(87)	Fall a sleep(58), sleep algorithm on(29)
		Stuck at home(17)	Stuck at home(17)
	Negative	Switch(299)	Stop using(166), change(133)
		Obsessed(647)	Obsessed(623), carried away by(24)
		Time killing(285)	Stay up all night(181), using algorithm endlessly(79), space out(14), lay Around(11)
		Postpone own work(34)	Postpone(34)
		Got a spoiler(128)	Got a spoiler(128)

betweenness, closeness and eigenvector centralities of each category based on semantic network analysis, as shown in Table 5. Degree centrality indicates the associations that are central to the network [12]. Similarly, eigenvector centrality refers to a word's overall location and importance in relation to other words in the semantic network [12]. The results of degree and eigenvector centralities indicate "intention for continued use" and "cannot understand" as the two most central words. Thus, these terms are important responses to the YouTube algorithm because they most frequently appear with other responses in the text.

Betweenness centrality calculates the degree of centrality between words. The larger the betweenness centrality of a word, the more it serves as a bridge between different words [13]. Closeness centrality indicates how close each word is to other words in the network [13]. Table 5 represents "healing" and "good" as high betweenness and closeness centralities. Thus, it appears that "healing" and "good" are key issues and reactions to the YouTube algorithm that have the greatest influence on the formation of the meaning of the entire network.

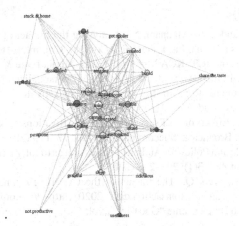

* using=intention for continued use; remind = reminding the past; sleep = sleep with algorithm; postpone = postpone own work
** The larger the size of each node, the higher the degree centrality is, and the node color represents the between centrality, high in the order of red, orange, yellow, and white.

Fig. 2. Results of social network analysis

Table 5. Each node of centrality

Node	degree (mean: 0.346560847)	betweenness (mean: 11.731314420)	closeness (mean: 0.010165088)	eigenvector (mean: 0.041410784)
intention for continued use	1	2	0.011627907	1
cannot understand	1	0	0.011235955	0.920363195
obsessed	0.888888889	2.25	0.0125	0.498012215
healing	0.592592593	50.62460317	0.019230769	0.048896645
good	0.666666667	39.82943723	0.018867925	0.047680076

*Table has shortened because of the page limitation.

5 Implications

In the post-COVID-19 era, as the lock-down period increases, the time spent on OTT services increases. To enhance consumer satisfaction, companies must prepare and manage an environment in which consumers can select, change, or maintain algorithms according to their preferences. Furthermore, for consumers who are wary of recommendation services provided based on personal information, the terms and conditions, and amendments thereof, should be fully specified, and efforts should be made to ensure the consumers' right to information. Conversely, consumers seem to enjoy the recommendation service provided by the OTT platform; however, they need to cultivate the ability to select content on their own, recognize how their information and records are used, and be able to use the recommendation service selectively.

References

1. Madnani, D., Fernandes, S., Madnani, N.: Analysing the impact of COVID-19 on over the top media platforms in India. Int. J. Pervasive Comput. Commun. **16**(5), 457–475 (2020)
2. Ministry of Science and ICT: KCA Monthly Trends, Media Issue & Trend, vol. 31 (2020)
3. Kim, M., Kim, M.: Influence a study on the effects of personalized recommendation service of OTT service on the relationship strength and customer loyalty in accordance with type of contents. J. Serv. Res. Stud. **8**(4), 31–35 (2018)
4. Kim, D.H., Park, N.: Effects of OTT service users use motivations on satisfaction and intention of continued use. J. Broadcast. Telecommun. Res. **93**, 77–110 (2016)
5. Joo, C.M.: Rationale and Policy for Audience Protection as to Interactive Digital Broadcasting Service. J. Commun. Sci. **3**(1), 207–238 (2003)
6. Chen, H., Qian, W., Wen, Q.: The impact of the COVID-19 pandemic on consumption: learning from high-frequency transaction data (2020). https://doi.org/10.2139/ssrn.3568574
7. Kang, M.: How YouTube became "GodTube", vol. 570, pp. 6–10. Korean Press Foundation (2018)
8. Chae, A.B., Lee, J.S., Kim, S.W.: A study on the recommendation method to induce users' participation of video watching in OTT service environment-focusing on the factors of gamification. J. Basic Des. Art **18**(6), 633–648 (2017)
9. Kwon, Y., Park, J., Son, J.Y.: Accurately or accidentally? Recommendation agent and search experience in over-the-top (OTT) services. Internet Res. **31**(2), 562–586 (2020)
10. Jung, M., Lee, Y.L., Yoo, C.M., Kim, J.W., Chung, J.E.: An exploratory study on consumers' responses to mobile payment service focused on Samsung Pay. J. Digit. Converg. **17**(1), 9–27 (2019)
11. Jo, T.H.: Concepts and applications of text mining. J. Sci. Technol. Knowl. Infrastruct. **5**, 76–85 (2001)
12. Jiang, K., Anderton, B., Ronald, P., Barnett, G.: Semantic network analysis reveals opposing online representations of the search term "GMO". Global Chall. **2**, 170082 (2017)
13. Gensler, S., Volckner, F., Egger, M., Fischnach, K., Schoder, D.: Listen to your customers: insights into brand image using consumer-generated product reviews. Int. J. Electron. Commerce **20**(1), 112–141 (2015)

A Comparative Study of Language Dependent Gender Bias in the Online Newspapers of Conservative, Semi-conservative and Western Countries

Jillur Rahman Saurav[1], Kezheng Xiang[2], Nikhil Deb[3],
and Mohammad Ruhul Amin[2(✉)]

[1] Shahjalal University of Science and Technology, Sylhet, Bangladesh
[2] Fordham University, New York City, USA
{kxiang1,mamin17}@fordham.edu
[3] Murray State University, Murray, USA
ndeb@murraystate.edu

Abstract. Newspapers are considered to be the mirrors reflecting what is happening within different societies. Thus, analyzing online newspaper contents across languages can help us to understand the language-dependent implicit biases, i.e. gender bias at a global scale. Implicit biases occur when someone consciously rejects stereotypes and supports anti-discrimination efforts but also holds negative associations in his/her mind unconsciously. In this research, we present a comparative study of gender bias in the published news from conservative (Arabic peninsula, and Pakistan), semi or lower-conservative (Bangladesh, Indonesia, West Bengal, and India), and western (USA, Canada, and UK) countries. As a result of the study, we present the current scenario of gender bias in different occupations in the above-mentioned countries. We evaluate the results of computational methods in the light of recent literature discussing gender biases in the regions of our interest. Finally, we present a list of occupations in which gender bias is more prevalent in those countries.

Keywords: Gender bias · Language dependent implicit bias · Gender inequality in occupation

1 Introduction

Gender is one of the main dimensions along which we separate humans in society across the world. Men and women are not merely viewed as different; men and women, including in advanced developed countries, experience unequal treatment in many areas, with men consistently holding more political, economic, and social power [1]. Although women worldwide have made and continue to make tremendous progress in education, work, politics, and economics, sociological research on gender differences and inequalities highlights and reveals multiple forms of discrimination against women. One area of positive accomplishment by

© Springer Nature Switzerland AG 2021
C. Stephanidis et al. (Eds.): HCII 2021, CCIS 1419, pp. 595–602, 2021.
https://doi.org/10.1007/978-3-030-78635-9_76

women is that the percentage of women in the paid labor force has been continuously increasing, but a severe gender pay gap exists. Many sociologists believe that sex segregation in occupations is the primary cause of the gender pay gap [2]. One reason is that gender stereotypes still work against women when it comes to occupations. Women are assessed negatively because they deviate from the norm of dominant male culture associated with power and are therefore less likely to be chosen for specific positions and professions [3]. Consequently, it is essential to observe cross-national differences to compare discriminatory biases against women in conservative, semi-conservative, and Western countries.

Both overt and subtle forms of discrimination against women characterize the employment market. Using the metaphor of "blindspot," Banaji and Greenwald [4] demonstrate the ways in which hidden biases shape our perceptions about different social groups, particularly of women. Cecilia Ridgeway, who used an experiment to test a theory about how status beliefs are formed [5], finds that people differ in pay levels for men and women. Maria Charles also discusses the role of cultural beliefs about gender play in occupational sex segregation [6]. In particular, she argues that while we have seen a decline in views of"male supremacy," essentialist beliefs that men and women are naturally better suited for different things have persisted. Similarly, based on empirical evidence, Paula England demonstrates how pervasive women and men's segregation into different occupations [7].

However, it is important to note that the disparities in Western nations, such as the United States, is pale compared to those in other nations, where gender bias and the cultural devaluation of women are widespread. Sociological research looks at how multiple forms of discrimination can differ based on various group members. For example, in the US, the experience of a black female may be distinct from a white female or a black male. Similarly, on an international scale, we must deal with both global structures, systems, and practices, as well local contexts that define such discrimination. To be specific, feminist scholars from developing and conservative countries argue that the Western versions of liberal and radical feminisms may not apply to most of the women in the world because they stem from the experiences of white, middle-class women in Western countries. Thus, gender inequality, as well as gender bias, must be analyzed by highlighting multiple lenses. In a conservative society, intersections among nationhood, gender, religion, sexuality, and economic exploitation may work in tandem as a source of gender bias [8].

In this paper, we study certain occupations to reveal how gender typing occurs in selected countries' employment markets. Even though women continue to do more domestic work than men, women hold positions that are lower in status and pay compared to men in the employment market. Men still dominate managerial and professional jobs, but implicit biases for certain occupations against women also remain a defining feature of the employment market in those countries. Consistent with this research's findings, although the number of women in professions previously dominated by men, such as doctors, lawyers, engineers, etc., has grown in Western nations, a severe form of gender discrimina-

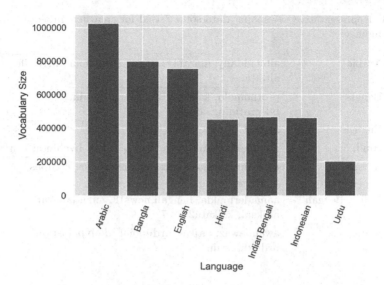

Fig. 1. The bar chart represents the vocabulary size of each of the Arabic, Bangla, English, Hindi, Indian Bengali, Indonesian, and Urdu languages. Here we see that Arabic has the largest vocabulary, while Urdu has the smallest vocabulary.

tion and biases against women exist. Cultural beliefs about gender differentially influence the career-relevant decisions of men and women. A significant part of this cultural belief is tied to religion's role in these countries [9]. It's thus no surprise that in countries, such as in the Middle East and Pakistan, where a conservative form of religion dominates most spheres of social life, implicit gender bias is higher there [8]. However, countries that adopted or in the path of adopting a liberal version of religion, such as Indonesia and Bangladesh, have less implicit gender bias [10] than those of thoroughly conservative countries. Moreover, since South Asian societies are typically similar in terms of gender bias and inequality, Bangladesh represents a similar form of gender bias against women as that of India.

2 Data Source

To compute implicit biases from the newspaper sources [11], we collected newspapers data from the online sources for the regions of our interest, such as Arabic, Bangla, English, Hindi, Indian Bengali, Indonesian and Urdu. Then for each of these languages, we created individual word embedding, representing respective words as a lower dimensional vector [12,13]. In our research, we kept the dimesnsion of embedding size as 300 following the popular implementations [14]. In Fig. 1, we present the vocabulary size for each embedding. To create the visualization plot, and generating a comparable results, we translated each of the

Table 1. Representative newspaper data source used for creating embeddings for different languages.

Arabic	albiladdaily, alarabiya, okaz, al-madina, alriyadh, alwatan
Bangla	prothomalo, kalerkantho, manabzamin, bd-pratidin, samakal
English	Statmt News Corpus [2018]
Hindi	abplive, amarujala, jagran, bhaskar, livehindustan
Indonesian	mediaindonesia, beritasatu, republika, kompas, jawapos
Indian Bengali	aamadermalda, bengali.news18, anandabazar, aajkaal, kolkata24 × 7
Urdu	awamiawaz, aajkal, urdupoint, dailypakistan, urdukhabrain

non-English words to English using google translator [15]. We have cataloged the data sources for different languages in the Table 1.

3   Methodology

Gender bias can be quantified reliably by using the contextual representations of words, i.e. word embeddings, created from massive corpora [16,17]. To know whether a word embedding has gender bias for a concept, in our case which is a word from the list of occupations, we compute the difference of associations of the respective word from male and female word groups. The representative example of male, female, and occupation word groups are shown below:

- **Male words**: he, his, boy, male, son, brother, nephew, uncle father, including the plural forms of some male words.
- **Female words**: she, her, girl, female, daughter, sister, niece, aunt, mother, including the plural forms of some female words.
- **Occupation words**: accountant, carpenter, clerk, dancer, doctor, driver, housekeeper, judge, librarian, mason, nurse, police, sailor, scientist, secretary, smith, teacher, etc.

Bias Computation: In formal terms, let x ($x \in X$) are words from the occupation group, X. And m ($m \in M$), f ($f \in F$) are the words from male (M) and female (F) word groups, respectively.

$$Female - Bias(x, M, F) = Association(x, \bar{f}_{f \in F}) - Association(x, \bar{m}_{m \in M}) \quad (1)$$

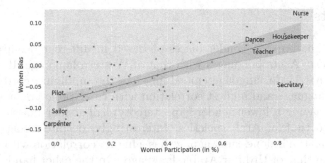

Fig. 2. Correlation between gender bias and women's participation in different occupations. This plot shows that occupations, such as nurse and housekeeper has more than 90% women participation, as well as higher implicit female bias. Similarly, sailor and carpenter having less than 10% women participation shows negative women bias or male bias.

Here, the above equation presents the female bias of the occupation x, whereas, $\bar{m}$ and $\bar{f}$ represent the centroids of the respective male and female word embedding groups. The associations or domain similarity can be measured using cosine similarity. We present the correlation between women participation in the workforce and women bias in Fig. 2.

Gender Bias Correlation Among Countries: To find the similarity in the implicit gender bias among conservative, semi-conservative and Western countries, we compute the Pearson's r correlation for each pair of the list of occupation biases of different countries.

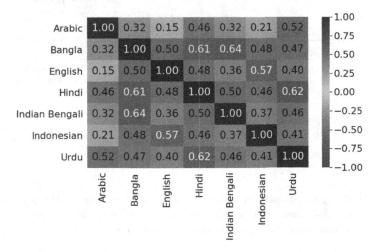

Fig. 3. Correlation of implicit gender bias in occupation for each pair of mid-eastern, Asian, and Western languages. The heat map shows that Asian languages have higher correlations for the implicit gender biases in occupations.

4   Results

We compare the implicit gender biases observed in different occupations from the mid-eastern, Asian languages with that of Western language. It can be seen from Fig. 3 that Urdu language embedding has the minimum correlation with the English language and highest correlation with the Arabic language, showing that despite having a lower gender gap, stereotypical gender biases in Pakistan are similar to that of Arab societies. Interestingly, despite being the largest Muslim nation, the Indonesian language has a higher correlation with the English language than that of Urdu or Arabic language. On the other hand, the Bangla language still has a higher correlation to the diverse languages of surrounding societies such as Hindi and the Indian Bengali language.

As word embedding represent each word using a lower dimensional representations, the bias computations depend on the quality of the underlying embedding, which in turn depend on the size of corpora from which the embedding was generated. This is why, the female-bias that we computed from the news sources are not a straight-forward measure of implicit gender bias, but a very good estimation of the gender gap inherent in the society reflected from daily news. In Fig. 4, we present a list of occupations that resulted in higher female bias, i.e., nurse, dancer, and midwife among all the different languages. Whereas, the words, such as driver, inspector, scientist, lawyer, soldier, and doctor ascertained higher male bias.

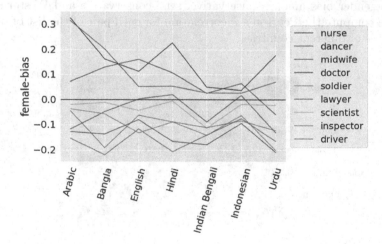

Fig. 4. Implicit gender biases are shown for some occupations for the seven different languages. The plot shows that nurse, dancer, and midwife has higher female bias, while scientist, inspector and driver has higher male bias.

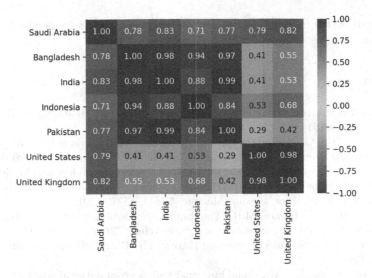

Fig. 5. The correlation between different countries using the gender inequality (GI) index of women share in parliament seats, female and male population with secondary education, male and female labor force participation. Here we present the GI index correlation among Saudi Arabia, Bangladesh, India, Indonesia, Pakistan, United States, and United Kingdom countries. Among which Arabic, Bangla, Hindi & Indian Bengali, Indonesian, Urdu, and English are the official languages of those countries, respectively.

5   Discussion and Conclusion

In recent studies, it has been shown that stereotypical gender bias in the English language is decreasing over time. But this is not true for all the other languages. In this research work, languages from three different parts of the world have been chosen in a way to analyze the differences among conservative, semi-conservative, and Western languages. Multi-lingual embeddings were generated to perform the bias analysis. The results reveal interesting observations other than that are visible in the gender inequality (GI) index. According to Fig. 5, Bangladesh, India, and Pakistan have the highest correlations among them in GI index. Whereas, implicit bias analysis shows that Bangla, Hindi, and Indian Bengali languages are highly correlated (Fig. 3), while on the other hand, Urdu shows somewhat different characteristics according to the implicit bias correlation than that of GI index. Implicit bias analysis for Urdu and Arabic language resulted in a higher correlation representing that the social practice as per their news articles in those countries is very similar despite their lower correlation in the GI index. Quite interestingly, although Indonesia resulted in a higher correlation with Bangladesh, India, and Pakistan in the GI index, the implicit bias analysis for the Indonesian language has higher correlation with that of the English language despite being the largest Muslim nation. We believe that this study will help to better understand the new development efforts we need to eradicate gender inequalities from the current world.

References

1. Staats, C.: Understanding implicit bias: what educators should know. Am. Educ. **39**(4), 29 (2016)
2. Dey, J.G., Hill, C.: Behind the pay gap. American Association of University Women Educational Foundation. 1111 Sixteenth Street NW, Washington, DC 20036 (2007)
3. Festing, M., Knappert, L., Kornau, A.: Gender-specific preferences in global performance management: an empirical study of male and female managers in a multinational context. Hum. Resour. Manage. **54**(1), 55–79 (2015)
4. Greenwald, A.G., Banaji, M.R.: The implicit revolution: reconceiving the relation between conscious and unconscious. Am. Psychol. **72**(9), 861 (2017)
5. Ridgeway, C.L.: Status construction theory. The Blackwell Encyclopedia of Sociology (2007)
6. Charles, M., Bradley, K.: Equal but separate? A cross-national study of sex segregation in higher education. American Sociological Review, pp. 573–599 (2002)
7. England, P.: The failure of human capital theory to explain occupational sex segregation. J. Hum. Resour. **17**(3), 358–370 (1982)
8. Shaheed, F., Equality, G.: Gender, religion and the quest for justice in Pakistan. Geneva: United Nations Research Institute for Social Development (UNRISD) and Heinrich-Böll-Stiftung (2009)
9. Koenig, H.G.: Research on religion, spirituality, and mental health: a review. Can. J. Psychiatry **54**(5), 283–291 (2009)
10. Islam, K.M.M., Asadullah, M.N.: Gender stereotypes and education: a comparative content analysis of Malaysian, Indonesian, Pakistani and Bangladeshi school textbooks. PloS one **13**(1), e0190807 (2018)
11. Caliskan, A., Bryson, J.J., Narayanan, A.: Semantics derived automatically from language corpora contain human-like biases. Science **356**(6334), 183–186 (2017)
12. Chaloner, K. and Maldonado, A.: Measuring gender bias in word embeddings across domains and discovering new gender bias word categories. In: Proceedings of the First Workshop on Gender Bias in Natural Language Processing, pp. 25–32 (2019)
13. Özdemir, P., Albayrak, T.: How to cope with second-generation gender bias in male-dominated occupations. In: Kitada, M., Williams, E., Froholdt, L.L. (eds.) Maritime Women: Global Leadership. WSMA, vol. 3, pp. 217–227. Springer, Heidelberg (2015). https://doi.org/10.1007/978-3-662-45385-8_16
14. Levy, O., Goldberg, Y.: Dependency-based word embeddings. In: Proceedings of the 52nd Annual Meeting of the Association for Computational Linguistics (vol. 2: Short Papers), pp. 302–308 (2014)
15. Google Translator. https://translate.google.com/. Accessed on 20 March 2021
16. Jones, J.J., Amin, M.R., Kim, J., Skiena, S.: Stereotypical gender associations in language have decreased over time. Sociol. Sci. **7**, 1–35 (2020)
17. Garg, N., Schiebinger, L., Jurafsky, D., Zou, J.: Word embeddings quantify 100 years of gender and ethnic stereotypes. Proc. Natl. Acad. Sci. **115**(16), E3635–E3644 (2018)

Pilot Study: Does Phonological Similarity of Words Enhance Humor in "Soramimi" Parody Songs?

Masaru Sasaki[1]([⊠]), Jiro Shimaya[2], and Yutaka Nakamura[3]

[1] Graduate School of Frontier Biosciences, Osaka University, Osaka, Japan
m.sasaki@fbs.osaka-u.ac.jp
[2] Graduate School of Engineering Science, Osaka University, Osaka, Japan
shimaya.jiro@irl.sys.es.osaka-u.ac.jp
[3] RIKEN, Wako, Japan
yutaka.nakamura@riken.jp

Abstract. Humor is essential to establish more natural and enjoyable human–computer interactions, and researchers have been working on developing a way to automatically generate humor. This study aims to explore a better way to automatically generate Japanese common humor "soramimi", and understand how the humor occurs. Soramimi is a type of parody song in which the original lyrics are replaced by different words that have similar pronunciations. Although a previous study proposed an algorithm to replace input text with homophonic soramimi text, the mechanism of soramimi humor is still unclear. Based on the incongruity-resolution model, we hypothesized that phonological similarity between the parody and the original lyrics enhances humor in soramimi. A subjective experiment was conducted in which the phonological similarity and humor of fifteen soramimi parody lyrics were evaluated. The results indicated that the phonological similarity of soramimi was positively correlated with its humorousness. Exploring other factors that affect humorousness and the development of an automatic generation system for soramimi lyrics based on the identified factors are topics for our future research.

Keywords: Humor · Soramimi · Incongruity-resolution model

1 Introduction

Humor is essential to establish more natural and enjoyable human–computer interactions [7, 8] and researchers have been working on developing a way to generate humor (e.g. [4, 8, 14–16]). Previous studies have suggested that the humor of computer agents can improve the quality of interaction with the agent [7, 8]. Ptaszynski et al. reported that conversations with computer agents expressing humor felt more natural and motivated the human participants to prolong the conversation [7]. Mashimo et al., 2016 suggested that information felt interesting and could be understood easily when it was provided by a system of two robots exhibiting a humorous dialog called Manzai [8]. The automatic

© Springer Nature Switzerland AG 2021
C. Stephanidis et al. (Eds.): HCII 2021, CCIS 1419, pp. 603–608, 2021.
https://doi.org/10.1007/978-3-030-78635-9_77

generation of humor is expected to be useful in involving the positive effect of humor into human-computer interactions.

Soramimi is a type of parody song in which the original lyrics are replaced by different words that have similar pronunciations. Soramimi has been enjoyed for decades in Japan through TV programs such as "Tamori Club", which introduces soramimi parody songs in which American pop music is replaced by homophonic Japanese sentences [12]. There is a type of soramimi parody song using only words in a particular vocabulary category (e.g. baseball players, footballers, stations, animals, and so on). This type of soramimi parody songs, for example, Japanese pop music sung only with baseball players or stations, are uploaded on the online video sharing platform and some are viewed over a million times. Exploring a better way to automatically generate soramimi parody songs can contribute to the development of entertainment culture.

Some researchers have focused on the automatic generation of puns (e.g. [1, 3, 6, 16]). Soramimi is similar to puns in terms of utilizing phonological similarity between different words, but the input and output formats of texts are different from puns. Soramimi is a sentence composed of words that are homophonic to the original, whereas pun is a sentence that includes a pair of homophonic words; thus, it is difficult to simply apply such pun generation methods to generate soramimi.

Few researchers have focused on Japanese soramimi generation. Sakakima et al. proposed the application of a Japanese automatic sound recognition system to English lyrics to generate soramimi [10]. Their system was not good at recognizing long sentences because of the instability of sound recognition in long sentences. Hajika et al. analyzed databases of English lyrics to generate soramimi and proposed using the edit distance of their phonetic symbols as a measure to be optimized, but they did not propose concrete algorithms for optimization [2].

In our previous study, we developed a prototype of an automatic soramimi generation system using words from a particular vocabulary category [11]. Our system transforms an input Japanese text into similarly pronounced word sequences of a particular vocabulary category using dynamic programming to investigate the suitable metrics on the parameters (e.g. the edit distance, concordance rate of phrase breaks) of it. In the previous study, we also investigated the types of parameters that could contribute to the subjective phonological similarity, but we did not consider which parameters could enhance soramimi humor.

In this study, we examined the characteristics of soramimi that influence its humor. We assumed that the incongruity-resolution model [9] can be applied to explain the occurrence of humor in soramimi parody songs. The incongruity-resolution model is a well-known theory that explains why humor occurs [9]. From this model, humor occurs when the incongruity of the presented stimuli is resolved. In soramimi, the phonological similarity with the original lyrics is considered to involve the resolution of incongruity generated by the unnatural use of words in parody lyrics. Thus, we hypothesized that the phonological similarity of the soramimi parody lyrics with the original lyrics positively correlated with the humorousness of the parody lyrics. In this study, we report the results of a subjective experiment to examine this hypothesis.

2 Method

In this study, a subjective experiment was conducted to verify the hypothesis that the phonological similarity of the soramimi parody lyrics with the original lyrics enhanced humor. In the experiment, the participants evaluated fifteen soramimi parody song lyrics regarding their phonological similarity with the original and humorousness, and then we tested their correlation.

2.1 Participants

A total of 56 college students (28 males and 28 females) participated in the experiment. The mean and standard deviation of the participants' ages were 21.5 and 2.0 years, respectively, and their minimum and maximum ages were 18 and 27 years, respectively.

2.2 Procedure

This experiment was approved by the Ethics Committee of the Graduate School of Engineering Science, Osaka University. Informed consent was obtained from all participants prior to the experiment.

To be presented in the experiment, fifteen soramimi lyrics were generated by converting five well-known Japanese nursery rhymes under three conditions (C1, C2 and C3). C1 and C2 were the conditions in which the weight of the parameter to increase the concordance rate of phrase breaks and that of the parameter to decrease the edit distance, respectively, were large. C3 was a condition that had in-between weights of C1 and C2. The original lyrics were replaced using only animal names based on the algorithm of the previous study, which could output the sequence of words to optimize scores related to phonological similarity with the input text using dynamic planning [11].

Each participant continuously listened to soramimi lyrics generated from a single nursery rhyme using the three conditions and ranked them across conditions in terms of phonological similarity and humorousness. The conditions were presented in a random order.

The following queries were presented to the participants to rank the phonological similarity and humorousness of songs: (1) Phonological similarity: "Please choose the parody lyric that you felt is the first/second/third most phonologically similar to the original song lyric", (2) Humorousness: "Please choose the parody lyric you felt the first/second/third most humorous".

This ranking evaluation was performed for each nursery rhyme. The nursery rhymes were also presented in a random order. Each soramimi lyric was sung by the singing voice synthesizer "UTAU-Synth" [13]. The default voice model was used for the synthesis. While the participants listened to the soramimi lyrics, both the soramimi lyrics and the original lyrics were displayed on the screen.

The average rank score of participants' ratings was calculated for each soramimi, and it was used as a measure of phonological similarity and humorousness for each soramimi.

3 Result

The correlations between the average rank scores of phonological similarities and humorousness for each soramimi lyrics were tested. The Pearson's correlation test revealed a significant positive correlation between them (Fig. 1, Pearson's r = 0.7849 and p = 0.0005).

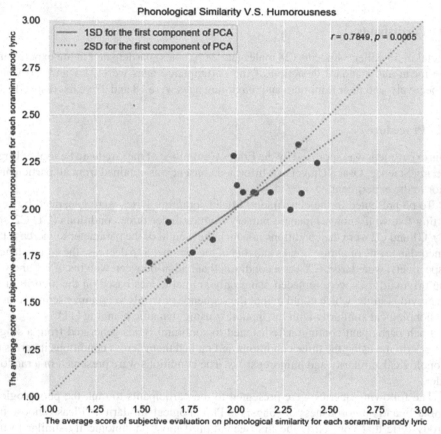

Fig. 1. Relationship between the average scores of the subjective evaluation of the phonological similarities of soramimi parody lyrics and humorousness.

4 Discussion and Conclusion

Our results implied that the more phonologically similar the soramimi parody songs were rated, the more humorous it tended to be. Thus, our hypothesis was supported. This result is consistent with our assumption that the generation of soramimi humor is explained by the incongruity-resolution model [9]. In other words, in soramimi, the phonological similarity between the parody and the original lyrics is considered to play a role in the resolution of incongruity. However, there are other possible candidates that caused incongruity in soramimi, and this study did not examine their role in causing incongruity. For example, the unnatural use of words in the parody lyrics and the gap in the meaning of words in the parody song lyrics and its original words might cause incongruity. The influence of these factors should be examined in the future.

The first contribution of this study is the proposal of a model to explain the occurrence of soramimi humor. Previous research has investigated the reasons for the occurrence of mishearing, but not the type of mishearing or humorousness of soramimi [5]. The second contribution is the proposal of a specific parameter to enhance soramimi humor, that is, phonological similarity, and indicating that the phonological similarity positively correlates with humor in soramimi through the subjective experiment. Although the previous study has developed an algorithm to generate soramimi, the influential parameter for humor has not been specified [11]. This study could be useful in improving the previously proposed algorithm.

However, there are other factors that can affect the humor of soramimi parody songs. Furthermore, in this experiment, it is difficult to conclude whether we were able to generate truly, not relatively, humorous soramimi parody songs because the participants evaluated the results by rank. These issues will be addressed in future studies.

The limitation of this research is that we presented soramimi lyrics that were composed using only animal names, and it is not possible to generalize these results to other kinds of words. It is important to verify that this relationship is met irrespective of the types of words and explore other factors that affect humorousness. Furthermore, the development of an automatic generation system for soramimi lyrics based on the identified factors is a future issue.

References

1. Binsted, K., Takizawa, O.: Japanese punning riddle generation system "BOKE." Artif. Intell. **13**(6), 920–927 (1998). (in Japanese)
2. Hajika, R., Yamanishi, R.: A study towards automatic generation of mishearing Japanese phrase from music lyrics in English. In: Proceedings of Entertainment Computing Symposium 2016, pp. 114–119 (2016). (in Japanese)
3. Hong, B.A., Ong, E.: Automatically extracting word relationships as templates for pun generation. In: Proceedings of the Workshop on Computational Approaches to Linguistic Creativity, pp. 24–31, June 2009
4. Labutov, I., Lipson, H.: Humor as circuits in semantic networks. In: Proceedings of the 50th Annual Meeting of the Association for Computational Linguistics (Volume 2: Short Papers), pp. 150–155, July 2012
5. Lidén, C.B., et al.: Neurobiology of knowledge and misperception of lyrics. NeuroImage **134**, 12–21 (2016)
6. Luo, F., Li, S., Yang, P., Chang, B., Sui, Z., Sun, X.: Pun-GAN: generative adversarial network for pun generation. arXiv preprint: arXiv:1910.10950 (2019)
7. Mashimo, R., Umetani, T., Kitamura, T., Nadamoto, A.: Human-robots implicit communication based on dialogue between robots using automatic generation of funny scenarios from web. In: The Eleventh ACM/IEEE International Conference on Human Robot Interaction, pp. 327–334. IEEE Press, March 2016

8. Ptaszynski, M., Dybala, P., Rzepka, R., Araki, K.: An automatic evaluation method for conversational agents based on affect-as-information theory. J. Japan Soc. Fuzzy Theory Intell. Inf. **22**(1), 73–89 (2010)
9. Graeme, R.: Developing the incongruity resolution theory. In: Wiggins, G. (ed.) Proceedings of the ASIB Symposium on Creative Languages, pp. 78–85. University of Edinburgh, Edinburgh (1999)
10. Sakakima, Y., Hori, K., Mizutani, Y., Hamakawa, R.: Automatic generation of Japanese which pronunciation is near from English voice file: mishearing automatic operation generation system. In: Proceedings of the 71th Symposium of Information Processing Society of Japan, Artificial Intelligence and Cognitive Science, pp. 101–102 (2009). (in Japanese)
11. Shimaya, J., Hanyu, N., Nakamura, Y.: Automatic generation of homophonic transformation for Japanese wordplay based on edit distance and phrase breaks. In: Stephanidis, C. (ed.) HCII 2019. CCIS, vol. 1033, pp. 61–68. Springer, Cham (2019). https://doi.org/10.1007/978-3-030-23528-4_9
12. Tamori Club, TV Asahi. http://www.tv-asahi.co.jp/tamoriclub/. Accessed 4 Mar 2021
13. UTAU-Synth, Ameya/Ayame. http://utau-synth.com/. Accessed 24 Mar 2021
14. Weller, O., Fulda, N., Seppi, K.: Can humor prediction datasets be used for humor generation? Humorous headline generation via style transfer. In: Proceedings of the Second Workshop on Figurative Language Processing, pp. 186–191, July 2020
15. Kota, Y., Minoguchi, M., Wani, K., Nakamura, A., Kataoka, H.: Neural Joking Machine: Humorous Image Captioning. arXiv [cs.CV] (2018). http://arxiv.org/abs/1805.11850
16. Yu, Z., Tan, J., Wan, X.: A neural approach to pun generation. In: Proceedings of the 56th Annual Meeting of the Association for Computational Linguistics (Volume 1: Long Papers), pp. 1650–1660, July 2018

Increasing Data-Knowledge Through Artistic Representation

Jayne Spence[1,2]([✉]), Ellie Schachter[1,3], Ayesha Saleem[1,4], and Bochen Jia[1]

[1] University of Michigan-Dearborn, Dearborn, MI 48128, USA
jespen@umich.edu
[2] Ford Motor Company, Dearborn, MI 48124, USA
[3] General Motors, Detroit, MI 48234, USA
[4] Quicken Loans, Detroit, MI 48226, USA

Abstract. In a data-driven world personal data is key to every business decision and strategy. Telling a story from raw data is a specialized skill gate-kept by graduate level data visualization education and occupational software. Lack of data literacy is increasingly perceived as embarrassing and detrimental to adults' understanding of the world around them. In this regard, an user experience case study was conducted to develop a method and tool to empower users to artfully tell stories with data. Robust human-centered design methodologies were employed to identify target users, develop deep user insights, and provide recommendations for a detailed design execution of a new creative data visualization tool concept. The results of this study demonstrated the potential of proposed tools in increasing user's data-knowledge through the medium of art. The new creative visualization tool developed could be further refined for children to increase their knowledge of the data-driven world and interest in STEAM careers.

Keywords: Data visualization · Human-centered design · User interface design

1 Introduction

Internet and connectivity are significantly and increasingly shaping human experiences with the world. Today, industries are collecting an exorbitant amount of data to inform strategic decision-making and to create personalized and contextual experiences for various users with digital products (Preoţiuc-Pietro et al. 2015). In this new connected world, it's vital to not only understand data concepts but also leverage data to skillfully communicate. The concept of "data literacy" is perceived as overwhelming, and even offensive, to many (Koltay 2015). Data visualization plays a crucial role in exploring data and communicating derived insights in an understandable way as "a picture is worth a thousand words". Data visualization requires application of familiar subjects, Math, Art, and Psychology (Aparicio and Costa 2015), but the barrier of entry remains high because it is not a part of early education. Art is a natural medium for increasing data-knowledge and practicing data visualization because it is accessible. Currently the skills for creating data-driven storytelling reside with professionals, but data-knowledge skills can be more widely shared through the medium of art.

© Springer Nature Switzerland AG 2021
C. Stephanidis et al. (Eds.): HCII 2021, CCIS 1419, pp. 609–624, 2021.
https://doi.org/10.1007/978-3-030-78635-9_78

1.1 Related Work

Within the realm of artistic data representation and human-centered data design, focus has been given to humanization and data literacy.

There is a growing movement to make understanding complex data more accessible. Humanizing data allows people to comprehend trends in the context of their personal experiences. Researchers created "data comics" to make graphic medicine more approachable, accessible, and relatable. The data comics created make understanding the story behind data more relatable and link users' personal experiences to the information conveyed. (Alamalhodaei et al. 2020) Researchers also noted the benefit of visual storytelling for populations with limited literacy or learning disabilities.

Many meaningful data visualization methods have been developed to convey information through relatable stories. Those are called information graphics. Jen Christiansen discussed the line between artist and infographer (Christiansen 2018). Christiansen identified a spectrum from figurative abstract representation to graphic data visualization. This continuum model is a useful mental model showing that even figurative models, like renderings of dinosaurs, use real data to inform their design. These abstract representations of data are used commonly in elementary education to convey information about abstract concepts to children.

Research on the data visualization capabilities of children has also shown that children are able to build visualization literacy skills from an early age (Bishop et al. 2019). Allowing children to explore their own ideas when visually representing a data set may lead to better understanding of how to represent and communicate using data, and how to use visualization to facilitate problem solving and decision making. There are three visualization activities for building visualization literacy skills: Reading Exercises: where children interpret a given visualization, Completion Exercises: where children fill-in or expand a given visualization template, Creation Exercises: where children create a visualization from scratch.

2 Methods

When increasing data-knowledge and practicing data visualization through art, an obvious tension exists between creating traditional and accurate data representations and creating artistic and abstract data representations. Through this study, human-centered design methodologies were applied to first identify target users, second to understand the prevalence of this tension for them, and third to design a tangible solution to relieve it.

There are six phases of the human-centered design process: Understand, Empathize, Define, Ideate, Prototype, and Test. These phases are not intended to be conducted strictly linearly, but instead cyclically. This is because new learnings will reform understanding derived from previous phases, requiring iterative cycles to ensure a tangible solution will deeply resonate. Figure 1 provides an overview of all methodologies applied throughout this research study, five of which are detailed: Empathy Interviews, Task Analysis, Ideation, Prototype Art, and Test Interactive Prototype.

Understand	Empathize	Define	Ideate	Prototype	Test

Iteration 1 Research Methods

Understand	Empathize	Define	Ideate	Prototype	Test
● Literary Review	● Empathy Interviews	● Define User Journey	● User Experience Ideation	● Create User Experience Storyboard	● Test User Experience Storyboard
● Develop "How Might We?" Question	● Affinity Diagramming			● Prototype Art	
● Mind-mapping project space	● Task Analysis 1				
● Benchmarking					

Iteration 2 Research Methods

		● Define User Interface	● User Interface Wireframing	● Create Interactive Prototype 1	● Test Interactive Prototype 1

Iteration 3 Research Methods

				● Create Interactive Prototype 2	● Test Interactive Prototype 2

Fig. 1. Overall illustration of study process

2.1 Empathy Interviews

Remote empathy interviews were conducted with ten subject-matter experts to understand key aspects and challenges for creating traditional data visualizations and for creating art. Of the ten subject-matter experts interviewed, one was the founder of a data-literacy start-up, three were data scientists with professional data visualization experience, one was an art teacher, one was a STEAM parent, and four were professional artists. Each empathy interview was conducted by three researchers that traded roles with each interview: a primary interviewer, a general note-taker, and direct quote note-taker.

The interview responses were clustered into fifteen recurring themes representative of this project space: Digital Literacy, Digital Devices, Data Visualization, Learning, Collaboration, Gamification, Data Privacy, User Interface, Inspiration, Ethical Representation, Exploration, Storytelling, Creating, and Process, and then were re-written as insight statements to better articulate learnings within each theme. Some themes were nuanced by subject-matter expert discipline, while others surfaces across multiple. Table 1 details five of thirty-four total empathy interview insights that were used to inform art creation method and the design of the tangible solution that will enable.

2.2 Defining a Target User

Many of the subject-matter experts interviewed enthusiastically considered themselves to be the target users for a tangible solution. Both artists and data scientists felt that a tangible solution designed to enable them to transform raw data into art would result in gaining valuable introductory skills in the opposing discipline and would help them think about their own work more creatively. One of the data scientists interviewed, who creates short data-literacy themed videos for popular social media platforms, explained, *"I wish I could get to the people, who in my opinion, need to be more exposed to data...but as it turns out my audience is mostly experts. They're the ones that most appreciate my content."* With this new understanding, researchers developed two user personas, a data scientist and artist, to keep their target user's knowledge, tool set, motivations,

Table 1. Example of empathy interview insights

Empathy interviewee	What they said	Insight themes	Insight statement
Founders of Data-Literacy Start-up	*"Another thing that I've found is that 'data literacy' is a touchy subject when talking to adults…when we go into an organization, and say only half your employees are data-literate, are we calling them not literate at all? And that's quite an aggressive stance to take…so maybe we should look at it from a slightly different angle when talking about it with the older generation. Probably 'data knowledge' works better than 'data literacy'."*	Data literacy, learning	"Data Literacy" is still a relatively new concept for many adults outside of Tech industries. Many even find it offensive as they feel they are being labeled as illiterate in a space. "Data Knowledge" is a more encouraging term for novices
Data Scientists	*"What I do try to teach people is that everything you're reading is an opinion, and they're trying to convince you, and tell a story to you. And you need to be able to detect that. Even when you first think of a question, by the way you are defining that question, you are already filtering and biasing yourself."*	Data visualization, storytelling, ethical representation	Data visualizations make data more accessible, but all data visualizations are both fact and opinion. Bias is everywhere
Art Teacher	*"Most are sometimes intimidated and afraid to make a mistake. Those that have a hard time understanding it will mostly not want to pursue it. When they are good at it, they feel very excited and want to do more projects with it."*	Learning, creating	When learning a new analog art concept, students are often intimidated and scared they will make a mistake

(continued)

Table 1. (*continued*)

Empathy interviewee	What they said	Insight themes	Insight statement
Artists	*"I can put something to the world and it's informed by my context, but someone else can look at it and be informed by their context. And you don't have any control over that."*	Storytelling	No matter their intention, artists don't have control over how someone interprets art. Everyone sees art in their own personal context

and frustrations at the forefront through project completion. With target users defined, researchers concluded that both data scientists and artists are passionate about working with a diverse digital toolset to create and communicate. Therefore, the new creative visualization tool concept should be developed as a user interface.

2.3 Task Analysis

In parallel to empathy interviews with subject-matter experts, researchers further empathized with target users by conducting a high-level task analysis. The goal of this task analysis was to understand the key moments a user would experience when translating raw data into art, which would inform the high-level information architecture of the new creative visualization tool concept. As shown in Fig. 2, several small personal data sets were recorded such as: coffee orders over a thirty day period and clothes hanging in the closet, then artistic representations of each variable and attribute within the data set were hand-sketched.

Fig. 2. Artistic visualizations of small personal data sets

2.4 Art Creation Method

As a result of the task analysis, researchers were able to define the key moments of the art creation method that the new creative visualization tool concept will enable. Users must first learn how to translate raw data into art. Second the user will identify the foundational data set: uploading an existing data set, creating a personal data set over time, or creating a new data set in one sitting. Third, the user must define the canvas size for their artistic representation. Fourth, the user must define relationships between variables in the data set and visual element type including the shape, size, color, texture, position. Some variables may be defined by multiple visual element types (i.e. in Fig. 2 above, latte is visually defined as a yellow circle) Fifth, the user must define how each variable will change across attributes, for example, defining the % of size, the color palette, or the texture associated with each attribute. Sixth, the user must create an artistic representation on the selected canvas from defined visual elements representative of the data set's variables and attributes. Seventh, the user may generate a key to decode artistic representation of the data set. Finally, the user must be able to share artistic representation with its intended audience.

2.5 Ideation

Before beginning to ideate researchers established three primary goals: 1. Enable the art creation method defined by the task analysis, 2. Appeal to both target users, 3. Identify aspects that should be nuanced based on the user's level of expertise in each discipline. With these goals, researchers created quick sketches, both hand-drawn and digitally drawn, to translate all prior insights into a number of diverse user interface ideations. Ideations ranged from a UI wizard designed to walk users through creating a piece of art step by step, the ability to set goals and earn rewards, randomly assigning shapes to variables for users to create a representative mosaic, a habit-tracking calendar that routinely prompts users to input data to create personalized data sets and collecting analytics from completed art pieces in order to generate an additional data set to create more art from. Each idea was vetted against each of the three goals, and prioritized by its feasibility, desirability, and viability. Prioritized ideations were incorporated into the user interface prototype to be evaluated by target users.

2.6 Prototype Art

Following ideation researchers further defined the art creation method by generating three pilot data-driven art pieces. Creating pilot art pieces enabled a deep understanding of how users would ultimately translate raw data into art through a user interface and ensure that the new creative visualization tool concept would be able to support creating something meaningful regardless of size or content. As an example, shown in Fig. 3, the largest of the three data sets detailed two hundred three Michigan wildflowers across twelve variables; provided by "Creating Sustainable Landscapes LLC" (2021). Because this data set can be categorized as large for this application, prior to beginning to visualize, researchers reduced the data set from twelve variables to the six variables that would be best translated into meaningful visual elements for this pilot: Wildflower Name,

Family, Average Height, Color, Months in Bloom, and Special Status. A researcher with professional design experience, representative of the research team's artist persona, leveraged Adobe Creative Suite products to create this piece which took over twenty hours to complete. Each visual element: shape, size, color, and positioning, in this piece is representative of one or more of the six selected variables. After completing the researcher reflected, *"As someone who comes from a design background instead of a technical background, in creating this piece, I came to know the data set much more intimately than I would have otherwise. And as a result, I was left with an artifact to be proud of."*

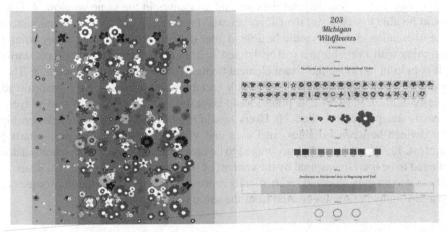

Fig. 3. Pilot data-driven art piece

The second data set used to create an artistic representation was a medium-sized data set exported from a researcher's Peloton app that detailed their workouts from January 2021 across four variables: Workout Discipline, Length, Instructor, and Calories Burned. A researcher with professional data analytics experience, representative of the research team's data scientist persona, leveraged Adobe Creative Suite products to create this piece which took eight hours to complete including their initial learning curve. Before beginning to visualize, the researcher also created a traditional data visualization of this data set, to strengthen their understanding. Each visual element: shape, size, color, and positioning, in this piece is representative of one or more of the four variables. The visualizations of this prototype art can be found in Appendix A.

The final data set used to create an artistic representation was a small, personal data hand-recorded by a researcher. The researcher took note of what they said out loud and to whom for five days in real-time. A researcher with professional design and data analytics experience, representative of both research team's personas, leveraged Adobe Creative Suite products to create this piece which took four hours to complete. Before beginning to visualize, the researcher translated their hand-drawn notes into a traditional matrix format digitally to sort the data and more clearly identify patterns. The visual representation was inspired by natural landscapes even though the foundational data detailed verbal communication. Due to its legend, the artistic representation can still be easily decoded. The visualizations of this prototype art can be found in Appendix B.

2.7 Prototype Art Insights

Twelve insights were gleaned from generating pilot data-driven art that directly informed the information architecture of the new creative visualization tool concept: 1. Users should be on-boarded to available digital creation tools if unfamiliar. 2. Before beginning, users should have a clear understanding of the scale of their foundational data set (i.e. 203 data points across 12 variables). 3. Users should be able to easily flip back and forth between their foundational data set and art canvas in the same window. 4. Users should be able to easily sort their foundational data set to begin to understand patterns prior to creation. 5. Users should be able to alter their foundational data at any point. 6. Beginning with a variable that will be defined by its shape is the easiest way to get started. 7. It is helpful to isolate the visual element being defined on its own artboard. 8. There should be clear visual indication of which variables and attributes have been already visually defined. 9. Every data point should be automatically saved on it's own layer to be easily independently edited. 10. Users should not be constrained to the relationships they defined between variables, attributes and visual elements as the piece starts to manifest. 11. Users should be encouraged to be creative. The artistic representation does not need to be literally inspired by the content of the foundational data set. 12. There are endless ways a data set could be artistically represented. It would be helpful for users to see a few unique examples created from the same foundational data set.

2.8 Interactive Prototyping

Researchers asked survey participants what platform they'd prefer to use to interact with this user interface. The majority responded with computers, leading the researchers to prioritize a web-based app interface over a mobile based app interface for the first inter-active prototype. Leveraging insights from all prior phases, researchers first sketched out a high-level information architecture. The prototype was made up of six distinct flows: No User Signed-In, Sign-In, Create Account/On-Boarding, Define Data Set, Create Art, and Settings. Because this is a new creative visualization tool, designing the No User Signed-In and Create Account/On-boarding flows was just as important as designing the Create Flow. It is a necessity to both entice and educate users before they begin creating. The Create Flow guides users step-by-step to define relationships between variables in their selected data set and visual element types, and then nuancing each visual element type by the number of corresponding attributes. Depending on the selected visual element type, complementary creative tools are available for users to define each visual element manually or automatically. Determining whether to define a visual element manually or automatically may be informed by a user's preference or familiarity with available creative tools.

Researchers used Adobe XD to first create a low-fidelity interactive prototype to easily navigate through the information architecture to refine. Adobe XD was then again used to create a high-fidelity interactive prototype. The high-fidelity prototype maintained a consistent style and theme throughout, resembling a real user interface as basic web design principles and accessibility considerations, such as recommended color contrast and text size ratios, were employed. The high-fidelity prototype also paid importance to educational content which was written with a sixth grade reading level to ensure understandability for most participants. To convey the Create Flow intent, researchers used "wizard of oz" prototyping techniques to simulate creating a piece of art that was previously created by a researcher during Prototype Art.

The prototype contained both an authenticated and an unauthenticated view of the app. All unauthenticated pages contained a sign-up call to action to encourage users to create an account. Creating an account is pivotal to save work and explore community inspiration. Unauthenticated pages also contained additional educational content to educate users on the different create methods.

2.9   Interactive Prototyping User Study

After completing initial prototyping, an online usability test tool (UsabilityHub, Collingwood, Victoria) was utilized to conduct user testing. UsabilityHub allowed researchers to conduct remote and unmoderated user tests to gain further insight into the prototype. Researchers set up a 32-question usability test that consisted of both quantitative and qualitative questions. The system usability scale (SUS) was used to quantify the usability of the prototype (Thomas 2021). Qualitative questions such as "how would you navigate this flow?" helped researchers determine user behavior and dig deeper into the attitudes of users and challenges of the prototype. Researchers asked users to elaborate on why they gave the rating they did. This allowed researchers to collect further information regarding usability and user experience. Questions such as the first click test, a test where a user is asked where they would click, was used to ensure the intended navigation was straightforward. Questions such as a 5 s test and preference test were used to determine the effectiveness of the copy and its role in educating users. Heat maps and tracking time taken on each task were collected through UsabilityHub to further quantify users' understanding. At the prototype's home interface, found in Appendix C, all participants gathered that the web-based application is a tool to create art and that the art would utilize data as an input. When asked where they would click to being, most participants clicked on "sample data" or "tutorials".

The average score for "Creating an account was easy to do" was 6.0 on a 7-point Likert scale. Users commented that they would like a confirmation page to verify successful sign-up and would like to be directed to a tutorial after completing the sign-up process. Users commented that the information about data should be a separate flow from the sign-up process.

When asked to differentiate between Sample Data, Data Diary, and Upload Data users were not clear on how these three features should function. There is no clear mental model for the users to reference when trying to understand these three functions. When asked to rate the level of understanding the differences between the three methods of creation the average answer was 5.0 out of a 7-point Likert scale. The three types of data entry must be simplified so there is a clear difference between presented options to avoid confusion.

Participants were asked to click through a Create Art flow to generate a piece of art using the wildflowers of Michigan data set. When asked to rate how intuitive the flow was the average response was 4.5 on a 7-point Likert scale. Users asked to have a back button on the page, in addition to more descriptions and examples. The design called out variables and attributes, which was hard to understand for some non-technical users, despite making an effort to limit jargon based on prior user feedback. At this point users want to see an example of what variables and attributes are and how their defined relationships correlate to the look of the final art piece. One participant commented "a visualizer on the side showing in real time how my decisions impacted output or end result" to describe how decisions made during the Create Art flow should be shown in real time.

One SUS question that had mostly poor results was "I found the site cumbersome to use" which scored a mean of 2.7 on a 7-point Likert scale. These results show that the Create Account/On-Boarding and Create Art flows require re-designing. Eight participants noted that they would need to learn something new before they could get going with this site, indicating that the jargon used on the site is not intuitive for some users. The full SUS score results can be found in Appendix D.

3   Discussion

By creating a tool for data visualization through artistic representation researchers were able to relieve the tension between accurate data representations and abstract data representations. The tool allowed users to create meaningful art pieces that can be translated to represent a the foundational data set or left as an artistic piece. The tool created is an effective way to increase data knowledge using humanized data visualization.

The barrier of entry to create and interpret data visualizations is high and this proposed new creative visualization tool can increase data-knowledge through the medium of art. A human-centered study was conducted to create a tool that can be easily used by all to create data visualizations using artistic methods. Insights derived from generating data-driven art include users should be on-boarded to available digital creation tools and should easily be able to flip back and forth between their foundation set and art canvas. Usability testing found that all test participants correctly identified the purpose of the app by just interacting with the home screen. User testing also echoed the importance of educating users and the barrier to entry with data concepts.

Despite the achievements in current study, a few limitations should also be acknowledged. First, because this is a new space and product, researchers were able to define the minimum viable concept with very limited time and resources. Researchers were only able to test this new creative visualization tool concept as a low-fidelity interaction prototype, leveraging wizard-of-oz techniques to demonstrate to participants the art creation method. Second, users could not actually create their own piece of art from data of their choosing using the current prototype, instead, all pieces of artwork were created by researchers rather than real users. Ideally researchers would have been able to give the assignment to unbiased users meeting target user criteria to help inform the art creation method and user interface design. Third, researchers' initial intent was to develop a tangible solution for users between the ages of ten and eighteen, grades fifth through twelfth, to increase their data-knowledge and further promote STEAM education. However, due to special IRB concerns and pandemic circumstances, no young participants were recruited in this study. Math curriculum in the US is designed to teach children at age ten to apply math concepts to the real world and link numbers to meaningful concepts in real life such as sizes and shapes of different objects (Morin 2019). At the same time, the art curriculum teaches ten-year-olds how to use different optical illusions and color techniques, such as shadow and negative space, to describe objects in different sizes and shapes. (Filmore 2020). Artistically and scientifically, ten-year-olds can identify meaningful concepts in spatial positioning and color, and start to learn to use numerical data to label objects that are perceived. Therefore, there is a clear opportunity to design a tool for children to develop an increased understanding of today's increasingly data-driven world through the medium of art. Therefore, future studies will be conducted to understand how the proposed application can be nuanced for children. In addition, as part of future study, various platforms will be developed to enhance flexibility and accessibility. Furthermore, future efforts will be made to test the ability of the proposed application to promote user-in-the-loop collaborative creations by enabling users to simultaneously collaborate on a large-scale art piece, either between friends or community-wide creations, with participating members only defining a few discrete visual elements of a larger art piece.

Appendix A: Prototype Art - Peloton Workouts

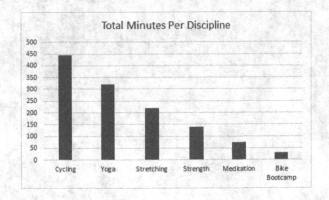

Appendix B: Prototype Art - Spoken Out Loud

Appendix C: Artful Interactive Prototype Home Page

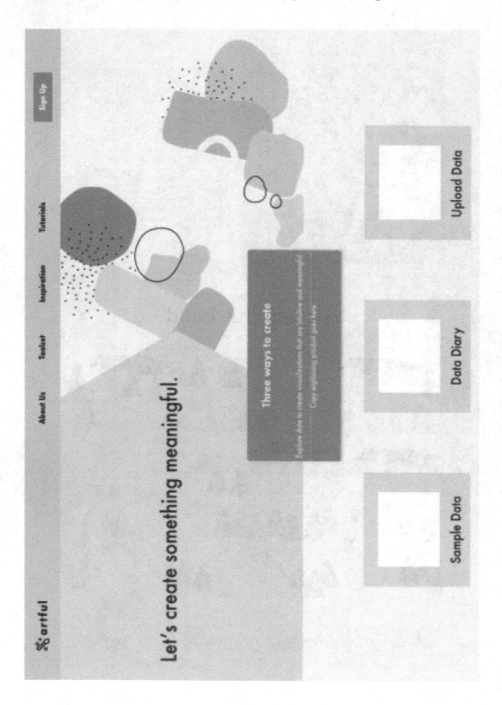

Appendix D: Artful Interactive Prototype SUS Results

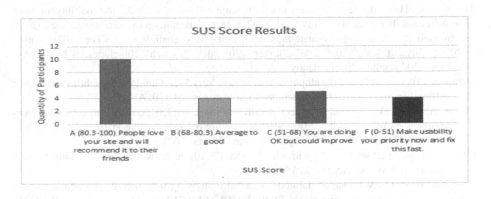

Participant	Score
Participant 7	32.14
Participant 23	41.07
Participant 14	44.64
Participant 22	44.64
Participant 21	57.14
Participant 3	58.93
Participant 18	62.50
Participant 2	62.50
Participant 4	66.07
Participant 13	69.64
Participant 16	73.21
Participant 10	76.79
Participant 12	78.57
Participant 9	80.36
Participant 5	80.36
Participant 20	80.36
Participant 15	82.14
Participant 17	83.93
Participant 6	83.93
Participant 1	87.50
Participant 19	91.07
Participant 11	92.86
Participant 8	101.79

References

Koltay, T.: Data literacy: in search of a name and identity. J. Doc. **71**, 401–415 (2015). https://doi.org/10.1108/jd-02-2014-0026

Aparicio, M., Costa, C.: Data visualization. Commun. Des. Q. **3**, 7–11 (2015). https://doi.org/10.1145/2721882.2721883

Alamalhodaei, A., Alberda, A., Feigenbaum, A.: Humanizing data through 'data comics': an introduction to graphic medicine and graphic social science. Data Vis. Soc. **21,** 347–366 (2020). https://doi.org/10.1515/9789048543137-025

Christiansen, J.: Visualizing science: illustration and beyond. Scientific American (2018). https:// blogs.scientificamerican.com/sa-visual/visualizing-science-illustration-and-beyond/

Thomas, N.: How to use the system usability scale (SUS) to evaluate the usability of your website usability geek. Usability Geek (2021). https://usabilitygeek.com/how-to-use-the-sys tem-usability-scale-sus-to-evaluate-the-usability-of-your-website/#:~:text=The%20System% 20Usability%20Scale%20is%20a%20Likert%20Scale%20which%20includes,1%20means% 20they%20disagree%20vehemently

Morin, A.: 10-year-old child development milestones. Very Well Family (2019). https://www.ver ywellfamily.com/10-year-old-developmental-milestones-620710. Accessed 25 Mar 2021

Morin, A.: Math skills: What to expect at different ages. Understood.org. https://www.unders tood.org/en/learning-thinking-differences/signs-symptoms/age-by-age-learning-skills/math-skills-what-to-expect-at-different-ages. Accessed 25 Mar 2021

Filmore 5th grade art lessons. Art with Mrs Filmore (2020). http://www.artwithmrsfilmore.com/ 5th-grade-art-lessons/. Accessed 25 Mar 2021

Preoţiuc Pietro, D., Volkova, S., Lampos, V., et al.: Studying user income through language, behaviour and affect in social media. PLoS One **10**, e0138717 (2015). https://doi.org/10.1371/ journal.pone.0138717

Bishop, F., Zagermann, J., Pfeil, U., et al.: Construct-a-vis: exploring the free-form visualization processes of children. IEEE Trans. Vis. Comput. Graph. **99**, 1 (2019). https://doi.org/10.1109/ tvcg.2019.2934804

Sustainable Landscape Design & Architecture in Ann Arbor, MI I Creating Sustainable Landscapes. Creatingsustainablelandscapes.com (2021). https://www.creatingsustainablelands capes.com/

Automatic Tagging of Food Dishes and Its Applications in Social Media

Durga Suryanarayanan[1] and Dvijesh Shastri[2]($\boxtimes$)

[1] Amazon Web Services, Houston, TX, USA
surydurg@amazon.com
[2] University of Houston-Downtown, Houston, TX, USA
shastrid@uhd.edu

Abstract. Eating is a social activity, and more so in the age of social media. It is estimated that 69% of millennials take pictures of their food before eating; many of these pictures end up on social media. Automatic recognition of food dishes from these images can be valuable, as it can increase the usability of the social media applications by automatically tagging the food items, and at the same time increase awareness of individuals' caloric intake. This paper presents a deep learning based approach for automatic recognition of food dishes. Specifically, we explored a set of convolutional neural network (CNN) architectures including the InceptionV3 and Xception architectures. Food-101 and Yummly datasets were used in the analysis. The results reveal that the Xception architecture works the best in classifying food dishes with a test accuracy of 79.66%. Broadly speaking, this highlights the role of the deep neural network technology for the newly emerging research field of Human-Food Interaction (HDI) which capitalizes the ubiquitous nature of technology to promote healthy eating.

Keywords: Deep learning · CNN · Food dishes · Social media

1 Introduction

Automatic tagging of food dishes is a classical computer vision problem where the goal is to classify a food dish from an image. The benefit of automatic tagging of food dishes is obvious; it minimizes user interventions, which can lead to improved usability of a software application. Social media and healthcare apps have been actively seeking this functionality to be integrated to their services so that users don't have to type or select a food dish manually. A case in point is Instagram, a popular social media site which has 500 million active users per day, and have 95 million photos uploaded per day [1]. It is estimated that 69% of millennials take pictures of their food before eating; many of these pictures end up on social media [11]. Automatic tagging of food dishes from these photos can save users from manual inputs.

D. Suryanarayanan—Student at the University of Houston – Downtown, Houston, TX – 77002, USA at the time of conducting the research.

© Springer Nature Switzerland AG 2021
C. Stephanidis et al. (Eds.): HCII 2021, CCIS 1419, pp. 625–630, 2021.
https://doi.org/10.1007/978-3-030-78635-9_79

Another application where this automatic tagging would be useful is in the healthcare-related apps. People are increasingly mindful of the food they eat and calories they consume. A large number of healthcare apps are available for tracking users' calorie consumption. The number of these apps has gone up by 50% on the Android platform and 20% on the iOS platform between the years 2016–2017 [12]. They collectively generate 26 billion in revenue. Currently, most healthcare apps require users to enter the food intake information manually. Automatic tagging of food dishes can offer an effective alternative in which food dishes can be predicted and calorie intake can be estimated from pictures taken via smartphones. Thus, it promotes healthy eating by taking advantage of two popular technologies, namely smartphones and deep neural network.

In this paper, we propose deep learning models to predict 1) food dishes (e.g., burger vs. taco) and 2) cuisine types (e.g., Italian cuisine vs. American cuisine) from food images. The rest of the paper is organized as follows: Sect. 2 describes previous work in this area. Section 3 discusses the datasets that we used for the analysis. Section 4 explains our CNN models and Sect. 5 discusses the study results. Section 6 concludes the discussion.

2   Previous Work

Since the ImageNet challenge in 2012 [7], researchers have been exploring CNNs in classifying images. Though CNNs have been successful in image classification, its application for food dish classification has not yet fully explored. One of the challenges of the food dish classification problems is high intra-class variance (e.g., different ways of preparing tacos) and low inter-class variance (e.g., noodles vs. spaghetti). Also, the number of classes for food images have not been definitively determined.

Traditional approaches of food image classification use feature detection followed by classification. In particular, Yang et al. exploited the spatial relationships between different ingredients in food images by calculating pairwise statistics between local features computed and obtained an accuracy of 28.2% [10]. Hoashi et al. achieved 55.8% classification accuracy with ten food items, using a two-step method by detecting candidate regions and classifying them by various kinds of features [8]. Bossard *et al.* gathered 101 classes of food dishes with 1000 images each for automatically recognizing pictured dishes [2]. Random forests was used to mine discriminative parts and achieved an accuracy of 50.76%. Kagaya and Aizawa tackle the problem of classifying food images from non-food images through convolutional neural networks, with an accuracy of 93.8% [6]. Recently, a CNN based approach is proposed to compute calories from food images [13]. However, their solution is a work-in-progress, requiring more research to improve the classification rate.

3   Datasets

We used two popular datasets in this study: 1) Food-101 dataset for classification of food dishes, and 2) Yummly dataset for classification of cuisine types.

3.1 Food-101 Dataset

The Food-101 dataset was used for classification of food dishes. It has 101 food dishes, with 1000 images of each dish, totaling 101,000 images [2]. The complete dataset was split into train-validation-test in 72-18-10 ratio, maintaining a balanced class ratio.

3.2 Yummly Dataset

The Yummly dataset was used for classification of cuisine types. The dataset is available on the website Yummly.com. The dataset that we downloaded for the analysis has 18,000 images with 6 cuisine types (Italian, American, Mexican, Asian, French, and Indian) and corresponding metadata files containing information that includes cuisine types and calories. The image files are of different sizes, and hence they were resized to either 100 × 150 pixels or 50 × 75 pixels. To increase the size of the input data, the images were flipped by 180° degrees, resulting into 36,000 images in the dataset. There were no other pre-processing steps involved.

4 Deep Learning Models

For the food dish classification and the cuisine type classification, four CNN models were prepared and ran on Amazon Web Services. The models were trained for multiple epochs to compare classification performance as well as model training time. The objective of the modeling process was to reduce the categorical cross entropy loss for the training set, and maximize the accuracy of the validation set.

Our first model is built based on the architecture proposed by Alex Krizevsky et al. [7]. The original architecture contains five convolutional layers, three of which are followed by maxpooling layers, and three fully connected layers with a final 1000 layer softmax activation function. The final layer has been modified to have 101 output neurons – one neuron per food dish.

Our second model is the Keras implementation of the ResNet architecture [4, 5] named ResNet50. For the food dish classification, the final layer was modified to have 101 output neurons – one neuron per food dish. For the cuisine classification, the final layer was modified to have 6 output neurons – one neuron per cuisine type.

Our third and fourth models are the Keras implementations of InceptionV3 [9] and Xception [3] architectures. A final layer of 101 fully connected neurons is added to the models for the food dish classification. Similarly, a final layer of 6 fully connected neurons is added to the models for the cuisine classification. The learning rate was set at 0.01 and softmax activation function was used.

5 Data Analysis Results

The data analysis results are discussed below:

5.1   Classification of Food Dishes

Table 1 summarizes the performance of each of the four CNN models that were developed for the food dish classification task. The AlexNet model (our very first model) performed poorly, predicting a single food dish for all 101 categories. The primary reason of the poor performance of the model's is that it is too simple to learn the complexity of the data. In particular, the complete model contained only eight layers – with one 11×11 layer, and one 5×5 layer followed by three 3×3 convolutions, and hence, could not successfully learn the complexities of shape and texture that are present in food images.

Table 1.   Deep learning model comparison for food dish classification.

Model	# of Epochs	Training time per epoch (min)	Training accuracy (%)	Validation accuracy (%)	Test accuracy (%)
AlexNet	10	15.80	1.00	1.00	1.00
ResNet50	20	41.33	21.88	19.32	19.05
Inception V3	32	66.67	99.98	80.26	79.77
Inception V3	8	66.67	93.73	70.59	71.69
Xception	16	98.30	99.99	80.77	80.77
Xception	8	98.30	99.36	79.28	79.66

In comparison to AlexNet, the ResNet50 model (our second model) showed improvement, with 19.05% test accuracy after 20 epochs, with a batch size of 32 images per epoch. Yet, the performance was far too low. Our third model, the InceptionV3 model took a bit longer time to be trained, but yielded 79.77% test accuracy after 32 epochs with batch size 32. Test accuracy after 8 epochs was 71.69%. Finally, Xception model (our final model) took about 1.5 h per epoch (with total training time is 8 epochs $\times$ 98.30 min) to be trained, and resulted in the best test accuracy of 79.66% after 8 epochs, with batch size 32. Any further tuning after 8 epochs resulted into insignificant improvement in the performance with twice the processing time (16 epochs $\times$ 98.30 min).

5.2   Classification of Cuisine Types

For the classification of cuisine types, we used the three CNN architectures: ResNet50, InceptionV3 and Xception. Table 2 summarizes the performance of each model. Overall, all of them performed suboptimal with validation and test accuracies in twenties. Furthermore, the Xception model suffered from the data overfitting issue as one may observe this from the accuracy gap between the training and testing sets.

We tried to tune the mode for epoch 1 to epoch 8. None of the three models improve the classification accuracy with the increase epochs, suggesting that they are unable to capture the data complexity. In case of the InceptionV3 model, a lowering training loss function without an improvement in the validation accuracy clearly indicates that the model overfits the data. The models' poor performance are primarily due to the fact that images from multiple cuisines may look similar (e.g., noodles - the Asian cuisine vs. spaghetti - the Italian cuisine), and a single cuisine may have multiple dishes that look completely different (e.g., burger vs. fries - in American cuisine).

Table 2. Deep learning model comparison for cuisine classification.

Model	# of Epochs	Training time per epoch (min)	Training accuracy (%)	Validation accuracy (%)	Test accuracy (%)
ResNet50	8	15.00	25.84	25.48	25.39
Inception V3	8	22.50	29.39	21.40	21.31
Xception	8	33.30	80.37	23.01	22.80

6   Conclusion

We explored a feasibility of using CNN architectures for automatic tagging of food dishes from digital images. Four CNN architectures were evaluated for this problem. Images from Food-101 dataset were used for training the models. A separate set of images from the same dataset was used to evaluate the models' performance. The results reveal that the Xception architecture performs the best with a test accuracy of 79.66% for classifying 101 food dishes. Furthermore, we explored the same CNN architectures for classification of cuisine types. Images from Yummly dateset were used for training the models. A separate set of images from the same dataset was used to evaluate the models' performance. The results reveal that none of the models achieved more than 25% of test accuracies in classifying 6 cuisine types.

In summary, the proposed research shows limitations of the CNN architectures in classifying *cuisine types* and at the same time, shows effectiveness of the architectures in accurately classifying *food dishes* from digital images of food. This opens possibility of promoting healthy eating by capitalizing two powerful technologies, namely smartphone and deep neural network.

References

1. Aslam, S.: Omnicoreagency.com, 1 January 2018. https://www.omnicoreagency.com/instagram-statistics/
2. Bossard, L., Guillaumin, M., Van Gool, L.: Food-101 – mining discriminative components with random forests. In: Fleet, D., Pajdla, T., Schiele, B., Tuytelaars, T. (eds.) Computer Vision – ECCV 2014: 13th European Conference, Zurich, Switzerland, September 6-12, 2014, Proceedings, Part VI, pp. 446–461. Springer International Publishing, Cham (2014). https://doi.org/10.1007/978-3-319-10599-4_29

3. Chollet, F.: Xception: Deep learning with depthwise separable convolutions (2016). arXiv preprint
4. Deng, J., Dong, W., Socher, R., Li, L.J., Li, K., Fei-Fei, L.: Imagenet: a large-scale hierarchical image database. In: Proceedings of the IEEE conference on Computer Vision and Pattern Recognition, pp. 248–255, June 2009
5. He, K., Zhang, X., Ren, S., Sun, J.: Deep residual learning for image recognition. In: Proceedings of the IEEE conference on Computer Vision and Pattern Recognition, pp. 770–778. IEEE (2016)
6. Kagaya, H., Aizawa, K.: Highly accurate food/non-food image classification based on a deep convolutional neural network. In: Murino, V., Puppo, E., Sona, D., Cristani, M., Sansone, C. (eds.) New Trends in Image Analysis and Processing -- ICIAP 2015 Workshops: ICIAP 2015 International Workshops, BioFor, CTMR, RHEUMA, ISCA, MADiMa, SBMI, and QoEM, Genoa, Italy, September 7-8, 2015, Proceedings, pp. 350–357. Springer International Publishing, Cham (2015). https://doi.org/10.1007/978-3-319-23222-5_43
7. Krizhevsky, A., Sutskever, I., Hinton, G.E.: Imagenet classification with deep convolutional neural networks. In: Advances in neural information processing systems, pp. 1097–1105 (2012)
8. Matsuda, Y., Hoashi, H., Yanai, K.: Recognition of multiple-food images by detecting candidate regions. In: IEEE International Conference on Multimedia and Expo (ICME), pp. 25–30. IEEE, July 2012
9. Szegedy, C., et al.: Going deeper with convolutions. In: Proceedings of the IEEE conference on Computer Vision and Pattern Recognition. IEEE, June 2015
10. Yang, S., Chen, M., Pomerleau, D., Sukthankar, R.: Food recognition using statistics of pairwise local features. In: Proceedings of the IEEE conference on Computer Vision and Pattern Recognition (CVPR), pp. 2249–2256. IEEE, June 2010
11. Amatulli, J.: An obnoxious 69 percent of millennials take photos of food before eating. huffingtonpost, March 2017. https://www.huffingtonpost.com/entry/study-says-69-of-millennials-take-photos-of-their-food-before-eating-us_58b73078e4b0284854b39105
12. Pohl, M.: 325,000 mobile health apps available in 2017 – Android now the leading mHealth platform. research2guidance, 7 November 2017
13. Meyers, A., et al.: Im2Calories: towards an automated mobile vision food diary. In: Proceedings of the IEEE International Conference on Computer Vision, pp. 1233–1241, (2015)

How Are Deepfake Videos Detected? An Initial User Study

Nyein Nyein Thaw, Thin July, Aye Nu Wai, Dion Hoe-Lian Goh[✉],
and Alton Y. K. Chua

Wee Kim Wee School of Communication and Information, Nanyang Technological University,
Singapore, Singapore
{nyei0004,july002,ayenu001,ashlgoh,altonchua}@ntu.edu.sg

Abstract. This paper describes an exploratory study of deepfake video detection from a user's perspective. Through semi-structured interviews, participants were asked to identify real and deepfake videos, and explain how they arrived at their conclusions. From the interviews, two sets of features were derived. One was associated with correct deepfake identification while the other was associated with incorrect identification. Interestingly, the two sets had overlapping features suggesting the difficulties associated with deepfake identification. Further, the majority of participants could not correctly identify all their assigned videos.

Keywords: Deepfake videos · Identification · Misidentification · Misinformation · User study

1 Introduction

The Internet and, in particular, social media platforms have made it easier for people to create and share content. Although this increased access brings about benefits, it also facilitates the spread of falsified content. One example is fake news, a neologism that denotes misinformation or disinformation packaged as legitimate news. Another even more recent example is the deepfake video (or simply, deepfake). Deepfakes are synthetically generated media that pose as an actual recording [1]. A typical example is the face of a person in a video being replaced by someone else who is originally not in it. Deepfakes use deep learning and artificial neural networks to generate falsified content, hence their name. Deepfakes have been used to create pornography where a hapless victim appears as an actor in the video. Similar techniques are used to attribute content to people in other areas such as news, politics and entertainment.

Due to the richness of content in videos when compared to articles that are primarily text-based such as news, the former are often more persuasive and hence have the potential to be perceived as more credible [2]. Consequently, deepfakes may cause more psychological, reputational, and/or physical harm to people than falsified textual content [3]. Unsurprisingly identification of deepfakes has recently attracted significant attention among researchers and practitioners. Extant work focuses primarily on the design,

© Springer Nature Switzerland AG 2021
C. Stephanidis et al. (Eds.): HCII 2021, CCIS 1419, pp. 631–636, 2021.
https://doi.org/10.1007/978-3-030-78635-9_80

implementation and evaluation of machine learning algorithms for deepfake identification (e.g. [4]). Typically, such algorithms aim to detect irregularities in video rendering or unusual behavior of people in the video content (e.g. [5]).

Research in the algorithm front has made significant strides. However, an important gap yet to be addressed adequately is from the human perspective, in particular, the characteristics of a video that people use to ascertain authenticity. This is an important area of investigation because it could lead to new insights that inform algorithmic research, as well as educational programs to help people spot deepfakes. In sum, the primary objective of the present study is to uncover the features that characterize a video as a deepfake. To accomplish this objective, we ask two research questions: (1) what features are associated with the correct identification of deepfakes? (2) what features are associated with the misidentification of deepfakes?

2 Methodology

Given the dearth of research, the present study was exploratory in nature, and a semi-structured interview was hence considered suitable. Questions asked in the interview comprised participant profile, features of deepfakes that made them believable as authentic videos, and features that made them unbelievable.

We further prepared four pairs (eight) of videos for use in our study. These were obtained through a search on the Internet, and we avoided content that may be considered offensive such as pornography. Each pair consisted of an original (real) video and its deepfake version. The first pair was about American actor Bill Hader doing impersonations on the Conan late-night television talk show. The second pair was American politician Nancy Pelosi speaking at the 2019 Center for American Progress Ideas Conference. The deepfake version falsely portrayed her as drunk while speaking. The third pair was a news clip by Tomio Okamura (a Czech-Japanese far-right politician and entrepreneur) while, the fourth pair involved a Kim Kardashian impression in which the deepfake version used face-swapping effects.

A total of 20 participants were recruited for the study using snowball and convenience sampling. Participants were either students or working adults. Each participant first watched two real videos and two deepfakes from the pool of eight. We ensured that no real/deepfake pair was assigned to the same participant to avoid comparisons of content. After the videos were watched, the interview commenced. We asked participants to identify which of their assigned videos were real and which were fake, as well as the aspects of the videos that led to their conclusions. At the end of the study, participants were told which videos they watched were real and which were the deepfakes to avoid any form of misrepresentation.

3 Results

The 20 participants in our study consisted of 11 males and nine females, between 21 to 40 years of age. Five participants were either undergraduate or graduate students while the remainder were working adults. The majority watched online videos at least once a day, and their top-three platforms were YouTube, Facebook and Instagram. Further, most participants reported watching and sharing videos they liked without considering their authenticity. They would also "do nothing" if they found out a video was fake.

We were surprised to find that only six of the 20 participants were able to correctly identify whether their assigned videos were real or deepfakes, and one participant had no correct identifications. The majority of participants (nine) made two correct and two incorrect identifications.

Table 1 presents the top 10 features were associated with the correct identification of videos as deepfakes. The two highest-ranked ones were blurred faces or those that seem to have special effects applied, as well as unnatural sounding voices. The third feature was a perception that no emotions were conveyed. The next three features were equally ranked by participants and included occurrences of face swapping within the video, familiarity with the actual person in the video, and background objects that seemed out of place. In seventh place was another subjective impression that the person in the video did not behave naturally. The final three features were eyes that were not rendered naturally, lack of facial expressions, and mouth movements that were abnormal or not in sync with speech.

Table 1. Features associated with correct deepfake identification

Feature	Number of participants
Faces blurred or with special effects	10
Unnatural voice	10
Lack of emotions	6
Face swapping	5
Familiar person in video	5
Irrelevant or out of place objects in background	5
Overall unnatural behavior	4
Poorly rendered eyes	3
Lack of facial expression	3
Abnormal mouth movements	2

Table 2 lists the top 10 features reported by our participants that were associated with deepfake misidentification. Put differently, these were the features that made a deepfake appear as an authentic, non-falsified video, or conversely an authentic video as a deepfake. The top feature, highlighted by 12 participants was a qualitative impression that the video appeared "natural". In other words, the video did not seem to be manipulated. Next, eight participants equated poor video quality (low resolution) with deepfakes, which turned out to be incorrect because authentic videos could also have such a characteristic. The next three features were ranked equally by participants. This included hands that were animated, a perceived lack of special effects applied to the video, and voices speaking at normal speed. Paradoxically, eyes that were misaligned, static facial expressions, and perceived lack of emotions in speech did not always mean that a video was a deepfake.

Table 2. Features associated with deepfake misidentification

Feature	Number of participants
Appears natural/realistic	12
Low video quality	8
Animated hand movements	5
No special effects	5
Voice at normal speed	5
Familiarity with video	4
Smooth voice tone	4
Misaligned eyes	3
Face remains at the same position throughout the video	3
Voice does not convey any emotions	2

4 Discussion

An interesting outcome of the present study is that despite knowing its purpose, the majority of our participants could not correctly identify all their assigned videos as real or deepfakes. In fact, participants mentioned that they were vigilant while watching their assigned videos due to the nature of the study, and remarked that if they watched such videos in actual social media platforms, they may not have noticed that there could be deepfakes.

One possible reason for the relatively poor identification success rate could be that the participants were unfamiliar with the content found in the videos and therefore had difficulty distinguishing between real and fake. In particular, the majority of the videos were Western-centric, while participants were primarily from Asian countries. Another could be the quality of the deepfakes that made them seem authentic. For example, in Table 2, it seemed that many participants had the wrong impression that deepfakes were typically poor quality videos. This was not the case, given advances in deepfake generation technology. A final possibility could be due to the profile of the participants. In particular, their reported video watching and sharing behaviors suggest a tolerance and low awareness of deepfakes. Our findings hence call for further investigations in these areas. Nevertheless, the results also imply that in the real world, it may be even more difficult for people to establish the authenticity of videos they encounter [6].

In terms of features that were associated with correct deepfake identification, we note that a number of them, such as blurred faces and poor rendering of eyes, are used by current algorithms. This finding provides further justification for using these features in algorithms for deepfake detection [7]. Features uncovered by our participants but not yet investigated adequately in algorithm development could be considered by researchers such as unnatural sounding voices, lack of emotions, and lack of facial expressions. Some of these features are however subjective in nature and may be challenging to implement.

At the same time, the features that were associated with deepfake misidentification demonstrate the difficulty of spotting such videos in the real world [6]. Specifically, there were some overlaps between Tables 1 and 2. This means that the very features that people use to correctly identify deepfakes may also result in false positives or false negatives, where an authentic video is incorrectly flagged as fake and vice versa. For example, while our participants associated low resolution videos (poor quality) with deepfakes, many authentic videos also suffer from such a characteristic, sometimes due to the need for small file sizes or to accommodate slow Internet connections. Likewise, a lack of emotions (Table 2) led a few participants to conclude a video was a deepfake. However, this could be an actual characteristic of the person in the video, rather than an indication of a manipulated video.

Our findings also suggest a need for digital literacy programs that inform people about deepfakes and how to identify the authenticity of videos [8]. In particular, this is demonstrated by the poor performance of our participants in distinguishing between real and deepfake videos. It should be noted that all our participants watched online videos on a daily basis, and would have been expected to be more familiar with this concept. In addition, the overlapping features in Tables 1 and 2 imply that our participants were relying on seemingly intuitive clues for deepfake identification that turned out to be insufficient.

5 Conclusion

Our exploratory study presents an initial understanding of how people perceive the authenticity of videos in response to the rise of deepfakes on the Internet. A couple of implications may be drawn from this research. First, our list of features in Table 1 could be used by other researchers to improve on existing deepfake detection algorithms or to implement new ones. Second, because people seem to have difficulty in correctly identifying deepfakes, there is a need for more education among Internet users to the dangers of such videos and how to spot them. Care needs to be taken to instruct people that the authenticity of a video cannot be simply evaluated based on one or two features. Instead, multiple video features should be taken into consideration since an authentic video may share a few similar characteristics as a deepfake.

Despite the potential usefulness of our findings, there are limitations that may limit their generalizability. One, we employed a qualitative approach using semi-structured interviews on a small number of participants. Two, our participant profiles were not sufficiently diverse due to the sampling method used. Hence, future work may adopt quantitative methodologies such as large-scale surveys to verify the stability and usefulness of our set of deepfake features in determining authenticity. Further, it would be instructive to understand perceptions of deepfake videos from a wider range of participant profiles include age, digital literacy and domain knowledge of video content. Finally, using videos from a greater variety of topics would better improve on the generalizability of our findings.

References

1. Chesney, R., Citron, D.: Deepfakes and the new disinformation war: the coming age of post-truth geopolitics. Foreign Aff. **98**(1), 147–155 (2019)
2. Ajukhadar, M., Senecal, S., Ouellette, D.: Can the media richness of a privacy disclosure enhance outcome? A multifaceted view of trust in rich media environments. Int. J. Electron. Commer. **14**(4), 103–126 (2010)
3. Burkell, J., Gosse, C.: Nothing new here: emphasizing the social and cultural context of deepfakes. First Monday **24**(12), (2019). https://journals.uic.edu/ojs/index.php/fm/article/download/10287/8297
4. Lyu, S.: Deepfake detection: current challenges and next steps. In: 2020 IEEE International Conference on Multimedia and Expo Workshops, pp. 1–6. IEEE Press (2020)
5. Yang, X., Li, Y., Lyu, S.: Exposing deep fakes using inconsistent had poses. In: 2019 IEEE International Conference on Acoustics, Speech and Signal Processing, pp. 8261–8265. IEEE Press (2019)
6. Wagner, T.L., Blewer, A.: The word real is no longer real: deepfakes, gender, and the challenges of AI-altered video. Open Inf. Sci. **3**, 32–46 (2019)
7. Tolosana, R., Vera-Rodriguez, R., Fierrez, J., Morales, A., Ortega-Garcia, J.: Deepfakes and beyond: a survey of face manipulation and fake detection. Inf. Fusion **64**, 131–148 (2020)
8. Hwang, Y., Ryu, J.Y., Jeong, S.H.: Effects of disinformation using deepfake: the protective effect of media literacy education. Cyberpsychol. Behav. Soc. Netw. (in press)

Author Index

642   Author Index

Printed in the United States
by Baker & Taylor Publisher Services